Hot Money and the Politics of Debt

R.T. Naylor

Hot Money and the Politics of Debt

McClelland and Stewart

McClelland and Stewart
The Canadian Publishers
481 University Avenue
Toronto M5G 2E9

Canadian Cataloguing in Publication Data

Naylor, R.T., 1945–
    Hot money and the politics of debt

Bibliography
Includes index.
ISBN 0-7710-6707-0

1. Money laundering. 2. Debts, External –
Developing countries. 3. International finance.
I. Title.

HG3891.N38 1987   332′.042   C86-094792-0

Design by Linda Gustafson
Printed and bound in the United States of America

Contents

Hot Money and the Politics of Debt

Acknowledgments

Although the bulk of the material in this book refers to a period of very recent financial history, specifically the period since the summer of 1982, when the world became mesmerized by the 'debt crisis,' the form and argument reflect more than a decade of concern about the politics of international finance. Hence, the author can have a special sympathy with developing countries struggling just to acknowledge their debts, let alone repay them – albeit my intellectual debts are genuine, whereas the central theme of this book is that many of the financial debts of the developing countries are not.

A few individuals made particularly useful contributions to specific sections. These include: Abbas Alnasrawi, George Archer, Pino Arlacchi, Paul Balfour, Anna and Patrick Brochard, Ayse Bugra, Paulo Carvalho, Stephanie Henley, the late August Hagedorn, Carlos Heredia, Arvind Jain, Jamal Kaffadir, Abdo and Maher Kassir, Martha Loutfi, Sam Noumoff, James Putzel, José Luis Robinson, my agent Bob Roistacher, Mel Rosenthal, Phil Sabetti, Julian Sher, and Steve Wasserman. And three individuals stamped their influence very strongly on the entire work. The project from start to finish had the warm and indispensable support of Michael Hudson, who understood immediately and fully what was at issue, and influenced strongly the general orientation of the research. J. C. Weldon combines an awesome theoretical acuity with a wider-ranging practical understanding from which a generation of colleagues and students at McGill have drawn. And the process of shaping what often seemed a tangle of digressions and formless detail into the present structure was handled by my editor, Charis Wahl (who also removed most of what I thought to be my best jokes). Not only are none of them responsible for any errors or misinterpretations, but some likely would not even agree with the bulk of the arguments of the book. Clearly, too, the project would have been much more difficult, perhaps impossible, without the pioneering efforts of a host of other investigators, too numerous to be mentioned individually here. Suffice it to note the names of: Jonathan

Kwitny, veteran prober of the American underworld, where high finance and low politics coalesce; Rupert Cornwell and Larry Gurwin, whose accounts of the Ambrosiano scandal will long remain classics of investigative journalism; Luigi DiFonza, whose biography of the larger-than-life Michele Sindona can only invoke as much envy as it does admiration; Thurston Clarke and John Tigue, whose 1970s investigations did so much to move the study of underground finance from artful anecdote to the science of hot-money movements, a process that Richard Blum did so much to further in the 1980s; Charles Raw and his associates, who applied that science to the enterprise of Bernie Cornfeld, and Robert Hutchison, who did likewise for the affairs of Robert Vesco; Nicholas Faith, who successfully demystified the world of Swiss banking for the English-language reader, and the much maligned and even-more quoted Jean Ziegler, who earlier did likewise for the French-language reader; Ugur Mumcu, whose explorations of the underworld of Turkish finance and contraband trade still remain largely unknown outside his homeland despite their global ramifications; and Jesus Ynfante, whose investigations into the world of Spanish hot-money movements blew the lid off one of France's most notorious postwar political affairs. And there are many more.

Because of the global nature of the issues under scrutiny, and the constraints of space, there are obvious gaps in the book. Earlier drafts contained complete chapters dealing with the experience of Chile under 'monetarism' and of the Philippines under the World Bank programs. Substantial cuts also had to be made in material dealing with African debt problems. Large sections had originally been drafted – then discarded – dealing with such issues as the rise and multiple falls of the South Korean 'curb' market, the crash of the Souq el-Manakh in Kuwait, why diamonds are often a contrabandista's best friend, the business of business on the Thai-Burma border, and how John Z. De Lorean invented a car so small it could fit into a Geneva mailbox. I had also planned to include a section on Lebanese banking in peace and war, with its notorious interface with the underworld of arms, drugs, and flight-capital movements. International debt and the politics of superpower rivalry, interacting with a complex of domestic ethnic tensions, form a particularly fascinating subject in present-day Yugoslavia. Another obviously 'missing' chapter is one on Brazil's experiences as a sovereign debtor. And the crisis in South Africa, which, given the imposition of 'sanctions,' is guaranteed to give black-market operations in goods and money yet another shot of economic adrenalin, reached dramatic dimensions only after the manuscript was completed. All these must await another day, and another book.

Prologue

This is a book about hot and homeless money – where it comes from, how it is used and abused, how the world of high finance, governmental and corporate, became hostage to it, and what price we will pay until the hostages are released.

This is also a book about international debt loads of crisis proportions – where they came from, how the borrowed money has been used and abused, and how the world economy can shed the crippling burden the debt loads have imposed.

And this is a book that explores the intimate relationship between the two. For ultimately hot money and international debt are the two sides of the coin of peekaboo finance – the arts and sciences of playing seek-and-I'll-hide with the fiscal and monetary authorities.

Logically, when some countries have pluses in their balance of payments, others have corresponding minuses. In actual calculations, there were always little discrepancies; things did not quite add up to zero. But the minor differences could be sloughed off as 'errors and omissions.'

However, in the late 1970s something began to change. Computations of the world balance of payments revealed systematic and growing discrepancies. One such calculation showed that by the early 1980s the world was running an annual balance-of-payments deficit with itself in the vicinity of $100 billion.[1] In other words, it was running a balance of payments deficit with the moon equal to about 10% of the total value of world market trade. The International Monetary Fund (IMF) had a useful explanation for such statistical holes. They were due to 'asymmetries.'

Therefore, this is also a book about asymmetries.

The most important of these 'asymmetries' is the stupendous growth in the amount of hot and homeless money ready at any time to leave its present abode for more hospitable climes whenever a tiny interest rate spread, exchange rate change, or shift in the political environment beckons. Today, foreign exchange markets turn over about $150 billion daily. And an ever-increasing percentage of international financial flows seems to be speculative funds seeking sanctuary in highly liquid, preferably anonymous, assets.[2] That growth in the volume of hot money needs explanation.

Since the late 1970s, when the world balance-of-payments statistics began to reveal those systematic and growing discrepancies, the world has also seen a dramatic rise in the organizational skills of white-collar criminals – specifically their ability to control illegal markets, to render the operation of legal markets illegal, and to debauch the political systems that are supposed to keep their power in check.[3] The financial counterpart of the growing power and scope of white-collar crime is the increasing use of the instruments of peekaboo finance, and a parallel expansion of its machinery.

Emerging first to handle the financial needs of a select group of covert operators – from ultrarich tax evaders to drug dealers to secret-service agents and their ilk – the methods and mechanisms of peekaboo finance have now been democratized, opened to the service of all, regardless of race, color, creed, or political affiliation, though decidely not regardless of income level. Thus, yet another of the IMF's unsung 'asymmetries' is the proliferation of havens, institutional and geographic, for hot and homeless money. In such havens funds can be stashed away for a rainy day or, preferably, 'recycled' into income-earning assets elsewhere, with the geographic or occupational origins of the money hidden from view.

Complementing the spread of financial havens has been a rapid development of banking technology, specifically of an electronic funds-transfer system that functions virtually instantaneously – while the regulatory apparatuses of the interested countries remain mired in a Gutenberg Gulag. As William Mulholland, chief executive officer of the Bank of Montreal, modestly claimed in the autumn of 1985 before a committee of the Canadian Senate querying him on the efficacy of the bank-regulatory apparatus, 'I can hide money in the twinkling of an eye from all of the bloodhounds that could be put on the case, and I would be so far ahead of them that there would never be a hope of unraveling the trail. I am not kidding you. Technology today means that that sort of thing can be done through electronic means.'[4]

Obviously it would be wrong to assume that the entire global pool of hot money derives from covert or criminal action. Dirty money is hot money, but the reverse is not true. And even within the genus of dirty money, there is an essential distinction between money that is dirty because of how it is earned and money that is soiled subsequent to being earned when its earners evade taxes and exchange controls.

Furthermore, much of that pool derives simply from the effects of misguided economic policy. In the late 1970s governments in the major Western countries declared war on inflation. Inflation usually won. The main effect of tight credit policies – of soaring interest rates and strangled capital markets – was to create an environment in which hot money, multiplying out of the control of any single actor, public or private, became a major determinant of economic and financial action. Tight credit encouraged, even forced, legitimate money into patterns of behavior historically associated with the cash hoards of drug peddlers, tax evaders, contraband traders, and others who have something to hide – namely, the search for short-term havens in highly liquid assets, instead of seeking opportunities for long-term productive investment. Today, the treasurer of the Wichita chapter of the American Red Cross might well find himself standing in line at the same offshore bank as the enforcer for the Milan chapter of the Italian Red Brigades. As a result, explicitly criminal activity is given the protective shield of a powerful financial lobby intent on defending the machinery of peekaboo finance from the probing eyes and itchy fingers of the judicial, fiscal, and monetary authorities.[5]

On the other side of the balance sheet stands a growing list of overground businesses, strapped for funds because of the credit squeeze. Hot money recycled through the machinery of peekaboo finance is often the sole means of keeping them in operation. Prominent among them figure banks desperate for deposit money to finance loans to their customers. The more bad loans they have on their books, the greater the need for deposits, a need that cannot be entirely unrelated to the growing scandal of major banking institutions actively laundering mob money.

Increasingly, too, among the recipients of hot money can be found governments. Tight credit, which puffs the supply of hot money, also undermines long-term investment and economic growth. It therefore subverts the capacity of economies to generate sufficient tax revenues to meet government expenditure requirements. And, in the ultimate in money-laundering operations, it forces governments to respond by offering fiscal sanctuary in the form of tax amnesties and 'bearer' bonds to the very pool of hot money that has created much of the fiscal problem.[6] Nor are such whitewash facilities offered only by obscure 'developing' countries. Even the US government has dipped its fiscal fingers into the hot-money pool.

Thus, another of the 'asymmetries' that the IMF failed to specify is the growing appetite of the United States for consuming the world's supply of hot money, an appetite that grew from the prodigious to the voracious with the capture of the American government by the apostles of Born-Again Capitalism in 1980.

The two central tenets of the Reaganite philosophy were combating the Bolshevik menace through increased military spending, and morally rearming American enterprise through the largest tax cut in American history. These principles combined with economic recession and the proliferation of offshore havens that facilitated tax evasion on a grand scale to produce a ballooning government budget deficit and a scramble to find a means of financing it.

It was quite reasonable to argue that, rather than being an economic problem, the public-sector deficit was responsible for lifting the US economy out of its worst recession since the 1930s. (Granted, it was a curious economic 'recovery,' with the 'service' sector booming, non-military manufacturing flat, and a farm economy mired in a Great Depression.) The deficit per se was not the problem: spending the funds acquired by government borrowing for military purposes, rather than for productive infrastructure, was. But it was politically impossible to offer the public such justifications of deficit spending and of a more socially rational use of the funds. The Reaganites had made too much political hay out of attacking both the Carter-era deficits and that era's allegedly weak-kneed response to the international Bolshevik menace.

Furthermore, no matter how beneficial the deficit might actually be in stimulating the economy, there was the problem of financing it. That turned the US toward increasing its dependence on international flows of hot and homeless money. A major function of that global pool became assisting the US government in general, and the Pentagon in particular, in financing the expansion of the US military machine, at home and abroad, without at the same time requiring that the US taxpayer foot the bill. In effect, the US had reversed the verdict of 1776, imposing taxation without representation on the rest of the world by redirecting the global flows of hot money.

The growing awareness by governments and financial institutions of the promises and, to a lesser degree, the problems of hot and homeless money has come at much the same time as, though for very different reasons than, public concern over the stability of the international financial system. These two phenomena – world debt and the global pool of hot money – are more intimately related than most citizens of the Northern creditor and Southern debtor countries are aware.

Whether most of the blame for crippling levels of international debt is put on the borrower ('living beyond his means') or the lender ('imprudent banking') or the OPEC countries ('greedy oil sheikhs'), there has been a consensus that the inability of debtors to carry their debt burden is *the* problem. In reality, it is merely a symptom of a deeper problem, one rooted in the very mechanism by which international financial relations are conducted.

By the time the 'debt crisis' broke into public view in the summer of 1982, international finance had degenerated into a global Ponzi game: banks aided and abetted the flight of capital from countries whose social and political fabric was subject to increasing strain, and then lent it back again to increasingly desperate governments to top up temporarily the level of foreign-exchange reserves out of which the borrowing country was to pay the interest due on its debt next time round. Some of the bankers were aware of the potentially suicidal game in which they were involved; but no institution could buck the tide, lest it be left high and dry by its competitors.

The US economy, too, developed a voracious appetite for flight capital, which puffed real estate values in major urban centers, helped balance trade deficits, and as noted above, assisted the government in financing its budget deficit. The US government found itself caught in an absurd situation. It was battling to ensure its notion of political stability and economic order in countries that it regarded as falling within its sphere of influence, while its budgetary mechanics and its balance of international payments were increasingly dependent on the spread of political instability and economic disorder, and on the flight of capital they engendered. This 'recycling' process, an elaboration of the process long used by black-market money to avoid detection, would periodically accelerate to a frenzy and then stop – leaving panic and economic prostration in its wake.

There will come a point at which the cycle must be broken. The aggregate sums grow, while the capacity of debtor countries to meet their increasing payment obligations shrinks. It is impossible to defer forever, perhaps not even much longer, the ultimate question of how to deal with about $400 billion of international bank debt, not to speak of an equal or even greater volume of nonbank debt, whose book value rises geometrically with each trip through the circuitry of peekaboo finance while its market value falls with each food riot and rumbling from the barracks. No matter how creative the accounting profession has recently become, there is a point below which the bottom line cannot be pushed.

The crisis is systemic and requires systemic solution, though the 'cures' offered thus far are, in general, worse than the disease. They involve virtually confiscatory income and resource transfers, either from the taxpayers of the Western industrialized countries or from the nominally sovereign debtor countries, or both. And they implicitly assume that the debt, and therefore the obligation to pay, is legitimate.

How the taxpaying public of the industrialized countries contracted an obligation to accept an attack on its living standards in order to offset the consequences of interest-rate decisions made by the unelected Federal Reserve Board of the US has never been adequately explained in terms of either democratic theory or the law of contract. How much more difficult will it be to find an adequate explanation when the same obligation is transferred to the debtor countries. How the population of the developing countries, beset by plummeting living standards and shattered expectations, incurred the further obligation to assume the burden resulting from the flight of capital staged by their elites in cooperation with the international banks that willingly served them must also be explained rather than assumed.

Of course, any individual resident in countries whose governments routinely make the Amnesty International all-star list has an incontrovertible right to try to better his circumstances in happier climes. But those left behind have an equally valid right not to be forced to pick up the tab left after the departure of their cocitizens and/or their fortunes.

While public attention has been riveted on the financial aspects of the sovereign debt crisis and on means of assuring that the Western banks would not have to write off large amounts of assets, something more important has been taking place – an attempt to legitimize the debt, converting it into an openly acknowledged public obligation of the developing countries. This would assure that whatever irregularity or even illegality with respect to the incurring of the debt is subsequently exposed, the obligation to service that debt to the best of the debtor countries' limited abilities is immutably entrenched in international diplomacy and law. Thus, disputes between debtors and creditors over rescheduling fees and grace periods have been, on one level, a smoke screen for a massive money-laundering operation. The most important question should not be *how* a developing country might pay the debt service charges being demanded but *why* it should – or perhaps should not.

Part One

The World According To Meyer Lansky

1

Capital Flight in the Jet Age

When Bernie Cornfeld, the architect of the world's largest and most successful offshore mutual fund, bought his first airplane, the joke went around his Investors' Overseas Services (IOS) that he was about to start 'Capital Flight Airlines.'[1] It was only partly apocryphal. If Bernie Cornfeld did not invent the modern technology of capital flight, he did far more than most of his contemporaries to put it to work in an imaginative, systematic, and profitable way.

Providing facilities for money to flee the scrutiny and, consequently, the grasp of any particular political authority may be the world's second oldest profession. But the capability of flight capital to threaten the stability of the international monetary system is much more recent, dating from the aftermath of the First World War. During the war, many countries imposed rigorous embargoes on movements of gold and foreign exchange. After the war, the major powers struggled to restore freedom of international financial movements – only to be defeated by the prophetic combination of massive international debt loads and an uncontrollable global swirl of hot money.

Itinerant pools of hot money in the 1920s were an important factor in the eventual collapse of the international financial system. During the subsequent depression and the concurrent rearmament race, and then with the renewal of war, came further tightening of restrictions on movements of gold and foreign exchange. The suspension of the free convertibility of national currencies into gold or other readily acceptable means of international payment caused those anxious to move their money to politically or meteorologically more desirable climates to select other vehicles for the trip: black-market gold, jewelry, valuable paintings, rare postage stamps, diamonds, and Swiss-franc bank notes. Missing from that roster of standard flight capital instruments of the 1930s was one that allegedly became of some importance in the hands of fleeing Iranian royalists during the late 1970s. Heroin[2] boasted a value in relation to bulk that rivaled that of diamonds; and its liquidity was, and likely still is, even greater.

By the late 1970s a sophisticated network of financial institutions specialized in channeling funds to places of refuge and/or convenience, with the trail lost to the prying eye of the authorities by a maze of shell companies, coded bank accounts, and other paraphernalia of modern peekaboo finance. Presumably some of the fleeing Iranian royalists had been denied access to these more orthodox channels, to which the royal family itself was no stranger. However, the use of heroin as an instrument of capital flight did point back to the days when the kingpins of American 'organized crime' played a trail-blazing role in developing the financial mechanisms for playing shell games with the fiscal and monetary authorities.

Meyer Lansky's Enduring Legacy
Despite the strenuous efforts of Hollywood and the FBI to equate 'organized crime' in America with southern Italians, whose slightly off-white complexions made them inherently suspect to the American mainstream, American 'organized' crime has never been the preserve of any ethnic group. Nor, apparently, has any major ethnic community lacked representation in the crime fraternity.[3] However, the 'Mafia,' with its blood oaths and vows of silence, made particularly good theater; and it came to dominate the public imagination just when big-time crime in America was about to undergo a transformation moving it even further away from the stereotype. Crime was big business, and it followed a general trend in American enterprise – the emergence of an elite of financiers several levels removed from the shop floor or the street action. Thus, the demarcation line between 'legitimate' and 'illegitimate' business blurred,[4] for, as Bernie Cornfeld so aptly put it some three decades later, 'Money possesses a strange kind of purity.'

Conditions were ripe for the change. During the Great Depression, banks crumbled and credit lines of legitimate businesses were cut. Governments reacted to the crisis by reiterating their faith in 'sound money,' further slashing credit and cutting expenditures. Businesses, starved for funds, saw bootleggers and other criminal entrepreneurs with cash surpluses to recycle into legitimate investments. Moreover, the eventual repeal of Prohibition prompted big crime, like any big business in crisis, to seek new enterprises[5] – preferably those that generated fast cash surpluses.

As big-time crime expanded into gambling and drugs, there evolved a parallel network of financial institutions to handle the flow of funds. No longer did it suffice to acquire a chain of laundromats or car washes whose cash-based business could hide and 'launder' the funds from illicit activities.[6] Instead the 'mob' was impelled to create its own subterranean financial system, one impervious to the effects of fiscal or monetary policy, as indifferent to the tax collector's outstretched paw as it was to the central bankers' squeeze. In fact, with each new application of the principles of 'sound money,' with each new contraction of credit, more otherwise viable enterprises might end up in the hands of cash-rich and crime-linked financiers.

The sentimental favorite for making all this possible is Meyer Lansky. After the Internal Revenue Service (IRS) succeeded in 1931 in obtaining a conviction of Lansky's ally Al Capone on charges of tax evasion, the mob bosses woke up to the urgent need for proper laundry facilities. That same year, Salvatore 'Lucky' Luciano, Meyer Lansky's business partner, led a coup against the old Mafia leadership, preparing the way for entry into the previously forbidden heroin trade. The flourishing activities of the Lansky-Luciano mob, and the subsequent necessity for sophisticated methods of hiding and directing the flow of cash, proved to be the mother of offshore invention.[7]

In 1932 Meyer Lansky made his first major foray into Swiss banking. The immediate objective was to set up an account for Governor Huey Long of Louisiana, who had allowed the syndicate to open slot-machine emporia in New Orleans.[8] That pointed the way for the general flow of mob money to overseas havens.

Although some syndicate cash followed the northern route – New York to Canada to Switzerland – most, particularly during the 1950s and 1960s, went by the southern route. From mob-run banks in Miami the funds went either directly to Switzerland or to the Bahamas for local deposit or for transfer to Switzerland.[9]

The Lansky operation perfected the technique of the 'loan-back.' The first stage involved moving funds out of the US. Although couriers carrying cash were the favorite vehicle, money could also be moved abroad in the form of traveler's checks, cashier's checks (payable to the bearer with no questions asked), stocks with nominee ownership, bearer bonds, and even blank airline tickets. Once abroad, the funds were deposited in secret bank accounts. Lansky's preferred institution was the aptly named Exchange and Investment Bank in Geneva.[10]

Once safely behind the screen of Swiss bank secrecy laws, the money was ready to return home, with its origins and nature in disguise. Sometimes it stopped off en route in a Liechtenstein *anstalt* (an anonymous company with a single secret shareholder). In the final stage, the initiator of the cycle 'borrowed' the funds from the *anstalt* or directly from the Swiss bank, repaying the 'loan' with interest – to himself – while deducting the interest from his taxable income as a business expense.[11]

These antics went merrily on until Chase Manhattan Bank discovered that two of its employees, quite independently of Lansky's activities, were using the Exchange and Investment Bank to hide money embezzled from Chase. Thereupon the Lansky mob merely set up similar arrangements with another Geneva-based operation, the Banque de Crédit Internationale, or International Credit Bank (ICB).

This bank had been founded in 1959 by the late Tibor Rosenbaum, a man who had been active after the Second World War running guns from Czechoslovakia to the terrorist Stern gang in Palestine. Subsequently leaving Israel for Liberia, Rosenbaum was rewarded for unknown services rendered to Liberia's head of state with a Liberian diplomatic passport – a document that conveys about as much information about the activities of its holder as a Liberian flag reveals about those of the ships that fly it.

The 'diplomat' and his bank appear to have been innovators in the development of the machinery of modern peekaboo finance. ICB's principal legitimate activities were the collection of funds for Israel from the Jewish communities of Europe and acting as banker to joint business ventures of European Jews and the state of Israel. But it also financed the acquisition and movement of weapons to Israel and its allies, particularly in Africa and central America, and reputedly acted as paymaster for Mossad, the Israeli secret service, in Europe.

Yet another function became that of Swiss depository for the skim from Lansky's casinos. And another was its role as banker to the couriers in Bernie Cornfeld's employ, who were busily spiriting tens, perhaps hundreds, of millions of dollars out of developing countries in defiance of their exchange-control regulations and to the detriment of their prospects for economic development.[12]

Pentagon Capitalism and the Dollar Glut

Perhaps unconsciously, Bernie Cornfeld had gleaned a special insight into the operational mechanisms of international finance during the 1960s. For over the decade between the creation of a post-Second World War financial order and Bernie Cornfeld's entry into the mutual-fund business, the international financial system had evolved in directions that promised remarkable profit opportunities to those who grasped the methods of 'recycling.'

After fifteen years of depression and war, of protectionism and exchange controls, in 1944 the allied powers began to plan the institutional framework for the postwar economic and financial order. At the top of the agenda was the need to reconstruct the international payments system. The prewar ideal (which had worked only very imperfectly) was a financial system in which each country fixed the value of its currency in terms of gold (e.g., so many paper piasters to a troy ounce of gold). It then allowed the free import and export of its national money, and guaranteed the convertibility of that money into gold on the demand of the holder. To the degree that the system really worked, the participating countries had no real control over credit conditions at home, as the domestic money supply would rise and fall according to the state of their international payments position.

In the postwar world, the return to such an 'ideal' system was impossible. So much gold had fled to the United States in the 1930s that most other countries' currencies could not support large-scale demands for conversion into gold. Moreover, many countries, scarred by the social and economic effects of the Great Depression, refused to surrender to an automatic international payments system their ability to influence domestic financial conditions.

Out of the 1944 deliberations came an alternative institutional structure, of which the most important components were the International Monetary Fund and the World Bank. The IMF was to provide short-term financing to cover temporary balance-of-payments problems. The bank was to provide long-term financial assistance, initially to support the reconstruction of Europe and subsequently to promote the economic development of countries emerging from the control of the old European imperial powers.

The IMF was to superintend the creation of a new international payments mechanism in which conversion of currencies into gold would occur indirectly – all countries would eventually fix the value of their currencies in terms of the US dollar, which would be convertible on demand into gold. Although gold was the foundation of the new international financial edifice, the arrangement reflected two practical realities: the concentration of ownership of the world's gold stocks in the hands of the US government; and the dominant position of the US economy (and therefore of the US dollar) in international economic and diplomatic affairs.

Such a system had to assure both stability and adequate liquidity. To achieve the first, the IMF was to supervise exchange-rate policies of member countries to guarantee that any exchange-rate changes they undertook would be 'orderly' and preceded by consultation. In practice, this meant that during the 1950s industrialized countries allowed the IMF to learn about changes in their exchange rates from the newspapers the morning after the event; and that during the 1960s, IMF officials had ample opportunity to browbeat the developing countries, which were beginning to queue for aid, into unwanted exchange-rate changes that suited the IMF. Developing countries facing balance-of-payments problems – whether caused by capital flight, by wars, by natural disasters, by collapsing prices of their commodity exports to the industrialized countries, by rising prices of their manufactured imports from the industrial countries, or by the IMF itself – could borrow from the IMF to finance the payments deficit. But to get IMF money they had to pay the price of allowing their economic policy to be shaped to meet the policy objectives of the IMF.

Central to the IMF's objectives were cutting down the size and influence of the public sector in developing economies and shifting productive resources from industries that served the domestic market to those oriented toward exports. Governments were to move from positions of budget deficits to surpluses, cutting down on the level of public-sector economic activity to free space for the private sector. At the same time, they were to try to produce a surplus in their international commodity trade and, therefore, a net inflow of foreign currency, which could then be used to pay interest and dividends to foreign creditors.

The techniques for accomplishing these objectives included credit squeezes; tax hikes; reductions of government expenditures on social services and of subsidies to essential goods and services; dismantling of controls that inhibited the export of foreign exchange, especially the payment abroad of interest and dividends to foreign investors; and devaluation of the currency to raise the cost of imports and reduce the price of exports.

For the developing countries, the programs were more often than not disastrous. They undermined prospects for long-term development and depressed living standards of all but the rich, who found their ability to stash funds in Swiss banks considerably enhanced by the IMF's prescriptions for 'liberalization' of foreign-exchange controls. Public-sector cutbacks, far from freeing space for private initiative, as the IMF theory argued they should, hampered business investment by forcing governments to cut down on essential infrastructure – roads, schools for training a skilled labor force, investment in public health, and so on. Those cutbacks helped generate waves of social and political unrest that encouraged yet more capital flight. Exchange-rate changes drove up the hard-currency cost of making payments on their foreign debt, and of purchasing essential imports. Yet such exchange-rate changes often did more to drive down export revenues through falling prices than to expand those revenues through increasing export volumes.

As a result, only the most desperate developing countries went to the IMF for financial aid. Most relied, whenever possible, on development aid from Western governments or on foreign investment by multinational corporations.[13] They would meet every new balance-of-payments crisis with pilgrimages to the aid agencies or supplications to the corporate giants, instead of by drawing on the resources of the IMF.

The second objective of the postwar reconstruction of the international monetary system was to create a large and potentially expandable pool of internationally acceptable money or monies to replace gold, which not only tended to be concentrated in the hands of the US government, but increased in supply only very slowly. The solution was for all IMF members to pay into a common pot of currencies, everything from afghanis to zlotys. The IMF would allow members in need to borrow from this pot, at a price that got steeper each time.

Again the reality was slightly different. Although all currencies were equal, some were more equal than others. It was not the IMF's casserole of currencies that provided the new money to fuel economic growth and the expansion of trade after the war. Rather, in the late 1940s and early 1950s, it was the Marshall Plan, the American government's emergency financial-aid program for saving Europe from the specter of communism and American industry from the specter of postwar recession. American aid financed reconstruction, underwrote European purchases of American goods, and relieved much of the world's shortage of foreign exchange. In the early 1960s, a much less important source of foreign exchange was Western aid payments to developing countries. Then another, initially unexpected, mechanism for supplying the world with liquidity emerged.

'Pentagon Capitalism'[14] in the 1960s was a tale of two deficits. Embroiled in an increasingly unpopular war in Southeast Asia, the American government refused to take the political risks associated with financing the war with higher taxes, particularly when there was a handy alternative. While the cost of military procurement at home helped drive the American government budget into deficit, military spending abroad had similar effects on the American balance of payments. However, since the US dollar was the currency on which the international payments system was based, it was the preferred instrument in which countries held foreign-exchange reserves. Finding themselves flooded with dollars by the US balance-of-payments deficit, other countries logically responded by investing the excess in treasury bills sold by the US government to help finance its budget deficit. In effect, the US Marines had replaced Meyer Lansky's couriers, and the European central banks arranged the 'loan-back.'

For the US, the system was a godsend. Instead of having to make the traditional choice between guns and butter, the US could have more of both, thanks to the way that the international monetary system unloaded much of the burden of financing the American budget deficit onto the rest of the world. While the artillery boomed, so did the domestic economy. When the mechanism was explained to the late Herman Kahn – lifeguard of the era's chief cold war 'think tank' and a man who popularized the notion that it was possible to emerge smiling from a global nuclear conflagration – he reacted with visible delight. Kahn exclaimed excitedly, 'We've pulled off the biggest ripoff in history! We've run rings around the British empire!'[15] Bernie Cornfeld must have been happy, too.

Swords into IOS-Shares

Tibor Rosenbaum, of Geneva's Banque de Crédit Internationale, claimed credit for suggesting the idea of an international investment trust to Bernie Cornfeld, who was searching for a way to make his dream – bringing capitalism to the little people – come true. Perhaps so; for in 1962 IOS established its first mutual fund, the International Investment Trust, in Luxembourg, that renowned refuge for the small and forgotten man. However, the real pioneer of the concept of an offshore mutual fund supported by 'banks' in appropriate locations was neither Cornfeld nor Rosenbaum. It was Allen J. Lefferdink, who moved offshore to Bermuda after the IRS and the Securities and Exchange Commission (SEC) broke up his onshore financial empire.[16]

Lefferdink was among the first to appreciate the potential for 'financial services' to American personnel in Vietnam eager to get their funds, however earned, out of the country. He also explored the capital-flight business in Latin America. And he ran mutual funds, as well as 'banks,' out of peekaboo financial centers. (Their precise location was periodically revised, depending on just where his creditors and 'bank' depositors were searching for him.)

Although he was a pioneer, the scale of Lefferdink's operations paled beside those of Cornfeld, the former Trotskyist turned B'nai B'rith activist turned international hot money operative.[17] Cornfeld's notion of 'bringing capitalism to the people' was a fashionable twist to the traditional game of bringing the people's money to the capitalists – though his definition of 'the people' seemed a curious one for a former Trotskyist. Less than 1% of the investors in his mutual funds accounted for over 25% of the total money put into them.[18]

With the Pentagon spending spree fueling a sustained domestic economic boom, a bull market swept the American stock exchanges. Conglomerates were the prevailing fad, and money for investment in their shares poured into the US from the offshore mutual funds. By the time the conglomerate boom collapsed in 1968, there were 165 offshore mutual funds representing assets of about $3.5 billion; of them the IOS group accounted for $2.5 billion. Apart from the attractions it offered by the use of its network of offshore banks and trust companies for laundering money and evading taxes, IOS was admirably suited to take advantage of the crosscurrents of international finance and the peculiarities of the postwar international monetary system.

While Allen Lefferdink was exploring the Vietnam market, Bernie Cornfeld was well established in Europe, peddling mutual-fund shares to American servicemen, particularly those stationed in Germany. His next big market was among the employees of the increasing numbers of American transnational corporations. By feeding off the growing pool of dollars resulting from US military expenditure abroad and US overseas investment, Cornfeld entrenched IOS as an integral part of the international dollar recycling mechanism. For many years, it was the largest foreign-based institutional investor on the American stock exchanges, and it was the largest private-sector vehicle for rechanneling the dollar overflow washing about European money and capital markets into industrial investments in the US, particularly during the conglomerate boom of the late 1960s.[19] The IOS 'recycling' activities received virtual government endorsement when, from 1968 to 1971, US officials suggested that countries politically and financially embarrassed by the flood of dollars put some of their excess dollars in the US stock market.

Recycling dollars from US servicemen and employees of transnational corporations was certainly not the only activity of IOS in the 1960s. Indeed, in the early part of the decade it may not even have been the most important of them, as Bernie Cornfeld added to his other distinctions that of anticipating one of the principal ways in which the recycling mechanism would work in a later era.

The capital-flight business was excellent in the 1950s and early 1960s. The Korean War had induced a commodities trade boom that temporarily filled the coffers of some developing countries with foreign exchange. A decade later, foreign-aid flows from the US and other Western countries kept them topped up. This was especially welcome in those recipient countries where it was simply assumed that the 'aid' would go more or less directly into the Swiss bank accounts of their heads of state.

The capital-flight business was also facilitated by the IMF pressing countries to dismantle exchange controls. In theory, the IMF focused most of its demands for liberalization on 'current account' transactions (the international trade in goods and services), allowing most countries to leave intact restrictions on capital movements (the international flows of investment funds). But there was a catch. Inflows of money resulting from overseas borrowing or foreign investment were defined as a capital movement. Logically, the outflow of interest and dividend payments on loans and investments should also have been defined as a capital movement, leaving countries free to control it. Instead, interest and dividend payments on foreign debts were defined as (nonrestrictable) current-account transactions – payment for investors' 'services.' Thus, the barn door was left wide open for capital to gallop out.

A country could still, in theory, impose exchange controls on the flow of repayment on the *principal* of its debt. But if interest rates were pushed high enough, the repayment of principal could be disguised as an outflow of 'service' payments on the debt. Besides, there was a plethora of techniques for simply evading the existing exchange controls.

One such technique, suitable for small sums, was the use of airline tickets. A first-class airline ticket to some faraway place would be purchased; but the ticket rather than the passenger would depart, to be cashed in for hard currency on landing. Another technique was the tried-and-true cash courier, wherever geography, smuggling, bribing of central bank personnel, and/or tourism provided a sufficient supply of hard currency.

A favorite technique appropriate to larger-scale movements was phony invoicing – reporting to the central bank and/or exchange authorities a higher price for imports than was actually paid, or a lower price for exports than was actually received. The difference was placed in secret hard-currency accounts abroad. At its crudest, this technique dovetailed into simple smuggling.

Most capital probably took flight through phony declarations to the central-bank and exchange-control authorities, or through smuggling commodities. But there was still lots of work for the cash courier. Some were free-lance professionals; others were salaried employees of Swiss- and Caribbean-based banks; yet ·others worked directly for organized crime. Indeed, some diversified, for it was easy enough to shift from carrying a heroin dealer's cash to conduiting flight capital.[20]

Just as the carriers and routes were the same as those used for hiding and laundering criminal money, so, too, were the techniques. Money was moved abroad for deposit in a secret account, then 'lent' back to the initiator of the transaction. He would declare it to his central bank, on whose books it would be entered as a legitimate foreign bank loan. The recipient of the 'loan' could legally draw foreign exchange sufficient to repay' the loan with interest. In effect, the country incurred an *increase* in its foreign indebtedness through the very act of exporting hard currency.[21] And 'repaying' the loan doubled the drain on its foreign-exchange resources.

In would come the IMF to examine the books, telling the country it was living beyond its means and prescribing a strong dose of austerity to assure that enough productive resources were diverted from domestic consumption and investment into exports to service the external 'debt.' Almost inevitably the treatment included further liberalization of exchange controls, which further facilitated the movement of funds outside the country.

In the 1960s, one of the top hot-money dealers was American mob 'paperhanger' Frank Peroff. Like Bernie Cornfeld, he literally had been in the flight-capital business. His fleet of small planes allegedly carried currency out of Chile, Peru, and Argentina in violation of exchange-control regulations, and emeralds out of Colombia in defiance of government export monopoly rules. He transported stolen diamonds from Europe to the US and carried the skim from the casinos from the US to Europe. He trafficked in all manner of hot and counterfeit paper – bank notes, securities, forged certificates of deposit and traveler's checks, even passports. Counterfeit US currency was in great demand. In Africa it was traded for the gold and diamonds that miners would smuggle out under the eyes of the mine security guards; and in the early years of the cocaine trade, counterfeit was cut half and half with real bills to purchase the drugs.[22] But even Peroff was a bush pilot in the international flight-capital trade compared to Cornfeld's IOS.

In the 1960s, with the great upsurge of interest in the problem of economic 'development,' IOS salesmen started combing the developing world for funds seeking anonymity and investment opportunities in American equity. Thus, as civil war ravaged Nigeria and international relief for the traumatized civilian population rolled in, IOS was on the scene to help: the international aid funds often wound up safe in Geneva. IOS men were also on the front lines during the military upheavals in the old Belgian Congo (Zaire), when the mineral-rich Katanga (Shaba) province attempted to secede. IOS men too saw service in Liberia; and it was when they tried to sell shares to 'diplomat' Tibor Rosenbaum that the capital-flight phase of IOS operations really got off the ground. By joining forces, Cornfeld and Rosenbaum could use a switch-sale tactic, offering customers both a Swiss bank account and participation in an American mutual fund. IOS salesmen doubled as cash couriers; coded accounts were created in Rosenbaum's ICB in Geneva (until IOS established its own comically named Overseas Development Bank); and ICB 'lent' the funds to the account holder to purchase a stake in a Cornfeld mutual fund.[23]

Latin America, not Africa, was the main field of operation. Although IOS appears to have pioneered the recycling of 'petrodollars' from Venezuela and perhaps cocadollars from Colombia, its richest market was Brazil. There IOS maintained safe houses where cruzeiros could be converted into hard currency and turned over to a network of airline employees who would arrange a pleasant flight. The money need move only to Montevideo, Uruguay, where the Foreign Trade Bank would arrange its wire transfer to Geneva.[24]

Unfortunately for IOS, a 1966 raid by the Brazilian police exposed a list of more than 10,000 customers whose funds had been illegally exported. Increasing and increasingly harsh clashes with host governments followed. Operations received another setback in 1967 when *Life* published its famous exposé of a joint IOS-Lansky mob courier carrying cash to Rosenbaum's Geneva bank. Then, in 1968, hopes for a major expansion into the Middle East were dashed by a conflict with Iran over violation of exchange-control regulations, and by the loss of Beirut, the Middle East's main capital-flight and hot-money mill, when the government of Lebanon applied to IOS the Arab League boycott of firms doing business with Israel.[25]

These events effectively marked the end of the developing-country capital-flight phase of IOS operations, though a few scandals were still to come. However, IOS was well established in the European market, and capital-flight activities were redirected to Italy. In short order IOS became a leading conduit for money contravening Italian exchange-control laws, as the firm brought to the Italian middle class the hitherto aristocratic art of capital flight.

Despite Cornfeld's periodic disclaimers, developing-country flight capital and conventionally criminal money seem to have been essential in getting IOS established. Investigators claimed that the firm operated on the assumption that 10% to 20% of the nearly $2.5 billion it had under management was effectively permanent capital – for the simple reason that the owners of the money could not risk exposure by withdrawal. This permanent capital gave IOS a greater capacity than other 'open-ended' mutual funds to gamble with the shareholders' money.[26]

IOS was a global empire, with hundreds of component companies and, at its peak, nine banks in its stable. Hiding behind the corporate secrecy laws of its nominal headquarters, Panama, and behind the bank secrecy laws of its operational headquarters, Switzerland, IOS was able relatively easily to swallow money and regurgitate it as loans or investments anywhere in the world. And before IOS came to a spectacular and scandal-racked end in the early 1970s, it had inspired other financial institutions, including major American banks, to follow its plunge into the global pool of hot money.

2

Eurodollars and Nonsense

Until the late 1960s, most banks in North America could still pretend to a pattern of behavior consistent with their public image. Bankers, no less than policemen, doctors, and lawyers, need to project a professional mystique to improve their cash-flow position and to cover up colleagues' periodic gross violations of professional ethics. Long before television created the stereotypes of the tough and incorruptible cop, the twenty-six-hour-a-day MD, and the razor-sharp lawyer brimming over with anger at the plight of the socio-economic underdog, the public was convinced that the banker was a sensible, staid, and conservative custodian of the widow's mite. Many a widow, and a multitude of orphans, came to regret that it was not so.

Once upon a time, there may have been some truth to the stereotype. Most banks used to be concerned with 'asset management,' taking deposits and finding safe, maturity-matching loans and investments to assure a modest but steady return on funds entrusted to their care. The public was partially protected because banks were required by law to hold fixed ratios of cash or immediately liquifiable government securities as reserves against possible demands for deposit withdrawals. And the ultimate collateral for depositors was the permanent capital invested in the bank by shareholders, against which bad loans and investments would be written off before depositors' funds were endangered. Sensible, staid, and conservative bankers voluntarily maintained high ratios of capital to deposits; while sensible, staid, and conservative governments entrenched the requirement in law.

From the early nineteenth century, US law was designed to block interstate branch banking and to defend regional savings from the Dracula instincts of the large banks of the principal urban 'money centers.' Furthermore, virtually alone among major Western countries, the US central bank was decentralized into several regionally based

31

Federal Reserve Banks. Although never as effective as its architects hoped, this partial decentralization lent some truth to the stereotype of small-town and regional banks and bankers. But in the large, urban centers of the US and in places such as Canada, where banks have long been allowed to run amok, this always was a myth.

Big banks are big-business bureaucracies in which the principal management concern historically has been its position in the hierarchy of power. Furthermore, the banks have been asset-growth-rate maximizers rather than profit maximizers. Thus, big banks, in their ambition to become bigger banks, were more concerned with their Fortune 500 ranking than with their credit rating. The faster a bank grew, the higher its shares traded. Perhaps investors had learned the historical lesson that political and financial power are inseparable; and that big banks, no matter how badly run, are always entitled to the free lunch at the public trough that the apostles of Born-Again Capitalism are so keen to deny to economically disadvantaged American schoolchildren. Moreover, the faster the bank grew, the faster was the rise through the bureaucratic ranks of those officers whose concern was with shoveling huge lumps of cash into the big borrowers' maw and then finding the deposits necessary to finance the loan.

The upshot was that big banks became liability managers, making high-profile loans and then searching for the money to assure that their commitments could be honored when the borrower attempted to spend the money the bank had lent him. As the obsession with competitive growth caused the 'quality' of loans to deteriorate, the banks' scramble for money intensified. At best, they became essentially unconcerned with the source of the deposits; and some American banks on some occasions consciously solicited money from dubious, if not overtly illegal, sources. The widow's mite and the temporary corporate working balance, the dictator's loot and the drug trafficker's suitcase of cash all glistened with the purity about which Bernie Cornfeld waxed so eloquent.

Chase-ing Flight Capital

The importance of flight capital as a potential source of deposits became increasingly evident to the big American money-center institutions during the 1960s. Flight capital had obvious advantages over other sources of deposits. The Swiss experience indicated that it was frequently possible for a bank to facilitate capital flight and to keep its subsequent whereabouts secret, in exchange for below-market interest rates on the deposits they received.

Moreover, as Bernie Cornfeld had discovered, flight capital, like criminal money, was often different in practical terms than it appeared to be in accounting terms. If its origins were sufficiently dubious, the need for secrecy might well make it behave less like a 'deposit' and more like the long-term capital resources of the financial institution. This was an attribute of flight capital that Swiss and Hong Kong banks had long appreciated, and in 1968 IOS created a VIP department to cater to the especially rich and/or politically influential. But American money-center banks were beginning to wake up to their potential as well. Citibank had already created a 'private international banking' division to help pull the money of wealthy foreigners into the US. Its major competitors were also eyeing the hot-money hoard.

Early in 1966, a draft memorandum on flight capital was circulating among economists at the New York headquarters of the Chase Manhattan Bank. Whether the contents had been seen by the bank directors is unknown, as is the level at which the memo was circulated, but its contents are revealing. The memo stated in part:

> The US is probably the second major flight money center in the world, but with little probability of rivalling Switzerland for the foreseeable future. Like Switzerland, flight money probably flows to the US from every country in the world. It is handled almost exclusively by the major New York and Miami brokers, lawyers, and leading commercial banks. Officers of CMB International Department and Trust Department confirm that CMB Home Office itself handles a reasonable amount of foreign flight money. However this is insignificant relative to the total potentially available.
>
> There is general consensus among CMB officers and both US and European experts in the field that *US-based and US-controlled entities are badly penalized in competing for flight money with the Swiss or other foreign flight money centers over the long run.* [Emphasis in original.] This is because of the following interrelated factors:
> (a) The demonstrated ability of the US Treasury, Justice Department, CIA, and FBI to subpoena client records, attach client accounts, and force testimony from US officers of US-controlled entities, with proper US court back-up.
> (b) The restrictive US investment and brokerage regulations and policies, which limit the flexibility and secrecy of investment activity.

(c) The US estate tax and US withholding tax on foreign investments.

(d) The role of the US as a major contestant in the Cold War, and resulting likelihood that investments through a US entity may be exposed to any hostility or freeze of assets occurring as a result of the Cold War.

(e) The generally held (and partly unwarranted) view of many sophisticated foreigners that US investment managers are naive and inexperienced in manipulation of foreign funds, especially in foreign markets.

Despite the above limitations, the US has broad appeal to flight money holders in other respects. These include: The largest and most active securities markets in the world, assuring both liquidity and diversification. Ease of transfer and mechanical handling of investments, partly through US banks' worldwide network. The world's leading reserve currency, the US dollar. In recent years, the unmatched financial stability and one of the highest levels of economic growth of any major industrial nation. Finally, negligible probability of revolution or confiscation, and low probability of inconvertibility.

Among the havens for flight capital that the Chase economists cited as worthy of note, if not emulation, was Beirut. After the creation of Israel in 1948, Beirut replaced Haifa as commercial center of the Mashreq (the Arab East). After the Suez crisis of 1956, it superseded Cairo as Europe's business beachhead in the area. Lebanon's geographic location, absence of exchange controls, and tight bank secrecy laws made Beirut well situated as a regional hot-money refuge and flight-capital center. It was soon hosting itinerant petrodollars, as the elites in Arabian-Persian Gulf states built up reserve funds for emergencies, political and economic; the Lebanese banks would recycle the hot money into local real estate and the American stock market.

At the time the Chase memo on flight capital was drafted, the doyen of Lebanese banks, holding 20% of the country's total deposits, was Intra Bank. It was created in 1951 by Palestinian refugee Yousef Beidas, and by 1966 the assets of the bank's parent holding company included control of the Port Authority of Beirut, Middle East Airlines, the Casino du Liban (the world's largest), the country's major radio station, hotels, movie studios, cement plants, and choice real estate on the Champs Elysées and Park Avenue. More than any other factor, Intra Bank had made Beirut the region's financial center.

But Beidas's creation was politically very vulnerable. The Lebanese financial establishment resented the control of a large part of the country's infrastructure by a Palestinian interloper. Furthermore, Beidas was funding the rise of el-Fatah, soon to be the principal military and political arm of the Palestinian Diaspora. Although el-Fatah was founded and controlled by men of intensely conservative social views, its supposed radicalism alarmed one of Intra Bank's major depositors, the late King Feisal of Saudi Arabia, whose pathological anticommunism would make Ronald Reagan blush.

In October 1966, the bank was short on cash: there had been losses in gold, copper, and American equity. It had tied up money in real estate, and a jump in eurobank interest rates on dollar deposits diverted hot money from Beirut. Saudi Arabia chose that time to pull its deposits. A general run began, forcing the Lebanese government to declare a three-day bank holiday. The Lebanese central bank and government, perhaps sensing an opportunity to strip Beidas of choice assets, refused aid apart from a small loan secured on Intra's shares in the casino, airline, and port. Chase Manhattan and several other American institutions then froze Intra's deposits in New York, declaring the deposits would be held hostage until Intra repaid loans from Chase.

Whether Chase's actions were designed to hamper the recovery of Intra Bank is unclear. But Beirut's major foreign banks did emerge strengthened from the affair, for the money fleeing Lebanese banks often merely ran across the street into the waiting arms of the foreign banks, Chase among them.[1] Beidas followed the hot-money trail to Switzerland, and a subsequent, politically convenient, demise.

Footloose and Reserve Free
Although Intra Bank was a mere 425th among world banks in total assets, its collapse represented the world's greatest bank catastrophe since the Second World War. And although the bank's rise and subsequent fall could be ascribed at least partly to 'political' factors, the situation should have highlighted the dangers inherent in financial institutions relying on hot and homeless money for funding their lending and investment activity.

In the wake of the collapse, there were many revelations of 'irregularities' in Intra's operations: payment of dividends by Intra-controlled companies that were losing money; loans to directors that greatly exceeded the maximum permitted by Lebanese law; illicit diversion of deposits; the use of shares held in trust to secure Beidas's personal loans from Chase and Banco di Roma (the money was then channeled back into Intra to cover the liquidity gap), and so on. All these accusations were likely true – and likely normal behavior for a Lebanese bank. After the crash they were given wide currency, probably to justify the failure of the Lebanese authorities to aid the bank. But Intra Bank's real problem was not its day-to-day irregularities; rather, it was the long-term regularities, namely its dependence on hot money for funding loans and investments.[2]

Furthermore, by the time of the Intra Bank affair, there had been a fundamental change in the rules of the hot-money game. Although hot money still had to hide its origins and sometimes its existence, that need for secrecy trapped it inside the system, but not inside any particular component of the system. The increasingly competitive scramble for this money caused the institutional and geographic choices of refuge to widen greatly. So, too, did the resulting threat to particular banks involved in the scramble.

However, few banks drew the necessary conclusions from the Intra affair; and the major Western banks, led by those of the United States, leaped headfirst into the whirlpool.

The critical innovation of the major American banks to gain access to the growing pool of hot and homeless money was a piece of paper called a negotiable certificate of deposit (CD). Introduced by Citibank in 1961, a CD in effect (though not in law) was a security the bank could sell to a corporation or individual with a temporary surplus of cash. The buyer could either hold it to maturity and pick up all accrued interest, or, if short of money in the interim, sell it back to the bank at a slight penalty or to a third party. The CD gave banks, which were traditionally confined in their search for deposit funds to the short-term money market, an entry into the long-term capital market. There, they could compete with governments and corporations trying to raise money through the sale of bills and bonds. Then, in 1964, the CD became cosmopolitan.

That year Bernie Cornfeld reportedly went to Citibank with a proposition. Observing that many wealthy Europeans wanted to 'avoid' taxes, IOS proposed that Citibank issue a 'eurodollar' CD to accommodate them. Thus emerged the financial instrument that would be critical to the banks' penetration of the offshore pool of dollar liquidity that subsequently became known as the eurodollar market.[3] Thus, too, the offshore pool of liquidity and the tapping of it by the major US banks became inextricably bound up with the search by hot money for a haven from the tax collectors' scrutiny and for ways to circumvent domestic monetary restrictions.

When a domestic banking system 'creates' money, in the form

of deposits against which its customers can draw checks, its creative urges are ultimately constrained by the need to hold reserves of cash (bank notes or deposits with the central bank). But the eurodollar market has had no such reserve requirement. Seemingly, banks can create deposits against which borrowers can draw, effectively without restriction. To some amazed observers euromoney appears to multiply even faster than the photosynthetic action of the trees on which it usually grows. The eurodollar thus seems like a snowball of liquidity rolling down an alpine slope.

The reality is a little more mundane. Far from representing liquidity multiplying without restriction, most of the more than a trillion dollars' 'worth' of assets/liabilities in the eurodollar market derives from transactions between banks. The net impact of interbank dealings on world purchasing power is virtually nonexistent. Because of the lack of reserve requirements, banks can lend deposits back and forth to each other, puffing the hypothetical value of assets/liabilities on their books almost with impunity. However, the result has little more effect on the real world than to increase the proportion of their salaries the banks' accountants spend on nostrums to relieve excess stomach acidity.

Nonetheless, apart from interbank transactions, hundreds of billions of dollars' worth of deposits have flowed into the eurocurrency system from depositors outside it, and similar billons' worth of loans have gone out again to final borrowers. The interesting questions are *from where, to where,* and *why*.[4]

The absence of reserve requirements is important to the market not because it permits the unrestricted 'creation' of money, but because it allows *all* the deposits to be rechanneled into interest-bearing loans. That in turn permits the eurobanks to offer depositors higher rates of interest than would be possible on domestically booked business. Lack of regulation also means complete anonymity could be offered to depositors, a significant factor in the creation as well as the subsequent growth of the market. The more often funds can be shifted from place to place and bank to bank, the greater the obscurity about their origin or ultimate destiny. Even the myth about the capacity of the euromarket to 'create' money plays a role in assuring anonymity, for it logically precludes anyone from asking whence the money actually came.

According to legend, the practice of holding and lending dollar-denominated deposits outside the US started when the USSR, fearing a possible freeze of the dollar component of its foreign-exchange reserves by the US government, opened dollar accounts in London banks. Although others followed suit, the eurodollar for some time remained a marginal legal oddity. Then in the late 1960s the market began to expand rapidly.

Part of the expansion was due to the growth of the US balance-of-payments deficits, which pumped increasing dollar liquidity onto world money markets. Part was due to measures taken by the American government to curb the inflationary effects of the Vietnam War and the capital outflow that went with it.

The US government tightened credit at home, which simply caused the big-money-center banks to finance more of their loans offshore by selling CDs in the expanding euromarket. It was an arrangement repeated all too often in the years to come. Illicit funds hiding in the euromarket could join legitimate money in loans to the international branches of American business firms. These, in turn, could lend the money to their parent companies in the US. Thus, the large US firms with international connections escaped the impact of the credit squeeze that hurt those competitors without such connections; and an array of tax evaders and flight capitalists might find themselves involved in an interesting variant of the old Meyer Lansky loan-back scam.

In addition, the US government tried to attack the capital outflow directly in order to prevent the balance-of-payments deficit from worsening. The gimmicks included measures to discourage foreign borrowing in the US, curbs on US bank lending abroad, and incentives for American corporations operating around the world to finance their expansion without drawing more funds from the US. In response, transnational firms kept more of their surpluses outside the US, and sought more dollar-denominated loans from offshore sources; and the US banks greatly increased both their branches and the proportion of their business conducted outside the US.

By the late 1960s the eurodollar market was neither exclusively European nor concerned only with dollars. Other countries and non-American businesses discovered the advantages of lending and borrowing offshore: avoiding taxes, evading exchange controls, and escaping the effects of domestic credit restrictions. 'Booking' branches of international banks proliferated in offshore centers offering tax concessions, freedom from regulation, tight secrecy laws, and a geographic position that facilitated the service of money escaping neighboring jurisdictions. For if anonymity was what the original eurodollar market offered the USSR, that same anonymity served asset strippers, drug peddlers, private arms dealers, tax evaders, and national intelligence agencies, not to speak of 'ordinary' citizens concerned with economic security in their declining years, free from the smell of the favela or the scent of the secret police.

Treasure Island

Tax havens, offshore banking systems, and peekaboo financial centers have long been essential to the financial aristocracy of Europe. Monaco has long housed treasures from France and Italy; Andorra taps the traffic of goods and money between Spain and France; the Channel Islands do likewise between Britain and the Continent; Luxembourg opens its bank doors to the secret savings of Belgium; until recently the Vatican bank blessed the flow of Italian flight capital that passed through en route to Switzerland; and Switzerland rolls out the welcome mat for the wandering wealth of the entire world, aided by a curiously itinerant tax haven.

When the tiny state of Liechtenstein emerged from the First World War, its economy was shattered and its financial system ruined. After breaking its old links with Austria in the 1920s, Liechtenstein set sail for more propitious waters, eventually mooring itself off Switzerland with a partial customs and currency union.

Liechtenstein was soon 'open for business,' offering a unique form of corporate structure, the *anstalt*, a single-shareholder company protected by the world's tightest corporate secrecy laws. By 1975, its capital city of Vaduz boasted 25,000 people and 50,000 cosmopolitan corporate citizens. The KGB and CIA allegedly established *anstalten* to handle covert funding of coups and revolutions; South Africa established one for its state arms company, ARMSCOR; Poland then apparently opened one in order to sell arms covertly to the South African regime it did not recognize; Israel ran much of its global arms dealing through Liechtenstein; the USSR allegedly used an *anstalt* for the secret purchase of strategic materials from Western companies. Not least, as the proceeds of white-collar crime poured into Switzerland, Swiss bankers would use *anstalten* to hide the money they were stealing from their clients.[5]

These European banking centers were joined in the 1960s and 1970s by a growing number of localities, whose association with hot money began when Spanish treasure fleets were transporting the loot of the Americas. Legends abound of pirates appropriating the treasure and burying it in the sands of some tropical island paradise in the Caribbean or, later, in the South Pacific.

The turning point in the modern history of peekaboo finance in the Caribbean came in 1959, when Fidel Castro unseated one of Meyer Lansky's principal business associates and closed the syndicate casinos and drug-trafficking facilities. Former Cuban strongman Fulgencio Batista flew off to a prosperous Miami exile on the money that Lansky had stashed away for him in Swiss banks while the Lansky mob dreamed of staging, with the aid of CIA-trained Cuban exiles, their own Douglas MacArthur-style 'return.'[6] But the failure of the Bay of Pigs invasion forced the mob to consider alternative locations, and set the CIA to haunting Caribbean and Florida-based financial institutions for funding of the continued military action against Castro. Operatives of both groups could periodically meet and exchange pleasantries while depositing hot money in the air-conditioned comfort of vacationland banks.

Among the favored locations was the Bahamas, where much of Bernie Cornfeld's IOS infrastructure was headquartered. There Lansky applied the lesson learned in Cuba, namely, that democratic regimes have greater potential ability than fading autocrats to guarantee the mob's rights to other people's property. He backed Lynden Pindling's Progressive Liberal Party, which attempted to articulate the aspirations of the black majority and promised desperately needed social reforms. A carefully concocted scandal discredited the incumbent regime and brought the Progressive Liberal Party to power: Lansky and his associates were in business. The casino boom coincided with the expansion of Bahamian offshore banking activities, and the subsequent growth of legitimate banking transactions provided ideal cover for a similar increase in money laundering.

Lansky was not alone in appreciating an island paradise that shared the time zone but not the weather of New York and boasted some of the world's tightest bank secrecy regulations. To the Bahamas came one Robert Vesco, then looting from IOS several hundred million of the dollars that Bernie Cornfeld had attracted through facilitating capital flight and tax 'avoidance' around the world.[7]

Robert Vesco was the whiz kid of the conglomerate craze that swept American equity markets in the late 1960s, partly sustained by Cornfeld's energetic 'recycling.' Vesco would take over one company with another, often one much smaller than the company acquired. The loans that funded the takeover would be serviced out of the treasury of the newly acquired company. Vesco's technique also worked for his acquisition of IOS, which had been swept with scandal and a wave of demands for redemption of its shares.[8]

Vesco was used to working the interstices of the international financial system. Between 1971 and 1973, hidden behind the bank and corporate secrecy laws of Switzerland, Panama, the Bahamas, and other, similar locales, Vesco forced IOS to sell off huge amounts of its blue-chip investments. He funneled the cash through his Luxembourg and Bahamas banks, and 'invested' it in a series of shell companies, which in turn 'invested' or 'lent' it to other shells. At the time, the loot was estimated at $224 million minimum; the SEC later jumped its bottom estimate to $392 million. Ten years after the event, the army of lawyers and accountants who were still unscrambling the dealings claimed to have retrieved $500 million, including some interest, leaving Vesco still holding at least $100 million. The uncertainty about the totals probably reflects both Vesco's skill in financial manipulation and the reluctance of some mutual-fund shareholders to reveal their stake in the companies.[9]

During his Bahamian exile, Vesco made unsuccessful bids for control of the local casinos, tried to buy the Exchange and Investment Bank of Geneva, and attempted to pick up Intra Investment Company, sensing that the remnants of Yousef Beidas's empire contained even greater opportunities for loot than did IOS.[10] He also busied himself with Bahamian politics, following Lansky's lead in funding the Progressive Liberal Party and lending money progressively and liberally to prominent party members. But American pressure on Premier Pindling forced his curious guest to flee to Costa Rica in 1973.

Before seeking asylum in the 'Switzerland of the Americas,' Vesco pondered the state of the offshore world. So, too, did one of his consultants, Richard Allen, expert in the emerging law of tax havens and offshore centers and a top aide to Henry Kissinger. Allen dreamed of a sort of offshore new republic, in which the only citizens would be transnational corporations.[11] It was Richard Allen to whom Vesco turned to explore the possibilities of establishing offshore facilities in the Azores, islands off the coast of North Africa over which Portugal (then in the midst of a left-wing revolution) claimed sovereignty. Allen lobbied Washington to pressure Portugal to call a referendum on independence or to support a unilateral declaration of independence, stressing the pro-American leanings of the big landlords on the islands.[12] Portugal demurred.

Others with similar ambitions were not deterred. In return for their aid in bringing the project to fulfilment, an event that never came to pass, a New York Mafia family was allegedly to get a bank, a casino, and the standard two diplomatic passports.[13]

Robert Vesco also turned his attention to Haiti and its strongman, François 'Papa Doc' Duvalier, 'President for Life, Protector of the People, Maximum Chief of the Revolution, Apostle of National Unity, Benefactor of the Poor, Grand Patron of Commerce and Industry, and

Electrifier of Souls,' this last a reference to his legalization of voodoo, whose 'priests' were stalwart supporters of the regime (provided that the practitioners paid performance taxes and conducted their rituals under a portrait of Papa Doc). The regime, and its infamous goon squad, the Tontons Macoutes, had a rocky relationship with Washington (not to mention the Vatican) and was blacklisted by President Kennedy. However, the Johnson administration succeeded in securing it a $2.6-million World Bank 'development' loan even though it was 'more or less taken for granted' that the proceeds would end up in Papa Doc's personal Swiss bank accounts.[14] However, some in Washington remained intent on reforming the regime, to prevent a repetition of the Cuban disaster; and for a time the CIA actively aided Haitian exiles training on Andros Island in the Bahamas for an eventual invasion.

Enter Mitchell WerBell III. A veteran of the Office of Strategic Services (OSS) (predecessor of the CIA) in China, WerBell owned a string of arms manufacturing and exporting companies, including the innocent-sounding SIONICS Ltd., an acronym for Studies in the Operational Negation of Insurgents and Counter-Subversion. He also operated a private training facility in Georgia, where military and intelligence officers, policemen, and right-wing political kooks were taught the arts of 'counterinsurgency.'[15] WerBell trafficked in arms to right-wing paramilitary groups in Central America and other parts of the world,[16] and designed the silencer for the machine gun used in Vietnam for the Phoenix Program, the CIA-planned mass assassination of up to 50,000 Vietnamese on the pretext of wiping out lower- and middle-level Viet Cong cadres. WerBell was also the commander in chief of the Haitian rebels training on Andros Island, until the Bahamian government cracked down. The US Coast Guard aborted the rebels' invasion plans, and WerBell ran afoul of the law in the United States.[17]

A few years later, Robert Vesco came calling on Jean-Claude 'Baby Doc' Duvalier, who had succeeded his deceased father in all his titles. Vesco tried to get Baby Doc to cede him the island of Gonâve as a headquarters for a global hot-money center, but Duvalier refused.[18] Vesco's camp followers suggested the little island of Isla Saona off the Dominican Republic as an alternative, but Vesco turned his attentions to Costa Rica.[19]

Costa Rica was then still under the sway of José Figueres (Don Pepe), who had blasted his way to the presidency in 1948, overthrowing one of the most left-leaning governments in Latin America.[20] In 1973 Don Pepe brought Robert Vesco to Costa Rica; Vesco returned the compliment by pumping a few million dollars of looted IOS funds into the Figueres family business, which was being rocked by a black-market-money scandal. In return for his safe haven, Vesco pledged to return tenfold whatever money IOS had siphoned out of Costa Rica, offering it the tantalizing prospect of becoming a headquarters for offshore mutual funds and a world gambling, banking, and financial center. All that was necessary was an autonomous zone within the country, modeled on the old contraband center of Tangiers, which, presumably, Vesco's entourage would run. Don Pepe enthused that Vesco's dreams represented the beginning of 'justice' for developing countries; and he presented Vesco with a Costa Rican diplomatic passport to assist in the fulfilment of those dreams and, coincidentally, to render him immune from arrest.[21]

Alas, Costa Rica's parliament, though willing to offer the country's hospitality to Vesco and his stolen fortune, balked at ceding him sovereignty to national territory.

Secession was all the rage among tax-haven advocates even before Vesco joined their ranks. In 1967 the population of the small island of Anguilla was angry over the terms of their forced incorporation into a British-sponsored merger of several island colonies, and rallied behind secessionist leader Ronald Webster. When Webster attempted to emulate Ian Smith's Rhodesia and declare unilateral independence from Britain, former US intelligence officer Jack Holcomb was on hand to write the new constitution in exchange for tax concessions and business monopolies. However, the British government took a dim view of the scheme and sent a military task force to abort it.[22]

A similar fate befell the schemes of Michael Oliver, a successful US real estate developer before he fell under the sway of Dr. John Hospers, guru of the 'libertarian' political movement in the US. Hospers inspired Oliver and his associates to create the Phoenix Foundation to proselytize and then to implement the libertarian economic and political creed of an earthly paradise characterized by zero government, a monetary system based on a strict gold standard, and no social welfare.[23]

In 1972 the Phoenix Foundation had attempted to effect the 'secession' of a tiny island in the South Pacific from the Tonga group to serve as a possible location for their new, governmentless republic, free, by definition, of the curses of taxation and banking regulations. Indeed, it was to be the ultimate peekaboo haven, as the entire island disappeared one meter underwater every high tide. When the king of Tonga sent an 'army' to wave spears at the invaders, Oliver took his dream of a global flight-capital and gambling center to Abaco, a small and long-neglected island in the Bahamas.[24]

Mitch WerBell was to provide an 'army' that could easily overwhelm any defense force Prime Minister Pindling could mobilize. But Mitch WerBell was in legal trouble again, for his efforts to sell Phoenix program machine guns to Robert Vesco in Costa Rica; and the plan was dropped[25] – though Oliver, like King Canute, kept trying.

Another opportunity to create an island fiscal paradise came when the French planters on Espiritu Santo in the New Hebrides (Vanuatu), fearful of approaching independence and the consequent threat to their land holdings that rule by the Melanesian majority might entail, began to plot secession. The planters were encouraged by the Phoenix Foundation, which at least partially drafted the independence prospectus and advised the leaders of the would-be new state on a gold-based monetary system. Phoenix heavily funded Jimmy Stevens, former bulldozer operator turned leader of the Espiritu Santo ('Vemarana') secessionist movement; the foundation was also marketing shares in the Vemarana Development Corporation, which was to run the island after secession.

The 1980 election in the New Hebrides delivered a decisive victory to the Vanuaaku party, which had denounced the 'American "Mafia" businessmen who use violence to promote their interests' in Vanuatu. That victory was the signal for the Espiritu Santo secessionists to spring into action.

However, nothing went right. New Hebrides Customs officials confiscated 1,000 'Vemarana' passports. The US government threatened to arrest the leaders of the Phoenix Foundation if they supported the secessionists, and a joint Anglo-French military unit put an end to the enterprise.[26]

One place where Oliver's influence seems to have persisted was Tonga, where American promoter John Meier became financial adviser to the king in the late 1970s. Meier seemed a curious choice – a business associate of Don Nixon, Richard's brother, and a former top adviser to billionaire Howard Hughes, he also raised funds for a variety of liberal political causes. Accused of swindling Howard Hughes of $8 million and hiding it in a Swiss bank account, and charged in the US with tax evasion, Meier bolted to Vancouver, insisting that he was the victim of a CIA-sponsored harassment campaign.[27]

From Vancouver Meier looked westward and saw Tonga. Together with William Waterhouse, Australia's foremost bookmaker and honorary consul of Tonga in Sydney, he promised the king of Tonga a new airport, aircraft assembly plants, luxury hotels, and a shipbuilding industry. In return Meier got a Tongan diplomatic passport and a ninety-nine-year monopoly on merchant-banking activities in the islands. The Bank of the South Pacific was soon functioning, its greatest asset allegedly being rumors about its Swiss and Middle Eastern connections. But Meier failed to deliver on his promises, and the US authorities began exerting pressure on the Tongan government. Tonga withdrew both the bank license and the diplomatic passport that had shielded Meier from arrest.[28]

Perhaps the attraction of the South Pacific for Michael Oliver and John Meier was that the Caribbean was being overrun by tax-haven and offshore-bank promoters. In 1978 North American promoters arrived in the tiny British colony of Montserrat, after being rebuffed in nearby Antigua, to push the idea of a free banking zone. The zone was to comprise a building at the airport to which Montserrat Customs and police would have no access. There, each client's valuables would be stored in a secret account. As each account would receive an individual bank license from the government, the clients could also launder any hot money that came their way.

The payoff to Montserrat would be 0.5% to 1% off the top of everything passing through the free banking zone. A law establishing such a zone was passed, but accusations of Mafia and corrupt union links, and rumors of bribes to members of the government led the British government to disallow it.[29]

Equally abortive was the scheme to create a peekaboo center on the island of Dominica. It all started with the overthrow of the strongman of Grenada, Sir Eric Gairy. Gairy was a visionary who had once wowed the United Nations General Assembly with a speech calling for UN funding for a major study of UFOs. But he was also sufficiently practical to have a paramilitary goon squad, the Mongoose Gang, modeled on Duvalier's Tontons Macoutes. When Gairy was deposed, he received an offer of help from a group of Americans and Canadians, including Nazis, Ku Klux Klan members, and an international arms dealer with a 'keen interest in mercenary adventurism.' But when they failed to come to terms with Gairy, they set their sights on Dominica, where Patrick John's Labour Party had just lost elections to Eugenia Charles's Freedom Party.

The deal was straightforward enough: the promoters' company, Nordic Enterprises, would arrange an invasion, put John back in power, and assure him and certain associates a share of the take. John would give them $50,000 in cash and an array of tax-free business concessions: the sale of passports, a gunrunning operation, casinos, resource wealth, and, of course, banks. Some of the partners also saw Dominica as a future refuge for 'pure white' colonists of confirmed Aryan stock.

But the US, which had helped to elect Eugenia Charles's government, objected. The merry band was arrested in New Orleans, just before putting the scheme into operation.[30]

In spite of these setbacks, however, there were so many refuges for hot and/or dirty money springing up that accountants specializing in tax evasion could barely keep track of them. And through them passed an ever-increasing portion of the international lending business of the world's major (and minor) banks.

3

Red Ink and Black Gold

The late 1960s and 1970s were happy days for the world's bankers. Not only was the machinery of peekaboo finance being set firmly in place, but there also seemed to be unlimited eager borrowers and inexhaustible funds to run through that machinery. The pop media had an interesting explanation why that should be so.

Perhaps drawing inspiration from the fable, common in the 1920s, of an international conspiracy of Jewish financiers, the updated version concerns an international conspiracy of Arab Oil Sheikhs. The story begins in 1973 when the wily Orientals of the oil cartel got together to undermine the moral and financial foundations of the Civilized World. That year the price of oil was quadrupled, resulting in a massive transfer of wealth to the A-Rabs. These A-Rabs, being primitive, could not use all the money. They traded their tents for luxury palaces and their herds of camels for fleets of Rolls-Royces. They even gobbled up prime real estate and industry in the Civilized World. But the money kept piling up. So the Arab Oil Sheikhs deposited the surpluses in the eurodollar market.

Organization of Petroleum Exporting Countries (OPEC) money was gleefully lent by the international banks to debtor countries, particularly developing countries, whose balance-of-payments deficits had soared because of the oil-price hikes. However, the avaricious bankers hustled more and more loans, virtually forcing the money on the developing countries, whose corrupt autocrats eagerly took the loans to finance their luxury automobiles and Swiss bank accounts. Then, one day, a new oil-price shock created a depression, caused unemployment and inflation to soar, and pushed the debtor countries (and their bankers) to, or even beyond, the brink of default.

And observing it all with a menacing sneer were the wily, burnoose-clad, hook-nosed Arab Oil Sheikhs of the 1970s, the spiritual descendants of the wily, gabardine-clad, hook-nosed Jewish financiers of the 1920s.[1]

There is another version of the story.

The Rise of the International Oil Standard

By the late 1960s Pentagon Capitalism had brought the financial world to the brink. The ultimate acceptability of the US dollar as *the* medium for effecting international payments lay in its convertibility into gold. But the world's stock of gold was relatively fixed, while the worldwide volume of outstanding US government financial obligations grew as overseas military expenditures rose. Once the foreign total of US dollar obligations exceeded the official domestic value of US gold reserves (then valued at $35 per troy ounce) it was evident that all claims could not be met if a 'run' occurred. In that eventuality, either only the earliest claims would be repaid in gold, or gold would have to be revalued upward. Both possibilities meant that a propensity to speculate against the US dollar and to cash dollars in for gold at the earliest opportunity was built into the system. The potential was particularly alarming after the French government of Charles De Gaulle started protesting American policy in Southeast Asia by demanding gold for its dollar holdings.

By 1971, on top of the war-induced capital outflow, the US economy saw its first commodity-trade deficit since the Second World War. That finally forced the US to stop all conversions of its currency into gold (a partial suspension had been in force since 1968), and to submit to the political indignity of devaluation. In effect, the world passed from a US dollar standard backed by gold to a US dollar standard backed by US dollars, and a massive flight of capital from the US followed. The capital flight eased in 1972, but accelerated again the next year, forcing another major devaluation.[2] But by then the US government had found another standard to which the dollar could be pegged.

In 1973, after years of bickering and ineffectuality, OPEC finally agreed to quadruple the world price of oil. There were two distinct elements involved: the largely symbolic, and virtually ineffectual, Arab embargo of the US because of its support for Israel during the October 1973 war; and the closing of OPEC ranks behind the traditional price hawks, Venezuela and Iran.

The success of the price hawks had less to do with immediate Middle Eastern politics than with long-term economic trends. For nearly three decades after the Second World War, the developing countries suffered a steady deterioration of their terms of trade with the West. The prices of their commodity exports from alumina to zinc rose, but the prices of the manufactured goods from the industrialized countries taken in exchange rose even faster.

For oil exporters the situation was worse; oil was the only major commodity to fall in absolute as well as relative price during the twenty-five years that followed the Second World War. And unlike avocados, bananas, and coffee, oil was nonrenewable. Thus, oil producers were consuming their national wealth to meet the demand of the West for cheap energy. Much of the rapid economic growth and rise in living standards in the postwar West was directly due to the free ride, or at least cheap trip, that the industrialized world enjoyed at the expense of the oil-producing countries.

Furthermore, as oil was traded largely (and, after 1975, exclusively) for dollars, its relative price dropped even further when the US dollar was devalued in the early 1970s. If oil's real purchasing power vis-à-vis essential Western-supplied goods had kept pace with that of other major commodities, its price would have reached just about the level that a tight market permitted the oil-exporting countries to push it to in 1973. Even so, the leading Arab producer, Saudi Arabia, lobbied in 1974 to try to push *down* the world price of oil, only to have its efforts apparently sabotaged by certain American interest groups.

While the oil-price hike was painful for most consumers and producers in the US, it did confer on some interest groups a number of economic, financial, and political advantages. Until 1973, American industry depended largely on domestically produced oil. But because of import restrictions, domestic oil cost more in the US than the Middle Eastern oil that the big US and British oil companies sold throughout the world.[3] With the US balance of payments under siege and American exports being increasingly threatened by the products of Japan and West Germany, the difference in energy costs was a luxury the US could no longer afford. The 1973 price changes eliminated the differential that had long disadvantaged American industry in export markets.

The major oil companies were not inclined to protest, as profits per barrel reportedly doubled. Those profits were justified in public by the insistence that they allowed the oil companies to finance the development of alternative sources of energy, thereby freeing middle America from the grasp of rapacious A-Rabs. In reality the profits funded a huge asset grab, as the big oil companies bought up vast existing holdings of coal, uranium, copper, and other minerals at home and abroad.[4]

In some of the OPEC countries, the oil revenues financed a development boom that opened markets for US consulting and construction companies. Even more important were the benefits to the US arms industry, then facing the specter of the end of the Vietnam War.

In 1972 President Nixon and Secretary of State Henry Kissinger assigned the shah of Iran the role of policeman of the Persian-Arabian Gulf that Britain had recently abandoned. They agreed to let the shah purchase any nonnuclear American weapons system he desired. The 1973 oil-price hikes assured him the means of paying the resulting bills. Aiding the process was the CIA's Operations Directorate (a clandestine operations wing), which ran a project – at the instigation of the Kissinger-controlled National Security Council – to retrieve some $20 billion the US spent on oil in the Middle East, by the surreptitious sale of high-priced military systems. The result was a shower of gold for desperate American war industries.[5]

Moreover, since oil was essentially a dollar-denominated commodity for purposes of international exchange, price increases sent virtually all other countries scrambling to find the US dollars necessary to meet their greatly enhanced oil bills. Not surprisingly, the US dollar quickly, if temporarily, recovered much of the exchange value it had lost in the previous years of dollar glut, crisis, and devaluation.

While Iran was pouring billions into the American arms industry, Saudi Arabia and the Arab gulf states were investing much of their surpluses in US treasury bills. (The exact sums remained a state secret.) Once more, the pressure on the US to close its budget deficit was eased. Instead of having to face the adverse political fallout from legislating tax increases, the US government could work through the intermediation of the oil-exporting countries, who could then be blamed for the resulting financial burden on oil consumers.[6]

Other beneficiaries of the price hikes were major US banks. Those most closely tied to the international oil companies were blessed directly with an enormous infusion of cash. Furthermore, the overall American international financial position so gained from the oil-price changes that the US could remove, a year ahead of schedule, the restrictions on capital exports imposed during the Vietnam War. Freed of operating restrictions, the US banks saw their foreign assets leap by 72% in one year as they rushed into international loan syndications in the burgeoning eurodollar market.[7]

The Crash of '74
Part of the credit for the rapid growth of the euromarket in the 1970s must be given to an unsung, though not unrecognized, pioneer of

peekaboo finance, Mafia financier and flight capitalist Michele
Sindona.[8] Not only did his enterprises provide substantial cash flows
into the market in the early part of the decade, but also efforts by
bank regulatory authorities to cover up a mess he helped to make
created a climate that encouraged the market's growth.

By the early 1970s there was nothing very odd about a major
mob figure controlling an American bank. After all, Lansky had
enough banks in his pocket to qualify for the presidency of the
American Bankers' Association.[9] Therefore, when Michele Sindona
set his sights on Franklin National Bank, twentieth largest in the
US, few people seemed concerned.

Sindona's background in Sicily was one of poverty and ambition
at a time when, despite a vicious campaign of suppression of the
Mafia by Mussolini, the island remained the joint fiefdom of the
Mafia and the church.[10] It was not unknown for priests to be local
Mafia *capos*, and more than one priest in recent years has been
charged with washing dirty money through the Vatican bank. It was
from his bishop that Sindona, then a young tax lawyer, heard the
parable of the New Worldly success of Amadeo Giannini, founder
of what became the Bank of America.[11]

During the Second World War, Sindona had an opportunity to
put his appreciation for things American to practical use. When
the American army invaded Sicily, it was with the support of the
Mafia, Sicilian and American. In one of the more bizarre and
portentous chapters of the diplomatic history of the era, the US
government in 1946 released Meyer Lansky's business partner, Lucky
Luciano, from jail. This was supposed to be in exchange for his
assistance in keeping the American waterfront unions in line during
the war, and in securing the active collaboration of the Sicilian Mafia
for the invasion of the island – though it has also been suggested
that it may have had something to do with a large check that the
mob allegedly wrote on behalf of the reelection campaign of crime-
buster Thomas Dewey for the governorship of New York.

Apart from using the occasion to resurrect the transatlantic heroin
trade,[12] the Mafia also requested American support for the independence of Sicily. Michele Sindona made himself useful to this dialogue
by trading lemons from Mafia-controlled suppliers to the American
forces on Sicily in exchange for grain for black-market sale. Allegedly,
too, he dealt in arms for the partisans fighting for independence.
Although the US refused to back the secession attempt, it did support
a compromise: regional autonomy under the joint auspices of the
Christian Democratic party, the Mafia, and the church.

In the postwar period, Sindona, a pioneer in the use of Liechtenstein *anstalten*, allegedly put his financial skills to work channeling CIA money to the church and the Christian Democratic party, and laundering and reinvesting heroin profits for the Mafia. Moving north to Milan, center of the Italian 'economic miracle' of reconstruction and industrial growth in the 1950s, Sindona teamed up with the Istituto per le Opere di Religione (IOR), the bank that serves the financial needs of the Vatican, to launch himself into the capital-flight business.[13]

All these enterprises required a particular financial infrastructure. In 1959 Sindona, the IOR in Rome, and the Vatican's principal American banker, Continental Illinois Bank and Trust Company of Chicago, acquired the Banca Privata Finanziaria (BPF), a small private bank in Milan with a long involvement in illicit capital movements. In 1964 he and the IOR bought the Banque de Financement (Finabank) of Geneva. It was then an easy matter for hot money to be transferred, first from Italy to Vatican City (as there was no real check on money moving between the two) and then from the Vatican into Switzerland.[14]

Sindona's dream of becoming the absolute monarch of Italian finance received a sharp setback when the Italian regulatory authorities blocked joint efforts by Sindona and the Vatican bank to take over two of Italy's largest holding companies. Hence, in the early seventies, Sindona set out to implement the lessons he had learned at his bishop's knee.

Sindona was certainly no mere deckhand when he plied the stormy seas of transatlantic capital flows in the early 1970s. Apart from numerous voyages spent scrubbing heroin-trade money through paper companies between the US, Switzerland, and Sicily during the 1960s, Sindona had floated a number of pulp-mill scams, taking over Italian pulp-and-paper firms and using them to strip money from North American partners. In addition to taking Celanese Corp. for $80 million, Sindona became familiar with Canadian logging. His skills in financial juggling proved remarkably adaptable to the game of birling pulp-and-paper companies' books, particularly those companies with government backing. Thus, as the government of the relatively poor province of New Brunswick pumped money into the South Nelson Forest Products project, Sindona cheerfully pumped it out again. After the failure of its giant Churchill Falls Industries Ltd. project, the government of Manitoba charged Sindona's accomplices with defrauding it of $93 million. What better experience for a foray into North American banking?

Franklin National was a large, sedate New York–area bank that had fallen on hard times before Michele Sindona looted enough money from Banca Privata Finanziaria to acquire it and turn it into the American vehicle for expanding the foreign-exchange speculations that had already yielded him great profit and personal satisfaction.

A cardinal objective of the postwar reconstructed world monetary order had been to assure stability of exchange rates. But by the late 1960s and early 1970s, pressures on the dollar made such an objective impossible. Commercial banks, including Sindona's, sensed an opportunity to profit heavily (at the expense of central banks) from the volatile foreign-exchange markets that developed, especially after the 1971 dollar devaluation.

Among Sindona's pioneering works before leaving Italy had been the establishment of Moneyrex, a money-brokerage operation to move money from banks with deposit surpluses to those in need of funds. With a client list that peaked at 850 international banks, Moneyrex also seemed an ideal vehicle for moving hot money out of Italy to distant and untraceable refuges. It was the instrument through which Sindona, Cologne's Bankhaus Herstatt, and several other institutions orchestrated a multibillion-dollar attack on the lira.[15] And Moneyrex became a partner with Franklin National in Sindona's subsequent forays into the foreign-exchange business.

Alas, the lack of honor among thieves. While Sindona's international department chief at Franklin National was making foreign-exchange trades based on information provided by Carlo Bordoni, head of Moneyrex, Bordoni was betting the other way. As Franklin National racked up massive foreign-exchange losses, Bordoni was secreting his profits in Switzerland. Rumors of losses and reckless speculation caused banks to boycott Franklin National; rumors of foreign-exchange losses led to runs, first on Sindona's Italian banks, then on Franklin National. The Federal Reserve pumped in more than $2 billion in loans to try to keep it afloat; but when Sindona's old partner in the attack on the lira, Bankhaus Herstatt, came crashing down in the summer of 1974, the Sindona empire on both sides of the Atlantic followed it to the scrap heap.

As was usual with mob-run banks in the US, the Federal Deposit Insurance Corporation (FDIC) picked up the tab. Sindona hid out in Switzerland for a while to avoid the Italian authorities, who wanted to charge him with, among other things, fraudulent bankruptcy. He turned up briefly as 'economic adviser' to the Taiwan government, but finally returned to the US and fought extradition to Italy. In 1980 he began serving twenty-five years in an American prison, a record for white-collar crime, and was finally extradited to Italy in 1984.

Sorting out Sindona's legacy was a protracted business,[16] but not as difficult as dealing with the wreck of Bankhaus Herstatt, whose losses on speculation against the US dollar were even greater than Franklin's. Most of Herstatt's foreign-exchange deals had been booked through affiliates in tax havens and offshore centers.[17] The losses to banks that had lent money to these affiliates therefore caused an obvious question to be raised: who was responsible for supervising their activities? The chief regulatory officers of the ten major Western industrialized countries, Switzerland, and Luxembourg pondered this question under the auspices of the Swiss-based Bank for International Settlements, a sort of central bankers' central bank.

They produced the Basle Concordat,[18] a set of agreements without legal force, assigning responsibility for supervising the international operations of banks. Under the terms of the concordat, assuring that a *branch* of a foreign bank was adequately capitalized was the responsibility of the country licensing the parent bank. However, supervision of the capital adequacy of *subsidiaries* of foreign banks was primarily the responsibility of the host country. The distinction was that a subsidiary is separately incorporated under the laws of the country in which it operates, whereas a branch is controlled directly by the parent bank.

The concordat was not very reassuring, particularly as the vague (and nonbinding) text remained secret for several years. But the belief grew that the major central banks had agreed to guarantee liquidity to internationally operating banks facing a deposit run. In other words, that the country hosting an international bank subsidiary was prepared to allow that subsidiary, even if it operated purely in the offshore market, to borrow from the host country's central bank when the subsidiary had no other source of emergency money.

Obviously, this was the interpretation the international banks wanted to believe, but some euromarket experts contend that the misunderstanding derived, at least in part, from misinformation spread by the Bank of England, which was facing a flight of dollar deposits.[19] England was particularly vulnerable to the euromarket panic that followed the Herstatt collapse. It was the largest euromarket center. It had also attracted fringe financial institutions that played the British real estate market. In 1974 a real estate boom came to a noisy end. Along with the Herstatt debacle, it set off a panic outflow of hot money.[20]

By conveying the impression that there was a firm deal to assure that eurobanks would have access to emergency funds from the central banks, the Bank of England allegedly hoped to, and apparently did, stem the outflow. That impression also puffed the growth of the euromarket, alleviating the uncertainties caused by the 1974 crisis. These sunny reassurances came just when banks in most major Western countries had more money than their domestic business required and when developing countries were anxious to borrow.

Setting the Debt Trap

For the developing countries, the expansion of the euromarket held out immediate financial and political advantages. After the dollar crises of the late 1960s, overseas investment by American transnational corporations fell off. Although that decrease had reduced one formerly important source of foreign exchange for the developing countries, it was not entirely unwelcome. The 1960s and early 1970s had seen major scandals, among them the role played by ITT in subverting the Chilean government of Salvador Allende Gossens and the intrigues of Union Minière of Belgium when Katanga (Shaba) province attempted to secede from the Congo. These and a host of less spectacular cases gave some developing countries second thoughts about welcoming transnational corporations.

Moreover, many of those corporations were facing vulnerable cash positions at home and the growing risks of expropriation abroad. New techniques were needed for selling developing countries access to industrial technology: joint ventures with developing-country-based firms and governments, plant-construction contracts and management arrangements, and the licensing of technology and industrial processes. These alternative arrangements, however, also required alternative sources of finance.

The second traditional source of foreign exchange, foreign aid, could not take up the slack. If anything, industrialized countries were cutting back on expenditures defended by weak political constituencies, especially those that the growing 'conservative' mood considered ideologically suspect.[21]

The third alternative was drawing more funds from the World Bank for development projects and from the IMF for balance-of-payments support; but potential borrowers ran up against the shortage of funds in and the conservative lending posture of the former, and the offensive loan conditions of the latter. A new generation of leaders had assumed political control in the independent Afro-Asian countries, in part on a wave of optimism about prospects of growth and development. Thus a visit from an IMF team preaching austerity was not welcome, no matter how highly advanced were local standards of hospitality. By the 1960s the phrase 'IMF riot' had a firm place in the lexicon of development politics.

The fourth alternative was the international banks, which were convinced that, unlike corporations, countries cannot go bankrupt, and which were eager to lend to developing countries on the security of future revenues from raw-material exports. The developing countries were eager to borrow without having to suffer the bullying of the transnational corporations or the perceived affront against national sovereignty of the IMF. The euromarket's attraction was even greater because, as the state sectors of the developing countries were trying to assert their leadership in the development process, the international banks preferred to have direct state guarantees and state involvement in projects they were funding.[22] This attitude seemed a pleasant contrast to that of the IMF, which was constantly badgering developing countries to reduce the state's economic role.

Nowhere was the new alliance clearer than in the natural-resources sectors. The developing countries followed the example of OPEC, whose governments had taken control of production from the transnational corporations. They frequently established state export monopolies that promised to give the lending banks the security of a de facto mortgage on their export receipts.

Briefly, the developing countries were able to play one syndicate of lending banks off against another. The banks cooperated, assuming that, even if the country was not really creditworthy, another syndicate of banks (or, if the country were strategic in a cold war context, Western governments) would lend the money it needed to repay its bank debts.[23]

All this was in progress well before the oil-price revolution of 1973. Although the oil-price increases did involve a huge transfer of resources to the OPEC countries it was temporary. By 1976 the OPEC balance-of-payments surplus had largely gone, and some members had growing deficits. Even though some OPEC countries continued to run surpluses, between 1974 and 1980 OPEC net deposits in the eurobanks totaled approximately $125 billion, while net lending out of the market was about $615 billion. Thus the OPEC funds joined with and were overwhelmed by a major infusion of liquidity coming in from the Western banking system, then flush with cash and seeking lending opportunities abroad.

Double Bubble

In 1979 the borrowing countries were hit with two severe blows. First, revolution in Iran overthrew the shah and sparked another dramatic jump in the price of oil. That permitted the Carter administration to bolster its sagging political fortunes by directing a hate campaign against a largely ineffectual OPEC.[24] The oil-price increases, sparked by market panic and inflation in the US, rather than by any mythical OPEC capacity to 'control' world prices, were painful to virtually every oil-importing country except the US, which could 'pay' for oil simply by turning on the printing press. The increases would probably have been manageable in isolation, but they coincided with other dramatic and adverse changes in international financial circumstances.

The second and, in the long run, more important change saw the main levers of government economic policy taken out of the hands of the elected Congress and given to an unelected clique of monetary technocrats.

During the late 1970s, central banks in the industrialized countries, including the US, responded to the crisis and financial confusion by reasserting a commitment to the principles of 'sound money,' principles that the Great Depression had proved unsound to all but crank academics. In particular, they resurrected the doctrine that to control inflation, it sufficed to control the supply of 'money.' Behind the revival of this formula was a long-discredited political theory – namely, that debtors, whenever possible, will use their allegedly superior political power to increase the money supply in order to inflate price levels, thereby reducing the real burden of their outstanding debts, which could be repaid in a depreciated currency.

Countering the process by which debtors historically have defrauded creditors requires that governments avoid inflationary gimmicks like budget deficits; and that the level of economic activity be allowed to rise and fall in order to stabilize the purchasing power of money, instead of the reverse. It is also necessary that the policy priorities of central bankers, who do not have to answer politically for the resulting costs, take precedence over those of elected representatives of the population.

The attempt to explain inflation by, and blame it on, an unwarranted increase in the supply of money was as absurd as arguing that influenza was caused by a high fever. Furthermore, controlling the 'money supply' was largely irrelevant and virtually impossible. With such advances in financial technology as twenty-four-hour electronic banking on a world scale, any restriction in the supply of 'money' simply caused the limited supply to circulate faster to offset the effect of the restriction. Moreover, every historical attempt by authorities to restrict the supply of 'money' simply encouraged societies to invent something else to take its place. The net result has been rather to change the definition of 'money' than to limit its amount.

Nonetheless, in 1979, the year that the Iranian Revolution sent oil prices soaring, the US Federal Reserve Board switched from attempting to stabilize interest rates to trying to limit growth of the money supply. As the Federal Reserve hit the brakes, interest rates soared and fluctuated wildly. Real rates of interest, which over long periods had hovered between 1% and 2%, and often dipped into the negative range, hit 6, 8, 10%, and more. Long-term capital markets virtually ceased to exist. Desperate borrowers turned to banks, thereby incurring huge short-term debt loads whose 'floating' interest rate seemed to float only up so long as the inflation rate continued to rise.

Latin America was particularly hard hit by the crisis. The positive effects of a decade of development were wiped out. The terms of trade of developing exporters of primary products deteriorated by an average of 30% between 1979 and 1982. Also down were the quantities consumed by industrialized countries, which were in their worst recession since the 1930s. With oil prices soaring, debt-service charges leaping, and commodity-trade receipts plummeting, the international-trade accounts of the developing countries crumbled. They began to borrow heavily, not for investment in development projects but to bridge the yawning gap in their balance of payments. And more and more of their borrowing was short-term, floating-rate loans. But this was not the end of their financial woes.

For almost any other country, a large and rising government budget deficit and a growing balance-of-trade deficit would have caused a sharp drop in its currency. But, since the US dollar was *the* instrument in which international exchanges were denominated, oil-price changes set off another scramble to buy dollars. Furthermore, the high interest rates available on US financial instruments caused a flight of funds to the US from around the world. Soon the dollar was rising in value again.

Prices of commodities such as oil, which were set in dollars, rose again in terms of almost every other currency. The appreciation of the US dollar and the collapse in price of export goods also greatly raised the cost to the developing countries of paying interest and repaying principal on dollar-denominated foreign debt. And not least of their problems was the announcement by the US banks, followed by the government, that they were open for the flight-capital trade when the speculative atmosphere generated by high and volatile interest rates had caused a great build-up of the hot-money pool both within and between countries.

Within the developing debtor countries, economic, and therefore the political and social, conditions worsened. This deterioration (often not unrelated to the activities of business and political elements directly profiting from illicit capital movements) caused more money to flee for safer havens. In turn, those countries needed to borrow more money to cover the resulting shortage of foreign exchange.

'Recycling' had taken a bizarre new twist. An ever-growing number of offshore banking centers and tax havens competed for the increasingly large supply of hot and footloose money fleeing the developing countries. The hot money was then lent through the eurobanking system, funding loans to developing countries in need of hard currency to bolster their foreign-exchange positions drained by capital flight.

4
Sheikhs in Sombreros?

Standing before the United Nations General Assembly on October 1, 1982, President José Lopez Portillo described Mexico as 'a living example of what occurs when that enormous, volatile, and speculative mass of capital goes all over the world in search of high interest rates, tax havens, and supposed political and exchange stability. It decapitalizes entire countries and leaves havoc in its wake.'[1]

President Portillo's lament came only some two months before his term of office expired. One might draw an obvious analogy to former US President Dwight Eisenhower's famous warning, during the last days of his administration, about the dangers inherent in the emerging military-industrial complex. In both cases, one might ask the esteemed presidents, where were you when all this was happening?

This is not to suggest that Lopez Portillo's complaint was in any way illegitimate. The financial collapse of Mexico made it dramatically clear that had there not been a massive flight of hot money, there would have been no general crisis of debt.

The Mexican debacle also demolished the myth that the debt crisis resulted from the ill-gotten gains extorted by the oil cartel from the world's oil consumers, and then lent to Third World countries whose finances had been shattered by the initial oil-price gouging. For in 1982, when Mexico put its economy into a tailspin to try to curb capital flight and service its external debt, it was both the world's fourth largest oil exporter and its second most heavily indebted developing country.

Capitalizing on a Capital Crisis
The collapse of the Mexican economy was particularly dramatic in view of its record during the 1970s. In 1975 Mexico had switched from being an oil importer to an oil exporter for the first time since

the nationalization of its oil industry in 1938. The flood of petro-dollars fueled a growth rate that hit 8% per annum. Oil revenues rose from 15% of exports in 1975 to 70% in 1981; during the same period the contribution of oil to government revenues rose from 6% to 55%. Massive government spending converted oil revenues into employment. From 1976 to 1981, Mexico created 500,000 new jobs per year.[2]

The external debt rose during the oil boom, though only modestly. But in 1981 the debt jumped 40%, as the government used funds borrowed on security of its oil revenues to keep up a 9% growth rate when the rest of Latin America was already in recession. That jump in the debt came just when Mexico's capacity to service it plummeted because of an oil glut and stagnant prices of other exports. Furthermore, the new borrowing was largely short-term, floating-interest bank debt, assuring high interest rates and the frequent need for renegotiation.[3]

Part of the problem derived from economic geography, from the fact that the US and Mexico are separated physically only by the Rio Grande, which Will Rogers once described as the only river in North America in need of irrigation. The extent and openness of the border, the lack of exchange controls, the high value of the peso against the dollar, and an abundance of petrodollars fed a growing appetite for American goods. Consumption of gringo products ceased to be a prerogative of the rich and spread not only to the middle class but also to the laborers who lived near the border or commuted across it for work. The restraining effect of Mexican tariffs was partially offset by the enormous volume of contraband, aided by a customs department allegedly among the most corrupt branches of a notoriously corrupt administrative apparatus.

In effect, the 'overvaluation' of the Mexican peso was a mechanism for recycling: the US paid for Mexican oil with dollars that returned home via Mexican purchases of cheap consumer goods and by a flow of Mexican money into real estate and bank accounts in the US. As long as there were also enough dollars for servicing the Mexican foreign debts, there were no complaints from gringo banks about the 'overvaluation'.

However, there was more involved. While the petrodollars were pouring into Mexico, they were being drained out again by asset stripping in both private and public companies – leaving the spectacle of rich entrepreneurs managing virtually bankrupt enterprises buried under dollar-denominated debt.

There were two traditional avenues for the flight of funds. One was directly across the border into certificates of deposit issued by southwestern American banks, undoubtedly many of the banks participating in syndicated loans to Mexican companies and government agencies. The other, favored by money seeking to hide its origin as well as its destination, was through secret bank accounts in peekaboo centers such as the Cayman Islands. From there, the funds were placed in trust with US institutional investors, who in turn invested them in real estate in the American Southwest.[4]

In 1981 there was a sharp drop in exports and a sudden upsurge in the volume and cost of borrowing. The traditional outflow of money was joined by torrents of 'fright capital.' This flow increased once more in August 1982, when the government doubled the price of tortillas and spread fears of a social explosion by the masses of urban poor. By then the character of the capital flight was changing. Mexicans were becoming increasingly sophisticated users of offshore facilities and ghost companies, and funds that did not go into real estate began to seek long-term investments in American stocks, bonds, and small businesses, rather than just in bank accounts.

Estimates of the total volume of capital that fled Mexico subsequent to the start of the oil boom vary. The political opposition claimed that in the few months prior to August 1982, when Mexico was forced to impose partial exchange controls, about $20 billion fled; others estimated $22 billion in the three years prior to August 1982. President Lopez Portillo's advisers put the total drain during the three years at a minimum of $39 billion: $25 billion invested in US real estate (an estimate later raised to $31 billion) and $14 billion in US bank accounts. Subsequent investigations estimated the loss to the end of 1984 between $33 billion and $60 billion, or roughly 50% of Mexico's total funds from export receipts and foreign loans during those years.[5]

Local bankers, who intermediated much of the outflow, insisted that they were simple clerks converting pesos into dollars at the request of their clients. But Lopez Portillo had a different opinion, denouncing 'the group of Mexicans ... headed, counseled and aided by the private banks [who have] taken more money out of the country than the imperial powers had exploited from us since the beginning of our history.' He accused the banks of actively fomenting the capital flight.[6] In effect, the local banks facilitated the flight of capital into foreign havens, arranged with international banks to borrow the funds back to replenish the foreign exchange being drained out, and collected at both ends of the process.

Mexico had pledged itself to the maintenance of a free-exchange market. Such a pledge was the price of purchasing middle-class support for the regime, and of assuring gringo businessmen that their profits could be freely remitted. Hence, when, in early 1982, the drain of funds seemed unsustainable, Mexico tried the standard IMF solution: a 30% devaluation. Like most IMF solutions, it made the problem even worse. It drove up the peso cost of imports but did nothing to affect the international price of Mexican oil, which was priced in dollars. And it caused more capital flight in anticipation of further devaluations. In August 1982, when Argentina's crumbling financial position had thrown a pall over all Latin American lending, Mexico imposed partial exchange controls and sent its finance minister, Jesus Silva Herzog, to Washington with cap in hand.[7]

Washington's stakes in Mexico were enormous. Mexican economic collapse would threaten the solvency of both the major American money-center banks and a host of smaller, regional ones in the Southwest.[8] Furthermore, there was a threat to the large and, until late 1981, growing flow of business from the US Southwest to Mexico. Apart from the sale of consumer goods to Mexican tourists and *contrabandistas*, much of the industry taking root in the American Southwest was built on the exploitation of illegal, cheap labor from Mexico. The pervasiveness of such labor was graphically revealed in 1980, when the US immigration service arrested eight illegal aliens who had been employed in landscaping the grounds of the immigration processing center near San Pedro, California. Indeed, by the end of the 1970s, there existed a border-area subeconomy – a virtual offshore industrial park – that straddled the Rio Grande but was economically part of neither the US nor Mexico.[9]

For the US, Mexican economic collapse could also be the prelude to social collapse in the country with which it shared a two-thousand-mile border. This could change the normal flow of illegal aliens from an economic blessing to a social curse.[10]

But any US bailout would be costly, for it would be a superb opportunity to knock into line Mexican policy on trade, oil, immigration, and foreign relations. Mexican concessions would be exchanged for financial assistance that did far more for American banks than for the Mexican population, just when Mexico faced its worst economic crisis and its first drop in per capita income since the Second World War.[11]

When the crisis erupted in August 1982, Thomas Enders, Assistant Secretary of State for Inter-American Affairs, made public internal documents stating that Mexico had 'the wind out of its sails' and would be 'less adventuresome in its foreign policy and less critical of ours.' As Enders put it, the tide of events in Central America was 'now running in our favor' and it was necessary to keep up the pressure on Nicaragua and Cuba. (The US had not forgotten that in April 1982, Mexico had negotiated the Nicaraguan revolutionary government's first euromarket loan,[12] and that it was supplying Nicaragua with oil on credit.) The Enders documents were explicit about the economic advantages to be drawn: the lowering of Mexico's traditional barriers to foreign investment; cooperation in curbing illegal immigration into the US; lowering of Mexican barriers to US goods; and more oil at lower prices.[13]

Oil had long fouled Mexican-US relations. The vastness of probable Mexican oil reserves had been well known at least since the end of the 1960s, when the World Bank came up with a plan for their rapid exploitation. President Luis Echeverria's refusal to accept the World Bank plan seems to have prompted the CIA to develop a plan of its own.[14]

It is not certain if the CIA plan to destabilize the Echeverria government was ever put into operation. Nonetheless, in 1975, when Alberto Sicilia-Falcon was arrested by the Mexican police on narcotics charges and tortured, he told a curious tale. Sicilia-Falcon, who had scurried from his native Cuba after the revolution, claimed to be a CIA agent, under orders to set up a heroin- and marijuana-exporting ring to finance the flow of weapons to paramilitary groups in the region, particularly the guerrillas of the Sierra Madre del Sur mountains, who were among Mexico's leading producers of marijuana.[15]

Upon Lopez Portillo's succession to the presidency in 1976, the oil fields were opened, and the boom was on, though the government tried to limit the percentage of total sales going to the United States.

During the 1970s, high and rising oil prices brought a 'recycling' bonanza to the US international banks. But as the 'debt crisis' unfolded, the critical issue became repayment. The US banks shifted from being net exporters of funds to being net importers. Since non-oil-exporting debtor countries often had to choose between meeting their oil-import bills or their debt-service obligations, falling oil prices became desirable, even necessary. And Mexico was seen as a potential battering ram for use against the OPEC price structure.

Mexico had overtaken Saudi Arabia as the single largest source of oil imported into the US. And the crisis of debt opened at much the same time as the 1982 bloodbath in Lebanon, which left the US prestige in the Arab Middle East in tatters. With the Reagan administration talking openly of increasing military cooperation with Israel in the early 1980s, there was the prospect of the US facing a drawn 'oil weapon.' In September 1982, the General Accounting Office of the US Congress warned the US government that its dependence on OPEC crude oil could increase 'dramatically,' and that the US had to work to prevent any new crisis of supply.[16]

The Mexican crisis gave the US a chance to lock Mexico's petroleum exports into the US market and Mexico into an extension of the US Strategic Reserve. Hence, part of the financial rescue operation for Mexico was a $1 billion advance payment for its oil (the interest was also to be paid in oil) at a price considerably less than the OPEC benchmark.[17] If the aid had been extended as a cash loan, the effective interest rate would have been 30%. This prompted US Treasury Secretary Donald Regan, formerly chief executive officer of Merrill, Lynch Securities, to explain: 'I just want to give the American taxpayer the same kind of service I gave to the stockholders of Merrill, Lynch.'[18]

Apart from using the deal as the first step toward Mexico's break with the OPEC price structure, the US announced that its strategic reserve would *not* be increased in size: any increase in imports from Mexico would be offset by a decrease in imports from Saudi Arabia.

Saudi Arabia offered a $12 billion loan on soft terms if Mexico agreed to join OPEC and to limit production. But Mexico refused both the loan and OPEC membership, and delivered a letter of intent to the IMF that presaged a further subordination of its petroleum policy to the US.[19] The right-wing business press in the US gloated, seeing Mexico's pledge to raise production during a time of soft oil prices as potentially 'the straw that broke the camel's back.'

The Moral Rearmament of Mexican Capitalism
The deal to increase US oil imports from Mexico at bargain prices was only part of the rescue operation launched in Washington in August 1982. The US also extended Mexico $1 billion in credits to finance wheat imports, and the Federal Reserve pitched in with $700 million in 'swap' loans. Before the crisis eased in 1984, the US had pumped into Mexico as much as $5 billion by some estimates. Moreover, the Bank for International Settlements pledged $1.85 billion, on condition that Mexico place its economic policy under IMF supervision. But that was the red flag waving in front of the Mexican bull.

Mexico has a long-standing antipathy to foreign financiers, dating back at least to 1853, when British gunboats bombarded Veracruz harbor and British banks took control of the customs house and its receipts. The IMF has also been regarded with suspicion, as a modern and somewhat more genteel gunboat.

There was no secret about the price tag an IMF deal would carry: reduced food subsidies and tariffs, cuts in public expenditures, hikes in prices, and less independence in energy policy. Lopez Portillo also knew that with the public denouncing his regime for its corruption, and blaming him for the economic crisis, he was about to leave office with his public stature at an all-time low. What was necessary was a gesture that would rehabilitate him in the public esteem, pass the buck, provide cover for the IMF, and placate the international bank creditors. It was a tall order, but there was a way to fill it.

Banks were natural targets for the politicians of the ruling Institutional Revolutionary Party [sic!] to attack in public and to foster in private. During the years of the oil boom, banks' unpopularity had grown with their power and profits.[20] Banks served as intake pipes for the foreign capital that funded major conglomerates that used the foreign loans collateralized on oil revenues to gobble up industrial sectors short of cash. Therefore, when a severe crisis struck in 1982, corporate debtors fell behind on payments, the financial position of the banks deteriorated, and the credit lines the Mexican banks had obtained from international banks were endangered.

For many years the left wing of the PRI and the independent political left had demanded nationalization of the banking system, while the PRI establishment had rejected it. Hence, there was both consternation and jubilation when Lopez Portillo ordered troops into the banks to prevent documents being removed or destroyed, cut telex lines between branches, had guards posted at the homes of the top bank executives, and then made his September 1 State of the Nation address in the House of Assembly, in which he imposed general exchange controls and nationalized the banking system.

There were many reasons for Lopez Portillo's dramatic move. It was a brilliant personal coup, reversing the decline in presidential prestige. He also hoped to enshrine his place in Mexican history. The nationalization of the banks was accompanied by comparisons to President Lazaro Cardenas's seizure of control of the oil industry from British and American companies in 1938, an event still celebrated with a national holiday.[21]

The nationalization also permitted Lopez Portillo to shift the blame for the economic and financial chaos: he denounced the bankers for sacking the national patrimony.[22]

For the PRI, nationalization paid big political dividends. The key to its long success had been its capacity to accommodate internally political diversity, as well as capturing labor and agricultural organizations as built-in bases of electoral support. In times of acute economic crisis, its inherent contradictions surfaced and threatened the establishment's hold on the party apparatus. With the bank coup, the IRP establishment countered the resurgence of the left, gained valuable breathing space for reorganization, and rehabilitated its claim to leadership in confronting the crisis.[23]

Under the aegis of the PRI-controlled labor and peasant organizations, 'spontaneous' demonstrations of support took place. The PRI called on workers to close their factories and hold pro-nationalization rallies at the presidential palace. The threat of the loss of a day's pay for failure to attend assured a massive turnout, and government agents organized the bussing of peasants to join the demonstrations. But however cynical on the part of the authorities, the move was extremely popular and assured that a party that had long 'ruled in the name of the poor but done the bidding of the rich' could continue its finest tradition.[24]

The *Wall Street Journal* saw through the farce quickly, noting that the PRI had to whip up nationalist fervor in order to get popular support prior to implementing a harsh IMF austerity package when the country was already crushed by debt and depression. The Argentine government had managed briefly to divert public attention from economic mismanagement by invading the Malvinas, but Mexico was hardly in a position to recapture the Alamo. Instead, it declared war on the banks. That permitted the PRI-controlled Mexican confederation of labor to 'agree' that the working class would defer demands for inflation-offsetting wage increases for four months as a quid pro quo for nationalization. The workers also 'agreed' to partake in the tradition of 1938 – when President Cardenas had called on the population to give their chickens and goats and wedding rings to the government to compensate the foreign owners of the oil wells[25] – by 'contributing' from their salaries toward the cost of nationalization.

Even more important than the political dividends was the reassuring effect of the nationalization on foreign banks. For when Mexico imposed foreign-exchange controls, it also established priorities for the use of foreign exchange.[26] First on the list came the servicing of public-sector debt. Once the domestic banks were nationalized, their debts to international banks also became a public-sector obligation, sharing first claim on the available supplies of foreign exchange. A spokesman for the Bank of America, the institution with the largest single 'exposure,' i.e., with the most to lose, in Mexico, declared, 'The decision announced by President Lopez Portillo has the merit of putting the Mexican state clearly behind its banking system.'[27]

Much more than the country's commercial banking system had fallen into the hands of the government. With the sixty banks came the shares (often large and controlling blocks) that the banks owned in industrial and commercial companies. Prior to the bank takeover, the government controlled nearly half of the GNP, acquired through major state initiatives in petroleum, steel, and railways, and by the acquisition of many companies through public bailouts. After nationalization, estimates of the state share in GNP ranged as high as 80%, though such extreme figures likely reflect the paranoia of American congressmen convinced that the Bolshevik hordes were assembling just south of the border.[28]

Mexico immediately followed the nationalization decree with explicit guarantees of interbank loans and credits. These were later extended to the international debts of many shaky private-sector companies as well.[29] Thus, whereas the 1938 seizure of the oil sector from British and American companies (to which the nationalization of the banks was being compared by friend and foe alike) had been followed by twenty years of international business boycott, the bank takeover seemed more likely to produce twenty years of international bank accolades.

With nationalization came calls to recapture the capital that had fled the country.[30] Lopez Portillo gave those who had sent funds out of the country thirty days to bring it back, thundering about penalties if they failed to do so. He called for the voluntary surrender to the government of the titles to real estate investments in the US worth as much as $31 billion. The government would pay for them in pesos and sell the real estate for dollars. So seriously were the threats taken that whenever dollars could be found they left the country just as before, with two possible exceptions: the government may have encouraged smaller-scale holders of assets to join their richer brethren in hightailing it for the border; and gold and silver coins and jewelry joined dollars as instruments of capital flight, even after the government banned that traffic as well.[31]

Although the government had seized the banks' records, virtually nothing was done to trace the departed wealth. Part of the problem lay in flight capital being routed through the offshore centers, which would hide the trail, and in the refusal of American banks to whom inquiries were directed to cooperate in the search.[32] But impolite speculation held that another reason for the gap between rhetoric and action was the number of prominent political figures who might be embarrassed by a successful hunt for buried treasure.

The initial domestic enthusiasm for the nationalizations soon calmed, perhaps dampened by the realization that the former owners were to receive a massive amount of compensation. Apart from producing a group of unemployed and angry former senior bank executives, the operations of the banks were unaltered. All but the top levels of management were left intact. Finance Minister Jesus Silva Herzog, who was regarded as essential to the successful conduct of negotiations with the IMF and the international banks, had threatened to resign over the exchange controls and nationalization. He made his continuation in office conditional on orthodox money men being appointed to head the banks.[33]

The left wing of the PRI demanded that the government either hold on to the stock of the companies picked up with the banks or resell it to unions, peasant organizations, and similar bodies to redress the maldistribution of wealth.[34] But once the new administration of President Miguel de la Madrid took office, the former owners of the banks were given first options on the stock. In the final analysis, over one-third of the equity in the banks was returned to the private sector once the international financial community had declared that Mexico had made a miraculous financial recovery.

The new administration wasted little time before making whatever concessions to the international financial institutions were necessary to obtain funds. Shortly after taking office, President de la Madrid purged the government of members of the left wing of the PRI, creating a cabinet and central bank staff more sympathetic to the IMF's demands,[35] and denouncing the 'financial populism' of his predecessor. Whipping up nationalist fervor against the banks, the IMF, and the United States had served its purpose, readying the mass of the population to accept a major attack on living standards: it was now time for 'responsible' statesmanship.

To maintain popular support in the face of further economic sacrifices, de la Madrid replaced Lopez Portillo's war on financial parasitism with a war on corruption. That had the virtue of making it appear as if the illegitimately rich would also bear a heavy share of the sacrifices necessary to pay the debts. Typical was the government's opening to public display the $2.5 million mansion of Mexico

City's fugitive $65-a-week police chief as a 'palace of corruption.'[36] Far more important, both symbolically and potentially, was the effort to bring 'moral renovation' to Petroleos Mexicanos.

Pemex was the doyen of Mexico's state enterprises, not least because it accounted for 25% of the public-sector foreign debt. Rather than Pemex being an administrative arm of the state, one could argue the reverse. Pemex was the country's leading source of foreign exchange (currently at least 75%) and the principal instrument of public finance. Created out of the foreign-owned oil companies expropriated in 1938, it exists as an important ideological component of Mexican nationalism. Pemex also had an important practical function in the Mexican political system; it spread its wealth geographically through development projects and socially through the sale of gasoline below cost. It was also a fat cow to be milked by politicians, bureaucrats, and union bosses.

When the cash crisis hit the Mexican economy, the state had to divert dwindling revenues from domestic development into external-debt service. The capital budget of Pemex virtually vanished, and the operating budget was slashed. Huge projects were canceled and massive layoffs threatened, as the state was forced to undermine its long-term foreign-exchange earning capacity in order to divert resources to the instant gratification of its foreign creditors. But such a diversion of resources required the weakening of union power, so the unions, too, were targeted for 'moral renovation.'[37]

Organized labor's crucial role in the 1938 takeover of the oil industry had been rewarded with participation in the operation of Pemex and the right of union-controlled enterprises to be preferred suppliers to Pemex. The Sindicato de Trabajadores Petroleros found its strength and its wealth increasing during the oil boom; by 1982 it numbered 150,000 members and controlled a 90-billion-peso treasury. Such a huge pool of funds enabled the union to dispense favors to politically useful individuals, including President Lopez Portillo, whose $2 million mansion in one of the most exclusive parts of Acapulco was reported in the press to be a gift from the union. Hence, when de la Madrid decided to take his war on corruption to the most powerful labor body in the country, he had no lack of ammunition.

Heading the union was Joaquin Hernandez Galicia ('la Quina') who ran a multimillion-dollar complex of companies that included a bank, food and department stores, a ranch, and a private militia financed by oil-company and union funds. La Quina was a close political ally of former president Echeverria, and it was his power that de la Madrid tried, unsuccessfully, to break. Another union boss, Hector Garcia Hernandez, better known as El Trampas ('the trickster') began his professional life as a chauffeur and built a financial empire using union and Pemex funds. According to El Trampas, when the 'moral renovation' campaign began, he agreed with the other union bosses to become the scapegoat: the union would press charges for defalcations against him alone. But the other bosses reneged on the deal, causing El Trampas to flee to the US, leaving charges of having embezzled 985 million pesos behind him. His stay in Texas was brief, for he was abducted, carted back across the border, and thrown in jail. The day of his abduction another union leader, who was also mayor of an important oil town, died in a mysterious car crash. His chauffeur was also found in the car, with a bullet in his head. Meanwhile El Trampas began telling his side of the story to the authorities, revealing, among other things, that one of his normal functions as 'education secretary' of the union was to handle the distribution of 'little gifts.' In the final analysis, the union lifted the charges against El Trampas in return for him giving his business empire to the union, which emerged from the fray little weakened.[38]

In all, union chiefs were alleged to have stolen as much as $1.5 billion. But if such union capers had actually happened, they followed the management example. Rumor puts the total drain from the Mexican national treasury (largely derived from Pemex) at more than $15 billion during the Lopez Portillo years – not far short of what was allegedly looted from the Iranian National Oil Company by the shah's entourage in the 1970s. Even before the change of administration, two deputy directors of Pemex were charged with a $97 million fraud involving deals to purchase equipment from US suppliers in return for bribes laundered through Swiss bank accounts. One of the two went to jail; the other hid out in Chile; and several executives of the US firms pleaded guilty to charges of corrupt practices brought by the US justice department. Even more important, the advent of de la Madrid to power was followed shortly by the jailing of the former head of Pemex, Senator Jorge Diaz Serrano, on charges of embezzling $34 million.[39]

It is likely, however, that Diaz Serrano's real crime was his aspiration to succeed de la Madrid in the presidency when other prominent PRI figures, notably Finance Minister Silva Herzog, also coveted the post.[40] Virtually every other investigation of Pemex defalcations was halted before any real conclusion could be drawn about the extent of the problem.[41] This reluctance to investigate might have reflected fears that the campaign would disrupt the functioning of the industry on which debt service depended.[42] It might also have been because of potential embarrassment to top figures in the PRI.

Behind this smoke screen, the government pushed up interest rates, devalued the peso, raised the prices of basic goods, and chopped state expenditures. Among the more useful economy measures may have been the grounding of some 750 executive jets used by government functionaries. Although the direct savings were of the foreign exchange required to keep the planes in service, a major indirect dividend was allegedly the removal from upper-level civil servants of a means of illegal currency export and contraband trade.[43]

The Mexican 'Miracle'

When President de la Madrid decried the 'financial populism' of his predecessor, he also repudiated Lopez Portillo's efforts to shift the blame for the crisis onto the international financial system. De la Madrid insisted – in language that could have come straight from any IMF-country report – that the causes of the problem were profligate government and consumer behavior, for which severe austerity was the obvious remedy. On the surface that remedy seemed to work. In 1981 there had been a $3.5 billion commodity-trade deficit; by the end of 1982 imports had been cut so much that there was a $5 billion trade surplus. During 1983 the surplus exceeded even the IMF-dictated target; and by 1984 Mexico was paraded as a model of fiscal and financial respectability.[44]

The oracles of 'sound money' exuded enthusiasm.[45] 'The medicine prescribed was as strong as it was effective,' The Economist proclaimed. A great to-do was made in the press over Mexico's repayment, by the summer of 1983, of its BIS and Fed loans (from the proceeds of new commercial bank loans!). A vice-president of the World Bank, Ernest Stern, contributed to the escalating nonsense by declaring that 'the way the people and government of Mexico have managed their crisis has filled the whole world with admiration.' But the prize goes to the Mexican economist who ventured that 'Financially things are going very well but economically things are going very badly'! That must have consoled the Mexican population: since 1982 they had experienced a 25% (by the end of 1984, 40%) collapse of real wages and an underemployment and unemployment rate of more than 50%.[46]

As incomes were squeezed, imports plummeted – from $24 billion in 1981 to $14.5 billion in 1982 to $8.5 billion in 1983. As Mexico lacked a real capital-goods sector, reduced imports translated directly into an industrial meltdown. Automobile production fell 70% in one year. Private domestic investment dropped by 23%. With so much idle capacity, domestic capital obviously chose to flee, with the US still the preferred final destination.

Unemployment in the smaller centers fed a migration to the cities and the further proliferation of slums. It also fostered the growth of petty crime. The employment crisis and sharply declining real wages increased the flow of illegal immigrants to the US, aided by 'immigration consultants' in the border regions. Congressional rednecks spoke of a plot by the international bankers to flood the US with illegal aliens in order to assure a flow back to Mexico of the dollars necessary to repay the debts.[47]

There actually was such a return flow of dollars, but not principally from clandestine remittances of Mexican unskilled laborers illegally at work in the US. After a series of IMF-dictated devaluations, Mexicans who had siphoned dollars out of the country could recycle them into real assets, their purchasing power enhanced sixfold. Speculators could pick up black-market pesos in the US for one-sixth of their former value and buy up Mexican real estate. Those who had incurred peso-denominated debts to secure the dollars they had parked abroad before August 1982 could discharge those peso debts for about 15% of the dollars they had previously obtained.

When, in 1983, Meyer Lansky died at a ripe old age, he must have been proud to see his influence stamped so strongly on the principles and practice of international finance, in Mexico and around the world.

Part Two

Parables of Peculiar Talents

5

Putting the Money Changers Back in the Temple

The world's most sanctimonious offshore banking center and tax haven sat, not on some idyllic Caribbean or South Pacific island, but in the heart of Rome. Nor did it originate in the plots and plans of American 'libertarians,' or in the schemes of Mitch WerBell's gunslingers. Rather it emerged from a fateful meeting in 1929 between Italian dictator Benito Mussolini and Pope Pius XI. That meeting laid the foundations for the creation of an institution through which Italian state finances could be subverted, capital flight encouraged, and Mafia money washed.[1]

Mussolini badly needed the support of the Vatican for a pending referendum to legitimize his seizure of power. To woo the church, he made the Vatican an offer it could not refuse. Under the terms of the 1929 Lateran Treaty, the Vatican was recognized as a sovereign state; the church was given the right to censor information reaching the Roman population even though the city was nominally subject to Italian civil law; the equivalent of $83 million at then-prevailing exchange rates was granted the church in compensation for lands seized by the Italian state; and church properties in Italy were exempted from taxation. In subsequent years, Mussolini was even more generous with the Italian taxpayers' money.

Another Kind of Fiscal Paradise
Aware that future economic (and therefore political) power would derive from financial assets rather than from landholdings, the Vatican's financial advisers put its Lateran Treaty wealth into gold, Swiss-based international financial holdings, and, especially, Italian financial and industrial assets. Among the latter were the burgeoning arms industry and the Institute for Industrial Reconstruction (IRI), the state-directed industrial-investment trust that formed the operational core of fascist economics.

In turn, Mussolini, about to rebuild the Roman empire, did what all good Roman generals did before embarking on a new campaign. He made an offering to the gods. Before his troops marched off to Ethiopia – an event some bishops hailed with waving flags – Mussolini exempted the Vatican from special taxes imposed on Italian corporations and real estate to help finance the war. In 1942 the Vatican received another exemption, from all taxes on dividends from its investments in Italy.[2]

At the end of the Second World War, the Vatican was concerned that the privileges it had won from Mussolini would be continued by the new, antifascist order. Part of the answer lay in fostering the growth, with the aid of the CIA (or, more precisely, its predecessor, the OSS), of the Christian Democratic party. When that party's hegemony seemed assured, and the Vatican had emerged from the war with its assets intact, the stage was set for the rapid growth of church wealth. It penetrated deeply and widely into the Italian economy during the boom of the 1950s and 1960s; then, however, things began to take a turn for the worse.

Since the late 1960s, the Vatican, like other sovereign states, has had a problem meeting its growing current expenditure obligations out of its current income. Like those of most other states, Vatican politics largely precludes serious expenditure reductions, apart from the possible savings to be derived from hampering the efforts of Vatican lay employees to unionize. The result has been increasing pressure on the Holy See either to sell off assets or to increase current revenues.

Although the 'wealth' of the church is indisputably enormous, much of it is in permanently illiquid form. The church cannot sell off its art treasures and buildings; many were bequests from the devout, often in the form of perpetual trusts. As for its investments around the world, estimated to total between $11 billion and $20 billion, which reputedly make the Vatican the most important single owner of equities on Earth,[3] the Vatican denies their existence as vehemently as it denies that its bank has functioned as a laundromat for Mafia money.

As the church's financial assets are, for one reason or another, sacrosanct, that left only the options of increasing income from ordinary budgetary sources and raising the rate of return on financial assets. Each of these, however, generated further difficulties.

During the Italian unification of the 1860s, the Vatican was stripped of most of its income-earning lands in Italy. To offset some of the loss an ancient source of revenue, St. Peter's Pence, was resurrected – a 'voluntary' contribution from believers for the pope's personal use. Its yield depends on the popularity of the reigning pope, which in turn has become a function of the number of his successful, high-profile public relations gestures. During the 1960s St. Peter's Pence were falling off; the Vatican, therefore, put pressure on its two main financial institutions to pick up a larger share of the bills.

One of those institutions is the Administration of the Patrimony of the Holy See (APSA), among whose functions is the investment of the money the church received under the Lateran Treaty. Traditionally, the investments were mainly in Italy; but at the end of the 1960s, that changed dramatically.

In 1962 the Italian government had announced its intention of lifting the tax exemptions Mussolini had granted the Vatican. The Vatican objected; the government backed down. A new government, led by Aldo Moro, pushed the issue again. The Vatican threatened to dump all its equity holdings; as Italian stock exchanges were notoriously thin, such an action would have caused a market panic. Again the government folded. But in 1968, a new government made it clear there would be no third reprieve, much to the delight of the political left, led by the Communist party, which had long lobbied for the end of the tax exemption.[4]

Although the Catholic orders and national church hierarchies immerse themselves to varying degrees and from varying perspectives in the political life of host countries the Vatican itself has a deeply entrenched political conservatism. True, there have been dissenting popes. One was John XXIII, who talked publicly of the immorality of the world capitalist order (thus, allegedly, causing the CIA to request that Italian military intelligence plant a listening device in the Vatican).[5] But such popes were aberrations. Even Pope Paul VI, who was in Vatican terms a 'liberal,' feared that the Bolshevik hordes gaining strength in Italian politics during the 1960s might seize, if not the Vatican itself, at least its assets.

Moreover, facing the church was the possibility of receiving a bill for unpaid taxes – that by some estimates could have run as high as $720 million. There was also the possibility of considerable embarrassment if the church were forced to reveal the extent of its financial-asset portfolio, not to mention some of its peculiar contents: in defiance of basic principles of risk diversification, the Vatican apparently simultaneously owned equity in firms making condoms and firearms.[6] Thus, in 1969, the Vatican turned to a trusted financial associate, a pillar of the Milan financial community, Michele Sindona.

While Paul VI, with Sindona's advice and prompting, publicly denounced 'the imperialism of money,' he privately was listening to Sindona's plans to move the Vatican fortune farther 'offshore.'[7]

Shifting Vatican assets abroad, together with the tens, perhaps hundreds, of millions lost in the 1974 debacle – when his banks came tumbling down – was not Sindona's only contribution to the Vatican's financial woes. Sindona also claimed credit for recommending Archbishop Paul Marcinkus as head of the Vatican bank, the Istituto per le Opere di Religione (IOR). Created in 1942, when Italy formally declared the Vatican a tax haven, the IOR had as its role the movement of funds out of Italy to support church organizations around the world. Today the bank accepts deposits of surplus funds from church-related organizations around the world and sends funds off to other church organizations so their schools, missions, and so on can avoid commercial bank borrowing. In between, the funds find their way into short-term loans in various national and international money markets.[8]

However, the IOR also has less ordinary banking functions. The great majority of its retail depositors have been laymen, principally though not exclusively Italians. The IOR would open accounts for persons recommended to it by existing account holders. Wealthy Italians seeking to render their money impervious to the triple evils of communism, taxation, and the declining lira came to the bank for assistance.

Italy has tight exchange controls. But there is no customs check between Rome and Vatican City. From the IOR, Italian money could be sent to the Swiss bank of the client's choice, perhaps the Vatican-controlled Banco di Roma per la Svizzera. Clearly, this was an open invitation not only to the tax dodger but also to organized crime: in 1978 a Roman priest was arrested and charged with buying marked ransom money for 70% of its face value and washing it through the Vatican bank.

The appointment of Paul Marcinkus as head of the IOR was an example of the growing concern of world bankers with the principles of liability management. At the time, the Vatican bank faced a falling-off of deposits from the US. Hence, the Vatican's financial advisers, David Kennedy of Continental Illinois Bank and Michele Sindona reportedly suggested that Archbishop Marcinkus of Chicago (perhaps the richest Catholic archdiocese in the world) could help reverse the deposit drain. More deposits meant more money to lend, and more profits, which meant a larger contribution by the IOR to cover the Vatican's operating deficit.[9]

Marcinkus was soon thinking like a true banker: the more money he made, the better able to conduct its business the church would be, and the higher he would climb in the hierarchy, perhaps all the way to cardinal, a rank that brought with it the financially useful perk of diplomatic immunity. Under the tutelage of his advisers, first Michele Sindona and then Roberto Calvi, Marcinkus launched the IOR on a stormy and tragic voyage in the unchartable waters of the euromarket, ultimately floundering and nearly sinking after an encounter with Exocet missiles in the south Atlantic.

Roberto Calvi's Expensive Ambitions

The Vatican had long involved itself in the tumultuous world of Italian banking. In the late nineteenth century, the church became increasingly concerned about the amount of Freemasonic influence in the 'lay' banks, a concern that reflected the powerful role played by Italian Freemasonry in the unification of Italy, in the subsequent stripping of church landholdings, and in demands for further secularization of Italian society. The response of the church was to encourage the creation of 'Catholic' banks, which often required the presentation of a baptismal certificate by prospective depositors or borrowers. Among these 'Catholic' banks was Milan's Banco Ambrosiano.[10]

Banco Ambrosiano became increasingly important in Italian finance during the 1950s and 1960s, as the Italian 'economic miracle' progressed. The geography of industrialization greatly increased the economic influence of the north in general, and Milan in particular. As the bank grew, so did the managerial authority of Roberto Calvi, whose earlier devotion to Mussolini and later devotion to 'Catholic' finance neatly symbolized what the Lateran Treaty had been about. In March 1982 an Italian lawyer was quoted in the glossy and prestigious *Euromoney* magazine as crediting Calvi with having built Ambrosiano into 'a big, solid, prosperous, well-run bank.'[11] Three months later it collapsed, in the greatest bank catastrophe since the Second World War.[12]

Before that event, Calvi had been busy remaking the Ambrosiano. Prodded by his business associate, Michele Sindona, Calvi sought to transform the staid Italian commercial bank into a top-level international merchant bank, an ambition requiring a major foray into the offshore world of peekaboo finance.

The Ambrosiano purchased one of Sindona's many Luxembourg ghost companies, which was renamed Banco Ambrosiano Holdings Ltd. Then Calvi acquired the Swiss Banco del Gottardo, which was strategically located to cash in on the steady flow of fiscal flight capital moving out of Italy for Swiss retreats. In 1971 what became Banco Ambrosiano Overseas Ltd. opened in Nassau with Bishop Paul Marcinkus on its board of directors. With a network that combined the fiscal advantages, bank secrecy rules, and freedom from regulation of Luxembourg, Switzerland, the Bahamas, and the Vatican, Calvi had a magnificent instrument for illegal capital movements for himself, his clients, and his eventual masters.

Calvi's close relations with the Vatican strengthened after Sindona departed for America. Not only was Calvi his natural successor as the Vatican's chief lay financial adviser, but after *il crack Sindona* (the 1974 debacle), Calvi's system reportedly replaced that of his former colleague as the main conduit for facilitating capital flight, and for financing the activities of the neofascist paramilitary organizations that were settling bloody scores with their left-wing competitors.

Calvi's succession was not entirely easy. The close financial association between him and Sindona was public knowledge. The noisy demise of Sindona in 1974, therefore, badly tarred Ambrosiano: depositors shied away, and its shares began to slide on the Milan market. Furthermore, the political environment in Italy was becoming uncomfortable for Calvi and his associates. The Communist party was making considerable gains, and Christian Democratic leader Aldo Moro began negotiations with the Communists with a view to bringing them into the government. Apart from posing a possible threat of nationalizing Ambrosiano, the Communists were on record as favoring a general cleanup of the banking system.

Calvi was therefore presented with a threefold challenge: how to assert a greater degree of personal control over the management of Ambrosiano in order to assure that his clandestine activities would remain unexposed; how to transfer the locus of control abroad, where it would be beyond the reach of an antagonistic government; and how to puff the value of Ambrosiano shares. For though in the short run the post-Sindona panic on the Milan market made the shares cheaper for Calvi to acquire, in the longer run declining share values would frighten away depositors. They would also threaten the bank's loan portfolio, because Calvi had already begun his own version of the loan-back scam.

In 1974, when shifting control of Ambrosiano offshore got well underway, the rapidly expanding euromarket provided excellent support. In conjunction with the IOR, Calvi had Banco Ambrosiano buy its own shares through the intermediation of offshore companies created for that purpose. Funds were moved from Milan to Banco Ambrosiano Holdings in Luxembourg, disguised as export-finance or ordinary interbank transactions, or were shifted by the 'sale' (to Calvi's companies abroad) of securities that were then 'bought' back at a higher price. BAH would then transfer the funds, along with hundreds of millions it eventually borrowed on the euromarket, to the Nassau affiliate, and subsequently to subsidiaries even farther afield. These companies, in turn, would lend the money to a string of Liechtenstein- and Panama-registered shell companies, technically owned by the IOR though controlled by Calvi, which would then buy the Ambrosiano shares via Banco del Gottardo in Switzerland or Banco Ambrosiano Overseas in the Bahamas.[13]

In the final analysis, some $1.3 billion were drained from Banco Ambrosiano or the euromarket borrowings of BAH Ltd. Between one-third and one-half of the total sum went to the shell companies to purchase the parent bank's shares, fulfilling Calvi's triple objectives. It supported share prices; it hid control from the Italian government; and it delivered to Calvi enough proxies to walk into shareholders' meetings holding 20% of the votes, more than enough for control. The rest of the money went through various channels for payoffs to the Vatican bank; illegal funding of political parties; financial support for Vatican-endorsed political causes, among them Pope John Paul II's favorite, the Solidarity trade union movement in Poland; building up secret Swiss bank accounts for Calvi and his political associates; and funding the activities of the Italian fascist secret society of which Calvi was the principal paymaster.[14]

Propaganda-Due
In 1738 the Vatican had responded to the anticlerical agitation of Freemasonic organizations by excommunicating Catholics who became Masons. In an effort to woo the Vatican (and to pander to the then-current paranoia about Freemasonic-Bolshevik plots), Mussolini also banned Masonic organizations and turned the secret police loose on them. Hence, after the war, Italian Freemasonry required reconstruction, an opportunity for the American OSS, which appreciated the potential of Masonic organizations for intelligence activity.[15] In 1948 a new Italian constitution legalized Masonic organizations, regardless of their attitude toward the Catholic Church, but banned secret societies, lay or religious.

The relationship between the Vatican and Freemasonry was contentious during the 1960s. Rapid industrial growth shifted demographic and economic power northward, away from Rome, thereby undermining the power base of the traditional right wing and the church. The left, particularly the Communist party, gained in strength. So, too, did demands for freeing Italian society from the influence of the Vatican, demands prominently voiced by Freemasons, among others. Nonetheless, one wing of Italian Freemasonry, the Grande Oriente, supported reconciliation with the Vatican. Although traditionalists within the church still fulminated at the very mention of Freemasonry, Pope Paul VI responded to Grande Oriente's overtures by watering down, though never eliminating, the Vatican's proscription of Catholic Masons, while prominent clerics talked about the possibility of 'Christianizing' Freemasonry.[16] Prominent among those 'Christianized' Freemasons was Licio Gelli.

A former Fascist party activist and veteran of the pro-Franco forces during the Spanish Civil War, Gelli also has on his curriculum vitae a stint as an SS Oberleutnant and 'interrogator' in Mussolini's short-lived Republic of Salo in 1944. After the war, Gelli got into the refugee and flight-capital trade. He allegedly helped to create the 'rat line' that moved fleeing Nazis and Fascists to South America, and reportedly relieved many of up to 40% of their wealth before the rest followed them into exile. He was also involved with supplies to NATO forces and free-lance arms-and-oil deals. He later served as 'economic consultant' to Argentine strongman Juan Peron. These activities laid the foundations of Gelli's personal fortune, which Roberto Calvi later estimated to be about $500 million. Gelli had been denounced as a spy and an arms peddler in 1949, but his reputation was laundered sufficiently that he operated in the 1950s as a go-between for the right wing of the Christian Democrats and the neofascist Movimento Sociale Italiano (MSI) party.

In 1965 Gelli was inducted into the Grande Oriente. Under its auspices he organized a special, ultrasecret, ultrarightist lodge, Propaganda-Due.[17] P-2 interfaced with other European right-wing political and paramilitary organizations in such 'Masonic' activities as international arms trafficking.[18]

Gelli's principal associate in the creation of P-2 was Umberto Ortolani, Second World War head of SISMI (Italian military intelligence) and confidant of the Vatican. It was in Ortolani's chateau that a cabal of cardinals planned the election to the papacy of a friend and admirer of Michele Sindona, Giovanni Montini, cardinal of Milan and subsequently Pope Paul VI. Ortolani, the 'Freemason,' was the recipient of Vatican honors, including the useful post of ambassador of the Knights of Malta to Uruguay, the main center for capital-flight operations in South America. By the remotest coincidence, Ortolani owned a Uruguayan bank.

The political ambitions of P-2 were to undermine liberal democratic institutions in Italy and parts of South America and to replace them with corporatist political systems inspired by Mussolini and Juan Peron. During the period up to 1974, P-2 perhaps initiated, and certainly assisted in, a threefold program. First, high-ranking military officers were recruited into P-2. Second, the group's bankers encouraged capital flight to put downward pressure on the lira; during the resultant financial chaos, the funds illegally moved out of Italy would be brought back again to buy up strategic parts of the Italian economy. And third, terrorist outrages from both extreme 'right' and extreme 'left' were fomented. The desired outcome was a psychological climate favorable to a military coup.

However, the plots failed, and the political environment in Italy blocked Gelli's plans. Christian Democratic Premier Aldo Moro opened political dialogue with the Communists. Success would have legitimized the Communist party, a development feared not only by the extreme right but also by the extreme left, which argued that street battles were the only path to political power.[19]

Hence, P-2 shifted from plotting a coup to constructing a parallel government in which the real power would lie.[20]

From 1975 until its exposure in 1981, P-2 infiltrated all facets of Italian public life: the state, the judiciary, the secret services, and the military. However, it did not completely abandon terrorist tactics. In the late 1970s, it was investigated in connection with right-wing terrorist bombings, assassinations, and kidnappings. It seems to have had a hand in the 1980 bombing of the Bologna railway station, which took the lives of eighty-five people. And it may have been involved in the 1978 kidnapping of Aldo Moro – the day after he invited the Communist party to join in a coalition government – and his subsequent murder. But the main thrusts of its activities were infiltration and manipulation.

In Italy, P-2 control of the secret services assured that infiltration could be kept clandestine, and that terrorist activities would be successfully covered up. Furthermore, P-2 made unprecedented invasions into strategic sectors of private business, particularly the mass media and financial apparatus. But the financial objectives no longer included wrecking the lira, at which Michele Sindona had been so adept. On the contrary. When the American Federal Reserve decided to fight inflation and the declining dollar by increasing interest rates, a flight of capital was induced into the US, and a sharp appreciation of the dollar relative to the lira resulted. This threatened and ultimately helped to destroy the grand schemes of Roberto Calvi, on whom P-2 relied heavily for funding.

Il Crack Calvi

To support his purchase of Ambrosiano shares and to finance P-2-controlled companies and projects, Calvi had to borrow, either from the euromarket or directly from Banco Ambrosiano. Yet the ultimate security for these loans consisted largely of shares in Ambrosiano itself. Calvi was incurring dollar-denominated debt to purchase lira-denominated assets while the dollar appreciated against the lira. Even worse, as borrowing rates shot up, funds were looted for payoff money, secreted in Swiss accounts, or plunged into money-losing propositions that the P-2 required for its subterranean political purposes.[21]

Finally, Calvi's bank could be saved only by an enormous infusion of capital. This could be done through the sale of new shares, but that might open the bank to the prying eyes of outsiders, including the Italian regulatory authorities. The sole alternative was a sharp appreciation of the price at which shares held by Calvi's offshore companies could be sold.

Bank of Italy inspectors were suspicious that the Banco Ambrosiano owned the companies that were buying its own shares. They were also convinced that some of Calvi's activities – selling shares to foreign-based companies and then buying them back at much higher prices – were a smoke screen for illicit capital exports. The meddlesome inspectors goaded Gelli into action: one of his captive judges ordered the jailing of a nosy Bank of Italy official on trumped-up charges. That bought Calvi time, which he used to rebury the bodies farther from the scene of the crime.

Among Michele Sindona's favorite business associates was the late Nicaraguan strongman Anastasio Somoza,[22] who combined an obsessive struggle against Central American communism with a strong desire to own as much of Central America as possible. These were complementary ambitions, for presumably whatever he owned was thereby rendered safe from communism. Somoza was also concerned with social justice, noting that 'poverty is a relative concept. It is not as hard being poor in Managua as it is in Bogotá, for example, where the climate is harsher.'[23] Roberto Calvi shared his view of the propitious climate in Managua. Among the loot that Somoza secreted in Switzerland were several million dollars paid to him, apparently on the advice of Sindona and Gelli, by Calvi in conjunction with the opening of Ambrosiano Group Banco Commerciale in Managua in 1977.

The Managua branch allowed Calvi's illicit dealings, formerly carried on through Nassau, to be shifted even farther from the scrutiny of Italian regulatory authorities; but it may have been profitable in its own right. Calvi had extensive, if shady, dealings in Central America, including a close friendship with the leader of the far right in El Salvador, Roberto d'Aubisson, the man accused of running death squads and arranging the murder of Archbishop Romero. In Nicaragua there was also much to do, especially once the Sandinista rebellion got under way. Ambrosiano allegedly bought property cheaply from fleeing Somocistas; it also financed the purchase of Israeli weaponry for Somoza in order to protect the bank's new investments.

The fall of Somoza did not immediately upset this comfortable arrangement. Even before the dictator's ouster, Calvi, evidently sensing which way the wind was blowing, had Banco Ambrosiano in Managua prudently diversify its investment portfolio. It apparently arranged the purchase of a large tract of land adjoining the Costa Rican border, across which arms could be smuggled to the revolutionaries. Once the new government was in place, it made a 'loan' to a failing meat-processing firm owned by the family of one of the members of the new ruling junta. Banco Ambrosiano was the only foreign bank not nationalized by the new government: nonetheless, it soon moved its operations to Lima.[24]

However, the parent bank was soon under fire from all directions: 1981 was a particularly bad year. In Spain, the Banco Occidente, a pillar of Catholic high finance, collapsed. Ambrosiano held a 10% interest, and the investment was wiped out. In Italy, a major P-2-controlled construction company, to which Ambrosiano had lent heavily, went under after it lost its Nicaraguan assets. Interest rates on the dollar-denominated borrowings by BAH Ltd. shot up. The Italian Guardia di Finanza – the police force responsible for investigating fiscal and monetary crimes – picked up where the Bank of Italy had left off and charged Calvi with illegal capital export.[25] After a brief stint in jail, Calvi was released pending appeal.

Nor were these the end of the bank's troubles. A police investigation into some of Sindona's tangled affairs led them to a factory owned by Licio Gelli. There, in a briefcase, was a list of nearly a thousand members of the P-2, a secret society banned under the Italian constitution. Among the names was that of Roberto Calvi. In the ensuing scandal, the Italian government, heavily infiltrated by P-2, collapsed; Gelli absconded; and Calvi's political and financial position was seriously weakened.

International banks cared little about either Freemasonry or Italian politics, consigning the first to the realm of the antiquarian and the second to the sphere of the occult. But the charges against Calvi for violation of exchange-control laws were a different matter. Banks shied from further lending to BAH Luxembourg, producing the ironic result that the only way to finance the various offshore operations was by draining more money illegally out of the Milan parent, intensifying the operation that had initially brought the charges against Calvi.

The ultimate security for many loans on the books of various Panamanian and Liechtenstein shell companies was shares in the Banco Ambrosiano; and by 1981 the hole in the parent bank's accounts had reached such proportions that it could be plugged only if the shares were to be sold for $200 each. Yet those shares had never risen beyond $40 on the Milan market. And the bank's desperate need for new capital gave the Italian securities commission a long-awaited opportunity to improve the efficiency of the Italian capital market.

The securities commission was a latecomer to the Italian regulatory scene, being created after *il crack Sindona* to prevent a recurrence of such a financial debacle.[26] It saw its function as improving the mechanisms for providing venture capital to Italian enterprises, for in Italy capital markets were weak and under-developed, which forced enterprises to rely heavily on bank credit; and the banks often lent more on the political affiliation of the borrower than on his creditworthiness.[27]

The securities commission had aimed to get the equity of Banco Ambrosiano, flagship of Milan finance, publicly listed on the Milan bourse. Calvi had long succeeded in confining trading in its shares to the over-the-counter market, which had much weaker disclosure requirements and could be more easily rigged, but he was finally forced to succumb to pressure to list the shares publicly. Desperate action was needed. As the shares could no longer be so easily puffed, the value of the security underlying the whole structure of borrowing was in danger. More ominous still, within a year of the opening of public trading, the consolidated accounts of Ambrosiano and its offspring would have to be submitted to public audit. When the shares opened on the Milan bourse, despite some prearranged support buying, they immediately fell 20%.

Early in 1982 a near-frantic Calvi had sought new shareholders to pump up the equity of the bank. One was Carlo Pesenti, another scion of 'Catholic' finance and owner of the largest financial holding company in Italy. But by the time Pesenti became the largest nominal shareholder of Ambrosiano, he was in perilous financial straits; and his shares in Banco Ambrosiano were bought with a loan – from Banco Ambrosiano!

The IOR's Paul Marcinkus assisted the rescue operation by announcing publicly that Ambrosiano shares were an excellent investment. It was far from a disinterested intervention.

When charges were laid against Calvi for violation of Italian exchange-control laws, and euromarket funds for the Ambrosiano group dried up, Banco Ambrosiano Andino in Lima began to worry about its exposure to the Liechtenstein- and Panama-based shell companies. Although Calvi had already been named as a member of P-2 and therefore theoretically in violation of the Vatican ban on Freemasonry, he appears to have had little difficulty getting Marcinkus to issue letters of comfort acknowledging the IOR's control of the shell companies. Although not legally binding, letters of comfort were – until the Calvi crash – widely used in international finance to accept responsibility for debts incurred by affiliated companies. And to all who queried the creditworthiness of the companies that borrowed so heavily from the Ambrosiano Group's offshore affiliates, the letters of comfort could be represented as a virtual Vatican guarantee of their debts.

However, as a precondition for issuing the letters of comfort – whose wording Calvi dictated – Marcinkus insisted on two conditions. First was that the letters not actually convey any obligation on the part of the IOR. Calvi therefore granted the IOR a secret absolution from all responsibilities to creditors that might be implied by the letters of comfort. The second condition was that Calvi have the mess cleared up by the end of June 1982, by which time he expected to find a buyer for the shares parked in the IOR shell companies. Indeed, he had already promised the Peruvian affiliate of Ambrosiano that the shell companies would repay their loans to the Lima and Nassau banks by June 13, 1982.

The June deadline was also important for another reason. Calvi was free on bail, pending appeal on charges of violating currency regulations; the new hearing was set for June 21, 1982. The Ambrosiano rescue had to be completed before the new hearings began, as there was no way to anticipate either what damaging information they would make public or their outcome.

The deadlines approached in a flurry of abortive salvage efforts.

One was headed by Robert Armao, a Rockefeller aide, whose experience in peekaboo finance allegedly included helping the Shah of Iran move money out of the country before the 1979 revolution. Armao's rescue package involved a consortium of Iranian royalists; hot money that had fled Iran was to plug the hole left by hot money fleeing Italy. Another involved Pierre Moussa, head of the most powerful French private bank, Banque de Paris et des Pays Bas, until the French Socialist government nationalized it – putting Moussa on the lookout for a new financial empire, as well as on trial for Calvi-style capital-flight charges. Yet another scheme involved financiers linked to the powerful and secretive Catholic organization, Opus Dei. It was apparently in conjunction with this last effort that Calvi, in early June 1982, rushed off to London to negotiate with potential buyers. His trip came to an abrupt end: he was found suspended under a bridge with a noose around his neck; but it was the bank, not the London bridge, that came tumbling down.[28]

Aftershocks

Only hours before Calvi's demise in London, his secretary allegedly jumped out a window of the bank headquarters building in Milan. These two 'suicides' conveniently eliminated the two parties most conversant with the inner affairs of Banco Ambrosiano. Soon afterward the bank itself followed them to its death. After its collapse, the BAH Ltd. debts went into default, and the shock waves in the euromarket measured about 9.5 on the Richter scale. For, though the Italian government was prepared to guarantee the domestic debts of the Milan bank, it refused responsibility for the $450 million (now swollen by compounded interest to $600 million) borrowed on the euromarket by BAH Ltd.[29]

The government of Italy had a simple and unassailable case. First, the Basle Concordat had never been intended to imply that central banks were obligated to guarantee the solvency of all banks in their jurisdictions; that would in effect be an obligation to guarantee all bank loans. Second, since BAH Ltd. was a holding company, not a bank, the central bank obligation to supervise the solvency of offshore affiliates and branches did not apply. Third, the Basle Concordat was not legally binding. A fourth, implicit argument was closer to the core of the issue – namely that if the eurobanks wanted the real culprit, they should knock on the gates of Vatican City, whose banker had refused to honor the letters of comfort issued to support Calvi's euromarket borrowings.[30]

While the major Western central banks tried to patch together the rags of the concordat, the international banks made a last-ditch effort to blackmail the Italian government. The major creditor banks of BAH Ltd. organized a carefully timed boycott of loans to Italy, just when Italy's balance-of-payments deficit needed external financing.[31]

The Bank of Italy organized a consortium of seven Italian banks to establish and manage Nuovo Banco Ambrosiano. To the new bank were transferred domestic business and most of the remaining assets of the defunct institution.

Again the international creditors cried foul, though not because a manager of the new bank decided to follow tradition and jump out a window.[32] Rather, the banks were upset because they had set their hopes on seizing those assets. They were joined by the shareholders of the old bank, who saw the last chance of recovering their investments disappearing with the assets. They blamed the securities commission for listing the bank on the exchanges, and thereby implicitly reassuring them that all was well. The securities commission in turn blamed the Bank of Italy for not giving it enough information about Ambrosiano's condition. The Bank of Italy rounded on the obvious target, whose machinations had provided the cover Calvi had used to plunder the bank into insolvency.

While fifty persons, including the three lay managers of the IOR, had their assets sequestered by the Milan magistrates as a result of their participation in the affair,[33] Archbishop Marcinkus was safe inside the walls of the Vatican, protected by its status as a sovereign country. Indeed, an effort by Bank of Italy inspectors to serve notice on the IOR that certain of its personnel might be implicated was stonewalled by the Vatican, which insisted that proper diplomatic channels be used to convey such information. The probings by Italian government financial officials did, however, end Marcinkus's other role, that of papal bodyguard and tour guide; without a cardinal's hat, he lacked diplomatic immunity from arrest should he step outside Vatican borders.

Inside the Vatican, Mussolini's legacy still provided protection; outside the walls, the Italian authorities moved to tighten safeguards against illicit capital movements. They also laid a political and diplomatic siege that ultimately brought down the IOR's freewheeling euromarket career, though not before the shock waves of the Ambrosiano crash were felt far and wide.

6

Of Dope, Debt, and Dictatorship

In October 1980, one month after a NATO-sponsored coup brutally ended several years of political turmoil in Turkey, the southern cornerstone of the NATO alliance,[1] London's prestigious *International Banking Report* made a cheerful announcement: 'A feeling of hope is evident among international bankers that Turkey's military coup may have opened the way to greater stability as an essential prerequisite for the revitalization of the Turkish economy.'[2] Those same international bankers were soon fondly contemplating the prospect of a Soviet invasion of Poland, the northern bulwark of the Warsaw Pact, with the same objective in mind – 'revitalization' of an economy shaken by civil unrest.

In the interim, the bankers were lending money to Banco Ambrosiano to assist it in its various business ventures. Among these were the handling of foreign-exchange transactions for the Italian company that supplied lethal ordnance to various Turkish paramilitary groups and the secret funneling of money, on Vatican orders, to the Solidarity trade-union movement to support its campaign to bring the Polish government to heel,[3] threatening the capacity of the Polish economy to service its international debts.

If politics makes for strange bedfellows, it has nothing on the perversity shown by international finance in selecting its conjugal partners.

Dry Run
In the aftermath of the First World War, the new republic of Turkey, under Mustafa Kemal (Atatürk), began the painful process of economic reconstruction, attempting to substitute economic nationalism for lost imperial grandeur. That strategy anticipated by several decades salient features of the 1950s and 1960s model of Latin American economic development.

Among those features were the economic leadership of the state and the encouragement – for a time under the influence of Soviet advisers – of heavy industry to serve the domestic market. To that industry flowed cheap credit from a state-controlled banking system, and cheap semimanufactured and intermediate products produced by state-owned industries. By the time the IMF intervened in the late 1970s, state economic enterprises accounted for 50% of Turkey's industrial output, and the state was responsible for 60% of the economy's investment.[4]

Another familiar feature was a financial crisis that served as a dress rehearsal for the international-debt debacle of 1982. By then, debt crises were sufficiently old news in Turkey that the country's manhandling by the IMF in the 1970s could be compared to the financial victimization of the Ottoman sultan by the banks of the great powers a century earlier.

The politics of debt in Turkey now, as in imperial times, turns on that country's strategic location in the geopolitics of great-power confrontation. Just as the Ottoman empire served as a Franco-British bulwark to keep the Russian navy out of the Mediterranean, so, today, Turkey deploys the largest NATO army, apart from the US, along its long land frontier with the USSR. Turkey is also a crucial military and political bridge between the Middle East and Western Europe.

This strategic role, enhanced by the fall of the shah of Iran in 1979, meant that the potential bankruptcy of the country and any consequent economic (and political) upheaval were considered by the Western alliance to be, in part, a security threat. (This was much the same view that the USSR took of economic disturbances in Poland in the late 1970s.) The security considerations prompted the government of West Germany to encourage its banks to lend heavily to Turkey in the 1970s; and ensured that when bankers' enthusiasm waned after 1978, economic and military aid was available from the West to fill in part of the hole.

Outside strategic pressures reinforced a propensity to militarization present in Turkey since the republican revolution of 1922; militarization in turn strengthened the tendency toward centralized economic planning.

Turkey's economic development strategy was in drastic violation of the canons of 'sound money.' In times of crisis, the banking system became loaded down with industrial loans that had gone sour. The state budget deficit had a built-in tendency to grow to finance the expansion, or merely the survival, of state enterprises. And ultimately the balance-of-payments deficit soared, as capital goods to sustain industrialization poured in, while manufacturing was trapped within the domestic market. Not surprisingly the Turkish military's principal battlefield experience came while under fire from the IMF.

For much of the 1970s, the IMF could only mouth platitudes about the virtues of the free market. Turkey secured adequate hard currency –

from the money sent home by its émigré work force in the Gulf and in Germany, and from international commercial bank borrowing – to ignore the IMF. But by 1978, Turkey was nearly a year behind on payments for imports; and the central bank admitted it had lost track of the size of the external debt. The international banks then shut off the tap. To the rescue came the IMF, assisting in a massive rescheduling of the debt and putting up the funds to allow many of the commercial banks to pocket their money and go home. That left the IMF holding the empty bag, realizing too late that future grand country-rescue operations would have to include measures to prevent the international banks from taking the money and running.

The 1978 rescue operation required the Turkish government to endorse the usual program of austerity and 'liberalization': cutting back on the growth rate of the money supply, slashing the public-sector deficit, curtailing public subsidies, and shifting resources into the export sector. The government's efforts to comply fed a wave of strikes through 1979, and the ensuing violence nearly culminated in civil war.

The fact that militias of all political tendencies seemed to be buying their arsenals from the same sources pointed to the possibility of a deliberate orchestration of the violence – of the sort P-2 had attempted in Italy a few years earlier – to prepare the psychological climate for a military coup. It also pointed to the link between rising street terror in Turkey and the revolution in the international heroin trade caused by the Soviet invasion of Afghanistan.

Resurrection of the Golden Crescent

Legend has it that when Meyer Lansky's old business partner, Lucky Luciano, was sprung from an American prison and deported to Italy, the stage was set for the French Connection. Turkish opium, refined into morphine, was smuggled with the aid of the Sicilian Mafia to Marseilles, where the Corsican gangs further refined it into heroin and arranged its transportation to the US.

During the Vietnam War, the most important source of America's heroin supplies became the Golden Triangle, the contiguous parts of Laos, Burma, and Thailand. Then, in the early 1970s, came the fall of the French Connection. The US and France broke up the trafficking rings, and Turkey suppressed opium production – much to the joy of the warlords of Southeast Asia, whose opium the CIA was merrily flying to market.[5]

At the time of the 'breaking' of the French Connection, nearly half a million Anatolian farmers depended on the opium poppy crop. It provided not only cash, but also cooking oil, animal feed, fuel, and other essentials. Suppression of the crop had to await a 1971 military coup that produced a government ready to trample on peasant rights in return for $100 million in American military aid. Actually Turkey's importance in supplying illicit drugs had been greatly exaggerated for public-relations purposes by the Nixon administration,[6] and the global supply of illegal narcotics actually rose in the following years. Nonetheless, the Middle East ceased to be a significant supplier, ceding place to Mexico and, especially, the Golden Triangle. Then, in 1979, events changed dramatically.

The Golden Crescent area, formed of parts of Iran, Afghanistan, and Pakistan, had long been a minor exporter of drugs. Pakistani opium would be refined into heroin in Iran.[7] This traffic expanded briefly at the time of the fall of the shah. The secret police, the SAVAK, allegedly stopped making arrests for drug offenses, permitting fleeing Iranian royalists (and SAVAK officers themselves) to buy heroin with Iranian currency for resale in hard currency abroad, thus assuring retirement funds for those close to the shah and building up a war chest for a possible counterrevolution.[8] But the Khomeini regime smashed the Iranian traffic, and the government of Pakistan closed many of that country's opium dens. Denied domestic and export markets, Pakistani producers faced an opium glut and a catastrophic price collapse.

The invasion of Afghanistan turned the situation around. As refugees poured into Pakistan, the CIA was on hand to organize resistance groups. Resistance groups needed money to buy arms, and in the international arms trade, heroin has long been hard currency. Soon a drug mafia in the northwest frontier province of Pakistan was converting the Pakistani opium into morphine and heroin for export. By 1984 Pakistan was supplying anywhere from 30% to 70% of American consumption, 80% of that of Europe, and, some claim, up to 90% of that of New York.

The drugs reached their final markets by several routes.[9] Some moved from Karachi across the Arabian Sea to Dubai, long the entrepôt for smuggling gold to and from the Indian subcontinent. From 1982 to 1983, seizures by Dubai customs of illicit drug cargoes jumped 600%. Some went southward via India and out through the flourishing contraband center of Bombay. And a not inconsiderable amount appears to have transited Turkey, through that country's thriving underworld. The drugs flowed out to European and American markets, and the weapons to sustain the rush toward civil war flowed back in.[10]

Sewing the Whirlwind

During 1979 and 1980, the Turkish unemployment and inflation rates rose while real wages fell. World recession reduced the chances of alternative employment in Europe; remittances to Turkey from émigré workers dropped off. Meanwhile, interest rates on its $20 billion foreign debt and oil-import costs climbed. By the end of 1980, the balance-of-payments deficit hit a record high.

In 1980 the government and the IMF negotiated a $1.6 billion loan, the largest to that date in the fund's history. The conditions were the standard ones: steady devaluations of the currency, a substantial hike in interest rates, and a sharp cut in public-sector expenditures. When Economic Planning Minister Turgat Özal pleaded with the parliamentary opposition for three years in which to turn the situation around, the opposition leader, Bulent Ecevit, commented, 'A model that has gone bankrupt in Latin America is now being imported into Turkey. Either it will not work or it will put constraints on democracy. It cannot be applied without bayonets.' A few months later, the military took power.

Özal's program had three explicit objectives. The first was to open the highly protected economy to international trade, promoting exports in the hopes of cutting back the huge balance-of-payments deficit. The second was to reduce Turkey's dependence on foreign credit by raising the level of domestically supplied investment funds through increased interest rates. The third was to chop the public-sector deficit, forcing 'efficiency' on state enterprises to restrain the growth of the money supply and hold down inflation.

This was standard IMF cant, ranging from gross oversimplification to simple error. But there was a fourth, implicit objective of the program. Reducing real wages would curtail domestic consumption of goods and services; it would free productive resources for the export sector, where they could earn the foreign exchange necessary to service the foreign debt. As the military banned strikes and arrested union leaders, some of whom were condemned to death, this part of the program was relatively easy to implement.

For the first two years, the program seemed a roaring success. The inflation rate fell from 130% in 1980 to 30% in 1982. Although GNP dropped 1.1% in 1980, it rose 4.4% in 1982. The public-sector deficit, 7.1% of GNP in 1980, was down to 3.2% in 1982. Most dramatic was the turnaround in the balance of payments. From the historically high deficit of 1980, export revenues were climbing rapidly by 1982, while import demand was held in check. The international banks were sufficiently impressed that Turkey was welcomed back into the syndicated loan market. The IMF mandarins beamed.

The only problem was that it was a sham. The sole reason for success was the achievement of the fourth, implicit objective of the IMF program. As the state-sector budget was slashed, state enterprises laid off workers en masse. As the prices of basic goods were pushed up and collective bargaining was abolished, the real income of the employed dropped. Credit stringency generated bankruptcies in the private sector and even more unemployment. The collapse of domestic purchasing power generated the exportable surpluses, and the Iran-Iraq war, which heated up after the middle of 1982, opened up a fortuitous and temporary market for those products.[11]

In the meantime, the balance sheets of the largest corporations deteriorated, and the Turkish banking system entered its worst crisis of solvency in the country's history.

As big business became increasingly estranged from Özal's policies, pressure mounted on the military to curb his enthusiasm for 'free-market' solutions. Factions of the bureaucracy also reacted defensively to the attack on the public sector's role. And within the military, which saw itself as custodian of the Atatürk tradition, there was a natural propensity to favor *dirigiste* over free-market solutions. But Özal had the backing of Washington, and was difficult to remove from power, until the pioneering endeavors of the Turkish underworld helped to produce a money-market panic that threatened the entire credit system.

The Long Arm of Bekir Celenk

Information on the alleged movement of drugs often reflects more about the physical location of paid informants of the US Drug Enforcement Agency and the US government's desire to blacken a regime's public image than it does about the realities of underworld activity.[12] Nonetheless, the Turkish phase of the reactivated Golden Crescent narcotics trade seems to be a monument to multinational cooperation. Heroin and morphine, manufactured in Pakistan by Pathan tribesmen of Afghan origin, are carried by Baluchi nomads into Iran and passed to Kurdish smugglers who transport it into Turkey.

From Turkey the underworld seems to move it along two main reexport routes. One crosses Syria to Lebanon, where the product provides its many paramilitary groups with the means to finance their imports of weaponry. While their followers were exhorted to selfless sacrifice for creed and country, the Christian warlords of Lebanon were murdering one another's offspring in clan vendettas inspired in part by the need to jockey for position in Lebanon's multibillion-dollar hashish, morphine, and heroin export trade.

Another route allegedly runs from northwestern Turkey into Bulgaria, across Yugoslavia, and over to Trieste. From there it splits in two. The most important subroute heads northward to Munich, European political and contraband center of the Gray Wolves, the terrorist arm of the

Turkish fascist movement. From Munich much of the continental European market is serviced.

The second subroute runs from Trieste to Sicily, and then across the Atlantic.[13]

Despite the small role it plays in feeding American habits, the Bulgarian route for transiting narcotics has made for excellent propaganda by cold war ideologues (particularly when enhanced by tales of attempted popicide by the joint forces of Bolshevik Atheism, International Terrorism, and the Islamic Jihad against Western Civilization).[14] The mundane truth seems to derive from Bulgaria's historic role as a transit trade route between East and West and from its need for hard currency. For all its Stalinist orthodoxy in domestic ideology and foreign policy, Bulgaria has the most open frontiers of the Eastern Bloc. Sitting astride one of the world's major overland trade routes, the country also sees millions of people crossing its borders each year. Adequate policing of the traffic is likely impossible, even if the Bulgarians were interested in trying, which they may not be.

The acute need for foreign exchange may blind Bulgarian customs officials to the contents of the bonded vehicles that cross their jurisdiction, provided the transit fees are paid. And some officials may follow the exhortations to entrepreneurial initiative they can hear over Voice of America and resell some of the heroin that they do confiscate. Bulgaria also mixes itself in the international under-the-counter arms traffic, which is a virtual mirror image of the international trade in narcotics.[15]

During the late 1970s, arms dealers smuggling their wares to Lebanon and Turkey were reported to be paying a commission of 12% to 15% to Bulgarian customs; Bulgaria was sufficiently impressed to get involved directly. If the arms went to destabilize a major NATO country, that would be the icing on the cake, but this evidently was not a primary motivation, for Bulgaria was happy to peddle arms to the fanatically anticommunist regime in Pretoria. When the South African state gunrunning operation, ARMSCOR, operating through its Liechtenstein *anstalt*, looked for weapons to bolster rebel groups in Angola and Mozambique, Bulgaria was willing to sell,[16] while the USSR, supposedly Bulgaria's master, was busily arming the government forces of Angola and Mozambique against the rebels.

Bulgaria's involvement in narcotics trafficking would seem to be an incidental result of its accommodating view toward the major Turkish arms smugglers, who reputedly transacted their business in Sofia at the fabled Vitoshi Hotel. All the major Turkish gunrunners arrested after the coup were found to have been also involved in drug trafficking under the protection of a domestic network of corrupted customs officials, police, and politicians of extreme right-wing views. The link between narcotics, arms dealing, gold and foreign-exchange smuggling, and Bulgarian customs was the subject of public speculation in Turkey. Indeed, Turkish Mafia godfather Abuzer Ugurlu allegedly became sufficiently worried about investigations being conducted by independent left-wing journalist Apdi Ipekci that in 1978 Ugurlu paid fascist militant and assassin-for-hire Ali Agça to put a permanent end to Ipekci's inquiries.[17]

Ali Agça spent only a short time in jail before a guard was bribed to facilitate his escape. And though Abuzer Ugurlu was subsequently convicted of trading drugs for weapons and jailed for fourteen years by the military authorities, one of Ugurlu's principal business associates, Bekir Celenk, beat a hasty retreat to Bulgaria, where his alleged relationship with Ali Agça gained him some unexpected notoriety.[18]

Son of a watchmaker from a small village near the Iraqi border, Celenk had a number of early brushes with the law. To get him out of trouble, his father arranged for Bekir to join the Turkish exile community in Munich, where he entered the 'import-export' business. His ostensible concern was shipping electrical appliances and automobiles to Middle Eastern markets; he added Swiss watches some years later. He also purchased a share in a small Panamanian-registered shipping company, and set up shell companies in the usual places. But officials claim that all these were merely a cover for his dealings in morphine and weapons.[19]

After decamping hastily from Switzerland, leaving behind unpaid debts amounting to 8 million Swiss francs, Celenk returned home in 1979, only to flee once more, charged by the military authorities with illegal capital export, fiscal fraud, and similar offenses. He did a brief stint in London, managing his shipping company. Business appears to have been good, and Celenk's ships were reputed to carry cargos on behalf of a Milan-based firm named Stibam International Transport Corporation. Celenk, however, soon found himself accused, over his vehement denials, of having paid Ali Agça to shoot Pope John Paul II.

Meanwhile, all was not well in the arms and narcotics business. When Italian authorities made a major drug seizure in northern Italy late in 1979, the drugs were found to have come from a new Middle Eastern source. The seizure also led to the arrest of Karl Kofler, who had been running morphine to Palermo by ship and the resulting cash to Monaco by taxi. There, obliging bank officials oversaw its onward travel, into Switzerland and Germany. While in custody, Kofler began giving information to the police. Although his testimony was abruptly terminated by a 'heart attack' assisted by a strategically inserted hat pin, his information eventually led police to Bekir Celenk's business associates at Milan's Stibam Corporation. Apart from a client list that included prominent members of the Turkish underworld, Stibam also had the curious fortune to have placed its headquarters in a building owned by Milan's Banco Ambrosiano, through which Stibam transacted its foreign-exchange business.[20]

Hanafi Arslanyan, head of Stibam, was truly a man of the world. A Syrian citizen, Arslanyan was an Armenian from Turkey, where he had cultivated a close association with the leading 'babas'[21] (the godfathers of the Turkish underworld). He lived in Italy, transacting his business throughout the Middle East and around the world. From Stibam Corporation flowed arsenals for the armies, private and public, that had turned so much of the Middle East into a charnel house. Back to Stibam flowed payment, sometimes in dollars to be washed through its Liechtenstein *anstalt*, and sometimes in narcotics moving from the Golden Crescent via Turkey for Western markets.

The main market for arms shifted among Turkey, Lebanon, and Iran, depending on the direction in which the trade winds and the fortunes of war were blowing. However, Stibam expanded its business beyond the Middle East. It was via Stibam that Taiwan allegedly acquired 238 tanks; the Philippines got an array of transport planes, missiles, helicopters, and even frigates; and Somalia acquired 116 tanks and 20 helicopters. The export goods in which the company dealt ranged from handguns and light machine guns to assault helicopters and Leopard tanks. In its final days, which were also the last days of the Malvinas War, the company was even reputed to have put Exocet missiles in its catalog. If true, this would have earned it the enmity of the British secret service and may have led directly to the company's demise as well as hastening that of its landlord.[22]

Five months after the Ambrosiano crash, Stibam was busted by the Italian police; they seized $690 million 'worth' of narcotics and arrested Arslanyan and two hundred others.[23] The size of the operation was so staggering that an Italian parliamentarian was moved to ask how Stibam could have operated for so long and on such a scale without the knowledge and/or intervention of the Italian secret services. To such an obvious question there were at least two answers.

Among those charged in the Stibam bust were individuals who combined high-level political influence with membership in Licio Gelli's P-2. As P-2 included fifty top-level military officers and the heads of the secret services, exposure of Stibam would logically have to await that of P-2.[24]

A second possible answer is Stibam's alleged operations on behalf of the CIA; the agency may have reciprocated by blocking Italian efforts to interfere.[25]

A third possibility may also have influenced the timing of the exposure. In 1982 the Italian government began a major drive to penetrate the Middle Eastern arms market; and this may have made it less tolerant of private competitors, particularly those whose foreign-exchange business was conducted through Banco Ambrosiano, one of the principal vehicles of evading Italian exchange-control regulations. The government's tolerance would be further tried by a private-sector competitor that was also earning foreign exchange for the Bulgarian government when accusations directed at Ali Agça's colleagues in Sofia had brought relations between Italy and Bulgaria to a postwar low.

Undoubtedly Hanafi Arslanyan could have shed much light on these hypotheses, but while in prison awaiting trial, he died of the usual heart attack. No hat pin was mentioned.[26]

Meanwhile, the Turkish government was struggling to placate the IMF and the international creditor banks by trying to weather the financial legacy of Hanafi Arslanyan and his Turkish, Bulgarian, and Italian associates. Through the financial storm and fury, it fought not only to keep the ship of state on an even keel, but sometimes to find and grasp the helm.

Money Brokers Take a Turkish Bath

In Turkey, as in many developing countries, big business was frequently organized in holding companies built around banks through which the bulk of the conglomerate's funding was done. Those banks raised money by begging (from the central bank), by borrowing (from international money markets), or by stealing (from depositors through interest rates lower than the inflation rate).

As the Turkish central bank, under IMF pressure, tried to curb borrowings by the commercial banks, and as the international banks cut off Turkey's credit, the depositors in the domestic banking system became the only source of funds. But Turkey had legal limits on interest rates. Nor were the banks eager to raise them, since that would adversely affect the rates at which they could lend to their associated companies. Hence, people with cash surpluses used them to buy real estate, to speculate in the black market, or to buy foreign currency or gold rather than effectively paying the banking system for the privilege of seeing their money lent to the big industrial corporations.

In the heart of the Istanbul souk, the so-called Tahtakele Central Bank, the illegal market in gold and foreign currencies operated openly. It converted hard currency and gold into Turkish lira, on behalf of émigré workers, black marketeers, and ordinary savers, and converted lira into hard currency and gold, on behalf of corporations desperate for imported goods and persons fleeing the police and military. Then the government came up with another idea.

In July 1980, Turgat Özal, then deputy prime minister, secured the repeal of the usury laws. Sharply raising interest rates on bank deposits and loans was supposed to encourage the public to bank more money, diverting the flow of savings from the black and speculative markets. The banking system could then make the money available for above-ground transactions. That was the theory.

The reality was that interest-rate hikes, together with IMF-dictated increases in the price of publicly supplied goods at a time of general recession, devastated the financial position of many corporations. They could pay interest on their bank loans only by borrowing more. The banks had to scramble for new deposits. They could bid to draw off one another's sources of money, but they preferred to avoid that. Or they could search for new money from outside the traditional banking system, notably the hoards of black-market money whether derived from smuggling, arms and drug dealing, or from routine tax evasion – if they could be laundered and cooled.

The banks were not alone in eyeing black-market funds. The government was under constant pressure from the IMF, which saw the growth of the money supply as a symptom, not of the breakdown of social order, but of the profligacy of government. Much of the hot money was held not in cash but in anonymous bank accounts payable on demand and as liquid as cash. Banks hankering after the hoards of hot money together with the government's desire to brush up the money-supply data to placate the IMF led to a large-scale laundry operation.[27]

It is purely coincidental that Bernie Cornfeld was born in Istanbul, though the technique chosen for the Turkish laundering operation might have been of his inspiration. It was the certificate of deposit in 'bearer' form. These CDs – anonymous, high-interest bearing, and transferable – would wash the black-market money and make the funds available on a medium-term basis to the banks' desperate corporate clients. Unlike cash and bearer-demand deposits, CDs did not count as part of the official, measured money supply. Therefore, any money shifted out of cash or deposits on which checks could be written would automatically reduce the money-supply figure that Turkey had to report to the IMF.

In short order the race was on, and the bidding war pushed up interest rates on CDs sufficiently that people hawked their jewelry, mortgaged their homes, and borrowed from one bank to acquire CDs issued by another. Puffing the process were professional money brokers who marketed the paper on behalf of small banks without extensive branch networks from which to sell CDs to the public.

Most prominent among these brokers was Cevher Ozden. Operating as Banker Kastelli, he became big in the 1970s as a stock and bond broker and foreign-exchange dealer. As marketing agent for ten small banks, Kastelli handled the savings of 300,000 people (totaling $700 million) and marketed 25% of all CDs sold in Turkey.[28]

The race for hot money was not without casualties. Late in 1981 the central bank, perhaps in response to the pressure of the big banks, raised the level of mandatory cash reserves of commercial banks; the resulting liquidity crisis wiped out several small money brokers: unlike Roberto Calvi, Istanbul's Banker Servat did not bother with rocks and ropes, but simply jumped off the Bosporus Bridge and drowned himself when his brokerage house began to founder.

It was a classic bubble in the making. As interest rates rose and business conditions deteriorated, corporations demanded still more bank credit. The banks could meet the demands of their corporate clients only by marketing more CDs, which required that they offer higher yields. The banks pressured Kastelli to sell more of their CDs and to speed up the turnover of the cash from the sales.

The government had insisted that CDs be sold strictly for cash, for only cash sales would achieve the bookkeeping objective of reducing the measured money supply. But banks sold the CDs for credit, accepting Kastelli's checks and agreeing to a certain delay before cashing them. In the interim, Kastelli could use the money to conduct his own lending business, the profits from which allowed him to offer a higher rate of return on CDs than his competitors. However, as economic difficulties deepened, firms to which Kastelli had lent money fell behind on their payments. He, in turn, had to ask the banks to further stretch the terms of payment.

At that point, the central bank chose to tighten up reserve requirements once again. The banks, desperate for cash, refused Kastelli the extension. With the market for CDs glutted by mid-June 1982, and with the banks pressing for payment, Kastelli requested aid from the central bank. When assistance was refused, he boarded a plane for Geneva, his collateral checks bounced, and his bank suspended payments.

Two other major money brokers followed suit. Runs began on several commercial banks, some of which were forced to close for several days. Tanks surrounded Kastelli headquarters, and the police cordoned off the premises of one of the banks on which the run was most severe. Finally the government intervened, guaranteeing the principal on all outstanding bonds, savings accounts, and CDs marketed by the brokerage houses. It also pumped anywhere from a conservative estimate of $200 million to a more likely one of $543 million into the commercial banking system – sufficient to send the money supply soaring well above the IMF target.

Down for the Count

Initially Deputy Prime Minister Turgat Özal tried to hang tough, refusing any bailout of the banks or big corporations. But if Özal balked at the sight of the growing queue of mendicant capitalists, others were moved, particularly the mendicant capitalists themselves and sympathetic military authorities. The crash and its aftermath gave the military a pretext to dismiss Özal and his finance minister.[29]

The new finance minister, Adnan Kafaoglu, faced the same problems: the need to launder black-market money, and how to reconcile IMF targets with corporate-sector demands for financial relief. But he approached them quite differently.

The government decreed an amnesty for the hot money of black marketeers, smugglers, and tax evaders. All that was required was that the funds be deposited in the state-owned Ziraat Bank[30] over the weekend, no questions asked. The state would charge a 1% laundry fee, about the same as Florida bank rates for handling drug money. On Monday morning the money would be returned to the depositors, squeaky clean.

It was a stampede. Fully 100 billion Turkish lira, equivalent to 25% of all cash in circulation, appeared for a cleansing. The commercial banks were hit with massive runs, as deposits were drained to participate in the cleansing. The commercial banks turned once more to the central bank and the money-supply targets went out the window again, once more calling forth the creative talents of government financial technocrats.

After Monday washday, Kafaoglu was still left with one of his problems: reconciling the strict IMF money-supply target with the ever-growing number of corporations requiring a life-saving infusion of public funds. The country seemed to face a grim choice: it could accept the IMF's constraints on the money supply and public-sector deficit and let its major industrial groups collapse, driving up an already appallingly high unemployment rate. Or it could bail out the companies, at the risk of pushing the public-sector deficit and money supply beyond the agreed levels, and consequently threatening the continuation of IMF loans needed to meet payments on its foreign debt. The IMF, badly needing a 'success' to flaunt before critics of its policy prescriptions, was publicly adamant.[31]

Yet both sides seemed to win. The money-supply figures were staying within their IMF-prescribed range[32] even though the state takeover of big industrial companies and ailing and failing banks must have been a heavy drain on the state budget.[33] What magic was involved in the Turkish solution to a common developing-country dilemma?

Once more it was Ziraat Bank to the rescue. Every Friday night from the end of July 1982, until December 1983, when the trick was exposed, funds were drawn out of Ziraat Bank and deposited in the central bank. Then the weekly money-supply calculations were made. As Ziraat was one of the largest banks in the commercial sector and operated all the private banks taken over by the state, the transfer of deposits made a dramatic dent, at least in the data. On Monday morning, the funds were shipped back to Ziraat for business as usual. For fifteen months, the secret transfers and cooking of the books went on, until brought to an end by the unexpected results of the first general election since the coup.

Despite the opposition of the military junta, the victor in that election, and therefore prime minister-designate, was Turgat Özal, in a political comeback. With 'sound money' now back in the saddle, the secret transfers were stopped and exposed.

But why had the IMF been so silent during months of statistical fraud? Either its technocrats were unable to detect it – good news, indeed, for developing countries everywhere – or the IMF had been privy to the scam, so it could continue to beat other developing debtor countries over the head with the example of Turkey's 'good behavior.'[34]

7

Playing Russian Roulette
with the Polish Debt

Good behavior among debtors was in short supply as the 1980s unfolded. Nor was the deportment of some creditors much better. After Ali Ağça pulled the trigger in St. Peter's Square on May 13, 1981, he neglected to put forward the one explanation that might have won him absolution, namely that he was defending the stability of the international monetary system against attempts by John Paul II and his bankers, Calvi and Marcinkus, to undermine it. (Nor did Ali then advance his subsequent claim to be Jesus Christ reincarnate, a claim that, if validated, might have given him the spiritual if not the temporal authority to dispose of popes at will.)

Ali Ağça initially chose to play dumb, claiming only that the botched assassination attempt was a purely individual enterprise. But after some prison visits from military intelligence officers, he changed his story dramatically. Ali's 'testimony,' which bore a textural affinity to Swiss cheese, gave birth to the Bulgarian Connection.

Connections: Loose and Bulgarian

According to this theory,[1] the KGB deployed its loyal Bulgarian assets, who in turn called in debts owed them by the Turkish underworld, to arrange the murder of a pope whose sponsorship of democratic freedoms in general and Polish trade union rights in particular threatened the totalitarian order. Central to the theory is that the KGB obtained as its agent a member of the fanatically anticommunist Turkish Gray Wolves, a collection of thugs who passed the time attacking left-wing, including pro-communist, political targets in Turkey, staging holdups, and running contraband in and out of the country.[2]

As to the Turkish babas' reputed recruitment of Ali on behalf of the Bulgarian secret service, it is quite plausible that the Bulgarian secret service would sometimes request their assistance for covert operations, in exchange for running cover for their smuggling activities. After all, there is nothing inherently improbable, or unique, about the association of the underworld of crime – covert economic action – with the underworld of 'intelligence' – covert political action. (The CIA tried to point Mafia hit men and their hardware in Fidel Castro's direction to try to curb un-American activities in Cuba – such as the closure of American-mob-owned casinos.)

Ali Agça, in his 'evidence,' claimed that Oral Celik, Turkish mobster, head of the Gray Wolves chapter in which Ali was enrolled, and allegedly the second hit man in St. Peter's Square, was actually an agent of Bulgarian intelligence. Furthermore, Ali claimed, his former mentor, Turkish crime czar Abuzer Ugurlu, held shares in Bulgarian companies manufacturing counterfeit goods for sale in the West, as well as in Bulgarian state enterprises dedicated to arms trafficking and drug dealing.[3] This was the first time the public was made aware that the Bulgarians were sufficiently advanced on the capitalist road to allow private foreign investment in their state companies.

One person who could have helped clarify the nature of the ties between the Turkish underworld and Bulgarian intelligence was Bekir Celenk, extradited to Turkey to stand trial for arms and drug dealing and exchange-control violations. Too bad about that heart attack.[4]

Apart from the oddity of a fascist assassin at the request of the KGB turning his professional attentions to a pope committed to undermining Bolshevism in Poland and around the world,[5] the theory of the Bulgarian Connection depends on one central assumption. The KGB apparently calculated that killing the Polish pope would crush the morale of Polish dissidents, rather than creating a martyr whose demise would inflame popular passions. The possibility that the murder of the pope would spark virtual civil war in Poland, undermine the regime the USSR was struggling hard to legitimize, and eliminate the last hope of a strictly internal resolution of the country's economic and political difficulties apparently did not occur to the dastardly Russians.[6] One wonders if it might have occurred to anyone else.

Why the East is in the Red

With the trigger-happy Agça tucked away in jail, there was no one to keep in check certain papal antics that were undermining Poland's international credit rating. By the end of 1981 Poland had a net foreign debt of some $24 billion – more than half owed to Western bankers, the rest to various governments. Poland's difficulties threw a pall over all the credits that Western bankers had been so keen to extend to Eastern Europe during the 1970s.

Several strong beliefs during that decade of heady euromarket expansion kept the bankers' cash flowing eastward (and fed the increasingly strident convictions of the American radical right that the international bankers, led by David Rockefeller, were part of a Bolshevik-inspired one-world-government conspiracy). The most important of these beliefs was the 'umbrella theory,' that behind the debts of Eastern European countries was ultimately to be found the guarantee of the Soviet Union. The USSR was assumed to be willing to underwrite with hard-currency subsidies and oil at below-market prices the Western-bank debts of its satellites. It was assumed that the Red Army would be both able and willing to play in twentieth-century Europe the role that the British Navy played in nineteenth-century North Africa and Latin America: rearranging the political order whenever and however necessary to assure payment of the foreign debt.[7]

Bankers were also convinced of the fiscal conservatism of communist regimes. Eastern European governments, being totalitarian, were assumed to not have to cater to the economic aspirations of their populations through the inflationary gimmicks that are the bane of sound finance in the democratic West.

Another myth insisted that centrally planned economies can shift resources rapidly into the export sector to assure the revenues for debt service. Prominent bankers fond of giving Rotary Club speeches denouncing the inefficiencies of socialist planning were equally at home approving loans on the assumption that the same planning mechanism, backed up by a totalitarian state apparatus, could deliver the goods.

Not least of the notions feeding the flow of cash was that in Eastern Europe governments could assure social peace and the flow of production – at gunpoint, if necessary. This was a particularly strange conclusion regarding Poland, where mass labor unrest had caused governments to tumble long before Solidarity came on the scene.

All these beliefs made for the view that Eastern Europe must be a terrible place to live in, but a very good one to conduct business in, while the opposite was presumably true for the West.

To cold war propaganda was added cold war realpolitik. The governments of the US and West Germany encouraged their banks to finance the acquisition by Eastern Europe, particularly Poland, of obsolete energy-intensive Western technology, in order to wean Eastern European economies from the USSR, and to create a dependence on Western supplies that could later be exploited for political purposes. Such loans assumed the open umbrella of cheap Soviet oil. It was an umbrella that was susceptible to abrupt closure because of shifting priorities of the USSR planning authorities, over which neither the banks nor the Polish government could have significant influence.[8]

In 1981 the USSR cut down its dollar subsidies and pushed its oil prices closer to world market levels, just when world recession had put the Polish economy in a sharp tailspin and exposed the creakiness of the Polish planning mechanism, including its inability to adjust effectively to change. With national income sharply falling, Solidarity won from the government major concessions, which caused the fiscal deficit to soar, reduced productivity, and undermined government efforts to squeeze domestic demand and shift resources into the export sector to generate foreign exchange. Grumbling Western bankers[9] could be heard discussing another aspect of the umbrella theory – namely, the ultimate obligation of the USSR to send in the army to ensure that Poland respected its international financial obligations.

Undoubtedly another topic discussed was how to call Pope John Paul II to order before his obsessive anticommunism brought down the whole house of cards.[10] This also appears to have been a subject of animated discussion inside the Vatican.

Which Road Leads to Rome?

The Vatican is one of the few places in the world that no one can criticize for covering its internal wrangling with a thick cloak of sanctimoniousness. But under the rhetorical wrappings are disputes about realpolitik, of which relations with the Soviet bloc and with Third World movements for social justice are among the most important.

The Vatican was not entirely displeased with the Bolshevik victory in 1917, for the Vatican was then facing a menace from the East that was graver than Bolshevism: its old rival for hearts and minds, and territory, the Eastern Orthodox Church. As the Orthodox Church was deeply compromised by its ties with the czars of Russia, the Bolshevik revolution provided one of the finest opportunities for the Church of Rome to smite its principal rival since an enterprising pope diverted a crusade to rescue the Holy Sepulcher from the Saracens into an assault on Constantinople, seat of the Orthodox Church.

For eight years following the revolution, the Vatican and Moscow negotiated for mutual recognition. When talks broke down, the Vatican switched to a policy of containment of communism, which in turn necessitated rapprochement with Benito Mussolini, whom it had formerly denounced.[11] And that secured for the Vatican the status of offshore center and tax haven that would prove so useful to Banco Ambrosiano's financial and political ambitions, including those in Poland.

In the 1960s the Vatican's attitude toward the East was again under debate. Vatican II, which conceded greater power to national episcopates, also included a policy of accommodation of the Eastern Bloc, and indirectly one of encouraging the theology of liberation.[12] Traditionalists inside the Vatican counsel the church's followers to be meek and mild with the established worldly order, promising them a better deal elsewhere in the universe as fast as poverty, disease, malnutrition, and military overlords can get them there. These traditionalists were outraged at Vatican II. And when the powerful Jesuit order, under the influence of its growing Latin American membership, embraced the theology of liberation and plunged into a worldly battle for social justice, it ran afoul of the American right, the Latin American family oligarchies, and the Catholic Church's answer to Freemasonry.

Sometimes called 'the saintly mafia,' Opus Dei[13] is a highly secretive organization in which religion, politics, and big business coalesce. Founded in Spain in 1929 by José Maria Escriva de Belaguer, it drew inspiration from three sources. The first two were organizations for which Escriva felt a repellent fascination: the Jesuits, from whom he took an organizational model, and the Freemasons, whence came secret initiation rites and recruitment methods. The third influence was Generalissimo Francisco Franco, beside whose monarchist-fascist forces Opus Dei's founder struggled against republicanism and Freemasonry during the Spanish Civil War.

From Franco's Spain, where it enjoyed great favor, the organization grew: today it may have more than 70,000 members worldwide. Undoubtedly the great majority are attracted purely by religious conviction. But the elite of the organization allegedly plays a powerful, right-wing role in the political life of those places where its membership is concentrated: in Spain, where the membership deeply penetrated finance, journalism, and political life; in Latin America; in Ireland; and, not least, in the Vatican.

For some time before his death, Escriva cultivated an obscure Polish cardinal, Karol Wojtyla, whose ultraconservatism on social issues, commitment to papal absolutism, and uncompromising anticommunism accorded with the views of Opus Dei, and were a comforting change from the detested opinions of John XXIII. When John Paul I died after only thirty-three days in office,[14] Opus Dei supporters helped to swing the support of the cardinals to Karol Wojtyla for the papacy.

Once elected, John Paul II lost little time before paying his political debts. It was a match made in heaven, and one of Wojtyla's earliest acts as Pope John Paul II was praying at the tomb of the founder of Opus Dei.[15] The political power of Opus Dei was considerably upgraded. John Paul II confronted the Jesuits and tried to knock them into line at home and abroad.[16] In Latin America, stirrings of liberation theology were met by a joint Vatican–Opus Dei counteroffensive; and the pope personally engaged in political search-and-destroy missions in Nicaragua, where Jesuit priests had joined the revolutionary government.

Part of John Paul II's concern with the Jesuits had to do with conditions in his native Poland, the sole country in Europe where the Jesuits were gaining in numbers and influence. This was disquieting in light of their demonstrated capacity to reconcile themselves with left-wing social ideologies, and particularly disturbing because John Paul II saw in Eastern Europe a new (or rejuvenated) source of pious Catholics to counterbalance his increasingly radicalized Latin American flock. Moreover, Opus Dei supporters had long argued for a confrontationist stance toward atheistic communism in Eastern Europe, as well as in Latin America. The Vatican, too, saw in the ongoing economic crisis in Poland a chance to enhance its own political power vis-à-vis the Polish state, not least by funding the Solidarity trade union movement in its battles against the Polish government.

Bankers Search for Solidarity

When Poland's financial problems became known early in 1981, they were the biggest shock yet to hit the euromarket. Five hundred banks were left with more than $12 billion at risk, and a similar sum was owed to Western governments.[17] Particularly vulnerable were the banks of West Germany, who had lent the most. They, like the other banks, faced not only the refusal of the USSR to continue to pick up the tab but also the Reagan administration's and Vatican's conviction that the Polish crisis could be turned to good political account.

At that time, the international banks had no real experience in rescheduling such large debts, and their record of cooperation across national and functional borders was very spotty. Merchant banks squabbled with commercial banks; American banks fought with German banks; little banks protested and squirmed when big banks tried to shanghai them into rescheduling deals. By early 1981 one small American bank had discovered a surefire escape mechanism. By threatening to call its portion of a Polish loan into default, thereby invoking the cross-default clauses that would put into default all the Polish debt to all the banks, the small bank panicked the big American banks into buying out its portion of the loan.

Apart from the sums at stake, Poland represented two other major problems. First, there was a long list of potential problem debtors who would watch carefully any precedent being set. Second, Poland was not a member of the IMF, whose cash would therefore not be available to fund the bankers' exit as it had done in Turkey. Moreover, as long as the banks were quarreling among themselves, Poland (or any other debtor country) could play one bank off against another to extract better terms. The Polish crisis of 1981 convinced the banks of the need to create formal means of coordination among themselves. Unfortunately that did not initially involve coordination with the US government or the Vatican.

Throughout 1981, under the scrutiny of an IMF adviser, the banks and Poland edged their way toward a deal. The government was to accept a technical adviser, appointed by the international banks, who would assist Polish planning authorities. Negotiations were to be conducted on a *political* level: the bank representatives would talk directly to the deputy prime minister for economic affairs, who would formally report every quarter. Poland's debts to *all* countries, including the USSR, were to be revealed.[18] Implied in the deal was a commitment by Poland to begin negotiations for membership in the IMF.[19] But the course of political events stemming from the deteriorating economic climate undermined the tentative arrangements.

Poland had experienced rapid economic growth until 1978, when it leveled off; then, beginning in 1980, it received a series of economic shocks. In the tradition of 1956 and 1970, food riots and demonstrations toppled the government. As a triumphant Solidarity faced a new, weaker administration, discussions among Union, Church, and State took shape. Open criticisms of the planning mechanism led to the most serious effort yet undertaken to decentralize the Polish planning model.

Then, in December 1981, the Polish authorities, partly in order to forestall direct Soviet intervention, decreed martial law and banned Solidarity. The US government (and its NATO allies) quickly imposed economic sanctions. The government that broke its air traffic controllers' union demonstrated its commitment to the principle of free collective bargaining by canceling the Polish national airline's landing rights in US airports. The government that, one year earlier, had responded to the Turkish military coup and its rounding up, imprisoning, and executing of unionists and opposition political figures by increasing foreign aid to the Turkish government, now responded to far less virulent repression in Poland by freezing government-to-government credits. It also banned exports of high-technology capital goods and canceled the relatively low tariffs on Polish exports to the US.

The Paris Club (the informal coordinating committee of creditor governments) followed the American lead by suspending discussions on the rescheduling of Poland's $12 billion government-to-government debt.[20] But they all stopped short of forcing Poland into formal default, arguing that default would relieve pressure on Poland to continue interest payments. For Poland there was to be no easing of the escalating burden of the terms of payment that had been a fundamental cause of economic and social breakdown. Yet any possibility that Poland could meet its original schedule of obligations was effectively destroyed by the international sanctions and the economic problems they intensified.

By 1982 productivity in Poland had dropped 11% below its 1978 peak, in part because of the shortened work week, which Solidarity had won, but in part because the banning of the union produced an increasingly sullen work force and economic sabotage. During 1982 national income dropped another 8%. Austerity made the economic crisis feed on itself. Lack of consumer goods exacerbated the deterioration in productivity; money balances piled up as there was nowhere to spend them except the black market. And lack of foreign exchange cut Poland off from the capital goods and essential raw materials necessary for industrial growth.[21]

All this must have been observed with some satisfaction in the Vatican, which was still pumping clandestine funding into the now-banned Solidarity. Before the church arrived at a partial accommodation with the Polish government in 1984, it reportedly poured more than $100 million into the union movement. Assuming the Vatican did provide so much money, its source becomes a matter of interest. Some fingers point to Chicago.

The late John Cardinal Cody, rumored to be an Opus Dei supporter, ruled over America's richest Catholic diocese, Chicago, the city with the world's largest Polish population outside Warsaw. He ruled it with an iron hand, which reputedly dipped into the collection plate for pressing theological requirements – such as an opportunity to speculate in Penn Central Railway shares, or baubles for his alleged mistress, or a little something to help his Vatican friends cover their budget deficits. A fellow ardent anticommunist, Paul Marcinkus, drew on the riches of his native Chicago to top up the IOR's deposits; Cody was one of the largest donors to the private budget of the pope; and much of the money for Solidarity was apparently mobilized in Chicago under Cody's guidance.[22]

Yet Cody would certainly not have been the only source of Solidarity's Vatican-inspired financing. According to Roberto Calvi, the contribution of Banco Ambrosiano to the cause was about $50 million.[23] Thus, were Ambrosiano to founder, the IOR would not only take direct losses, it would also lose a donor to John Paul II's favorite tax-exempt charity. This consideration may have signaled Opus Dei to try to save the bank.

In his last days, Calvi was seen in the company of two priests sympathetic to Opus Dei, including John Paul II's personal chaplain; and he discussed with close associates a plan to move the headquarters of Ambrosiano to Rome.[24] According to Calvi's family, these desperate last-minute efforts to save Ambrosiano landed Calvi in the middle of a vicious Vatican power struggle. Although Paul VI had made sympathetic noises about reconciliation of Catholics and Freemasons, this was not a sentiment that Opus Dei shared.[25] The Opus Dei faction had been strengthened by the election of John Paul II, as well as by the P-2 scandal, so it was in a position to demand its ton of flesh when Ambrosiano began to crumble. Reportedly Opus Dei supporters agreed to arrange the takeover of the 16% of Ambrosiano shares held in the offshore shell companies, thereby rescuing the bank and the IOR simultaneously. Opus Dei financiers in Spain, whom Calvi planned to visit early in 1982, were to pump $1 billion into the IOR. In return Calvi was to create a sort of 'Bankus Dei,' a banking institution that would link Opus Dei–allied groups from South America to Eastern Europe, thereby helping to tilt the balance of power within the Vatican decisively in favor of Opus Dei. In return, also, Opus Dei–allied financiers demanded that Archbishop Marcinkus be replaced as head of the Vatican bank, and that dickering with the Polish government cease in favor of open confrontation. This arrangement allegedly won the support of John Paul II, but was opposed by Marcinkus, naturally, and by Cardinal Casaroli, the Vatican secretary of state and architect of the policy of seeking accommodation with Eastern European regimes.

Allegedly Calvi's final flight to London was to close a deal with financier members of Opus Dei. Instead it took the portly, un-athletic, aging Calvi on a late-night stroll through London with ten pounds of rocks in his pockets. Miles from his room (where an ample supply of potentially fatal drugs was at his disposal) Calvi, in spite of his vertigo, seems to have clambered down a complex network of bridge scaffolding so he could commit suicide by hanging himself from it.[26]

Selling Out Solidarity to the Creditors' Cartel

Despite the loss of Calvi and his bank, the church won major victories in Poland. But this time the international creditor interests were happier over the result.

Central to the 'reform' of the Polish finances that creditors demanded was a further squeeze on domestic consumption. The immediate target was the workers' savings, which could not be converted into real goods because of rationing and shortages. The 'inflationary' potential of these soft-currency hoards was neatly eliminated by a series of price hikes, while devaluations of the zloty encouraged the diversion of production into foreign or foreign-exchange-financed sales. Savage cutbacks in hard-currency-financed imports further injured the manufacturing sector, which was already severely affected by the Western sanctions. By the end of 1983 Poland had achieved a record balance-of-trade surplus, at a cost of three successive sharp declines in living standards and in investment.

Between 1978 and 1983, national income fell 18%; from 1980 to 1984, investment in the Polish economy declined by 40%. The forecast was more of the same until 1990, as long as the banks and the IMF could keep the military dictatorship from giving in to popular demands to reflate the economy.[27]

Deflation and the search for foreign exchange went hand in hand; after wiping out the purchasing power of those who had saved money in zlotys, the government followed the example of many fellow debtors and tapped the black market. Polish citizens had long had dollar-denominated bank accounts. In the 1970s there were plenty of dollars floating around from the remittances of émigrés and from black-market activity. The government had coaxed them into the banking system by offering competitive interest rates and freedom from taxation, thereby acquiring about $1 billion to add to its foreign-exchange resources. It also attracted hot dollars by offering spot delivery of automobiles paid for in dollars – there was a five-year wait for cars bought with zlotys. In addition, the state maintained stores that sold all manner of consumer goods for hard currency only.[28] The military government banned further dollar-denominated bank accounts, but its desperate need for foreign exchange forced it to increase the number and importance of the dollar stores.

The decision to encourage the black market while wiping out zloty-denominated purchasing power meant that production for local sale was to be secondary to the demands of Poland's foreign creditors. As domestic manufacturing for the local market shrank, there were 'success' stories in the primary sector, in coal and in agriculture, which could generate foreign exchange for the international banks and political capital for the Vatican.

Poland's coal mines are legendary, not least to the miners subjected to notorious working conditions in them. Poland is the world's fourth largest coal producer (after the US, the USSR, and China) and the second largest exporter (after the US). The coal goes east to trade for oil; it goes west in exchange for hard currency; or it stays at home to fuel 80% of Polish industry and produce 95% of the country's electricity. In the event of shortages resulting from the breakdown of antiquated mine equipment, the first two demands will likely be satisfied before the third.[29]

The mines were also important politically. The miners were very religious, which allowed John Paul II to stage some of his most aggressive intrusions into Polish politics from the mining centers. They were also determined supporters of Solidarity, which had won important gains in miners' working conditions. Banning the union was essential to the turnaround of the Polish balance of payments, for only with Solidarity out of the way could production be accelerated and the six-day workweek reinstated. Any additional revenues generated were immediately eaten up in foreign-debt payments.

Another stronghold of the church was the agricultural sector. In Poland virtually all farmland is in private hands, and some 25% of the population is involved in primary production; however, the state controls marketing, credit, and the provision of capital equipment. And it was toward reducing government power in those sectors that the church and the Western governments directed their attention.[30]

Polish agriculture had been severely and deliberately squeezed by the NATO sanctions. The end of government-to-government commodity credits cut off the supply of US grains and feedstocks on which much of the sector depended. In 1982 alone, poultry production fell 80%. Farmers, like the labor force in secondary industries, began to challenge the regime's directives. The resulting shortages were an additional factor in increasing resentment against the military government. When students in the state-run agricultural college, incited by the priests, protested government refusal to permit the hanging of crucifixes in their classrooms the North American press denounced the government's stance with the same righteous vehemence with which it defends the principle of separation of church and state at home.

The resolution of the 'crucifix war' paved the way for a major accord between church and state, and for the establishment of an agricultural foundation endowed with as much as $2 billion from various churches, Western governments, and the Rockefeller Foundation.[31] This fund was to be administered exclusively by the church, in effect enforcing the political position of the church in a country that was officially atheist. As the money was to be invested only in private agriculture, it would tilt the balance of economic power toward the private sector and away from the state, while reorienting the Polish economy toward primary production. Solidarity's leader, Lech Walesa, subsequently hailed by the *Wall Street Journal* as a convert to the principles of supply-side economics,[32] showed his understanding of the situation by contributing his Nobel Prize money to the agricultural fund – just when hardliners in the Polish planning department were discussing the need to phase out 'inefficient' industrial sectors such as the Gdansk shipyards, where Solidarity was born.[33]

Curiously enough, as church and state in Poland inched toward an understanding, as the international creditor interests and the US government began to be more flexible, and as the ground was prepared for Poland to join the IMF, Solidarity remained illegal, its leadership subjected to continued official harassment.

8
Paradise Lost?

Solidarity may have been an unwitting victim of the Ambrosiano debacle. If so, it had plenty of company, including some two hundred creditor banks with loans totalling $450 million due from Banco Ambrosiano Holdings of Luxembourg. Someone had to pay. That called into question the future of one, indeed two, of the world's offshore centers, and highlighted the shaky financial position of some of the Vatican's principal allies at home and abroad.

At the time of the Italian government's refusal to honor the debts incurred by BAH Luxembourg, complex negotiations with the Vatican were in progress. At issue was a new pact to replace the Lateran Treaty, which had granted the Vatican offshore status. The Italian negotiators sensed that the circumstances worked to their advantage: to help put an end to the anomalous position of the Vatican and the IOR under Italian law; and to force the Vatican to assume part of the $1.3 billion or more in losses from the Ambrosiano collapse.[1]

Initially the Vatican tried to play tough, disclaiming, with the aid of a blue-ribbon committee of eminent Catholic financiers, responsibility for the affair.[2] It insisted that it had received no financial benefit from its involvement, and that although it may have owned the shell companies through which the looting occurred, it did not know it owned them and therefore could not be held accountable![3] When each of these evasions had been debunked, it tried its cheapest ploy: it blamed the Bank of Italy for inadequate inspection of Ambrosiano, neatly sidestepping the real issue, which was the Bank of Italy's inability under the Lateran Treaty to inspect the IOR. That inability, however, was not destined to last.

Decline and Fall of Another Roman Empire
While the Italian government was trying to get the IOR to pick up the tab, it, too, was being subjected to considerable international pressure.

The major creditor banks of BAH Ltd. organized an unofficial credit cutoff, just when Italy was under severe balance-of-payments pressure, and capital flight and tax evasion had driven its budget deficit to a record 15% of Gross Domestic Product.

Italy responded by rationing foreign exchange, by tightening exchange controls, by increasing pressure on the Vatican to revise the Lateran Treaty, and, not least, by opening negotiations with the US for a new extradition treaty that would get Michele Sindona back to stand trail.[4] As Sindona threatened, 'If I ever make it back to Italy, if they don't kill me first, I will turn my trial into a circus. I will tell all.'[5]

Gradually the Vatican's resistance crumbled, and it began preparing for the day of reckoning. In December 1982, it published a full budget for the first time, including income from diocesan contributions; but it carefully excluded income from financial assets and from the IOR. It seems to have wanted to convey the impression of poverty, to shame the creditors into accepting a lower settlement and to coax more money out of the faithful.[6] The Vatican also began to generate cash flow from traditionally nonperforming assets such as art treasures, which were, for the first time, exhibited to the world's paying public.

Traditional sources of revenue were milked to the full. Much of the Vatican's money comes from the creation and exploitation of cults, the most important of which is the cult of St. Peter. In Rome the alleged remains of St. Peter act as a magnet for tourists (pilgrims, they are politely called), and for the revenues they bring in, while reasserting the political status of the Vatican over its theological competitors. Similar cults around other Catholic religious sites generate surplus cash that is siphoned off through the IOR. Bits and pieces of various saints are put on display, despite the fact that, if the reputed remains were reassembled, they would rival the handiwork of Dr. Frankenstein.[7]

In the same spirit, John Paul II made two important announcements on the same November day in 1982: the Vatican agreed in principle to cover part of the hole in Ambrosiano's assets; and 1983 was to be a Holy Year, 1,950 years after the crucifixion of Christ. That 1983 by some counts misses the 1,950th anniversary by several years was beside the point. A Holy Year could be expected to increase the flow of pilgrim-tourist revenues and the inflow of Peter's Pence.[8] Nor could it be said that John Paul II's objectives were purely mercenary; 1983 was the six hundredth anniversary of the Cult of the Black Madonna, which in his native Poland is a symbol of national resistance to barbarian invasions from the East.[9]

Also significant was the pope's decision to pass over Archbishop Marcinkus for promotion to cardinal; the Roman curia had demanded the unpopular outsider as a scapegoat. A cardinal's hat would have brought him diplomatic immunity; without it he could only ignore the magistrates' warrants piling up at the gates of the Vatican by staying inside.[10]

After the Vatican conceded the principle of the Ambrosiano claims, progress toward revision of the Lateran Treaty and on the amount the Vatican would pay the Ambrosiano creditors went much faster.[11] It was also, no doubt, aided by the fact that, for the first time in Italian history, a non-Christian Democrat – Socialist party chief Bettino Craxi – headed the government while a non-Italian headed the Vatican.

Under the revised treaty, Catholicism ceased to be the state religion of Italy; Rome ceased to be a sacred city over which the Vatican could exercise powers of ideological censorship; and, perhaps most important, the IOR was to establish a branch in Rome outside Vatican City. It was through that branch that the Vatican was to conduct all its financial transactions with Italian citizens. That branch would also be subject to the scrutiny of the Bank of Italy, which could hamper the future usefulness of the IOR in money laundering, tax evasion, and exchange-control violation.[12]

Indecent Exposure

The Vatican was not the only center of peekaboo finance to come perilously close to being caught with its private participants exposed in the Ambrosiano crash. So, too, was Luxembourg, which had hosted BAH Ltd. and an array of other offshore banks and holding companies.

Luxembourg had forged a monetary union with Belgium in 1922 and passed Swiss-style bank-secrecy laws in 1935. Therefore, it was ideally placed to provide Belgian citizens with tax-evasion facilities. In the 1950s it also became a major booking center for the eurobond market, a notorious laundromat for hot money. In the 1960s Franco's reign in Spain produced showers of gold for the Luxembourg banking system. Thus it had a long history as a peekaboo center before the first West German bank set up operations there in 1970.

The impetus to Luxembourg's growth came from two sources, the first being the dollar crises of the late 1960s and early 1970s, which saw the deutschmark gaining in value and popularity as an international currency. As a result, Luxembourg became a major center for booking West German bank loans to Eastern Europe, including the Polish loans that Banco Ambrosiano had been undermining. The second was the collapse of steel, virtually its only industry, in the early 1970s. The government promoted the banking business to replace the lost jobs, foreign-exchange earnings, and tax receipts. By 1984 Luxembourg had one bank for every 3,000 citizens; and its offshore banks had $115 billion in loans on their books, 50% denominated in deutschmarks.[13]

To its traditional role as a fiscal parasite feeding off Belgium, Luxembourg in the 1970s added that of helping highly paid West German and French citizens working in the Gulf oil states to hide their incomes from tax collectors.[14] And through Overseas Development Bank, Luxembourg, Robert Vesco ran much of the cash he was stealing from IOS clients, unperturbed by the 1971 arrest of two of its employees for activities on behalf of a Mafia-backed counterfeit-securities ring run by the son of a British peer.[15] Despite such curiosities, the largest share of Luxembourg's banking business was in the wholesale interbank market, at least until the Ambrosiano affair.

The refusal of the Italian government to stand behind Banco Ambrosiano Holdings was a severe shock to Luxembourg's status as an offshore center, especially as it came just after the West German banks had written off much of their Polish debt.[16] To stem the resulting flight of funds, Luxembourg authorities demanded that all parent banks of Italian subsidiaries operating in Luxembourg unconditionally guarantee their affiliates' borrowings. And they requested letters of comfort from parents of all other offshore banks. But just when the aftershocks of the Ambrosiano affair seemed to be subsiding, a fresh scandal shook the system.

A German landed aristocrat of ancient lineage and an upstart son of a welder should have little in common; but they eventually found enough to share responsibility for West Germany's greatest banking disaster since the Herstatt collapse.[17]

Count Ferdinand von Galen was at the helm of Schröder, Munchmeyer, Hengst & Co., Germany's most reputable private bank, when it found itself dragged deeply into the funding difficulties of IBH Holdings Ltd., a major construction-equipment manufacturer headed by Horst-Dieter Esch. IBH had seemed to be one of the great industrial successes of the era, picking up and integrating other, weaker firms until it was the world's third largest in its field. Not until after the crash did it become clear that much of the conglomerate's 'earnings' were based on 'selling' unsaleable inventories to its own subsidiaries and crediting the proceeds of the 'sales' on its books, even though the equipment had not left the inventory yard.

None of the establishment banks would touch Esch, who had a reputation as a 'vulture capitalist.' But Schröder's, which held some equity in IBH, filled the gap. West German banking law limited a bank's exposure to any one borrower to 75% of its basic capital. Schroder's lending to IBH – some $300 million – exceeded that limit by a mere 500%. The excess was hidden by booking the loans through Luxembourg shell companies and having the various IBH subsidiaries pose as independent borrowers.[18]

Late in 1983 an allegedly random audit by the German Bankers Association supposedly exposed the operation; but given the cover of the Luxembourg shell companies, it seems more likely that someone on the inside tattled to the authorities. By then IBH was hopelessly insolvent, and only a desperate rescue effort by the German banks, anxious to avoid another Herstatt-type debacle, saved Schröder's. IBH was declared bankrupt, Esch charged with fraud, von Galen was unseated and subsequently also so charged, and the bank was sold off to Lloyd's, a British bank seeking an entry into the German market.[19]

The timing of the crash could not have been worse. Schröder's had been a private bank that managed old family fortunes and peddled securities. It had no retail deposit base. It therefore had raised 40% of its money on the interbank market. The interbank debts of BAH Luxembourg had barely been settled. The trial of the directors of Bankhaus Herstatt was still under way. And fears over the American plan to establish Pershing missile bases in West Germany were making the deutschmark vulnerable. Luxembourg was battered with yet another flight of funds, much to the delight of the West German bank regulators who, like their Italian colleagues, had long looked askance at offshore booking centers being used to evade regulatory requirements.[20]

In the aftermath of the crash, West Germany reduced the permitted exposure of a bank to any one borrower to 50% of capital, and raised the capital requirements of its banks. It also forced its banks to publish consolidated accounts, which would prevent them from hiding infractions of banking law behind a network of shell companies in offshore havens. The result was to threaten to turn a short-run panic flight of funds from Luxembourg into a long-term decline in its offshore business.[21]

Luxembourg, however, was determined to fight back. If the interbank market was to pass it by, there was an alternative that its bankers had long dreamed of: stepping up its business in handling the affairs of 'private clients.'[22]

Meanwhile, back in Italy, the government's move against the IOR and its offshore operations was not an isolated event. At the same time there came a concerted effort to deal with one of the most notorious customers of offshore and underground financial facilities.

Financial Tricks from the River Styx?

It had long been suspected that much of the street violence that shook Italy in the 1970s and early 1980s reflected an informal coalition of interest groups. The Communist party was particularly vehement in denouncing the links between the crime syndicates (especially the

Sicilian Mafia and the Neapolitan Camorra), P-2, paramilitary groups, and foreign intelligence agencies, all of which were enthusiastic users of the machinery of peekaboo finance.

In a sense, the rejuvenation of organized-crime syndicates, particularly the Mafia, was a tribute to the enterprise of Bekir Celenk and his associates. Throughout the 1950s and 1960s, the role of the old village-based Mafia in Sicilian life diminished as the economy grew and diversified, as emigration to the Italian mainland increased, and as the political left grew at the expense of the Mafia-infiltrated Christian Democratic party. But in the 1970s rising unemployment and the revival of the heroin traffic encouraged a Mafia renaissance.[23]

Sicily was ideally placed to broker the movement of Golden Crescent narcotics to the North American market, as well as to organize much of the flow of South American cocaine into Western Europe.[24] As a result, a new underworld took shape, urban and entrepreneurial in character, and tightly interfacing with the overworld of high finance and national as well as regional politics.[25]

The flood of liquidity from the drugs business not only saw cash-rich banks proliferate across Sicily, but also permitted the new criminal money to penetrate ever deeper into the Sicilian economy. Crime-linked businesses had a number of advantages over their competitors. They had no serious labor problems; they had access to guaranteed sources of cheap credit; and they carried lower tax loads as they exempted themselves from paying employee security benefits. By the early 1980s 'Mafia'-linked business was estimated (probably greatly overestimated) to account for nearly one-third of the Sicilian economy, with the percentage control of public-works contracts estimated as high as 50%. The flood of drug-based liquidity, however, plunged the crime families into particularly bloody vendettas and prompted assassinations of opposing politicians, judges, and journalists.[26]

Among the new enterprises that attracted the attention of organized crime was the NATO plan to install cruise missile bases in Sicily. These planned missile bases had set off a war of words between Italy and Bulgaria even before Ali Agça and his Turkish mobster friends brought their relations to a postwar low.

Sicilian crime-based entrepreneurs were enthusiastic about the plan: the Mafia controlled prostitution, which would thrive around American military bases; crime-linked construction companies hoped to get the plum contracts; and the crime elite reportedly controlled 30% of the land around the projected base sites, which could be expected to soar in value when the ultimate in security was provided for it by the US military installations.[27] The one major threat to such plans was the power of the Communist party, which was vocally opposed to the militarization of Sicily.

Perhaps coincidentally, in 1979, the year before he was finally forced to start serving his twenty-five-year prison sentence in the US, Michele Sindona arranged his own 'kidnapping' back to Sicily to participate in the planned secessionist coup of which he and certain other Mafia-linked figures had long dreamed. It was a monumental fiasco, not least because Licio Gelli, the man who had helped to arrange Sindona's flight from the US, refused to support the plot; and it was an investigation of Gelli's role in the Sindona 'kidnapping' that led the police to his chateau and office in Arrezzo, and to the discovery of the P-2 membership lists.[28]

To some degree, the P-2 scandal was a watershed in the war against the crime syndicates. The exposure of P-2 weakened, if only briefly, their protective coloration in the top levels of the judiciary, police, secret services, and financial establishment. The collapse of Banco Ambrosiano also helped, for it sent Calvi's principal business 'consultant,' Francesco Pazienza, fleeing from Italy.

Pazienza had a colorful career before being arrested in the US and extradited to Italy to face charges, among them of fraudulent diversion of funds from Banco Ambrosiano. Pazienza was hired in 1979 by General Giuseppe Santovito, the head of the Italian military intelligence force, SISMI. Among Pazienza's alleged accomplishments was the creation of Super S, a superspook agency that arranged smuggling and dirty money operations on behalf of the Italian secret services. Other SISMI functions apparently included joint action with organized crime to hamper the rise of the Communist party. It was allegedly in his capacity as liaison with organized crime that Pazienza's path crossed that of Ali Agça.[29]

The prison to which Ali Agça had been confined after his arrest in Rome turned out to be within the sphere of influence of the Camorra, the Naples-based counterpart of the Sicilian Mafia. Among its occupants was Don Raffaele Cutola, chief of the so-called 'new organization-Camorra' whose members had been involved in a three-way bloodbath with the Guardia di Finanza and rival gangs for control of the lucrative cigarette-smuggling business into the Bay of Naples. If Giovanni Pandico, a Camorra kingpin who later turned state's evidence, is to be believed, the new Camorra saw in Ali a potentially useful ally for future operations, and began cultivating him, including giving him the television set from which he derived some of the 'evidence' he read into the court records during the trial of the Bulgarian Connection. Then SISMI seized the opportunity to strike a propaganda blow against both the Warsaw Pact (then making a fuss over the planned installation of cruise missiles in Sicily) and the Italian Communist party, by turning the papal assassination attempt into the tale of of Ali Agça and the Forty Spies. The head of SISMI allegedly made a deal with the imprisoned Camorra chief to get Ali to implicate the Bulgarians. Although Ali denies being coaxed, he insists that among his visitors in jail was SISMI spook Francesco Pazienza.[30]

After the P-2 scandal ended the career of his boss, Pazienza also lost his job, and was subsequently hired as special 'consultant' to Roberto Calvi. It was allegedly Pazienza who tried to bribe a judge in Calvi's exchange-control-violations trial, using money embezzled from Banco Ambrosiano. Pazienza was also the broker for the attempt to rescue Ambrosiano with refugee Iranian money. But that and other rescue attempts failed, and in 1982 Pazienza followed Calvi out of the country, though not to the same fate.[31]

In the year of the Ambrosiano affair two assassinations drew public attention more closely to the issue of hot and dirty money. One was the murder of Sicilian Communist party chief Pio La Torre, who had been calling for an end to bank secrecy and for the confiscation of property originating in criminal activity. A few months later, carabiniere General Carlo Alberto Dalla Chiesa was gunned down in Sicily, where he had been sent to lead a crackdown against the Mafia. Dalla Chiesa had made two fatal mistakes. He had spoken openly of the importance of following the trail of dirty money right to the top in order seriously to deal with the Mafia menace. His second mistake was admitting in public that he did not have the support of top politicians for his efforts to crack the secrets of money laundering. If anything, he felt the opposite to be true.[32]

After the two murders came a new anticrime law that focused on finances and gave to police the power to probe bank accounts. The law permitted limited penetration by the police and judiciary of that gray layer of entrepreneurial activity where underworld and overworld business interact.[33] But the law was ten years too late, for the big money, following Michele Sindona's lead, and allegedly with the subsequent assistance of Roberto Calvi's Banco Ambrosiano and the IOR, had long been hiding out in the eurodollar market. This was a pioneering role that the Italian authorities saluted when they added a twelve-year sentence for the fraudulent bankruptcy of Banca Privata Finanziaria to the twenty-five years the American courts had given Sindona for looting Franklin National into insolvency.[34] They saluted it, too, by the clause in the revised Lateran Treaty that forced the IOR to open a branch on Italian soil.

Last Rites?

The Italian government and the Vatican combined the revision of the Lateran Treaty with the final settlement with Ambrosiano's international creditors. Part of the money came from unearthing secret accounts that Calvi had established. That, however, was a near thing, for a few months after the Ambrosiano crash, Licio Gelli turned up in Switzerland waving a Chilean passport and trying to make off with $60 million from one of the accounts. He was identified by the Swiss police, but his extradition to Italy was the subject of long judicial delays.[35] Then, ten days before the Swiss courts were to settle the matter, Gelli proved that what flies into the cuckoo's nest can fly out again. With a little help from his friends in Argentine naval intelligence, who provided phony papers and an escape route,[36] Gelli was sprung from his Geneva jail, apparently driven over the French border, taken by helicopter to Monaco and then moved to Uruguay, long the financial headquarters of the P-2 in Latin America. However, the money stayed behind, to the financial relief of the Vatican.[37]

One month later, Brazil freed the P-2's cofounder, Umberto Ortolani, from jail. He was a naturalized Brazilian citizen, and untouchable by extradition proceedings.[38] But not all Ortolani's assets were similarly amnestied. Two years after his release, a Quebec superior court seized the money that he had tucked away in Montreal bank accounts.[39]

The proceeds of the sale of Banco de Gottardo, the contents of Calvi's secret accounts, and assets seized from persons charged in the affair netted international creditors about 70% of their loans. While still disclaiming legal responsibility, the Vatican agreed, in recognition of its 'moral' involvement, that it would pay about $250 million to the creditor banks. The Vatican also passed to the international bank creditors ownership of all those offshore shell companies it had claimed not to own. In return, the banks agreed not to serve writs against the IOR.

Apart from the huge financial cost, the Vatican was hurt in another way by the agreement. It contained a clause stipulating that the agreement was to be interpreted according to Italian law, which further undermined the political independence of the Vatican.[40]

The Vatican now had to seek and find $250 million. Some assets were put up for sale, including the Vatican's remaining Swiss bank, Banco di Roma per la Svizzera. Available liquid assets were mustered, and John Paul II stepped up his remunerative jet-setting.[41]

In the summer of 1984 John Paul II went on the road denouncing 'imperialism' and economic systems in which profit is the only motivation, in speeches that sounded like recycled drafts of those Michele

Sindona dreamed up for Pope Paul VI. Ivory-tower leftists swooned at the prospect of the Vatican becoming an ally in the struggle against the world capitalist order, forgetting that among the traditional enemies of the free-market system could be found feudal landlords and medieval theocrats.

In his crusade for clean banking, John Paul II called for a larger role for voluntary contributions (and therefore a lesser role for IOR earnings) in covering the Vatican deficit. He demanded that governments in the West provide more public money to support religious schools. All of this was expected to increase the flow of voluntary contributions to the Vatican.[42] The pope's efforts were understandable because the Ambrosiano collapse had cost the Vatican more than just the financial support of Roberto Calvi.

While Italian magistrates were prying into the affairs of Archbishop Marcinkus, they were also becoming increasingly interested in those of Ambrosiano's largest domestic shareholder, Carlo Pesenti, Italy's leading private banker, who saw $50 million evaporate in the crash. Even before his name became associated with the illegal parking abroad of Ambrosiano shares, Pesenti's financial arrangements with the IOR were the subject of criminal investigation. Of particular interest was a 1972 'loan' to Pesenti from the IOR. It was indexed to the Swiss franc and, when repaid, cost him three times the sum originally contracted. Whether it was a smart business operation by the IOR, a cover for Pesenti's pumping money into the Vatican bank, or simply a device for the IOR to help Pesenti illegally move a large sum of cash abroad will likely remain a mystery. In the autumn of 1984, on a visit to Montreal, Carlo Pesenti died of a heart attack. His companies' shares immediately rose 3% to 4% on the Milan bourse.[43]

Nor was Pesenti the only staunch church ally to find himself financially embarrassed just when the Vatican needed him most. The fate of another may be connected with the rumored last-minute attempt by Opus Dei – linked financiers to save Banco Ambrosiano.

The Spanish Connection

Although Opus Dei deeply penetrated Spanish business, particularly banking and the mass media,[44] it had not been universally welcomed in Franco's Spain. Opus Dei was enthusiastic about the regime's anti-communism and its commitment to Catholicism as a state religion. But in its economic philosophy, Opus Dei stood for a neoliberal technocracy, which contrasted sharply to the statist orientation of the old fascist Phalange, with whom it became a major rival for power.[45]

Spain emerged from the Second World War with an autarkic and technologically backward economy, as the rest of Western Europe was beginning a period of rapid economic growth and development. With Western Europe and the US pushing Spain toward modernization from without, Opus Dei was shoving from within. During the 1950s the organization's power grew rapidly; and in 1958 some of its members produced El Plan del Estabilizacion Economica, a watershed in Spanish economic policy. El Plan could have been drafted by the IMF: it called for austerity, trade liberalization, an export drive, and convertibility of currency.[46]

It also set off a massive flight of now-convertible currency through Andorra and Gibraltar en route to Switzerland, as Spanish capitalists discovered how to use accredited diplomats as cash couriers to evade Spain's exchange-control laws.[47]

During the 1960s, as Opus Dei increased its influence in the banking system and on the economic ministries, the state swung behind industrial modernization and export promotion. Symbolizing that new economic policy was a company called Maquinaria Textil del Norte de España SA (MATESA), whose owners claimed to have made major breakthroughs in textile technology that would put the Spanish industry on the world map. The state, egged on by the Opus Dei sympathizers, poured in 10 billion pesetas worth of subsidies while the company merrily exported not its machines but the subsidies. Using state funds to build a network of overseas affiliates, MATESA arranged to 'sell' machines to its affiliates abroad. It shipped off state subsidy money in cash, recycled it back as 'payments' for the supposedly exported machines, and on the basis of the resulting 'export' receipts, claimed yet more state subsidies.[48]

Although under El Plan, the peseta had become convertible, Spain still had tough controls on the export of capital, which required an increasingly sophisticated apparatus to circumvent. Luckily there were American pioneers to show the way.

In 1967 the failure of a Barcelona savings bank led investigators in two directions along a paper trail: to Andorra at one end and to Bernie Cornfeld's IOS at the other. The Spanish IOS operation was shut down. Its absent chief was eventually given a fine of 22 million pesetas (about $330,000) and a three-year jail sentence; nineteen other absent salesmen and clients were also fined.[49] By that time MATESA had also learned modern flight-capital techniques. Instead of cash in suitcases, it moved the state subsidies through a network of shell companies in Luxembourg, Panama, Liechtenstein, and Switzerland, until a 1969 scandal put an end to the operation and tossed the company's owner in jail.

Although Opus Dei's dream of MATESA putting Spain in the forefront of modern industrial technology failed, indigenous capitalists learned the modern mechanisms of capital flight. Perhaps that was why Roberto Calvi turned to them for help in June 1982. If so, he came calling at the wrong time, for in the heartland of Opus Dei, bank failures had become almost routine. Another of its top protégés, one whom Calvi had tried to contact, was soon on the lam, following a long trail of absconding Spanish hot-money men,[50] and leaving behind a bill that ultimately came to $3 billion.[51]

In 1961 Andalusian sherry manufacturer José Maria Ruiz Mateos landed an exclusive contract with Harvey's of Bristol for the purchase of his products; and the next year he bought his first bank. From then on he seemed unstoppable until, early in 1983, the new Socialist government expropriated his RUMASA Group of companies. Its constituent parts then numbered 800 – in wine, food processing, advertising, computers, construction, cosmetics, pharmaceuticals, thirty-two hotels, twenty farming operations controlling thirty-four landed estates in Andalusia alone, twenty banks, and a host of ghost companies in the usual places. At their peak these enterprises produced goods and services estimated at between 2% and 3% of Spain's GNP.

There were two fundamental reasons for this spectacular growth. One was political: Ruiz Mateos long had the active support of Opus Dei, and therefore of the Franco government. The second reason was financial. Banks in the group broke with Spain's bank cartel by aggressively bidding for deposits, and poured the money into RUMASA companies, ultimately financing 80% of their operations. (After expropriation it was found that some banks had as much as 80% of their assets in loans to group companies.) The remaining 20% of group financing came from the acquisition of cash-rich businesses – hotels, retail outlets, and so on – that could be drained to assure a flow of liquidity to the group even if it threatened the particular company's solvency.

The loose state of Spanish disclosure law made it easy to cover the trail. RUMASA never in twenty-two years of operation published a consolidated account. All the banks in the group were existing institutions that RUMASA had taken over. Thus the scrutiny that an application for a new banking license would have brought could be avoided.

Nevertheless the Bank of Spain, facing escalating bank failures and concerned about the condition of the eighteen known RUMASA banks (ownership of the other two was a secret), began pressuring Ruiz Mateos for information. Ruiz Mateos then tore a leaf from P-2's book and tried to bribe politicians to remove the deputy governor of the Bank of Spain in order to halt the inquiry. He also decided that it was time to create a personal safety net outside the country, which required some imaginative circumventing of Spanish exchange controls.

Ruiz Mateos was not without experience in such matters. In 1977 his companies were twice fined a total of 170 million pesetas for evasion of exchange controls.[52] But the 1980s called for something more elaborate for Ruiz Mateos, though for the peekaboo centers it was merely business as usual.

Ruiz Mateos would order his local banks to ship deposits to their London and Amsterdam branches, and the receiving branches would ship the money off, some as fictitious loans to Panamanian shell companies, some to shell companies in Liechtenstein, Luxembourg, and Curaçao. Funds were then paid back into coded accounts at Nordfinanz in Zurich. Nordfinanz pumped the money into a London subsidiary of a Curaçao holding company; and the London company would invest the funds in appropriate overseas locations. The government initially charged that more than $600 million had been illegally exported from Spain, much of it crossing the Atlantic and rematerializing in everything from Argentine wineries to Uruguayan banks.[53]

Meanwhile, the Bank of Spain was struggling to cope with what was likely the worst and most protracted banking crisis in Western Europe. When recession hit in 1978, the year the RUMASA Group acquired its last bank, the entire Spanish banking system began to totter. There followed a series of crashes, occasionally accompanied by some new recruits to Spain's ranks of absconding financiers. Some of the crashes were minor; but others were major, and their importance was enhanced by their political implications. Banco Occidental failed in 1981, after an officer and $125 million hurriedly departed for Houston, wiping out Roberto Calvi's investment in the bank. Even more serious was the scandal over Banca Catalana and the $1.8 billion bailout it required, for it added seven banks – the entire group of which Banca Catalana was the flagship – to the sixteen being cared for by officials of the deposit-guarantee fund.[54]

Banca Catalana had been founded in 1958 by Catalan nationalist leader Jordi Pujol. Apart from the seven years he had spent in Franco's jails in the 1960s, Pujol ran the bank until he resigned in 1977 to commit himself full time to fighting for Catalan sovereignty. When the area was finally granted autonomy, he became head of the regional government. For Pujol, the bank had been an instrument in the struggle for autonomy – standing bail and paying fines for Catalan nationalists, funding Catalan cultural activities, and making loans to enterprises run by fellow nationalists. Apart from the suspicion its political activities engendered among Spanish establishment banks, Banca Catalana was also resented because, like the RUMASA banks, it would not abide by the interest-rate cartel, pushing up deposit rates aggressively to generate needed money.[55]

After the group was forced into the care of the bank hospital, and subsequently sold off to the big establishment banks, charges began to surface that the executives had been setting up phony payroll accounts to embezzle at least $130 million. It was an open secret in Spain that most banks engaged in under-the-table deals. Banca Catalana was certainly not the only one with dubious accounting methods and two sets of books; therefore, the charges were seen as politically inspired. Their aim, it was felt, was to undermine the credibility of the leadership of the Catalan nationalist movement and to exact revenge for its victory at the expense of the then-ruling Socialist party in local elections in the spring of 1984. That feeling was given some support by the fact that the government set out to suppress all information coming out of the trial, and leaned on a publishing house to withhold publication of a manuscript entitled *Banca Catalana: More Than a Bank, More Than a Crisis.*[56]

That description could also apply to the banking arms of RUMASA, and to the circumstances in which they fell under government control.

The protracted recession in Spain had helped bring the Socialist party to power at the end of 1982. It lost little time in demonstrating its commitment to socialist principles by imposing a harsh austerity program, abolishing the usury laws, and negotiating Spain's entry into NATO. Austerity and soaring interest rates shook RUMASA off its cash-flow tightrope. Yet Ruiz Mateos still refused the Bank of Spain's request for an audit. A political slanging match between Ruiz Mateos and Miguel Boyer, the new Socialist finance minister, touched off a major run on the RUMASA banks. This and overcrowding at the bank hospital sup-posedly caused the government's decision in early 1983 to expropriate the entire RUMASA Group. It has also been suggested, however, that the expropriation had something to do with the Socialist party's desire to break the hold of Opus Dei sympathizers on the Spanish financial apparatus.[57]

Unscrambling the accounts and operations was no easy task. Ruiz Mateos was hiding out in Britain, which had no extradition treaty with Spain,[58] and executives of the group apparently had been able to destroy many records before the police arrived to enforce the takeover order. But in April 1983, police, allegedly hunting for a kidnap victim taken by Basque-separatist (ETA) guerrillas, claimed to have stumbled on 15,000 kilograms of RUMASA files hidden behind a false wall at a RUMASA-owned garage in Madrid.[59] Using information from these files, the government claimed that in 1982 RUMASA had lost $515 million, and that it had arrears of taxes of $500 million plus another $100 million in unpaid social-security levies. These figures were later scaled down considerably.[60] The files also revealed companies, including two banks, that had been secretly acquired. They documented the capital flight, in violation of Spanish exchange-control law, that had permitted the buildup of an overseas empire. And they referred to large donations to Opus Dei.[61]

The government charged Ruiz Mateos with smuggling, accounting fraud, tax evasion, fiscal fraud, social-security fraud, and even – most heinous of all – insulting the king. This last straw referred to a London interview given by Ruiz Mateos in which he implied that the king was implicated in the 1981 bribery attempt to block further enquiries into RUMASA's affairs. To most of the charges, Ruiz Mateos had a simple but eloquent reply: 'There isn't a company in Spain that doesn't have two sets of books ... one for tax functions, one for themselves.'[62]

In April 1984, just when the scandal over the Banca Catalana was coming to the boil, Interpol found Ruiz Mateos in Frankfurt, carrying a pistol and a phony Panamanian passport; they arrested him. Freed on $3.5 million bail (a record for Western Europe), he spent the next eighteen months playing host to politically disenchanted Spanish military officers, denouncing the government, accusing leading Opus Dei-linked financiers of betraying him, fretting about the possibility of poison in his food, and fighting extradition on the grounds that his conservative social views precluded a fair trial in Spain, while insisting to reporters that he had no fear of going back to Spain to defend himself.

In the meantime, the cost of rescuing and reviving the RUMASA banks and companies was being reckoned in the multibillions of dollars. Even the big banks were forced to foot a share of the bill, but their reward came quickly: the resurrected RUMASA banks followed those leaving the bank hospital into the clutches of the established giants.[63] The rest of the RUMASA empire was also sold to the private sector, though not before some rearguard action from Ruiz Mateos. Blaming Mariano Rubio, deputy governor of the Bank of Spain, for his downfall, Ruiz Mateos reportedly employed a former police officer to implement a campaign of harassment against him. The campaign's most imaginative feature came during a time of very high interest rates: newspaper ads were planted that gave Rubio's home address as that of a business specializing in low-interest loans. Ruiz Mateos also was alleged to have hired thugs to try to dissuade potential buyers of his companies, and to stir up labor unrest in them. 'Unfounded lies,' Ruiz Mateos insisted.[64]

In the wake of the crisis, the government moved to stiffen accounting procedures and to tighten barriers to capital flight and illegal-currency movements through offshore peekaboo financial centers[65] (a tightening that was of little use, as matters turned out). And it kept up the pressure to get back at least one of its fugitive financiers.

It was in the autumn of 1985 that Ruiz Mateos lost his last court appeal. He was virtually kidnapped by West German police and bundled back to Spain amid recriminations and a bomb threat, to face charges of fraud and the possibility of a twelve-year jail sentence.[66] But before he left he confided to reporters the real source of his reluctance to return. The problem was, he insisted, that some people 'want to shut me up.' But, he threatened, 'If I am killed or disappear, the secret documents of RUMASA... will see the light.' And he underlined his fears by rolling his eyes, turning pale, and whispering the name of a former business associate, 'Roberto Calvi,'[67] whose legacy had shaken the world.

9

What Went Down with the Belgrano?

In the spring of 1982, a British war fleet set sail for the Malvinas Islands in the south Atlantic. In the diplomatic scramble that followed, negotiations intermediated by President Fernando Belaunde Terry of Peru seemed to be successful. The Argentine military forces, which had occupied the islands, were to be withdrawn in exchange for a commitment by Britain to continue the process by which sovereignty over the Malvinas was being gradually ceded to Argentina.

However, for reasons to do with the need to bolster her government's then-sagging electoral fortunes, with lingering British imperial xenophobia, and with the desire to 'demonstrate' the need for a British long-distance strike force (undermining those calling for reductions in British military expenditure), Margaret Thatcher ordered the torpedoing of the Argentine heavy cruiser *Belgrano* after it had begun to steam away from the combat zone.[1] Torpedoed along with it were prospects for a peaceful resolution of the dispute. And the international financial community waited in dread to see if several hundred billion dollars worth of assets in potentially defaulting debtor countries would go down with the ship.

Southern Exposure
Out of tiny cells are mighty cancers grown, a poetic banker might have said, casting a jaundiced eye over the financial ruins of Argentina. At the end of the Second World War, Argentina, with its population largely of Italian extraction, seemed to have much in its favor. Strongman Juan Peron was preaching his peculiar mixture of Mussolini-style corporatism and Latin American anti-imperialism whose radical rhetoric served the conservative purpose of assuring social peace. Argentina therefore became a favored refuge not only of ordinary citizens fleeing postwar economic and social uncertainty but also of fascist sympathizers on the run. With them came whatever funds they could carry or arrange

to have transported. They were followed in the 1950s by investments of major Italian companies.

How so much money moved out of Italy when the country had exchange controls in force remains to be explained, perhaps by Mr. Licio Gelli or some of his associates in the Vatican.

Gelli joined those Italians ready for a change of ambience after the fall of Mussolini. He ingratiated himself with the Peron regime and saw Argentina as a base for an Italian political renaissance. Although Gelli returned to Italy in 1955, after Peron was ousted, he reportedly remained a confidant of the dictator during his long Madrid exile.

With a similarity to contemporary Italian developments (and those of Turkey a short time later) that was too close to be entirely coincidental, political violence racked Argentina during the late 1960s and early 1970s. Elements of the military became convinced that only Peron could halt the slide toward civil war. In 1972 Peron was summoned home. Licio Gelli soon followed and was rewarded with the post of 'economic adviser,' a diplomatic passport, and the immunity it brought.[2]

Although the Latin American financial headquarters of P-2 was in Uruguay, Argentina was the South American country in which P-2 had penetrated deepest into business, political, and military life, facilitated by Italian family and business connections. It was a man who later figured on the P-2 membership list, General Carlos Suarez Mason, first army chief and commander of the Buenos Aires military district, who swung the military to accepting Peron's return. His reward was appointment as head of the state oil company, subsequently said to be the most important instrument for moving hard currency out of the country. Peron also appointed another P-2 man, Admiral Emilio Massera, as navy chief, from which position he would become, a few years later, head of the newly installed military junta.

When Peron died in 1974, the presidency passed to his widow, 'Isabelita'; but the real power lay with another P-2 man, Juan Lopez Rega. Popularly known as 'El Brujo' (the magician) because of his fascination with the occult, Lopez Rega divided his leisure time among astrology, politics, gunrunning between Libya and Argentina, diverting money from social programs into Swiss banks, and murder, perhaps with some drug dealing on the side. As minister of social welfare in Isabelita's government, Lopez Rega signed, on behalf of the Argentine government, a 1974 agreement with the US to fight drug trafficking in South America. The war on drugs, the American ambassador proclaimed, with Lopez Rega standing at his side, would also be a war on left-wing guerrillas, the real source of the drug scourge. The arms he received from the US to prosecute the war on drugs equipped his Argentine Anti-Communist Alliance (AAA), a paramilitary death squad, much publicized for its largely ineffective assassination campaign against 'Communists,' but little publicized for the more effective support some of its members provided for the South American leg of the French Connection heroin ring.[3]

After Peron's death, economic and political conditions took a sharp turn for the worse. Investment fell off and capital flight accelerated; the IMF was banging on the door. The armed forces were openly chafing for an opportunity to turn their talents loose on the Montoneros. This guerrilla movement had come into the open on the return of Juan Peron, attempting to assert itself as the legitimate voice of the Peronist revolutionary left by cultivating close ties with the Peronist-dominated unions. On his death the Montoneros returned to guerrilla action. Their most spectacular coup was the kidnapping of industrialist Jorge Born, for whom a $60 million ransom was paid – a handsome contribution to the cause. The army was outraged, denouncing both the guerrillas and those who authorized the ransom payment in contravention of Argentine tax and exchange-control laws! An army offensive followed, first against the Montoneros and then against bigger game.[4]

By late 1975 it was obvious that a coup was in the works. In the midst of the turmoil the IMF demanded austerity measures. But the government wavered, fearing a popular backlash from the Peronist union movement, for the unions had not forgotten that among Juan Peron's proudest accomplishments from 1945 to 1955 was purging from the government, including the central bank, persons who seemed too chummy with the international bankers. He had also kept the IMF wolves from the door, although they got inside in 1956, the year after his ouster. It looked as if 1976 would witness a repeat of the 1956 scenario.[5]

Early in 1976, as a last effort to undermine the military plotters, Isabelita's government dreamed up the cute idea of an invasion of the Malvinas. But the coup intervened; Isabelita was deposed, and the IMF program was approved.[6]

Austerity was greatly assisted by the rounding up of trade-union leaders, which blunted the resistance to wage rollbacks and weakened the power base for a Peronist countercoup. The old regime was further discredited by stories of corruption. Just before the coup, Argentine military intelligence unearthed – or perhaps simply invented, for reasons of political expediency – a network of smugglers shipping cocaine to the US. Prominent among its alleged participants were several top-level figures in the Peronist right, including Lopez Rega,[7] who by that time had fled.

Lopez Rega was not the only interesting individual to depart hurriedly after the coup. Banker David Graiver had practiced a curious version of the banking principle of spreading risk. Graiver handled the subterranean financial requirements of the Argentine navy (including payments allegedly made to Argentine naval officials by the Atomic Energy Commission of Canada to secure orders for its nuclear technology), and banked the treasury of the Montoneros guerrillas, particularly that $60 million from the Born kidnapping. When the military coup occurred, Graiver decamped for Belgium, where he established the Banque pour l'Amérique du Sud, and then made for the US, where a financial plum was waiting to drop into his eager hand.

When José Klein, a Chilean mining and shipping magnate, went into a Geneva exile (after the government of Salvador Allende had nationalized his property), he turned his talents to activities other than merely financing the right-wing backlash against the government. Through his Continental Trade Bank of Geneva, Klein controlled the American Bank and Trust Company, which had got itself into deep trouble over coal deals by the mid-1970s. Klein transferred control over ABT to Graiver's Belgian bank, and the fun began. As a *Barron's* magazine exposé later put it, 'BAS in Belgium was not a bank at all, but merely a conduit for laundering and stealing any funds deposited in it.' From ABT Graiver looted $40 million, passing it through BAS en route to another Graiver-controlled bank in Luxembourg, along with 40% of the assets of BAS, frolics that ended only when he supposedly died in a 1976 plane crash in Mexico. The money was never recovered, and both ABT and BAS collapsed, inadvertent victims of the overthrow of Peronism.[8]

An Offer They Couldn't Refuse
The military hierarchy in Argentina had long seen Peronism as a greater enemy than communism, for the Bolshevik Menace was largely a myth, while Peronism, with its organized blue-collar base, was all too real. After the coup, the military launched a three-pronged attack. First came the kidnapping and murder of top opposition political cadres and union leaders. Then came the 'dirty war' in which as many as 30,000 people disappeared. Finally came the destruction of the breeding ground of mass support for Peronism, the industrial base itself, by the application of long-term 'liberal' economic policies.

The shift of economic policy coincided with a profound militarization. Argentina had always had a strong tradition of military involvement in politics, but after 1976 the officers took charge of ministries and sat on the boards of every major state company. Nor were the traditional military pursuits neglected.

American eagerness to encourage firmly anticommunist regional power in the south Atlantic coincided with Argentina's Beagle Channel dispute with Chile, its aspirations in the Antarctic, and, of course, the running sore of the national psyche, British control of the Malvinas. Seized by the British from Spain in 1763 as a base for intercepting Spanish imperial trade from across the Pacific and around Cape Horn, the Malvinas represented more than just a territorial dispute Argentina inherited from Spain after independence. In the 1970s, raw material shortages, real or imagined, caused states to position themselves for control of the Antarctic region,[9] to which the Malvinas Islands were a logical stepping stone. The combination of geopolitical ambition and complete control over the instruments of government caused the armed forces to go on an arms-importing spree, and to hold out a new opportunity for the irrepressible Mr. Gelli.

Gelli survived the coup handily and quickly formed a profitable working relationship with Admiral Massera, who headed the junta. Gelli brokered three-way oil and arms deals among Libya, Italy, and Argentina through the quaintly named Agency for Economic Development, which he and Umberto Ortolani owned.[10] In 1976 Italy sold Argentina $239 million worth of arms; by 1978 the total had hit $1.27 billion. Gelli also honed his contacts on the international arms black market, providing Argentina with equipment from a variety of sources, much of which, the military complained, did not work properly.

The 1976 coup led to Argentina being buried under foreign debt in two ways. 'Liberalization' of the financial system opened the private sector to a flood of overseas borrowing to finance domestic speculation; and the military seized on the absence of significant civilian bureaucratic restraints to make massive arms purchases with borrowed funds. And both were made simple by the high foreign-exchange value of the Argentine peso.[11]

The principal architect of the strategy was Finance Minister José Martinez de Hoz, a former protégé of David Rockefeller's Chase Manhattan Bank and Trilateral Commission.[12] Martinez de Hoz, who invited international bankers to 'call me Joe,' presided over an economic team thoroughly infused with doctrines of 'sound money.' Interest restrictions were lifted, and a credit squeeze caused the rates to soar, making foreign borrowings cheaper than domestic ones. Tariffs protecting domestic producers were sharply lowered. Imports, increasingly financed by foreign borrowing, rolled in; together with the tight credit policy, they wiped out droves of domestic firms. The result, as in Chile at about the same time, was to foster the development of an economic system in which speculation was more profitable than production and the industrial core shrank.

The high value of the peso was essential to political support. As working-class living standards deteriorated, the middle classes could join the military in enjoying cheap imports, and in spiriting funds out of the country. But the price tag was enormous.[13] The debt load escalated rapidly. Firms switched from production to peddling imported goods; industrial production fell sharply between 1976 and 1981, while speculation flourished and the financial sector grew by 35%. Argentina saw the emergence of financial empires controlled by instant millionaires with access to cheap foreign credit, who plunged into the business of buying and selling banks, finance companies, and commercial and industrial enterprises.[14]

Early in 1980 a large number of industrial, agricultural, and commercial firms crumbled under the weight of debt, taking major banking houses with them. Following the collapse of the country's second largest finance company, a liquidity crisis struck the Banco de Intercambia Regional, the country's largest private bank. Its chief executive fled to Mexico, and the government closed the bank down. Three more major banks and an array of other financial institutions followed it into trouble. Within a month of the liquidation of the banks, the government had pumped the peso equivalent of $1.7 billion into 100 financial institutions.[15]

As the financial system disintegrated, the balance-of-payments position worsened: imports soared and exports stagnated. By the end of 1980 capital flight had drained $6 billion from the national reserves. To try to sustain the balance of payments, to finance the import bill (including the arms import and nuclear programs), and to cover the capital flight, more and more funds were borrowed from abroad – $11 billion more by the end of the year. The result was that Argentina's external debt, which had stood at $7.8 billion in 1976, was about $35 billion by the end of 1981.

Despite an emergency devaluation and the imposition of exchange controls, capital flight continued. So, too, did heavy foreign borrowing, until the Malvinas War caused an international credit cutoff.

The invasion of the Malvinas followed the script written six years earlier by Isabelita, though this time it was designed to perpetuate, rather than to prevent, military rule. Economic disorder was feeding popular unrest as surely as it was failing to feed the populace. By early 1982 the only hope of a daily meal for 250,000 families in Buenos Aires was the soup kitchen run by their local parish churches. The invasion promised a diversionary circus, if no bread; it came just after a mass rally denounced the government and called for a drastic change in economic policy.

Britain had encouraged various Argentine governments to believe that the transfer of sovereignty was only a matter of time. With British approval, Argentina had steadily taken over an increasing share of the burden of maintaining social services and infrastructure on the islands, for the island economy had been run as a company colony, with little investment by the owners. It was close to collapse when the Argentine armed forces stumbled ashore.

The diplomacy of Peru's president, Belaunde Terry, held out hopes that armed conflict could be avoided. Belaunde Terry even publicly announced the pending end of hostilities only hours before the torpedoing of the *Belgrano*.[16] Apart from the loss of several hundred Argentine sailors, the torpedoing may have subsequently cost the lives of scores of British soldiers and sailors. For, allegedly, President Belaunde Terry was sufficiently angered by British duplicity that Peru played a crucial role in the supply of Exocet missiles to the Argentine air force. It was at this point that the shadow of Licio Gelli once again fell across the Argentine stage.

When the P-2 scandal broke in Italy, calls were heard for an investigation into arms trafficking between Italy and Argentina, and into the payment of 'commissions' to prominent military figures; but in Argentina there was little scandal. This reflected both the powerful position P-2 had achieved in the Argentine mass media[17] and tight press censorship. Several prominent magazines were shut to prevent exposure of the affair. Only one newspaper braved death threats and published the names of Argentine P-2 members, which included many ambassadors, politicians, and military figures.[18] Also on the list was the head of Banco Ambrosiano's Buenos Aires representative office.

In 1981, when Roberto Calvi arrived in Buenos Aires to celebrate the official opening of a full-fledged Ambrosiano branch, he was asked about his involvement in P-2. His reply was that 'politics and banking should be kept separate.'[19] Yet Calvi's concept of exclusivity was compatible with renting to General Suarez Mason, a P-2 member who was head of the state oil company, an office in the Banco Ambrosiano headquarters.

Initially the breaking of the P-2 scandal made Gelli persona non grata in Argentina and in many other places where the publication of the list caused embarrassment. For a time he was forced to hide out in Honduras.[20] But several months later, a second group of officers, closer to the P-2 organization, took power in Argentina. The way may then have been cleared for Gelli's rehabilitation in return for certain favors.

Rumor has it that when the outcome of the Malvinas War hung in the balance, and when Argentina faced an official international arms embargo, Gelli instructed Calvi to lend Peru (where Banco Ambrosiano had an important affiliate) the funds to finance the purchase of black-market Exocets for Argentina. Although the deal was never consummated, among Calvi's last acts before leaving Italy was to instruct that about $100 million be sent to Switzerland, perhaps for eventual use by the Argentine air force. One theory holds that when Calvi fled to London, apart from any Opus Dei dealings, he asked highly placed Masonic brothers there for help in rescuing his bank, using as a bargaining chip a threat to release the funds for the Exocets. If true, it was a futile, and possibly fatal, act.[21]

Aftermath

The military debacle destroyed the remaining moral authority of the Argentine armed forces in the domestic political arena. And, by precipitating an international credit cutoff, which quickly degenerated into a generalized flight of funds from Latin America, the Malvinas War made the 'debt crisis' a global phenomenon in a way that the financial problems of Turkey or Poland could not.

Inside Argentina, defeat shattered the flimsy unity of the armed forces. Junior and middle-ranking officers turned their wrath on the senior officers, long despised for their corruption and now for their incompetence; and the air force, glorying in its relatively creditable performance, made a bid for greater power. The military junta underwent a quick face-lift, and then attempted to defuse the anger with some reflationary measures and exchange controls, whose main effect was to irritate the IMF.[22]

The official unemployment rate stood at 14%; unofficially it was double that. GDP had followed its 6% 1981 drop with a 7% decrease during the first half of 1982. Such manufacturing as had survived 'liberal' economic policies was at half capacity under a crippling debt load. Bankruptcies were at record levels. The banking system was hit by a major withdrawal of funds, as hot money poured into real estate, durable goods, and hard currency. This internal flight from financial assets exacerbated the external flight of capital.

The IMF's central economic objective in Argentina was the restoration of 'liberal' economic policy. But that required that three political conditions be met.

One was the containment of the power of the Peronist-led unions, which could be counted on to resist sacrifices in domestic living standards in the interests of servicing the external debt.

A second precondition was a rapid return to civilian government. This necessity had been brought home to Washington in May 1982, when the junta informed the US government that, in light of the post-Malvinas economic and diplomatic situation, repudiation of the external debt was a distinct possibility. A civilian government would eliminate the banks' prevailing fear that, should the military, especially the air force, gain the upper hand in domestic politics, it would try to raise its domestic prestige by dropping a debt bomb on the banks of those NATO countries that had stood by Britain and voted sanctions against Argentina.[23]

Another advantage of a civilian government would be that it would be forced to take a proper inventory of the debt, consolidating all the secret and under-the-table military dealings into the public accounts, where they would become a recognized and legally accepted Argentine public responsibility.

Certainly not least, the bankers must have realized that a new civilian government stood a better chance than did the discredited military of getting the population to acquiesce to the further drop in living standards that would be necessary to meet external payments obligations. A civilian government could blame the austerity measures on the mess inherited from the military. The junta was more likely to resist the IMF than would a new civilian administration, particularly as the military, after the defeat, had been trying to win back public favor through reflationary measures.

Success in Argentina was critical to international creditor interests. Success would, of course, help in dealing with other debtors; but failure in Argentina was particularly dangerous because, unlike other major debtor countries, it was self-sufficient in food and fuel. Argentina was the one country in Latin America that could survive a credit cutoff, should it decide to repudiate its external debt – a possibility increasingly under public discussion. What was at issue was not the country's physical but its moral ability to resist a credit cutoff; and that ability could be expected to be greater under a civilian administration, especially if a resurgence of Peronism could be stopped.[24]

The third prerequisite to achieving IMF objectives was the most immediate: to browbeat or bribe Argentina into lifting its economic sanctions against Britain, especially its freeze on British assets.[25]

The freeze was an especially delicate matter as London was the center of the euromarket. The British government insisted it would not lift its freeze on Argentina's assets until Argentina lifted its freeze on British ones and declared a formal cessation of hostilities. The banks, for their part, would not participate in rescheduling Argentina's debt until arrears were cleared. And the only way for Argentina to clear its arrears was to borrow – on the euromarket. Jacques Delarosière, the IMF chief, extracted a secret promise to work on a thaw from the Argentine minister of finance and the head of the central bank at the 1982 IMF meetings in Toronto.

But the military was in no mood to lift the freeze, fearing this would be interpreted by ambitious junior and middle-ranking officers as a sign of weakness or a concession of defeat. It might provide the pretext for a coup by precisely that layer of the military hierarchy most likely to repudiate the debt.

The outcome was a 'compromise' similar to that of Poland. The British banks participated in debt renegotiations with the Argentine government, while the British government maintained a freeze on public-sector dealings with Argentina.[26] And to criticisms of the British banks' participation, the chairman of Lloyd's Bank replied that the 'new' loans to Argentina were in fact simply a rescheduling of old loans, from which Argentina derived no real benefit; the 'new' loan format was a legal ruse to eliminate the danger of some banks invoking the dreaded cross-default clauses. Furthermore, as Margaret Thatcher pointed out in the banks' defense, the alternative, allowing Argentina to default, would harm Britain financially and would free Argentine export earnings to be diverted into further arms purchases.[27]

The Price of Power

When Argentine Economy Minister Jorge Wehbe made his promises to the IMF in September 1982, no one was sure he could deliver. The military was resisting further austerity; the air force and Peronist unions were publicly pledged to fighting a debt deal that would erode living standards while the country was in the midst of its worst economic crisis of the century. Union leadership boasted 85% to 90% participation in a spring 1983 general strike; there were riots over tax hikes in a working-class suburb of Buenos Aires; and the middle class was in an uproar over the accelerating inflation rate.

What was at stake for the creditors was the successful implementation of two distinct but related agreements. The first was a deal between Argentina and the IMF to impose the usual deflationary policies in return for the money, which, released in installments conditional on progress toward negotiated targets, would go directly to the international banks to discharge the arrears on Argentina's debt-service obligations. That deal paved the way for the second accord, with the banks themselves, rescheduling the debts falling due in the next year. As the chairman of Lloyd's had boasted, the agreements promised no new money for Argentina, simply some housecleaning of the banks' books. In exchange, Argentina pledged to maintain steep real rates of interest, implement regular devaluations, slash its public-sector deficit from 12% to less than 8% of GDP, and, of course, resume interest payments to the British banks.

No sooner was the deal completed, however, than it began to fall apart in the face of stubborn resistance from the unions, small business, and the air force.[28] A return to civilian government was urgently required.

Contesting the elections for a civilian government were the Peronist and the so-called Radical parties. Both pledged to reverse the direction of economic policy: to raise tariffs, to ease credit conditions, and to take a tough line on the external debt.[29] But there were major differences between them. The Peronists demanded that domestic economic recovery take precedence over the foreign debt. They called for a return to 1974 living standards within five years; state ownership of major industries; far-reaching reform of the banking system; building up domestic industries to replace imports; and, not least, after denouncing NATO for supporting Britain in the Malvinas War, a return to the Peronist ideal of international nonalignment.

The Radicals soft-pedaled the nonalignment question, downplayed questioning of the legitimacy of the external debt, and put their principal financial spokesman, Eduardo Grinspun, on record as calling for quick renegotiation of public-sector companies' debt.

No matter who won the pending elections, a major concern would be determining just how much external debt there actually was. Argentina was reputed to be the third most heavily indebted developing country in the world. But was it? If the IMF and international banks were overestimating the debt load, they were also demanding more severe austerity policies and greater diversion of production into the external sector than the actual debt load justified.

It was generally accepted that, during the heyday of 'liberalism' in Argentine economic policy, the debt load rose astronomically. But the actual figures were only working estimates. Late in 1982 Jorge Wehbe declared the debt was $43 billion. The air force insisted it was no more than $37.8 billion. In 1983 AmEx Bank estimated it at $43.7 billion, adding the significant insight that of $63 billion of debt 'missing' among the twenty-four largest debtor countries, Argentina had 'lost' a quarter of the total.[30]

Part of the problem was inadequate records. It proved difficult to determine the volume and purpose of, or interest rate and maturity on, loans that had been contracted both by the government and by state- (often military-) controlled companies on their own authority. During a period of acute tension with Chile over the disputed Beagle Channel, arms imports totaled about $9 billion. The nuclear program, also under military control, cost about $6 billion, mainly financed by foreign borrowing. After the Malvinas War, another splurge of military expenditure to replace lost equipment added $1.5 billion to the military component of the debt.[31] But much of this 'military' component had less to do with defense than with creating sinecures for officers. And it was generally felt that in some cases the military had run up debts without the money ever entering the country. As an investigating judge put it, 'It is not clear whether we are dealing with the results of massive looting or chaos or both.'

Sorting out the civilian-sector debt was also complex. Most of it had accumulated when there was an overvalued exchange rate but no exchange control. In a variant of the loan-back scam, an Argentine citizen could import dollars and sell them to the central bank with a guarantee of rebuying the dollars in future at the original rate of exchange. The capital importer could then sell the pesos on the open market for dollars, repay the external debt, and leave the original transaction on the books of the central bank as a guaranteed foreign-exchange credit for future use.[32]

Just prior to the elections, a team of Peronist economists concluded that '40% to 50% of the private-sector debt is fictitious.'[33] Yet late in 1982, under IMF and bank pressure, the government had guaranteed all private-sector external debts, converting them into a public responsibility. The Peronist economic team also calculated that of the total private and public debt on the books, fully $11 billion was impossible to verify.[34]

Thus the debate over the size of the debt also inevitably raised the question of its legitimacy, and therefore of the degree of public responsibility for honoring it.

Notice was served on the international credit institutions that the legitimacy question would be a thorny one when in 1983 ex–finance minister José Martinez de Hoz was accused of fraudulent administration of the foreign debt. Peronist lawyers accused the Martinez de Hoz team of accepting commissions from those receiving foreign loans, and of complicity in the diversion of funds from the projects for which they were allegedly intended into speculation on local financial markets. In addition, Martinez de Hoz was accused of involvement in a multibillion-dollar scam at the state oil company. The company had borrowed $5 billion, even though Argentina was self-sufficient in hydrocarbons and all company expenditures were peso denominated. According to his accusers, none of the $5 billion entered the state company's coffers.

The air force, conducting its own investigation into the debt question, and seeing the issue as a club with which to beat the army representatives in the junta, made great hay of the Martinez de Hoz affair.[35] And as the debate over the legitimacy of the public debt intensified, the air force had other cute tricks up its sleeve.

Judge Kramer's Coup d'Etat

In ten days that shook the banking world in October 1983, a judge in the remote town of Rio Gallegos, 2,000 miles from Buenos Aires, suspended payments on the external debt. He also ruled that Argentine law superseded that of New York, in a case that was to be the model for the renegotiation of $5 billion of state agency debt, and he ordered the arrest of the head of the central bank on charges tantamount to treason.[36]

Before Judge Kramer made his move, negotiations with the foreign creditors had been bumping up against Argentine bankruptcy law. In Argentina, companies having debt-payment problems can have recourse to a court-supervised renegotiation of debt; this can lead either to bankruptcy or to a rescheduling agreement. During such proceedings involving the debts of a pulp-and-paper conglomerate that owed foreign banks $100 million, international creditors discovered to their horror that Argentine law required that the claims of domestic creditors take precedence over those of foreigners.[37]

When the international banks demanded that the bankruptcy laws be revised, the government tried to rush through a draft bill to abolish the offensive clause, lest new credit be withheld by the banks. But the air force blocked the change. Economy Minister Jorge Wehbe then tried to get the law altered by presidential decree; but the president, fearing a clash with the junta, refused. There was, however, another possible way out of the impasse.

Late in September the state airline, Aerolineas Argentinas, signed what was to be a model rescheduling deal with its creditors in New York. The contract stipulated that Aerolineas Argentinas did not have 'sovereign' immunity; that New York law was to take precedence over that of Argentina in enforcing the terms of the contract; and that, in the event of default, creditors of the airline would have the right to seize assets of any and all state companies. In effect, the state was to guarantee, with a pledge of all its existing assets, the debts incurred by the many publicly owned but autonomously operated companies.

Military opposition to the deal, led by the air force, was strong. The Peronists, too, publicly denounced it. Then, when Wehbe and central bank chief Julio Gonzalez del Solar were in Washington trying to pry loose $830 million promised by the banks and the IMF, Judge Kramer made a decision that threw the negotiations into a tailspin.

Kramer ruled that the airline debt deal was null and void because of the stipulated precedence of New York law. He ordered the government to desist from further negotiations with respect to company debt until the report of a Buenos Aires judge investigating the origins of the debt was completed. As Kramer put it, 'The debt of all firms is in question until we know the overall debt.' The decision halted all foreign-exchange dealings; the central bank officially ceased to sell foreign exchange (of which it had actually run out); and local banks stopped foreign-debt payments.

Panic spread. Rumors that the government was going to seize private dollar accounts led to runs on the banks; even safety-deposit boxes were emptied. Capital flight to the peekaboo financial havens accelerated.[38] And when central bank chief Gonzalez del Solar arrived back from Washington, there was an arrest warrant awaiting him. After a night in the Buenos Aires police station, he was flown to Rio Gallegos to face an ebullient Judge Kramer, who had not had so much fun since the days when he used to capture headlines for arresting Chilean political refugees on charges of espionage.[39]

The judge's decision no doubt derived partly from his right-wing, nationalist political beliefs, and partly from his links to the air force hierarchy, who hoped to use his decision and any crisis it provoked to grab more political power. Unlike the senior staff of the army and navy, that of the air force took a hard line on the debt question. Kramer, a military appointment, might also have been trying to cultivate a new constituency to safeguard his job when the expected civilian government took over.[40]

However, the Court of Appeals ruled him legally incompetent to judge on such matters and reversed the decision within two weeks. This was enough time for foreign exchange to begin flowing into the country again, and therefore for some payments on the debt to resume flowing out.[41]

There remained the two basic and closely related questions: how much debt was there, and how much money had been, and continued to be, looted? As inflation accelerated, the gap between the official and black-market exchange rates widened. The smuggling of export goods became endemic, as did the underinvoicing of those exports passing through legal channels. In the first nine months of 1983 illegal exports – mainly of wheat – were estimated at over $1 billion, a huge blow to the foreign-exchange reserves. Private Argentine bank accounts in the US, Panama, Uruguay, and other havens were estimated at $11 billion (subsequent estimates put the figure as high as $28 billion), in addition to Argentine holdings of foreign real estate and other physical assets. From the coup of 1976 to late 1983, the estimated total of funds secreted abroad reached as high as $35 billion, a sum that seemed perilously close to guesstimates of the country's total external debt load. The rather obvious implications made the question of who was to do the counting, and the accounting, particularly important.[42]

Heads ... You Lose

The result of the presidential campaign, to the great relief of the bankers,[43] was an unexpectedly strong victory for the Radical party led by Raul Alfonsin. The Peronists had entered the contest divided; and unsuccessful efforts by Admiral Massera to secure Isabel Peron's endorsement of him as party candidate did them little good, especially as Massera ended up not in the presidential palace but in jail, charged with covering up a murder during the 'dirty war.' Nor were the party's fortunes aided when one of its candidates for a state governorship was charged in connection with a drug-smuggling and prostitution ring.[44] Also important was a rallying to the Radicals of the middle class, frightened by the Peronist unions' show of strength in the streets. 'Liberal' opinion also feared a Peronist sellout to the military: there was evidence of a tacit alliance between some union leaders and nationalist factions of the armed forces over the debt question. No prosecution for crimes committed during the 'dirty war' might well have been a quid pro quo.[45]

But perhaps most important in explaining the extent of this first-ever Peronist defeat was the fact that Martinez de Hoz seems to have had the last laugh.

The traditional electoral base of Peronism had always been in the industrial working class. But the industrial sector of the economy was devastated by 'liberalism.' Some important producing sectors vanished entirely; industrial production fell 16% in a decade. Surviving firms regressed to about 50% capacity on average. Fixed investment dropped by 4.3% per annum after 1981, as funds fled into speculation or abroad. Overall employment in industry fell sharply as workers shifted to 'self-employment' and the 'services' sector – manning 300,000 cigarette and candy kiosks, driving taxis, or working as semiskilled or unskilled labor outside formal establishments (and therefore outside the protection of social security).[46] One consequence was the permanent erosion of the Peronist blue-collar electoral base, which helped to turn the global battle between the bankers and the debtors sharply in favor of the former.

Although negotiating the rates and maturities at which Argentina would pay the debts and calculating how resources could be diverted from the domestic economy into debt-service payments would be difficult, the principle was settled. The triumph of democracy in Argentina was also the triumph of those political elements intent on taking a 'responsible' attitude toward international debt. Deals could still be struck over terms, but the legitimacy of the debt was no longer subject to serious challenge. With such an outcome in the most self-sufficient of the global megadebtors, the bankers had won more than just a battle; they had considerably enhanced their odds of emerging triumphant from the war.

10

Born-Again Banking

Both the upheavals in Catholic finance in Italy and Spain and the defeat of Argentina in its twin wars – for the Malvinas and for a rational resolution of its debt problem – provided an opportunity for another group of practitioners of the arts and sciences of peekaboo finance. And they brought into the limelight yet another flourishing hot-money mill.

These participants viewed Central America through red-tinted glasses. The Argentine military, protesting American support for Britain, had ceased to aid the antigovernment guerrillas in Nicaragua and to bolster the juntas in the surrounding states. Argentine 'advisers' and arms were soon replaced by a motley collection of mercenaries. These forces drew financial sustenance from an increasingly bizarre combination of 'religious' organizations in a competitive crusade to undermine or overthrow the Nicaraguan regime. While the bells in St. Peter's Square were tolling for Calvi, Gelli, Ortolani, Pesenti, and Ruiz Mateos, Protestant fundamentalists were flexing their political and financial muscle.

Hence, in Central America, theological politics became a three-way struggle. John Paul II and Opus Dei denounced the Jesuits for their involvement in the fight for social justice, while supporters of evangelical churches infiltrated governments, plotted and executed coups, and assisted counterinsurgents. Support for the evangelicals came from two crucial sources. The first was tax-free funding made available in the US for the promotion of 'religious' activities and laundered through a network of peekaboo financial facilities. The second was the Pentagon, which saw the 'free churches' as more reliable than Catholicism in the battle against communism in the region.

Gimme That Prime-Time Religion ...
The seeds of that Pentagon-'free church' alliance can perhaps be traced to the early 1960s, when one of many CIA schemes to overthrow Castro was dreamed up by General Edward Lansdale, veteran organizer of

counterinsurgency campaigns in the Philippines. Lansdale proposed that, after an intensive propaganda campaign identifying Castro with the anti-Christ, a procapitalist Christ arrive in Cuba aboard an American submarine as star shells exploded in the sky. This would spark a spontaneous combustion of anticommunist fervor that would cause the overthrow of the regime – 'elimination by illumination' as the CIA called it.[1]

The spirit also touched Guatemalan strongman General Ephrain Rios Montt, who, in 1979, became a convert to the Church of the Word, set up in Guatemala three years earlier by Gospel Outreach of California. Coming to power in a coup, for which he thanked God and the government of Israel,[2] Rios Montt drew additional sustenance from an alliance of American fundamentalist churches, which raised the money he needed to buy Israeli arms for his 'beans and bullets' campaign. The campaign was such a roaring success that his officers spoke of the 'Palestinian-ization' of the rebellious Indian population.[3]

Rios Montt certainly needed all the support the churches could give him. Since 1954, when the CIA and the United Fruit Company staged a coup to depose the government of Jacobo Arbenz Guzman and put an end to its program of land reform, the Guatemalan political system had been rotted by corruption and the ranks of the politicians periodically thinned by death squads. Only the fractious army held the country together.

In 1977 the Carter administration cut off official funding to the regime in protest against its human rights record.[4] But in early 1983 the US rolled out the barrel and reopened the spigot on military aid. The Guatemalan regime's reputation, President Reagan insisted, was a 'bum rap.' After all, who could object to a government headed by a man who declared, 'We don't have a policy of scorched earth. We have a policy of scorched Communists.' The regime then stepped up the 'counterinsurgency' operations that, by some estimates, left between 30,000 and 100,000 dead by 1985.[5]

Nonetheless, Rios Montt had his detractors. The Catholic Church, long resentful of the preferential treatment granted Protestant evangelicals, was outraged when, on the very eve of a visit by John Paul II, Rios Montt executed six 'guerrillas' whom the pontiff had asked him to spare. The military hierarchy detected an increasing reticence in Rios Montt to extend the Guatemalan counterinsurgency campaign into a regional crusade. Local businesses were irritated at his charges that they were paying protection money to the guerrillas and upset at his efforts to do the will of the IMF – to close the budget deficit by raising taxes.[6] Local businesses included much of the army's officer corps, who owned some of the banks the IMF measures would squeeze and who opposed cutbacks in the distribution of luxury imported goods at low prices through the commissary stores.[7]

In 1983 an army coup dumped Rios Montt and the Church of the Word.[8] The next year an attempt by exiled rightists to sell cocaine to finance a countercoup was busted by the Miami police.[9]

Elsewhere in the region, notably in Honduras, Protestant fundamentalism was also thriving. Honduras, too, had been on President Carter's blacklist; but in 1982 a civilian president was put in office. Although the real power remained with the army chief of staff, General Gustavo Alvarez, the facelift was enough for the Reagan administration to step up military aid. Fundamentalist church activists mobilized money and support for Alvarez, organized anticommunist propaganda in the Honduran university and army, and facilitated the acquisition of Israeli arms and technical advisers to realize the Honduran air force's lofty ambition to become the strongest in the region.

General Alvarez understood the nature of his country's social problems: 'Our people are used to hunger. If they revolt it is because someone incites them.' Presumably, this analysis applied in 1984, when reformist junior officers and an air force hierarchy nervous about Alvarez's increasingly strident anti-Nicaragua rhetoric followed the Guatemalan example and chased Alvarez off into a Costa Rican exile.[10] Also on the Guatemalan model, a group of exiled supporters collected 320 pounds of cocaine in Florida for purchasing military equipment to stage a comeback, only to run afoul of the FBI.[11] By then, however, Alvarez's sponsors had already turned their attentions elsewhere.

How High the Moon?

The story of those peculiar sponsors begins far from Honduras of the 1980s. In 1936, on an obscure farm in northern Korea, Christ appeared to sixteen-year-old Sun Myung Moon and told him he had been selected to finish His work on earth. To drive the point home, Buddha and Moses came calling on Mr. Moon in 1954. The result of the visits was the launching of the Holy Spirit Association for the Unification of World Churches, under whose auspices the curriculum at the Honduran national university would be restructured.[12]

At the time Buddha and Moses dropped in to chat, Korea was emerging from a particularly brutal civil war, in which the social fabric and faith in traditional secular and religious institutions were rent. Korea became an ideal recruiting ground for evangelical 'Christian' movements. They were undoubtedly encouraged by the American military, for such sects usually included staunch anticommunism in their creed. Frequently they also embraced a Born-Again Capitalist ethic that blamed the failure of traditional Christianity on its excessive concern with the ethereal kingdom at the expense of the worldly one. Apparently the leaders of these sects had never met Archbishop Marcinkus.

Some of the Korean sects are strictly local. The Olive Branch Church of Reverend Pak Tae Son, operating out of his 'Millenium Castle,' aims at economic self-sufficiency: followers are encouraged to place their worldly goods at the command of Reverend Pak.[13] Other sects are regional. Singapore, long a stomping ground for American evangelicals, has become a favorite for Korean ones as well. In early 1984 Chui Yonggi drew 40,000 people on each of five consecutive days. One drawing card was Chui's downplaying of Christian poverty. Chui and others in the revival business assure their followers that making money is not only permissible but wealth is a blessing given by God to the faithful. As one local recruit enthused, 'We [Singapore] can become a Christian center for the same reason we are a commercial center – our geographical position, our infrastructure, our financial resources.'[14]

Some Korean cults go beyond the local, beyond the regional, to the global, on the way to becoming celestial. Certainly the ecclesiastical notions of the Reverend Sun Myung Moon are worthy of universal attention. Claiming to be a descendant of God, he insists that his mission includes the creation of a divine race that will take over the world on behalf of a Holy Trinity (God, Moon, and the War on Communism) and destroy Satan, a rather broadly defined concept that seems to embrace all Moon's political and ecclesiastical opposition.

Other prominent individuals in the region, particularly those with South Korean investments to protect from a communist takeover, seem to share at least part of Moon's vision of Satan. In Japan two powerful Moon sponsors set up Win Over Communism (WOC) as a virtual subsidiary of Moon's Unification 'Church.' The chairman of WOC was Ryoichi Sasakawa, who had led his own black-shirted party in Japan in the 1930s and once flew to Rome to hear Mussolini. He was interned, though never prosecuted, by the US occupation forces in Japan, as a 'Class A War Criminal.' After the war Sasakawa, aided by his political connections, built a massive business empire, both at home and abroad – including a recent effort to break into the action in Atlantic City. In his spare time he was a major funder of the ruling Japanese Liberal Democratic party, created after the Second World War by the CIA, who had embraced Sasakawa as a friend. His other friends included former president Ferdinand Marcos of the Philippines, the late Anastasio Somoza of Nicaragua, and of course Reverend Sun Myung Moon.[15]

The second chief adviser to WOC was Yoshio Kodama, a leader of the ultrarightist faction in Japan, who parlayed prewar underworld experience into a wartime fortune based, it has been claimed, on raw materials looted from occupied China. Closely tied to Japanese military intelligence during the war, he inevitably emerged unscathed, free to continue such activities and his agitation for the remilitarization of Japan, leading to his role in the great Lockheed Corporation bribery scandals in the early 1970s.

In the search for military contracts, Lockheed scrubbed bribe money for Italian politicians through a Liechtenstein *anstalt*. Funds for Japanese politicians took two routes. Some were carried to Hong Kong by cash courier – a Spanish Jesuit priest – for laundering through obliging banks. The second route was by telex to the Hong Kong office of Deak & Co., the foreign-exchange dealership set up by a former OSS China operative. The telex order was converted into cash and taken to Kodama, who was busy funding the rise and spread of the Moonies.[16]

Reverend Moon set up shop in South Korea after the 1948 partition. Although he had a rocky early career,[17] his organization was soon adopted by the Korean CIA and the military establishment, who appreciated its potential in the war on communism and for positioning pro–South Korean propagandists in strategic positions abroad, especially in the US. This relationship paid dividends to the Moon organization. Revealing a better grasp of the principles of risk diversification than did the Vatican, Moon included in his Korean business operations control over the export of ginseng to the world's vegetarian pacifists and the manufacture of M-16 rifles, machine guns, and grenade launchers for the South Korean army.

In 1972 the Korean CIA set out to improve the public image of President Park Chung Hee, then under attack for his human rights record (another 'bum rap,' as there were no human rights to record). The Moonie operations base shifted to the US. Paving the way was Colonel Bo Hi Pak, one of the officers responsible for the coup that had put Park in power, and subsequently military attaché to the South Korean embassy in Washington. Indeed, some have suggested that Bo is the real mastermind behind the Moonie organization.[18]

But Moon soon followed, called to America by God, he claimed, to deal with its moral and political decay – not to mention the need to head off American plans to pull troops out of South Korea. As he told admirers in 1985, '...this country continues to ignore the monumental will of God. America is withdrawing more and more from its global responsibilities, preferring to enjoy false comfort as if this nation were a world unto itself. This attitude, of course, merely multiplies America's problems. Deterioration of social, ethical, and moral values, decline of religious life and Christian faith, and the rise of materialism and communism will not disappear just by ignoring them.'[19]

Interesting thoughts from someone who had just been released from jail after serving time for tax fraud and perjury.

In the US the Moon cult prospered. Indeed, the vigor with which the cult expanded in the US may not be completely unrelated to problems that befell it in South Korea. In 1977, one year after the notorious 'Koreagate' scandal in the US, the South Korean regime decided to disassociate itself partially from the sect, which had become somewhat of an embarrassment. The South Korean authorities leveled a number of charges of fiscal fraud against the management of Moonie-controlled enterprises.

The sect responded by creating the Unification Church International, a nominally religious and charitable foundation whose real function was to pump money out of South Korea and to build up an American business empire, in contravention of exchange-control regulations. Some of the money was moved to the US in cash, using sect members as couriers; some moved laterally as 'loans' to South Korean foundations, which were 'repaid' in the US.

On top came a flow of cash from its Japanese associates, to finance Moonie political and business growth, while the Moonies adroitly applied to their recruitment program the science of mind control developed by intelligence agencies during the Korean War. The cult was endorsed by prominent members of the American political establishment, undoubtedly encouraged by the Moonies' public defense of Richard Nixon during the Watergate scandal.[20]

Moonie finances were further enhanced by the organization's official 'church' status. Revenues from its empire and contributions from converts were tax free. This encouraged converts to turn over their incomes to the 'Father' to further his sacred objectives – proselytizing, evangelizing, and redeeming the world from communism.

Adequate financing was the key to world domination. Tax-free revenues were soon flowing from Moonie-controlled travel agencies, restaurants, real estate, shipbuilding, food processing, jewelry, and fishing fleets. With such diverse interests falling under the influence of the Moon, a logical addition was a bank.

The target was the Diplomat National Bank of Washington. The sect and the Korean CIA (which used the bank as a conduit for covert funding) eventually attracted 53% of the stock – and the attention of American bank regulators over attempts to hide ownership and over apparent infractions of lending regulations.[21] Through Diplomat National

Bank the Moonies broke into the newspaper business in the US and around the world.[22] Their big media drive, designed to counter 'communist' propaganda, led to their ultimate political triumph. Shortly after his election as president, a smiling Ronald Reagan was photographed holding a copy of the Moonie publication *News World*. The Moonies' penetration of Central and South America thereafter assumed a new energy.

The Empire Strikes Back

The success of the evangelical churches in Central America caused considerable alarm in the Vatican, not least because, though the Catholic Church remained overwhelmingly dominant in South America, there were signs of revolt from both right and left. In Argentina, political and military leaders had refused to meet with Bo Hi Pak; but the archbishop of La Plata, in keeping with his struggle against communism and his rigid opposition to liberation theology, endorsed Moon and cooperated openly with him.[23]

In Brazil, the various cults reached such proportions by 1985 that the National Council of Brazilian Bishops sponsored a study of the phenomenon, which it sent to the Vatican for consideration. That study called for deeper investigation into the reasons for their growth and for an investigation of the alleged role of the CIA in fostering them.[24]

John Paul II's counteroffensive had two thrusts. One was the attempt to 'reevangelize' Catholicism,[25] a process already established inside Italy.[26] The second was to step up the attack on Latin American liberation theology, which had been gaining acceptance as economic and social conditions in debtor countries deteriorated. Voices were being heard ever higher up the church hierarchy pointing to the debt crisis as a fundamental cause of the deterioration of the living conditions of the people. During a conference on regional debt problems in Havana in the summer of 1985, a Brazilian bishop argued, 'The Old as well as the New Testament clearly condemns debts causing hunger, dependency, the lack of conditions essential to life.'[27]

Those were brave words; for a full year earlier John Paul II had denounced the stance of some Latin American church leaders as Marxist and therefore incompatible with Christianity. The pope declared that there could be no solidarity between the church and the meek who were supposed to inherit the earth if that solidarity derived from notions of class struggle or even of class distinction. John Paul II's words must have been heavenly music to the ears of the military government in Brazil, which had been hauling increasing numbers of priests before military tribunals to answer charges of subversion. Early in 1985 the

Vatican applied the coup de grâce by ordering Father Leonardo Boff, Brazil's leading exponent of liberation theology, to observe a period of 'obsequious silence to allow him serious reflection.'[28]

The Brazilian church was not the Vatican's only target. Applauded by Opus Dei, the Vatican had been directing warnings with increasing frequency at the Peruvian church.[29] The Vatican quarreled publicly with the Nicaraguan government, which had Jesuits in cabinet,[30] and important Vatican allies began funding, in cooperation with Sun Myung Moon and about twenty private US-based organizations, the anticommunist governments and guerrilla movements of Central America.

The rallying point came when the US Congress rejected a 1984 bill authorizing $27 million in economic aid to the Contras. The money was not the issue, for the US government continued to funnel clandestine money through private American businesses in the area or allowed it to be quietly diverted from American military aid to El Salvador or Honduras or Israel. Moreover, the Reagan administration could always rationalize the absence of official, overt funding as being in keeping with its philosophy of encouraging free enterprise and the privatization of existing government activities. What was important was the legitimacy that Congressional aid would have given the Contras.[31] They certainly needed it.

The leadership of the Contras stationed in Honduras though less so in Costa Rica were former National Guardsmen who had assured Somoza peaceable enjoyment of private estates allegedly equal in area to all of El Salvador. These and other businesses put his personal fortune, just before his overthrow, at about $600 million.[32] The Guardsmen were bolstered by various foreign mercenary groups.[33] Apart from squabbling among themselves over the division of the aid monies, they found useful employment, while waiting to invade Nicaragua, acting as enforcers for big landlords and merchants in the Honduran countryside.[34] They became such powerful regional warlords that their host governments came to take almost as dim a view of their presence as did Nicaragua.[35]

With the refusal of Congressional aid (reversed a year later),[36] the slack was taken up by the Moonies and other private groups, including evangelical churches, the Taiwan-sponsored World Anti-Communist League, and *Soldier of Fortune* magazine. Not the least of the participants was a 'private, humanitarian organization' called Americares Foundation, which formed a cooperative program with the Opus Dei–linked Order of the Knights of Malta to channel money to El Salvador, Honduras, and Guatemala. Most of the money was earmarked for hospitals but some reportedly went for funding the Contras and creating Vietnam-style 'model villages' for the Guatemalan Indians.[37]

With such cooperation, perhaps Reverend Moon's dream of the unification of world churches in the struggle against Satan was becoming a reality.

Despite such successes abroad and President Reagan's endorsement at home, the Moon organization had its problems.[38] Like the Vatican's a decade and a half earlier, its tax-free status was being threatened. In 1981 the New York State Supreme Court ruled it more a business than a church, hardly a startling finding given that annual gross revenues from Moonie global businesses were then apparently topping $500 million. The township in which much of Moonie property was located sued for back taxes, and other lawsuits followed. In 1982 Moon was personally convicted of tax fraud, perjury, conspiracy involving false documents, and obstruction of justice.

While Moon's lawyers appealed the verdict and kept the case before the courts for another two years, danger signals prompted the 'church' to move its financial headquarters to more hospitable climes. Their choice proved to be that of the Latin American headquarters of Licio Gelli's P-2, and one of the principal havens through which Opus Dei's protégé Ruiz Mateos had moved money spirited out of Spain.

Two, Three... Many Switzerlands

Uruguay is often referred to as the Switzerland of the Americas. So is Costa Rica. The comparison is assumed to be flattering to the people of Uruguay and Costa Rica.

Granted, Uruguay's political violence in the 1960s and 1970s, its long and only recently altered status as a military dictatorship, and its prostrate economy are remarkably un-Swiss. But it does have a freewheeling banking system that operated as a laundromat for drug money and is still the most important South American depository for flight capital and tax evaders' funds.[39] What could be more Swiss than that?

Hot money has long sought sanctuary in Uruguay's capital of Montevideo – or Moon-tevideo, as it is now sometimes called. Uruguay was a major American stop on the escape route Licio Gelli created for Fascist family fortunes escaping Italy after the war, and many a European family gold hoard wound up in exile there. Apart from offering an attractive urban environment and freedom from extradition, Uruguay offers bank secrecy laws sufficiently appealing that, in 1971, the US narcotics bureau found Uruguay to be a pivot of financial operations associated with the French Connection heroin route. But Uruguay blossomed as a peekaboo financial center after a military coup in 1973.

The coup followed a sharp deterioration of economic circumstances in the 1960s and a civil war between the army and the Tupamaros urban guerrilla organization. The polarization provided an opportunity for major French heroin traffickers in Uruguay, who bought the protection of Uruguayan military intelligence by infiltrating the Tupamaros, promising them arms while informing the Uruguayan military about their activities.[40]

The military coup was followed by 'liberalization' of the sort subsequently practiced in Chile and Argentina. Exchange controls were dismantled; interest-rate restrictions were eliminated; and the welcome mat was rolled out for foreign capital. Uruguay became a major American center for tourism and gambling and a refuge for fiscal flight capital.

In the run-up to the Spanish elections in 1982, an estimated $3.2 billion fled Spain, frightened by the Socialists' dramatic threat to close budget deficits through tax increases. During the 1960s and 1970s, tax evasion and the privilege of holding secret bank accounts within Spain swelled the deficit to such a degree that the government simply gave up trying to keep them in check. To finance the deficits, the authorities developed a domestic variant of the loan-back scam. Hot money was welcomed into bearer bonds issued by both corporations and the government.[41] When the Socialists threatened an end to the internal laundromat, black money streamed to foreign havens, particularly Uruguay and Switzerland.

Even more important for Uruguay was its role vis-à-vis its South American neighbors, who found funds legally due their governments as tax revenues secreted in Montevideo banks.

Uruguay fed heavily off Argentina. Part of the capital inflow took the form of direct investments by corporations; Argentina ranked second to the US in direct foreign investment in Uruguay. But the much larger part was speculative and flight capital. During the days of *plata dulca*, when Argentina's exchange controls were liberal or nonexistent, and the international banks were lending heavily to the country, Argentine tourists flocked to the Uruguayan casinos and Argentine money poured into beach resorts and luxury holiday retreats. Any time the tax collector came knocking on the Argentine door, more money fled out the Uruguayan window. Every crisis in Argentina sent suitcases of currency across the estuary separating Buenos Aires from Montevideo. The ease of capital flight goes far to explain why fully 50% of the Argentine economy is 'underground.' It helps to explain why, by 1984, Argentine citizens were estimated to have piled up as much as $28 billion in foreign bank accounts. And it explains the phenomenal real estate boom in Uruguay.[42]

During the decade that followed the coup, 60% of buyers of Uruguayan land were foreigners, most Argentine. Thanks to Argentine money, Punte del Este became the fastest appreciating piece of urban real estate in the world, while the traditional peasant economy was thrown into upheaval by land speculation. By mid-1985 Argentine land holdings in Uruguay were conservatively estimated to be worth $7.5 billion.[43]

This was a hot-money bonanza too rich to be ignored. Between 1973 and 1983, as the banking and currency arrangements were further liberalized and bank-secrecy laws tightened, twenty of Uruguay's twenty-two banks fell into the hands of foreign investors. In an example of efficient recycling, as foreign bank loans poured into Argentina and, to a lesser degree, into Chile, the dollars flowed right out again, first via the Uruguayan banks and then through the increasing numbers of foreign banks setting up shop in Montevideo.

Prominent among the foreign financiers was Umberto Ortolani, Licio Gelli's chief Italian P-2 lieutenant, and Vatican-appointed ambassador of the Knights of Malta to Uruguay. From Uruguay, Ortolani could manipulate the contents of the Argentine newspapers he controlled through a Panamanian ghost company. The main financial instrument of the P-2 in Uruguay was Ortolani's Banco Financiero Sudamericano (Bafisud), which boasted minority participation by Banco Ambrosiano and other P-2–linked Italian financial institutions. Among Bafisud's functions was securing loans from Banco Ambrosiano and recycling the money back to Italy, with its origins obscured. Gelli is also alleged to have created a substantial personal retirement fund in Uruguay, in addition to acquiring a $5 million villa in the country.[44]

Also among the foreign financiers moving into the Uruguayan banking system was José Maria Ruiz Mateos, head of Spain's RUMASA Group, favorite son of Opus Dei, and one of the major conduits for capital fleeing the incoming 'Socialist' government of Spain.[45]

Initially the impetus for foreign financiers was a desire to cash in on a good thing in one of the globe's most flourishing hot-money centers. But after 1981, when the international environment began to deteriorate, the objectives shifted toward capitalizing on weakness. In the face of global recession and the attractions of the US, cash began to flow directly out of Uruguay, too, and the country was forced to join its neighbors in borrowing to replenish its foreign-exchange reserves. As in Argentina and Chile, economic 'liberalism' imposed on Uruguay both the iron boot of military rule and a heavy sovereign debt load. It also left it, by 1984, with an unemployment rate exceeding 16% and an inflation rate of over 70%.[46]

After the crisis of 1981, virtually all Uruguayan banks were forced to borrow from the central bank and to unload bad debts on the public sector. The central bank, in the guise of bolstering the capital of weak banks, intermediated the sale of local institutions to foreign financiers, among them the indomitable Reverend Sun Myung Moon.[47]

The local Moonie chief, Julian Safi,[48] quietly bought up small blocks of stock in the Banco de Credito, the third largest in the country, using funds provided through Kami Ltd., a Moonie-controlled Cayman Islands bank that Bo Hi Pak had established for the sacred purpose of keeping funds transfers from the prying eyes of the fiscal authorities.[49]

The context and timing were ideal. On the one hand, the financial crisis in Uruguay made the government keen to attract foreign capital, particularly to a banking system that generated so much foreign exchange. If that foreign capital came with an ideological bent with which the military government felt highly sympathetic, so much the better. President and former commander in chief Gregorio Alvarez (a member of Gelli's P-2) defended the Moonie encroachment as a matter of religious freedom. 'Also, we share their ideas as people involved in the struggle against communism.' As the Moonies were under siege elsewhere, particularly by the American tax authorities, and as they had targeted the Americas, particularly the southern parts under military dictatorship, for intensive proselytizing, Uruguay was the ideal financial headquarters.

Eschewing evangelism to avoid conflict with the local church hierarchy, they concentrated their Uruguayan activities on making money and influencing the right people. By 1983 it was estimated that Moonie investments in Uruguay totaled about $100 million. They had acquired the third-largest bank, the largest hotel, and local distribution facilities for Moonie-produced goods from all over the world: French jewelry, canned tuna, porcelain vases from Taiwan, and Korean ginseng and weapons. They also owned two local printing companies and prime real estate.[50] In 1983 they began planning a new forty-one-story hotel and conference center. The military government contributed a declaration that the hotel complex was 'of national interest' and therefore exempt from import duties.[51] The military also assisted them with tax breaks and public advertising revenues in their takeover and operation of one of the three local newspapers.[52]

The Moonies reciprocated by conducting promilitary and anti-'Communist' propaganda, just when the Uruguayan population was demanding, sometimes in mass street demonstrations, democratization of political institutions; the military government responded with more repression.[53]

Ultimately, however, 'democracy' returned to Uruguay. The main contenders in the 1984 election to succeed the military regime were the Blanco (center-left) and Colorado (right) parties. One of the differences between them was their attitude toward the Uruguayan banking system: the Colorados were committed to maintaining capital-flight facilities, while the Blancos argued for tighter controls.[54] The military weighed in to assure a fair contest, jailing the popular leader of the Blancos on his return from exile, and forcing the party to field a relatively unknown alternative. After a vote that the chief electoral officer described as showing 'irregularities previously unknown in Uruguay,' the will of the people prevailed, and the Colorado candidate assumed the presidency, assuring that at least one peekaboo financial center would be available for further Christian service.[55]

Part Three

High Finance in Cocaine Country

11

On Coca-collateral and the Andean Debt

At the 1981 Academy Awards ceremony, Johnny Carson quipped, 'The biggest moneymaker in Hollywood last year was Colombia. Not the studio – the country.'[1] His comment was only partially flippant. From the trendsetting denizens of Hollywood and other high-income, high-profile social groups,[2] cocaine use spread through American society.[3] By 1984 the US was guesstimated to be importing about sixty-five tons per annum, worth between $30 and $65 billion on the street, a sum sufficient to provoke an American administration campaign insisting that the spread of drug use was a communist plot.[4]

It is a long way from the Beverly Hills mansions of elite North American cocaine dealers to the Bolivian Indian peasant villages in Chapare where the manufacture of the drug begins. Snow blows north: from the high Andean plateaus of Bolivia and Peru, where most of the coca crop is grown, to Colombia, where historically it has been refined into cocaine, to Panama and the Bahamas whence it is transshipped via southern Florida to final markets across North America and, increasingly, Western Europe. The blizzard leaves behind a revolution in the structure and geography of finance, within and among the countries involved.

The cocaine economy forms the biggest component of an international drug complex whose gross annual revenues in the US alone may top $100 billion (though, by definition, all such numbers are 'soft'). That drug complex, in turn, is probably the largest single component of a global black economy that makes nonsense of conventional financial statistics. And the complex feeds the growth of 'narcocracies' whose financial power overwhelms the economy of small countries, undermines the fiscal integrity of large countries, and subverts the political and judicial process everywhere it reaches.[5]

Atahualpa's Revenge

Bolivia is the ultimate source of about half of the world's supply of illicit cocaine and most of its legal coca, albeit during the past few years its lead has been challenged by Peru.[6] Coca leaf has been Bolivia's most important product – except, briefly, silver – since Inca times, and played a central role in the Indian diet and religious rituals.[7] A small amount of cocaine began entering North America almost from the time it was first synthesized from coca in the mid-nineteenth century. But the snowstorm really began in the mid-1970s, built on a political infrastructure put in place right after the Second World War.

In 1945 US Army intelligence acquired Klaus Barbie, the 'Butcher of Lyons,' from the Gestapo. He was put on the payroll to mold clandestine Nazi cells in Eastern Europe into anticommunist spy rings. In 1951 he was given a new name and a false passport and sent to Latin America to help the US to combat 'communism,' particularly in Bolivia.[8]

Bolivia entered the postwar period in the throes of a popular insurrection against the elite of landowners and tin barons. Until 1952 the largest tin mines had been the fiefdom of the Patino family, which paid the miners sufficiently to assure Bolivia the highest child mortality rate in Latin America. When the revolution succeeded in 1952, the Patinos followed their money to a peaceful Swiss village near Geneva, and the Bolivian state mining monopoly, COMIBOL (Corporacion Minera de Bolivia), was born.

After the revolution, the government abolished the army, a virtual private guard for the old elite. But in 1956, under US pressure and with heavy Pentagon aid, the popular militias were replaced by a regular army. The results of army reconstruction showed in 1971: a populist government fell to army putschists. Colonel Hugo Banzer took power, appointing Barbie special security adviser.[9] During the next few years, the drugs mafia began flexing its muscle.

From the start, the US campaign against the drug traffic ran afoul of an internal contradiction. The US government wanted to stamp out the sources of illegal drugs imported into the US, but it was also intent on its crusade against the international communist menace. The major traffickers bought US complicity by posing as bulwarks of freedom against the Bolshevik hordes. Elements in the US intelligence agencies came to appreciate the importance of the dope trade in financing covert action and paying for arms to equip right-wing paramilitaries, who also drew recruits from the trafficking gangs. The stage was then set for the American war on drugs to run afoul of subversive activities conducted not by the international communist conspiracy but by America's own nominal allies at home and abroad.[10]

In 1978 Hugo Banzer was forced from office; after years of political chaos came a civilian regime headed by Hernan Siles Zuazo, one of three leaders of the 1952 revolution. However, the reform-minded administration would never take office. In its stead came a military regime headed by General Luis Garcia Meza. A combination of practicality and humor led to the appointment of Colonel Luis Arce Gomez as minister of the interior. Arce Gomez had excellent credentials: a cousin of Roberto Suarez Gomez, the country's leading producer of coca paste, he also allegedly claimed membership in Licio Gelli's P-2.

Although the direct instigator of the 'cocaine coup' was the alliance of senior military officers and drug producers – who pulled back some cocadollars hidden abroad to support the regime and to offset the adverse impact of Western governments cutting off aid flows – it also had moral support from outside. One month before the coup, the Reverend Sun Myung Moon had another vision, which predicted the event. That must have been good news to Garcia Meza, who had presided over a dinner in La Paz in honor of a visit by Colonel Bo Hi Pak. Moon's organization reportedly offered money to the putschists, and after the coup some 50,000 books extolling the principles of the Unification Church arrived in La Paz, allegedly on US Air Force planes.[11]

The core of resistance to the coup had been the trade union central, the Central Obrera Boliviana (COB), and especially the miners' unions. Cleaning out COB headquarters was the task of Stefano Dalla Chiaie, the right-wing terrorist wanted in Italy for the bombing (allegedly on Licio Gelli's orders) of the Bologna railway station. As union leaders were rounded up and murdered by paramilitary forces speaking with Argentine and Italian accents, air force planes strafed the mining camps that were union strongholds.

The real prize from the coup was the coca trade, the yields from which made canceled aid payments from Western governments seem like petty cash. To secure the prize, the putschists called in a special paramilitary force, quaintly called the Fiancés of Death, whose leader liked to parade around headquarters in an SS officer's uniform. It was given a list of small drug dealers to be put out of business – the Fiancés did not apply their peculiar concept of courtship to the really large-scale operators. Allegedly the generals managed to collect, in the form of a 10% levy on the major coca producers, upward of $1.5 billion. And as the paramilitary force retired the small dealers, the new government could pose to the outside world as actively suppressing the drug trade, while converting it into a virtual state industry.[12]

Armed resistance by growers and small dealers prevented a complete takeover by the narco-fascistas of La Paz. There was actually plenty of business for all, given the rapidly growing market. Indeed, the pretense of policing the traffic was formally abandoned by Garcia Meza in May 1981, when he announced that Bolivia would cease further action 'because of the poor reception given its efforts by the consuming countries.'[13]

American pressure led to another military coup later that year, which produced a government somewhat less sympathetic to the ambitions of Reverend Moon and less directly compromised by the coca trade; but it did little to lessen the influence of the major dealers – albeit they stopped recycling cocadollars back to the now less-overtly friendly government and caused yet another financial crisis. However, in 1982, in the midst of depression and international financial crisis, a joint effort by the Bolivian opposition, the US embassy, and the international banks pulled down the military regime and a new civilian coalition government headed by Hernan Siles Zuazo took its place.

Dope, Debt, and Democracy

That change of government reflected, at least partly, the financial legacy of the Hugo Banzer regime,[14] which had adopted an odd definition of economic 'development.' The state, controlled by the military, borrowed heavily and lent the proceeds to private Bolivian firms with which the military leaders were associated.[15] If a project was successful, everyone came up smiling. If it was not, the state picked up the bill, and everyone still came up smiling. In both cases most of the funds went to import consumer durables (with the trade accounts scrupulously falsified to assure a fair return to the intermediating official), or were spent on arms purchases, or were diverted to banks in Uruguay, Panama, Miami, or Switzerland.[16]

The fall of Hugo Banzer began an era of remarkable political instability.[17] As coup followed coup, bank lending dried up, and creditors fretted as arrears on debt-service charges accumulated. The 1980 coup aborted a tentative rescheduling agreement, and Bolivia survived financially only because Argentina's Martinez de Hoz approved of the entrepreneurial spirit of the new government enough to extend it credit. A major rescheduling of bank debt in April 1981 was supposed to be followed by an IMF deal; but between the cocaine coup in 1980 and September 1982, ten IMF missions came and went without real progress.

The end began in 1981, far from Bolivia. An attempt by the Malaysian government to rig the world tin market failed, and tin prices fell. Natural gas briefly replaced tin as Bolivia's principal legal export, but the main market for gas was Argentina, which ran out of hard currency after the Malvinas War. Then a July 1982 coup put in power a group of officers described by international bankers as 'incapable and incoherent,' completing Bolivia's ostracization from international credit markets.[18]

In September the military government made one last attempt to impose a severe austerity program, in spite of militant dissent from the powerful COB, the peasant organizations, and the employers' association. By this time foreign-exchange reserves were technically negative; the drain was so severe the banking system was paralyzed.[19] As business, labor, and peasant groups were mobilized against austerity, the international banks refused a grace period on overdue payments in order to step up pressure for the resignation and replacement of the military government. The American embassy was also growing insistent.[20] Together they backed Hernan Siles Zuazo, whose previous presidency had been marked by a successfully implemented austerity program. The bankers hoped that Siles Zuazo could use his high-level political prestige to persuade the population to accept renewed austerity; the US hoped that, as he was coming to power untainted by association with the cocaine mafia, Siles Zuazo could make some progress in suppressing the traffic.

Shortly after the new administration took power, the military leaders most implicated in the cocaine coup, Garcia Meza and Arce Gomez, fled to the safety of Argentina's military rule. Some of the Italian neofascists active in Bolivia were captured, though the most important, Stefano Dalla Chiaie, escaped; Klaus Barbie was arrested on charges of defrauding COMIBOL and extradited to France.[21]

Because Bolivia had no extradition treaty with France, right-wing Bolivian politicians seized the occasion to accuse Siles Zuazo's government of kidnapping Barbie and selling him to France in exchange for increased financial and military aid. Nor did it escape notice that when Siles Zuazo, on a state visit to France, placed a wreath on the grave of Barbie's best-known victim, French Resistance leader Jean Moulin, he made a direct reference to the burden of the Bolivian foreign debt.[22]

To cope with that burden, the government declared a state of economic emergency. The peso was massively devalued, exchange controls were imposed, taxes were raised, subsidies on basic goods were lifted, banks were forced to convert from dollar to peso transactions at a time when 70% of bank accounts were in dollar form.[23] The banning of dollar-denominated contracts aimed to isolate the dollar-based underground economy from the peso-denominated legal one.[24]

Instead, falling real wages fueled the growth of the underground economy; tax evasion rose with the tax rates; and the government resorted to the printing press. The devaluation set the inflation rate soaring, while doing little to improve overseas markets for Bolivian products. The balance-of-payments deficit worsened; and any hope of meeting debt-service obligations had to be deferred once more. By the end of 1982 the government deficit was running at 40% of (legal) GDP; private consumption was down 10%; manufactured goods production was off 15%; mineral production had fallen by 12%; and construction dropped 40%.[25]

However, coca production grew dramatically. In 1983 the amount of coca diverted into illicit channels was triple that of 1981. Although prices had dropped markedly owing to huge production increases in Bolivia, Peru, Colombia, and even Brazil, the effect of the price drop on Bolivia may have been partly offset by Bolivian producers increasingly undertaking full-scale processing of cocaine, rather than exporting coca paste to Colombia, as had been past practice.[26]

The new government was in an impossible situation. The US was demanding action against the cocaine traffic, yet the cocaine business had become so deeply entrenched as to constitute a parallel state and a parallel economy. The total revenues from drug exports were estimated to be running at upward of $2 billion per annum, an enormous sum for such a small and impoverished country, even though perhaps no more than 20% of the total earned from Bolivian drugs returned home (the rest being stashed in the usual banks in Panama, Miami, Nassau, Geneva, Moon-tevideo, and so on). The limited moves made by the Siles Zuazo government to curb the trade served only to shift production into more remote areas, where the government's writ has rarely run.[27]

There the uncrowned king of cocaine is Roberto Suarez Gomez, who may account for half of the total output. Theoretically the most wanted man in Bolivia, and pursued by the American police, Suarez Gomez claims to be a victim of intrigues by the US DEA, which has forced him in self-defense to create a private army of 1,500 soldiers, an elite guard allegedly trained in Libya, and an air force of three vertical-takeoff Harrier jets, twelve fighter bombers, some reportedly equipped with Exocet missiles, and/or twenty-eight other aircraft.[28] This is no mean accomplishment for someone who insists he is a mere cattle rancher.

Suarez Gomez cultivates a Robin Hood image in areas the government largely neglects. Thus, in mid-June 1983, he entered a bank in a jungle town with twelve machine-gun-toting guards, cashed a check for the equivalent of $150,000 (all the money there was in the bank), gave the local authorities enough money to build a school and repair the airport road, and vanished when the government ordered an alert.

Nor is his philanthropy merely domestic. When his son and heir, Roberto, Jr., was arrested in Switzerland and extradited to the US on charges of cocaine trafficking, Suarez Gomez offered to turn himself in to the DEA in exchange for his son's release, provided the US paid off the Bolivian foreign debt of $5 billion. When 'Bobby' was acquitted, Suarez Gomez flew over the Indian villages in his domain, dropping $5 and $10 bills to the children below.[29]

He also apparently felt generous on the debt question, publicly offering aid from his personal fortune. In a secret meeting in June 1983 with the Siles Zuazo government minister in charge of suppressing the drug traffic, Suarez Gomez allegedly made a specific offer of a $2 billion loan from his foreign bank accounts. When news of that meeting became public a year later, the scandal nearly brought down a government already weakened over dope, debt, and dissension.

The government's efforts to deal with the coca trade were checked by the lack of alternative economic activity, and by the deep entrenchment of drug-mafia allies in the state apparatus. Even nature conspired with the trade: in the summer of 1983 Bolivian agriculture was devastated by the El Niño weather disturbance, alternating bouts of drought and deluge that wiped out millions of animals and nearly half the food crops, precipitated peasants' revolts and looting of food stores, and forced massive emergency imports of food. The only areas unaffected were the coca-producing regions, which therefore drew destitute peasants from other areas.[30]

At the very time when one-quarter of the population had been adversely affected by El Niño, and domestic and external finances had been thrown into greater than usual upheaval, the IMF demanded another cut in food subsidies. It also demanded a major hike in utility charges, although some towns had been without water for months.[31] The IMF insisted that the market mechanism would alleviate the food shortage. It was never specific whether this would occur because rising food prices would improve weather conditions, because the coca planters would switch to cabbages, or because pricing food beyond the capacity of the population would lessen demand as it reduced the demanding population. The US government, irritated by Siles Zuazo's lack of progress against the coca traffic, contributed to the solution by suspending all emergency food aid until food subsidies were lifted.

The coalition government looked increasingly precarious,[32] torn asunder by the demands of right and left factions, while facing periodic defections. It was under constant pressure from the US over debt, dope, and communist participation in the government; it was under attack by the IMF and the international banks, while the military plotted coups.

Much of the political action shifted to the streets, where the Communist party–led COB could make its strength felt.[33] At the head of the COB was Juan Lechin Oquendo, another of the three leaders of the 1952 insurrection. Lechin had severed political relations with Siles

Zuazo in the late 1950s, when Siles Zuazo, as president, had imposed severe austerity measures. By mid-1983, the country was set for a reprise: the COB was demanding wage hikes that compensated for inflation; nationalization of the public-service industries; labor comanagement of all state companies; tighter bank supervision; an end to negotiations with the IMF; and a moratorium on debt-service payments until economic health was restored.[34]

On the other side, the IMF was demanding the end of indexation of wages and the elimination of the subsidies on essential products; the dismantling of state monopolies, particularly in mining; phasing out exchange controls and other state interventions in the free international flow of goods and money; and priority of the external sector in the allocation of productive resources.

The US government made major infusions of aid conditional on an IMF deal; the international banks refused further credits until Bolivia recommenced service payments on past loans (which required that an outside source of foreign exchange be found); and the IMF dangled a $350 million credit line before the hungry population. But each effort to increase austerity precipitated strikes and threatened the coalition. Meanwhile, Hugo Banzer, the military, and the drug mafia plotted a political comeback.

Some of the more respectable elements of the right-wing opposition received encouragement from the US embassy,[35] for Washington was concerned over the specter of Latin American eurocommunism. The embassy insisted that capital fled Bolivia not because of paramilitary thugs or massive drought, or because of the partial dismantling of exchange controls demanded by the IMF – not even because Bolivia was the fastest undeveloping country in Latin America. Rather, it was because of Communist party members in the ministries of labor and mines. They 'soured the investment climate.'[36]

Presumably the investment climate sweetened dramatically in April 1984, when a reshuffling of the coalition weakened the influence of the Communist party and set the stage for the successful negotiation of an IMF deal. The peso was further devalued by 75%; bread prices were increased by 480%; public transportation tariffs were pushed up 180%; fuel costs were raised 400%. The only wage earners granted sufficient increases to cover the price hikes were the police.[37]

Once more the COB took to the streets and the labor leadership staged a hunger strike. The strike movement hit the government in a particularly vulnerable area when employees of the central bank refused to apply the devaluation of the currency, or to process applications for foreign exchange, or to administer new interest-rate structures. The central bank strike froze the entire credit system, forcing private-sector banks to shut down, until the government sent the police into the central bank to restore operations. But by then the government had partially capitulated to the unions.[38]

By May Bolivia was in default on its obligations to the international banks. Its foreign-exchange reserves were again completely exhausted. As the government had nothing to lose, it accepted COB demands that not more than 25% of export earnings go to interest on the foreign debt.[39] This concession allowed the COB to order its members back to work while proclaiming victory. Over whom that victory occurred was unclear, as 25% of foreign-exchange receipts was a considerable change from the 0% Bolivia had been paying. Moreover, the US banks had long since moved Bolivian loans into the nonperforming category and set aside special reserves against them in order to safeguard their earnings position.

The most dramatic result of the 25% rule was to allow Hugo Banzer, whose 1972–78 government had contracted two-thirds of the country's debt, to rise again. Banzer demanded that Siles Zuazo resign, on the grounds that the de facto moratorium violated international treaties, closed international financial markets to Bolivia, and threatened to precipitate an economic blockade. And, though the government and the unions fell out again almost immediately over the question of wage and salary adjustments, before a new strike movement could get under way President Siles Zuazo was kidnapped – causing acute embarrassment to the US-sponsored war on drugs.

The creation of a special paramilitary force to deal with the Bolivian drug mafia may have originated in the Nixon administration's decision to apply a sort of Phoenix-program solution to the American heroin plague. An assassination squad was to knock off the major dealers, with the help of exotic devices from the creative engineering of Mitch WerBell.[40] In a similar spirit, in Bolivia, there was to be a new police unit, ostensibly free of dope-mafia influence. This was particularly important in light of experiences elsewhere, not least in the US, where members of elite, undercover antidrug strike forces often emerged as leading traffickers once the competition was gone. The Bolivian force also had to be free of the political aspirations that seem to come naturally to all uniformed Bolivians above the rank of lieutenant, albeit by 1984 the state coffers were completely empty, and therefore the material incentive for coup-making had disappeared.[41]

The elite unit, called the Leopardos, was to be equipped with special French-made communications equipment and machine pistols to lessen the equipment imbalance between government forces and drug-mafia militias. Allegedly the French equipment was part of the reward Bolivia negotiated for arranging the 'kidnapping' of Klaus Barbie. To avoid provoking the prodrug-mafia elements in the regular armed forces, the equipment was shipped to Bolivia in crates marked 'Food,' only to be hijacked by the army. The weapons seizure was the signal to mutiny in one of the southern garrisons commanded by a general who accused the government of acquiring the machine pistols to equip a left-wing paramilitary force. That seemed to incite a group of army officers and policemen to kidnap Siles Zuazo.[42]

The attempted coup was a fiasco. The US embassy refused to endorse the putsch; the population and loyalist police and army units rallied to the regime; and the plotters fled in panic to the Venezuelan embassy, where they were offered sanctuary only in return for revealing the abducted president's whereabouts. The net result was to heighten the president's prestige and give him a few more months in office,[43] but it also threw the antidrug war into disarray, for the kidnappers turned out to be members of the elite, supposedly incorruptible, Leopardos.[44] Deep in the interior, Roberto Suarez Gomez probably smiled, though his Colombian former associates were not laughing.

What Flows Downstream?

Nothing better illustrates the financial advantages of a developing country insisting on full downstream processing of its natural resources than the contrast between Bolivian and Colombian finances in September 1982.[45] While Bolivian banks simply shut down for lack of cash and international creditor banks began writing off their Bolivian exposure, Colombia's rosy prospects were being lauded by the financial press. What that press rarely mentioned was why Colombia was in such an enviable position when bankers were fleeing from Latin American syndications as fast as their telex machines could carry them.

Johnny Carson had provided one explanation. Throughout the 1970s Colombia was flush with cash from exports of its major crops: coffee, cotton, marijuana, and cocaine. By some estimates the last two contributed to Colombia's foreign-exchange receipts a minimum of $2.5 billion for each of the five years prior to 1982. (By 1985 there was talk of a $5 billion drugs export business.[46]) Much of that money, perhaps half, did not actually enter the domestic economy, but was salted away in deposits in offshore banks or converted into US real estate.

Nonetheless, as exports rose in volume and in price during the late 1970s, Colombia, unlike most developing countries, ran balance of payments surpluses and government budget surpluses; it rapidly accumulated foreign-exchange reserves, about half of which were imputed to inflows of hot money. It also began to accumulate external debt to banks happy to lend at relatively low rates. By early 1982 its debt totaled $10 billion; but its foreign-exchange reserves were a remarkable $4.5 billion. However, cracks were appearing in the seemingly solid financial edifice. Partly it was the normal shocks – rising oil prices and interest rates, and recession in the consuming countries that caused coffee exports to drop sharply in volume and in price. But Colombia also suffered from US entrepreneurs' implementation of import substitution, a strategy long favored by developing countries as an instrument of economic growth; and it suffered further from the vagaries of Bolivian politics.

The Colombian marijuana boom actually had innocent origins. Just after the Second World War, Colombia had difficulty providing its textile industry with adequate raw cotton. Hence, the government encouraged the cultivation of hemp. It produced a poor raw material for textiles but an excellent one for smoking, something that Columbia's old landed aristocracy quickly came to appreciate. But the export boom really started in the early 1970s, when Mexico and Jamaica were trying to suppress production. The Mexican eradication program was effective for a while, though one late 1984 raid in northern Mexico yielded marijuana stocks several times the estimated total annual production for all Mexico. However, Jamaica's success can be measured by the DEA's assessment that in 1984 the 'ganja mafia' was grossing $1.4 billion per annum from a crop which, if all marketed, would have been worth more than the official GNP.

But Jamaica's decision to remain on the ganja standard and the rebirth of Mexico's drug trade were not the main problems for Colombian producers. Rather, it was the development of US home-grown varieties. While Colombia still dominates the US import market, and may earn as much from marijuana as from coffee, its share of the total US market dropped sharply after 1980.

The modern, organized Colombian cocaine trade has roots in quite different social strata than that of the marijuana traffic. In 1966, a financial crisis forced the government to impose exchange controls and import restrictions. This created a new skilled class of *contrabandistas* and currency black marketeers, based especially in the city of Medellin. In 1974, the leading black marketeers joined forces to organize and promote the cocaine export trade, which, like the marijuana traffic, flourished until 1980, when it was sharply checked. Until the 1980 cocaine coup, Bolivians had been largely content to grow coca and reduce it to paste for export to, and refining in, Colombia. Colombia would market the final product in the US and, increasingly, in Western Europe. But after 1980 Bolivian production was more frequently diverted into local refining, for export through new trafficking rings. By the end of 1983 even Roberto Suarez Gomez was refining as much as 40% of his coca output – for which his Colombian former associates are rumored to have kidnapped and mutilated his son and heir, 'Bobby.'[47]

Nor was this the only source of new competition. Historically *the* contraband center of South America has been Paraguay, the entrepôt for marketing American whiskey and electrical goods, and cigarettes on such a scale that Paraguayans believed the country's *contrabandista* system had been created by the American tobacco companies. By the early 1970s the government of Paraguay was deriving one-third of its revenues from transit duties, while top military men who controlled the land on which the runways were built were collecting transit duties of their own.

Initially it was largely a one-way flow. But in the early 1970s, under the aegis of exiled Corsican mobsters, the inflow of American consumer goods began to be complemented by return cargos of heroin. Although French-produced heroin ceased to flow through Paraguay after the breakup of the Corsican rings in 1972, the legacy of the partnership facilitated the flow of Colombian cocaine to European markets.[48] It was apparently on the basis of that infrastructure that Nazi exile Dr. Josef Mengele took a leaf (or, perhaps, several thousand tons) from Klaus Barbie's book and entered into the Paraguayan drug traffic as early as 1971; however, it was not until the early 1980s, when officials close to President Alfredo Stroessner came to appreciate the growth potential of the trade, that Paraguay seems to have become an important refiner and exporter.[49]

Peruvian production also expanded sufficiently that local coca baron, 'el mosquito loco,' could offer to pay off the entire Peruvian foreign debt in exchange for a pardon. (Alas, when he died in a prison riot in 1984, hope for the restoration of Peru's flagging financial fortunes died with him.)[50] On top came the successful breeding of new strains of coca more at home in the humid and hot lowlands of Brazil's Amazon Basin than in the cool highlands of the traditional Andean growing areas.

Not surprisingly, prices collapsed. In Medellin, Colombia's second largest city and principal black-market center for drugs, cigarettes, and emeralds, a kilogram of pure cocaine was selling for $20,000 in 1982; by early 1984 the FOB price had dropped to $4,000. Allegedly, too, the price fall almost precipitated major international gang warfare until an agreement on division of the market was worked out by major traffickers meeting, naturally, in the Vitoshi Hotel in Sofia, Bulgaria.[51]

The Colombian cocaine king is reputed to be multibillionaire Pablo Escobar Garvira, who, in the 1970s, persuaded veteran smuggler Fabio

Ochoa to diversify his entrepreneurial efforts from 'importing' cars, liquor, and electrical appliances to exporting cocaine. That was the beginning of an organizational shift from which Escobar emerged controlling a de facto cartel of major exporters. Like his Bolivian counterpart, Escobar cultivates a Robin Hood image among the poor, erecting low-income housing, providing free hospital care, building a zoo, and donating a soccer field to Bogotá. He also sat in the Colombian House of Representatives on behalf of Medellin.

Equally patriotic is Carlos Lehder Rivas, who set up his own rightist Latino Nacionalista party, encouraging attendance at its meetings by handing out 1,000-peso notes. His private militia also encouraged grassroots participation by giving money for urban redevelopment. The party's election platform called for the rejection of an extradition treaty with the US on the grounds that it would be an affront to national dignity.[52]

In the 1970s, under presidents Alfonso Lopez Michaelsen and Julio Cesar Turbay Ayala, the government decided that it could do nothing to control the traffic. Hence, it might as well put the cash to public good by encouraging it to flow into the financial system as security for international borrowing. Unlike Bolivia, Colombia permitted no dollar-denominated bank accounts. Returning money was converted into pesos in two ways. One was through US branches of Colombian exchange houses, which accepted dollars in the US and issued equivalent pesos in Colombia, at the black-market rate. Dollars could also be converted inside Colombia at the *ventanilla siniestra* of the Banco de la Republica, where dollars were exchanged for pesos with no questions asked.[53]

In effect, the government accepted a dual economy and a dual state apparatus. The cocaine mafia directly accounted for a large and growing share of Colombian economic activity; the cash flow also fostered other activities outside the officially recognized economy. Allegedly thousands of businesses came into existence – everything from contraband imports and illegal emerald mining and exports to simple textile production – that were not captured in the official data. It was an arrangement the local bishop saw fit to bless. In accepting the traffickers' gifts of cash for the church, he insisted that the alternative was for the money to go into funding prostitution, racketeering, and influence peddling. Certain of his colleagues at the Vatican would have understood.

Local banks bridged the underground and overground economies, channeling 'narcodollars' toward local real estate and on-lending drug money to other components of the parallel economy: smuggling, illegal mining (the state has a legal monopoly on the purchase of gold and precious stones), and general black-market dealings.[54] Banks feeding off hot money were also the financial base for huge business conglomerates.[55]

All this was cheered by the National Association of Financial Institutions, whose chief took on extra duties as campaign manager for Lopez Michaelsen in his last election effort, and as chief lobbyist for the legalization of marijuana.[56] And the process must have been further encouraged by the substantial funding of both political parties by the drug dealers.

Snow Storms and Asset Freezes

While the drugs mafia created a parallel economy, they also created a parallel state, with their own militias and captive sectors of the judiciary.[57] However, one part of the state apparatus they chose not to duplicate was the tax collector's office. With 50% of Colombian economic activity officially belonging to the 'underground' sector, it is little wonder that the budget surpluses that made Colombia so popular with international bankers in the 1970s were replaced by 1982 with increasingly severe deficits, equal by 1984 to half of all government spending.[58] By mid-1982 a declining portion of hot money was coming home, and by the end of 1984 foreign-exchange reserves were down by 75% from their 1981 level. A Peruvian central bank official could have been speaking for all the coca-belt countries when, in 1985, he said, 'Coca is our first export product. It is illegal, but it provides us with needed reserves. It helps the country's balance of payments.... The problem with hot money is that these funds could leave in a second and the country would be without reserves.'[59]

As in Bolivia, the emerging financial crisis coincided with political changes in Colombia. The Liberals, who had held office during the golden years of the drug trade, lost the presidency in 1982 to the Conservatives led by Belisario Betancur.[60] Washington backed Betancur in the hope that he, like Siles Zuazo in Bolivia, would clamp down on the drug trade.[61] In short order, however, Betancur was struggling with twin problems: keeping the drug-fueled financial system from exploding, and bringing peace to an interior overrun with paramilitary groups of all political persuasions,[62] whose single common characteristic appeared to be a propensity to dip into the hot-money pool that the drug traffic produced.

The fiscal and financial problems Betancur inherited derived from the fact that hot money was both notoriously unpatriotic and the foundation of the Colombian credit system. Hot money also helped keep the peace between the old landed and military elite and the upstart *clase emergente*; but in so doing it also may have perpetuated the absurd political order in which two parties representing the same elite interests alternated in power and drove opposition groups into armed insurgency.[63]

Unlike such predecessors as Turbay Ayala, who had insisted that jailed guerrillas were torturing themselves to make the government look bad, President Betancur called for a full pardon for all guerrillas who turned in their arms; but the amnesty fell afoul of the army and Washington's demands for action against the drug trade.

The major guerrilla groups had a history of kidnapping and shaking down the drug dealers, imposing 'war taxes' on them.[64] That led the major traffickers, early in 1982, to collaborate with the army in the creation of a paramilitary death squad called Muerte a los Secuestradores ('Death to Kidnappers'). The group protected the plant and equipment of the major traffickers against guerrilla raids and unleashed a wave of assassinations and kidnappings of antigovernment activists, trade union and peasant leaders, opposition journalists, and politicians and lawyers campaigning against the drug trade. MAS also lent an important hand to right-wing efforts to sabotage the presidential amnesty by kidnapping and murdering amnestied guerrillas.[65]

Early in 1984 the US government intensified pressure on Colombia to move against the cocaine traders. The Colombian government was caught in a bind: US financial and political pressures were impossible to fight; but ordering the army into drug traffickers' terrain would violate pledges to the guerrillas that their territories would be demilitarized.

To step up pressure on Betancur, the US government and the Colombian army concocted the notion of an alliance between the guerrilla groups and the drug dealers: allegedly, the left-wing guerrillas were not merely 'taxing' the traffic as well as all other businesses in their areas, but were actively guarding the cocaine refineries and clandestine airstrips against the army.[66]

The story got increasingly complicated with each telling. Fidel Castro was supposed to have brokered a deal between the Colombian drugs mafia and the pro-Cuban M-19 guerrilla group; the drugs mafia provided arms in exchange for assistance in marketing drugs, and the Cuban government took its cut in hard currency. This tale was later embellished by bringing into it Robert Vesco, then hiding out in Cuba. According to this version, Vesco (the former exporter of machine guns to right-wing paramilitaries in Central America) had joined forces with the government of Nicaragua (then combatting a US-armed and -funded right-wing insurgency) in a conspiracy to export Colombian cocaine to the US.[67]

Whether the major traffickers also planned, during their alleged meetings at the Vitoshi Hotel in Sofia, to finish the job Ali Agça left uncompleted has not yet been revealed. But an interesting and strangely familiar twist came in 1985 when Jorge Ochoa, Pablo Escobar, and

Carlos Rivas were tried in absentia in Miami for importing drugs into the US via Nicaragua. Ochoa, who was arrested in Spain while trying to establish refining facilities to service the European market, told reporters that the idea of implicating Nicaragua had been given to him after his arrest by a US DEA agent who was a former CIA man.[68]

President Belaunde Terry of Peru also decided to get into the act. Peru's 'underground' economy was larger and more sophisticated than that of Bolivia, and the government had always turned a profitably blind eye to the coca boom. When the drug trade was building up steam in the late 1970s, Peru deliberately abolished exchange controls to attract cocadollars, exchanging them for pesos or for dollar-denominated certificates of deposit with no questions asked. Peruvian banks expanded rapidly into cocaine country to sop up the flow. By the early 1980s Peru's cocaine trade was reputedly worth $1.5–3 billion per annum, of which about $800 million returned home to a warm and officially sanctioned welcome.[69] Yet Belaunde Terry insisted that Peru's Shining Path guerrilla movement was part of a vast international narco-subversive network[70] undoubtedly controlled by the KGB.

Logically, Belaunde Terry may then have had to conclude that the KGB had infiltrated to the top of his own government, for in the summer of 1985 an explosion in a Lima cocaine refinery brought to light a network of such refineries operating in suburban villas controlled by Peru's largest trafficker. The coca king's legal adviser was found to have a direct phone line to the police branch in charge of drug investigations; and he also operated as the liaison between the coca king and the minister of the interior in Belaunde Terry's government.[71]

Meanwhile, Colombia had bowed under US pressure. Justice Minister Rodrigo Lara Bonilla cooperated with the army in two major raids on complexes owned by traditional drug mafia kingpins[72] who immediately denounced Lara Bonilla as a tool of the US government. On April 30, 1985, a hit squad recruited in Medellin assassinated the justice minister. That eliminated the major architect of the war against the drug trade and its allies, paramilitary groups and official corruption, and the cabinet minister with the best relations with Cuba. It also provided the army with a means of pressuring Betancur into declaring a full-scale state of siege,[73] and ultimately ended any serious hope for peace with the guerrilla movements.[74]

After the assassination, a much-publicized sweep arrested hundreds, bombed clandestine airstrips, and allowed the government to seize the assets of those proved by military tribunal to be implicated in the traffic. But apart from briefly disrupting the real estate market in Atlantic-coast resort towns when owners of luxury villas and flats precipitously left, it made little difference to the cocaine trade. Most of those arrested were street peddlers, and most of the handful of middle-ranking traffickers who were picked up bribed their way to freedom shortly afterward. In fact, the regional government of Medellin found itself with a new fiscal problem: how to pay for the gourmet tastes of the animals in fugitive Congressman Pablo Escobar's private zoo.[75]

The major traffickers, who were enjoying an open-ended vacation in Panama, may not have been disconcerted by the drug seizures, as any destroyed by the government would help relieve the glut that was depressing prices. And the likely longer-term result of the campaign would be merely to cause more production to shift to Peru, and into the Brazilian interior, where the vast, impenetrable Amazon jungle would ensure the industry immunity from such inconveniences in the future.[76]

The war on drugs received yet another setback from the deterioration of Colombian external finances. In 1982 Betancur had tried to amnesty black money, provided that it would be invested in productive (i.e., legal) enterprises. But local banks objected, presumably because legalization of the money would force them to pay higher interest on any of these funds deposited with them. Moreover, the Supreme Court ruled against the amnesty. Then, less than three weeks after the Lara Bonilla assassination, Betancur's attorney general and former president Alfonso Lopez Michaelsen went to a meeting in Panama City. There they met the three drug dealers who represented 80% of the traffic to consider an offer that was difficult to refuse. The government would grant a truce and a pardon to the drug dealers, and would oppose any extradition to the US; in return the cocaine kings would lend the government $3 billion to help reactivate the economy.[77] News of the negotiations coincided with a major scandal in Bolivia, in which Siles Zuazo was formally censured by the Senate; a year earlier his minister in charge of suppressing the drug traffic had held a secret meeting with Roberto Suarez Gomez. Subject – the economy, and a $2 billion loan to revive it.[78]

Andean Free-fall

There was certainly a lot to discuss. In Bolivia the IMF-style 'economic recovery' had continued throughout 1984. Official GDP was down 10% from its 1982 level; per capita income had dropped 30% during the previous four years; the inflation rate hit 2,500% while wage increases were running at 300%; the peso had depreciated from an official rate of 44 to the dollar to 45,000 to the dollar, while the black-market rate stood at 170,000 to the dollar by the end of 1984. Legal exports had dropped to $700 million per annum; debt service charges, had they been paid, would have added more than $800 million per annum to an import bill of, at the very least, $500 million. Production levels in mining, manufacturing, and food-oriented agriculture dropped in absolute as well as in relative terms.[79]

As Bolivia lacked formal mechanisms for capturing the returns from the coca economy, the fate of the tin and silver mines was crucial to the country's future foreign-exchange earning capacity. Successive military regimes had systematically run down the equipment, and the most accessible lodes were depleted. While world metal prices stagnated, costs soared, with austerity and the IMF replacing military diktat in keeping investment in the publicly owned mines at or below zero. Moreover, between smuggling and phony invoicing, little of the proceeds of the private mines made its way into the economy.[80]

Of course, there were exceptions to the economic collapse. By mid-1984 it was estimated that there were 500,000 people dependent on the coca business. They were led by a group of former army officers who found plying the drug traffic more rewarding than plotting and executing coups to control a bankrupt state. Austerity fed the coca business, as unemployment and the decline of capital-intensive industry encouraged the shift toward the 'informal' economy. In the interior, US-sponsored attempts to suppress the trade were countered by the conviction that cocaine-refining brought new jobs into the area. If the products also killed gringos, so much the better. In any event, as Bolivians like to point out, the main traditional product of Bolivian industry, tin, is destined primarily for the American arms industry, and therefore routinely kills far more people than cocaine ever could.

In mid-1984 the Bolivian government was pressured by the US to declare Chapare a military zone and to order in the army. This was done over the loud objections of the peasants' organizations and the COB, but not a sound was heard from the drug dealers, who had had plenty of time to vacate.[81] As an antidrug move, it was a farce; and the first casualty of the campaign was not the drugs mafia but the peso. Fear of political backlash and the cutting off of the black-market dollar inflow sent the peso into free-fall.

A longer-term casualty of the war was the government itself.

At the beginning of 1985 Siles Zuazo still battled on. His 'coalition' was reduced to feuding pieces of his own party. It faced a Senate in which a majority was held by parties of Hugo Banzer and another former president, Victor Paz Estenssoro, who agreed on the need to unseat Siles Zuazo. Juan Lechin deployed his forces, each attempt to tighten austerity precipitating more street demonstrations and strikes. Inflation jumped to an annual rate of 34,000%, and bank notes became Bolivia's second most important import, as domestic presses were unable to keep up with demand. It became a standard joke that there were no more bank robberies since no one could cart off enough cash to make one worthwhile.[82] In the meantime, the US government was denouncing Siles Zuazo for his lack of enthusiasm in the war on drugs; and the international banks and IMF were pressing for a deal on the debt. With the balance of political advantage swinging to Hugo Banzer, Siles Zuazo gave up, resigning one year before his term officially ended.[83]

One of the most important concessions wrung by the unions from the Siles Zuazo government had been an agreement for increased labor comanagement of state-sector companies, particularly the mines. Hence, added to the right wing's ideological antagonism to state ownership of the mines was an immediate political objection: the comanagement deal had strengthened the power of the communist-led unions and had helped to swing the local business community behind Hugo Banzer.

Banzer had been denouncing the government's failure to honor the foreign debt, the bulk of which was a legacy of his term in office (the money had usually ended up in the offshore retirement accounts of his government associates). His rising star so frightened the left that they rallied behind Victor Paz Estenssoro, the third grand old man of the 1952 revolution.[84]

The seventy-seven-year-old Paz, seeking his fourth term as president, had a spotty political record. In the 1940s he and his political associates in the MNR (the Revolutionary Nationalist Movement) had plotted the overthrow of the military regime that protected the tin barons and their foreign partners, and had called for agrarian reform and the unity of the workers, peasants, and middle classes. But by the time he resurfaced in active politics, most of the radical rhetoric had vanished. Granted, as the first president after the 1952 revolution, he had presided over the nationalization of the mines. But that had been forced on his government by the COB; and Paz ensured that it was a lucrative deal for the tin barons. He also fought demands for worker management of the mines. He had backed Hugo Banzer's military coup in 1971, and consistently opposed Siles Zuazo's efforts to secure election.[85]

With the center and left rallying to Paz, the only obstacle to his victory was the possibility of a pro-Banzer army coup, which was averted by a deal that the presidents of Argentina, Uruguay, and Colombia hatched with the two contenders. Revealed in autumn 1985, in what was ironically called the 'New' Economic Policy, the deal proved a shock: the newly elected Paz handed cabinet posts to supporters of the old and bloody military regimes, jettisoned all his left-wing backers, and imposed the most severe austerity package ever attempted in Latin

America. He then arrested and exiled union leaders who objected.

The IMF-dictated program saw the peso devalued by yet another 95%, from the official rate of 75,000 to the dollar to the black-market rate of 1.5 million; gasoline prices rose tenfold; price and exchange controls and subsidies were abolished, and wages frozen; all comanagement deals won by the unions were wiped out; the state-owned smelting company was abolished, and COMIBOL itself, symbol of the 1952 revolution, was to be 'decentralized,'[86] pending the appropriate moment to return it to private ownership, likely with foreign participation. But that would require a further improvement in the investment climate, one that another facet of the New Economic Policy hoped to achieve.

The Bolivian state and the banking system officially went into the laundry business. In an appeal for dope money to come home – all would be forgiven – the New Economic Policy decreed that 'No proof need be given, at the national, departmental, or municipal level, of the origins of assets invested' during the next four months. The central bank began marketing bearer CDs in dollar denominations with a guaranteed 10% rate of return; and the commercial banks were to be allowed to open accounts without reserve requirements, in order to provide domestic competition for the offshore banks.[87] In effect, the black-market money of the narcocracies was officially invited to swallow the overground economy.

The Colombian government, too, was forced to capitulate formally to the 'underground' economy. The deterioration of its international financial position was partly due to the general flight of funds from Latin American lending. Another impetus may have been political in origin, as elements in the military and the old oligarchy cooperated with the narco-financieras to spirit what they could out of the country and to undermine the Betancur government's policy of 'war on drugs and peace with the guerrillas.'[88] Although Colombia remained the sole Latin American country to continue to service its foreign debt without rescheduling, international banks cut back on their bank-to-bank credit lines and never fully restored them.

Capitulation to the hot-money pool came in two stages. In February 1984, to try to bolster the foreign-exchange reserves, the government was forced into a bizarre arrangement for the purchase and sale of gold. It would buy gold domestically for pesos, at a rate nearly $100 above the world market price, with no questions asked about the origin of the gold. It would resell it abroad for dollars at the world market price. Most of the gold originated in the Bolivian and Brazilian interiors, coming into Colombia along the coca-paste trade routes; and the gold-wash facility benefited the underworld financiers responsible for the cocaine traffic.

They could use dollars earned abroad by the export of cocaine to purchase gold, which they could import into Colombia and sell to the central bank for a 30% markup on the official fixing.[89] Then, in the spring of 1985 the central bank's *ventanilla siniestra* reopened. This arrangement anticipated Bolivia's moves by a few months, and meant that drug money was to be welcomed back to Colombia, no questions asked.[90]

But whether hot money would return to either country depended on developments farther north, where Panama jockeyed with Florida as premier flight-capital center and hot-money laundromat in Latin America.

12

Country of Convenience

While Costa Rica and Uruguay competed for the title of 'Switzerland of the Americas,' Panama bore a closer resemblance to Hong Kong.[1] There has been a long spiritual and political relationship between the two areas. Both Panama and Hong Kong were created, by the US and Britain respectively, as commercial and financial centers to serve their broader ambitions. While Britain and the other major powers of the late nineteenth century carved up China, the US fostered the emergence of Panama as an 'independent' country.

In 1898 the US launched the Spanish-American War, acquiring from a decadent Spanish empire the Philippines and Puerto Rico, and making a client state of what became a nominally independent Cuba. The Philippines gave the US control of Manila harbor, an excellent base for its Far Eastern trade. Cuba and Puerto Rico were important for business opportunities and for the naval presence in the Caribbean they gave the US. This presence was essential to the defense of the projected canal across Central America that would link the American eastern seaboard with the burgeoning commercial interests in the Pacific.

To complete this grand design, in 1903 the US sponsored a revolution in Panama, then a province of Colombia. A year later W. H. Taft, US secretary of war and commissioner of the projected canal, drafted the law that formed the basis of the Panamanian financial system, including provisions that made US currency legal tender. That year, too, the predecessor of Citibank opened in Panama, inaugurating it as an international financial center. Panama so grew into this role that at present it is Latin America's largest offshore center, hosting 130 banks from thirty countries, with combined assets in the vicinity of $50 billion.

Shell Collectors
The key to Panama's growth as a peekaboo financial center lies in a combination of geography and legislation. It is an ideally located conduit

186

for financial flows and trade, legal and contraband, mainly between South and North America, but also between Latin America and the Far East and Europe. In addition to capturing a large share of the flight-capital business out of Latin America, Panama is close to the main drug-trade route from Bolivia and Colombia to Florida.[2]

Legislation and administrative procedures evolved to enhance this geographic advantage. Panama accorded the usual advantages to offshore banks; it also copied corporate anonymity laws from Liechtenstein and bank secrecy rules from the Swiss, including jail sentences and heavy fines for bank employees violating secrecy provisions. (Panamanian bank employees may not be able to find out anything about accounts they are administering even if they want to, as a depositor does not have to give a name or address.)

Panama boasts a double layer of additional defenses. One of the principal occupations of Panama City's several thousand lawyers is to create and subsequently to administer shell companies on behalf of offshore clients who designate 'nominee' directors. The turnover reached such proportions in the early 1980s that shell companies were being manufactured a hundred at a time and turned over to brokers for resale.[3] A shell company capitalized by the issue of bearer stock, and therefore with no owner of record, could deposit money in a bank account protected by the world's tightest secrecy laws. Once international hot-money flows became tidal waves, Panama was right on the crest.[4] Riding a wave of enthusiasm was Minister of Justice Jorge Riba: 'There is no such thing as good or bad money. To me, money is neutral.'[5]

Of course, the system is subject to legal scrutiny. There is a government banking commission, over whose decisions representatives of the private banks have a veto. And there is a national bank, which has few of the powers of a central bank and cannot audit bank activities except in cases involving crimes under Panamanian law. Nonetheless, bank audits are mandatory; they must be conducted by the bank on itself once a year whether it needs it or not. These private audits follow no set procedures; one banner day in 1983 the Banco de Ultramar published its audited balance for the year, showing everything was in order, and promptly collapsed.[6]

Flight from Freedom?
Among users of Panamanian banking facilities and corporate secrecy laws were the major financial holding companies of Chile, during the period when it was declared to be the century's most radical 'experiment' in free-enterprise economics. That 'experiment' followed the overthrow of the left-wing regime of Salvador Allende Gossens by a coalition of

Chilean business interests, domestic and expatriate,[7] American multi-nationals,[8] and the Nixon administration.[9] In its wake came a military regime commited to 'free enterprise,' later joined by a collection of trained-in-Chicago hard-money ideologues eager to 'experiment' with the crank lessons their professors had taught them.[10]

The 1976 'Chicago' program had two fundamental, mutually rein-forcing, policy objectives. One was the opening of the domestic economy to the world 'market'; the second was an extreme privatization of economic life. The main tools for achieving the first were reducing tariffs, abolishing exchange controls, and eliminating political and financial obstacles to foreign investment. The main tools for achieving the domestic objectives were slashing public-sector activity and a drastic credit squeeze. This involved selling state companies to private enterprise and opening to private-sector exploitation parts of the economy, such as social services, where the 'market' had never before intruded.

Private capital responded appropriately to the 'incentives.' Throughout the Chicago era, Chilean domestic investment dropped to roughly half the Latin American average, well below the lowest levels of the supposedly antibusiness Allende era. Money avoided productive activity in favor of speculation and commerce in imported goods, prodded by high interest rates, low tariffs, and easily available foreign credit to finance imports. As Chilean goods lost ground to imports, as the industrial and agricultural sectors were squeezed, the well-to-do enjoyed cheap Scotch whiskey and imported cars. And the military, eyeing with envy and fear their Argentine neighbors, went on an arms-importing spree, financed by euromarket borrowing.

The 'spendthrift' socialist government had left behind a foreign debt of $3 billion and a debt-service bill that took 15.5% of export receipts. As the Chicago era of 'free enterprise' drew to a close late in 1982, the cost of servicing Chile's $19 billion foreign debt, in per capita terms the highest on the continent, had climbed to 85% of export receipts.

A pronounced change in the economic power structure accompanied the Chicago-era 'reforms,' particularly in bringing to the fore an elite of speculators and financiers popularly known as 'piranhas.' Their emergence was directly linked to efforts to close the state-sector deficit and open the Chilean economy to international financial flows. With interest rates in Chile kept above world levels, Chilean banks borrowed heavily abroad, often through Panama, and re-lent to companies in the conglomerates to which they belonged. The conglomerates could thus grow rapidly, not through real domestic investment, but because of their ability to gobble up existing assets.

These assets fell into their clutches from two sources. Smaller domestic companies, without captive banks through which to tap the eurocurrency market, were crippled by high domestic interest rates, making them easy prey for the piranhas. Moreover, efforts to close the state-sector budget deficit by selling off public assets put many companies on sale to politically favored individuals at bargain-basement prices. In 1981, Javier Vial, head of BHC Corporation, the largest Chilean conglomerate, estimated that the companies he had acquired from the government were worth eight times the purchase price.

The conditions that made capital inflow easy also simplified capital outflow. After acquiring assets thrown on the auction block by credit stringency or state-sector cutbacks, the wealthy could loot the companies and stash the cash abroad in Panama and other peekaboo financial centers from which the purchase price had originally been borrowed in anticipation of a rainy day.[11] It was soon pouring.

Chile, which had helped precipitate the Malvinas War by forging a secret military alliance with Thatcher's Britain,[12] was the Latin American country most severely affected by its financial aftermath. Chile, like the rest of Latin America, was deprived of new bank loans; its economic recession set a continental record; and capital flight through the peekaboo centers accelerated.

To try to halt capital flight, interest rates were pushed to 70%, double the inflation rate, but the only discernible result was to hasten bankruptcies of smaller firms, as funds continued to seek offshore resorts. Only when capital flight topped $45 million a day did the government reinstate exchange controls.[13] An IMF-imposed emergency devaluation drove up the cost of servicing international bank-to-bank debt until, in conjunction with the effects of domestic austerity, it brought the Chilean banking system to the point of general insolvency.

Early in January 1983 Finance Minister Rolf Lüders declared a bank holiday. Three banks and finance companies were liquidated; five others were nationalized. Three of the five banks seized belonged to the BHC Corporation, the largest of the Chilean conglomerates. The takeover cut off credit from the banks to companies in the group, causing several to default. Mobs of worried savers gathered outside the conglomerate's banks and finance companies until dispersed by police. Suspensions of payments by numerous finance houses continued throughout the next few months, threatening the savings of the middle classes.[14]

With the financial system tottering on the edge, Chile's international bank creditors decided they had had enough of free enterprise for a while. After Lüders nationalized part of the banking system and guaranteed domestic deposits, international bankers demanded similar insurance, insisting that the government unconditionally guarantee dollar-denominated debts contracted abroad by the nationalized part of the banking system. When Lüders hesitated, the government, seeking both a handy scapegoat to domestic debtor unrest and a means of currying the favor of international bankers, overruled and sacked him. It subsequently barred him and thirty other top financiers from leaving the country while their private financial affairs were under investigation. Fifteen business and opposition leaders sued the unfortunate former finance minister for mismanagement of public finances, and within a year of losing his position, Lüders was in jail.[15] Unfortunately for him, the government had discovered what he had under his Panama hat.

Prior to assuming the finance ministry, Lüders had been vice-president and virtual operations chief of the BHC Group, among whose fifty or more companies could be found four banks (including Banco de Chile, the largest private bank in the country). In 1981 the government had tried to curb intragroup lending, but the BHC devised a simple stratagem to evade the regulations. The BHC banks established a Panamanian subsidiary, Banco Andino, in which another, independent Chilean bank, Banco Sudamericano, took a minority interest. The BHC banks then 'lent' money to Banco Sudamericano in Chile, which lent the money to Banco Andino, which lent the funds back to companies in the BHC Group. These companies would record the loans as new international bank borrowing, which would increase the size of the Chilean foreign debt. Ultimately BHC Group accounted for more than 11% of Chile's total foreign debt.

When the government was forced to seize control of several private-sector banks, including three in the BHC Group, it uncovered the Panamanian money-go-round. The superintendent of banks, Boris Blanco, issued a stinging indictment of the BHC, neglecting to mention that, prior to entering public life, he had been vice-president of Banco Sudamericano when all the frolics were taking place. After Lüders was arrested, other financiers were picked up; and finally, in the spring of 1984, Boris Blanco joined them in prison.[16]

Not that prison constituted much of a hardship. While debt was driving farmers and small businessmen in Chile to suicide, the offending financiers were housed in a special annex of the Santiago prison inhabited chiefly by delinquent upper-class debtors. Conditions were described by visitors as 'more than tolerable.' Prisoners with means could 'rent' private rooms with color television sets, and the prison had a swimming pool.[17]

On Guard for What?

Finance is not the sole base of the Panamanian 'service' sector, though it accounts for 9% of GDP and was growing faster than all other elements including shipping, revenues from the canal, and, formerly, US military expenditure. Panama boasts the fifth largest merchant marine in the world, making it a leader in flag-of-convenience shipping as it is in flag-of-convenience banking. (Among the more illustrious users of these Panamanian corporate facilities is the government of South Africa. After the Ian Smith regime in Rhodesia declared unilateral independence from Britain, the international community reacted with economic sanctions. Then Freight Services sprang into action: jointly controlled through a Panamanian ghost company by the South African state shipping company and Anglo-America, the gold and diamond consortium, Freight Services established a network of companies in the usual places to run oil and other strategic supplies to Rhodesia. In the early 1980s, when it seemed that South Africa itself might face sanctions, Freight Services resurrected its covert trading network.) Around the canal is the second largest free-trade area in the world, a boon to the *contrabandistas* of neighboring countries.[18] And until recently, Panama hosted SouthCom, the US military's southern command headquarters, which serves as the US supply and intelligence center for Central America.

It was a far from comfortable arrangement. Local strongman Omar Torrijos, who came to power in 1968, made recovery of the canal his foreign-policy priority, particularly after 1971. That year the US Bureau of Narcotics and Dangerous Drugs (predecessor of the DEA) took aim at Panama's controller of air traffic, who allegedly took a cut of all contraband running through the area. US agents lured him into the Canal Zone, where they arrested him on narcotics charges.[19] The result was an explosion of nationalistic anger in Panama, which likely sealed the fate of the canal. It may also have prompted President Nixon to add Torrijos to his list of heads of state slated for assassination, ostensibly for involvement in the heroin traffic. If so, the outbreak of the Watergate scandal saved Torrijos, at least for a while.[20]

Panama's importance in American military strategy increased during the late 1970s and early 1980s as regional tensions grew. Torrijos incurred American displeasure (apart from offering a brief sanctuary for the itinerant shah of Iran), first because of rumors of a deal with Castro for Cuban troops to aid him in the event of a military confrontation with the US, and then by supporting the Sandinista rebels against Somoza, to the extent of funneling them arms.[21] But to counter official American displeasure, Torrijos had cleverly cultivated a powerful constituency – the American banks and transnational corporations that had set up under Panama's hospitable banking and tax laws – which supported him in disputes with the US government.[22]

With the coming to power of an administration headed by Ronald Reagan (who in 1976 had declared that if he were president he would keep the canal[23]), relations soured again, particularly as Torrijos continued to try to moderate tensions in the area by mediating between Nicaragua and its neighbors.[24] Torrijos died in a plane crash in 1981; afterward, one of his brothers claimed the CIA had sabotaged the plane.[25]

Under the Panamanian constitution, the National Guard is equal in importance to the executive, legislative, and judicial branches of government. But after Torrijos's death, the Guard demonstrated that some branches are more equal than others. First, it prevented his elected successor from taking office; then it sacked an attorney general found to be cooperating with the US in certain criminal investigations. During the following three years it imposed or deposed three more heads of state.[26]

By the early 1980s bank secrecy had replaced the Panama Canal as the main source of tension with the US. Panama's committed defense of its banking system can be attributed to a number of factors apart from the rumor that Panamanian banks take 12% of funds they launder (an even larger cut than that taken by the Vatican bank).[27] One factor was a general economic crisis in the productive sectors of the Panamanian economy after 1981,[28] which made Panamanian authorities anxious to safeguard the only sector that was still flourishing.

Allegedly, too, the Guards' commitment to bank secrecy reflects the close relationship between them and organized crime. A self-perpetuating elite, the Guards interact with the locally based traders in drugs, arms, gold, and rich refugees. Local business allegedly puts an officer on the payroll; the alternative might well be pillaged warehouses or worse. Drugs on their way north and cash flowing back are reputedly warehoused by the National Guard, which will obligingly arrest dealers who have not paid the transit fee in advance, and obligingly release them again when the appropriate sum has been paid to the appropriate officer.

Another reason to defend the banking system was the burden of foreign debt – $3.5 billion of it. (Panama ties Costa Rica for the highest per capita foreign debt in the Americas.) However, Panama had three special lines of defense. Its dollar-based economy was, by definition, immune from pressures to devalue that elsewhere forced up local-currency carrying costs of the sovereign debt load. International banks were also willing to continue cheap credit to defend the financial health of an important offshore center. Finally, Panama had collateral, in its capacity to attract financial inflows.[29]

This was partly due to Panama's ability to reverse its role from that of a center for negotiating loans and investments flowing to the rest of Latin America to that of a major conduit for capital flight out of the continent. Virtually all Latin American banks that did international business maintained a Panamanian subsidiary – useful for circumventing the home countries' exchange controls and lending regulations. Principal among these banks, and long an important source of liquidity for the Panamanian financial system, were the subsidiaries and affiliates of cash-rich Colombian banks that, in happier times, were net lenders to the rest of Latin America of $2 billion through the Panamanian syndicated loan market.

Nor was that the only service Panama provided them.

Former gas-station owner turned real estate broker turned venture capitalist Felix Correa Maya built an upstart conglomerate that eventually came to control fifty-six companies. He put it to work in peekaboo finance, establishing a series of Panamanian shell companies to siphon $150 million in depositors' money from Banco Nacional to advance his and other major shareholders' private business interests. When, in the spring of 1982, the superintendent of banks moved to stop the drain of deposits, the publicity spread panic; and a run on the group's banks forced the government to pump in emergency cash. One of Correa Maya's banks was forcibly liquidated; and the group's largest finance company collapsed on top of the savings of 18,000 people. Correa Maya was jailed; nine of his associates fled the country and a tenth was murdered. It was the worst Colombian financial crisis in fifty years, but it was only the beginning.[30]

Next came an Ambrosiano-style scandal at the Banco de Bogotá, the oldest and most establishment-oriented financial institution in the city. In 1981 the owners of the bank had to avert a takeover. They borrowed heavily from international banks on the basis of falsified documents, diverted the money through Panama, and used it to buy up the bank's shares at greatly inflated prices. This ultimately forced the state to take the bank under its trusteeship and to guarantee the foreign loans.

Then, in August 1982, came revelations that the president of Banco del Estado had been using a Panamanian bank he controlled to drain off Estado's deposits; meanwhile, the bank's shareholders had borrowed from the bank in order to buy up outstanding shares. Ultimately the bank president was jailed, and the bank was nationalized under the terms of an economic emergency law proclaimed by incoming President Belisario Betancur.[31]

The law came too late to save Grupo Grancolombiano, the largest conglomerate in Colombia, which two Liberal party presidents had aided by blocking investigations into its affairs.[32] The group was an avid euromarket borrower, running up a foreign debt of $550 million by the time of the crash. More than one-third of the money had been borrowed by a Panamanian subsidiary of the group's flagship bank; another third was owned by a Curaçao ghost company controlled directly by the group's president. By the time the group's tangled affairs had been unscrambled, some $250 million had fled through the network of shell companies to a Panamanian haven and Grancolombiano's president, Jaime Michaelsen Uribe, cousin of the former Liberal president, had taken flight to Miami.[33]

By 1984 the percentage of foreign deposits in the Panamanian banking system seemed destined to decline. Flight capital bypassed Panama, going straight to Miami, which had long aspired to be the true banking and financial center of Latin America. When reschedulings of Latin American debt occurred, the US banks involved in the syndications rebooked them to Miami and New York, where most of the refinancing occurred. Furthermore, major US banks began scaling down their local and offshore operations in Panama.[34]

Nonetheless, Panama still seems secure as a peekaboo financial center, for new Japanese and Latin American banks continue to open. And Panama is still important to strictly inter-American financial flows. Thus, in the spring of 1985 the M-19 guerrilla movement faced a renewed army offensive and heavy losses among its leaders. It attempted to withdraw the $50 to $60 million that M-19's late and legendary leader, Jaime Bateman, had deposited in the Tower Bank in Panama. The owner of the bank refused to cooperate until the guerrillas carried *him* off to Colombia instead of the cash.[35]

Panama has always had a sense of opportunity. When concern over the expansion of the drug trade and of tax evasion finally prompted the US government to try to find out what was really going on in the peekaboo centers, its first major success was a 1977 convention with Switzerland, which facilitated the penetration of bank secrecy in the event of a criminal investigation – of drugs, but not of tax evasion. Panama responded by discovering that its bank regulators did not have the legal power to make examinations, thereby putting an end to the joint inspections that they used to conduct with US regulators.[36] Then came major crackdowns on those Florida banks that were the most notorious laundromats. After 1981 more and more pressure was applied to the Caymans and the Bahamas.[37] The result was to reinforce Panama's position as probably the most important regional center for financing drug trafficking, depositing the profits, and laundering the take. This role was graphically illustrated in 1985, when US pressure forced the closure of First Interamericas Bank, the vehicle through which Jorge Ochoa, then in jail in Spain on cocaine-trafficking charges, had allegedly run cash earned from the New York leg of his enterprises.[38]

In 1980 Panamanian banks shipped $200 million in surplus US bank notes back to the US. In 1981 they sent back more than $500 million. In 1982 excess cash topped the $1 billion mark, where it stayed through to 1984. US government officials made considerable public to-do over the disproportionate number of $20 bills, supposedly the denomination in which retail cocaine and marijuana deals are commonly conducted in the American market. Of course, in a country in which the US dollar circulated in lieu of a national currency, other explanations of the phenomenon were certainly possible, but politically less useful.

Perhaps even more important, by the early 1980s Panama could take the next giant step forward, by reversing an existing role as a conduit for investment flows from the Americas to the Far East. When Chinese intentions to reintegrate Hong Kong into the mainland economy caused a massive crisis in the colony, Panama stood to gain no small part of the peekaboo financial business fleeing its East Asian soul sister.

Part Four

What Gets Washed in the Pacific Basin?

13

Some Like It Hot

In 1839 William Jardine, a Canton-based drug trafficker, seized on the Chinese government's confiscation of illegal opium stocks to steer the British government into the first Opium War. At the end of that conflict, the Chinese empire was forced to pay a cash indemnity covering the costs of the war and the confiscated opium; and it was forced to cede Hong Kong to Britain as a permanent trading and smuggling base. William Jardine moved his business to Hong Kong, becoming the new colony's first landlord.[1] From such roots grew Jardine-Matheson, the major multinational conglomerate engaged in commerce, real estate, and financial services, among other businesses, in Hong Kong and around the world.

In March 1984 Jardine-Matheson, the *hong* that was synonymous with British presence in the colony, shocked local business and caused stock exchanges to plummet by announcing the shift of its international headquarters to Bermuda. To *The Hong Kong Standard*, it was as if the Queen had announced that she was immigrating to Australia. Behind the announcement lay not only the shadow of China's intentions for a usurped part of her territory, but also the ravages of two years of business chaos: plunging property markets, financial upheaval, and the ignominy of capital fleeing one of the world's premier flight-capital centers.

As early as 1966 Chase Manhattan Bank economists enthused over Hong Kong's unique role in regional finance and hot-money flows:

> Hong Kong has long been the flight money center for Southeast Asia and the Far East. Its stature in the postwar era has apparently grown year by year with the intensification of the cold war and mounting revolutionary crises in the area. All the trouble spots, Indonesia, Vietnam, Thailand, Burma, Malaysia, Singapore, India, now contribute to the flow. One of the largest contributors is the relatively

stable and prosperous Philippines, whose smuggling operations are a continued source of funding. Hong Kong is also Communist China's major foreign-exchange earner and window on the Free World, and Communist China has encouraged its prosperity despite the fact it could be shut down at any time. Although Hong Kong, like Beirut, is an imperfect flight center in comparison to the relative security of Switzerland or the US, it has the advantage of physical closeness and cultural similarity to the flight areas it serves.

Because of those advantages, by 1982 Hong Kong ranked third among world financial centers, surpassed only by London and New York.

Hong Kong's International Financial Position

Hong Kong is, or was, a free-marketeer's dream in Technicolor. A complex of banking institutions operate in a legal system combining some of the world's tightest confidentiality laws with one of its laxest regulatory frameworks. Hong Kong also boasts one of the world's largest gold markets, an active diamond exchange, four freewheeling stock markets (now merged), and a market that deals in shell companies.[2] Historically the names of company shareholders need not be divulged – they can hide behind nominees – and the most blatant insider deals are legal. Publicly quoted companies can be so tightly controlled by unknown major shareholders that they might as well be private. For outsiders, share trading is more a game of chance than an investment decision. It was often impossible to know who owned what until it was too late to avert a major swindle and ensuing crash, and sometimes not even then. Even a company's managers may not know who its owners are; they can honestly disclaim knowledge of the origins of the property they are administering.

Hong Kong began its spectacular growth as an international financial center during the Vietnam War. Foreign currency, particularly dollars, flooded into Southeast Asia at a time of intensifying military and political upheaval. A regional capital-flight center was needed, in which freedom of financial movements and anonymity were assured. Financial facilities were also required to service the proceeds of increased arms smuggling, narcotics trafficking, and general black-market activity. To meet those needs, the Hong Kong banks undertook a rapid extension of their international operations, and the Hong Kong property market welcomed the resulting inflow of funds. By the end of 1965 Chase Manhattan Bank economists estimated the percentage of Hong Kong bank deposits resulting from flight money at between 30% and 50%, 'one of the highest components of flight money in any banking system outside of Switzerland,' and about the same percentage invested in Hong Kong real estate came from similar sources.

After the Vietnam War, Hong Kong continued to grow as a financial center and as the commercial hub of the rapidly expanding Pacific-Basin economy, which was linked by an old and extensive web of overseas Chinese family ties that drew business to Hong Kong.

One reason was its strategic position: it was able to act as China's window on the world and the world's window on China. While the bamboo curtain was still tightly drawn, Hong Kong business could grow fat by charging both sides for a political peep show.

Hong Kong controls the transit trade of China, estimated to be worth $34 billion per annum, and provides China with an entrepôt from which to conduct economic relations with countries China does not recognize, such as Taiwan and South Korea.[3] Hong Kong is China's source of high technology and modern managerial techniques, and provides 80% to 90% of the foreign capital invested in its New Economic Zones, where capitalist methods are welcomed.

Hong Kong also provides a milieu for Chinese business and investment activities, including huge gold and foreign-exchange dealings. The role of the Chinese government-owned banks in the Hong Kong financial system is second only to that of the old, establishment Hongkong & Shanghai Bank. China has also invested heavily in the Hong Kong property market, and in the establishment of manufacturing capacity. Chinese-owned factories exploit cheap Hong Kong labor to contribute to the flood of textiles exported to the US, which formed the backbone of Hong Kong's rapid industrial growth in the 1970s. All these activities made Hong Kong the source of about 40% of China's foreign-exchange earnings.

The Hong Kong financial system also grew rapidly because the colony remained the area's premier flight-capital center and money laundry. As late as 1984, when Hong Kong had seen its position as a peek-aboo financial center eroded by competition and a confidence crisis, one-sixth of the gold production of the noncommunist world still found its way to Hong Kong. There much was resold to smugglers, who use it to finance contraband trade and to facilitate capital flight throughout the region.[4]

A third factor must also take some credit for the continued expansion of the Hong Kong financial system: the colony is heir to Marseilles as the hub of the international heroin-trafficking business, aided by the colony's freewheeling financial system and the world's most powerful and secretive criminal societies.

Triads

The Triads began as secret patriotic societies. Their avowed purpose was the restoration of the Ming dynasty after it was overthrown by the Manchu invaders from Mongolia.[5] But criminals and adventurers also found Triad membership useful. The Green Gang of Shanghai, a Triad that controlled the opium traffic and most of the city's organized crime, cooperated with another eminent Triad member, Chiang Kai-shek (whose Kuomintang was a merger of several Triad-style secret societies), to massacre the communist cadres and trade union leaders of the city in 1927. This confluence of anticommunist and organized-crime interests was remarkably similar in motive, and in results, to the smashing of the communist-led Marseilles waterfront unions by the CIA and Union Corse two decades later. In that case, the result was the birth of the nefarious French Connection.

In 1949 Kuomintang (KMT) rule collapsed. Much of the Shanghai underworld moved to Hong Kong, and some remnants of KMT forces retired to northern Burma. Inside Hong Kong, the Green Gang ran afoul of the entrenched secret criminal societies of the *chiu chao* ethnic group and was quickly neutralized. But the KMT 'army' found itself in far more hospitable territory: Britain had long encouraged the rulers of northern Burma, the area known as the Shan States, in the cultivation of opium, which provided profits to British traders and a means for the British authorities to keep the population under control.

When British rule ended, the KMT army stepped in to protect and encourage opium production, and to tax the trade. International trafficking was handled by *chiu chao* syndicates in the Chinese émigré communities throughout Southeast Asia; the financing went through Hong Kong.

The northern Burmese hill tribes and their KMT overlords were not the only opium producers in the area: the French in Indochina had actively promoted its cultivation by the Meo tribesmen of Laos. Much of the financing of the French colonial administration and the regional war to defend the French empire came from the proceeds of legal opium dens. After the French regime, the Meo turned for marketing assistance to the CIA. (Meanwhile, the French intelligence officers who had been active in the Southeast Asian drug business plugged into the Turkish dope network; when the French Connection was broken, more than half of those arrested allegedly had ties to French intelligence.[6])

By that time the hundreds of thousands of American soldiers in Southeast Asia had created a rich hard-currency market for the local products. And the fuse was lit for an explosion of narcotics trafficking out of Southeast Asia. As the late General Tuan Shi-wen of the KMT eloquently summed up the situation in 1967: 'We have to continue to fight the evil of Communism, and to fight it you need an army, and an army must have guns, and to buy guns you must have money. In these mountains the only money is opium.'[7]

The Vietnam War also aided the trade indirectly, by demonstrating the virtues of the lateral-transfer technique for financing the traffic without the risks of cash couriers or cable transfers. During much of the war, the black-market rate for dollars was nearly double the official rate. Local money changers would purchase dollars for South Vietnamese piasters at the black-market rate; the dollar exchange would be sent to Hong Kong, then transferred to Switzerland or Dubai to purchase gold. The gold would be reimported to South Vietnam, where it was in great demand as a flight-capital vehicle and brought a higher rate than the original black-market price for dollars. But a crackdown by the South Vietnamese government in the late 1960s led to a change in technique. A US citizen seeking black-market piasters would tell his bank to wire funds directly to an account kept by his money changer in Hong Kong, while he would collect his piasters in Saigon. (Among these American users was the CIA, which, to finance its activities in Vietnam, allegedly paid dollars to the currency- and bullion-dealing company of Deak & Co. in Washington, and picked up the proceeds in black-market piasters in Saigon.) After the war, heroin smugglers all over the world adopted the technique of indirect, lateral financing. However, the Hong Kong–based underground banking system – built on a combination of family ties and paperless authorization of transfers via private radio or scrambled telephone lines – remained the most sophisticated.[8]

Even before the fall of the French Connection, Hong Kong had become a refining base and smuggling entrepôt for the region's opium production. During much of the 1960s and 1970s Burma was the main producer of opium, which was sent across the border by mule caravan and reduced to morphine base, one-tenth the bulk, in Thailand. The morphine went to Hong Kong for refining into heroin and for export – by syndicates directed by Triad members of the Hong Kong police force.[9] This inspired the British satirical magazine *Private Eye* to refer to the Royal Hong Kong Police Force as 'the best police force money can buy.'

In 1975 a major shake-up of the police force sent wealthy sergeants to distant havens, and some of the prominent civilian organizers were identified; but most escaped to Taiwan, which had no extradition treaty with Hong Kong. Hong Kong's role as a refining and distribution center was taken over by Thailand; and the city of Chiang Mai became the commercial center of the traffic. Throughout the upheavals in production and distribution, Hong Kong continued as financial metropolis of the narcotics trade. Only in Hong Kong could the traders be assured complete freedom of international financial movements, access to the gold used to barter for opium, and absolute anonymity.

The Structure of the Hong Kong Financial System

At the top of the financial power structure in Hong Kong[10] is not the government but the Hongkong & Shanghai Bank,[11] the *primus inter pares* among the colony's commercial banks. Starting as the banker to the old Anglo-Scottish trading *hongs* in the 1860s, Hongkong Bank developed and diversified until it came to dominate both private and public finances. It controls 50% of the domestic retail business; dominates the interbank market; markets securities through its merchant-banking arm; and manages corporate assets through its holding company. It also controls Hong Kong's gold market.

In its public functions, Hongkong Bank is virtually synonymous with the colonial government. It issues 75% of the currency notes (the Chartered Bank, also privately owned, issues the rest); it operates the clearing house and is fiscal agent to the government. In a colony without an official central bank, Hongkong Bank is informal lender of last resort. With the government virtually abdicating control over credit conditions to a legal cartel of commercial banks, Hongkong Bank, by far the largest, is the dominant domestic force in setting interest rates.[12]

The ordinary commercial banks number about forty. Thirteen, controlling nearly 40% of domestic retail deposits, are owned by the People's Republic of China. Entry into the banking game was a virtual free-for-all until 1965, when the collapse of a major trust company and a subsequent run on the banks prompted a government moratorium on new bank licenses.[13] It may not have been entirely coincidental that the moratorium, which effectively shut out new foreign banks from the domestic deposit and loan business, came just when the Vietnam War was flooding the area with dollar liquidity and the major American banks were waking up to the profit potential of the flight-capital business in and around Hong Kong.

For the commercial banks, the situation seemed unbeatable: an absolute barrier to new entrants and a legal price-fixing cartel. But as Hong Kong grew, so did the demand for credit facilities, and soon a side door opened.

Hong Kong law defined a bank as an institution that did a *checking* account business. But other deposit-taking companies (DTCs) could operate if the deposits accepted were for a term longer than three months. As the demand for credit grew, the number of foreign banks looking for a piece of the action grew. DTCs, varying in character from merchant banks to glorified pawnshops, proliferated outside the interest-rate cartel run by the commercial banks.

The counteroffensive came in two stages. In 1978 the moratorium on new bank licenses was lifted. The colony could appear to be bending to pressure from foreign banks to liberalize its laws. But any new full-scale bank came under the jurisdiction of the interest-rate fixing cartel, which would prevent it from bidding deposits away from the older established banks. Then, in 1981, severe restrictions were imposed on the DTCs.[14] No new DTC could operate unless it was owned by a bank, and existing ones found that they were being barred from the retail deposit business, the source of over half of the funds they used to finance their lending.[15] But the commercial banks' self-congratulations were short-lived.[16]

New foreign banks and bank affiliates flowed into Hong Kong with the flight capital of the region. The new banks, awash with funds but short on domestic customers, began lending on the wholesale market, from which the DTCs borrowed heavily to fund a booming property market. DTC deposits dropped 40% in one year; their assets rose 35% over the same period. Their growing reliance on the interbank market meant that any liquidity squeeze on the lending banks originating from anywhere in the world, or any nervousness about their exposure in Hong Kong, would be reflected quickly in the colony's credit market.

Secrecy, freedom from regulation, and extensive international financial connections can be awesome problems when hot-money movements slam into reverse. World recession, a huge property swindle, and the aftermath, financial and political, of the Malvinas War precipitated, in the autumn of 1982, Hong Kong's worst financial crisis. And the Hong Kong government lacked effective instruments with which to deal with it. Its long-standing laissez-faire attitude toward the financial sector left it particularly vulnerable to any deep-seated crisis, let alone one deriving from a shattering of confidence in the colony's very raison d'être.

China and Hong Kong: Unstable Symbiosis

The People's Republic of China has an enormous financial stake in Hong Kong.[17] The largest of its thirteen Hong Kong retail banks, the local branch of the Bank of China, is also powerful in the foreign-exchange and syndicated-loan markets. Between 1979 and 1982 it poured $3.5 billion into local industry, commerce, and real estate. Between 1977 and 1982, total PRC investment in Hong Kong in property alone was more than $5 billion. There is also Chinese capital in manufacturing, insurance, trade, shipping, retailing, and many other concerns.[18] This seemed an excellent insurance policy for Hong Kong, until Margaret Thatcher came on the scene.

The future relationship of China and Hong Kong depended on the interaction of two strategic factors and one tactical element. The strategic factors were the Chinese attitude toward the treaties with Britain and the evolution of the economic ideology of the Chinese leadership. The tactical element was the degree to which Britain and China were willing to battle indirectly by passively accepting or actively inducing crises in the Hong Kong financial and property markets.

There were two distinct types of treaties. The first, which had led to the permanent cession of Hong Kong Island and Kowloon to Britain, derived from the Opium Wars. China had been forced to accept British hegemony over Hong Kong, British opium peddling, and the resulting impoverishment and debauching of its population and finances, and British kidnapping of Chinese labor for the mines, plantations, and construction camps of its colonies throughout the Pacific. While China protested the 'unequal' nature of the treaties, the British demanded that China adhere to 'international law.'

The second type of treaty came some fifty years later, when the great powers were scrambling for spheres of influence. China yielded Britain a ninety-nine-year lease on, rather than absolute property rights to, the New Territories, 80% of the current land area of the colony. China had merely to point to the letter of the law and the 1997 expiry date on the lease, and the British case was lost. So, too, was Hong Kong, for the colony could not exist without the New Territories.

But it was not the politically and militarily indefensible British claims that would determine the fate of Hong Kong. Rather, it would be the official Chinese view of how Hong Kong would fit into its development strategy for China, including Hong Kong, Macao, and Taiwan. That view was summed up when Hu Yao-bang, the head of the Communist party of the People's Republic, made a speech commemorating the centenary of the death of Karl Marx: he devoted much of it to outlining what he saw to be Marx's mistakes. It was more than a history lesson. As he spoke moves were being made to dismantle the 'people's communes' and decentralize economic planning.

In the mid-1970s China integrated itself rapidly in the expanding commerce of the Pacific Rim. Between 1976 and 1981 its trade surplus trebled; it replaced Taiwan at the World Bank and the IMF. With gross foreign-exchange reserves of $17 billion (since raised to $20 billion) and a foreign debt of only $4 to $5 billion (since reduced to about $3 billion), it was well placed to become an important participant in international money markets. Its surpluses found their way into euromarket deposits in London, and the Bank of China participated in all manner of syndicated loans. By early 1985 China was even welcomed back into the eurobond market despite (as debtor developing countries should carefully note) its refusal to honor defaulted debt predating the Communist victory in 1949. Apart from an estimated $5 billion in the euromarket, China boasts a growing inventory of direct foreign investments all over the world, designed to secure access to industrial raw materials it cannot find at home.[19]

China's rules on foreign investment have been steadily liberalized as the Special Economic Zones have developed. These zones are intended to encourage local production, to facilitate integration into a world economy, and to prepare the way for the reassimilation of Hong Kong, Macao, and Taiwan. In them foreign investment, even 100% foreign-owned plants, is welcomed with tax and tariff concessions, exchange-control waivers, soft loans, and assurances of low wages.[20] When the Communist party chief called for reforms in the economic planning mechanism, including the use of profit criteria and the end of wage equality, he also called for an end to the doctrine of continuous revolution under the dictatorship of the proletariat.[21]

China's desire to participate in the most dynamic features of the modern world capitalist economy is aptly symbolized by decisions by Club Med and Coca-Cola to open for business in China.[22] It is also lent credibility by the growth of an 'underground economy' involving massive tax frauds and currency black markets,[23] and by the return of the Triads, which are setting up shop in the Special Economic Zones after three decades of exile in Hong Kong. The Triads have been attracted by an increased flow of cash into the hands of individual farmers and merchants after the communes were abolished in favor of individual enterprise,[24] and by the potential of the liberalized customs and exchange rules of the zones for moving Southeast Asian heroin to European and North American markets.[25]

Chinese accommodation of the capitalist world was undoubtedly watched with little enthusiasm by that stronghold of free-enterprise capitalism across the bamboo curtain, for Hong Kong's economic raison d'être derived in good measure from the absence of capitalist-style incentives inside China. But as long as China trudged along the capitalist road, the future of Hong Kong became increasingly doubtful. Such deep-rooted political anxieties certainly exacerbated the economic crisis in the autumn of 1982 by laying bare the artificial foundation of the colony's prosperity.

In a sense Hong Kong was another victim of the war for the Malvinas. On her visit to China in August 1982, fresh from her triumphant defense of the sovereign right of 250,000 sheep to graze, strong and free, on British soil, Margaret Thatcher talked tough. By chiding the Chinese for their lack of respect for international 'law,' Thatcher changed the climate of Anglo-Chinese relations. Formerly, China had two objectives: resumption of sovereignty over Hong Kong and defense of the colony's prosperity. After Thatcher's bellicose defense of the Opium War treaties China's second objective became the total eviction of the British. The Chinese government would play games with the fragile prosperity of Hong Kong to drive the point home.

The Hong Kong Property Bubble

While much of the credit for Hong Kong's prosperity in the 1970s must go to the commercial ruthlessness of its entrepreneurial class and the existence of a docile labor force, much of the income gains registered in the colony came from inflows of speculative capital. This included flight money and funds searching for safety, anonymity, and automatic laundering, as well as legitimate money seeking to participate in the great wave of real estate speculation that increased Hong Kong property prices fourfold between 1978 and 1981. The Hong Kong banking system was swimming in liquidity; and the government had no means to curb the phenomenal growth of credit even if it wanted to, which it did not. The government interpreted the boom as an indicator of the success of the colony's economic policy, not only because the boom directly profited the ruling elite, but also because the government derived more than 30% of its revenues directly from property taxes puffed by speculation.[26]

For a time the boom was self-regenerating. As banks and international companies crowded into Hong Kong to participate in the rapid growth of the Pacific Rim, the demand for office space shot up. And the new financial firms brought with them funds to finance the real estate mania. Much of the lending nominally earmarked for other purposes went into the property market as individuals and firms drew to the limit of their credit to speculate on property.

Also feeding the property market were DTCs that functioned as cheap credit arms of property firms. In theory, lending by a DTC to any individual or group, including its parent firm, was limited to 25% of its capital. However, this limit could be legally exceeded if the parent firm provided the superintendent of banks with a letter of comfort 'recognizing' the obligation. If issuing a letter of comfort was too much trouble, the 25% rule could simply be ignored – after all, in Hong Kong, who would bother checking? (And even if they did check, the colony's notoriously opaque business practices would assure that proof of illegality was hard to find.)[27]

At the center of the boom, and of the subsequent bust, was the Carrian group of companies. The Carrian saga tells how good luck, good timing, good connections, and the laissez-faire Hong Kong environment permitted the creation out of nothing of a multibillion-dollar conglomerate involved in shipping, insurance, and banking, with real estate at its core.

It began in 1974, when George Tan fled bankruptcy proceedings in Singapore, leaving behind a wrecked investment company. Tan started over in Hong Kong, as a site engineer for the Chung family, who controlled a big property firm called EDA Investments. In 1979 Tan made his big move, somehow acquiring for HK$700 million – twice its book value and four times its market value – a holding company that became his Carrian Investment Limited (CIL). Behind the publicly traded CIL stood Carrian Holdings Limited (CHL), a private company that controlled 53% of CIL equity. And behind CHL was Carrian Nominee, a company that held 100% of CHL shares. But who owned Carrian Nominee? That was one of the mysteries that made Carrian the greatest contemporary success story in Hong Kong business, and then its gravest scandal.

Hong Kong's accommodating attitude toward nominee companies was fully exploited by the Carrian group. Rumors abounded about Tan's possible backers – from Imelda Marcos to Southeast Asian warlords to Arab oil sheikhs. These rumors and the decision by Wardley's, the prestigious merchant-banking arm of Hongkong Bank, to back Carrian when it went public account for at least part of the banks' enthusiastic lending to Tan once he launched himself into heavy property speculation. So, too, does his impeccable timing, starting the snowball rolling just as new banks were rushing into Hong Kong in pursuit of local business. His meteoric rise just may have been assisted as well by his practice of passing out millions in jewelry and cash as presents, presumably to those in a position to appreciate the gifts.

The deal that put Carrian on the corporate map was the purchase, with other prominent developers, notably the Chung family of EDA Investments, of Gammon House (later the Bank of America Tower). It was the most expensive real estate transaction in the colony's history, but how it was financed remained a Carrian mystery until after the crash.

Part of the funds came from Tan's secret backers, but part came from nowhere, because the deal was never actually completed. The Carrian group was a complex of companies whose interrelations could often be hidden from public view quite legally. CIL, the publicly quoted flagship of the group, had more than a hundred subsidiaries poetically named Deciding Deed, Outwit, Perfect Combination, Knife and Dagger,

Beat the Bush, and so on; CHL had a hundred more. Together with Tan-controlled companies not formally part of Carrian, but handy for purposes of peekaboo finance, there were more than five hundred companies whose affairs any loan officer intent on understanding the structure of the borrowing entity would have to unscramble. In the end, however, he would still not know the identity of the mysterious owners of Carrian Nominee who were the ultimate security for money lent to Tan's empire.

The property bubble Tan did so much to create was assisted by the Hong Kong practice of selling commercial real estate on a floor-by-floor basis. Carrian went one better, 'selling' particular floors of its buildings to its own subsidiaries. Another tactic was for two separate property companies to 'sell' assets back and forth. Each would thereby puff the books, reporting 'profits' that could then justify more borrowing for yet more property purchases. As the excitement spread and prices rose, acquired properties could be mortgaged for more than their purchase price, thus encouraging the spiral. False book profits also allowed real estate companies to float more equity on the Hong Kong stock markets, which provided more capital to buy more property. For fiscal year 1981, fully 40% of Carrian's profits turned out to be fictitious, based on reported sales for which no payment was ever received.[28]

First to fall was EDA Investments, the vehicle of the Chung family, who had used it to run up $195 million in corporate debt and many millions more in personal borrowing. As the major bank creditors picked over the corpse, Chung Ching Min, the patriarch of the family firm, visited Taiwan, which, as an earlier generation of dope peddlers knew, had no extradition treaty with Hong Kong. After a brief stint in a Hong Kong jail, his son joined him.[29]

The stock market, on which property companies were the premier securities, heaved and plunged; and other companies and private speculators followed developers, big and small, into disaster.[30] The textile industry, Hong Kong's largest manufacturing sector, in trouble because of the depressed state of world commerce, had contracted an additional debt burden in order to play the real estate market.[31] The game ended in forced liquidations, an occasional jail sentence, and a few more absconding financiers.[32]

Malaysian Fallout

Watching these merry events were bank depositors, whose runs shook the financial institutions in Hong Kong and abroad. Particularly vulnerable was Malaysia's largest bank, Bank Bumiputra, whose Hong Kong affiliate was heavily involved in the property-market disaster.

Bank Bumiputra was established in 1966 with funds from the

Malaysian finance ministry to aid the economic ascent of the native Malays ('bumiputras') in the business sector dominated by ethnic Chinese. The bank was a key instrument in the government's New Economic Policy, whose intent was to transfer control of strategic parts of the economy to indigenous Malays. The bank's virtually open credit line from the government meant easy money for borrowers; and each successful loan was heralded as proof of the government's concern for the Malay entrepreneur.[33]

When Bank Bumiputra's Hong Kong subsidiary, a DTC called Bumiputra Malaysian Finance (BMF), announced that its position had shifted from a profit of HK$10 million in 1981 to a loss of HK$53 million in 1982, there seemed little cause for financial alarm. The loss was considered to be a normal effect of the property-market collapse, and surely could be taken in stride by so wealthy and prestigious a parent. Nonetheless, the whispering began. Why did Bank Bumiputra, established to aid the indigenous Malays, plunge so much money (just how much was still unknown) into Chinese financiers' speculations on the Hong Kong property market? The ethnicity of the recipients of the funds, the place, and the type of investment were all wrong.[34]

The political embarrassment became a roaring scandal when the real extent of Bank Bumiputra's exposure became known. As each knot in the tangled affairs of the big property companies (notably but by no means exclusively George Tan's Carrian group) was undone, estimates of the money (virtually all coming from the Malaysian parent) that BMF had pumped into the bubble seemed to increase. In the final analysis, BMF had committed more than $1 billion to property speculation in Hong Kong. Some 90% of its total loan portfolio was accounted for by three troubled firms, of which Carrian took about 70%; and much of the money lent to Carrian had disappeared through two Liberian-registered ghost companies.[35]

Here at last was the solution to the mystery of Tan's start-up money. It did not originate with Imelda Marcos or oil sheikhs or dope-dealing Southeast Asian generals. Rather it came from the public revenues of Malaysia and from the savings, via Bank Bumiputra, of ordinary Malays who had been assured that the government was committed to their economic advancement.

But before the fall, Bank Bumiputra's directors had sent Jalil Ibrahim, head of its Internal Audit Department, to Hong Kong to probe BMF's operations.[36]

The unraveling of the property-market scandal seemed to raise endless embarrassing questions about the behavior of BMF, and even more embarrassing answers. Why were the loans made, even though officials of the Malaysian central bank recommended against them on the grounds that they were poor risks? Why were huge sums lent to Carrian and other Tan companies after the property market had already collapsed, and the collateral for existing loans had depreciated by 50% to 75%?[37] Could the lending to Carrian be related to large personal overdraft facilities (personally guaranteed by George Tan) held by directors of BMF at certain Hong Kong banks? Could the loans be related to alleged 'consulting fees' paid to bank officials by Tan companies? Was it coincidence that the executive director of BMF, who owned a Hong Kong company appropriately called Silver Present, received on behalf of that company a check for HK$3.4 million from the wife of Chung Ching Min, head of EDA Investments? Was it serendipity that the check was received two days before BMF approved a $40 million loan to that property firm? Clearly these and other transactions needed clarification quickly, for the growing questions, and speculation about the answers, set off the worst run in Bank Bumiputra's history.

Perhaps Mr. Jalil, who had been quietly investigating the situation in Hong Kong since February 1983, could provide the necessary clarification? Alas, no. On July 18, 1983, Jalil responded to a phone call on his private line, and rushed out of the office with HK$50,000 in his pocket. Two days later he was found on a banana plantation in the New Territories, a judo belt twisted around his neck.

The Carrian Crash

In an oblique way the ensuing murder investigation was the ultimate cause of the Carrian crash, for that investigation revealed information that wrecked the Carrian-rescue operation the banks were mounting.[38] A raid on Carrian offices by agents of the Organized Crime Bureau, the Commercial Crime Bureau, and the government's Independent Commission Against Corruption revealed that Tan and his nimble accountant, Bentley Ho, had been draining off money and lending it back to the company to puff the books. Also revealed at the time was the extent to which the fabulous profits that had set off the property mania were fraudulent.[39]

The major creditors petitioned the court for a winding-up order. Tan and Bentley Ho were charged with various counts under the Hong Kong theft ordinance, and charges were subsequently extended to some of the firm's auditors, lawyers, and merchant bankers. Tan, architect of the greatest bankruptcy in Hong Kong's history, had the additional distinction of seeing his HK$51 million bail set a new record for the colony. The police discreetly impounded his various passports.

For Bank Bumiputra, yet more embarrassments were in store.[40]

Participating in the raid on the Carrian offices had been the Hong Kong Securities Commission, suspicious that assets were being siphoned off and parked abroad as special security for one unidentified creditor. Hundreds of millions of dollars borrowed by Tan had disappeared without a trace,[41] which called for a reexamination of some of the curious antics of BMF. Why had the bank initially grossly understated its exposure, claiming publicly to have lent only $35 million when the real sum was closer to $1 billion? Why had the bank continued to lend heavily even after it was obvious that Carrian could not pay its existing debts? Why had it secretly channeled large sums to Tan through a complicated network of offshore and onshore companies? Why had it put funds into an offshore investment company of mysterious parentage to enable the company to bid for the profitable insurance arm of the Carrian group, thereby shifting control offshore? Why had it rewritten its records to shift the debt to the parent bank in Malaysia? Surely there was a logical explanation of these anomalies.

What if Bank Bumiputra's actual net exposure to Tan's operations was less than the enormous sum publicly recognized? This was just possible if Bank Bumiputra was the mysterious beneficiary of the Carrian assets spirited abroad. If so, the bank would be a covertly privileged creditor, with part of its exposure covered by assets hidden elsewhere, and part covered by its participation with the other – unsuspecting – creditors in the carving up of the carcass.[42] Obviously, should such an arrangement have been made, the authors would take great pains to cover the trail, pains that might just have been connected with the fate of the unfortunate Jalil Ibrahim and that of at least one other principal in the affair.

Death of a Banker ... and a Lawyer

The trial of Mak Foon Than, the Malaysian-Chinese businessman accused of killing Jalil Ibrahim, took some time to get under way, for Mak had to recover from a crash of his own, which resulted from a leap out a third-floor window when the police came banging on his apartment door.[43]

Once the trial started, Mak insisted on his innocence. As he told the story, Jalil, who was responsible for clearing further loans to George Tan, was an obstruction. Hanging on the edge was a loan Tan wanted BMF to grant an offshore investment company bidding for some valuable CIL assets. Nominally owned by unidentified Malays and headquartered in a Channel Islands tax haven, the investment company was actually Tan-controlled, and appears to have been a device for moving good assets offshore before the crash. Jalil, who had approved earlier loans to Tan's companies in an effort to keep them afloat, appeared to balk at the latest request, allegedly causing George Tan to refer to him as 'a pain in the ass.'[44] Mak claimed to have placed the call to Jalil, requesting that he come to the hotel to cash traveler's checks for a prominent visiting Malaysian businessman. Why was Jalil so quick to respond to Mak's call? According to Mak, it was because of Mak's alleged position as political bagman for Malaysian Finance Minister Tengku Razaleigh Hamzah, who had supposedly sent Mak to Hong Kong frequently during the previous eight years to collect cash from rich Hong Kong businessmen. Nor were the funds exclusively for use in electoral contests; according to Mak, 'The finance minister must get his cut.'[45]

In Malaysia the politicians were well aware of how potentially explosive was the scandal. The prime minister had denounced BMF's participation in the Hong Kong property bubble as 'a heinous crime' and ordered a purge of top management. But there were also serious political and financial aftershocks.

The most important Malaysian elections are not the general ones, which the ruling National Front coalition routinely 'wins,' but the contests within the ethnic parties – the United Malay National Organ- ization (UMNO), the Malaysian Chinese Association, and the Malaysian Indian Association – that make up the coalition. Of them, UMNO is the most important in terms of numbers and power.[46] At the time of Mak's revelations, Finance Minister Tengku Razaleigh Hamzah was fighting for the position of UMNO vice-president. Although Mak subsequently repudiated his accusations, they accomplished their apparent aim of leaving Tengku a loser in the contest. Tengku noted bitterly that in 1981 his bid for power had been similarly aborted by a conveniently timed scandal regarding United Malay Banking Corporation.[47]

Ultimately the cost of the Carrian affair fell heavily on Malaysian state finances.[48] The government was forced to cut back on expenditures on the New Economic Policy,[49] and to sell Bank Bumiputra to the Malaysian state oil company, which alone had the cash resources to rescue the bank. Malaysia's natural-resource wealth was thus frozen in Hong Kong office towers, monuments to the late Jalil Ibrahim.[50]

As for the rest of Mak's story? In the hotel when Jalil was summoned was also a Korean hit man named Shim, who claimed he worked for 'George.' Mak was sent out to buy a large suitcase. In the interim, Jalil arrived at the hotel and telephoned BMF. The general manager, Henry Chin, informed him of pressure from the top to clear the loan to the investment company before the close of that business day. Chin reported receiving a note from the executive director of BMF saying, 'Henry, please proceed to implement at once.'

Jalil, the normal channel through which such loan requests were cleared, queried the authorization and advised delay. Chin waited until 4:30. When Jalil failed to arrive, he cleared the loan, hiding it, on the instructions of the executive director, as a foreign-exchange transaction. By then Mak had returned to the hotel, where he claims to have found Jalil already dead. He then helped Shim load the body into the suitcase and dump it on a banana plantation out in the New Territories.[51]

Undoubtedly Mak's earlier retraction of the allegations about Tengku Razaleigh Hamzah damaged his credibility, for he was found guilty of the murder.[52]

By the time Mak's trial was drawing to a close, another was in progress. The revelation that the initial Gammon House 'sale,' which had set off the boom, and much of Carrian's subsequent 'profits,' which had fed it, were really creative bookkeeping, led to four partners in Deacon's, Hong Kong's second-largest law firm, and two accountants from Price, Waterhouse being charged with conspiracy to defraud. Other Deacon's lawyers were named as unindicted coconspirators, including a former senior partner named John Wimbush. Wimbush, apparently one of the major architects of the Gammon House deal, responded to the investigators' requests for assistance by returning from a leave of absence in England in order to 'commit suicide' by tying a fifty-five-pound concrete manhole cover around his neck and leaping into his swimming pool.

14

Birds of a Feather...

Just as Margaret Thatcher's post-Malvinas bellicosity in the summer of 1982 helped precipitate a property-market collapse that autumn, so her insistence in the summer of 1983 on a continued British presence in Hong Kong after the treaties expired helped bring on a financial crisis the next autumn.

As the banks reeled from the property-market collapse, China fed the panic to demonstrate that if its two objectives, recovery of Hong Kong and preserving the colony's prosperity, were unobtainable on its terms, it was prepared to sacrifice the second for the first. In so doing, China turned a 1982 squeeze on the DTCs into a 1983 commercial bank panic.[1]

Banking on Trouble

When the property bubble burst, the DTCs were affected in two ways: they experienced direct losses from depreciating assets, and the cost of money rose as hot money fled from the interbank market.[2] These two problems, and more, were at play in the curious tale of the fall of Dollar Credit.

At first it all seemed normal enough. A property firm owned by directors of the Dollar Credit DTC did what many others had done – it passed its dividend and shook its main banker. But Dollar Credit managed to call on friends for assistance.

Among those friends were the directors of Hang Lung Bank, who quickly extended credit to the DTC. Why this eagerness to oblige? The DTC's chairman, Willy Yu, was also a major shareholder in the commercial bank; the managing director and the general manager of that bank, along with Willy Yu, dominated the board of directors of the DTC; and the trio collectively held more than half the bank's shares.[3] Thus rehabilitated, the DTC poured money into some 'trading' companies owned by one of the DTC's directors. Then Willy Yu absconded to Taiwan, leaving behind HK$900 million in debts, of which perhaps two cents on the dollar were recoverable. Other banks panicked, pulling in credit lines. In short order some twenty DTCs saw their checks bouncing all over the colony.[4]

Market panic quickly precipitated a flight of funds by those who could move them, a category that included the owners of Axona International Credit. In theory, a DTC could not lend more than 25% of its capital and reserves to a single borrower or 'group' unless the lending was secured by letters of comfort from the parent institution. Axona had no such 'parent,' but it did have a relative, an offshore bank established by the owners of Axona in the Pacific peekaboo center of Vanuatu. As the 25% limit did not apply to interbank loans, the DTC 'lent' its entire capital of $47 million to the Vanuatu bank, and its owners followed the cash out of Hong Kong.[5]

Collapsing DTCs meant work for the Hongkong & Shanghai Bank as unofficial central bank. By mid-November it had bailed out more than thirty. As Hong Kong had no deposit insurance, money frightened out of smaller institutions took refuge either abroad or in the vaults of big banks such as Hongkong & Shanghai, whose size and connections assured unlimited government support should it ever be in need. Hongkong Bank, however, reserved the right to select whom to assist; and if Hongkong Bank refused aid to an illiquid DTC, the Hong Kong banking commission could revoke the DTC's operating license. The deposit money would then have to go elsewhere – for example, into the commercial banking system.[6]

However, the commercial banks did not entirely escape the maelstrom. When, in September, a prominent jewelry firm that had been speculating heavily in the property market collapsed, it caused a one-day run on its bankers, the Hang Lung Bank. When a line of credit was secured from another bank, confidence seemed to be restored, and deposits began to return. But Willy Yu, chairman of Dollar Credit, picked that moment to decamp with what he could carry, setting off another run on the Hang Lung Bank.

Just why Willy Yu ran off is interesting, and not yet officially resolved. It has something to do with the efforts of John Mao Kai-yuan, owner of the famed 'trading companies,' to raise money for the family shipping business. Just what his family 'shipped' was subject to some dispute. Apparently his father had been active since 1950 helping the government of Taiwan use the cover of Hong Kong to hide assets from the People's Republic of China. Mao and six other officers and directors of Dollar Credit and Hang Lung Bank were involved in what may have been the greatest check-kiting scheme in history. Mao would write checks on accounts that three of his Panamanian-registered companies kept in New York and Chicago and present them to Dollar Credit, which in turn would send them to Hang Lung. The checks would then go to the US, to American Express, Banque Indo-Suez, or Citibank for payment. But before the check got there, Mao would cash yet another check and use the money to cover the first. Each check had to be larger than its predecessor to cover the basic sum, the bank handling charges, and the amount Mao claims officers of Dollar Credit and Hang Lung were stealing on each pass. From 1977 to 1982 as much as $21 billion in bad checks was floated between the participating institutions. Initially Mao and his associates obtained hundreds of millions of dollars worth of interest-free credit; but over time he was trapped, losing money because of the thieving of his confederates.[7] American Express and Banque Indo-Suez grew suspicious and stopped accepting his business. But Citibank was eager to expand its Hong Kong business, as it had not taken part in the property boom, and continued to accept the checks.

When, after the September 1982 run, the bank inspectors were due to examine Hang Lung's books, it pulled out of the check-kiting scheme and left Dollar Credit holding the bad checks. This is what seems to have prompted Willy Yu, Mao, and several others to take a Taiwan vacation, and it nearly collapsed sectors of the banking system of neighboring Macao.

Macao functions as an offshore center for Hong Kong. In the Macao banking system, 75% of deposits and 70% of loans are denominated in Hong Kong dollars. Much of this seems to be money avoiding Hong Kong taxes, particularly a withholding tax levied on interest paid to investors by Hong Kong financial institutions. Customers of a Hong Kong bank could deposit their money in an affiliated Macao bank and withdraw it on demand in Hong Kong, thereby circumventing the tax. As a result, the banking system was so closely integrated with that of Hong Kong that Macao felt immediate and direct effects from financial shocks to its neighbor.

The runs on Hang Lung Bank nearly brought down Macao's Banco do Pacifico. The two banks held shares in each other, and Pacifico provided Hang Lung's facilities for avoiding the Hong Kong withholding tax. When Pacifico was forced to suspend payments, the run spread to the other Macao banks. Only a major rescue operation by the government of Macao and the bankers' association stopped runs on most of the banks.[8]

Back in Hong Kong, Hang Lung's problems were far from over.[9] After Willy Yu's abrupt departure, the remaining partners paid off some of the debts, borrowed enough to brush up the balance sheets, had their reputations laundered by the ever-vigilant banking commission, and plunged their rehabilitated bank back into the property market, pouring money into shaky firms run by close business associates. The consequences went unnoticed for some time, not least because Hong Kong became preoccupied with more DTC disasters[10] and the shadow of its awesome neighbor.

As negotiations with Britain stalled, China made a public show of drafting laws to turn Hong Kong into a special administrative region with no guarantee of financial autonomy. Panic fed by pessimistic rumor shook the colonial financial system throughout early 1983. More DTCs crumbled, and capital flight accelerated.[11]

Once more Hongkong & Shanghai Bank tried to restore confidence in the colony's financial future. It announced an 11% increase in profits and unveiled plans for the most expensive corporate headquarters in the world: the final cost estimates were $1 billion. The bank also financed the construction of a mansion to house its chairman, Michael Sandberg. The mansion, officially named Sky High (a reference to its location rather than its price), was placed on one of the world's choicest pieces of real estate; included in the design was a modest twelve-car garage.[12] Few people apart from Mr. Sandberg were impressed.

In the autumn of 1983 the business climate deteriorated further. The vice-chairman of the Foreign Relations Committee of the Chinese Congress publicly declared that 'Only when Britain agrees to return sovereignty, including administrative power... will China be willing to cooperate with Britain and adopt all kinds of active measures to stabilize the economy of Hong Kong.' The stock market plummeted again, capital fled faster, and intense pressure built up against the Hong Kong dollar. Runs began on several commercial banks as depositors rushed to convert to foreign exchange.

Once more Hang Lung Bank was in trouble, but this time the other commercial banks refused assistance. Late in September, for the first time, the Hong Kong government took over an ailing institution.[13] But less than a month later, another pillar of the Hong Kong financial establishment came under attack.

The Setting Sun

Back in the spring of 1982, some months before the property market crash, Sun Hung Kai & Co., the largest securities firm in Hong Kong, announced a deal that was to be Hong Kong's financial swan song. Already linked to Banque de Paris et des Pays Bas, France's most powerful private banking firm, Sun Hung Kai had just added Merrill, Lynch to its shareholder register. The tripartite alliance of Parisbas, Sun Hung Kai, and Merrill, Lynch would have enabled them to span the globe with twenty-four-hour trading and, in the opinion of *The Banker*, 'confirms Hong Kong's position as the world's number-three financial center.'[14] The only problem was how to keep Sun Hung Kai alive long enough to consummate the financial *ménage à trois*.

Sun Hung Kai had an important political role in Hong Kong. Its founder, the late Fung King Hey, represented the new generation of Chinese entrepreneurs, who were challenging the traditional Anglo-Scottish business elite, and formed the economic cadre on which the People's Republic of China was relying to assure a smooth transfer of sovereignty. But the securities firm also had a rocky history. In 1978 speculation in gold and rumors of losses set off a deposit run that nearly brought down the firm's DTC. It was saved by an infusion of liquidity from the Hongkong Bank and the Bank of China, and by a major injection of capital from Parisbas. In 1981 it was the property arm of the company that came close to sinking the fleet. (In 1983 that honor would again go to the DTC.)

In 1981 the property arm bought a building from EDA Investments at an absurdly high price. Unable to resell on the open market, it arranged to 'sell' the building to its own DTC. The price was sufficiently modest to absorb a mere 70% of the DTC's funds. There were two results: a DTC with a liquidity crisis waiting to happen whenever credit conditions tightened or more than the usual numbers of depositors demanded their money back; and a big but bogus increase in profit of the property arm of the company, which in turn puffed the book profits of the parent firm. For a time, all seemed well. Then, only two months after *The Banker's* tribute, Sun Hung Kai came close to collapse again, when the company was hit with the usual double play. The property arm lost money, and the DTC was squeezed between the depreciation of its main asset and a deposit drain caused by new regulations pushing the DTCs out of the retail deposit field.

But Mr. Fung was well connected, and the Hong Kong government gave him the first new bank license issued in the colony since the moratorium of 1965. His DTC was thus dignified with the status of commercial bank just in time to be hit by a depositors' run that nearly brought it down. Yet another major rescue was mounted by the Hong Kong authorities, and Sun Hung Kai's two foreign partners pumped in more capital. But the dream of a twenty-four-hour global financial supermarket died when Parisbas sold out, and the banking arm was sold to Arabian Gulf investors looking for a place to park their money before the Ayatollah came calling.[15]

While the commercial banks were facing runs, DTCs continued to falter and fall. By the end of 1983 thirty had closed their doors: some crashed, some had their registrations revoked, and some just gave up in the face of the shrinking market and changing regulatory environment. The government finally moved to tighten up on lending practices, and also introduced desperate measures to curb and reverse capital flight and to maintain the Hong Kong dollar. The withholding tax on interest paid to overseas depositors was abolished; interest rates were pushed up sharply; and the Hong Kong dollar was pegged to the US dollar. The big banks made a public show of building up their foreign-exchange reserves in order to help the government defend the dollar. For a financial center whose historical raison d'être lay in its capacity to attract flight capital from regional trouble spots, the new regulations symbolized the end of an era.[16]

Flying High

For several years prior to the crises of the early 1980s, major corporations had been quietly diversifying out of Hong Kong, while rich individuals had been parking assets abroad and picking up foreign passports.[17] The quest for foreign citizenship was a particularly pressing issue, because the 'British ' passports carried by Hong Kong residents were virtually worthless. Britain had decreed that holders of 'British' passports issued in Hong Kong did not have the right to live in Britain; only British-born persons had such a right. Of course the British sense of fair play demanded there be exceptions, and indeed, exceptions could live in Britain when accompanied by an investment of £150,000.

In theory, the devaluation of the British passport applied to everyone. In reality, the white elite was protected; they had only to park their wealth abroad, which most of them had already done. The rich Chinese had to find a parking space that could accommodate both themselves and their wealth; the latter was usually more welcome than the former.

Hence, the smart money in Hong Kong quickly linked investment with citizenship, offering itself as a package to various suitors. The worse the state of the Hong Kong stock market, the better was the market in exit insurance; 'investment counselors,' 'immigration consultants,' and similar carpetbaggers arrived in droves. Indeed, it was with an almost audible smack of the lips that the Taiwan Economics Ministry estimated that, by 1997, when the lease on the New Territories expires, Hong Kong would lose $30 billion. Needless to say, Taiwan was determined to find a share.

Perhaps it reflected the lingering influence of Michele Sindona, who had taken refuge there briefly and functioned as an 'economic adviser' to the government, when in 1984 Taiwan launched itself into the offshore banking game, suitably protected against exchange controls, interest-rate ceilings, reserve requirements, and taxes. However, a more compelling reason was the desire to attract business fleeing a commercial rival and ideological competitor.

The antagonism between Taiwan and Hong Kong went back to 1950, when Britain formally recognized the People's Republic of China. Apart from resenting Hong Kong for being 'soft on communism,' Taiwan was jealous of its success in the regional hot-money game. Indeed, the lack of an extradition treaty between the two reflected not only ideological antagonism, but also an effort to encourage reciprocal raids on hot-money pools through the capers of refugee financiers. The Hong Kong heroin-trade scandals in the mid-1970s permitted Taiwan to pick up more rich refugees and provided a unique opportunity for indigenous entrepreneurs to break into the business.

When Chinese-American author Henry Liu was gunned down in California, the spotlight was thrown on another manifestation of the confluence of interests of organized crime and government agencies responsible for 'intelligence' activities. Liu had just completed a critical biography of Taiwanese strongman Chiang Hsiao-wu; and Taiwanese military intelligence decided to give the renegade author a 'lesson.' According to US prosecuting attorneys, Chen Chi-li, international operations chief of the crime syndicate known as the Bamboo Union, volunteered to administer that lesson.

The Bamboo Union had come a long way since the mid-1970s when it was merely a handful of street thugs. By the time Chen Chi-li was incarcerated for his role in Liu's murder (as were top figures in the Taiwan military intelligence agency), the Bamboo Union had a membership estimated at anywhere between 15,000 and 40,000. It was centered in Taiwan but active in Japan, the Philippines, Hong Kong, Saudi Arabia, and the US in drug dealing, gambling, extortion, bribery, kidnapping, and paid assassination. Its activities were well protected, not only by the secret induction ceremonies and blood oaths of its members, but also because many of its top people were sons of prominent Chinese Nationalists who had fled with Chiang Kai-shek to Taiwan in 1949. Just how well placed was the Bamboo Union, or at least its chief, became evident when Chen was charged by the FBI with having arranged, from his prison cell in Taiwan, for the importation of 300 kilos of heroin into the US, and for the Bamboo Union to break into the Las Vegas gambling scene.[18]

All this meant that Taiwan was in need of modern peekaboo financing facilities. But its position was highly vulnerable because of the notorious corruption of its corporate practices and because it was on China's hit list as well.

China, too, was an aspirant to at least part of Hong Kong's former role, as it created tax havens and decentralized banking zones in the Special Economic Zones and in its own in-house version of an offshore center. When, on top of the profit incentives offered to small-scale, private enterprise, China called for the unleashing of the 'creative urges' of its aspiring entrepreneurs,[19] some of those avidly listening were the party apparatchiks and business managers on the island of Hainan.

Like Caribbean contraband and offshore banking centers, Hainan was once famed as a haunt of pirates and exiles; it was subsequently renowned for its backwardness. In 1983, in an effort to stimulate economic development, the tax and exchange-control incentives awarded the Special Economic Zones were extended to Hainan in the expectation that this would encourage investment. What it encouraged was local officials who borrowed 4.2 billion yuan – $1.5 billion at the official exchange rate – from local banks, which received kickbacks for their cooperation. The yuan were then sold on the currency black market in the Shenzen Special Economic Zone near Hong Kong. The hard currency was then used to import, among other items, 89,000 cars and trucks, 2.9 million color televisions, 250,000 VCRs, and 122,000 motorcycles, which were resold at fat markups throughout China. The ensuing scandal sent many party functionaries into disgrace, caused the central government to retighten exchange controls, and led to the planning of a special anticorruption commission modeled on that of Hong Kong. Clearly China still had some distance to travel along the free-enterprise road.[20]

That was not true, however, of the most obvious aspirant to Hong Kong's regional role. Singapore was the largest offshore banking center in the Asian-dollar market (the Pacific equivalent of the eurodollar market), and the development of its entrepreneurial instincts was attested to by the nature of its banking system. Singapore bank-loan officers were notorious for their greasy palms, and Singapore banks equally notorious for evading restrictions imposed by the regulatory authorities.[21]

Apart from whatever regional banking business it could pick up from Hong Kong, Singapore aspired to replace Hong Kong as the Pacific-Basin center for loan syndications and fund management. The Singapore authorities made serious efforts to attract longer-term investment funds by cutting taxes on investment income and shaving the management fees on nonresident investment portfolios.[22]

Elsewhere in the area, Macao in theory was facing the same fate as Hong Kong, reincorporation into China. But it looked forward to competing with Hong Kong as a financial center for the Special Economic Zones in southern China. In the interim, it made a grab for flight capital.

Perhaps Macao saw the opportunity to reverse historic roles, for Macao had once been the broker for most of China's external trade, and the host of the major Southeast Asian gold market. It was subsequently eclipsed by Hong Kong and reduced to a marginal and anachronistic Portuguese enclave, hobbling along as a gambling and tourism center, and offshore to Hong Kong's offshore facility, until the 1980s when its financial system was shaken by events in Hong Kong, and it was forced to strike out on its own.[23]

Further afield was Vanuatu, a Pacific island chain with a long-established Chinese commercial community. Since achieving independence in 1980, Vanuatu had launched itself into the Southeast Asian capital-flight business, on the advice of Michael Oliver and his Phoenix Foundation. It was a natural haven for hot Hong Kong money, as the owners of Axona International Credit had realized.[24]

Even farther afield, Australia was swapping citizenships for investment funds; Tonga peddled its passports to anyone willing to pay the price, including George Tan; and Hawaii opened its heart and its vaults to those in need of refuge. Hawaii had become happy host to an 'investment company' with the impressive title of Bishop, Baldwin, Rewald, Dillingham and Wong, and the equally impressive functions of laundering money for CIA covert operations in Southeast Asia and providing flight-capital facilities for anyone nervous about the results. This esteemed corporate citizen made a bid for Hong Kong hot money, until it came to an undignified end in bankruptcy court in the summer of 1983.[25]

There were many other eager entrepreneurs channeling Hong Kong flight capital to eager recipients. Canadian government officials swooned at the possibility of welcoming itinerant Hong Kong capitalists,[26] some of whom had set their sights on Vancouver, which had hosted an earlier wave of millionaire Hong Kong retirees, including former sergeants from the narcotics and vice squads.

California offered a sunny climate, political security, the strength of the US dollar, high interest rates, and the services of banks such as American Express. Although some left home without it, Amex enthusiastically helped others express their hot money out of Hong Kong.[27]

Even Texas tried to get into the act, when two university professors dreamed up the ultimate in recycling schemes: land was to be leased in perpetuity from Mexico in exchange for the liquidation of its sovereign debt; and on the territory, which would become a commercial appendage of Texas, would be settled one million Hong Kong refugees. When there proved to be little general enthusiasm to add the Yellow Peril to the existing Hispanic Menace, they tried again. This time only Hong Kong capital would come in, and be settled in a new industrial zone near San Antonio. Here, in the world's most elaborate sweatshop, would work cheap Mexican labor.[28] Their remittances back home, presumably, would facilitate the service of Mexico's sovereign debt.

The Caribbean, and Central and South America were certainly not going to be left out in the scramble, particularly after the US government launched its Caribbean Basin Initiative, which offered tariff concessions in the US market in exchange for good political behavior.[29] Jamaica bid to relocate part of the Hong Kong textile industry, whose major market had been in the US; the Cayman Islands hunted fund-management business; Panama looked for banking business and an inflow of long-term investment funds for its free-trade zone; Costa Rica peddled its passports for cash; and even distant Paraguay allowed George Tan and other Hong Kong–based entrepreneurs to diversify their portfolio of passports through shared citizenship with the ex-Nazis Paraguay had already welcomed. Perhaps because of declining export markets for its marijuana crop, Belize hit upon the idea of diversifying its access to the hot-money pool by selling citizenship. Not to be outdone was Stanley Randall, a former Ontario minister of economics and development, who had given the world this poetic sentiment: 'Selling is like shaving. If you don't do a bit of it every day, you're a bum.' He therefore decided to clear the world's streets of vagrants from Hong Kong by promoting a scheme to sell them Netherlands Antilles 'alien' passports.[30]

Of all the American havens for Hong Kong capital, none achieved the distinction of the Dominican Republic, racked by debt and depression, and desperate for foreign money. The island was solicitous of Hong Kong entrepreneurs willing to help build the tourist trade, and in 1985 made itself the center of Hong Kong's most dramatic financial scandal since the Carrian collapse.[31]

Overseas Trust Bank (OTB) was the third-largest privately owned bank in Hong Kong. Founded in 1955 by Chang Ming-thien, it remained firmly under the control of the Chang family, which provided it with a secretive network of business associations throughout Southeast Asia and beyond. Family ties had long been the means by which OTB and many other Hong Kong–based financial vehicles drew in hot money from abroad. But such a network had the potential of working in reverse when the economic and political environment worsened.

Inside Hong Kong, OTB had a far from glorious history. It found itself involved in a price-rigging scandal in 1974; it was the center of a securities scandal in 1981; it had had holdings in Dollar Credit and Hang Lung Bank and was involved with these two institutions in John Mao's check-kiting scam. These events and more took place behind the usual wall of secrecy, until the unfortunate suspension of Dominican Finance in January 1985.

After the events of the summer of 1982 the Chang family decided to shift their assets out of the colony. Simon Yip, chairman of Dominican Finance, was also the honorary consul of the Dominican Republic in Hong Kong; and Patrick Chang, son and heir of the founder of OTB, carried a Dominican diplomatic passport. Among the prominent assets on the books of OTB was an unsecured loan of HK$900 million to Dominican Finance.

In early June 1985 the International Monetary Conference was meeting in Hong Kong. That elite gathering, including the heads of the world's most powerful banks, had as an implicit objective the bolstering of confidence in Hong Kong as an international financial center. Alas, that failed to impress the chairman of the collapsed Dominican Finance, Simon Yip, who had decided to follow the money out of the colony. OTB was declared insolvent and taken over by the Hong Kong government. Some $500 million was found to have been misappropriated, less the $1.5 million in cash, negotiable securities, diamonds, and jewelry found in the possession of a bank officer arrested at the airport while attempting to implement the true principle of capital flight.

In the aftershock, the Hong Kong government guaranteed the deposits, and the Hongkong & Shanghai Bank, along with the Bank of China, pumped in the liquidity necessary to keep the panic from spreading. Indeed, so shaken was the Hong Kong financial system that the government was forced to consider the ultimate capitulation: the abolition of bank secrecy laws, the end of the system of nominee ownership, and the integration of DTCs into the bank regulatory apparatus. And when the tiny Ka Wah Bank got in trouble a few months later, it was quietly sold off to the People's Republic. By that time China was willing to help shore up confidence in the Hong Kong financial system because it had imposed its terms for the reintegration of the colony.

Throughout the storm and fury of 1982 and 1983 China had played a clever game, turning the money tap on and off to make political points. After the Hong Kong property-market collapse, China bought property and offered long-term low-interest loans to manufacturers, thereby demonstrating to the business community that it, not Britain, held the key to future prosperity. In the autumn of 1983, when Britain tried to toughen its negotiating stance, China simply stoked the fires of panic, egging on another financial panic and flight of capital.

Indeed, when China opened its stockbrokerage operation in Hong

Kong, it engaged in an exercise that would have been unlawful in almost any country with a modicum of regulatory pride. Because every growl or purr from China made the stock market fall or rise, it would take but little coordination between the Chinese foreign ministry and the new PRC-owned stockbrokerage firm for the brokers to sprint off with half of the colony in their pockets.

By the spring of 1984 the situation seemed to have stabilized. China and Britain were largely agreed on the shape of the colony's future. It was accepted that there would be no formal British presence, but capitalist structures and their legal framework would remain in place for fifty years after the transfer of sovereignty. Chinese long-term capital was stabilizing the property market, and short-term funds were returning.[32] But before the climate became congenial enough for local entrepreneurs to reactivate their long-term investment plans, Jardine-Matheson threw the colony into turmoil once more.

Noble House?

The most spectacular casualty of the property-market crash, and of the political tug-of-war between Britain and China, was the *hong* that had long symbolized the British presence in Hong Kong. Jardine-Matheson had diversified from trading and real estate into an international conglomerate involved in shipping, construction, energy development, and financial services; and it had reduced its exposure in Hong Kong. Nevertheless, in 1982 the colony still generated 70% of Jardine's business. Hong Kong Land, its property arm, was the largest single component of the group, and its massive holdings of downtown commercial real estate made the group very vulnerable to changes in the colony's business environment.

Jardine-Matheson was also vulnerable precisely because the conglomerate effectively symbolized the British presence. It had been the target of takeover bids by aspiring Chinese entrepreneurs, backed by the PRC-controlled banks, during the boom of the 1970s. As these Chinese entrepreneurs assumed greater political influence and increased weight in colonial business and financial affairs, Jardine-Matheson, heir to the drug-peddling operation out of which Hong Kong was torn from China, could be forgiven a touch of paranoia.

During the 1970s the fastest-growing arm of the Jardine-Matheson group was the international component of the financial-services wing. For despite the spectacular growth of Hong Kong as a financial center, Jardine-Matheson was being squeezed out. When Sun Hung Kai Finance applied for a banking license in 1982, so, too, did Jardine-Fleming, the DTC run by the Jardine-Matheson group. Sun Hung Kai got the license;

Jardine-Fleming did not. Something fundamental had changed in the politics of Hong Kong business; and the change was not to the liking of William Jardine's heirs.

Hong Kong Land had been one of the most active participants in the later stages of the property mania. When the bubble burst, it left Jardine-Fleming with a HK$350 million exposure to Carrian, threw Hong Kong Land for a $1.6 billion loop, and blew a huge hole in the earnings of the parent company,[33] whose shares tumbled on the Hong Kong exchanges. The ensuing power struggle within Noble House culminated in its decision to join the general exodus.[34]

A coup d'état replaced top executives committed to rapprochement with China and defense of Hong Kong as the base of operations. The new top management sought a fifty-fifty diversification between Hong Kong and the rest of the world, and a strategy to bolster the financial-services arm, particularly in the North American market.[35] It also decided to shift its international headquarters to Bermuda.

Coming in the spring of 1984, when the economic climate seemed to be improving rapidly, the announcement of the shift of headquarters was a particularly severe shock. The stock exchange took a nosedive; only the peg of the Hong Kong dollar to that of the US and the mobilization of huge foreign-exchange reserves prevented the currency from following. Even the old Anglo-Scottish business elite expressed surprise at the decision. As one banker put it, 'All the *hongs* have doomsday scenarios ready to go, but nobody expected Jardine would be the first.'[36]

The Chinese angrily insisted that the move had been coordinated with Britain to raise the stakes in the bargaining just when the political odds were swinging in favor of China. Romantic journalists speculated that novelist James Clavell, author of two sanitized Jardine sagas, *Noble House* and *Tai-Pan*, could now complete a trilogy. But Clavell may already have written that big, allegorical novel – *King Rat*.

Part Five

What Flies into the Cuckoo's Nest?

15

Swiss Contributions to Economic Development

There is an old proverb that the best defense is a good offense. And who could be expected to be more conversant with old proverbs than a pope? With one financial scandal after another spinning around his head, Pope John Paul II had a ready reply. On a 1984 state visit to a place where popes, if not angels, had formerly feared to tread, he boldly declared:

> Tiny Switzerland has today become a world power in business and finance. As a democratically constituted society you must watch vigilantly over all that goes on in this powerful world of money. The world of finance too is a world of human beings, our world, subject to the consciences of us all; ethical principles apply to it too.[1]

Presumably if the Swiss banks[2] applied to their business the standards of ethical deportment that the Vatican bank traditionally applied to its, the pope would have no complaint. Neither would the Swiss banks.

Fat but Still Hungry
Switzerland vies with Hong Kong for third place among the world's financial centers. In 1984 it had 527 operational banks, employing 100,000 people, with assets totaling more than three times the country's gross domestic product. The major Swiss banks are megabanks, combining commercial and investment banking, commodity and foreign-exchange dealings, stockbroking and investment counseling within a single institution.[3] Thus, if Swiss Bank Corporation is typical, about half the profits of Swiss megabanks come from lending activity; and the rest from fees for 'services' to clients, domestic and international. There is also an array of 'private banks,' who discreetly handle personal fortunes.

Nearly 40% of the balances on the books of Swiss banks are denominated in foreign currency, attracted by the security and secrecy with which 'Switzerland' has become synonymous. A 1984 estimate of the foreign assets controlled in various ways and forms by the Swiss banks puts the total at more than $350 billion, approximately equal to the net foreign bank debt of the world's developing countries – a coincidence pregnant with implication. Domestic opponents of Swiss bank secrecy estimated that at least $70 billion of the assets could be attributed directly to looting by dictators currently or formerly in control of developing countries; and this estimate was made prior to the enormous burst of capital flight after the summer of 1982. But the foreign-currency-denominated assets of Swiss banks are no indicator of the amount of their business generated in international financial markets. The Swiss banks run the world's largest gold market; and the Swiss franc has been more important than the US dollar as a global currency of refuge, a situation the US has been seeking – successfully – to change.

Thus, during 1982 to 1984, when the world financial system trembled on the brink of the abyss, when debtor countries groaned under the burden of their debt-service obligations, when capital flight entered the space age, and when financial centers, fly-by-night havens and long-established capitals alike, were shaken to their foundations, guess who came up smiling? The year 1983 was a very good one for Swiss banks, the most profitable in their history. The next year their performance was almost as strong.[4]

Unlike other banks in Western Europe, those of Switzerland functioned as a magnet for capital fleeing shaky debtor countries, yet they had relatively little loan exposure to those debtors.[5] Their main problems appeared to be political, as fiscal authorities in Italy, Spain, France, and the US, and an opposition movement at home sought to pry the lid off of bank secrecy.

When Silence is Golden

In Switzerland, bank secrecy is protected by both civil and criminal law. As tax evasion is not a crime in Switzerland and there are no restrictions on currency movements, Swiss banks are prohibited from communicating information about tax or exchange-control violations to foreign governments. In April 1978 the Council of Europe, concerned by the growing problem of capital flight and tax evasion, not just from developing countries but also from France and Italy, asked member states to cooperate in curbing such practices. The Swiss politely declined on the grounds that such cooperation would violate bank secrecy.[6]

If the Swiss public prosecutor has information that bank secrecy has been infringed, he *must* investigate and, if appropriate, prosecute. This mandatory prosecution rule, which can result in long jail sentences and heavy fines, means that bank-secrecy rules are much stronger than the professional secrecy rules for doctors and lawyers, for example, for in such instances prosecution will result only if an injured party lodges a complaint.

Swiss banks are famed for their stability and conservatism. Their stability is attested to by the highest bank-failure rate per capita of any country in the industrialized world;[7] and their conservatism is well demonstrated by their record of fleeced clients. Swiss law protects the banks not only against curious or angry foreign governments but also against their customers. Swiss bank secrecy is often a trap for depositors. As they often have something to hide, *their* lips are effectively sealed, no matter if they are robbed by the very institution to which they have entrusted their money.

Money on deposit in Switzerland comes from a variety of sources and seeks refuge there for a variety of reasons. Its ultimate origins and final destinations are often deliberately murky. This obscurity is increased because at least 40% of Swiss bank dealings are with other bank havens; and that rises to more than 50% if the City of London is included.[8]

Certainly one of the largest sources of foreign funds for Swiss banks has been ordinary, everyday flight capital from developing countries. Foreign money also pours in to evade taxation in developed countries such as France and Italy and, in the case of American money, also to circumvent margin requirements imposed on domestic but not on foreign purchases of US stock. Historically, these monies have been joined by a flow of funds from gunrunning, drug dealing, insider trading, commodities fraud, and covert operations of intelligence agencies and/or underground political organizations. All is washed through the Swiss banking system and emerges gentrified in overseas real estate investments, in stocks and bonds of legitimate corporations and governments, and even occasionally in euromarket loans to countries trying to cover government budget or balance-of-payments deficits caused partly or entirely by tax evasion or capital flight.

Although Swiss hospitality to refugee money dates back to early modern times, it was systematized during the 1930s. According to the mythology recited by the Swiss banks, the stringent secrecy laws that date from 1934 were passed to protect the funds of Jewish clients from the Gestapo. In fact, the laws were passed because the French government was becoming increasingly belligerent about tax dodging via Geneva banks by its rich citizens during a time of general austerity. A scandal following a 1932 police raid on a Paris branch of a Swiss bank led in

1933 to a tightening of French laws against exchange-control violations; the Swiss responded the following year with their reinforced bank-secrecy provisions.[9]

In 1935 the Swiss did react to Nazi probes, but with a law to counter industrial espionage. This is something that the Swiss continue to stand guard against, as the unfortunate Stanley Adams discovered.

In 1973 Adams was a director of Hoffman–La Roche, the Swiss pharmaceutical giant. He found that the firm was forcing clients to sign contracts making it their sole supplier. He did two things: resigned from the firm, and turned incriminating documents over to the EEC in Brussels. EEC officers also did two things: fined Hoffman–La Roche for violations of European commercial law, and told the firm where they got the information. Adams was then residing in Italy. When he unsuspectingly crossed the border one day late in 1974, he was seized and hustled off to Lugano prison, where he was held incognito until a released prison mate informed the EEC of his fate.[10] Hoffman–La Roche was guilty as charged, but so was Adams. That was the same equality before the law that the Swiss applied to their dealings with Nazi Germany.

Swiss 'neutrality' before and during the war meant a roaring business with Hitler's Germany. Switzerland was the home of the Bank for International Settlements (BIS), the central bankers' central bank, whose Nazi-influenced directorate provided cover for financial operations essential to German objectives. Ordinary Swiss banks also performed vital functions: financing much of the trade necessary to keep the German war machine operating; laundering German gold (most of it loot from occupied countries); serving as a conduit for funds officially secreted abroad by top Nazis as they planned their postwar careers; and, after Stalingrad, assisting other, less privileged orders with unsanctioned capital flight as they prepared for the worst.[11]

The Swiss concern with political neutrality has a contemporary context, as well, for Switzerland is for the USSR rather what Hong Kong is for the People's Republic of China. It has been alleged that, through the intermediation of Swiss banks, the USSR has gained controlling positions in some American corporations producing strategic goods, including armaments.[12] Much of the commodity trading and foreign-exchange activities of the USSR are conducted through its Swiss affiliates, which have given the USSR a reputation for being among the shrewdest commodity traders. (That reputation took a blow recently when Wozchod-Handelsbank AG, the USSR's chief gold-trading bank, fired its chief trader for losing as much as $390 million in unauthorized trading in gold futures and foreign exchange. The USSR then shut down the bank.)[13]

The USSR is not the only country to appreciate the potential of Swiss secrecy for cloaking the volume and destination of its gold sales. In the 1960s the USSR was joined in the Swiss gold market by staunchly anticommunist South Africa, which moved the locus of its gold sales from London to protest Britain's joining the international embargo on arms sales to South Africa.

That change of locale proved fortunate in 1985, when South Africa's international financial position came under fire: military expenditures had driven up its budget deficits; gold prices were falling in the early 1980s (as sovereign debtors dumped gold reserves and as hot money took refuge in high-interest US-dollar-denominated securities instead of gold); and capital inflows dried up in the face of a deteriorating internal political situation. By 1983 South Africa had been forced to go begging to the IMF. Two years later, a new round of political conflict forced it to suspend payments on its $12 billion international bank debt and ask for a rescheduling. When the British and American banks refused to manage the rescheduling deal, it was Swiss neutrality to the rescue: the task of reordering South African finances fell to the three big Swiss banks. Their spokesman, former BIS chief Fritz Leutwiler, explicitly rejected the idea of asking Pretoria for political changes as a prerequisite to renegotiating the debt.[14]

That gave the Vatican yet another reason to appreciate the Swiss notion of neutrality in world politics. For, while the black townships burned and the pope publicly denounced apartheid, the IOR, through its Swiss affiliate, Banco di Roma per la Svizzera, was participating in syndicated loans to South Africa. The Vatican later pointed out that these were not loans to the South African *state;* and it was the state that the Vatican was criticizing. Apparently the Vatican's definition of 'state' does not include recipients of the loans' proceeds such as the city of Johannesburg and the South African state telephone, telegraph, and postal corporation.[15]

South Africa, like many other countries, makes use of Swiss bank secrecy for conducting aspects of its international relations that require particular discretion. South Africa's secret service launders through fiduciary accounts at the Union de Banques Suisses payments for espionage and such special functions as an abortive attempt in 1977 to buy control of prestigious European publications to silence their criticisms of the regime. Similarly, the CIA ran secret accounts through Swiss Bank Corporation and Lloyd's Bank International in Geneva, to finance covert action in NATO countries. Such accounts also held the money that the CIA, together with the Reverend Sun Myung Moon and assorted US rightist groups, had been banking for the Contras. Italian military intelligence paid Francesco Pazienza through coded Swiss accounts for services rendered in maintaining communications with Italian organized crime. France's Service de Documentation Extérieur et Contre-Espionage (SDECE) was certainly no stranger to the coded accounts that French customs was constantly trying to crack. And there was Tibor Rosenbaum's Banque de Crédit Internationale (ICB), a quintessential Swiss bank.

ICB of Geneva was paymaster for the Mossad, and at one point it was estimated that 90% of the Israeli Department of Defense overseas arms-purchase budget passed through it. It also functioned as a laundromat for Meyer Lansky, and was in the capital-flight business with Bernie Cornfeld's IOS. So enterprising was its spirit in the capital-flight trade that it allegedly pioneered the creation of clients' accounts denominated in gold bars and coin. There were many satisfied customers.[16]

The Wealth of Other Nations

Switzerland traditionally has opened its doors to absconding autocrats and their cash with the same facility with which it closes those doors behind evicted Yugoslav and Turkish guest workers. Looted foreign-aid payments make their way to Switzerland in sufficient amounts that, in the interests of efficiency, US-AID, the World Bank, the African Development Bank, the Inter-American Development Bank, and so on, might well eliminate the middleman and pay the money straight into Swiss accounts. But perhaps there is a logic to the exercise, for those aid agencies and development banks borrow on the eurobond market via Switzerland. Thus, with superbly efficient recycling, Swiss banks can offer secrecy in return for less than market rates, and then invest part of the proceeds in the triple-A bonds floated by the development agencies backed by Western governments.

Thus, in the 1960s, while Bernie Cornfeld's IOS was busy in Nigeria recycling foreign-aid payments into Geneva bank accounts, it had important competitors. One was the Geneva branch of Yousef Beidas's Intra Bank, in which Ahmed Obellow, secretary-general of Nigeria's ruling party, banked the commissions paid to him by Lebanese traders operating in the country. When Obellow was killed in a 1966 military coup, Swiss bank secrecy proved useful once more: Beidas and the main Lebanese intermediary simply split the contents of the account. After all, who was going to find out – or to complain in public, if they did?

A similar process is at work recycling the proceeds of many eurocurrency market loans. Some of the funds borrowed in the name of developing countries top up the retirement savings plans of well-placed individuals. Guatemalan Archbishop Prospero Penado summed it up: 'If you give a $10 million loan, perhaps half is used. The other half goes to Switzerland or Miami.'[17]

Argentine strongman Juan Peron was a double boon to the Swiss banks. Peronism frightened the Argentine rich, and their money took flight to Switzerland via Uruguay. Although Peron was exiled to Madrid, his money, and, allegedly, $140 million belonging to the legendary Eva, preferred Switzerland. According to Lopez Rega's girlfriend, El Brujo's fascination with the occult extended to the study of the secrets of banking in Switzerland, where he also de-astralized himself after vanishing from Argentina in 1975. There, too, Fulgencio Batista stored his spare cash. By the time of his assassination in 1961, the Dominican Republic's Rafael Trujillo was rumored to have tucked away in Switzerland between $180 million and $840 million, in gold, diamonds, currency, securities, and titles to real estate holdings all over the world.[18] Whatever the exact figure, the Trujillo family fortune was sufficient to precipitate a major banking scandal.[19]

Nicaragua's Anastasio Somoza also liked saving for a rainy day. His concern with the vagaries of nature was borne out by the 1972 earthquake that devastated his country's capital city. Foreign relief poured in, and his Swiss bank balance grew *pari passu*. His balance was allegedly aided by a contribution by Roberto Calvi to assure that Banco Ambrosiano Managua continued to enjoy Nicaraguan hospitality.

Political earthquakes had similar effects. The 1974 revolution in Portugal sent more than one billion escudos out of the country; much of it was subsequently tendered to the Portuguese central bank by the Swiss National Bank for gold and hard currency.[20]

Also in 1974, Honduras tried to impose its first income tax. The result was a flight of funds to Switzerland via Panama. The next year the US Securities and Exchange Commission halted trading in United Brands shares on the New York stock exchange after allegations spread that the company had funneled bribes to prominent Honduran officials through Swiss banks.[21]

However, 1974 had its sad moments for Switzerland. The banking system was shaken by scandals, some related to the fallout from *il crack Sindona* and the Tibor Rosenbaum affair, and one of Switzerland's most important deposit clients faced a cash-flow crisis. When Ethiopian Emperor Haile Selassie was deposed, the revolutionary government reportedly found among his personal papers a letter from his Swiss bankers asking him to hold off shipping gold bars, for they had run out of storage space. Small wonder. Since 1948 Haile Selassie had been buying the entire output of the gold mines in southern Ethiopia at one-half the world market price, and adding it to the proceeds of his other tax-free holdings, such as 20% of the arable land in the country. While subsequent estimates of his personal gold reserves were put at a scarcely credible $6 to $9 billion, they were reportedly sufficient to permit him to withdraw $600 million from his Swiss accounts to help the Ethiopian government finance its war with Somalia.[22]

The oil-price increases of the 1970s also paid handsome dividends to the Swiss financial system. Switzerland was a favorite piggy bank for the shah of Iran and his family; some oil traders claim that a standard 15% of payments for Iranian oil went into Pahlavi accounts.[23] These payments appear to have blazed an Alpine trail for cabinet ministers, generals, SAVAK officers, and so on, who allegedly moved $4.5 billion through Swiss accounts in a matter of months after the revolution broke out in 1978.[24]

None of the above is intended to belittle Mobutu Sese Seko, whose Swiss accounts are not likely to be significantly smaller than Zaire's foreign debt.

Bringing Light to the Heart of Darkness

During the 1970s Zaire was boomtown, Africa, a major coffee exporter, with mineral reserves – copper, cobalt, chromium, zinc, gold, tin, platinum, cadmium, uranium, and diamonds – that were legendary. The cobalt, chromium, and industrial diamonds, not to mention the uranium reserves, were essential for the aeronautics and rocket manufacturing industries of the Western powers.[25] So, too, was Mobutu Sese Seko.

Officially known as the 'savior guide,' Mobutu ruled Zaire with US, French, Belgian, and West German military aid, Israeli arms and advisers, and armed gangs to terrorize the opposition. His popularity was furthered by his star qualities: every evening the national TV news opened with pictures of the 'guide' descending from heaven against a background of flashing lights and exploding rockets.

Zaire had little initial difficulty running up its foreign debt. The 1970s boom in international bank lending, preferably to projects in which the state was involved, coincided with Mobutu's taking control of many foreign-owned companies in Zaire. (He turned them over to his political henchmen or nationalized them or both.)[26] For some time French, Belgian, and American banks, with a nod from their governments, pumped in money secured on the huge output of Zaire's Shaba province, whose mineral resources are unparalleled. Allegations that Mobutu was draining half the commodity-export receipts into his own pockets or those of his clan did not deter the banks. But in 1975 the price of copper fell sharply on the world markets, and bank lending largely dried up. That left only the question of how to secure repayment of the several hundred millions in bank debts already contracted.[27]

In 1977 an even graver crisis faced Zaire's creditors in the shape of a secession attempt by Shaba province, and a subsequent invasion by Angolan-based rebels. After the military threat was quelled by Moroccan, French, and Belgian forces, the IMF seized the opportunity to impose some order on the country's finances. It forced Zaire to accept its nominee, a German banker named Erwin Blumenthal, to head the central bank, with instructions to keep the public-sector deficit under control and the foreign-debt-service payments in order.

Blumenthal spent two years facing threats and intimidation, trying to curb the appropriation of foreign-exchange receipts by the president and his relatives and to force Zairian companies to repatriate capital shifted abroad. He also fought the diversion of funds to the president in favor of diverting them to Zaire's international bank creditors. According to Blumenthal, the president for life was *the* obstacle to budget control. Some 12% to 18% of the national budget was routinely earmarked for his personal expenses (allegedly four times the budget of rich Shaba province); and Mobutu treated the central bank as a personal cash dispenser: for example, he took ninety personal guests on an all-expense-paid visit to Disneyland. Blumenthal's efforts to curb the appetites of some of Mobutu's generals for 'project finance' sometimes led to withdrawals from the central bank at gunpoint.

Apart from shifting funds abroad through manipulation of the exchange rate – purchasing zaires at the black-market rate and reselling them to the Mobutu-controlled national savings bank at the official rate – Mobutu is also alleged to have been busy diverting diamonds from the state mining monopoly for private sale in London, smuggling gold to Europe, and selling strategic minerals through South Africa, with the proceeds sent to his foreign, mainly Swiss, bank accounts.[28]

The net result is subject to dispute. According to former prime minister Nguza-Karl-I-Bond, by 1982 Mobutu had stashed in Swiss, Belgian, and French bank accounts about $4 billion. Others put the current total at $5 billion, the rough equivalent of Zaire's total foreign debt. Mobutu is also reputed to have eight houses and two chateaux in Europe, as well as a Swiss estate, a big Paris apartment, three hotels in Dakar, and villas scattered across Africa.[29]

Sugar and Rice and Everything Nice ...

Switzerland's position as a global financial center has also made it a major entrepôt for world commodity trading. Thus, in a neat parallel to its role in the global flight-capital business, Switzerland, headquarters of the International Red Cross, also hosts a brokerage firm that specializes in buying blood from Zaire and other impoverished nations of central Africa and selling the plasma in the United States.[30]

Switzerland shares with Hong Kong the honors of the multibillion-dollar business of global maritime fraud. Panamanian ghost companies provide a cover for entrepreneurs operating out of Greece and Hong Kong, hijacking and diverting perhaps $15 billion worth of cargoes per annum, and laundering the receipts through Hong Kong and Swiss bank accounts. But in keeping with its principle of strict neutrality, Switzerland also hosts the Société Générale de Surveillance, the world's largest company in the business of tracking smugglers, verifying commodity movements, and preventing maritime fraud.[31]

Nigeria, for many years the world's most frequent victim of maritime fraud, until 1984 employed the Société Générale de Surveillance to monitor its trade flows.[32] There was a lot to monitor.

Africa's most populous country had long been able to thumb its nose at meddlesome IMF missions. Its oil wealth not only provided 90% of its foreign exchange and 80% of its government revenues but also fueled ten years of economic growth at an annual average rate of 6.5%.

The enormous influx of cash and the growth of industry and trade that it financed caused peasants from depressed rural areas to pour into burgeoning urban centers, along with hundreds of thousands of immigrants from neighboring countries. The resulting shantytowns were a social powder keg, kept from exploding by the distribution of imported food at subsidized prices, and by the slum dwellers' lingering hope that someday they would be the lucky ones into whose outstretched palms some of the oil wealth would tumble.

There were such lucky people, but they did not live in the slums and shantytowns. The heady days saw a huge increase in 'corruption,' though pious denunciations of 'corrupt' practices were rarely heard in the West as long as there was enough cash left over to maintain external debt-service payments. Allegedly, under President Shehu Shegari, the average rake-off on public-sector deals hit 14%; it was routine for oil traders to kick back a cut into the foreign bank accounts of government officials. The government reportedly issued import licenses to reward political service; the recipients could resell them to genuine importers of goods.

Looting of the national patrimony was facilitated by a high value to the exchange rate. As hundreds of thousands of immigrant workers flowed back and forth across the border, the currency was readily available from money changers in neighboring countries, despite exchange controls. Therefore, the Nigerian elite with access to central-bank-issued exchange forms could obtain dollars for nairas inside Nigeria, export them to neighboring countries, use part to buy nairas on the black market at much less than the official rate, and smuggle them back into Nigeria to repay the central bank. The excess dollars would be parked abroad in secret accounts. Early 1983 estimates of the amount looted by phony invoicing and exchange fraud ran as high as $7.5 billion, a sum equal to about 40% of the Nigerian foreign debt.[33]

When oil revenues collapsed and the party ended, Nigeria was left with a multibillion-dollar unpaid trade bill, mainly due British suppliers, and an industrial recession as imported inputs and capital equipment were cut off.[34] The government's response was a mass deportation of foreign workers (estimates range as high as two million) to whip up a nationalist backlash against the 'alien' source of the economic crisis. The exodus also opened up jobs for the locals, who could be expected to respond enthusiastically in the forthcoming elections.[35]

President Shegari was returned to office in December 1983 with a large majority and ample accusations of vote rigging. He immediately imposed the harshest austerity measures in the country's history. But before negotiations with the IMF and the creditor banks could progress,[36] General Mohammadu Buhari, formerly minister of petroleum, launched his New Year's Eve coup.[37]

The military government – headed by a man who had overseen the operations of the national company during a time when a yawning hole emerged in its books – proclaimed its intent to clean out corruption, leading some to observe that the main effect would change the hands pilfering from the public purse without affecting overall volume. Others were less pessimistic, pointing out that military governments tend to be leaner, if not cleaner, with no party hacks to support.[38]

The new government, too, was soon quarreling with its international creditors over the huge arrears of trade debts and imposing one austerity measure after another; however, it resisted signing an IMF deal or substantially devaluing the currency.[39] Instead it hatched a more imaginative plan for alleviating the trade debts, a plan that took it to Geneva and then to London.

To prepare the psychological climate, the government floated more stories about corruption, denouncing a 'mafia of Nigerians in collusion with foreigners' who were allegedly smuggling oil – as much as 100,000 barrels per day, worth an annual $1 billion – out of the country. About 475 former politicians and business leaders were arrested. Illicit currency exporters were linked to illegal arms importers, implying that an organized subversive movement was at work in both areas,[40] as it may well have been. A sudden, complete recall and conversion of currency wiped out the black market in nairas conducted by petty smugglers. It also neutralized the savings of countless ordinary people who did not understand the mechanics of the conversion.[41] But the military government had bigger game in mind.

Among those international commodity dealers who rode the oil boom in Nigeria was Rajendra Sethia, an Indian expatriate with corporate headquarters in London. His specialty was sugar; an alleged subspecialty was the forging of documents to get loans from Indian banks to finance sugar exports to Nigeria. The New Year's Eve coup cost Sethia and his Indian bankers heavily, for the new government repudiated $60 million in debts incurred by the old regime to Sethia's commodities empire. The financial aftershocks won Sethia distinction as one of the largest private bankruptcies in history and an honored place in a high-security New Delhi jail.[42] And Sethia's discomfiture also assured that among the victims of Buhari's New Year's Eve coup would be one of the City of London's most prestigious banking institutions.

When the City of London fraud squad was probing the use of phony invoices to defraud Nigeria of $7.5 billion, it allegedly found the trail blocked by officers of Johnson-Matthey Bank. One of five London institutions that meet daily to fix gold prices, JMB was also heavily into financing Nigerian imports, particularly sugar. JMB would make payments in sterling for nonexistent imports on the basis of fraudulent bills of lading and forged inspection certificates. Customs officials in Nigeria collected bribes for cooperating, Rajendra Sethia and other Indian traders secured huge payoffs, and Nigerian politicians hid the take in British bank accounts held in the names of offshore companies. JMB officers allegedly accepted bribes and provided cover and tipped off suspects when the fraud squad came snooping. But the Buhari coup and Sethia's collapse brought down the bank, which had to be rescued by a massive infusion of funds from and takeover by the Bank of England. The debts of the Indian traders had to be written off.[43]

Whether it was these long-unrestricted antics by Nigeria's sugar daddy that caused the military government to cancel the contract of Société Générale de Surveillance is difficult to say, but the government, or rather the Nigerian secret service, asked another Geneva-based business to help sort out the mess.

Also among the commodity traders participating in the Nigerian boom was Nessim Goan, a Sudanese Jew who, from a Geneva base, had built a billion-dollar empire from commodity trading and construction. During the Nigerian oil boom, huge amounts of rice were imported; Goan soon had a virtual monopoly on the supply. That also made him one of the largest holders of Nigerian government promissory notes, prospects for repayment of which were increasingly in doubt. Furthermore, the military government suspended many of his contracts, accusing him of price gouging. By early 1984 he was rumored to have lost as much as $100 million in Nigeria. His business was kept afloat by a large loan from the big three Swiss banks. Goan also had political assets far from Nigeria.[44]

Among the uses to which Goan put his personal wealth were investments in Israel, one of the most notable of which was his funding of the Tami party, a right-wing Israeli political organization based largely in the Sephardic community. After the 1977 elections, the Tami party gained considerable influence, forming an essential part of the coalition that kept Menachem Begin in power.

Nigeria had been among the many sub-Saharan African states that broke relations with Israel after the October 1973 Middle East war. However, this did nothing to hamper close commercial relations between the two countries. Nigeria was Israel's biggest customer in Africa, and Israeli businesses existed in many sectors of the Nigerian economy.[45] But Israel wanted Nigerian oil, and Nigeria wanted Israeli expertise: to train its secret services, and for another special job.

Among those prominent Nigerians who beat a hasty exit after the New Year's Eve coup was Alhaji Umaru Dikko, brother-in-law and campaign manager of ex-president Shegari. He was also the former minister of transport and head of the regulatory agency that controlled rice imports. Dikko was known as the principal fixer, to whom all deals involving transportation contracts and import licenses had to be referred; he was also the man in charge of organizing food supplies. Companies wanting contracts would allegedly send suitcases stuffed with currency notes to Dikko's residence. Part of the take went for domestic political purposes; part of it was purportedly shipped abroad with the assistance of some of his foreign business associates.

The agency controlling rice imports had been set up ostensibly to assure that Nigeria's huge and growing appetite for imported rice could be met at a reduced cost. Under Dikko, the cost was reputedly reduced to about double world-market levels. Accusations about how much Dikko is supposed to have taken vary from $1.7 billion to $5 billion. Whether the allegations are true, or whether Dikko was just being used as a convenient scapegoat for defalcations by persons remaining in politically powerful positions in Nigeria has not been determined; nonetheless Dikko took refuge in Britain,[46] leaving Nessim Goan and other commodity traders to fret over unpaid bills and the Nigerian government to fend off bank creditors.

Dikko became the most wanted of the postcoup fugitives, in part because the military regime feared that Dikko and other wealthy exiles would use their loot to raise a mercenary army to topple the new government, but getting him back for a show trial and shakedown was difficult. The British courts would permit extradition only if they considered that the extradited individual faced a bona fide criminal trial, a category that did not extend to Nigerian military tribunals. Moreover, relations between Britain and Nigeria were particularly bad: the British government was unhappy over the coup; Nigeria and Britain were battling for the same shrinking oil market; and the British banks, to whom the largest part of as much as $8 billion in arrears on trade credits was due, were angry at the Nigerian government's refusal to meet IMF conditions for a major loan.[47] Hence, a faction of the Nigerian secret service put in place another plan of repatriating Dikko.

In jail in Nigeria were a number of European businessmen reputed to have participated in some of the looting operations. To secure release, some had offered to cooperate with Nigeria in getting Dikko back. Other European businessmen were reportedly offered priority in settling their claims on the Nigerian government if they assisted.[48] With the aid of the Mossad connections of some of the European businessmen, an Israeli snatch team was assembled.

The bait for Dikko was a phony film company. To increase its credibility, the architects of the scheme tried to get Dikko's old associate, Nessim Goan, to appear for an 'interview,' which was then to be shown to Dikko. Goan refused, but the company asked Dikko for an interview, at which he was drugged and stuffed in a crate labeled 'Diplomatic Luggage' and taken to London airport. There the crate was joined by another, in which the Mossad men were hiding. But the crates were not correctly marked to verify their diplomatic status, and they were opened. Dikko was retrieved and the Mossad men arrested.[49]

Nessim Goan denies that he was privy to the plan or that he agreed to take part in the hope of retrieving some of his overdue debts and thereby saving his Swiss commodity empire. Indeed, accusations against him were met with full-page ads in Nigerian and Swiss newspapers denying his participation, and with the threat of lawsuits against Israeli media.[50] His financial circumstances continued to deteriorate. At one point he turned to Israel for assistance but an application for a $35 million loan was refused.

Perhaps the last victim of the hot-money chain linking Nigeria, London, and Geneva was in Jerusalem. Shortly after the loan was refused, the Tami party pulled out of the governing Israeli coalition, and the Likud government, then headed by Yitzhak Shamir, was forced to call new elections, which ended with Labor leader Shimon Peres installed as prime minister.[51]

Switzerland and World Trade

The Dikko affair was not the first time that Israel's need for a secure petroleum supply had taken it to Switzerland. It was there that oil-poor and arms-rich Israel met oil-rich and arms-poor Iran, then under a Western boycott.

A number of businessmen had tried to cash in on the war in the Persian-Arabian Gulf. One Swiss firm run by Lebanese businessmen allegedly sent Stefano Dalla Chiaie, Italy's most wanted right-wing terrorist, to negotiate an arms deal with Iran's Deputy Prime Minister Sadegh Tabatabai. But President Bani-Sadr blocked the deal before the hostage crisis gave the Iranian mullah-cracy a pretext for unseating him. Also rumored to be in the market was the Freibourg-based Dreikot Trading and Financial Corporation, owned by Hans Kunz. This businessman added to his arms-trafficking business at least one foray into the commerce in refugee financiers. For, when Roberto Calvi made his escape from Italy bearing a falsified passport, it was Hans Kunz who was credited with arranging the trip.[53]

In 1980 representatives of the Israeli and Iranian governments had met in Paris to work out a deal. The US had embargoed arms shipments to Iran, which desperately needed parts and ammunition to keep its American-supplied military machine in operation. Israel agreed to supply the American equipment in return for Iran's facilitating the emigration of Iranian Jews. As cover, the Israeli arms were to be reclassified as 'surplus' and sold off to Swiss intermediaries. As all this was negotiated while the American hostages were still captive in their Tehran embassy, the CIA pressured Israel to delay the first deliveries until the hostages were released.[54]

Israel was to get cheap oil from Iran in exchange for weapons: the oil fueled Israel's invasion of Lebanon in June 1982, and the weapons helped Iran's major assault on Iraq one month later. Profiting at both ends were the various Swiss intermediaries, which allegedly bought Iranian oil at $22 a barrel and resold it at $27, as well as brokering the movement of weaponry. They also helped to create yet another client for the machinery of peekaboo finance. After the destruction of the PLO infrastructure in Lebanon – its factories, banks, media, and assorted other businesses – the organization followed the lead of many govern-ments and businesses and shifted from fixed investments to short-term money-market assets, whose existence could be protected by the corporate and banking secrecy laws provided by peekaboo finance centers.[55]

However, Iranian experiences in the Swiss arms market do not appear to have been entirely happy. In May 1983 a Swiss prosecutor charged that Swiss arms peddlers had swindled Sadegh Tabatabai of the advance paid on fifty American tanks. The tanks never arrived, and 30 million Swiss francs disappeared to Luxembourg, never to return.[56]

Swiss law actually forbids the sale of arms to any country at war or located in a troubled area. So seriously do the Swiss take that law that during the summer of 1984 the Swiss government apparently entered the trade, selling planes flown to Iran by pilots of the Swiss air force. Switzerland claims the planes were trainers and therefore not 'war materiel.' Converting the trainers to war planes required reference to a detailed conversion manual, which the Swiss included in the terms of sale.[57]

To be fair, Switzerland was not alone in clandestine arms sales to Iran, public or private. Sweden shared Switzerland's commitment to remain neutral in the Gulf war. Thus, while the late Swedish prime minister, Olaf Palme, was part of a UN-sponsored effort to mediate the conflict, Sweden's number-one arms producer, Bofors, was selling weaponry to both sides.[58]

Also benefiting from Swiss facilities to assure that despite politics the business of business remains business was South Africa's ARMSCOR. Seeking weaponry for the war against Angolan-based insurgents, it obtained American, British, and West German parts through a British front company. When British customs caught on in 1980, ARMSCOR ran the traffic through Switzerland's Sweizerrische Industrie-Gesellschaft for the next four years.[59] In a similar spirit, when the Reverend Sun Myung Moon decided that Germany, like Korea, was a country rent asunder by the machinations of the Communist Satan, it was through a Zurich holding company that the Moonies moved Japanese money en route to taking control of major industrial assets in the West German arms industry.

South Africa also followed Israel's lead in exploring for oil in Switzerland. The nuisance of an OPEC embargo against South Africa provided an opportunity for the Lebanese-American owner of a Liberian-registered oil tanker, the *Salem*, to turn a dollar or two from an honest day's work off the west coast of Africa. A load of Kuwaiti oil ostensibly for a European destination was secretly unloaded in South Africa. The ship then proceeded up the coast, where it had an 'accident.' After the ship's crew had ample time to change into street clothes and stow their possessions into lifeboats, a distress signal was sent. The ship sank on schedule, and the $43.5 million received for the oil also disappeared, refined through a network of Swiss and Italian bank accounts.[60]

Trouble on Oiled Waters

The owner of the *Salem* could plead in his own defense that his foresight in offloading the cargo in Durban saved West Africa from ecological catastrophe. But if he did so plead, it failed to impress the American IRS, which charged him with tax fraud. Perhaps it had just had its fill of the fiscal shenanigans of slick traders, particularly if their operations were as oily as those of Switzerland's Marc Rich & Co.[61]

While the world was watching oil-price changes in 1973, a less noticed development was that OPEC countries broke the stranglehold of the major oil companies on marketing. They began negotiating with buyers through commodity traders, who had hitherto stayed out of the oil business. Pioneering the entrée of those traders into oil were two former employees of Philipp Bros. (Phibro), Marc Rich and Pincus Green. Marc Rich became known as 'El Matador,' not because his earliest oil deals were with Spain, but because he gained a reputation for killing bull markets when they did not suit his corporate interest. Within a decade Marc Rich & Co. grew into the world's largest single commodity-trading firm. At its peak, it ran an annual $15 billion worth of commodities through its operations. The profits wandered through a maze of shell companies in the Bahamas, Caymans, Liberia, Panama, Liechtenstein, and elsewhere.[62]

Marc Rich & Co.'s power over commodity markets determined the fate of small countries and large banks. Virtually all Bolivia's mineral exports, except smuggled gold, passed through the company's hands; and in 1981 Marc Rich & Co. joined with Marc Rich's personal friend Abdul Ramhin Aki, head of the Malaysian state tin monopoly, in an effort to rig the world's tin market by stockpiling the output, financed by Bank Bumiputra. The scheme worked briefly. However, the US government released its strategic stockpile and the bottom fell out of the market, sending Marc Rich & Co. for a $60 million loop and ravaging the earnings of Bank Bumiputra, on the eve of the Hong Kong property-market debacle.[63]

Commodity trading is a highly secretive business, and the skilled traders weave their way through an obstacle course of exchange controls, blockades, embargoes, and unfriendly taxation structures. But Marc Rich & Co. was undeterred. Maintaining the neutrality of the marketplace, they sold Saudi Arabian oil to Israel, Soviet oil to Western Europe, and Nigerian oil to South Africa. The exposure of that last deal caused considerable corporate discomfort, until a payment of $1 million was allegedly made to Alhaji Umaru Dikko (with whom they also traded rice) to settle the issue.[64] However, problems with the American government were not so easy to settle.

Marc Rich & Co. was essentially an American operation, but it kept its official headquarters in the tiny Swiss town of Zug. There Marc Rich & Co. was a pillar of the fiscal community, paying $12 million per annum in taxes. The tax collectors of Zug were happy: those of America were not.

After the oil-price hike of 1973, a window of opportunity opened. Firms could sell oil from old wells, which had been profitable at pre-1973 prices, at the new prices. To prevent such sales, the US government set price ceilings on old oil. But according to charges filed by the US government against Marc Rich & Co., the company acquired oil from old price-controlled wells, passed it through a daisy chain of intermediate 'sales' to hide its origin, and then resurfaced it falsely labeled as new oil, which could then be sold at world market price. During the Iranian hostage crisis and the American embargo on trading with Iran, Marc Rich purchased Iranian oil, passed it through subsidiaries marketing Nigerian, Algerian, and Peruvian oil, and sold it to desperate American refiners for several dollars per barrel above the already skyrocketing spot price. Part of the payment for the Iranian oil was allegedly made in arms.

The alleged 'fraud' label posed an additional problem. In order to funnel the profits to its Swiss headquarters, Marc Rich reportedly would buy tanker loads of crude oil from its own Swiss parent and resell them at a much lower price to the American affiliate, 'losing' tens of millions of dollars on the deals. According to the US government, the result was the largest American tax fraud to date.

As the American government leveled charges against it, Marc Rich & Co. tried to delay a grand jury investigation long enough to liquidate American assets, to prevent their seizure by the American government. Before the US authorities froze liquidations, many millions were funneled out via the Cayman Islands and the Bahamas. Yet another defensive action involved securing a loan from the Rothschild's Bank in Zurich. The loan was collateralized by a mortgage on a company tanker, the lien preventing the US from seizing the tanker in partial compensation for the tax arrears.[65] And Marc Rich renounced his US citizenship for that of Spain, whose extradition treaty with the US prohibited the extradition of a Spanish citizen who has committed a crime in another country before becoming Spanish. (Pinky Green chose Bolivian citizenship for much the same reason.) In the meantime, the best Swiss resources were mobilized to block the American investigation and to defend Swiss secrecy laws.[66]

In Switzerland, tax evasion is not a crime. Tax fraud is, but it is virtually impossible to prove, particularly as laws block the release of the necessary documents. The US tried to force Marc Rich & Co. to release information pertinent to the case by imposing fines of $50,000 a day. But the Swiss authorities seized documents from the company to prevent them from falling into American hands; just by happy chance, this gave Marc Rich an alibi for failing to comply with the US court's order. According to the Swiss authorities, its actions were taken under Swiss laws forbidding economic espionage and defending corporate secrecy. They denounced the US for trying to encroach on Swiss sovereignty, and formally refused to approve the extradition of Marc Rich.[67]

Marc Rich did not come out entirely unscathed from the affair, for the US government and the company struck a deal: the company would plead guilty and pay the US government close to $200 million (with legal and other costs, the deal may have set the firm back $350 million). The personal indictments against Rich and Green, potentially adding up to three centuries in jail for each of them, would remain in force. However, the US government would unfreeze the assets. Marc Rich & Co. could then reopen, and the business secrets that had generated enough profit to permit the company to survive such a massive penalty would remain safe with the partners – in Switzerland.[68]

16

Good Neighbor Switzerland

By the time of the Marc Rich affair, many sets of inquiring eyes were focused on Switzerland, for its role as a refuge for fugitive American financiers, or at least for their money, was based on long experience with its European neighbors, particularly those that could least afford it.

Preying on the Italian Miracle

Italian money began moving to Switzerland well before the First World War. In the 1920s Swiss banks established branches in the south of Switzerland specifically to service Italian flight capital. During and after the Second World War the Swiss business in Italian flight capital was aided by a special partner. That partner's relationship to Switzerland is graphically symbolized by the last remaining contingent of those famous mercenaries that once dominated the gun-for-hire business in Europe: the Swiss Guards at Vatican City.[1]

The Istituto per le Opere di Religione (IOR) had been conceived as an instrument for mobilizing the surplus cash of church organizations around the world, and for rendering the church and its subsidiaries free of external brokers and bankers. But by the time of its actual creation, the IOR had another function.

The danger of an Allied victory and fears about the potential strength of the Communist party encouraged the movement of assets out of Italy. As church agents could pass freely across most battle lines, some priests, and their banking facilities, reportedly became couriers for the cash and valuables of privileged individuals.[2]

After the war it was business as usual for the Vatican bank, albeit with an expanding group of competitors and partners. The 1950s and 1960s were the era of the Italian economic 'miracle,' to celebrate which Swiss bankers must have been tempted to light votive candles. Apart from intermediating the cash flowing to Argentina and other favored foreign resorts, Swiss banks were the key to loan-back deals. Because interest and dividends earned by 'foreign' investments in Italy were exempt from exchange-control regulations, money could be smuggled out of Italy, deposited in Swiss banks, and then 'borrowed' from the bank, to which tax-deductible 'interest' and tax-free dividend payments could be made without restriction.[3]

Italian exchange-control laws dated back to Mussolini's time, but they were eased slightly in the 1950s and 1960s. As a result, Ticino, the Italian-speaking canton of Switzerland, seemed to boast more banks than pizzerias. Among them was Weisscredit Bank, run until 1977 by Emilio Zoppi, who had been in the fruit and vegetable business: his trucks crossing the border loaded with the bounty of nature provided excellent cover for the bounty of man.[4]

By the time Weisscredit Bank was shut down, three lira devaluations, a sharp drop in foreign-exchange reserves, and the strengthening of the political position of the Communist party had caused an acceleration of the rate at which the rich or their couriers were rowing money across Lake Lugano or hiding the transfers through shady financial deals. In 1976 the Italian government tightened controls, made the banks responsible for phony invoicing, and declared unauthorized capital export a criminal offense. The main result was increased 'discretion' by Swiss bankers handling Italian accounts.[5]

The most important technique for discreet transfers, apart from the simple cash courier, was the fiduciary contract. It cannot be entirely coincidental that during the 1970s, when there was an apparently tremendous increase in volume and value of global white-collar crime, the fastest-growing item in the Swiss banks' balance sheets was the fiduciary deposit.[6] For example, Michele Sindona's Banca Privata Finanziaria in Milan would transfer a customer's funds to Switzerland, recording the transfer as a normal interbank deposit, and naming itself as owner of the funds. In the meantime, a secret agreement would have been concluded with the recipient Swiss bank – perhaps Sindona's own Finabank of Geneva, which was acquired from the IOR for just such purposes, or the IOR's Banco di Roma per la Svizzera – under the terms of which the Swiss bank would lend the funds to the real owner, relieving it of any obligation to repay the 'interbank' deposit to BPF.[7] En route, Sindona would divert some of the money for his own purposes, and the IOR, when participating, could skim some off the top. Since the entire transaction was illegal, the client was in no position to object.

Such capital-flight activity grew sufficiently that by the time of the Ambrosiano collapse the IOR was accused of earning $100 million a year through charging 10% of the principal shifted out of Italy on behalf of wealthy Italian individuals and corporations in violation of Italian exchange controls.[8]

The IOR was certainly not alone in working the capital-flight business out of Italy to Switzerland during the Italian economic miracle. By the late 1960s, the single most important illegal-currency exporter may have been Bernie Cornfeld's IOS. One of its former managers later estimated that IOS conducted $20-to-$30 million in illegal Italian sales each month, of which half were strictly cash. After establishing its close relationship with Tibor Rosenbaum's Banque de Crédit Internationale in Geneva, IOS operated through banks in Chiasso, a town said to be in the flight-capital business the way Detroit is in automobiles.

In Chiasso, the main partner of the IOS was Finter Bank. Long active in flight-capital trade and the subject of a 1960 scandal, Finter Bank fell into the financial orbit of Carlo Pesenti in 1967. Pesenti, one of the deans of Italian Catholic finance, teamed up his new bank with Cornfeld's IOS to revive the flight-capital business.[9] Their success can be indirectly indicated by the estimate that, between 1964 and 1974, capital flight out of Italy via the Lugano area may have totaled $15 billion.

The problem of tax evasion and capital flight did not die with IOS, for Bernie Cornfeld had democratized his old dream, lighting the way for others interested in bringing flight capitalism to the 'people.' One interested party was Ernst Kuhrmeier, the manager of the Chiasso branch of Crédit Suisse, who built it into the institution's most profitable arm. Traditionally, Swiss banks in the area relied on Italian banks for client referrals; but Kuhrmeier and his associates would go to Italy to solicit flight capital. Normally, too, Italian money, unlike that from developing countries, goes to Switzerland for exchange speculation and tax evasion. The Swiss bank then reinvests it in Italy – at the clients' risk. Kuhrmeier and his associates went one better. They offered a Crédit Suisse guarantee to depositors, channeled the money into a Liechtenstein *anstalt*, and reinvested it on their own behalf inside Italy.

The problem they faced was the same one that subsequently wrecked the schemes of Roberto Calvi. With capital flight and tax evasion occurring on a massive scale, the lira depreciated with respect to harder currencies. Kuhrmeier faced Swiss-franc deposit obligations with assets denominated in depreciating lire. The only way to cover the drain was to solicit more flight money – some two billion Swiss francs' worth, in the final analysis – and to add to it a credit line he gave himself from the parent bank. Finally, in 1977, his Ponzi game collapsed in one of Switzerland's biggest bank scandals.[10]

Italy was well aware of its vulnerability to capital flight and the tax evasion that often accompanied it, and of the associated damage to both the lira and public finances. Preventing such violations was the duty of the Guardia di Finanza. Being head of the Financial Guard was therefore an important responsibility, and candidates had to be carefully screened. On a recommendation from Cardinal Ugo Poletti of Rome, Giulio Andreotti, prime minister and confidant of Licio Gelli, appointed as head of the Financial Guard General Raffaele Giudice, whose name figured on the list of P-2 members later unearthed in Gelli's office.[11]

Giudice, Gelli, and Sindona then worked out a cute scheme. In Italy, oil used for heating is taxed at only 2% of the rate at which the same oil is taxed if used as diesel fuel. Allegedly with massive complicity by businesses and tax officials, Giudice fiddled the papers to get oil sold in service stations reclassified as heating oil. The difference between the tax paid by motorists and the tax eventually paid to the Italian state was shipped off to the IOR, for transfer to Sindona's Finabank in Geneva. When the scam was finally exposed, it was estimated to have cost the Italian government between $200 million and $2.2 billion in lost taxes. Giudice was eventually sentenced to seven years in jail; and in 1983 two priests were arrested and charged with accepting bribes to help arrange the transfer of funds via the IOR. Several other Vatican officials, including Archbishop Marcinkus and two members of parliament, were put under investigation.[12]

Considerably aided by the proximity of Switzerland, tax evasion by all levels of society became an Italian national sport. By 1984, with the budget deficit ballooning and the IMF stepping up its pressure, the Italian authorities decided that it was time to crack down. Although wage and salary earners had little or no opportunity to evade taxes, which were deducted at source, Italy's 900,000 shops and 1,000,000 self-employed artisans were notoriously reluctant to declare their incomes. The government responded by a bill permitting tax collectors to base assessments on estimated profits, which provoked a series of protest strikes. Very rich evaders, however, were held to have a stronger sense of civic pride. For a time, the Finance Department published the names of prominent tax evaders in newspapers in an attempt to shame them into paying up. But the only beneficiaries turned out to be those elements in Italian organized crime specializing in high-level kidnapping, so the campaign was abandoned.[13]

Kidnapping wealthy Italians is actually a well-organized part of the Mafia money cycle. Kidnappings yield ransom money, but usually in marked bills. These can be taken to the casinos in the north of Italy, near the Swiss border, and converted into chips. The chips can then be cashed, and the marked bills end up in the hands of some unsuspecting tourist. The unmarked money, after being thoroughly washed through Switzerland, can become seed money for heroin deals; the heroin deals in turn might fund arms for export, causing yet more hot money to flow from the recipient countries to Switzerland.[14]

Swiss Banks Are Bullish on Spain

Hot-money flows from Western European countries other than Italy graced the balance sheets of the Swiss banks in the postwar period. Switzerland was also a favored resting place for the treasure troves of Spaniards fleeing taxes, evading exchange controls, and anticipating adverse changes in the political environment.[15] Although London was his first retreat, and Frankfurt the place where he fought extradition back to Spain, it was through Zurich that José Maria Ruiz Mateos wove himself a social safety net abroad.[16] And it was through Switzerland that a group of high-society people conducted the capital-flight scam for which they were arrested early in 1985.[17]

When the various pieces of the RUMASA empire were put on the auction block, among them was a New York commercial company. An anonymous bid for the company caught the eye, and subsequently the ear, of the Brigada de Delitos Monetarios, who were tapping the phone of Francisco Javier Palazon. Until 1981 Palazon had been Spanish consul in Geneva. Subsequently, while still retaining diplomatic status, he became a consultant to Equitas S.A., an investment company affiliated with the Rothschild's bank, through which he began managing clients' portfolios. His new career was ideally timed to cash in on the Red Scare that swept Spanish hot-money markets in 1982 and 1983 before and after the Socialist victory. When his flight-capital ring was broken, about forty-two people, including seventeen diplomats, were arrested (although only seven were ultimately convicted).

The money moved in two ways. The first was the traditional suitcases carried by couriers protected by diplomatic passports. The second was through a string of companies Palazon ran in Spain: filmmaking, real estate, agribusiness, import-export, and Catalonian casinos. Clients in Spain would 'invest' in his companies, and the money would reappear in Swiss accounts under his management. Clients earning hard currency outside Spain would turn it over to Palazon in Geneva and collect the tax-free pesetas inside Spain. But some of the money making its way to Palazon in Geneva would be allegedly recycled back to Spain, without the clients' permission, to expand Palazon's business holdings there. More money was allocated to businesses owned by Palazon and his clients in the Dominican Republic, Argentina, and elsewhere in Latin America.

The sums involved in Palazon's traffic were not very great – some 10% of the total capital flight *detected* in 1984. His operation paled beside that of the Costa Rican consul in Barcelona. The consul had been merrily pumping the spare tire of a Renault 30 full of large-denomination bank notes with such zeal that when he bolted to Switzerland, some forty Catalonians, mainly businessmen, were collectively charged with smuggling out 23 billion pesetas. But the Palazon affair was more dramatic, in that it involved several diplomats, including the first secretary of the Spanish embassy at the Vatican and a number of noblemen close to the royal family. And it culminated in Palazon's jumping bail and joining the long line of Spanish flight capitalists applying the principle of *toma el dinero y corre*.[18]

The Palazon affair came hard on the heels of a heated debate over the future of hot money. Spanish government efforts to ban secret bank accounts were met by bankers' protesting that such a move would simply cause more hot money to bolt for distant havens. Their opinion was not entirely ingenuous; a Finance Ministry official put his finger squarely on the fundamental rationale for bankers' pursuing hot money all over the globe: 'It is clear,' he said, 'that the banking community earns good money with black money, which is also very stable because it has few opportunities for alternative investment.' In the final analysis, the government imposed heavy withholding taxes on bearer bank accounts and bearer bonds, exempting from disclosure requirements and withholding taxes only one type of financial asset – government treasury bills.[19]

Meanwhile, back in Switzerland, a spokesman for the Union de Banques Suisses (UBS), which had handled Palazon's accounts, replied to reporters' probes with typical Swiss stalwartness: 'We do not know if this person has opened accounts for the presumed capital evaders. Even if we knew, we could not tell you because of bank secrecy. The banks have nothing to do with capital flight. It is the private affair of the capital evaders.'[20]

A Sniff of Scandal

The Italian and Spanish governments were not alone in their dim view of Swiss 'private affairs.' The largest single source of hot money in Switzerland likely came not from working the loan-back scam out of Italy or the travel agency business out of Spain, or even from selling retirement savings plans to Latin American generalissimos. Rather, it had some connection with the degree to which movements of the Swiss franc on foreign-exchange markets correlated with changes in the political climate inside France.[21]

Proximity and language had long served to make Geneva a natural haven in which well-to-do Frenchmen could hide money from the *fisc*. Even before the French Revolution, Geneva private banks were working a variant of the loan-back: accepting French tax evaders' money and lending it to the French government when it was unable to raise enough taxes to meet its expenditure obligations. Swiss perseverance in that time-honored game reached such scandalous proportions in the 1930s as to prompt the French crackdown that in turn led to the entrenchment of Swiss bank-secrecy provisions.

After the Second World War, France, like Italy, saw tax evasion and capital flight racking its domestic and external finances. In 1954 French probes into the external bank accounts of its citizens led the Swiss government to arrest eleven Swiss bank employees. But by the mid-1950s, under the influence of Finance Minister Antoine Pinay, a fiscal conservative and right-wing pan-Europeanist, France announced an amnesty for black-market money, cutting taxes and opening treasury bonds for no-questions-asked investments.[22] In 1967 France abandoned exchange controls altogether, on the IMF-style theory that where there is no law, there is no crime. But the May 1968 insurrection forced their reimposition.

One estimate put capital flight out of France between May and December 1968 at 4 billion Swiss francs.[23] Three types of capital movements were involved. One was normal fright capital. A second was speculative capital, moving out in anticipation of a devaluation of the French franc. A third was the war chests of political factions, preparing for the day when their disputes would be settled in the streets.[24]

Throughout the next decade the toughened exchange controls taxed, but failed to daunt, the imaginations of French flight capitalists. In a period of political calm, the illicit movement of money out of France was estimated at the equivalent of $1 million a day. The techniques employed varied from simple cash couriers to border-area casinos (an exchange of French cash for chips for Swiss cash); the vehicles included diamonds, precious artworks, rare stamps, and, not least, gold.[25] Indeed, many French and other European citizens who declared to their fiscal authorities that they were en route to Switzerland for 'heart surgery' would likely be found to have hearts of gold.[26]

Among those French citizens making use of secret Swiss accounts was Samuel Flatto-Sharon. When his close friend, the gentleman ruling Dahomey, managed to negotiate the country's first World Bank loan, worth $10 million, they allegedly split the proceeds. Flatto-Sharon, still sporting his Dahomey diplomatic passport, then got involved in Paris real estate. He would organize ghost companies to handle transactions, 'selling' properties from one to another, puffing the value, and therefore the amount of money he could raise on a mortgage loan. Some of the borrowed funds would be used to cover the original purchase cost of the building while the rest would be sent in suitcases to the Banque pour le Commerce Suisse-Israel. The funds would then return to France, or go to Israel, for investment.[27]

The opening of an inquiry in France in 1972 aroused in Flatto-Sharon an urge to visit Israel, thereby avoiding a fifteen-year jail sentence and a $200 million lawsuit by bilked investors. Like Meyer Lansky a few years later, he claimed Israeli citizenship as a 'returned' Jew. Unlike Lansky's, his request was granted. When the French government started extradition proceedings, Herut party leader Menachem Begin offered Flatto-Sharon immunity from extradition if he would help fund the party's electoral campaign. In 1977 Flatto-Sharon assumed a place of honor among that party's members of the Knesset, sponsoring a bill prohibiting the extradition of Jews, and promising to put his financial genius to work solving Israel's pressing financial problems. And in 1982, shortly after Israeli bombs, artillery shells, and rockets had reduced much of West Beirut to rubble, Flatto-Sharon turned up in occupied Lebanon to promote a bank to handle Israeli-Lebanese commerce. Alas, Flatto-Sharon subsequently lost his seat in the Knesset, was found guilty of electoral fraud,[28] and then found himself an inadvertent victim of the Ambrosiano affair.

When, in the late 1970s, Michele Sindona was in the US fretting over how to get needed money to fight Italian extradition efforts, he turned to Luigi Cavallo, confidant of various secret services and publisher of a news sheet specializing in sensational and politically inconvenient disclosures. Together they launched a blackmail campaign against Roberto Calvi, airing his various misdeeds in public posters and print until he agreed to make heavy protection payments to Sindona. Unfortunately Cavallo had underestimated the power of the press, including his own, and his revelations brought snooping inspectors from the Bank of Italy, who eventually landed Calvi in jail, charged with violation of exchange-control laws.[29] Cavallo had moved his headquarters to Paris, but he was arrested by the French authorities in 1984, released, then rearrested late in 1985. The Italians had by then arrested Flatto-Sharon on an Italian visit. All that was missing was a little exercise in international trade. But, alas, after spending a few months in the luxury of an Italian prison – the private room and amenities provided, at a price, by the Mafia – he was released on bail and promptly absconded back to Israel, where he was suitably protected from extradition.[30]

By the time Flatto-Sharon had absconded from France, customs officials were stepping up their snooping into the offshore finances of French citizens. They bribed an employee of the Swiss Bank Corporation to turn over lists of thousands of clients. The ensuing crackdown on tax evasion set off a virtual war between French customs and the Swiss police. Then, in 1980, French customs and police officers raided the department of the Banque de Paris et des Pays Bas that handles private clients' accounts, turning up what French authorities claimed to be evidence of a massive illegal currency-smuggling network. However, it was not until after the victory of the Socialist party in the 1981 presidential elections that charges against Parisbas officials – for arranging the illegal export of $3.2 billion – were pressed.[31] The reluctance of the former government of Valéry Giscard d'Estaing to push ahead on the Parisbas case may well reflect that, with the government's approval, ELF-Aquitaine, the French state oil company, had been using secret Swiss bank accounts to pour funds into the hands of the promoters of the notorious *avion renifleur*.[32]

The story of the sniffer airplane begins in 1965 with a Belgian count (Comte Allain de Villegas) and an Italian TV repairman-turned-self-proclaimed nuclear physicist (Aldo Bonassoli).[33] Both 'scientists' had a passionate belief in alchemy and UFOs, and they established a Geneva-based company to finance 'scientific discoveries.' Their first project was to develop desalination technology, which made Geneva a natural place for their headquarters. (The Swiss association with oceangoing enterprises is well-known, and informed observers never fail to be amazed at what can wash up in Switzerland from far offshore, begging to be salted away in that Alpine redoubt.)

The failure of the desalination scheme led logically to their next one. If they could not get the salt out of water, the next best thing was to find new sources of fresh water through a device that could 'sniff' underground reservoirs. It was at this point that their paths crossed that of Jean Violet.[34]

Violet's political formation came in the 1930s in le Comité secret pour l'action révolutionnaire (CSAR). A far-right political cult modeled on a Freemasonic movement, complete with Masonic-style rites and rituals (although committed to ridding France of the left-wing subversion the bona fide Freemasons allegedly represented), CSAR was a sort of French predecessor of Licio Gelli's P-2. It was intensely secretive in all but its admiration of Franco and Mussolini, and after the war some of its members were accused of being Nazi collaborators. In the 1950s, with his own record pronounced clean, Violet became a close collaborator of French intelligence, and an active supporter of Opus Dei. He was also the central figure in a rightist political grouping, linked to various intelligence agencies, whose inspiration was the right-wing pan-Euro-peanism of Antoine Pinay. In fact, Violet's objectives in teaming up with the two 'scientists' may well have to do with the need to find funding for clandestine political action.[35]

Violet's Vatican connections gave the inventors the financial backing they required to proceed with their experiments. The first stop was Spain, where Opus Dei supporters in the Franco government assured official aid for the project. Financial backing also came from another Vatican-linked source.

The foundations of Carlo Pesenti's business empire were set in concrete by an uncle who was close to Mussolini. He thereby secured privileged treatment in the export of cement to Italian-conquered Ethiopia. At the end of the war, Carlo tried to clean up the family firm's image; and under his direction, and with the spiritual and material support of the Vatican and the Christian Democratic party, the firm became a financial empire involved in banking, insurance, newspapers, and a host of other enterprises. However, it was the cement, and, more specifically, the need to assure fresh water supplies for its manufacture, that permitted his friend and legal adviser, Jean Violet, to arouse Carlo Pesenti's interest in the sniffer airplane.

Pesenti's financial involvement with the inventors appears to have been episodic, perhaps because his empire was already on the skids. It was Pesenti's financial holding company, Italmobiliare, and more specifically its finance and insurance subsidiary, Bastogi I.R.B.S. S.p.A., that Michele Sindona had targeted for takeover in the early 1970s, when he was trying to fulfill his ambition of becoming financial overlord of Italy. Pesenti rescued his firm from Sindona with the aid of another prominent Catholic financier, Philippe de Weck, chief of the Union de Banques Suisses. But Italmobiliare emerged from the fray considerably weakened, forced to sell off assets, including a string of banks, and dependent on the IOR and subsequently on Banco Ambrosiano for infusions of funds to keep it alive.

Alas for inventors and investors alike, no water was found: but that dampened the enthusiasm only of Carlo Pesenti, who by then was more concerned with the water in his stock than the lack of it in his cement. For the others the failure simply whetted their appetites for further discoveries. In the tradition of the medieval alchemists, the team of inventors set out to convert a base material, namely water, into black gold. The supposition was that if the sniffer device could not smell water, perhaps it could smell oil.[36]

The international situation was certainly favorable. Synchronizing the launching of the new scheme with the oil-price revolution of 1973,

the syndicate attracted other associates. Among them was the government of South Africa, whom Jean Violet and friends regarded as a bulwark
of Western Christian civilization. South Africa needed oil self-sufficiency
as insurance against the embargo orchestrated by the heathen hordes
into whose hands the world's energy lifeline had fallen. However, early
experiments with the sniffer device failed, and the South Africans lost
interest. No matter, for Jean Violet had even more distinguished and
generous patrons to take their place.

For the government of France in general, and the French state oil
company ELF-Aquitaine in particular, the project held out many attractions – if it worked. ELF-Aquitaine could secure sources of crude oil of
the sort lost after the Algerian Revolution, making it a major world
supplier, and the invention would put it at the forefront of world
petroleum technology. France itself would be relieved of the dollar drain
of paying for imported oil if sources could be found either domestically
or in France's African tributaries. Furthermore, incumbent President
Valéry Giscard d'Estaing was close to Violet's political and Opus Dei
circles. Violet was also well connected with French intelligence, which
in turn had influence with ELF-Aquitaine.[37]

With the president himself giving the clearance for ELF-Aquitaine
to ignore normal government accounting procedures and exchange
controls, it pumped hundreds of millions of Swiss francs into the project.
Under the supervision of the inventors' financial agent, UBS chief Philippe
de Weck, the funds earmarked for payments to various Italian 'creditors'
were allegedly funneled via a Zurich company called Ultrafin, owned
by Milan's Banco Ambrosiano.

Interestingly, Philippe de Weck was one of four Catholic experts
that the Vatican later called on to report on the IOR's involvement with
the Calvi catastrophe, and to devise reasons why the Vatican should
not share the resulting costs. That task he undertook with distinction;
but when the French government asked him to explain his sniffer airplane
financial maneuvers that made so much French taxpayer money disappear, he declined – good Swiss banker that he was – to violate client
confidentiality.

The sniffer enterprise was a complete fiasco – a fact that may have
had some influence on the 1981 crash of the Opus-Dei-influenced Banco
Occidental in Spain. French President Giscard d'Estaing managed a cover-
up, in which his successor, François Mitterrand, cooperated. But late
in 1983 a tax-department clerk, investigating the route by which 800
million French francs had left the country (340 million without a trace),
inadvertently blew their cover. By then, however, the French government
had more important things on its mind.

France, an Endangered Sovereign Debtor?

By the time the sniffer airplane scandal broke, the financial environment around the new French government had drastically deteriorated.[38] The balance-of-payments deficit soared; and between the election of the Mitterrand government in 1981 and the summer of 1984, the French foreign debt tripled to about $80 billion. The conventional explanation for the increase went as follows: the government tried to keep its campaign promises to reflate the economy and to nationalize certain industries. The result was to drive up the budget deficit and to price French goods out of world markets, while the additional purchasing power caused imports to rise sharply. The government therefore had to borrow heavily to cover the twin deficits.

All this is standard IMF cant, which neatly sidesteps most of the important issues – namely, the need to replace capital stripped from the nationalized industries by their former owners; the usurious levels to which interest rates on existing debt were driven by factors outside the French government's control; the impact of the rising US dollar in pushing up the French-franc cost of purchasing oil; the effect of the debt crisis in drying up markets for French goods, especially arms, among developing countries. And there were two more deep-seated reasons for the deterioration of French finances.

One was the fact that, precisely when the French oil and debt-service bills were shooting up, France's international assets were depreciating. During the 1960s and 1970s French credits abroad were largely denominated in French francs and tied to the purchase of French goods. But as the dollar gradually replaced the franc in international exchanges, and even in dealings between France and its former colonies, French exporters and official aid agencies found themselves borrowing dollars in order to lend dollars to the ultimate purchasers of French goods.

Moreover, developing countries started asking for credits, not merely to cover the cost of purchases, but also to provide funding to cover the local cost of working up French goods into final form or to make capital equipment operational. Then they added demands for general balance-of-payments support as part of the package. By the 1980s, for every $100 worth of French goods being exported to some developing countries, France was providing $250 in financing, borrowed on the euromarket. The more France exported, the deeper in debt it got. Furthermore, the French euromarket debt began rising in cost just as France's developing-country customers were falling behind on their payments to France.[39]

A second fundamental cause of the deterioration of the finances was the increased productivity of the Swiss bankers and their French associates.

There had long been professional agents who handled illegal transfers of money across the border to Switzerland. The volume of their business varied with the perceived probability of incumbent governments increasing income taxes. When the Socialist-Communist party coalition won the 1981 elections, capital flight naturally accelerated, as wealthy Frenchmen anticipated tax increases to pay for nationalization of industry and banks and for improved social services. That, in turn, led to tighter border security and closer administration of exchange controls, which produced more crooked accountants who would falsify invoices in order to move the money.[40]

Capital flight was also exacerbated by the international political climate. The US and France engaged in their bitterest public quarrels, political and economic, since De Gaulle had attempted to stop the US from passing on to the rest of the world the costs of the Vietnam War. However, this time most of the aces were in the American hand.[41]

In late 1981 the French external financial position took a sharp turn for the worse; and in 1982 a major crisis forced the first of three devaluations and the need for emergency borrowing to cover the gap. The fiscal deficit also continued to climb, despite the success of the Socialist-party government in settling at least one outstanding political score.

Among those political forces inclined to see red at the prospect of a victory for the Socialist-Communist coalition was the local affiliate of the Unification Church International. For many years Moon had put his French resources at the disposal of the political right, in return for which the governments serving President Valéry Giscard d'Estaing had given Moonie operations a fiscal whitewash. With Mitterrand's victory in 1981, the Moonies quickly tried to render themselves less conspicuous. But early in June 1982 the new government struck, with a massive police sweep of Moonie establishments. Arrests followed, and in 1985 the sect was presented with a bill for unpaid taxes totalling Fr 35.5 million.

Despite this happy windfall, French finances remained in a perilous condition. The devaluations and austerity simply fed the flight of funds. As capital fled faster, pressure was mounted on the government to sell off some of its gold. In the spring of 1983 an austerity package, shocking in its unexpected severity, was unveiled; massive demonstrations followed. Despite the austerity and the success of the government in halving the 1983 trade-balance deficit, more hot money beat a retreat to Geneva. This forced yet more emergency borrowing, sufficient to cause another major hike in the French external-debt load.[42] Then came another twist in the capital-flight business.

Most flight capital operations revolve around one or a few bank accounts; but Pierre Moussa, head of Parisbas, managed – quite legally – to make an entire bank vanish. As the Mitterrand government nationalized those parts of the French banking system not already in state hands, Pierre Moussa, Canada's Power Corporation, and Schlumberger of Luxembourg decided to pull off a Roberto Calvi-type operation. They created a Luxembourg ghost company, to which was transferred control of Parisbas Suisse, which held large blocks of shares in Power Corporation, in Schlumberger, and in Sun Hung Kai of Hong Kong. The objective was to keep these assets out of the French government's hands. Though the ploy was perfectly legal, the Mitterrand government was furious and, in revenge, prosecuted Parisbas officials for the 1981 illegal capital export.[43]

While the trial was in progress, French customs continued the crackdown. In 1983 they uncovered a list of 5,000 French citizens using the Union de Banques Suisses to evade taxes. Shortly afterward, two employees of that bank were arrested by the Swiss government on suspicion of having disclosed the client lists to the French authorities. The next year French customs broke a computer code, spreading panic among an estimated 50,000 holders of secret accounts. The result of all these moves was to cause capital flight to fall somewhat; to a degree it even went into reverse, as heavier wealth taxes forced some rich Frenchmen to bring cash back from Switzerland.[44]

But that was about as far as the crackdown went. Early in 1984 Pierre Moussa was acquitted, although several officials and clients of the bank were not.[45] French government finances deteriorated further, and its gross debt jumped another 17% in 1984. For the 1985–86 fiscal year, the French government was forced to impose yet harsher austerity measures, including the most severe cuts in public expenditure since the Second World War.[46] And yet another scandal revealed just how difficult – and dangerous – following the trail of hot money could be.

All in the Family?

With the right staging a strong comeback, and demanding denationalization and an amnesty on black money, the political handwriting was already on the wall for Socialist Prime Minister Laurent Fabius when, late in 1985, his close friend, lawyer Jacques Perrot, was murdered. At least one person besides the murderer had anticipated the event: a few days before his death Perrot had told friends, 'If I have an accident, have an autopsy done.'[47]

The motive seemed obscure. Perrot was not a political activist. Nor was robbery an apparent motive. Perhaps the murder had to do with his activities as an intermediary between the French government and companies facing problems with the fisc. Perhaps it had to do with his passion for gambling on the horses. But perhaps one police investigator was right in suggesting that the trail might lead into the inner sanctum of the P-2.[48]

L'affaire Boutboul began innocently enough. Perrot and his estranged wife, famed jockey Darie Boutboul, were engaged in a custody battle over their son that set Perrot off on a search of the family background of his spouse. Two shocks quickly followed. The first was that his wife's father, who had allegedly died in a plane crash, was alive and well and living in Paris. The second was that his mother-in-law, a rich business-woman, Elizabeth Cons-Boutboul, had been a lawyer, but was disbarred in 1981. According to her ex-husband, the story about the plane crash was to prevent their divorce causing Elizabeth Cons-Boutboul embar-rassment with one of her major clients.

The story of that client began in Hong Kong in 1920, when a French banker resident in Hong Kong died. His family asked Father Robert, local head of Missions étrangères de Paris, to take care of settling the estate. Father Robert reported that there was nothing to settle – it had all been squandered. But in 1968 the heirs took legal action against Missions étrangères, accusing it and Father Robert of having fraudulently diverted the deceased banker's money. Missions étrangères then hired as legal counsel Elizabeth Cons-Boutboul, who allegedly bilked the religious organization of, and siphoned off to Switzerland via Liechten-stein, some 14 million francs during the following years. In 1981 she was disbarred, but Missions étrangères took no action to recover the money. Its explanation – the desire to put an end to a sordid affair – produced general skepticism, not least from Elizabeth Cons-Boutboul, who pointed out that if she really had embezzled the money, Missions étrangères would be unlikely to be so hesitant to try to get it back. It was suggested that a more likely reason was its desire to keep from further legal scrutiny its own financial arrangements, the trail of which appears to have led in some curious directions. It was, perhaps, that trail onto which Jacques Perrot stumbled when investigating the reasons for his mother-in-law's abrupt retirement from her legal career. Certainly Jacques Perrot's enthusiasm about his discovery of his mother-in-law's alleged financial dealings would have been dampened a little if he had consulted her. As Elizabeth Cons-Boutboul subsequently told reporters, 'If Jacques had spoken to me about the dossier, I would have told him – don't touch it. It's dynamite.'

Just why the dossier should have proven sufficiently explosive to detonate several .22 caliber bullets, remains obscure. Perhaps it has something to do with a longstanding curiosity of the French police about the accounts of Missions étrangères. For it seems that, for some time, American Mafia figures had been using the religious organization's international network as a cover for spiriting dirty money out of the US, where international transfers greater than $5,000 required the filing of a report to the government, explaining the reasons for the transfer. With the cooperation of the IOR, the ultimate custodian of surplus funds of all Catholic organizations worldwide, though apparently not with the knowledge of Missions étrangères itself, the mob made 'contributions' to Missions étrangères in the US. The funds were transferred to the IOR's Swiss affiliates and correspondents; and the money was then returned to the mob, less a 3% to 10% cut for the Vatican bank. If this was indeed the twist in the hot-money trail onto which Jacques Perrot had wandered, it might explain why, some time before his death, a former British commando-turned-mercenary-turned-general-hired-gun was approached with a contract on Jacques Perrot's life, which he declined because of the political heat its execution would generate. On the other hand, the connections between the mob and the Missions étrangères were sufficiently old and well known to the authorities as to make them an unlikely motive for the assassination.[49]

Not so old was another possible lead. Jacques Perrot enthusiastically reported to a friend, shortly before his murder, that he was convinced his mother-in-law had been moving money on behalf of Banco Ambrosiano and the P-2. Or perhaps it was, as the right-wing French press speculated, his association with yet another set of experts in the arts of peekaboo finance that brought about his abrupt demise. If so, Jacques Perrot may have been a victim of the same set of strategic considerations that landed France in the malodorous affair of the *avion renifleur*.

At least since the time of Charles De Gaulle French governments have been passionately committed to the preservation of the country's independence in energy. When the Algerian Revolution cost France her absolute security of oil supply, France set off on the search for whatever alternative sources it could 'sniff out' at home and abroad. She also fostered the development of a huge nuclear industry, which in turn fed the growth of France's independent nuclear *force de frappe*, much to the consternation of certain Pacific island paradises, which would periodically become ground zero *pour la gloire de France*. Among those taking exception were the indigenous populations, who demanded independence, and Greenpeace. According to the right-wing press, anxious to further embarrass the government of Laurent Fabius, the hand chartering the sailing ship that carried the French *barbouzes* off to bomb the *Rainbow Warrior* in a New Zealand harbor belonged to Jacques Perrot. And, according to his wife, Perrot had expressed the wish to act as attorney for the French agents arrested and jailed in New Zealand.[50] Whatever the truth, the *Rainbow Warrior* affair delivered an unexpected victory to Opus Dei in its long and bitter struggle against French Freemasonry: it forced the resignation of French defense minister Charles Hernu, the powerful masonic representative in the French cabinet.

Elizabeth Cons-Boutboul's own response to inquiries was that she had no desire to end up suspended under a London bridge. Certainly not, when the alternative was to continue to enjoy the fruits of her French business endeavors in Switzerland, where voters had already given an overwhelming endorsement to their government's efforts to keep their country the world's most genteel laundromat.

Behind the Bank-Secrecy Referendum

Swiss banking is not an entirely risk-free profession, and 1974 was a particularly difficult year. In the wake of *il crack Sindona* and the Bankhaus Herstatt debacle, Geneva's Finabank crumbled. Tibor Rosenbaum's ICB shut down, much to the distress of thousands of rich French Jews who had used the bank to shift the cost of their conscience-money payments to Israel onto the French exchequer. Several other banks also folded. Then, just when the damage seemed to have been repaired, came 1977, an even worse year.

Swiss authorities merely looked on with disdain when banks controlled by foreigners periodically crashed. But it was another matter when peekaboo finance – specifically Ernst Kuhrmeier's antics at the Chiasso branch of Crédit Suisse – nearly brought down that most Swiss of banks. The bank did survive, but Kuhrmeier had blasted a $615 million hole in its books and an almost immeasurable gap in its credibility.

On top of the Chiasso affair and its impact on the flow of Italian flight capital came a disaster in Geneva that wiped out a host of French family fortunes.

Geneva has long been the operational center for those Swiss private banks that specialize in the discreet handling of personal asset portfolios. As late as 1983, nine of Switzerland's twenty-one private banks, half of their partners, and two-thirds of their employees were in Geneva.[51] Until 1977 Geneva had also hosted MM Leclerc & Cie., a private bank whose principal partner, 'Bobby' Leclerc, had a long career in the peekaboo-finance business.

Former French finance minister Antoine Pinay was a man to practice what he preached. After his place in French financial history was established in his amnesty of black-market money, Pinay was installed by Bobby Leclerc in 1969 as president of the Compagnie de Guarantie des Investissements Industriels et Financiers in Geneva, which used Pinay's name to attract French funds.[52] Leclerc also had good relations with finance minister, subsequently president, Valéry Giscard d'Estaing.

Not least important of Leclerc's activities was his role, with Prince Jean de Broglie, cofounder of Giscard's Independent Republican party, in the administration of Sodatex, the Luxembourg-based holding company through which the principals of the notorious MATESA were looting Spanish government subsidy money in the 1960s.

It may have been partly personal greed, but de Broglie seems to have had political motivations for involving himself in the MATESA affair. These may have included using money siphoned out of the Spanish treasury to fund the rise of Giscard's Independent Republican party, which top French Opus Dei figures endorsed.

After the MATESA scandal broke, de Broglie engaged in long negotiations with the Spanish government over the return of the loot. Financial pressures also appear to have involved him with some notorious French white-collar criminals. Then came charges that Sodatex was the center of a huge arms- and drug-dealing operation across the French-Luxembourg border. All this assured that, when de Broglie was gunned down in a Paris street in 1976, the subsequent exposure of links to Sodatex set off a run on Bobby Leclerc's bank.[53]

The liquidity problem itself would likely have been manageable, but Leclerc had been applying the Bernie Cornfeld principle that those who seek secrecy have something to hide. Therefore, between 1970 and 1977, he diverted his French clients' funds from secret accounts in his bank to even more secret accounts elsewhere, and then used the money for real estate and for financing the building of a sports complex. In 1977 the Swiss Federal Banking Commission closed him down after they found a 394 million Swiss franc shortfall in his books.[54]

As if this were not indignity enough, in 1977 the Swiss banks also found themselves embroiled in a scandal deriving from a presidential succession campaign in Mexico.

Until Alberto Sicilia-Falcon was arrested in Tijuana in 1975 and charged with masterminding the most important marijuana and cocaine smuggling operation yet uncovered, he was living in regal splendor. He was also boasting that he had extensive influence in the government, and that many top figures in the Mexican administration and police were on his payroll. One person who was smeared in the aftermath was the presumed successor to President Luis Echeverria, Mario Moya Palencia, Minister of the Interior. In the scandal that followed Sicilia-Falcon's American-sponsored arrest, Moya Palencia, who was sympathetic to Echeverria's policies of restricting American investment and keeping the oil fields closed, was passed over in favor of Lopez Portillo. Two consequences followed: one was the great Mexican oil boom; and the second was the launching by the DEA and IRS of Operation Goldfinger, a worldwide search for Sicilia-Falcon's treasure troves, which some estimates put at $500 million. Under American pressure Switzerland agreed to its first-ever freeze on the assets of a major drug dealer, thereby paving the way for the 1977 general accord between the two governments. In future Switzerland promised cooperation with the US in drug cases, as well as a closer watch on the origins of the funds flowing its way. It was the first major chink in the armor of Swiss bank secrecy, even if it came after Sicilia-Falcon's money had already escaped.[55]

After Chiasso, Leclerc, and Sicilia-Falcon, the Swiss banking community was faced with the task of laundering not routine suitcases of currency but the reputations of Swiss banks. To cover the damage, the bankers concocted a new 'code of conduct' in which they pledged not to actively support capital flight and promised to take a closer look at the identity of clients. With subsequent modifications, the code called for the screening of over-the-counter cash transactions involving more than 50,000 Swiss francs. Furthermore, in future only Swiss-domiciled attorneys, notaries, and so on, would be permitted to vouch for a client without disclosing his identity. And, if this weren't stringent enough, safes would be rented only to clients whom the bank felt to be trustworthy.

With such a tough code of conduct, compliance was to be voluntary; equally voluntary was the payment of fines the Arbitration Commission might levy for infractions. So tightly was the code enforced that in the first eight years of its existence a total of three banks, whose identity had to remain a secret, were fined equally unidentified sums of money. By chance the code was 'tightened' a few months before a general referendum on bank secrecy; and two of the three fines assessed were publicly unveiled just before it.[56]

The 'People's Initiative against the Abuse of Bank Secrecy and Banking Power' was the product of a number of political influences, which the 1977 scandals served to crystallize. For some time certain strata of Swiss society had been embarrassed, morally or financially, by the antics of the bankers. Businessmen complained about the effect of huge capital inflows in pushing up the exchange rate and therefore pricing Swiss products out of world markets. Manufacturers claimed that they were unable to obtain bank loans on tolerable conditions because of the Swiss banks' zeal for international lending activities. Others saw the proliferating rumors about shady deals affecting Switzerland's international reputation. And the Social Democratic party at last found an issue that might help restore its flagging political fortunes.[57]

The bankers mounted a powerful counterstrike, pointing out that the financial sector was producing jobs while the industrial sector was in crisis. (That, if taken to imply causation rather than coincidence, was tantamount to conceding the opposition's case.) According to the bankers' logic, Switzerland was not a flight-capital haven, as most of the foreign deposits in Swiss banks were legal ones. (Under Swiss law, they certainly were.) They cited the rigorous checks on illicit-money flows that already existed as a result of the post-1977 code of conduct. They claimed that the end of bank secrecy would lead to a massive capital outflow (but did not reconcile this contention with their insistence that the vast majority of money in the banks was legal in origin), and this would cause interest rates to soar, the stock market to plummet, and tens of thousands of upright Swiss citizens to lose their jobs, because, unlike Turks or Yugoslavs, they could not be deported whenever the business cycle turned down. The bankers also insisted that the loss of bank secrecy would be the first step in undermining the Swiss social order. (Undoubtedly they were right.)

Of course, no one really expected the referendum to win, not even the Social Democratic party, which endorsed it but whose representatives in the Swiss coalition government, including the finance minister, campaigned against it! Victory in a Swiss popular referendum – a relatively rare occurrence – requires a majority of votes in a majority of cantons. The bankers' campaign was effective and well funded: could it be that profits from washing Mafia money were being employed in a campaign to convince the electorate that the banking system was clean and healthy? The bankers campaigned vigorously, not because they really feared defeat, but because they wanted an overwhelming victory in order to reconfirm Switzerland's commitment to bank secrecy.[58]

The problem was that Switzerland was no longer alone in the peekaboo business. Its competitors were busy denigrating the traditional Swiss virtues of solidity and discretion, and governments were becoming increasingly concerned over tax evasion and flight-capital movements. Furthermore, despite efforts to blunt criticism by agreements to cooperate with the US and other governments in drug-dealing cases, some deputies in the Swiss parliament were arguing that bank secrecy should be waived when requests came in from foreign governments in cases of suspected tax fraud and capital flight. As the reputation of the Swiss banks deteriorated, some former Chase Manhattan employee(s) must have been pleased with his (their) powers of prediction. They would also be gratified by their ex-employer's decision to purchase from the IOR its last Swiss holding, the Banco di Roma per la Svizzera. Certainly some London and New York bankers waited eagerly to 'clean up' from Swiss discomfiture.[59]

A striking victory in the referendum was therefore necessary though not sufficient to turn the tide. Just when the US government was prying the lid off the Cayman Islands, Bahamas, and other peekaboo financial havens, the Swiss banks could not only hope to gain money fleeing other financial havens coming under US scrutiny, but could also use the 73% to 27% victory to fight increasingly strong American pressures being directed at them.

Part Six

The Grim Reaper

17

Economics for the Moral Majority

When a recently elected Ronald Reagan was photographed holding a copy of *News World*, there were two possible interpretations. One was that the Moonie publication had replaced *Reader's Digest* as the president's main source of hard information on the state of the world. The second was that Reagan was engaging in a gesture of solidarity toward fellow believers – not in the divinity of the Reverend Moon, but in the legitimacy of the worship of the golden calf.

To the advocates of 'supply-side' economics, that old-time economic religion preached by the Reaganites, government meddling with the distribution of income undermines the American social fabric, sapping entrepreneurial initiative. Not only are businesses hampered in their efforts to produce more and different goods, not only is the supply of investment funds to the private sector preempted by government borrowing, but also the poor lose their incentive for self-improvement. The key to the rejuvenation of the American economy, and thereby the society, is cutting the burden of taxation that drives the poor onto welfare, the entrepreneur into the underground economy of illicit and nontaxed activity, and the rich into exile in the Bahamas.

The traditional fear that cutting taxes would push the government budget deficit to new and more dangerous heights was brushed aside. The supply-siders replied that the reactivation of the economy generated by a tax cut would produce an increase in total tax receipts that would more than offset the tax-rate cut. Besides, it should force the government to shave spending on nonessential items such as food supplements for the poor, which only encourage the perpetuation of the problem.

However, it is not always easy to turn the water of faith into the wine of hard cash. To the task of morally rearming American enterprise with the largest tax cut in American history, the Reaganites joined the necessity of combating the Bolshevik Menace through a jump in military spending. The joint result was a ballooning government budget deficit. Soon the fiscal position was haunted by the specter of $200 billion per annum deficits stretching as far as the eye could see, prompting a scramble to find a means of financing them.

What's Good for General Dynamics Is Good for the USA

By the 1980s secular growth of the military component of the budget seemed an inevitability,[1] given the political forces demanding it. Industry lobby groups were reinforced by the ever-growing tendency of military officers and Pentagon officials to retire into industrial careers, not least in defense contracting.[2] Furthermore, pork-barrel politics had invaded the 'defense' industries with a vengeance. Congress has been accused of forcing extra spending on the Pentagon, converting it into a massive public-works program.[3] But no one in Congress forced the Pentagon deliberately to overestimate the impact of inflation on its costs, and then to refuse to readjust the numbers downward. (Between 1980 and 1984 the Pentagon got an extra $35 billion to play with.[4]) Hence, when the uproar over Pentagon waste forced the Reagan administration to freeze the 1986 military budget at the 1985 level with a cost-of-living adjustment[5] (a trifle denied social security recipients), someone in the Pentagon hierarchy probably had difficulty suppressing a smile.

During the Reagan-era expansion of the military budget – $300 billion by 1985 – political contributions by the twenty largest US defense-contracting firms doubled. During the same period, these firms managed to increase their share of defense contracts by 150%.[6] The concentration of contracting in a few favored giants also increased their dependence (measured by their ratio of defense to nondefense-sector sales) on the federal government. Not surprisingly, those military-industrial behemoths showed consistently higher profit rates than other sectors of American industry. They were awash with cash when nonmilitary companies were penurious, and had substantially better stock-market performance. After the 1981 military spending expansion, firms engaged in both military and civilian business found their profit rates higher on the military component, a reversal of the situation during the 1970s.[7]

And why not, with payroll padding, secret swapping of classified documents obtained by sleuths hired to penetrate the Pentagon, rigging bids, charging $640 for a toilet seat, and billing for Halloween parties to boost 'employee morale.' So intensely was the game played that, by early 1985, 45 of 100 of the largest military manufacturers in the US were under criminal investigation. The military consequences seemed summed up in one of the air force's new air-to-ground missiles. It proved lethal to telephone poles but had a disquieting tendency to ignore the targeted tanks.[8]

However much the Pentagon pork barrel spread corruption into American public life, and spearheaded a general debasement of corporate practice,[9] the budget deficit it exacerbated was not *per se* a major economic problem. As a percentage of GNP, the US deficit was not far out of line with general Western experience; and the rise in the public-sector deficit was actually one of the main reasons the US began to climb out of a deep recession in 1983. Moreover, when a sensible view was taken of public-sector accounting, with government debt offset against public-sector assets, the US government still came out with a substantial positive net worth.[10]

However, such rationalizations for a deficit were politically unacceptable to the Reaganites. And no matter how much economic stimulus the deficit might produce, there was certainly a problem financing it. This was true partly because (contrary to supply-side rhetoric) by 1985 the US personal savings rate had plunged to about half its normal level, partly because periodic increases in the interest charges on the public debt wiped out savings achieved by chopping social expenditures, and partly because financing the budget deficit interacted with concern about the American balance of payments.

Double Trouble
During the Vietnam War, the US had faced the problem of the war-bloated budget deficit and the gap in the balance of payments caused by US direct foreign investment and military expenditure overseas. The answer lay in the transformation of the international financial system, shifting it to a US-dollar standard and forcing the central banks of the major Western countries to accumulate unwanted inventories of US treasury bills. One offshoot of dollar liquidity had been the emergence of the eurodollar and eurobond markets, and the proliferation of peekaboo financial centers, the foundation of the explosive growth of international bank lending in the 1970s. Another result had been an increase in the net flow into the US of profits from the international lending activities of American banks – these 'service' items on the balance-of-payments account provided some cushion with which to finance a continuing deficit in merchandise trade.

During the Reagan era, the US merchandise-trade deficit deepened. Exports to developing countries plummeted as a result of the debt crisis, and falling oil prices hurt US markets among the OPEC group. Much of the former strong surplus in 'service' items dried up.[11] Yet the US dollar continued to appreciate, rising by 80% against a basket of other major convertible currencies between 1980 and the end of 1984. Not until well into 1985 did the US and other major Western central banks coax and bludgeon it down again. The perverse performance of the dollar reflected the fact that the US currency unit had added to its traditional role of the main international medium of trade and financial flows increased demand as *the* currency of refuge.

Between 1977 and 1982 US banks had been net capital exporters of $140 billion; in 1983 they became net importers of more than $26 billion.[12] Developing debtor countries saw their foreign-exchange reserves depleted by flows of hot money into the US. Other financing came from the savings of industrialized countries: during the 1970s central banks of Western Europe, Canada, and Japan had bought up huge amounts of surplus US dollars and recycled them into US treasury bills; but by the early 1980s, the movement of funds into the US, into public- and private-sector securities and in direct investment, came increasingly from private investors abroad. Despite strong trade surpluses with the US, major Western countries found their foreign-exchange reserves stagnant, as they sold off billions of dollars to combat the rise of US currency against their own. The dollars sold were then recycled by private investors back to the US.[13]

From January 1980 to June 1984 an estimated $417 billion in foreign capital flowed into the US, from Europe, Canada, Japan, and the developing countries.[14] The share of Japan, and of the developing countries, was rising fastest. After all, according to a top-level Moonie, between 1975 and 1984 the sect moved no less than $800 million from Japan to the US. In 1984 Japan financed nearly half the US trade-balance deficit, pouring into the US $33 to $50 billion per annum; much of it moved into US treasury debt.[15]

That led to a new Yellow Peril to compete with the Islamic Hordes as a threat to the American Dream. Fed chief Paul Volcker warned of America's 'addiction' to foreign capital. CIA chief William Casey denounced Japanese investment in the US computer industry as a Trojan horse. Governor Richard Lamm of Colorado told Americans to ask themselves, 'How much can we afford?' without suggesting the rest of the world do likewise. William Proxmire, the ranking Democrat on the Senate Banking Committee, adopted the philosophy of the radical left in Latin America: 'As time goes on,' Proxmire intoned, 'as foreign investors get a larger and larger share of the national debt, they get into a position where they can impose tough terms or cut off credit. You lose part of your sovereignty under those circumstances. You lose your independence.' To these sentiments Felix Rohatyn, of the Lazard Frères merchant-banking firm, added the fear that Japan could suddenly yank out its money, causing the US dollar to plummet, and then return to buy up American industry at fire-sale prices.[16] Perhaps he had been observing the activities of US commercial banks in Latin America.

In reality, the percentage of foreign-held to total US government debt was no larger in the mid-1980s than it had been a decade before – perhaps smaller. Less than 1% of US tangible assets and real estate were in foreign hands, along with 5% of all private and public securities. And the US was the world's only 'debtor' country that could pay off its foreign debt simply by cranking out more paper. Irving Kristol of the American Enterprise Institute called for the Federal Reserve to accommodate the demand for US dollar assets: 'If foreigners are so eager to buy dollars, a commodity we can produce very cheaply, why should we obstinately frustrate them.'[17] Herman Kahn would have approved.

The US was also the only country that could unilaterally influence, if not determine, the rate of interest on its foreign debt. And much of that capital inflow went into investments that were effectively locked into the US, not susceptible to being easily pulled out again, by virtue of either their legal terms or their illegal character. Flight capital generally had the happy feature of not really increasing the host's net foreign obligations.

Nonetheless the rate at which foreign capital was flowing into the US was increasing. Hence, even if the twin deficit was not a domestic economic problem, it was a political one: the US entered 1985 in a – illusory – net debtor position for the first time since 1914.[18] To combat that inflow several options were available.

One option not available – particularly after Reagan's second victory – was a tax rate increase to close the budget deficit and to reduce the need for foreign financing. An alternative strategy was to step up collection of taxes at the given rates. This would mean attacking the burgeoning underground economy that the tax cut was supposed to have helped extinguish.[19]

Lost Horizons

By definition, the size of the underground economy in the US is impossible to ascertain.[20] Whatever the precise figure, it is huge, in the hundreds of billions; it is growing rapidly; and if it could be brought within the tax collector's grasp, it would cover a hefty part of the budget deficit, perhaps even converting that deficit into a surplus.[21]

In order to tap that money, two separate but related problems had to be tackled. One was the detection of illegal incomes; the second was the detection of tax evasion (including fraudulent tax exemptions) on legally earned incomes. For fiscal purposes, the value of legally earned components of the underground economy is far larger than the criminal parts. But tax evaders' hoards follow the routes through the circuitry of peekaboo finance explored by the drug peddlers.

Size estimates of the illegal component of the underground economy vary greatly. In 1985 the take of the drugs economy alone has been placed as high as $110 billion.[22] The public hysteria directed against illicit drug trafficking is proportional not only to its purported size but also to its usefulness in confirming stereotypes about tightly organized criminal conspiracies (whose masterminds rarely bear honest-sounding 'American' names).

Actually few major components of the criminal economy seem to have a significant 'Mafia' presence. In drug dealing, Mafia activity seems mainly in heroin, but is far from dominant. Of the boom drugs of the 1970s, illicit LSD was the product of American-born enterprise and was marketed, first to the 'sixties' generation of peace-loving flower children, and then beyond, by a network of biker gangs reinforced by unrepentant Vietnam War veterans. At first, wholesaling marijuana was the preserve of Colombian and Mexican gangs and the Jamaican ganja mafia. Then, as domestic American production displaced imports, the 'Dixie mafia' emerged, with an industrial organization that more closely resembled the Keystone Kops than it did the adversaries of Charlie Chan. Cocaine importing seems to include a small Italo-American Mafia presence; but it is largely controlled by Miami-based Cuban and Colombian gangs whose degree of organization can be gauged by the murder rate in the major urban centers of Florida: in any other country it would be interpreted as the beginnings of civil war.[23]

The great bulk of the cash that results from retail drug dealings and routine tax evasion can be handled by virtually any lawyer or money broker or accountant, and certainly by any banker. The major distinction seems to be not between organized and unorganized crime, but between big- and small-scale dealers operating in a highly competitive environment. The rich returns to the dealers tend to blur the boundaries between underground and overground economies; and the number of bankers involved helps the blurring process.

Illegally earned tax-evaded money is a fraction of the legally earned but illegally evaded portion.[24] For 1986 the IRS estimates the net tax loss from nonreported income will exceed $100 billion.[25]

Much income is illegally tax-sheltered in schemes such as one developed by a Fort Lauderdale promoter who, with a group of like-minded American and Swiss citizens, set up a series of Liechtenstein companies, ostensibly to trade in gold. No bullion was bought, but the appropriate receipts for writing off losses against taxes were generated, and the money passed back to the principals through banks in the Cayman Islands and Bahamas.[26] Not to be outdone even by Marc Rich, another entrepreneur pleaded guilty in 1985 to marketing $445 million in phony income tax deductions, mainly through false trading in government securities and precious-metals contracts. The results allegedly cost the federal government $250 million in lost tax revenues.[27]

The Moon Is Down

In the drive against tax evasion, some traditional tax exemptions came under scrutiny, including one whose technique was aptly summed up by former faith healer-turned-TV-evangelist Pat Robertson, when he advised his followers to avoid the stock market and give to his church. As he put it, 'Funds used to build God's kingdom and help others are always secure. The bank of heaven is not subject to business cycles.'[28] It is, however, subject to the demands of the Pentagon budget. Hence, among the most prominent victims of the attack on the budget deficit was the Reverend Sun Myung Moon.

In July 1983 the tax authorities of Norfolk, Virginia, seized a flotilla of eighty-three never-launched fishing boats belonging to the 'Ocean Church,' the Moonie affiliate that has a presence in thirty coastal towns in the US. The Moonies protested that the purpose of the boats was strictly religious, that 'We go to sea and we pray at sea, where it is quiet.' To this the Norfolk tax assessor retorted, 'Well, when I go fishing, I pray a lot, too, and I pay taxes.'[29]

Moon's appeal against his personal conviction for tax fraud failed, despite major lobbying by fundamentalist groups, which Moon characterized as 'God's dispensation working behind the scenes.' And although Moonie publications are essential reading in the White House, *realfinanz* triumphed over *realpolitik*; Moon received no administration assistance. When he was sentenced to eighteen months in prison, he professed his astonishment, given how much he had done for the American economy.[30] To ascertain the extent of his contribution would likely require a close scrutiny of the books of that bank the Moonies reportedly own in the Cayman Islands.

The late L. Ron Hubbard, founder of the Church of Scientology, ran into similar difficulties shortly after Moon's incarceration. Scientology, its founder claimed, is unique in its use of a one-to-one counseling technique called 'auditing.' According to former officials, money was extracted from converts through intimidation and blackmail based on information received during 'auditing' sessions. Recent accusations at a Montreal press conference by former Scientologists added charges that the 'church' entrapped its converts in debt-bondage by selling them on credit 'courses' of instruction.[31]

In the late 1960s, to escape persecution by law enforcement officers of several countries, Hubbard moved his operation offshore to a large yacht called the *Apollo* and, like Moon, allegedly created a special group of followers to infiltrate government agencies and suppress investigations. Also moving offshore, according to former officials of the organization, was more than $100 million from 'religious' endeavors diverted into Swiss, Liechtenstein, and Liberian bank accounts that Hubbard controlled. Sometimes the money moved in the traditional way, using church officials as cash couriers; sometimes it followed a more sophisticated calling, at the Religious Research Foundation, a Liberian-incorporated shell company. In 1984, on the basis of testimony of former officials, Scientology lost its 'religious' tax-exempt status in the US.[32]

Also in 1984, the IRS raided the offices of a tax 'planning' service in eight American cities. Among the tax shelters being peddled was a tax-deductible contribution to the Cayman Islands–based Congregational Church of Human Morality. Allegedly, once the funds were paid in, and the tax deduction claimed, the money was returned to the contributor.[33]

Alpine Outings

The trail of hot money escaping the tax collectors' grasp often pointed not merely offshore but all the way to Switzerland. Since Meyer Lansky made his first foray into the peekaboo world of Swiss banking in the 1930s, the American IRS (not to mention the DEA, the FBI, and the SEC) had been frequently stymied by Swiss bank-secrecy laws. Indeed, it was precisely because US government agencies had had such discouraging results in their search for illicit money flowing through Switzerland that it was mainly – though far from exclusively – through Swiss banks that the Nixon administration laundered illegal corporate contributions to the president's reelection campaign. To secure access to bank documents, the authorities had to demonstrate that the offense being investigated was also a crime under Swiss law. Obviously such proof was often impossible without access to the documents that were the object of the search. Moreover, even if the US agency convinced the Swiss federal authorities that a crime under Swiss law had been committed, the Swiss federal government simply passed the US request for information to the relevant cantonal governments, which could respond according to their particular administrative practice.

During the 1970s the US pressured Switzerland into toughening its public attitude toward drug money, though Switzerland stood firm on funds from tax evasion, unless another crime were associated with it. The Swiss also agreed to a cooperative treaty with the US for joint investigations in overtly criminal cases.[34] Although the deal may have chased much drug money off to the Bahamas, Panama, and the Caymans at first, a lot could return to Switzerland in the form of interbank deposits.

Furthermore, most American hot money going to Switzerland was likely tax evaders' funds, which could return to the US in the form of Swiss bank purchases of American securities on behalf of anonymous investors. As such, the subsequent capital gains and dividends earned also escaped taxation. Such tax evasion could be combined with evasion of margin requirements and with insider trading through use of a Swiss-bank fiduciary account.

When New York stockbroker William Mellon Hitchcock used the Bern-based Paravicini Bank to avoid margin requirements, it was not until the bank suspended that the operation stopped. Similarly, the Weisscredit Bank of Chiasso was reputed to be a vehicle for circumventing margin requirements until its demise in 1977. Since at least the 1960s, when Swiss banks accounted for as much as 15% of all activity on Wall Street (undoubtedly much of it recycling of hot money), insiders could place stock orders through Swiss banks which could also collect the profits on behalf of the client.[35] Despite some steps toward cooperation,[36] by the mid-1980s insider trading, often via Swiss banks (with or without the additional paraphernalia of Panamanian ghost companies and Liechenstein *anstalten*), was rampant on American stock exchanges.[37] So, too, was the alleged use of Swiss banks for recycling tax evaders' money at a time when 'foreign' investment in US equities, as well as in government and corporate bonds, was climbing rapidly.

In 1984 the SEC proposed to institute a 'waiver-by-conduct.' Under its terms, any purchaser of American securities automatically waived the protection of foreign bank-secrecy laws. While proposed to deal with the specific problem of insider trading, 'waiver-by-conduct' could have been the means to a general attack on tax-evading loan-back deals conducted through Swiss and offshore banks. In retaliation, the Swiss threatened to abandon all cooperation with the US government in tracing criminal transactions. Early in 1985 John Fedders, chief of the SEC's enforcement division, resigned and the SEC abandoned the 'waiver-by-conduct' principle to the joy of the Swiss bankers.[38]

Global Laundromat

Despite some well-publicized success stories, the taxable sums uprooted from underground have been a pittance compared to the deficits that needed funding. (Or, indeed, the legalized tax evasion practiced by the wealthy corporate individual. General Dynamics, for example, a corporation whose operational philosophy was described by Navy Secretary John Lehman as 'catch us if you can,' made a double contribution to the US budget deficit, padding its bills and paying no taxes since 1972.) The US government looked farther afield, not only to curb the use of offshore banks by Americans hiding money from the tax collector, but also to tap the international pool of hot and homeless money known as the eurobond market, and to channel it into American government securities.

While decrying offshore tax havens and peekaboo financial centers as instruments of a KGB-directed organized-crime cartel, the Reagan administration set out to convert the US Treasury into a laundromat for the world's dirty money.

Under American law, a 30% withholding tax was levied on interest paid to foreign holders of American bonds. But in 1948 the US and the Netherlands had signed a tax treaty that exempted from the withholding tax interest paid to investors or companies resident in the Netherlands Antilles. As US corporations tapped the growing pool of dollar liquidity abroad, the logical approach was to incorporate a Netherlands Antilles paper subsidiary to issue bonds guaranteed by the parent corporation. Using the Netherlands Antilles loophole, US corporations could raise long-term capital at lower than domestic rates. Foreign investors found several attractions on this scenic route. Not only were foreign investors in such US corporate bonds exempted from the 30% withholding tax, but the eurobonds could be issued in bearer form, invisible to the snooping gaze of the tax collector in the investors' home country.[39]

Among the pioneering users of the facilities was Bernie Cornfeld's IOS, whose banks, acting on behalf of the mutual funds, participated in many of the early eurobond issues, most of which had to be drastically written down if not entirely off.[40] Nor could Cornfeld have been much pleased, in retrospect, to have numbered among his early eurobond purchases securities issued by an upstart conglomerate-maker named Robert Vesco.

However, others found the eurobond market less problematic. From 1973 on, US corporations made growing use of this tax-avoidance route. From 1980 to 1983 there was a sharp increase in company formation and bond issue, as US domestic interest rates soared and the volume of hot money available greatly increased.

While US corporations were setting up shop in the Netherlands Antilles, especially Curaçao, so, too, were foreign individuals and corporations hoping to invest in the US and avoid the withholding tax. Another great attraction of the Netherlands Antilles was that corporations could be established and owned through bearer shares, leaving virtually no trail for those checking on the use of the area by US citizens. It became a favorite haunt not only for tax evaders and flight capitalists but also for drug dealers and arms traffickers seeking to shift their money into legitimate investments in the US. Close enough to Venezuela to profit from its great petro-boom and subsequent capital-flight bonanza, the Netherlands Antilles were also the conduit for most of the billions of dollars Latin Americans – not to mention Imelda Marcos – were moving into Florida and New York real estate.[41]

By 1984 the many thousands of 'corporations' in Curaçao generated 50% of government revenue and were responsible for much, if not most, of the livelihood of the area's legal and accounting professions. The Netherlands Antilles suffered a severe shock when fiscal pressure moved the US administration to increase its share of the pool of hot money into which US corporations had long been dipping.[42]

Government officials began quiet inquiries among euromarket underwriters to assess how much it could pull out of the eurobond market each year. The response was that there were two major impediments to US government participation on a par with US corporations. One was the 30% withholding tax (as the US Treasury could not, like American corporations, establish paper subsidiaries in the Netherlands Antilles); the second was the inability of the US government to issue its bonds in bearer form. With these two impediments removed, however, some estimates put the possible take at upward of $60 billion.

First Boston Corporation calculated that without the 30% withholding tax, the US could finance its entire budget deficit offshore.[43] This might cause a reduction in US interest rates and an easing of the competition between US business and the government for domestic savings. Of course, it also meant that the US would be raiding the pool of savings on which Europe was drawing to finance its own economic recovery. As well, it held out the possibility of further downward pressure on major European exchange rates. By combining this with the introduction of anonymity for foreign holders of US government securities, the US government would be joining private US corporations in the encouraging of foreigners to evade taxation.[44]

When the US announced that it was contemplating lifting the 30% withholding tax, the eurobond market was badly shaken. And when in May 1984 the managing director of Morgan, Stanley of New York announced before the general meeting of the International Bond Dealers' Association in Nice that such a US action would wipe out the eurobond market and shift business to New York, European investment bankers called it 'a declaration of war.'[45]

The American offensive came in two stages. First came the actual abolition of the 30% withholding tax. Western European governments responded by moving to repeal their own withholding taxes. Then the US Treasury stated its intent to issue bearer securities.[46] The US government, like those of many other countries, was so eager to cut the interest cost of the bonds it was issuing to cover the deficit that it officially accepted the fundamental rules of the hot-money game. As the prestigious *Institutional Investor* affably put it: 'Many European investors are willing to accept a lower interest rate if they are able to buy securities anonymously.'[47]

Reaction in Congress was adverse. For the introduction of bearer bonds and bills by the US government opened up more opportunities for American residents to launder criminal funds through nominee companies and fronts in the various peekaboo centers. Hot money could move into US government financial instruments, just when the US government was supposedly committed to the death of big-time crime.[48] But a compromise was worked out. Investment dealers marketing the US government securities simply had to attest annually that none of the tax-free bonds were held by US residents, without revealing their clients' identities. The US government in turn pledged that it would only investigate the certification if it felt there were strong grounds for suspecting fraud. That arrangement left the US government free to tap the global pool of fiscal flight capital and black-market money, while retaining some impediments to American citizens exploiting the facilities.

After some initial hesitation, the measures seemed eminently successful, helping the inflow of foreign investment into US treasury bonds. It also eliminated the need for US corporations to maintain Netherlands Antilles subsidiaries, thereby hurting an economy already suffering from the drying up of petroliquidity from Venezuela. And the new regulations helped to make the US public treasury a huge suction pump for capital from countries struggling to mobilize enough foreign exchange to meet the debt-service demands of American banks.[49]

18

Buddy, Can You Spare a Billion?

During the 1970s many American banks had grown by leaps and bounds. But as the 1980s unfolded, the US banking system[1] found itself in a precarious position. Major banks with double or treble their equity tied up in loans to delinquent debtor countries became household gossip. Moreover, world energy and agricultural prices were soft, and, until late 1985, the high dollar was pricing American manufactured goods out of world markets. As a result, equal or worse was the threat to banks that had lent to the domestic farm, energy, and manufacturing sectors. Banks were forced into a scramble for deposits to finance loans to domestic and international borrowers having trouble repaying existing credits on time.

Michele Sindona's Last Laugh

In July 1982 Penn Square Bank, a high-flying Oklahoma City operation with an appetite for energy-sector speculation, collapsed with more than $2 billion in worthless loans on its books.[2] The ensuing tremors shook and eventually collapsed the sixth largest bank in the US, an institution with a history of odd domestic and international associations.[3]

Continental Illinois Bank and Trust (Conti) had long prided itself on being the largest bank in Archbishop Marcinkus's hometown. Their mutual admiration was highlighted when one of Michele Sindona's Italian aides became a father, and the boy was named David, after David Kennedy, then chief executive officer of Conti and subsequently Nixon's secretary of the treasury and American ambassador to NATO. Marcinkus baptized the baby, and Sindona, appropriately enough, became his godfather. Conti was a partner in Sindona's main capital-flight vehicle, Banca Privata Finanziaria. And it was a former vice-president of Conti whom Michele Sindona hired to run the foreign-exchange department of Franklin National, whose subsequent foreign-exchange speculation losses set off America's greatest-ever deposit run – until Conti broke that record ten years later.[4]

Perhaps Continental Illinois had been blessed for its alleged funneling of money from the Chicago diocese to Solidarity in Poland. In any event, it was one of the glamour boys of American banking during the 1970s, aggressively pushing loans, particularly in the energy and industrial sectors. By 1982 it was the largest industrial lender in the US. But the ban on interstate banking meant that Conti, like many other major American banks, had a relatively weak retail-deposit base. Its asset growth was funded by borrowing hot money, domestic and foreign, making the bank highly vulnerable to shifts in the mood of the money market. In mid-1982 it was hit from three directions at once.

Recession played havoc with its industrial customers, among whom were some of the most notorious basket cases of the era.[5] It also found its oil and gas loans in trouble as prices came under downward pressure; and fully $1 billion of those energy-sector loans were the bequest of Penn Square.

Conti's rapid growth came to an abrupt end. Its cost of funding in the euromarket jumped;[6] its old rival, First National of Chicago, replaced it as top banker in the region; and the federal regulators quietly put it under particular scrutiny.

After the 1982 debacle, domestic-money managers began to avoid Continental Illinois, and it was forced to rely more heavily on the international interbank market. At the same time it was dropped from the top run of American banking, those largest institutions that automatically got best terms for their paper. By early 1984 Conti was able to show a profit only by selling off assets. Then rumors, apparently originating in a Chicago bar frequented by money-market traders, had it that Conti was about to file for bankruptcy; the 'hot tip' was picked up by the international news agencies and flashed around the world, and a massive flight of wholesale deposits from Conti began.

In an effort to stop the run, the US comptroller of the currency issued a public declaration denying that the bank was in trouble, but it did not escape notice that this was the comptroller's first such public declaration since the time in 1974 when he issued the same sunny reassurances about Franklin National. The Federal Reserve Board poured in $4 billion, arranged multibillion-dollar standby credit from a consortium of other banks, and the Federal Deposit Insurance Corporation (FDIC) publicly guaranteed all deposits – of any size, domestic or foreign – although the law stipulated that the maximum deposit insured by the federal agency was $100,000. The FDIC also pumped in more than $2 billion in capital, assuming control of the bank. It dismissed senior management, wrote off or sold billions of dollars worth of assets. In the end, Conti was virtually halved and 80% of the capital was owned by the FDIC, an agency of the American government whose administration was committed to getting that government out of the marketplace.[7]

Initially the rescue was presented as a special case to prevent a massive flight of interbank funds from the American banking system. But it became policy when the comptroller of the currency announced publicly that the US government would not allow the top banks to fail, effectively guaranteeing all their deposits. This delighted the big money-center banks, half of whose funding came from overseas deposits on which they paid no insurance premiums. Large interbank deposits in US money-center institutions had become functionally equivalent to government securities. The US had been forced into the same humiliating public guarantee of international interbank debt that its banks had been forcing on developing countries.[8]

It also meant that the US effectively had two banking systems: the giant institutions where deposits were completely safe, and the smaller and regionally based banks where the depositer of more than $100,000 still had to beware. That produced an irony: any future panic originating from the antics of a large money-center bank might end up causing a flight of deposits away from well-managed regional institutions toward the big money-center institution that was causing the problem.

Conti was spectacular, but it was certainly not alone. In the 1960s an average of 4 US banks failed a year; in the 1970s the average was 8; in 1981 10 US banks fell; in 1982, 42; in 1983 the casualties hit 48; in 1984 the figure was 79; in 1985, the total was nearly double that of 1984. FDIC payments from 1934 to 1980 totaled $500 million; from 1981 to mid-1985 they were ten times that total. About 800 US banks were on the regulatory agencies' 'problem list.'[9]

Some of the failures could claim 'special' circumstances, such as the farm crisis that wiped out numerous agricultural debtors and, sometimes, their bankers. (It also fed the recruitment efforts of far-right political cults condemning usury, and provoked assassinations of bank officials.)[10] But most of the failures reflected strains within the mechanics of the system. Nor were all of the endangered banks small.

First Chicago, Conti's traditional rival, and Bank of America were forced in 1984 to pledge to the comptroller of currency to shore up their capital and reserves (or have their top executives removed by court order). And a few months after Michele Sindona was finally extradited to Italy to face charges ranging from fraudulent bankruptcy to murder, European American Bankcorp, the holding company that had taken over the wreck of Franklin National, posted one of the largest quarterly losses ever recorded by an American bank.[11]

Conti's collapse and the sovereign-debt crisis together spelled the end of the phase of American banking characterized by a race for asset growth, a race in which the top corporate honors went to the officers who could hustle the most loans. Instead, concern focused on two issues. One was the question of capital adequacy. The second was the flow of deposit funds to finance loans, which at least implicitly yielded corporate brownie points to those bank officers and branch managers who could attract the greatest deposit surpluses.

Liable for What?

Extra deposits for banks strapped for funds could come from offering laundry service. There was certainly ample opportunity during the 1980s as the underground economy grew rapidly in size and sophistication. The situation was reminiscent of the 1930s: legitimate businesses needing money in a time of recession and a credit crunch turn to bootleggers- now-become-drug smugglers flush with cash and eager to launder it through legitimate businesses. The process was obligingly intermediated by banks, whose deposit hunger made it easy for them to turn a blind eye to the sources of the money washing through the system.[12]

American official awareness of the problem had produced the Bank Secrecy Act of 1970, which required the specific reporting by banks and financial institutions of cash movements exceeding $10,000. But the act accomplished little: exemptions were granted many retail businesses that routinely generated large amounts of cash – the very businesses that were prime vehicles for illicit money movements. Exemption was also granted casinos, some of which added laundry service to the traditional game of skim-the-cash for their secret mob-linked owners.[13]

Nor did the Bank Secrecy Act seem to do much to impede the banks. Exemptions were granted for wire transfers, which soon far surpassed cash, cashiers' checks, and money orders for large-scale movements. And other options were available: breaking the money down into amounts of less than $10,000 and washing it through several banks;[14] bribing deposit-hungry banks to ignore the required paperwork; and/or simply finding a bank that found the paperwork inconvenient or 'difficult' to understand.

For example, in the famed 'Pizza Connection' heroin affair, the alleged traffickers used both cash couriers and wire transfers as a take-out service for the dough picked up from retailers across the northeastern US. Part of the money was deposited in New York banks, wire transferred to Switzerland, and from there invested in Italy. Some of it, however, was moved out of the US in cash by private jet to Bermuda, and then wired to Italy. Some of the money transited major investment dealers. Merrill, Lynch and E. F. Hutton invested the funds in the New York bullion market, and transferred the proceeds of subsequent sales to Switzerland. While Merrill, Lynch grew suspicious about the origin of the funds and stopped dealing, E. F. Hutton informed the account holders that the FBI was snooping, despite being asked not to make such a disclosure. The company's spokesman called it a 'misunderstanding.'[15]

All manner of financial institutions 'misunderstood.' Late in 1984 the Presidential Commission on Organized Crime aired the dirty-money issue in public. It not only brought down several affiliates of the bullion-dealing and money-changing firm of Deak-Perera, but also set off a run on a bank in New York's Chinatown controlled by a former Hong Kong police sergeant who had relocated in 1975, the time of the police corruption scandals.[16]

Although a variety of institutions participate, most laundering is conducted through the commercial banking system. Even though many banks had been named in the past in criminal actions,[17] the issue moved from transgressions by the occasional, usually obscure, bank to a systemic scandal with the Bank of Boston affair. The sixteenth-largest US bank, the Bank of Boston also had the third-largest overseas network. Through it, apparently, ran shopping bags of cash, accepted on deposit on behalf of persons later charged with racketeering and loan-sharking. Through it also (in what the bank says were unrelated transactions) ran more than $1.2 billion in cash, deposited in Swiss banks, and then returned neat, clean, and unreported to the federal authorities. The bank subsequently admitted, as well, to failing to report $110 million in transfers between its Miami branch and the Caribbean.[18]

In the aftermath of the affair, banks scrambled to avoid prosecution. Other New England banks admitted to having 'omitted' filing some of the required declarations. Prominent New York banks such as Manufacturers Hanover, Chase, Chemical, and Irving Trust also joined the line in front of the confessional. Nor was the action limited to the East Coast.

California's Crocker Bank negotiated a fine of $2,250,000 for its failure to report $4 billion in cash transactions between itself and six Hong Kong banks, and failing to report similar transactions at its Mexican border branches. When the assistant secretary of the treasury, John Walker, publicly speculated that drugs could have been the source of the cash, Crocker denied it furiously, claiming that the Hong Kong money was the normal return of cash taken abroad by American tourists and the equally normal flow of flight capital from Hong Kong to the US.

Bank of America, the inspiration for young Michele Sindona, negotiated a fine of $4.75 million for having failed to disclose transfers of over $12 billion.[19]

All this made for work for the American Bankers' Association: in 1985 it was reported to be negotiating with the US Treasury on behalf of about 45 banks, while the federal government had put some 140 banks under scrutiny.[20]

Banks in need of deposits could also draw on the services of the money brokers that had sprung up all over the US. The boom in brokered deposits came as an incidental result of partial 'deregulation' of the financial system. In the late 1970s the big American banks found themselves under pressure from other financial institutions, which were bidding away their deposits. They lobbied successfully for the removal of the interest-rate ceilings under which they had formerly stooped. But for many of the American banks, deregulation was more a curse than a blessing. In the 1980s the easing of interest-rate restrictions allowed the development of a massive wholesale-deposit market.[21] Into that domestic pool of hot money the money brokers plunged.

Some brokers would make deposits with banks in return for assured loans to specified borrowers, who could be close business associates or even officers of the brokerage firm. An increasing number of bank failures were linked directly to these tied-in loans.[22] But even more important was the threat the brokers posed to the deposit-insurance system.[23]

Brokers generally dealt in deposit bundles of $100,000, the maximum covered by insurance. Smaller deposits would be lumped in $100,000 bundles and sold to the highest bidding bank; similarly, deposits exceeding $100,000 would be divided and placed in several smaller acccounts. Using such techniques, Merrill, Lynch, the largest money broker in the US, had placed $2.5 billion in fully insured, and therefore risk-free, deposits in troubled banking institutions by September 1984.[24]

Brokered deposits meant hot money; and in the wake of the Continental Illinois debacle, federal regulators and big money-center banks decided that the banks needed a cool and stable retail-deposit base to allow them to bypass the brokers and to rely less on the euromarket.[25] That required the dismantling of the functional distinction between savings and commercial banks, which would open the deposit base of the savings banks to the big money-center institutions. It also required that the barriers to interstate banking be lowered, opening up the rich deposit surpluses in California and Florida.

While Congress dithered over the question of barriers, various states approved regional interstate banking in order to develop large, regionally based banks strong enough to repel the advances of the big money-center institutions.[26] A lawsuit by Citibank to void the laws permitting only regional interstate banking, on the grounds that they constituted discrimination and a restraint on trade, failed in the Supreme Court in June 1985.[27]

The big money-center institutions had also tried to get around such barriers with 'nonbank banks,' affiliates that did not do a demand-deposit or commercial-lending business. Although the situation was initially checked by court rulings in Florida and Georgia, the US Supreme Court found in the banks' favor. Early in 1986 the door was opened to nonbank banking;[28] the next step would be interstate full-service banks.

Some progress in that direction had been made even before the Supreme Court's ruling. After the Continental Illinois crash, the state legislature rolled out the welcome mat for an interstate takeover, to avoid closure of the bank and the loss of thousands of jobs, when unemployment was already high.[29] Then came the great 'thrift' crisis of 1985.

When interest-rate deregulation hit the US, first on the chopping block were the savings banks, whose main function had been to convert retail-savings deposits into householder mortgages. High interest rates offered by other institutions threatened to drain deposits from the 'thrifts'; and they were forced to push up their own rates and offset the cost by high-risk ventures.[30] Some went under in the interest-rate wars; others survived by speculating in financial futures and pouring ordinary depositors' money into luxury real estate. However, that strategy also took its toll.

In March 1985 came the failure of a small Fort Lauderdale dealer in government securities. ESM Government Securities had a long history of doctoring its balance sheets, allegedly with the aid of an amply remunerated auditor,[31] to hide heavy losses in the options market. The crash nearly wiped out the Ohio savings-banking system. Marvin Warner, owner of Home State Savings Bank of Ohio, had lent the bank's money heavily to the Florida securities firm, while his son-in-law, Miami attorney Stephen Arky,[32] kept the SEC from looking too closely at ESM's activities. Fears over ESM losses set off a depositors' run, first against Home State and then against other Ohio thrifts.

Once the runs were stanched, the failed thrifts were put on the auction block. The Chase Manhattan bought up three and offered to buy four more if the Ohio legislature permitted them to be converted into commercial banks.[33]

Two months later, it was the turn of the Maryland thrifts. Old Court Savings and Loan Association, a hot-money mill pulling in deposits from all over the US, had been pouring money into a Florida real estate market puffed by flight capital and dope money. When Old Court suspended payments, the crisis quickly spread to other thrifts with the usual result. Emergency funds were mobilized, and the big commercial banks, particularly Citibank and Chase, negotiated to purchase the weakened institutions, conditional on federal subsidies and state banking-law changes.[34] The former owner of Old Court faced a $200 million civil suit by the state insurance fund. He was also convicted of embezzlement and misappropriation of trust funds, for which he was jailed.[35]

Whiter Than White

The American savings-bank system's classic role was financing the postwar American Dream – the single-family home in a clean suburban neighborhood, with two cars in every garage and diapers billowing on every clothesline. But as the Home State and Old Court affairs demonstrated, by 1985 that system's fate was bound up with events in a part of America where a rather different concept of wash-and-dry prevailed.

Miami's commercial and financial position is built on history and geography.[36] Southern Florida was a major port of entry for bootleg liquor in the 1930s, a pivot for the southern leg of the French Connection heroin route in the 1960s, and the early 1980s entrepôt for 70% to 80% of the marijuana and cocaine entering the US. (So great was this inflow that doubts were cast on the integrity of the American air defense system, and governors of the Gulf Coast states called for military action against the importers.)[37]

Southern Florida is also a major refuge for Latin American flight money, which pours into the Florida banking system and local real estate.[38] The flight-capital-into-real-estate business is an old one. In the 1950s and 1960s, Kuomintang money from Thailand and Burma came via Hong Kong to be washed through Lansky-related property firms. The Trujillos, Somozas, and their confrères from South America bought up Miami mansions and filled up local banks. But during the 1970s the inflow became a flood, as the middle classes aspired to the oligarchy's standards of secure retirement. Money flowed from Latin America into offshore havens such as Panama, the Bahamas and, particularly, the Netherlands Antilles, whence it poured into Florida real estate.

By the end of the decade one-third of all money entering southern Florida's property market was foreign, especially Latin American, in origin – $3.5 billion in 1980 alone. One Florida real estate expert estimated, perhaps with considerable exaggeration, that of all foreign purchases in the first half of 1979, only 20% were the product of legitimate money.[39]

Southern Florida in general, and Miami in particular, is also a prime location for banking facilities. In 1978 foreign banks were admitted to Florida, and in 1980 Florida granted major tax concessions to encourage the inflow. Soon 40% of the money on deposit in Miami banks was reckoned to be of foreign origin, particularly Latin American.[40] Insurance companies followed suit, putting their head offices for Latin American business in Miami.[41] The hope was to make Miami, rather than Panama City or Montevideo, the financial center of Latin America. One incidental result was to make Florida a principal battleground for American money-center (especially New York) banks trying to expand into deposit-rich regions, as the local banks defended their territory against their incursions.[42]

From 1970 to 1980 Florida's population grew 43%; during the same period deposits in Florida banks grew 186%. Since 1976 Florida bank region showed the only persistent and growing cash surpluses of any Federal Reserve Board's divisions (an honor it must now share with California). Although much of the deposit growth came from the influx of wealthy retirees, it also prompted the launching of Operation Greenback, a 1980 combined IRS, DEA, and FBI crackdown on illicit cash movements. The main results seem to have been to drive some small operators out of business, to increase the importance of brokers' accounts for disguising domestic dirty money, and to deliver more business to banks with a wide wire-service network overseas.

The financial flows from the explosive growth of the Colombian drug trade through southern Florida required a particular financial infrastructure. Certain limitations on Colombian banks' international dealings did not apply to exchange houses: a Colombian bank required a specific license to deal in foreign exchange, and could only exchange dollars for pesos domestically, at the official rate; however, an exchange house could buy dollars for pesos without special licenses, pay more than the banks, guarantee anonymity, and deal more easily with the US.

Hence, cash generated from drug sales in the US could be deposited with the American branch or correspondent bank of a Colombian exchange house and the peso equivalent issued within Colombia, a variant of the 'lateral-transfer' technique used by heroin traffickers in Southeast Asia. Exchange houses also became a major financing facility for general contraband. To finance illegal imports, dollars would be purchased from Miami exchange houses and converted into goods. The goods would be sold in Colombia and the pesos handed over to the exchange house to purchase more dollars in Miami for the next round. The exchange houses could also scoop up any excess dollars in Colombia and ship them off by cash courier for deposit in Miami banks.[43]

Hernan Botero Moreno of Medellin was charged by the FBI with conducting one of the largest illegal-currency operations on the Colombian-Florida circuit. Allegedly, suitcases of currency were presented to a branch of the Landmark First National Bank in Florida. The branch charged a 1% fee to transfer the funds as interbank loans to four Colombian banks, which in turn converted the dollar deposits into cash pesos through the money-exchange house that Botero Moreno operated out of a Medellin hotel that he owned. In 1980 several bank officials, though not the bank itself, were charged with accepting bribes to falsify documents and with not filling out the forms required by the Bank Secrecy Act. In 1985 Colombia extradited Botero Moreno to the US, where he was found guilty of seven counts of laundering $57 million.[44]

For Florida banks the returns were tempting, indeed. Florida may be the only state in the US where many banks can get a fee for accepting demand deposits. One of these banks was the Great American Bank of Dade County; the bank was convicted of accepting money from Colombian traffickers and wire transferring it to other banks on their behalf.[45]

Of course, Florida bankers reject the accusation that they are more open to deposits of dirty money than other banks in the US. In October 1983 the president of the Florida International Bankers' Association declared, 'We probably exercise more scrutiny on deposits here than anywhere else in the world.' And he ominously added, 'We research depositors to death.' However, in 1980, of twenty-two full-scale investigations underway in the US under the terms of the Bank Secrecy Act, twelve involved Florida banks.[46] And in 1982 the comptroller of the currency estimated that between sixty and seventy Florida banks accepted deposits of drug money. Interestingly enough, when, in the autumn of 1984, the Reagan administration unveiled a new legislative program to deal with money laundering, among the opponents of intensified scrutiny was the head of the Florida Bankers' Association.[47]

One of the more sophisticated efforts to avoid that kind of scrutiny was conducted by a branch of the Garfield Bank in collaboration with a former SEC attorney named Nathan Markowitz. Markowitz was a tax lawyer and business broker specializing in distribution systems for Colombian marijuana, selling complete packages, including drug sources, airplanes, and street peddlers. He received cash from clients, paid bank officers to accept cash deposits without filing the required currency reports, and had the funds wired to the Bank of Bermuda. That bank wired the funds back to the US with fictitious loan documents prepared by Markowitz to allow the money to be classified as nontaxable business loans to phony Liberian- and Panamanian-headquartered investment-counseling companies created by Markowitz on behalf of his clients. These corporations could provide such perks as expense accounts, salaries, pensions, and company cars. But when Markowitz turned police informant, he became just another bank depositor that got researched to death: his bullet-riddled body was found in a Miami garage.⁴⁸

Obviously not all deposit surpluses in the Florida banking system can be imputed to drug dealing.⁴⁹ As Florida's population is now one-third Hispanic, and as one-third of American exports to Latin America go via Florida, the area has naturally strong ties to Latin America. This factor feeds the concurrent boom in flight capital. Florida's large inter-national banks are concerned to accommodate the needs of the 'high net-worth individual,'⁵⁰ while general trade and flight-capital flows likely prompted Colombian financiers to accept Florida's invitation to set up shop.⁵¹

Before he was thrown in jail, charged with plundering his Banco Nacional, Felix Correa targeted for takeover the Bank of Perrine (sub-sequently renamed Florida International Bank), perhaps unaware of its previous reputation as a two-machine laundromat for the Lansky mob and the CIA.

Also making the excursion into Florida banking was Jaime Michaelsen Uribe of the Banco de Colombia. Michaelsen took over the Central National Bank of Miami by means of a Netherlands Antilles holding company, and changed its name to Eagle National Bank. When the bank scandals in Colombia broke in the early 1980s, Michaelsen soon followed the money trail into a Miami exile.

Yet another Colombian entrepreneur who became active in Florida banking was Alberto Duque. Originally sent to New York to run the local branch of the family coffee business, he soon moved his business interests southward and took control of City National Bank in Miami. Duque also acquired control of the Chase and Sanborn coffee company, allegedly using as security for the necessary bank loans fraudulent bills of lading drawn on nonexistent inventories of coffee beans.

In 1982 Duque ran into several problems. In Colombia, the presidential elections went against Lopez Michaelsen, whose campaign Duque's father had been funding in the expectation of government support for his troubled coffee business. For several years Duque had been going against the tide, borrowing in the US and shipping the funds to Colombia, usually via Panamanian banks, to support the family enterprise. Somewhere between $28 million and $75 million was alleged to have been so diverted.

Then, in November 1982, Duque's former New York partner, a commodity dealer named Eduardo Orozco, was arrested, charged, and later convicted of running the largest money laundry ever uncovered in the US.[52] Although some of the funds that passed through Orozco's laundromat were of Colombian origin (allegedly some arrived in the US in Colombian air force planes), most were raised in the US and passed through banks and currency-exchange houses. Citibank of New York was reported to have been offered 1% to accept the deposits of cash; but, according to the presidential commission on money-laundering, the biggest recipient seems to have been the exchange house and bullion dealer Deak-Perera.[53]

Meanwhile, Alberto Duque was being sued by some twenty banks for $125 million he had borrowed on the basis of the allegedly fraudulent bills of lading. Duque and some of his associates were indicted by a grand jury and, early in 1986, found guilty on sixty of sixty-one counts of fraud and conspiracy.[54]

Florida banks and financial institutions are certainly not the only ones to engage in hot-money transactions; nonetheless, until recently, Florida banks were likely the primary beneficiaries of hot money moving into the American banking system. Florida's international banking operations were the fastest growing in the US,[55] a source of considerable annoyance to the big New York banks, which lusted after the deposit surpluses available in Florida.

These surpluses were theoretically available to the money-center banks through money brokers, but using brokers had serious disadvantages: banks had to bid competitively for the surplus deposits, driving up the cost and reducing the certainty of supply. And, of course, the reliability and longevity of individual money brokers was a worry. In 1983 a Miami money broker found his diversified career terminated on being charged with sending $150 million in hot cash to Panama during an eight-month period. In his office were found sixty-four pounds of cocaine, $40,000 in counterfeit bills, and various firearms.[56]

For the money-center banks it was better to establish local branches from which to dive into the hot-money pool. Hence, louder demands were heard to end barriers to interstate banking; and the Florida legislature became the site of major battles between competing bank lobbies. As one Florida state senator put it:

> Why in the name of reason should we make ourselves prey for those big New York money-center conglomerates that want to come in here and drain the capital of Florida to fund loans to Abu Dhabi, Afghanistan, and everywhere else?[57]

Florida banks engaged in court battles to halt the nonbank banks, and in regional mergers with banks of neighboring states to impede takeovers.[58] Nonetheless, in the long run, the balance of power favors the big money-center banks, who undoubtedly have watched gleefully as FBI and IRS agents exposed Florida money-laundering activities. So much for defending the integrity of the local banking system from outside encroachment. Early in 1986, twenty years after members of its economic staff wrote their memo on hot-money flows, Chase Manhattan may have rung the death knell of Florida's independent banking system. It outbid rivals by a wide margin to buy the bankrupt Park Bank from the FDIC and became the first New York bank to acquire a fully licensed banking operation in Florida.[59]

19

What's Better in the Bahamas?

Florida was not the only target of the big American money-center banks. They also cast a critical eye at the offshore booking centers of the euromarket. After ten years of lobbying by the banks, in 1981 the Fed had given first to New York and subsequently to other major centers permission to open International Banking Facilities (IBFs). These permitted the big banks to operate in the offshore sector, unencumbered by domestic regulations, without leaving home. The money-center banks of New York hoped to lure back much of the hundreds of billions of dollars' worth of loan business that US banks had booked offshore.[1] This antioffshore sentiment was encouraged by the entrenched position of major Canadian and British banks in the Bahamas and Caymans.[2]

The big banks' hopes of building up the IBFs were strengthened after 1982. The debt crisis caused them to rebook sovereign loans to New York or Miami, where the refinancing was taking place. By mid-1983 US IBFs ranked second only to London as euromarket centers. Furthermore, after the Continental Illinois collapse, the money-center banks cut back even further on their euromarket exposure.

The US government had its own reasons for trying to bring the offshore onshore. It hoped to use the IBFs as a bludgeon to force other countries to relax restrictions on the entry of US banks into their domestic financial markets. Such an opening would defend the flow of 'service' items that helped finance the adverse balance of commodity trade. Moreover, there was a fiscal problem posed by budget deficits that were ideologically, if not economically, out of control. Denunciations of illegal tax dodging through foreign bank havens diverted public attention from the much more massive legal tax evasion in which rich individuals and major corporations routinely indulged at home.

Thus, breaking down offshore bank secrecy might not only dig up some of the tax evaders' treasure, it might also frighten offshore business to the deposit-hungry New York banks.[3] And how better to start the assault than to dress it up as a battle against organized crime, particularly if the target couldn't fight back?

In 1983 a US Senate investigation declared that the flow of criminal money between US and offshore havens was so huge that it posed as great a threat to the American banking system as did bad and doubtful sovereign debt. The investigation also suggested that much of the $75 billion 'errors and omissions' in the US balance-of-payments statistics could be accounted for by the operation of money laundries, particularly in the major Caribbean havens.

Treasure Island Revisited

During the 1970s increased drug trafficking through the Caribbean, particularly the Bahamas, paralleled the expansion of its offshore banking.[4] (By 1982 it was estimated that 50% of the cocaine and much of the marijuana entering the US transited the Bahamas.) In 1980 it apparently dawned on US authorities that street-level dealers were in virtually infinite supply – particularly given their government's commitment to fighting inflation by driving up youth unemployment, especially in minority, ethnic communities. Officials turned their concern to those who financed the trade through banks and trust companies in the Caribbean financial havens. For, the more the US government pressured domestic financial institutions to curb their wash-and-dry activities, the more important the diversion of funds through offshore facilities became. Over all of this hung the politically useful legend of Robert Vesco.[5]

During his Bahamian holiday, Vesco had kept busy looting IOS and funding Lynden Pindling's political career. After he was chased off to Costa Rica, and later to Cuba, his reputed wealth multiplied with each telling, and his business interests allegedly diversified into arms trafficking, LSD manufacturing, underwriting heroin trading,[6] smuggling US machinery into Cuba,[7] and even financing the Carlos Lehder cocaine ring (though why a multibillionaire cocaine king of Colombia would require outside financing was never explained). There even emerged tales about Vesco joining with members of the Nicaraguan government to sell cocaine in the US to generate the cash to buy arms, from Libya of course.

All this proved good cover for Contra elements who supplemented Moonie funding with pin money from dealing drugs.[8] Moreover, rumors of Vesco's payoffs to the Pindling regime, and of his 'ownership' of Norman's Cay, a small island well situated for drug running, continued underground, awaiting a convenient moment to surface.[9]

In 1980 the US launched Operation Greenback. Perhaps coincidentally, that same year the Bahamas tightened its bank-secrecy code.

On the advice of a resident former Canadian finance minister, Donald Fleming, the Bahamas passed the Bank and Trust Regulation Act, which closed most of the loopholes through which confidential client information could be obtained.[10] When the United States instituted its Caribbean Basin Initiative, offering tariff concessions and aid to regimes with appropriate political credentials, it made participation conditional on cooperation with US authorities in tracing illicit money flows. One place that did not respond enthusiastically was the Bahamas, where finance is second only to tourism as a source of legal income, where by the mid-1980s drugs might have been the ultimate source of 25% or more of its GNP, and where the bankers used to hold 'Round Table' discussions on techniques for money laundering.[11] Protestations about national sovereignty were code for a confession that the Bahamas literally could not afford to cooperate.

Like the Caymans and other offshore centers, the Bahamas had two distinct banking systems. International banks used them as booking centers, to avoid regulations that might impede their effectiveness in bidding for deposits and offering loans. In 1983 US banks had 189 branches in the Bahamas, virtually all corporate shells whose business could theoretically be handled through domestic IBFs. The second level of banking was the domestic business, in which the US banks had only a marginal presence. The four biggest Canadian banks controlled more than 80% of increasingly lucrative Bahamian domestic business. (In 1983 the Royal Bank of Canada's branch on the tiny and impoverished island of Bimini saw $12 million in cash deposits, a sum that the central monetary authority of the Bahamas believed could have originated only from drug deals.)[12]

US authorities had been interested in the activities of certain Bahamian-based institutions at least since 1965, when they forced the closure of the Bank of World Commerce. But during the early 1980s their curiosity grew considerably. One object was the venerable Columbus Trust, which had once had a shareholder named Robert Vesco.

Vesco apparently severed all ties with the company after his departure, yet some peculiar corporate behaviour of Columbus Trust kept idle and/ or legal tongues wagging. It maintained the usual inventory of shell companies for clients who needed an instant 'corporation.' The trust company then operated the 'corporation' on behalf of the client to assure that his money was invested in the location and/or instrument of his, rather than the tax collector's, choice. Columbus's reputation was not helped much in 1980 when its officers attracted a string of indictments in the US on charges of tax evasion and drug trafficking. Some of the soil on its reputation was bound to rub off on its minority shareholders, including one Lynden Pindling. Finally in March 1983, under US pressure, the Bahamian government suspended its operating license.[13]

By then there were more prominent targets for the American investigators. The US Senate's Permanent Subcommittee on Investigations pointedly stated in its report on criminal use of offshore banking facilities that a certain unnamed 'major Canadian international bank has a consistent reputation for encouraging dirty money.'[14]

The most important of the five major Canadian international banks in terms of the total amount of business it did in the Caribbean was the Bank of Nova Scotia. The Bank of Nova Scotia had come a long way since the early nineteenth century when it followed the rum trade from Halifax to the British Caribbean. By 1982 more than 50% of its profits came from international business. Of all Canadian banks, it therefore had the most to lose from US pressures to shrink the Caribbean offshore centers in favor of New York and to break down the wall of bank secrecy.[15]

Drawing unwanted attention from US grand juries was the Miami branch of the Bank of Nova Scotia, whose main function seemed to be to help US citizens set up accounts in one of the ten Scotiabank branches in the Bahamas.[16] According to major traffickers, the proceeds of retail drug deals – including those from the notorious Pizza Connection case (later described as the most important heroin operation since the breaking of the French Connection) – were flown to the Bahamas in cash, and deposited in the name of shell companies in at least one Scotiabank branch. The money was then wired to accounts in the Bank of Nova Scotia Caymans Islands branch, and then to its New York office, whence the funds could be made available to the persons who initiated the operation. Allegedly from some of these deals, one Bahamian branch took a 2% handling fee, and appropriate 'tips' were paid to bank personnel.[17]

In 1981 a Fort Lauderdale grand jury subpoenaed the records of a Bahamian branch of the Bank of Nova Scotia as part of an investigation of a drug-smuggling ring. When the branch refused to yield the records, the US court imposed a fine; eventually the branch surrendered, much to the ire of the Bahamian government. In March 1983, in connection with another drug ring, more demands were made on the bank to surrender branch records, along with the imposition of a $500-a-day fine for contempt of court. But the bank variously argued that the documents requested did not exist or were not germane to the case, that compliance with the court's demands would violate Bahamian law, and that the court request represented an infringement of Bahamian sovereignty. However, the US court remained unimpressed. The previous year, the

US had passed the Tax Equity and Fiscal Responsibility Act (TEFRA), which gave the IRS the power to secure records of US taxpayers, including resident foreign corporations, operating in foreign jurisdictions. When the court raised the fine to $25,000 a day, and gave the bank to understand that its US assets could be subject to seizure, the bank was quite impressed, and capitulated.[18] In January 1984 twelve persons were indicted on charges of importing marijuana into Florida. The leader of the ring later claimed to have incorporated businesses in Florida and the Bahamas and washed the funds through several secret accounts in the Bahamas and Cayman Islands branches of the Bank of Nova Scotia.[19]

Even before the second Bahamas case, the Scotiabank found itself at odds with US investigators and courts over its activities in the Cayman Islands. The Caymans were latecomers to the offshore banking game, springing into action when the Bahamas seemed to be getting into financial and political difficulties, and accepting business that the more 'respectable' offshore centers would not touch.[20]

Financial havens tend to tier by age and 'quality' of business. As the older and more established ones gentrify, they can afford to become selective about the business they accept, though governments tend to leave the selection process to the 'professional ethics' of individual bankers. Switzerland, entrenched as *the* capital-flight and tax-evasion center, and benefiting from every flight of funds out of other flight-capital centers, could afford to chase out drug money in the 1970s. Similarly, the sun had not yet set on London as the first refuge of funds derived from large-scale corporate fraud committed elsewhere in the world[21] – or what's an empire for?

The *arriviste* Cayman Islands soon made up for lost time. In 1964 the islands had two banks, whose business was domestic. In 1983 there were 450 banks – 250 of them booking branches of major international banks, 100 locally incorporated subsidiaries of international banks, and 100 locally chartered 'private' operations. Euromarket bookings in 1983 totaled $127 billion. In addition, the islands boasted 270 insurance companies, and thousands of other 'corporations' (by some estimates as many as 14,000, nearly one for each islander).

All this was nurtured by the IMF, which helped the Cayman Islands and other offshore centers to draft banking regulations and assisted in their application – thereby facilitating tax evasion from countries under IMF attack for their public-sector deficits, and abetting capital flight from countries under IMF pressure to meet their debt-service payments. The Caymans banks quickly acquired a reputation for turning suitcase currency into cashiers' checks. The islands' proximity to Miami allowed couriers to return to the US on the same business day to begin the checks' long and cleansing voyage through the US domestic banking system.

The Cayman Islands, which had rejected independence from Britain, was naturally willing to defend its 'sovereignty' stubbornly. The first major blow came in the 1970s, when the managing director of the Cayman Islands branch of Castle Bank & Trust, a notorious conduit for CIA money and evaded taxes, was refused fifth-amendment protection by a US court. He had argued that any information he gave US courts would put him in violation of Cayman Islands banking law and would expose him to prosecution there. The court refused to extend fifth-amendment protection in a situation in which criminal prosecution was imminent in a foreign jurisdiction. Then another major test came in the summer of 1980, when a notorious Australian drug-money and CIA laundromat, the Nugan-Hand merchant bank of Sydney, crashed, taking with it dozens of affiliated companies, most of them shells. And in a hasty effort to cover the trail, Nugan-Hand's Cayman Islands branch voluntarily surrendered its banking license; the government could then tell investigators that no records could be surrendered, as the bank did not exist. Howls from the Australian government led to relisting by the Cayman Islands, but the whereabouts of some $20 million from the Cayman Islands branch remained as deep a mystery as that of $30 million missing from other dark corners of the Nugan-Hand empire.[22]

The US battle against Cayman Islands bank secrecy, begun in earnest in 1981, scored significant victories the following year. The first came during the investigation of a businessman charged with padding a shipping contract and splitting the overcharges with several confederates. The funds were washed through the Swiss accounts of Liechtenstein corporations before coming to rest in the Bahamas and the Caymans. The Cayman Islands court refused information to the prosecutors, but an appeal to the Jamaica courts (which handle Caymans appeal cases) proved successful, and the Cayman banks were ordered to divulge the information.[23]

In October 1982 the US Justice Department brought down a criminal indictment against, among others, the Bank of Nova Scotia for tax and mail fraud. A Cayman Islands branch was accused of participating in a scheme to defraud the US government through $122 million in phony tax-shelter claims. The 'payments' necessary to justify the tax write-offs were reputedly generated by check kiting between the bank branch and the other conspirators.[24]

The next year the Florida grand jury investigating a drug-trafficking case demanded records of the bank's Caymans, as well as its Bahamas, branches. Drawing fire and $25,000 a day in fines, the bank decided that discretion regarding customers' accounts was no longer the better part of valor. It applied to the Cayman Islands government for exemption from the rigorous secrecy laws. Not only was this refused, but the government also secured an injunction prohibiting the bank from surrendering the records. However, the US court was unmoved by the bank's poignant pleas that its hands were tied. It denounced the bank for deliberately delaying the surrender of the relevant documents. Fines for contempt of court eventually reached $1.8 million.[25]

It seemed that every time the postman rang, the bank was being served with another subpoena. The other major Canadian banks had been on the receiving end of US court demands, but none had Scotiabank's track record.[26] The Canadian government, mindful perhaps of the approaching federal election and of the need to win support from the country's strongest business lobby, added its voice to the chorus, lamenting that the US courts were violating Canadian sovereignty – whereas allowing the Pentagon to test cruise missiles on Canadian soil apparently did not. Robert Mackintosh, head of the Canadian Bankers' Association, argued that US court demands would put the international banking system under tremendous adverse pressure, threatening its foundations. (Apparently the cement used disintegrates on contact with light.) The cartel denounced the US court for its 'flagrant' violation of due process. The bank itself reacted by instructing its branch managers to be prepared to explain large fluctuations in their cash balances. It began training senior managers in the art of detecting suspicious accounts, and hired a special adviser to oversee a program to curb laundering activities at its Caribbean branches.[27]

Although the government of the Caymans felt even more threatened than that of the Bahamas, seeing in the case the potential end of its burgeoning euromarket business, it buckled and granted the bank a special exemption, permitting it to release the records.[28]

A formal deal on drug money cases followed. The Caymans agreed to tighten up on banking procedures and to require that its banks accept cash deposits of no more than $10,000 (though enforcement is virtually impossible even if the government of the islands wanted it). The Caymans held tight in refusing information on tax evasion; according to a government official, inhabitants of the tax-free islands regard taxation as 'repugnant' in principle. It did, however, agree to exchange information with the US in drug cases. Subsequent to the autumn of 1984, US authorities could request information from the Cayman Islands government for use by particular agencies in specific investigations, with the understanding that the information could not be passed to other agencies or used in cases other than the one that prompted the request. The demand would be passed on to the bank or trust company concerned, and the islands' government would prosecute company executives who did not comply. The agreement was a model that the US planned to impose on other British tax havens and peekaboo financial centers in the Caribbean,[29] whether they liked it or not.

One that certainly did not like it was the Bahamas, which continued to resist. In December 1982 Lynden Pindling stated that US interference in Bahamian banking operations constituted a threat to the islands' living standards. And the Bank of Nova Scotia's 1983 decision to surrender documents in the Florida drug case brought Bahamian threats of criminal charges down upon it – not to mention a subsequent threat by a drug dealer convicted on the basis of its documents that he would sue the bank for violating its contractual commitment to secrecy. The Bank of Nova Scotia affair brought relations between the US and the Bahamas to such a low ebb that the time was right for the US to move against its next Bahamian target.

In September 1983 NBC-TV alleged that Prime Minister Pindling was receiving more than $100,000 a month to protect Robert Vesco's drug-trafficking operations. Carlos Lehder was also allegedly paying off top Bahamian officials. Charges were being made, as well, that Bahamian tax-shelter facilities were washing criminal money and that the islands' lawyers were getting fat on fees paid by criminals.[30]

Such 'charges' had been Bahamian street gossip for years. The only mystery was why the US chose this time to unveil them. One answer undoubtedly lay in Pindling's resistance to the US assault on the secrecy laws that underlay the Bahamian banking system. A scandal over the prime minister's personal finances could combine with the general economic crisis to weaken his government and, therefore, his will to resist Washington's demands – not least, its demand that the Bahamas allow the US to establish a base for its nuclear submarines.[31]

Pindling's response was to accuse Washington of conspiring with the opposition Free National Movement to discredit him and force him from office. As to the Vesco connection, Pindling may well have revealed something the US government had not bargained for when he suggested that Vesco had his own deal with Washington as an integral part of its Caribbean and Central American intelligence-gathering network. He then appointed a Royal Commission of Inquiry into his own conduct.

Although the Royal Commission found no direct evidence to implicate him in drug money, its investigation caused him no small amount of embarrassment, not least because its report came on the heels of

Miami prosecution of two top Bahamian government officials on drug charges. In the Royal Commission report, one of Pindling's cabinet ministers was denounced as a front for US Mafia figures, and another was charged with accepting money from smugglers. The two were sacked; and some peculiarities in the prime minister's personal finances came to light.[32]

To the question, how had Pindling managed to spend more than eight times his annual salary seven years running, came two possible answers. One was that Pindling may have received substantial payoffs from casino operators for services rendered.[33] One witness, a convicted marijuana smuggler, claimed to have withdrawn $100,000 from his account in the Bank of Nova Scotia and passed it to Vesco, who, the witness claimed, said he was going to give it to Pindling.[34]

Some of the excess income undoubtedly came from the earnings of Pindling's private businesses, such as the catering company to which Vesco's Bahamas Commonwealth Bank had lent money. After Vesco's departure, the loan was refinanced through the Bank of Nova Scotia. There was also another loan of more than $1 million from Scotiabank, which seemed to do little to annoy Pindling with interest payments. Nonetheless, the loan appeared to be secure, as cash deposits had been made into the bank in the name of Pindling and his wife to the tune of $2.4 million.[35]

Prime Minister Pindling survived the investigation. He hired US lobbyists and public relations consultants to fight back, and brushed up his image by hosting the 1985 British Commonwealth prime ministers' conference.[36] The main effect of the Royal Commission report was the sacking of two more cabinet ministers who tried in vain to use it to dump Pindling from power.

Not so fortunate was the chief minister of the Turks and Caicos Islands, who was arrested with two senior officials in Miami early in 1985 and charged with conspiracy to smuggle cocaine into the US. A scramble to confer on him retroactive diplomatic immunity failed to secure his release. The Turks and Caicos plan to introduce offshore banking foundered after the jailing of its principal advocates.[37]

Then, late in 1985, the US began applying a new, more effective technique for extracting information. Faced with the fact that the deal with the Cayman Islands covered only drug cases, US courts began ordering persons under investigation to waive their rights to confidentiality. First applied to a tax-evasion case involving the Cayman Islands, it quickly resulted in the surrender of documents to a Florida court by the Bank of Nova Scotia.[38]

Go West, Young Promoter, Go West

US victories in the Caribbean were only a beginning. A tax haven, and an offshore bank to occupy it, can be made to order. By the mid-1980s, peekaboo financial centers spanned the globe. As fast as US fiscal authorities could move on established havens, new havens serving other hot-money circuits sprang up.

Some of the drug money fleeing the Caymans and Bahamas headed for Panama, mitigating the deposit loss the area had suffered when flight capital began going directly to Miami. Though the US put pressure on Panama, its authorities merely shut down the occasional particularly notorious bank, such as that owned by the top Colombian drug dealers. In general, the National Guard firmly defended their banking system, despite US brandishing of the old 'waiver-by-conduct' weapon.[39]

Panama was a canal joining the hot money flowing out of the old and declining Caribbean circuit with that from the rising trans-Pacific drainage system. San Francisco was soon rivaling Miami, drawing in flight capital from Hong Kong and the Philippines and attracting dirty money for laundering in sufficient quantities that its local Fed was soon awash with surplus cash. Undoubtedly, part of the boom reflected the fact that, after the collapse of its legal economy in 1982, Mexico was soon back in the big leagues as a source of illegal drugs for the US market, pouring out marijuana, cocaine, and heroin, apparently with the ample assistance of some police and government officials; hot money followed the drugs into neighboring US states, particularly California. With the temperature rising along the Pacific Basin, it cannot be entirely coincidental that two of California's biggest banks, Crocker and Bank of America, drew record fines in 1985 for failure to report cash transactions. Nor can the flows of hot money fail to have been a factor in New York pressuring California to lower barriers to interstate banking.[40] And, as the Pacific hot-money circuit took on greater importance, it encouraged the flowering of bank havens on exotic Pacific isles.[41]

Thus the roving eye of offshore bank promoter Jerome Schneider scanned location after location, claiming to be able to detect whenever a particular haven had had its day. As US government pressure mounted on the Caribbean, he shifted his salesmanship efforts to the South Pacific. In 1982, Guam, Palau, and the North Mariana Islands passed bank secrecy laws, allegedly because of Schneider's influence. Schneider's promotional brochures reportedly extolled the islands' location for capturing a share of the East Asian flight-capital market. These islands, especially the North Marianas, were reputed to combine the advantages of being beyond the scrutiny of the IRS and bank regulators and benefiting from Federal Deposit Insurance Corporation coverage. For $25,000 one could get the complete package: a box of legal documents including preprinted CDs and letters of credit. There was no need for a bank owner to make the long and arduous trip to its island headquarters, many thousands of miles from the mainland US. A local trust company could handle the few mechanics of its operation.[42]

However, American bank regulators insisted that US law *did* apply to American trust territories in the Pacific, and Washington began to exercise the leverage that comes with providing 50% of the Mariana Islands government budget. Obviously the US government could hardly take seriously charges that it was infringing on the sovereignty of its own trust territories in demanding information. (Nor were the territories likely to argue that the US should manage its deficit through reduced expenditures rather than through increased tax revenues from eliminating loopholes.)

Schneider's enterprise was set back somewhat when the government of the Marianas refused to renew the license of the First Bank of North America. It had been opened in Toronto and Miami by a man convicted in 1979 of mail fraud involving two Florida banks. First Bank's letters of credit and CDs turned out to be worthless, and the government of Ontario searched in vain for the proceeds of two small-business development grants awarded the owner's other enterprises.[43] Early in 1986 indictments were brought down against the owners of another Marianas bank, alleging that they used the bank to defraud people trying to get money out of Mexico after the imposition of exchange controls.[44]

Also problematic was the financial future of another US Pacific trust territory, the Marshall Islands, the largest of which, by early 1985, hosted more than 100 'banks.' Violations of security law, bad checks and phony CDs, and 'investment' programs promising impossible returns were drawing lawsuits and the scrutiny of the US comptroller of the currency.[45]

Could it be that the heyday of the US Pacific trust territories, like that of the British Caribbean havens, was over? Maybe, but Jerome Schneider, like Michael Oliver before him, had another idea: Vanuatu, with its booming satellite-linked and Hong Kong–fed international financial center, its instant Panamanian-inspired corporation-manufacturing business, and its Liberian-style ship 'registry.'[46] And Vanuatu was not alone.

In 1981 the Cook Islands, impressed by Vanuatu's success, decided to follow suit. The Cook Islands found its geographic position in relation to the US of special benefit. The adviser to the government of the islands who framed their banking laws, put it this way: given the distance and travel expense, there was 'no possibility of an American IRS man flying to the Cook Islands with petty cash – as they can to the nearby Caymans –

to bribe clerks into letting them see accounts which are then used to prosecute.'[47]

Geographic distance and the proliferation of new havens were not the only obstacles faced by American regulators. Although the IRS, the DEA, and the FBI took an interest in following the trail of dirty money, the CIA contended that such pursuits were outside its field of competence. However, as far back as 1975 two former investigators from the US Department of Justice suggested another possible explanation for the CIA's reluctance to get involved: 'It is widely believed that the agency itself uses Swiss and offshore banks to finance its covert operations in much the same manner as organized and white-collar criminals.'[48]

20

Ghost Companies and Haunted Banks

In the spring of 1982 the CIA issued an unprecedented public denial: 'The CIA has not engaged in operations against the Australian government, has no ties with Nugan-Hand, and does not involve itself in drug trafficking.'[1] At the time 'the Company' was being haunted by the specter of a bizarre scandal surfacing from the underworld of international banking – the collapse of the Nugan-Hand merchant bank of Sydney. This institution, which passed its time laundering drug money, trafficking in arms, and funding CIA covert operations, was described as having enough former top-level military personnel on its staff to be able to conduct a small war.

Although the Nugan-Hand affair threw the issues into sharp relief, the interface of the three underworlds – 'intelligence' or covert political action, criminal enterprise or covert economic action, peekaboo banking or covert financial action – was hardly new.

Curious Company
It was precisely such a coincidence of interests between Bulgarian intelligence and the Turkish babas – the former offered cover for the smuggling of arms, drugs, and hot money in exchange for clandestine 'services' rendered by the latter – on which the Italian military intelligence (SISMI) spooks built the theory of the Bulgarian Connection. Similarly, when Taiwanese military intelligence, which operates a paramilitary force in the heart of the Thai-Burma narcotics-producing region, needed special talent for a political hit, it was to the dope-dealing Bamboo Union to which it apparently turned. And certainly not the least of the intelligence forces with a history of drawing on the services of the underworld for skilled personnel was France's General Directorate of External Security (DGSE). In fact, after 1962, when the military unit that had provided the bulk of the personnel needed by DGSE for covert action was disbanded by President De Gaulle – its officers having been found conspiring to assassinate the president after he began negotiating

Algeria's independence – the French government began heavy recruiting of replacements from the ranks of the French, especially the Corsican, underworld. This practice stopped only when De Gaulle's successor, Georges Pompidou, realized that both the US-sponsored war on narcotics trafficking and his own need for a secret service loyal to him rather than to De Gaulle pointed to a massive purge of the DGSE.[2]

In a similar vein, one organization alleged – perhaps fancifully – to share covert objectives with the CIA, the Irish Republican Army, has been a long-time user of clandestine mechanisms of money transfer. Much of the money for IRA activities is raised by contributions from supporters in the US. Historically the money moved across the Atlantic through cash couriers – often, apparently, those employed by 'organized' crime. But to these traditional methods have been added cashiers' checks issued, for example, by the New York branch of the Bank of Ireland, and bank-to-bank wire transfers.[3]

According to former Italian spook and Calvi consultant Francesco Pazienza, the IRA (though perhaps not the Provisional Wing) also received money, on Vatican orders, from Banco Ambrosiano. This allegation, if true, might help explain why $30 million of the missing Ambrosiano money turned up in a small Dublin private bank in 1984.[4] Yet another alleged source of IRA money is drug dealing. For example, US prosecutors in the trial of John Z. De Lorean on charges of cocaine trafficking claimed that the IRA had provided seed money for his alleged (and unproved) efforts to save his Irish industrial enterprise by dealing in Colombian cocaine.[5]

One source of money that appears to be subject to no such doubts is that derived from kidnapping and ransoming Irish businessmen delinquent in their protection payments. One 1983 kidnapping saw the ransom money washed through Switzerland, transferred to the New York branch of a Swiss bank, moved to the New York office of the Bank of Ireland, converted into cashiers' checks, and sent back to Ireland.[6]

Of course, not all the money need move back to Ireland, for much of the Provisional IRA's arms purchases are effected in the US, through such varied partners as the Mafia and the CIA, either of whom could undoubtedly assist in moving any unspent surpluses discreetly abroad.[7]

With or without such fellow travelers, America's spooks have long haunted the corridors of domestic and international financial institutions.[8] During the 1970s rapid inflation and post–Viet Nam paranoia caused the US intelligence budget to jump considerably – by 1984 it totalled $24 billion. Of this, the CIA got about 15%, on top of whatever it earned from its portfolio of commercial and financial assets.[9] Given the magnitude of CIA operations, a worldwide financial network is necessary. Given the nature of those operations, the modus operandi of that network must be secret. The need for secrecy has been particularly acute since 1981, when William Casey, Reagan's appointee as CIA chief, began rebuilding the covert-operations wing of the CIA, which had fallen into disfavor during the scandals and purges of the mid-1970s.[10]

There are three levels on which the CIA and other intelligence agencies interact with the overworld of business and finance. One derives from the need for facilities for transferring funds to finance covert operations, military, political, and economic – including handling insurance and social benefits needed by deep-cover agents who cannot be covered by normal social-security provisions. The second, closely related, level derives from the need for the clandestine investment of the agency's earnings from its front companies. The third, that of corporate cover, derives from the need to generate the illusion that agents engaged in covert action are actually ordinary employees of legitimate businesses.[11]

All three levels can be handled by CIA-owned companies. Sometimes these are merely shell companies, essentially mail drops managed by friendly lawyers. Sometimes they are actually operating companies: import-export firms, shipping companies and airlines, insurance companies and, not least, banks. But even wholly owned CIA proprietaries would rarely be used solely by the agency. Haunted companies require the public cover of legitimate business activities in order to service their clientele of spooks. And the clandestine services that intelligence agencies require can also be of benefit to certain forms of private enterprise that share the need for secrecy.[12]

They can also share personnel. The CIA-produced instruction manual for the Contras in Nicaragua advising on the proper techniques for sabotage and assassination and recommending the hiring of experienced criminals for 'selective jobs'[13] was part of a tradition going back at least to its contract with the Florida mob to murder Fidel Castro.[14] As the agency's help-wanted ads proudly proclaim, 'The CIA is an Equal Opportunity Employer.'[15]

The agency can also work through private-sector companies. After the Vietnam War, the agency began scaling down its proprietary companies in favor of more extensive dealings with the private enterprise that it was charged with defending around the world. Subsequently, some of America's best-known corporations and banks have allegedly acted on behalf of the Company, moving its money and providing cover for its agents.

It was a former operative for the OSS (predecessor of the CIA), Nicholas Deak, who, shortly after the Second World War, founded a currency- and bullion-trading company that soon became the largest in America.

The firm apparently served the Company well. It allegedly shifted the funds the CIA needed in the 1950s to finance the overthrow of Iranian Prime Minister Mossadegh when he attempted to take control of his country's oil wells. Deak also apparently moved funds to finance CIA operations in the old Belgian Congo (now Zaire), when secessionists made their play for the mineral-rich Shaba province. During the Vietnam War, Deak provided the CIA with black-market Vietnamese piasters in exchange for dollars deposited with it in the US.[16]

Similarly, Bernie Cornfeld's Investors' Overseas Services, with its specialists in underground financial movements, allegedly cooperated with the CIA, which used its banks to run money and apparent employment as mutual-fund salesmen as cover for agents.[17]

Michele Sindona may also have put his institutions at the service of the CIA, running through his Banca Privata Finanziaria $4 million (from Continental Illinois) to help the colonels' 1967 coup in Greece, and $10 million to finance anticommunist activities in the 1972 Italian elections.[18]

Such private-sector companies might even be direct outgrowths of former intelligence-agency proprietaries. Thus, when Edwin Wilson was ostensibly forced out of the CIA in 1971 for using CIA proprietaries for private business, he was taken under the wing of the Office of Naval Intelligence. There he operated a commodity-trading firm, Consultants International, which provided cover for global intelligence gathering. In 1977, Wilson was apparently sacked from ONI, but he took Consultants International with him into the private sector.

Operating out of London, the world center for arms trafficking, and Geneva, where he banked, Wilson used the cover of Swiss and Liberian companies to run arms and military trainers to Libya, and to assist Mouamar Qadhaffi in disposing of exiled opponents. Tricked into returning to the US in the belief that his services were required to set up a new intelligence-gathering system in the Caribbean under the cover of a commodity-trading firm, Wilson was arrested and jailed in 1981, all the while protesting that his Libyan operation had the sanction of US intelligence.[19]

In spite of the appeal of the Crusade against the Bolshevik hordes, governments and their law-enforcement agencies are sometimes reluctant to let intelligence agencies run roughshod over their financial and fiscal regulations, not to speak of their narcotics laws. Yet the last thing the CIA wants is the IRS probing the origins and destinations of financial flows of its associated companies. Nor does it want the Bureau of Alcohol, Tobacco and Firearms looking into the export business of some of its contract agents; the bureau's officers complain that just when they are about to crack a gunrunning ring, the case is blocked by the CIA.[20] And the CIA certainly does not want the FBI or DEA questioning the extracurricular activities of some of its associates. Embarrassing conflicts and revelations could sometimes result, though in most contests between the Justice Department, IRS, DEA, FBI, and customs on the one hand, and the CIA on the other, the other agencies, even with the help of the Firearms Bureau, are usually outgunned.

In the early 1970s the FBI probably had evidence to implicate Archbishop Marcinkus in a bizarre scheme with American mobsters and professional paperhangers, by which the Vatican bank would buy $1 billion worth of counterfeit American securities.[21] One theory about Marcinkus's remarkable longevity in the Vatican, notwithstanding this and many subsequent scandals, is that he is its principal contact man for the CIA.[22] Similarly, one of Michele Sindona's unsuccessful joint ventures with the Vatican – an attempt in 1975 to purchase a small New Jersey bank, whose main asset seemed to be a list of 300 FBI agents who owed the bank money – may have been intended to short-circuit FBI probes of the sort that caused embarrassment over the stock deal.[23]

Neatly avoiding such embarrassment was one of the pioneers of the Florida banking boom in the early 1970s, Guillermo Hernandez-Cartaya, who had learned his banking in Cuba before the revolution. In exile, in 1970, he organized the World Finance Corporation (WFC), which leaped into international lending. It established offices all over Latin America and beyond, a bank in Panama, another in Costa Rica, and in 1976 acquired control of the National Bank of South Florida. WFC soon attracted FBI attention as a possible drug-money laundromat. The FBI tried to crack it; but WFC had CIA protection. Furthermore, one IRS agent reportedly told FBI investigators that WFC was a legitimate company: if it dealt in drug money, so much the better; narcotics money that stayed in the US was good for the American economy.[24] Many Florida banks would agree.

Despite this cheerfully accommodating view,[25] wrecking the tax agency's voyages of discovery on the shoals of offshore banking is normally a high priority for the CIA. Therefore, the CIA has long prowled Caribbean peekaboo centers, particularly since Castro's revolution. Nor was it unacquainted with some of the creators and principal users of those centers for the practice of the arts and sciences of peekaboo finance.[26] The specter of Cuba led the CIA to undertake a wide range of covert actions – assassinations, bombings, naval raids, and the equipping of paramilitaries for Central American countries whose shaky finances required a communist 'threat' to stimulate the flow of US aid money. To finance these activities, the CIA turned to Castle Bank & Trust of Nassau.

The bank was established by Paul Helliwell, a former OSS China hand with a background in drug-trade intelligence. After the war, Helliwell had run CIA front companies in Florida. Through his Bahamian bank, and a companion institution in Florida, millions of dollars were funneled for covert military operations[27] staged off Andros Island in the Bahamas. Castle also facilitated tax evasion, and, in its trust-company capacity, voted the shares of certain nonresident owners of Resorts International, the top Lansky-era casino operation on Nassau. When one of those shareholders so strongly objected to the way Castle was voting his shares that he sued the bank, the scheme began to unravel.

The shareholder was William Mellon Hitchcock, the New York stockbroker who had been using the Paravicini Bank of Berne, Switzerland, to circumvent the New York Fed's margin requirements.[28] Allegedly, Hitchcock also put his business experience to work in 'high finance,' along with the Brotherhood of Eternal Love, whose clandestine California laboratories reportedly produced more than half the LSD that levitated political debate on American campuses in the 1960s. It was Hitchcock's friend Timothy Leary, the era's most publicized advocate of the chemical lobotomy, who got him involved with the LSD operation. The profits were laundered through the Paravicini Bank until its demise and through the IOS-controlled Fiduciary Trust in the Bahamas.[29]

After Hitchcock's lawsuit, the IRS made its move, anticipating the biggest tax-evasion bust in American history. But the CIA successfully lobbied for the inquiry to be buried, and many IRS veterans quit in disgust. But Castle Bank shut down its Caymans and Bahamas operations in 1977, and moved to the more congenial environment of Panama.[30] The resulting vacuum in the Caribbean may have sucked in Australia's most haunted bank at the end of its strange career.

Antipodal Ambrosiano?

Australia is a prize cold war asset. Its strategic mineral resources include about 20% of the world's uranium, and its geographical position makes it the ideal host for at least ten American military installations, including the world's most elaborate electronic espionage station. Given this strategic importance, the CIA maintains close ties with the Australian Secret Intelligence Organization (ASIO).[31] Allegedly, their close relations included a 'dirty tricks' campaign in the 1970s to discredit certain Labour party politicians.

US covert operations in Australia were carried out by Task Force

157. The organization was set up in the 1960s under the umbrella of US Navy Intelligence after the Bay of Pigs fiasco revealed glaring deficiencies both in CIA intelligence gathering and in the hopes for a frontal assault on the Castro regime. TF 157 was a collection of super-spooks whose two major functions were monitoring Soviet shipping and operating more than 100 front companies. To these was added respon-sibility for ultrasensitive covert operations in gunrunning, money laun-dering, and political espionage. TF 157 funds to buy political support, infiltrate unions, and maintain an anti-Labour party media blitz report-edly were passed through the Nugan-Hand merchant bank in Sydney.[32]

Victory for the Labour party in the 1972 federal elections was seen as a strategic threat. The Labour government was committed, as was that of Salvador Allende in Chile, to restoring national control over mineral resources by buying out the US transnational corporations. It broke with the US foreign-policy line on Southeast Asia and the Middle East; and it began investigating ASIO subversive activities performed on behalf of the US.

Task Force 157 concocted a scandal over loans the minister of energy was seeking in the Middle East, providing a pretext for the governor general, who had very close intelligence links, to dismiss the government. After this bloodless coup d'état, a right-wing government came to office. Australia acceded to US requests for port-of-call facilities to US nuclear warships; and it announced its intention of lowering obstacles to US investment in the mineral and energy sectors. When the now-opposition Labour party picked a new chief, approved by Business International, a private club of twenty giant American transnational corporations,[33] the CIA could relax – until shaken awake by the crash of the Nugan-Hand bank.

Frank Nugan began his business career in the family fruit-packing business in a region famous for its marijuana crops. Despite his other activities, he took sufficient interest in the family business that, at the time of his 'suicide' in 1980, he was accused of illegally diverting $1.6 million of Nugan-Hand money into it, and of making large payments out of it to persons linked to drug trafficking.

His future partner was American Michael Hand, a former Green Beret who had taken part in the Phoenix Program, the mass assassination program in Vietnam, planned by future CIA chief William Colby, with hardware specially designed by Mitch WerBell. As an employee of Air America, the CIA-owned airline often accused of carrying opium from the Golden Triangle to market,[34] Hand worked extensively among the Meo people. As mercenaries, paid in gold, Meo men provided the CIA with its most important irregular force in Southeast Asia; and as opium growers, Meo women helped consolidate the fiscal foundations of pro-American regimes.

The first Australian business ventures of Nugan and Hand were selling land to American soldiers in Australia on R&R during the late 1960s. Once R&R ceased, the two partners established a Panamanian company to buy the land back at perhaps one-third of its value. Of nineteen founding shareholders of their real estate company, at least ten had some association with the CIA.[35] So, too, did many of the officers of their future 'merchant bank.'

Until recently, Australia has maintained fairly tight restrictions on commercial bank activity, limiting entry and legislating functional barriers. For this reason, merchant banks, like deposit-taking corporations in Hong Kong, could exploit areas barred to commercial banks.[36] This was normal enough, but Nugan and Hand took a rather Swiss view of merchant banking.

In its history, Nugan-Hand engaged in negotiations with US mob figures to launder their funds back to them in the form of an international bank 'loan' to finance a Las Vegas casino project. Facilitating tax evasion was another service Nugan-Hand reportedly offered its private clients.[37] As a regional paymaster to the CIA Nugan-Hand supposedly funded covert action against the Australian Labour party and other regimes in the area. It was even reported to have been a conduit for CIA money moving to the Italian Christian Democratic party. As a funder of covert action, it could help destabilize areas, for a price; as a capital-flight vehicle, it could service the money fleeing the consequences, for a fee. Nugan-Hand was also said to have been involved in helping to move part of the shah of Iran's fortune into an Alpine resort. (Probably no other monarch in history has had as many purported assistants to cart off his cash as had the late shah; but then perhaps no other monarch in history had so much baggage to be carried.) Nugan-Hand also found irresistible a foray into the international arms-trafficking business, which, almost by definition, required participation in the drug trade, its virtual mirror image.

There was nothing illegal about Nugan-Hand's gunrunning out of Australia. It was merely acting (seemingly with the assent, if not active instigation, of Task Force 157) as broker between two or more outside parties, including the CIA-backed UNITA guerrilla movement in Angola and the Ian Smith regime in Rhodesia. Funds to purchase the arms were apparently moved from the Nugan-Hand Hong Kong affiliates to Switzerland; the return flow of payments came partly in gold and partly in ivory and tiger skins.

The bank's involvement with the drug trade can be traced at least to 1977, when it came to the attention of the Sydney police. Investigations in Australia were blocked, and the US DEA seems to have done nothing, though the US was the ultimate destination of much of the heroin being moved by Nugan-Hand's clients.[38] Yet, when a proper investigation was finally undertaken, an Australian government inquiry found that the bank had links with at least twenty-six different individuals or groups known to be associated with drug trafficking.

As regional banker to the dope trade, Nugan-Hand provided a laundromat for domestic distributors, passing the cash through controlled companies. It also arranged international remittances for foreign clients, notably from Chiang Mai, Thailand. There, in the center of the Golden Triangle opium network, Nugan-Hand had its office in the same building, on the same floor, as that of the US DEA. Its Bangkok office included one employee known to be involved in running guns to the Kuomintang forces in the Shan States, and Nugan-Hand appears to have entered into fruitless negotiations for a sale of arms to the government of Thailand.[39]

The bank also operated extensively in the secondary market for trade paper associated with the narcotics business. It used the lateral-transfer technique favored by the Southeast Asia traffickers. Cash would be accepted in Sydney, and Nugan-Hand's Hong Kong DTC would issue a cashier's check for the same sum; the check would be cashed at the Hong Kong office of Deak & Co. and the cash would be used to buy heroin for export back to Australia. Similarly, money could be sent to Hong Kong from Thailand by cash courier to be washed through the DTC and a string of Hong Kong companies. Nugan-Hand also raised money in Hong Kong by issuing CDs, whose proceeds would be recycled to Australia. And it considered going into the trade-insurance business, projecting, though never establishing, a $1.4 million bail fund for couriers caught in the US.[40]

The bank grew rapidly and spread widely in the late 1970s, in good measure because of the astounding number of former armed forces and intelligence personnel it showcased. Among them was Admiral Earl Yates, formerly of US Naval Intelligence, who initially headed the Cayman Islands branch and later the overall international organization. The man in charge of the Bangkok office was the former CIA station chief for the city. The former commander of US forces in Thailand became Nugan-Hand's Hawaiian representative. Several other generals, admirals, and top-level spooks figured among its staff and business associates, including William Colby. After he retired as head of the CIA, one of Colby's hobbies was acting as legal adviser to Nugan-Hand, helping it with tax matters and with banking projects in Florida and Panama.[41]

The army-and-navy team was still in charge when, in 1980, Frank

Nugan performed a 'suicide' that was almost as acrobatic as that of Roberto Calvi. The bank and related companies, including its Hong Kong DTC,[42] came crashing down with $50 million missing from its accounts. None of the missing money was ever recovered, nor, curiously enough, did the depositors try to get it back. Also missing were most of the Hong Kong and Sydney records and Michael Hand, who vanished.[43]

The investigation into drug trafficking conducted by the federal and New South Wales governments after the Nugan-Hand collapse tended to downplay the backgrounds of the bank's staff. It stressed that the boys had been colleagues in military and intelligence life before becoming so in private business, and that their association in such large numbers came late in the bank's career.[44] It is true that the rapid growth of personnel with a military and/or intelligence background came just at the time when the Office of Naval Intelligence was shutting down TF 157, and when the CIA was engaged in a massive purge of its clandestine operations branch – which would put many ex-spooks in the private-sector job market. However, that fails to explain why a merchant bank preferred a staff trained in espionage and counterinsurgency to one versed in interest-rate futures and currency swaps. The roster of personnel with intelligence and military backgrounds was effective window dressing – it did attract depositors – but it was also of obvious value for arms trafficking. And although most of the personnel of the bank might have been largely unaware of what was going on, arms trafficking and narcotics dealing in Southeast Asia are Siamese twins.

Nor did the investigators seem to convince the New South Wales Corporate Affairs Commission, which called for a formal Royal Commission of Inquiry into trafficking in drugs and arms, tax evasion, the CIA link, and the obstructionist behavior of US government agencies, which stonewalled requests for information.[45]

Last Flight of the Phoenix Program?

One of the most intriguing aspects of Nugan-Hand's business career was its decision, just before the crash, to increase its Caribbean presence beyond a branch in the Cayman Islands and a representative office in Miami. Its objective was not merely a new location for peekaboo facilities, but an island sanctuary defensible by a specially trained guerrilla army, composed of Meo tribesmen displaced after the fall of South Vietnam.

Following in Robert Vesco's footsteps, the bankers put at the top of the shopping list a small Haitian island, threatening to overthrow Baby Doc if the cession were not made peacefully. The bank's officers went calling on none other than Mitchell WerBell with a contract to test the suitability of the waters for their new hot-money dump site.

It was only after WerBell advised against the scheme that Nugan-Hand opened negotiations with the government of the Turks and Caicos Islands.[46]

On Grand Turk Island was a former US naval base where some 3,000 Meo were slated for resettlement. It was an expensive and troublesome installation for an island that could barely find enough fresh water for its existing population; and Nugan-Hand's reasons for conceiving the resettlement proposition were probably not entirely altruistic. At stake was much more than an ordinary tax haven and offshore banking center – albeit the IRS and DEA were putting pressure on the nearby Cayman Islands, where Nugan-Hand located much of its international business. Grand Turk would be a particularly attractive alternative if, manned by one of the US's most experienced foreign mercenary forces, it could also become a paramilitary center for pursuing US foreign-policy aims in the Caribbean. The island's attractions were enhanced by the refusal of the Pindling government to permit further use of Andros Island as a staging point for anti-Castro operations, which the defunct Castle Bank & Trust had funded.

But for entrepreneurs as imaginative as Frank Nugan and Michael Hand, there was another intriguing possibility, not entirely unrelated to the economic function Meo women had performed in Southeast Asia. The cocaine trade from South America was ripening, and the heroin traffic from Southeast and Southwest Asia often went through South America en route to final markets in the north.

In brief, the Turks and Caicos[47] – complete with a private army of experienced mercenaries and opium traders, and with Nugan-Hand, heir to the Castle Bank & Trust, to oversee financial arrangements – could double as a peekaboo financial center and drug-transshipment point. If such a scheme was afoot, however, it collapsed after Frank Nugan got himself suicided, precipitating the failure of the bank.

Hawaii's Worst-Kept Secret

While Australian investigators agreed that the plethora of personnel with intelligence backgrounds in the Nugan-Hand affair was disturbing, they had found it difficult to accept a direct CIA link in Nugan-Hand's activities. They preferred to believe that the bank simply used its officials' former connections to assist in and cover up the illegal acts it undertook purely for profit. The most logical basis for that position was not the association of the bank with drug peddlers (an association that might be interpreted as clinching the case for the prosecution) but rather the fact that Nugan-Hand seemed to be so amateurish. Surely, the commissioners dithered, a CIA enterprise would conduct its business in a far more professional manner.[48] But would it?

In the summer of 1983 the Hawaiian investment company, Bishop, Baldwin, Rewald, Dillingham and Wong,[49] was forced into involuntary bankruptcy by four clients who claimed to have been victimized by the firm. That was the beginning of a saga whose similarities to the Nugan-Hand affair were so great that the CIA seized the files on grounds of 'national security.'

Donald Rewald, principal of the firm, apparently began his association with the CIA in his college years during the turbulent 1960s, informing on campus antiwar activists. In 1977 he arrived in Honolulu carrying one conviction for theft and one personal bankruptcy. He soon ingratiated himself with the local CIA and military hierarchy, abundant in Hawaii because of its strategic location, its military bases, and its comfortable retirement facilities for ex-soldiers and former spooks. He then set up, allegedly with CIA aid, an investment company, one of whose interests was hyped in a pamphlet entitled, 'Capital Flight from Hong Kong and How Hawaii Can Benefit.' The five-barreled company name was created by combining his name and that of his partner, Sunlin Wong, with the names of three of Hawaii's best-known families, none of whom had any connection with the firm. Observers later remarked that it was a little like establishing a New York firm named Rockefeller, Roosevelt, Rewald, Vanderbilt and Mellon.

Among Rewald's clients and associates could be found the recently retired head of the US Air Force's Pacific Command and two former CIA station chiefs for Honolulu. After the crash, Rewald faced prosecution; by 'pure, utter coincidence,' the attorney assigned to prosecute his case was a former chief of the CIA's litigation branch at the Langley, Virginia, headquarters.

Like Nugan-Hand, Bishop, Baldwin had expanded rapidly, with offices in Taiwan, Singapore, Tahiti, Jakarta, and elsewhere. Soon it had, at least on paper, a corporate empire from Hawaii to Europe via the Far East, and was picking up more CIA and military associates en route. With things going so well, Rewald cultivated a flashy lifestyle, purchasing twelve limousines and luxury cars for his personal use, buying ranches, a villa, and similar essentials of his craft. Investors were attracted by his guarantee of a 26% return, by his boasting of FDIC coverage of deposits of up to $150,000 (a double deception, for FDIC limits were $100,000 and his firm was not eligible for coverage), and not least, by his ostentatious flaunting of his CIA links. (Rewald seemed to work on the same principle as the White House special spook corps, whose officers can be found at functions in distinctive uniforms with Secret Service emblazoned on the chest.)

In a classic Ponzi game ploy, high returns were paid to the initial investors out of the funds paid in by subsequent ones. Some 400 people, including several CIA men and their relatives, ultimately had $22 million at risk, of which the liquidators could initially locate only $300,000.

Like Castle Bank & Trust, Bishop, Baldwin had problems that began with the IRS when, in the autumn of 1982, a Hawaiian agent noted a discrepancy between Rewald's lifestyle and his reported income. Initially the investigation was blocked by the CIA, though it used the occasion to order some of its agents to pull their money out of Rewald's firm. There was good reason for blocking the investigation. Although the books were adequate to coax more investors into putting money in the firm, they would not have survived expert scrutiny, despite the best efforts of the firm's bookkeeper, who (also by 'pure, utter coincidence'?) was a former employee of the National Security Agency. But IRS persistence, and the four angry clients, pushed the firm into bankruptcy. Rewald was subsequently charged with fraud, perjury, and tax evasion.

Instead of being a routine trial of the firm's principals, the case became a closed circus. The CIA impounded and censored the books and documents, and the courts were persuaded initially to set Rewald's bail at an incredible $10 million, to assure that he remained out of circulation. Nor were visitors allowed to carry paper or pens when they went to see him. This was curious in view of the CIA's public admission of only a 'low level' association with Rewald. One officer insisted that 'This idiot provided a cover for some of our guys'; and the CIA disclaimed all responsibility for the actual conduct of his business.

But if Rewald is to be believed, the 'low level' association included the following: his chauffeur drove around Hawaii dozens of agents and foreign dignitaries the agency was entertaining; CIA operatives across the Pacific used 'employment' with the firm as cover and its offices as information drops; the firm monitored flows of money arriving from outside; it acted as a conduit for funding covert action and for the establishment of retirement accounts for foreign potentates, held against the day when they might have to leave home in a hurry. Also benefiting from Bishop, Baldwin's services were Southeast Asian businessmen whom the agency wanted to favor. Nor does Bishop, Baldwin appear to have been a complete stranger to clandestine arms trafficking and weapons intelligence. In all, it was scarcely surprising that Rewald was once introduced to Vice-President and former US top spook George Bush as 'an invaluable friend' of the agency.[50]

After surviving a suicide attempt, Rewald filed a $600 million damage suit against the CIA. Fifteen California investors also sued, claiming it was the CIA connection that had persuaded them to risk their money in the firm. Rewald insists that the firm was set up specifically on CIA orders as a cover for covert financial operations and that the agency told him to live high in order to mingle with and spy on wealthy Asian politicians and businessmen. Even his phony law degree, he claims, was a gift from the CIA. Alas, that law degree was little help; and in the autumn of 1985, Rewald was found guilty on ninety-four of ninety-eight counts.[51]

Deak's Last Stand

The jury was still out on the Bishop, Baldwin affair when charges of laundering cocaine money brought down a far more prominent US firm long associated with US overseas intelligence operations. By the time of its collapse, Deak & Co. was parent to a global empire based on currency and bullion dealing, with a forceful presence in the Hong Kong gold market, and a Swiss bank, the Foreign Commerce Bank of Zurich, in its stable.

Within the US, the most important subsidiary was Deak-Perera, the foreign-exchange and bullion dealer. In October 1984 it attracted accusations in connection with laundering hundreds of millions of dollars for Colombian cocaine traffickers. But it was in two obscure subsidiaries that the financial aftershocks of the accusations first manifested themselves.[52]

Deak Perera Wall Street and Deak-Perera International Banking Corporation were two Connecticut banks that were not banks. They dealt only in foreign deposits attracted by high interest rates and, undoubtedly, the appeal of anonymity. The funds were used to speculate in foreign-exchange and bullion markets. While the great bulk of the deposits came from Latin America, especially Argentina, the nonbanks had no branches there: they worked a sort of mail-order capital-flight business. It was a run on the Latin American deposits of these two subsidiaries, following the Presidential commission's revelations about Deak-Perera, that forced them to file under US bankruptcy law for protection from creditors. Why the depositors panicked is unclear. It may have been fear of the US government freezing the deposits; it may have been fear of the possible collapse of the companies; or it may have been fear of exposure of the names of depositors, likely of more interest to their home governments than to that of the US.[53]

Also shaken by the crisis were Deak's Hong Kong affiliates, which had been important for Nugan-Hand's dealings in the heroin trade paper market and in the Lockheed bribery operation. In Hong Kong there were five subsidiaries, of which the most important were a DTC, Deak-Perera Finance, and a bullion dealership, Deak-Perera Far East. The company was also present in Macao through Deak & Co. Macao Ltd.

Between Deak-Perera Far East and the Macao affiliate some odd transactions took place. Deposits were solicited in Hong Kong for transfer to Macao, though neither company had a DTC license. When the American subsidiaries filed under US bankruptcy law, the Hong Kong depositors panicked and tried to withdraw their money. It did not exist, at least not on the books of the Macao company that was supposed to be its custodian. Inquiries as to its whereabouts were hampered by the disappearance of the managing director. The Macao operation was closed. In Hong Kong, the government revoked the license of Deak-Perera Finance, a court ordered the liquidation of Deak-Perera Far East, and the police issued an arrest warrant for Nicholas Deak. And some quick changes of hand for the Foreign Commerce Bank of Zurich set off another tiff between Switzerland and the US Justice Department seeking to subpoena the bank's records of transactions of US clients.

In the autumn of 1985 Nicholas Deak was gunned down by one of those lone nuts that do for US politics what heart attacks do in Italian jails.[54] The remnants of the empire went up for grabs. Among the bidders was Beirut's Bank El-Mashreq, part of the original Yousef Beidas Intra Bank group,[55] the financial holding company that in 1966 had been the first prominent victim of the global hot-money whirl and narrowly escaped falling into the eager clutches of Robert Vesco. But finally Deak & Co. emerged from under Chapter-Eleven proceedings, paying off its creditors at 48¢ on the dollar, in the hands of a Pacific-based business group intent on plunging the rehabilitated company into the booming North American market in 'financial services.'[56]

Part Seven

Strange Harvest

21
Capital Punishment

The 1970s were, to some degree, a decade of development. Aided by foreign loans and strong commodity markets, many developing countries made impressive gains. While 'waste,' 'corruption,' and diversion of money to the military were amply evident, public works and industry did take shape.

The 1980s have been, to a considerable extent, a decade of undevelopment. Past income gains have often been erased, economic diversification regressed, and capital cannibalized,[1] as the IMF and other creditor interests decided that the developing countries should learn to live below their means.[2]

In 1982 GDP in Latin America fell 1.2%, the first absolute drop since the Second World War. In per capita terms the decline was 3.4%. Yet during the previous decade real growth had averaged 3% per annum. The situation was especially grim in Argentina, Bolivia, Chile, and Uruguay, where per capita income fell 10% between 1980 and 1982.[3] Even worse, real investment fell on average by 13%, a guarantee that the next year would show an even worse economic performance.

In 1983 absolute GDP fell in seventeen of nineteen countries by an average of 3.3%. The per capita decline averaged about 6%, returning to its 1977 level; in some countries it dropped to the level of the 1960s.[4] During those two grim years, net capital inflows ceased; net transfers of interest and profits out of the area hit $20 billion in 1982 and $29 billion in 1983. These transfers were made possible by a record merchandise-trade surplus, about 40% of which was directly remitted abroad as profit and interest payments.[5]

Nor was there any respite in 1984. Overall debt-service charges ran at 61% of export receipts; and net financial transfers were still more than $25 billion. During 1980 to 1985, inclusive, GDP in Latin America as a whole rose 3.9%, translating into a per capita decline of 8%. For fourteen countries the drop exceeded 10%; for seven it exceeded 15%.

Similarly, even as massive famines racked sub-Saharan Africa, the banks siphoned $3 billion net from the area, helping to bring the continent's 1984 per capita income to 90% of that of 1980. To the obvious suggestion that the area's debts be cancelled, the US ambassador to the United Nations, Vernon Walters, replied that such action would undermine international cooperation and economic development.[6]

During 1984 the developing countries put double the amount into the international banking system that they took out of it.[7] The Bank for International Settlements estimated that the net injection of funds into the banks of the major Western countries and the bank havens, from outside (mainly from developing countries), considerably exceeded the infusion of funds into that banking system produced by the oil-price hikes of 1973 and 1979.[8]

The dramatic turnaround in the trade balances of developing countries in Latin America and Africa came not through the expansion of exports, as IMF policy programs had envisaged, but by a collapse of imports. Money once spent on imports and investment went into interest payments on the external debt. By the end of 1984 the interest on that debt amounted to a burden on the developing countries double that imposed on Germany by the notorious post–First World War reparations bill.[9]

Most of the lost imports were not arms and luxury goods but industrial parts and equipment and food. Their loss meant enormous amounts of productive capacity were idle, and tens of millions of people faced malnutrition and famine[10] – and all to service a debt load that stemmed mainly from factors outside the control of the debtor countries: interest-rate increases, rescheduling fees, terms-of-trade deterioration, and, not least, the need to replace foreign exchange lost by capital flight.

Flying Lessons

The techniques of capital flight had not changed much since the golden years of IOS. Cash couriers, briefly out of fashion after hijackings by Palestinian guerrillas in the late 1960s and early 1970s, staged a professional comeback after electronic scanning devices replaced body searches at airports. And flight capitalists probably still accounted for a good share of the $200 million per annum traffic in phony and stolen airline tickets.[11]

Lateral transfers also remained a viable technology. In Mexico the major US banks, allegedly led by Citibank and Bank of America (though Citibank denies it), would accept pesos from local customers and make the dollar equivalent appear for their customers elsewhere – until

November 1985, when the Mexican government banned the practice and reimposed partial exchange controls.[12]

Among the most important techniques for illicit transfers remained those that required no cross-border movements of money – particularly phony invoicing, overvaluing the cost of imports and underreporting the receipts from exports, with the differences stashed abroad. In Nigeria, manipulation of invoices and fraudulent use of exchange-requisition forms cost the government billions.[13] In 1985 Paraguay was rocked by 'the greatest fraud in the country's history,' as an investigation by the Société Générale de Surveillance led to half a dozen leading banks and finance companies being accused of an invoicing scam equal to 20% of annual imports. The problem of phony invoicing soon caused Colombia to begin auditing coffee exports, and Ecuador and Venezuela to negotiate general inspection contracts with the Société Générale de Surveillance.[14]

These figures do not include the foreign exchange lost by trade conducted with no invoice at all. Argentina was losing about $1.2 billion a year from wheat smuggled out to avoid export taxes. Brazil loses perhaps $250 million per annum from smuggled coffee. After first trying to destroy the Nicaraguan coffee crop on which the Sandinista government depends heavily for foreign exchange, the Contras offered growers higher prices and payment in hard currency if they would avoid the official export monopoly. And Nigeria added hundreds of millions of dollars lost from smuggled oil to the billions looted by phony invoicing; the combined loss is estimated to have been equal to 20% of oil revenues between 1975 and 1983.[15]

In Southeast Asia the smuggling trails and the peekaboo-financial machinery pioneered by the opium and heroin traffickers could be put into general service. While Thailand busily exported drugs and guns to Malaysia, back came cheap oil and tin, evading the Thai excise taxes on the first and the Malaysian export royalties on the second. Thai traders in the border areas handled the payments through their unofficial check-clearing system, beyond the scrutiny of the monetary authorities, or by lateral transfers. The proceedings were allegedly encouraged by big Western commodity-trading firms who bought up enough of the smuggled tin concentrates to destroy the tin cartel run by the producing countries. The situation became so serious that in 1985 the Malaysian government began work on a wall along the Thai border to block the smugglers.[16]

More traditional capital-flight vehicles were also well used in the 1980s. From Turkey gold was smuggled abroad and sold for foreign exchange, which was smuggled back and resold, sometimes for more gold with which to repeat the process. The consequent drain of between sixty and ninety tons of gold between 1980 and 1983 sent several top bank executives to jail.[17]

By the early 1980s Brazil, the world's third most important gold producer, was losing $250 million annually in gold smuggled along the routes and in the light planes that serve the burgeoning cocaine trade of the Amazon. (Bolivia's gold production similarly evaded the official monopoly.) Even larger may be Brazilian losses from illicit exports of gemstones. Brazil has the world's largest reserves of topaz, tourmaline, and agate, as well as an abundance of emeralds; much of the production moves through tightly organized contraband rings protected by corrupted officials. In March 1985, US customs in Miami intercepted a courier carrying more than $2 million in emeralds. The trail led to a man already accused of fiscal fraud, whose Rio home contained eighteen tons of gem-bearing rocks. This was only part of the annual loss of hundreds of millions of dollars' worth of uncut and unpolished stones whose final market value might be as much as $10 billion,[18] even as Brazil is paying $12 billion a year in interest on its foreign debt.

Another traditional vehicle for illicit asset transfers is diamonds. From South Africa to Tel Aviv to Amsterdam and Antwerp[19] to New York, much of the trade is normally done without paper. There are also some extraordinary incentives to secrecy. Prior to its 1974 revolution, Portugal encouraged colonists fleeing Angola to use diamonds for flight-capital purposes by legislating that sellers of diamonds did not have to account for the gems' origins.

Angola, reeling from the virtual obliteration of its coffee production in the ongoing war against the CIA-backed UNITA guerrillas, found its state mining company drained by diamond smuggling. In 1984, one ring, working through the VIP lounge of Luanda airport, was accused of having stolen $140 million worth of diamonds during the previous two years. (Intriguingly, two of its members were also accused of having CIA associations.) From Luanda the diamonds proceeded to Lisbon, where a club of clandestine diamond dealers received and resold them, under the protection of the prerevolutionary secrecy law.[20]

Estimates of foreign exchange fleeing developing countries are bound to be tentative, variable, and likely conservative, particularly as they do not take into account losses from smuggling. The Bank for International Settlements, whose figures seem particularly conservative, put the amount leaving Latin America alone between 1978 and 1982 at about $55 billion. This is equal to about one-third of the region's total borrowing, and added $6.5 billion in 1983 debt-service charges for new borrowing to replace it. The US Federal Reserve estimated capital flight from Latin America for the same period at $84 billion; the Organization for Economic Cooperation and Development (OECD) ventured that in 1982 alone some $70 billion fled Latin America, double the interest payable on the entire Latin American debt for that year. The Bank of England's estimate was more modest, putting capital flight between 1981 and 1984 at only $80 billion, a mere 2.5% of Latin America's total debt.[21]

Manufacturers Hanover Bank calculated late in 1983 that during the previous four years, Latin America lost $100 billion. In 1979 $4.4 billion fled Mexico; in 1981 the figure had risen to $12.3; and by 1982 it hit $13.2 billion. Between 1983 and 1985, another $17 billion fled. Brazil lost $4.8 billion in 1982, three times its 1981 loss, and another $6.6 billion during 1983–85. Argentina lost $3.2 billion in 1982; Venezuela lost $9.7 billion.[22] The World Bank estimated that between 1979 and 1982 Mexico lost $26.5 billion, Venezuela $22 billion, Argentina $19 billion. It found Brazil's losses were 'only' about $4 billion,[23] though others put Brazil's 1982 loss at $12 billion.[24]

The net results are also subject to dispute. Mexican economists claim that at least $45 billion and perhaps as much as $60 billion in flight capital was stashed in US banks and real estate, while Morgan Guaranty Bank put total capital flight from Mexico by the end of 1985 at $85 billion, nearly equal to the country's total debt. Venezuelan assets abroad by 1984 were claimed to be as great as $35 billion, more than its total foreign debt. In 1985 Argentine external assets were estimated by some to be as much as its $50 billion total foreign debt.[25] In the aggregate, Morgan estimated that, in the decade before 1985, the 18 largest-debtor countries had added $450 billion to the foreign debt and had seen nearly $200 billion of it flee.[26]

To such sums pouring into the global hot-money pool must be added the flows from France and Spain, and certainly from Italy, whose flight capitalists received a new lease on life when one of their principal servants lost his. After receiving a life sentence for the murder of the liquidator of Banca Privata Finanziaria, Michele Sindona decreed that his appeal would be the moment when names would be named. Sindona allegedly knew the contents of the legendary list of 500 top illegal capital exporters. Alas, two days later, his memory was impaired – by a fatal dose of cyanide.[27]

And what about the wily A-Rabs of the oil cartel who supposedly caused it all? The OPEC group saw their total balance of payments go into deep deficit. And some of the individual members still running surpluses found themselves prominent victims of the global swirl of hot money. After a major bank failure shook the United Arab Emirates, capital flight accelerated until, by late 1984, it was running at an annualized rate of $5.5 billion.[28] Kuwait's $100 billion in foreign-exchange reserves are invested across the world and yield nearly as much revenue as does oil; yet even in Kuwait recession and the shadow of the Ayatollah brought to an abrupt end perhaps the greatest stock bubble in history, leaving a frozen credit system, a prostrate economy, and capital flight of such dimensions that the country was forced to impose emergency exchange controls.[29]

Whatever the total of capital flight from developing countries, it is sufficient to make nonsense of conventional financial statistics, and therefore of the economic-policy prescriptions based on them. From an approximate equilibrium during the early 1970s, the world balance of trade was showing increasing and logically impossible deficits by the end of the decade. According to IMF data, in 1981 the world was running a balance-of-trade deficit with itself of over $50 billion; this estimate approximately concurred with that of the Bank of England. The next year, the world payments gap was put between $76 billion and $100 billion. The OECD calculated the 1982 gap at $95 billion; Henry Wallich, a governor of the US Federal Reserve Bank, estimated a figure of $112 billion. In 1983 the IMF, traditionally conservative in its estimates, announced a hole in the world balance of payments of about $70 billion; its figure hit $100 billion by 1984.[30]

It seems only apt that the OECD should now divide the world economy into four sectors – the three traditional ones comprising the industrialized countries, the oil-exporting developing countries, and the nonoil-producing developing countries, and a fourth, offshore sector, with resources in excess of OPEC surpluses at their peak.[31]

But every cloud has a silver lining. In 1982 the US Commerce Department estimated that flight capital entering the US was $40 billion. By one estimate, in 1981 and 1982 when capital flight was just beginning to accelerate, Latin America lost $100 billion to the US and to Western Europe through black and gray transfers.[32] In 1984 alone, the Commerce Department calculated a net influx of foreign capital into the US at about $100 billion. All this must have struck terror into the hearts of Manhattan tenants, who faced landlord rampages as the inflow of flight capital sent the dormant real estate market of the 1970s into a dizzying speculative boom.

Helping the process are the growing number of American consultants and brokers specializing in capital flight. Flight capital was an especially welcome addition to a bank's funds, for bank officers handling it could usually insist on full discretion – the client was in no position to resent or complain of the results.[33] Hence, too, the growing number of 'private banking' departments of major American financial institutions, modeled on Citibank in 1966 and IOS in 1968. 'Private banking' represented a major American incursion into the territory of European, particularly English and Swiss, institutions that got their start handling the financial affairs of old, wealthy families for whom discretion was paramount.[34]

Merrill, Lynch Securities explained, on entering the field, that its private-banking department would cater worldwide to the 'ultra high net worth' client, whose minimum net assets were $10 million. This no doubt gladdened the heart of its former chief executive officer. On a 1983 tour of Arab Gulf states shaken by the Iran-Iraq war and the collapse of oil markets, Don Regan, then secretary of the treasury, promised that Arab assets would be safe in the US: 'We have become a haven currency and a haven country not only for people but also for their money.'[35] The 1966 dream of certain Chase officers had become a reality.

That certainly seemed to be good news for Ferdinand Marcos, family, and friends.

Of Coconuts and Queens

Marcos seems to have been accumulating money in his offshore retirement account almost since he became president of the Philippines in 1965; but the nature of the accumulation process changed in 1972. After a clandestine meeting between Marcos, two close civilian associates, and the military hierarchy, martial law was declared, ostensibly to deal with left-wing insurgency. Marcos used the cover of martial law to entrench his political power, and his associates captured the commanding heights of the Philippine economy. The IMF battled to 'liberalize' the financial system, and the World Bank deployed its technical forces to implement a new strategic plan for the country's economic development.[36]

At that time American and Japanese transnational corporations were searching the world for cheap labor. The Philippines was an ideal location, as some corporations apparently acknowledged by funneling payoffs to the presidential entourage (via Switzerland, if the one paying were American; through Hong Kong, if the company were Japanese). Marcos and the military assured a docile labor force; the IMF helped to maintain a financial system that permitted the unrestricted export of profits; and security was provided by the two largest US military bases outside continental North America.

US control of the Philippines dates from the Spanish-American War in 1898 and the resulting dual conquest of the islands, first from the Spanish and then from indigenous political forces demanding independence. The principal American objective was Manila harbor – America's answer to Hong Kong – as a center for trade with China. Despite the Philippines' becoming independent after the Second World War, the US maintained its military presence. The importance of the bases, and of the Marcos regime in defending them, assured that the US long turned a blind eye to the economic and military aid that got diverted into the first family's business empire at home and abroad.

Martial law made two major economic contributions to the Philippines. It permitted the civilian economy to be increasingly infiltrated by army officers with large numbers of progeny or Hong Kong bank accounts to feed. (After the overthrow of the Marcos regime, a new government alleged that as much as one-third of all military expenditures in the Philippines had vanished in bribes and commissions during the Marcos era.) And it abetted the emergence of a virtual parallel economy run by and for the president and his close associates.[37] Foreign bank loans, guaranteed by the state-owned development banks, were made available to selected entrepreneurs, permitting them to gain control of specific sectors of the economy. These sectors would then be favored by presidential decrees raising or lowering tariffs. Allegedly many of the loans were for rather more than the projects required; the difference, less the presidential tithe, would be diverted into the pockets of the borrowers.[38]

Associates controlled banks, insurance companies, basic manufacturing, commodity exporting, automobile importing, construction, and many other sectors, often built up and kept operational by massive infusions of state aid. Indeed, some enterprises were actually state owned, but operated as the personal property of Marcos's family and friends.[39]

Most notorious was that of former beauty queen and Eva Peron moral look-alike, Imelda Romualdez Marcos. Hardworking Mrs. Marcos ran the Greater Manila area (in which the bulk of the foreign investment occurred) and thirty government-owned corporations. As Minister of Human Settlements through whose department American economic aid was channeled, Imelda had a curiously limited definition of the spectrum of humanity deserving of settlement. Convention centers and luxury hotels sprang up around Manila, funded by borrowing abroad under government guarantee or by diverting the rent paid by the US government for its military bases. This aspect of the development strategy was so successful that by 1985 Manila was estimated to provide employment for 20,000 underage prostitutes.[40]

Despite such advances, the backbone of the Philippine economy remained agriculture – rice for domestic consumption and sugar and coconuts for export. Political power in the Philippines had long rested with the sugar barons, particularly after the Cuban Revolution, which saw the US grant the Philippines the privileged entry to the US sugar market that had formerly been extended to Cuba. But after declaring military rule, Marcos set out to centralize control over the sugar sector and to tap its wealth for his own political purposes. He created a vertically integrated, centrally controlled sugar sector, and placed it under the aegis of Roberto Benedicto, who also handled most of Marcos's personal bank accounts and ran the Marcos party machine on the island of Negros, the main sugar-growing area.

After indulging his sweet tooth in the sugar sector, Marcos got a hankering for a lovely bunch of coconuts. The Philippines is the world's leading producer of coconuts, and the structure of the industry changed dramatically under the military government. At the secret meeting at which imposition of martial law was planned, two tycoons and regional party bosses, Eduardo Cojuangco and Juan Ponce Enrile, were present. Thereafter, the coconut industry was reorganized under the able direction of Eduardo Cojuangco and Juan Ponce Enrile. The latter also became minister of defense, itself an entrepreneurial opportunity as the coconut regions were hosting the only growing communist insurgency in Southeast Asia. What made the coconut coup particularly propitious were the petroleum price hikes of 1973, which drove up the price of substitutes such as coconut oil. The proceeds of an export levy sent a flood of cash into Cojuangco's bank, driving up the value of the shares – not least those apparently allocated to President Marcos – and funding, sometimes through the quiet intermediation of Hong Kong ghost companies, further expansion of Cojuangco's corporate empire.[41]

The oil crisis of 1973 also turned the regime's fancy to thoughts of assured energy supplies. In 1973 the government created the Philippine National Oil Company. Typical of post-1973 developments, most of its operations were government-to-government deals. It was later charged that its Marcos-appointed chief not only skimmed off a percentage of each deal but also took kickbacks from ships chartered to carry oil to the Philippines and a cut on the insurance premiums; the money was allegedly siphoned off to Hong Kong and to the US.[42]

Nor was the oil supply the only energy-related question under consideration by the regime. In 1976 General Electric and Westinghouse got into a competition to build the country's first nuclear reactor; Marcos personally intervened to throw the contract to Westinghouse. Not only did the country get one reactor for the price of two, as cynics later described it, adding an estimated 8% to its total foreign debt, but Marcos allegedly received another $80 million for his retirement fund.[43]

All in all, it was a tidy arrangement. The government-owned development banks borrowed money abroad and 'lent' it to favored companies;

their owners would divert some of that money through Hong Kong bank accounts held in the name of Panamanian ghost companies or through the peekaboo centers of the Caribbean. The take, along with whatever could be skimmed from more than 300 government-owned and largely unaudited corporations, would come to rest in Swiss bank accounts – sometimes through the intermediation of Liechtenstein 'foundations' – or in ownership of California banks, Texas and New York real estate, and shares of corporations listed on the Zurich or Luxembourg stock exchanges.[44] The Redwood Bank of San Francisco fell into the hands of two Marcos cronies via a British Virgin Islands holding company. The Oceanic Bank of San Francisco, whose staff was graced by the presence of the former CIA Manila station chief, was taken over by a Marcos business associate.[45] And Imelda Marcos built a handsome New York real estate empire through a Netherlands Antilles shell company, whose power of attorney was allegedly held by the New York Land Company of Ralph and Joseph Bernstein. Much of their expertise in foreign real estate investment was imparted at 'family' gatherings by Nessim Goan of Geneva.[46]

Money was also diverted from US military aid. Three California companies bidding for contracts to provide communications equipment for the Filipino army were owned by the aptly named Golden Asset company of Hong Kong. It, in turn, was quietly owned by a Filipino businessman whom Marcos had allegedly designated as go-between with companies wanting to do business with the Philippine military. As funds for the California equipment ultimately came from US military-aid payments to the Philippines, the art of recycling had reached perfection.[47]

The consequences of cronyism in economic action were ably demonstrated by the Philippines' foreign debt. In 1972 it was $4 billion; in 1984 it had hit $27 billion, mostly incurred by the public sector. Yet one major New York bank estimated that between 1978 and 1983, when the Philippines foreign debt rose by $19 billion, about $9 billion fled the country in defiance of its exchange controls. Others have estimated the drain at between $10 and $30 billion, the latter figure exceeding that of the country's total foreign debt.

The 'Radical' Response

Faced with the staggering sums on the global money-go-round and the sacrifices demanded of developing countries to pay their debts, the international banking fraternity confronted two critical questions in the early 1980s. One was a political issue: *would* the debtors agree to accept their debts as legitimate? The second was economic: assuming that they did, was it possible for them to fulfill that agreement? Argentina, which led the way into the global debt crisis in the spring of 1982, pointed the way out again two years later, by answering the first question in the affirmative.

'Radicalism is practical antiimperialism. And Raul Alfonsin has begun the battle against imperialism and international financial usury,' crowed Finance Minister Eduardo Grinspun, without evident embarrassment, even as his government connived with the IMF to break its election promises.

Within weeks of coming to office on a reflation platform, the new civilian government rolled back wage demands and slated massive cutbacks in state-sector expenditure. As cover, a commission of inquiry was established to investigate economic crimes of the previous regime, including wasteful and costly public expenditure and the nationalization of crippled companies. The Radical hierarchy, like many new regimes in developing countries before and since, realized that one way to win public acquiescence to a drop in living standards would be to tie the public-sector cutbacks to a war on the corruption of the former government.

After an unsuccessful effort to break the hold of the Peronist power brokers on the unions, the government also began to tar the Peronist unions with association with the military. In this way, the ongoing investigation into the fate of the 'disappeared' might reduce the effectiveness of union claims that the government had failed to honor its campaign promises.[48]

Certainly the new government inherited a financial disaster; and in its initial fumblings could be detected a genuine commitment to limiting the adverse impact that external-debt payments would have on living standards. But the party leaders must have known that some adverse impact was inevitable; that their election promise of rapid reflation was impossible to reconcile with the demands of the IMF and the banks, and that, in the final analysis, it would be living standards, not debt-service payments, that would give way.

In a sense Argentina, like the rest of Latin America, was trapped by the idiosyncrasies of the accounting methods used by US banks. To keep their stock prices high, the banks had to report good quarterly earnings. Yet until accounting methods were modified late in 1984, those 'earnings' were often the result of a statistical subterfuge.[49] As interest on loans was calculated frequently, yet only paid at much longer intervals, perhaps quarterly, US banks reported as earnings interest accrued but not yet received from their borrowers. But when a loan had not paid interest for more than ninety days, it had to be reclassified as 'non-performing.' Thereafter, interest on the loan could only be recorded as earnings when it was actually paid. Furthermore, the bank had to deduct from its previously reported earnings all interest accrued but not received. The result could be a major drop in its reported earnings for the quarter in which the adjustment had to occur. Nonperforming loans had also to be disclosed in the quarterly report. The net result could be a sharp drop in stock prices. That not only reflected adversely on management but could set off a depositors' panic, as the equity was the ultimate security for those deposits too large to be covered by insurance.[50]

The Argentine negotiations dragged on, and, once a quarter, Wall Street held its breath. If, somewhere, money would be found to permit Argentina to reduce its arrears to eighty-nine days, the banks could continue legally to misrepresent their earnings position. And each quarter, Argentina, like other debtors in similar circumstances, found the necessary money – from the IMF, or from the commercial banks themselves, which created 'new' loans to Argentina on their books, and credited the money to themselves as interest on their previous loans. But each time the charade was played, Argentina paid a heavier price. And each time more and more people wondered why Argentina did not use the moral authority of its new and clean government, and the power of its food and energy self-sufficiency, to lead Latin American debtors collectively to demand that creditors scale down the debt load and dramatically improve the terms of repayment.

The Creditor Cartels

Certainly the creditor interests saw little moral or practical impediment to forming a united front of their own: actually there were several. One was the Paris Club, where Western governments met to coordinate strategy with respect to countries that owed them money from official loans and export credits.[51]

Another was the Bank for International Settlements, where central bankers from the major industrial countries met monthly in secret to coordinate policies for strangling global credit conditions and to plot the strengthening of the political position of central banks vis-à-vis the governments they were supposed to serve. The BIS excludes finance ministers from its deliberations – politicians have an irritating habit of putting the demands of their constituents ahead of the principles of sound money. As banker to the central banks, the BIS could function as lender of first resort to countries awaiting IMF loans, but en route it often took the opportunity to relieve them of their gold reserves,[52] and to browbeat their governments into increasing the power and independence of their central banks. This it did in Latin America, in the three largest debtor countries, with great success during the early 1980s.[53]

There was also the US government's Interagency Country Exposure Committee, made up of representatives of the Federal Reserve Board (charged with assuring banks of adequate liquidity), of the comptroller of the currency (whose role was to safeguard solvency by monitoring the capital of banks), and of the Federal Deposit Insurance Corporation (which would pick up the tab after the first two failed to prevent a disaster). This committee had the power to order commercial banks to reclassify loans as substandard and nonperforming, whenever it was convenient to reduce a country's credit rating and force it into the waiting arms of the IMF.[54]

Then there was the IMF itself, visibly pleased at its return to the center of the world stage after being marginalized during the lending boom of the 1970s. Like the World Bank, with which it coordinated efforts,[55] the IMF was anxious to plant its 'experts' in positions of power in the developing countries in order to assure their continued commitment to public-sector austerity and 'free' financial markets.

There also evolved a mechanism by which the international banks themselves could coordinate strategy independently of the official cartels.[56]

Informal coordination among banks has rarely worked effectively. In 1976 an effort by a group of banks to impose an IMF-style program on Peru, without the participation of the IMF, flopped in the face of creditor wrangles. During the Iranian hostage crisis of 1979, Chase Manhattan Bank infuriated the international banking community by unilaterally declaring Iran in default and making a preemptive seizure of its assets. During the Polish crisis of 1980–81, the US banks, under government pressure, played it tough, refusing to compromise on the terms of a rescheduling in which they had little at stake. And when the debt crisis had broken, after the summer of 1982, interbank squabbling assumed dimensions sometimes out of all proportion to the potential revenues of the countries over which the fracas occurred.

Some commercial banks had made to Costa Rica the usual syndicated loan; some had made a loan specially secured on the sugar crop; and some merchant banks had bought Costa Rican eurobonds. Normally, the claims of bondholders rank first, secured creditors second, and unsecured creditors third, when it comes to carving up the carcass. But, in the Costa Rican case, the main beneficiaries appear to have been the lawyers of the contending claimants, as Costa Rica had played peekaboo with its foreign-exchange reserves using a secret bank account in Panama.[57]

Sometimes it was the banks of individual countries that were at loggerheads. For example, when the Malvinas War erupted, a British freeze on Argentine assets and an Argentine freeze on those of Britain set the banks off on a replay of the Iranian crisis. Since the loans to Argentina were syndicated, in theory all interest payments made to the banks managing the loan were to be distributed pro rata to all members of the syndicate. The US banks, citing the freeze, initially refused to give the British banks a share of the interest payments that Argentina still occasionally made.[58]

In Cuba, apart from a brief and unsuccessful effort by British banks to open the old umbrella theory and dump Cuba's financial responsibilities on the USSR, 1983 negotiations for a rescheduling seemed to go well. There were no US banks involved in Cuban loans, until the US dealt a double blow. US customs broke up a scheme, concocted with the aid of Robert Vesco, to smuggle into Cuba US machinery that would convert sugar cane fiber into fuel oil. This could reduce Cuba's dependence on the USSR for the oil that drove up its soft-currency debt or allow Cuba to divert some of the redundant oil into hard-currency sales, which could help service its debts to the West. Then, American Express bought out Geneva's Trade Development Bank, which was a party to the negotiation of the Cuban hard-currency debt. Likely deferring to pressure from the Reagan administration, which hoped to use the debt squeeze to encourage Cuba to pull its troops out of Angola and to cease aiding the government of Nicaragua, AmEx scuttled the deal.[59]

Even within the ranks of the US commercial banks, feuds hampered negotiations with debtor countries. Small banks were ever on the lookout for ways to bail out of loan renewals that the big money-center banks, the IMF, and the US government were leaning on them to accept. Michigan National Bank produced widespread consternation when it sued Citibank for unlawful extension of its participation in a loan to Mexico's Pemex. Michigan National had agreed three times to Citibank's requests for renewal; but it refused a fourth. Citibank went ahead with the renewal despite the refusal, locking in Michigan National's funds.[60]

Nor was that Citibank's only contribution to smooth interbank relations. In August 1984, the US government decided to send a 'signal' to its increasingly prodigal client regime in the Philippines in the form of the 'return' of exiled opposition leader Benigno Aquino. A former protégé of the CIA's Edward Lansdale in the anticommunist campaign of the 1950s, Aquino was also a representative of the old sugar baronry, whose political power Marcos had crushed. His assassination on the tarmac at Manila airport set off a massive flight of funds. When capital flight from the Philippines reached intolerable heights and the government froze all foreign-exchange transactions, Citibank gave the international interbank market one of its worst shake-ups since the Ambrosiano collapse. It responded to the public freeze by freezing all payments on $1 billion in interbank loans extended to its Manila branch by banks around the world. When Banco Ambrosiano repudiated the debts incurred by BAH Luxembourg, it could cite as justification the separate incorporation of the Luxembourg company. But the Citibank freeze was the first time a major international bank had repudiated an obligation to make good on loans extended to one of its branches, legally a direct extension of the American parent.

The other banks howled in outrage and hinted that Citibank was playing doubly foul. The suspicion emerged that Citibank, sensing trouble, had reduced its own lending to its Manila branch and told it to step up its borrowings from other banks. When the freeze came, it would be other banks' cash that was caught out in the cold.[61]

While the banks were squabbling in public, bankers were planning in private to create machinery that would obviate such quarrels in future. A cartel arrangement, the Institute of International Finance (IIF), gave the banks a number of advantages. Headquartered in Washington, it could lobby the Fed, the World Bank, the IMF, and the US Treasury. It could help prevent debtors from playing one bank against another to negotiate improved terms. It could serve as a means for big banks to pressure small ones into continued participation in international loans. It would work to improve the data pool available on economic and financial conditions in the borrowing countries. And it could evolve into a forum wherein creditor banks and debtor countries could meet and negotiate, thus metamorphosing the debtors' adversary from a school of piranha into one big shark. This would help to create both a methodology and a common law with respect to debt-negotiation agreements to assure that dealings with one country did not create unfortunate precedents on which other countries could seize. The IIF could also act as a collective bargaining agent on behalf of the banks should the debtors ever get *their* act together.[62]

Let Them Eat Platitudes

As the bad news from Latin America got worse, the financial community and the population of the debtor countries waited for governments there to declare an 'OPEC of the indebted.' While world debtor countries faced diverse economic and political circumstances that largely precluded an effective global united front, the Latin American countries were reasonably well placed to create a regional one.

It was Venezuela that, during a massive flight of funds in the autumn of 1982, first issued the call for collective bargaining. The next spring Ecuador put the need for collective action on the agenda of the annual meeting of the Inter-American Development Bank and hosted a conference of Latin debtor countries. After Quito came meetings in Caracas and in Cartagena, all of which produced enough smoke to assure the suffocation of the fire.

Most of the Latin American politicians were playing to domestic audiences when they huffed and puffed and blew their own houses down. The larger debtor countries such as Brazil were convinced that they could make better deals on their own. They paid lip service to collective negotiations only when domestic pressure mounted or when they needed a minor concession from their creditor banks. Regimes that were completely dependent on the US for their survival, such as the military junta in Chile, avoided any declaration of support for the notion. The small debtors and those Latin American technocrats convinced of the need for collective action found their efforts sabotaged from within and without.

Although Latin American, Javier Perez de Cuellar, the Secretary General of the United Nations publicly appealed to Latin debtors, just before the Quito meeting, to follow an 'orthodox' course, austerity and one-country-at-a-time negotiations.[63] World Bank Vice-President Ernest Stern, on a visit to Mexico, announced shortly before the Caracas meeting that any country declaring a unilateral moratorium would find itself blacklisted from international credit markets 'for many years.'[64] His threat was endorsed by BIS chief Fritz Leutwiler.[65] When the Organization of American States (OAS) met to consider problems of external financing, the US sent a hard-line US Treasury official, Beryl Sprinkel, to lay down the law, to reject categorically all collective dealings, and to insist on the IMF route to national salvation.[66]

Within the debtor countries there were more problems. Former Peruvian finance minister and Rockefeller associate Manuel Ulloa,[67] who chaired the OAS meeting on external financing, insisted at the outset that 'We have mismanaged our affairs in a gross manner and we are paying the price.' After this bold assault on the privileges of international financial monopoly, the meeting culminated in 'an exercise in damage control,' as a former Colombian finance minister afterward described it. 'This was an initiative that could have degenerated into the creation of a debtors' cartel. The fact that it has not is a positive development.' His words were echoed by the incumbent Peruvian finance minister, who declared, 'The fact that we have had this meeting closes a chapter in the debt crisis. It will help quell the political pressure in many countries to do something drastic. That is very beneficial.'[68]

Perhaps most important in giving the coup de grâce to prospects of hemisphere-wide negotiations was the capitulation of Argentina's Radical party government in its historic deal of March 31, 1984.

Solidarity Deferred Forever

It was that time again. By March 31, 1984, the US banks had to get interest arrears on their Argentine loans down to no more than eighty-nine days. Argentina, they insisted, had the money to cover the arrears, for its foreign-exchange reserves had been rebuilt to a respectable level (at an enormous cost in living standards). But with the unions in rebellion against an almost unbroken record of broken campaign promises, the Alfonsin government balked at using the reserves for interest payments. After all, those reserves were perhaps the only cushion the government had on which to set a modest reflation. The banks were adamant: no rescheduling without the arrears being cleared. In public, the Argentine government refused to bend. Would March 31 mark the beginning of the end? Would the US banks be forced into drastic writedowns, precipitating depositors' runs and financial Armageddon? Then came an eleventh-hour deal in which Argentina found $500 million to clear enough of the arrears so that the sham could be continued.

Behind the deal could be found the hand of eighty-three-year-old Raul Prebisch. He had had a vital role in the 1933 creation of the Argentine central bank, which he ran until a radical nationalist member of the government named Juan Peron chased him out on the grounds that he was too chummy with the international financiers.[69] Yet he gained much of his subsequent reputation as dean of Third World development economists from public IMF-bashing.

After the restoration of civilian government, Prebisch became a special adviser to President Alfonsin.[70] It was allegedly Prebisch who handled negotiations for a secret IMF accord that was the prelude to the spectacular rescue. The deal with the IMF involved enormous cuts in public expenditures, a big leap in interest rates, more drastic devaluations, and a lid on wage concessions, at a time when real wages were the same as they had been a decade earlier. In return, Argentina 'received' the $500 million needed to clear enough of the interest arrears that the US banks would not have to reclassify their Argentine portfolio. But whence came the $500 million?

Argentina stalwartly refused to draw down its foreign-exchange reserves to clear up the arrears – except for $100 million. The eleven banks negotiating with Argentina on behalf of the creditor banks put up another $100 million on what seemed remarkably easy terms. But those terms reflected ironclad security, for Argentina had quietly pledged yet another $100 million of its supposedly sacrosanct reserves as collateral. (As these reserves were on deposit with the New York Fed, they could be easily seized if any future government tried to change its mind.) Brazil, Mexico, Venezuela, and Colombia pitched in with a $300 million loan. In yet another example of the Ponzi Principle in international finance, the $300 million was effectively guaranteed by the US Treasury. For as soon as Argentina reached a deal with the IMF, the US Treasury would 'swap' Argentina $300 million for an equivalent amount of pesos; the dollars could be used to repay the Latin American lenders. If Argentina then used IMF money to repay the US Treasury when the swap came due, the circle would be complete, as much of the IMF's money came from the US.

The loan by the continent's first, second, fourth, and fifth heaviest debtors to its third heaviest was indeed a remarkable event, though not because of the 'hemispheric solidarity' participants tried to imply. Precisely the reverse. The deal represented the death knell for a debtors' cartel. Argentina had used its potential self-sufficiency not to bludgeon the banks into easier terms but to coax the other Latin American countries, who could not so easily survive a credit cutoff, to pick up part of the tab. The much-touted debtors' cartel had degenerated into a mutual insurance plan financed by the debtors on behalf of the creditors. Moreover, as Argentina's prospects for repaying them depended on a deal with the IMF, the other four debtors had hundreds of millions of good reasons to pressure Argentina to settle. As Mexico's Finance Minister Jesus Silva Herzog, along with Prebisch the principal architect of the scheme, exulted, 'Here is a cartel organized to pay, not not to pay!'[71]

All Washed Up

Small wonder that a vice-president of Manufacturers Hanover Bank had once declared, 'Thank God for Mr. Silva Herzog.'[72] At the time of the minister's enthusiastic outburst, Mexico was back in the limelight as a model of fiscal and financial respectability.[73] The balance of commodity trade was in substantial surplus; foreign-exchange reserves were on the rise; and the stock of companies nationalized along with the banks had been returned to their former owners.[74]

Mexican President de la Madrid had made his economic priorities clear – slashing the public-sector deficit in anticipation of IMF demands (so he could tell the population it was a made-in-Mexico policy), and arranging a strictly Mexican accommodation with the creditors' cartels. When asked by the *Wall Street Journal* if he favored paying back loans at less than the rates demanded even if this risked having the banks declare them nonperforming, he replied, 'I do not believe it would be convenient for Mexico to lose its credit standing.'[75]

It certainly would not be convenient for President de la Madrid, if Washington newspaper columnist Jack Anderson's accusations about the size of de la Madrid's Swiss bank account have any foundation.[76]

In the summer of 1984 serious bargaining began on a deal that both sides knew would be a precedent. Creditors sought to use their most pliant pupil to create a long-term model for restructuring and rescheduling debt. Not only would such a deal eliminate much of the uncertainty (and consequent volatility of bank share prices) that frequent negotiations produced, but it would also go far toward settling the first of those two critical questions, namely, whether the debtor countries would agree to pay the full principal of the outstanding debt, no matter what its origin. Each time a debtor country signed a new accord on a piece of its debt, it was legitimizing it, even if that debt had been incurred by discredited military dictatorships to finance repression, or by thieves in public office to offset their Swiss retirement accounts. A long-term deal covering a large part, perhaps most of the debt, and effected by a government that had itself been legitimized by recent elections, made the origins of the debt 'academic.'[77]

The stakes were large, and the banks kept Mexico on a short leash. Mexico was not meeting its IMF targets and was anxious for a quick deal before the quarterly review of its performance would make that failure official. And behind the whole operation was powerful Fed Chairman Paul Volcker, who had called for a strategy of rewarding, with slightly more lenient terms, countries that made good progress toward deflating their economies.

Consummated in September 1984, the Mexican deal involved a fourteen-year restructuring of nearly 75% of the Mexican public-sector debt. It included concessions by the banks – in reduced interest rates and waived rescheduling fees – worth about $400 million. This left Mexico with an annual interest bill of about $12 billion. In exchange, Mexico agreed to lock in for a long term and therefore to legitimize the bulk of its public debt. Under the terms of the accord, the IMF undertook to conduct twice-annual reviews of the Mexican economy – the previous practice was an annual one – and to turn over the hitherto-confidential results to the banks. This deal became the model for negotiations with Brazil and Venezuela and served as a reference point for the terms of Argentina's final capitulation three months later.[78]

March 31, 1984, had been Raul Alfonsin's version of the Malvinas disaster – a defeat followed by a retreat that soon degenerated into a rout and an unconditional capitulation. In June the Argentine government made one last effort to preserve some self-respect. In a gesture of public 'defiance,' it broke off negotiations with the IMF team and delivered its 'own' letter of intent directly to the Executive Board of the IMF. What then got lost in all the public-relations hype was that the letter of intent promised a program of austerity only slightly milder than the one the

IMF team was attempting to impose – from a government electorally bound to reflation.[79]

Also in March 1984, the Radical party government had attempted to undermine its most important domestic opposition. Taking advantage of an ongoing dispute between Isabel Peron and the local Peronist party bosses, many of whom were union leaders, Alfonsin negotiated an accord with Isabel Peron in which she pledged support for his economic program. The accord called for increases in real wages, and it resurrected questions about the legitimacy of part of the foreign debt. In theory, the accord should have strengthened Alfonsin's hand against the IMF; in reality it strengthened his hand against the unions, for it isolated the Peronist left wing and its union base, while Isabel Peron created a new party superstructure.[80]

After the IMF refused Argentina's letter of intent, new 'negotiations' saw Argentina ceding more austerity, tighter credit, and a larger trade surplus, though 'insisting' on being able to raise real wages.[81] Even that last gesture of resistance had vanished by September, when the Alfonsin government set wage increases at 16% a month, although the monthly inflation rate was 21%. (Albeit the government tried to beg another $1 billion from the creditor banks as a partial offset.)[82] With the IMF placated, the stage was set for a deal with the banks in December.

Given Argentina's history of 'defiance,' the creditor banks decided that the terms of the accord should not be as 'lenient' as those granted Mexico.[83] The banks refused to waive the traditional rescheduling fees, and the interest spread was set at a higher level. But the crucial issue was the size of the deal, a long-term stretching of $17 billion in principal falling due within two years. Thus, about 40% of the total debt of that country with perhaps the best evidence of a fraudulent incurring of that debt, effectively vanished from the political agenda. The long-term rescheduling essentially laundered the tens of billions of dollars stashed abroad. Argentina began work on, and eventually unveiled, a five-year austerity plan that closely followed IMF prescriptions. And Eduardo Grinspun began jetting about the world to lobby the financial community, replacing his speech about his government's war on 'international financial usury' with another asserting that Argentina had opted for an 'orthodox solution' to its debt problem.[84]

22

Taking Stock

The legitimization of the debt, its conversion into a recognized public-sector obligation, was only the first step. Next came the task of finding a means by which the debtors could actually pay.

The creditors faced a grim dilemma. They could maintain their façade of liquidity, by forcing developing countries to slash imports and investment yet further to divert foreign exchange into debt-service payments.[1] But this would endanger their own solvency by undermining the long-term capacity of the debtors to service their debts.

Furthermore, the substitution of interest payments for import purchases cost the industrialized countries and the creditor banks' domestic customers too high a price. The US had become particularly dependent on export markets among developing countries in the 1970s, and the drop in their imports spelled serious trouble for major smokestack industries already hurt by domestic recession and heavy debt loans.[2]

Nor were the debtors likely to be able to bear the squeeze much longer. By mid-1985 trouble was brewing.

Economic Australogy

As one Argentine austerity program followed another, inflation accelerated, to no one's surprise except the IMF's, until by early 1985 the annualized rate was 1,000%. Argentina was also $900 million in arrears. Although a new loan of $2.4 billion was negotiated, it was conditional on $500 million of IMF money; and the IMF responded to Argentine inflation by cutting off credit.[3]

In February, Finance Minister Grinspun, whom the banks mistrusted, was sacked, along with the head of the central bank; they were replaced by a team whom the international financiers welcomed as more inclined to impose 'economic discipline.' Further concessions were squeezed from Argentina by the IMF refusal to release funds, and by US regulators, who downgraded the status of Argentine loans, decreasing the likelihood and increasing the cost of new money.[4]

In June 1985 Argentina poured cold water on an effort to revive the concept of a debtors' cartel and made its peace with the IMF. On the third anniversary of the Malvinas surrender, Argentina declared war on its own economy. Under the 'Austral Plan' (prepared 'in consultation' with the IMF and the Fed) wages and prices were frozen, public expenditures were chopped even more than the IMF had demanded, and higher taxes and forced savings took the equivalent of 2.5% of GDP out of the economy (GDP was already predicted to drop 3% to 5% for the year). Argentina also found a sure cure for inflation. It introduced a new currency unit called the 'austral,' worth 1,000 old pesos, and put spies in the streets to inform on price-freeze violators.[5] Soon Argentina was declared a model debtor again. Early in 1986 major banks lent Argentina more money to clear its interest arrears. This permitted them to upgrade the status of its loans and to return them to an accrual basis, which in turn allowed the banks to falsify their books and to declare a large jump in profits.[6]

Elsewhere, however, the news was not so rosy. There were growing signs of revolt against the IMF. The banks became sufficiently nervous that the IIF approached the Cartagena group of debtors, proposing a formal dialogue that bypassed the IMF.[7] Brazil became the test case.

For a while Brazil's $100 billion external-debt load had rested relatively lightly on the shoulders of banks' accountants. Brazil achieved its balance-of-payments targets with relative ease – apart from a prostrate economy and famines that threatened millions of lives. Capital flight was not as severe in relation to debt as it was in Mexico or Argentina – for the simple reason that Brazilians had never had their long-term pride in and commitment to their country, or their faith in its future, shattered. Tancredo Neves, victor in the presidential elections that had heralded the return to civilian rule, insisted that Brazil had to take 'a realistic position which cannot ignore the basic rules governing international financial operations.' He had already endorsed the efforts of the outgoing government to arrange long-term rescheduling like that of Mexico and Venezuela. And he denounced 'xenophobia' with regard to foreign investment.[8]

The new government responded to IMF bullying with more concessions. The budget deficit – which during 1984 assured that the legal economy showed its first real growth in four years – was cut. The financial administration was tightened, making the central bank more independent, which delighted the BIS. To the joy of the IMF, power was shifted from the planning ministry, staffed by progrowth technocrats, to the finance ministry, which, like the central bank, was manned by hard-core monetarists. President Neves told the international creditors that his first priority was the fight against inflation.[9] Neves died before he could effectively take office, but his successor, José Sarnay, quickly reassured the banks that his government would adhere to the agreed-on debt-negotiation framework.[10]

However, by the summer of 1985 revolt began. Brazil had achieved its balance-of-payments targets and was up to date on interest payments; each effort to use that success to ease domestic austerity was met by the IMF pointing an accusing finger at accelerating inflation figures. After the IMF cut off credits, stalling new commercial bank loans, total breakdown threatened. In the autumn the planning ministry reasserted power against the finance ministry: the government purged the central bank and finance ministry of hard-money men and, to the undoubted horror of the BIS, made the central bank once again subordinate to the finance department. President Sarnay denounced the IMF for fostering social strife and weakening democracy.[11]

To the consternation of the banks, Sarnay called for a new initiative on the debt, and Paul Volcker's pet pupil, Mexico, responded. After overachieving its IMF targets in 1983 and 1984, Mexico was in deep trouble. Partly because of the need to buy support in congressional elections in the summer of 1985, the government deficit was rising again. Inflation was accelerating; capital flight worsening – during the election period alone $4 billion fled. And further downward pressure on world oil prices forced Mexico to admit publicly that the debt was unpayable.

Within the Mexican government, a war of words broke out between the finance ministry and the central bank. The finance ministry demanded lower interest rates to ease the burden of the internal debt; the central bank, which had recently become more independent, wanted higher rates to discourage capital flight and make more foreign exchange available for paying the external debt, then $900 million in arrears. Even Jesus Silva Herzog, grooming himself as successor to President de la Madrid, picked up on an increasingly popular slogan – 'grow to pay.' The IMF responded by threatening a credit cutoff.[12] But just when things looked blackest, a devastating earthquake, followed by a burst of capital flight, provided a pretext for the creditors to defer the payments Mexico could not make, while claiming that no basic principles had changed.[13]

Yet another problem was the intrusion of a new and unwelcome participant in the great debt dialogue. Sensing that debt and not Central America was of paramount concern in Latin America, Fidel Castro seized on the debt crisis to raise his profile in the region. While Cuba assured its bankers that its own debts would be honored, Castro declared the general debt burden to be 'not only unpayable, but also uncollectable,' and urged partial repudiation as the ultimate weapon if Western governments refused to lighten the load. Cutely denouncing the US for 'exporting revolution' by fomenting social unrest through its financial policy, Castro called for a hemispheric meeting on debt for Havana in the summer of 1985.[14]

The meeting was hardly a roaring success. Few top-level politicians attended. Of those that did, former Colombian president Alfonso Lopez Michaelsen set the tone by arguing against Castro's line; and a former Argentine central-bank chief publicly rejected the concept of a moratorium. Outside, President Sarnay of Brazil denounced the 'politicization' of the debt question; Jamaica's Edward Seaga endorsed the case-by-case approach; Jorge Blanco of the Dominican Republic called Castro's ideas 'emotional and unrealistic'; and Uruguay's Julio Maria Sanguinetti called on the region to forget about moratoria and repudiation.[15]

Nonetheless, by the IMF annual meetings in Seoul in September 1985, even Jacques Delarosière was bowing to the inevitable, allowing the formerly obscene word 'growth' to pass his lips. However, his eleventh-hour recantation came too late to save him from the wrath of the Reaganites.[16]

The IMF had perhaps forgotten that its philosophy – slashing imports and squeezing private investment, and raising taxes to close deficits instead of lowering them to stimulate growth – ran counter to the political priorities and economic ideology of the Reagan team. With supply-side economics triumphing again at home in the 1984 presidential elections, it was time to take the show on the road. And the catalyst proved to be the collapse of the ancien régime in Peru.

Economic crisis and the failure to make progress against the Shining Path guerrilla movement swept to power the 'populist' Allen Garcia, who had pledged to do what populist governments do best: push up taxes and slash public expenditures. The bankers were initially enthusiastic. The old government had made three abortive attempts at an IMF deal, interest arrears hit $500 million, and it looked as if the Peruvian debt was going to join Bolivia's in the cooler. 'We want to pay,' Garcia assured them; and, in an Andean version of 'Happy Days Are Here Again,' he insisted that 'The Belaunde government spoke of austerity without recession. I propose austerity without pain.'[17]

No one really took Garcia's public posturing very seriously, even his threats to pull out of the IMF and to restrict payments on the public part of the foreign debt to 10% of total export receipts. After all, that was more than the banks had been receiving, and, in any event, the private-sector debt continued to be serviced as usual. Furthermore, as some of the 'Garcia Plan' boosters enthused, the idea of fixing debt payments to export receipts would help stabilize the flow of payments to the banks, reducing fluctuations in their earnings and their stock prices, and decreasing the danger of repudiation. Garcia raised no serious question about the legitimacy of the debt: he insisted that Peru would pay ('because we are honest and assumed a responsibility to do so'), though on a slower timetable; he shelved many public-sector projects to curb the need for future borrowing; and he denounced Castro's call for partial repudiation as 'infantile, unrealistic and extremist.'[18] But what *was* important was that Garcia's inauguration provided an opportunity for Latin American heads of state to impress on US Treasury Secretary James Baker the need for a fundamental change of policy.

The Rush for Spoils

From competing paper mills had already come abundant alternative schemes for 'solving' the crisis. The most definitive was that of William Rhoades, senior vice-president of Citibank, who simply declared the debt crisis 'over.'[19] So much for the debt crisis.

An equally simple approach was that of Malaysian Chinese entre-preneur Lee Ah Sin, known as King Kong because of his girth and body hair. When the US Secret Service and the Malaysian police shut down his counterfeiting business, the Secret Service declared his bills to be among the best it had ever seen. Alas, when, in 1986, the US announced plans for redesigning the currency to make copying much more difficult, it squelched a straightforward resolution of the debt problem.[20]

However, other plans afloat bore an affinity to that of Lee Ah Sin. Foreign-exchange shortages in developing countries had forced some to introduce special soft-currency payment facilities for debt. The mechan-ics varied, but essentially a soft-currency trust account was created with the central bank for a sum equivalent, at the prevailing 'free' market rate, to payments due on the hard-currency debt of the company or bank concerned. The government of the debtor country would guarantee payment of the debt to the creditor bank when/if hard currency became available. Some US government officials, such as Commerce Under-Secretary Lionel Ulmer, advocated that soft-currency payments be accepted as bona fide debt service. But even if US bank regulatory authorities agreed, as they had in the case of Mexico for a few months in 1982, there remained the question of what the banks would do with the soft currency if there were long delays in conversion – besides playing the lateral-transfer game and formally speculating against their own borrowers.

Some plans wrestled with how to restructure the flow of payments. Herman Kahn's old think tank came up with a variation on the old theme of debt bondage. It proposed shifting forward the stream of payments: keeping interest payments low and increasing the principal in line with inflation.[21] The New York Fed and others suggested 'capping' interest rates; the difference between the capped level and the market level would be added to the principal, or deferred while accumulating interest at the market rate.[22]

Some talked of a publicly funded International Lender of Last Resort on which the international banks could dump nonperforming foreign loans when a liquidity squeeze threatened. Such an institution might even purchase the loans at heavy discounts and sell them back to the original debtor.[23] Others preferred a mechanism for selling bank loans to private investors, in effect converting them into securities.[24] Yet others called for converting existing bank debts into bonds owned or guaranteed by an international institution such as the Inter-American Development Bank or World Bank or some new entity.[25]

Felix Rohatyn, a partner in the private banking firm of Lazard Frères, proposed an extension of his Municipal Assistance Corporation (MAC) of New York, which had taken over the city's short-term debts using money from the sale of its own federally guaranteed bonds. The state government allocated a stream of tax revenues from the citizens of New York City to service the MAC bonds. The administration was under the control not of the citizens subject to the tax but of an externally appointed body. Rohatyn suggested a similar Big-MAC attack on the global debt problem, with the new funding entity buying up the bank loans with money from its own international bond sales. Why would anyone purchase Big-MAC bonds? Because the developing countries would give the agency a mortgage on the income from their primary product exports.[26]

The possibility of securing for the creditor institutions privileged access to the foreign-exchange earnings of the developing countries was itself the subject of debate. The CIA think tank, the Georgetown University Institute of Strategic and International Studies, came up with the concept of Exchange Participation Notes, by which debtors would pledge to creditors a specified percentage of their future foreign-exchange receipts in lieu of immediate repayment of principal. This plan would encourage banks to shape future lending to enhance borrowers' capacity to earn foreign exchange.[27] This and similar plans might solve the immediate cash-flow crisis; they would also lock debtor countries into a future emphasis on the export of primary products and would also guarantee Western countries a supply of raw materials below prevailing world prices.

Some plans focused not on assuring the service of ex
on how to restore the flow of money to the developin
trade credits, balance-of-payment loans, or project finan
Lever, a former British Chancellor of the Exchequer, pus
of a super-trade-credit agency that would help to restor
while enhancing the ability of the creditor countries
monitor aggregate borrowing and to control economic policy in the debtor
countries.[28] Fed chief Paul Volcker proposed a superbank to disburse
loans to developing countries. The superbank would be headed by the
chief officers of the megabanks, (i.e., those already in the IIF) and it
would operate on a one-dollar one-vote principle to preclude smaller
banks from vetoing participation in loan syndications.[29] And Henry
Kissinger proposed a Marshall Plan for Latin America in which a new
paper mill, the Western Hemisphere Development Institute, would use
money provided by Western governments to pump long-term low-interest
loans into Latin America.[30]

All these schemes sidestepped the question of the legitimacy of the
debt, and focused exclusively on the mechanics of payment. All would
lead to increased creditor power vis-à-vis the developing debtor countries.
Yet despite such evident merit, there was a problem: none of them fitted
the political agenda of the Reagan White House.

From the IMF's Frying Pan into the Baker's Oven

When Argentina's Raul Alfonsin and Uruguay's Julio Sanguinetti took
the occasion of Allen Garcia's inauguration to whisper in US Treasury
Secretary James Baker's ear, he had already inclined it at a sympathetic
angle. 'Growth' was the new buzzword not only throughout the developing
world, but also in Congress, where redneck and liberal members alike
distrusted the IMF and the World Bank.[31]

After succeeding Donald Regan at Treasury, James Baker launched
several interrelated financial initiatives. His tax plan called for decreasing
the rates, especially on investment income, but increasing the take
(thereby cutting the budget deficit) by eliminating loopholes and shelters.
And he pushed for lower interest rates, which would reduce the burden
of the federal debt and would lessen the US's attraction for, and dependence
on, foreign flight capital for financing the deficit.[32] Such flight capital
drove up, and kept up, the exchange value of the dollar, thereby worsening
the developing countries' debt problems and pricing US goods out of
world markets.[33]

There were three essential elements to the Baker Plan:[34] first, an
additional $9 billion over three years from the multilateral development
banks, especially the World Bank;[35] second, the squeezing of $20 billion

more from the international banks. (This money would come not from all banks, as before, but mainly from the 100 international banks most committed to international lending, chiefly members of the IIF.) The third and most crucial element was the policy package that would go with the new money. While the IMF was still to monitor developing countries' finances, its traditional policy of resuscitation by asphyxiation was to be replaced by a supply-side version of the 'grow to pay' philosophy. Compliance would be judged by the Reagan administration, which held the keys to the strongbox.

Returning to the Victorian distinction between the deserving and undeserving poor, the Baker Plan envisaged economic assistance for those who met aggregate credit, inflation, and deficit targets, to be sure, but more important, who created a propitious climate for private-sector investment. That came to mean a reversal of the trends of the 1970s, when international bank loans and a strong state presence in economic life had allowed the developing countries to reduce their dependence on the transnational corporations and foreign ownership of their productive capacity.[36]

An 'Equitable' Solution?

During the 1970s many countries had erected barriers, psychological and legal, against increased foreign ownership. In the 1980s the psychological barriers were crumbling. Increasing destitution and the explosive social environment in many debtor countries sent their governments on a scramble for new investment. The legal barriers, such as the jurisdiction of local courts in disputes involving foreign investors,[37] were reduced by outside pressure; one country after another ceded de facto extraterritoriality to foreign investors.[38] Another barrier was the legacy of the economic nationalism of the 1970s: state-owned companies that often dominated the most potentially lucrative spheres of investment – something with which supply-side economics could easily deal.

Government budgetary expenditures had already been sliced to the bone in most debtor countries. Yet public-sector deficits remained, in part because the deflation caused by cutbacks in state spending so reduced economic activity that it also dried up governments' tax receipts. The IMF demanded higher tax rates. But to the Reagan administration the key to cutting the deficits (and simultaneously improving the atmosphere for private profit) lay in a policy that Lord Harold Macmillan once described, with British experience in mind, as 'paying down the mortgage by selling off the family silver.'

Just as Margaret Thatcher precipitated the debt crisis in the spring of 1982, so, too, after winning reelection on a wave of post-Malvinas xenophobia, her government showed developing countries how to 'solve' their budgetary problems by a massive sell-off of public assets. The sale of state companies would serve three objectives. The revenues generated would help to reduce deficits and allow cuts in tax rates. Turning the assets over to the private sector would create a new class of minicapitalists with a stake in the political status quo – the Conservative party. And a sufficiently massive sell-off would ensure that it would be too expensive for any future Labour government to renationalize the companies. Of course the Iron Lady's enthusiasm for generating stock market bubbles may not be completely unrelated to her own portfolio of shares, in which the Labour party alleged she had dealt heavily during her preceding years in office.[39]

By the end of 1985, public assets (Jaguar, British Aerospace, British Petroleum, and others) had been sold for a bargain $10 billion; the next year other companies would join them, including British Gas (expected to fetch $10 billion) and all the waterworks of England and Wales. At the back door of the fire sale stood the ragged figure of British social overhead capital – declining educational standards, dilapidated industrial infrastructure, and a stock of public housing that needed some $25 billion to restore it to decent standards. The British government responded by putting the public housing, too, on the auction block.[40]

To be fair, Britain was not alone in its craze for 'privatization' of public assets. In Canada, a band of bumbling yahoos headed by Brian Mulroney celebrated its election by winding up the agency that screened direct foreign investment, selling off state companies to foreign and domestic investors, and planning the reprivatization of the national oil company.[41] And in France, the right, savoring their victory in the National Assembly elections, planned to close a deficit, caused in part by tax-evading capital flight, by means of a major denationalization. This would prove particularly difficult for a future Socialist government to reverse, as exchange controls would also be dismantled, making tax-evading capital flight even easier in the future.[42]

Thus, there were many precedents to follow when developing countries from Argentina to Zaire put their family silver up for sale. But who should buy it?

There were two potential sets of scavengers. One was traditional transnational enterprises. However, during the 1970s they had ceased to be primarily concerned with natural resources for export and manufactories to service local markets for secondary products. Rather, they became preoccupied with the search for cheap labor to manufacture goods for export to the industrialized countries, and with investments in local 'service' industries – hotels, tourism, information, and, increasingly, finance.[43] They were also reluctant to increase their exposure in developing countries, apart from those in Southeast Asia, which did not need their financial assistance.[44] But if the terms were sufficiently lucrative, perhaps they could be tempted.

The second set of would-be buyers was the big banks themselves. By focusing on the top 100 banks, the Baker Plan publicly acknowledged that international lending had been concentrating more and more in their hands. A secondary market in developing-country debt had sprung up. Brokers and merchant banks would quietly, indeed secretively, arrange to swap or sell loans on behalf of banks, especially smaller US regional ones, who wanted out of the international-lending business. These swaps and sell-offs would take place at heavy discounts. In early 1985 Mexican paper traded at 80% of face value, Venezuelan at 85%, and Brazilian at 75%. Bolivia set the record; its debt was available at 20% of its face value – though in subsequent months, the Peruvian debt came close.[45]

The purchasers were sometimes private investors. Sometimes they were large money-center banks, who bought the loans in the conviction that the government would bail them out of any difficulty. They also feared that if they did not acquire the loan participations, the smaller banks would invoke the cross-default clauses and sink not just their own ship but the entire armada.[46] Despite the risks, the acquisition of loans from other banks[47] produced exciting possibilities – if such debt could become an instrument for obtaining assets worth much more than the purchase price of the loan.

In February 1984 a financial study group affiliated with David Rockefeller's Society of the Americas – regarded in Latin America as *the* voice of US big business, especially of the money-center banks – articulated the new philosophy. Pointing to a looming funding gap, which the banks could not or would not meet, the commission made the usual demands: more IMF financing, more Western government money for export financing, more aid from the World Bank for private investors, and lower barriers against direct foreign investment. But it went one important step further. To ease the burden of their existing debt, and to encourage more inflows of bank loans, the commission affably suggested that 'In general, highly indebted countries would benefit from converting a portion of their debt into equity.'[48]

Thus, every increase in developing-country indebtedness – whether through bona fide borrowing or phony invoicing, whether to finance essential imports or to cover the foreign-exchange drain from capital flight, whether to pay for irrigation systems used by rural development agencies or interrogation systems used by secret police, whether to provide credit to domestic industry or to accommodate the results of US monetary policy – would be laundered and converted into income-earning factories, mines, agricultural land, infrastructure, and so on in the debtor countries. Ownership of these assets would rest with the foreign creditor banks.

The implementation of a strategy that reduced barriers to direct foreign investment, sold off state assets, and converted debt into foreign-owned equity ran up against much opposition – from threatened enterprises and from nationalist elements, military and civilian.[49] Nonetheless, desperation for foreign exchange, creditor pressure, and the political and economic discrediting of regimes that had effected the 1970s strategy of euromarket borrowing and state-led economic growth assured that resistance could often be surmounted.

Many state industries ran at commercial (though not necessarily social) losses, and many had become means of looting the public purse. Where military regimes fell into disrepute, subsequent civilian governments might start dismantling the military-industrial complexes that served as much as sinecures for officers as instruments for industrial development. A war on corruption became cover for a dual program: 'publicization' of private liabilities, whereby the state guaranteed and therefore legitimized debt incurred by private actors; and 'privatization' of public assets, whereby the government sold off the state companies to pay down the debt it had legitimized.

Global Pawnshop

From its earliest days, the Alfonsin government in Argentina took the offensive against the military, revoking their self-amnesty laws, arresting and trying top officers, and slashing the military budget. This last had a trebly useful effect: it cut the level of state expenditure and therefore helped to meet IMF targets; it undermined the power base from which nationalist elements, especially in the air force, meddled in the debate over the foreign debt; and it resulted in the sale of a host of industrial companies, generating revenue for the government and attracting the attention of foreign investors.[50] When José Maria Ruiz Mateos and a group of other Opus Dei–linked Spanish financiers began looking for overseas havens for their money, on the list were Argentine military industries being denationalized.[51]

With each austerity package more public assets were slated for sale,[52] with the acquiescence of the population, weary of depression and of the state-sector privileges typical of the military regime. In vain did Peronist economists point out that the real issue was not private versus public investment; that Argentine private firms were as 'inefficient' as the public ones; and that the problem was really the economic policy, instituted by the military and continued by the IMF, that made speculation and capital flight more profitable than domestic investment. But in mid-1985 came the 'Austral Plan,' which achieved a budget surplus through massive spending cuts and tax increases, a surplus the government tried to preserve by putting 350 state companies, including major public utilities, up for sale.[53]

During 1985 Alfonsin personally went to the US and to Europe to beg for foreign investment. Even oil companies were on his itinerary, as Argentina abandoned its policy of keeping the petroleum sector the exclusive preserve of its state oil company.[54]

In Bolivia, most state companies, including COMIBOL and the state oil company, were products of Victor Paz Estensorro's 1952–56 government. But in 1985 Paz rammed through the New Economic Policy, angrily dismissed by the left as *pinochetismo economica*. He jettisoned the statist development model that the revolution of 1952 had put in place, and began the process of 'reprivatization' by 'decentralizing' COMIBOL, the symbol of the revolution and a political stronghold of the Communist party. Aptly summarizing the triumph of supply-side economics, the smuggling of tin, which broke the efforts of the producing countries to maintain prices, also encouraged Bolivian miners to join the peasants previously ruined by El Niño in moving to the coca-producing areas, where employment seemed more secure and wages better.[55]

Brazil, too, joined the Latin American scramble to attract new foreign investment and to privatize public assets. Restrictions on foreign investment began being rolled back in 1983, though not without resistance.[56] And with the rollback came an attack on 'corruption' and 'inefficiency' in the public sector, and calculations of budgetary economies possible from shedding money-losing enterprises. The Ministry of Commerce called for the abolition of the state companies it ran; and the IMF pushed for the complete sell-off of state enterprises. Among those under scrutiny was Petrobras, the state oil company, some of whose creditor banks became enthusiastic advocates of 'privatization.' Prophetic perhaps was the decision of Volkswagen, Brazil, to buy up its own debt and convert it into equity.[57]

Chile was among the first to take the concept of a debt-equity swap to its logical conclusion. Among the 'triumphs' of the Chicago era was the privatization of social security. Public pension plans had been dismantled and replaced by exclusively worker-financed schemes run by special pension trusts controlled by the giant conglomerates. The Thatcheresque logic for privatization of social insurance was to give individual workers a stake in the political and economic status quo.[58]

Originally the pension trusts could invest only in government bonds and bank CDs. But the crisis of 1983 forced the nationalization of collapsing conglomerates and left the Pinochet regime in the embarrassing position of holding a higher percentage of GNP than had Allende's socialist government.[59] The pension trusts used for privatizing social security became vehicles for denationalizing companies. By 1985 30% of pension-trust money was in blue-chip stocks and equity of state-owned enterprises.

The conglomerates that owned the pension trusts had another potential role in privatization and the encouragement of foreign investment. Much of the foreign debt was due to their borrowing; so, too, was much of the capital flight. When Chile formally proposed the idea of directly swapping debt for equity with foreign bankers, the *grupos* saw an opportunity for the ultimate loan-back scam, buying up Chilean paper abroad at big discounts on the secondary market and using it to regain control of their former empires.[60]

Colombia did not sell off state assets, but joined the queue for foreign investment, setting up 'free trade zones' modeled on those in Asia, where cheap labor and freedom from taxation might attract companies manufacturing for the North American market.[61]

Similarly, when Costa Rica abandoned Robert Vesco and his dream of a global flight-capital haven, it opened its doors to US transnational firms, offering sweeping tax concessions, preferential interest rates, and a guarantee that foreign investors would have first call on the foreign-exchange reserves to send their profits home.[62]

Even Cuba tried to get into the act. As relations with the banks became strained in 1983, it offered, unsuccessfully, to host joint ventures with foreign investors in profitable sectors such as tourism.[63]

Ecuador paid a high price for hosting the 1983 meeting of Latin American debtor countries. The commercial banks, after sabotaging prospects for a debtors' cartel by promising special deals to the major debtors, cut further lending to Ecuador. The next year its ruling center-left coalition was ousted by a right-wing antinationalist regime that capitalized on the economic recession and on opportunities for denouncing 'communist' influence in the former government.

The new regime was headed by pistol-packing Léon Febres Cordero, Latin America's answer to Ronald Reagan. Febres Cordero and his sidekicks sauntered into the central bank and proceeded to hold up the depositors, raising reserve requirements to force cuts in commercial-bank lending. The government also lost little time putting a cap on state-sector expenditure, eliminating subsidies on basic goods, abolishing price controls and programs of import substitution, and liberalizing exchange controls – all in the name of a war on corruption. It also denounced OPEC and 'subversion' by Nicaragua in Ecuador. Then it let fly with both barrels. First came the attack on Decision 24 of the Andean Pact Agreement among Ecuador, Venezuela, Bolivia, Colombia, and Peru. Decision 24 set limits to foreign ownership and restricted profit remittances by foreign investors. The old regime had already reopened the oil sector, nationalized in 1974, to foreign investors; the new government declared a virtual open house and lobbied its Andean Pact partners for the dismantling of all restrictions.[64] Then it invited the hot money from out of town to belly up to the bar – interest rates were pushed up to lure back flight capital, and the black market was legalized.

One unexpected casualty of the Baker Plan was Haiti's Baby Doc Duvalier, heir to his father as America's guardian of the Windward Passage against the Bolshevik Menace, for which service he, like his father before him, took a personal cut of US economic and military aid. The proceeds of special 'military' accounts at the central bank, from which he could draw $1 million each month in petty cash, and the standard rake-offs from the government-owned flour mill, sugar refinery, cooking oil plant, and cement factory – let alone the cash flow from the institutionalization of voodoo – netted the first family of the Americas' poorest country an overseas retirement fund variously estimated between $200 and $900 million.

When, in the winter of 1985–86, antiregime riots erupted, Jamaica's Edward Seaga joined the US government in pressing Baby Doc to leave in a hurry. Seaga found his thuggish neighbor bad for business in the Caribbean, and Jamaica was scrambling to attract foreign investment. Furthermore, Haitian businessmen detected a unique opportunity in the 50% unemployment rate and the $3-a-day average wage of the other 50%. After Baby Doc flew off to France, the head of the local manufacturers' association enthused that 'US companies facing fierce competition with Asia for production of cheaper and better-quality goods can come here.' And the investment climate was further improved by the dismantling of the state monopolies that had formed the fiscal foundations of the old regime and by a bloody vendetta, encouraged by some Catholic priests, against the voodoo priests who had politically bolstered it.[65]

The real prize for foreign investors in the Americas was the very place that had been curbing its operations the longest. During the 1970s the Mexican government of President Echeverria passed laws restricting foreign ownership to 49%, except by special permission, and closing certain sectors completely. But under de la Madrid, attracting foreign investment became a top priority. First, more projects were classified as 'exceptions,' then the legal restrictions were rolled back. Every sector except oil and electricity was opened to majority foreign ownership, and the takeover of Mexican-owned assets by foreigners was permitted for the first time. The agency set up to screen foreign investment actively solicited newcomers; state companies were put up for sale; and, finally, foreign creditors were offered a straight debt-equity swap. In 1984 one of Mexico's major industrial conglomerates, the troubled Alpha Group, decided to sell off equity to relieve its debt load.[66] In 1985 it was the turn of the state companies.

In March a new austerity program envisaged putting 236 of 900 state companies up for sale, although protests forced the government to cut the auction list to 82. Then, as the IMF austerity demands tightened, the debt-to-equity scheme was officially unveiled. The state would directly take over the debts of some state-sector companies and offer equity in them in exchange for annulling the debt. The international creditor banks received a draft list of forty companies being considered for such treatment, including manufacturers of steel, trucks, chemicals, mineral products, and paper. The petroleum industry, national airlines, telephone and telegraph companies, and electrical utilities were at least temporarily excluded, though creditor banks made no secret about the one state company they really coveted: Pemex, the proudest symbol of Mexican economic nationalism.[67]

Such developments – the invitation to foreign ownership; the dismantling of state-sector natural resource monopolies; the phasing out of government participation in industrial development; and the moves toward an exchange of international debt for equity – were not limited to Latin America.

Nigeria, for example, had not been one to put its money where its mouth was, as trade debts from food imports attested. But creditor pressures proved irresistible. Even before General Buhari's coup, the government had agreed to sell off state companies in the hotel, brewing, and other sectors, the national airline, and the 60% government ownership in the major banks. After the coup the military government used the cover of a war on corruption to speed up the privatization of the state companies, whose profitable shares could be sold to loyal servants of the new regime.[68]

In the Philippines, privatization of state industries was complicated by the fact that Marcos and his cronies seemed so well entrenched. Despite strong pressure from the IMF, which complained of the profligacy of the government and of the 'demoralizing' effect of the state monopolies on private investors, Marcos continued to bail out cronies' firms using money from the state development bank, to treat the central bank as a political slush fund, and to stonewall efforts to dismantle the sugar and coconut monopolies. During one period of particularly acute foreign-exchange shortage, Prime Minister Cesar Virata had opened the Philippines to 100% foreign-owned investments for the first time; but pressure from the Marcos cronies caused a retreat.[69]

Then, early in 1986, with international creditors at the end of their patience, noncrony business in an uproar, and Washington angry that Marcos had proved more adroit than the US government at rigging elections, a political-military coup organized by presidential aspirant Ponce Enrile sent Ferdinand Marcos scurrying for safety. The new regime, headed by the widow of Benigno Aquino, had campaigned on a program of better terms from the creditors. But once in office it announced a policy of strict conformity to IMF guidelines and of 'reorganization' of the sugar and coconut sectors to stimulate private production, much to the joy of the old sugar barons and of the American government, whose Secretary of State, George Shultz, quickly congratulated it on its sense of fiscal and financial responsibility. The new regime picked as finance minister a man already on record as favoring a swap of debt for equity; and investors showed their approval by a rush to buy the stocks of Philippine companies listed on American stock exchanges. With power delivered to an anticommunist, business-dominated, reformist regime, the credibility of the Communist-led insurgency as the only viable alternative to Marcos was severely undermined. The Georgetown University International Institute of Strategic Studies could justifiably refer to the coup as 'a small miracle' – and not merely because of the important role the Philippine church hierarchy, headed by the improbably named Cardinal Sin, had played in bringing it to pass.[70]

In Poland there was equally good news for the banks, the Western governments, and, not least, that intrepid Polish entrepreneur, John Paul II. Poland joined the IMF and World Bank, thereby qualifying for loans; Solidarity remained banned so as not to disturb the value of the lien on the coal output that secured much of the bank debt; 'privatization' of the agricultural-service sector proceeded rapidly; and a black market flourished.

As early as 1981 Communist Poland had shown the way for other debtors in soliciting private, direct foreign investment. The target was the many millions of people of Polish origin living abroad, especially in the US and Germany, who were given three-year tax holidays, the right to repatriate 50% of their profits in hard currency, and flexibility in relating wages to productivity in exchange for their investments in the export sector. By the end of 1984 some 650 privately owned firms financed from abroad were in operation.[71]

The Rockefeller Foundation, which had participated in the church-sponsored aid fund for private farmers, proposed an International Foundation for Polish Agriculture. Under its aegis, private Western investment would join the Polish government in manufacturing agricultural products for export, with the assurance that part of the profits would be reinvested and part would be freely repatriated in hard currency to the private Western investors.[72]

But debtor countries from Argentina to Poland still had a lot to learn about 'privatization,' and the logical teacher was Turkey's Turgat Özal. For if anyone wanted to buy a bridge or an electric-power plant or a solvent and fully operational national airline or two, he had them for sale.[73]

Turkey *seemed* to be in better financial shape than Latin America. Its export sector did seem to be booming. However, much activity was of doubtful durability. In 1984 the Turkish state textile firm was working at full capacity manufacturing burial cloth for Iranian soldiers. Nor should the balance-of-payments statistics be taken at face value. In 1984 as much as 10% of recorded exports may have been fraudulent. Businesses registered exports with the fiscal authorities at several times their actual value and collected the generous tax rebates that the government offered as encouragement to 'free enterprise.'[74]

By early 1985 the gloss was off. The export boom was fading and the budget deficit was growing; the government was under pressure to step up the program of selling off the state assets and opening the economy to foreign investment. Paralleling efforts that had failed abysmally in the Philippines five years earlier, the government poured money into creating the infrastructure that would serve the foreign investment still to come. The government then set off the big BOOM – Build, Own and Operate Model – offering foreign investors a guaranteed market if they would take the lead in creating electrical and nuclear plants. On top came the sell-off of existing state-owned industry.[75]

There were actually two schemes for generating revenue from the 'sale' of public assets. The first was to sell transferable 'revenue participation certificates' for dams, bridges, power plants, highways, railways, telecommunication facilities, ports, and civilian airports. These allowed the public an initially tax-free share in the net revenues of a particular piece of infrastructure. First to be privatized was the Bosphorus Bridge, assuring that future bankers leaping from it would have to pay a toll.[76]

The second device was the sale of equity in the state-owned companies, many of which had been acquired in bailouts of private firms. On the advice of top consulting and investment-banking firms from the US and France, the national airline, banks, the state textile agency, cement plants, fertilizer factories, and many others, including the national post, telegraph, and telephone company, were slated for dumping. The sell-off was to be accompanied by the opening of the first stock exchange in Turkey in fifty years.[77] Not only would foreign investment be welcome, but also some companies' shares would be listed on the New York and London stock exchanges.[78]

Similar visions seem to have appeared to Zaire's Guide during one of his descents to earth. His September 1983 austerity program descried a devaluation of a mere 500% – with the usual program of 'liberalization': removing price controls, eliminating subsidies, abolishing major import restrictions, cutting government expenditures, and phasing out public-sector companies. Some forty-seven state companies were scheduled for liquidation or reorganization on commercial lines, including Air Zaire, the Compagnie Maritime Zaïrois, and Petrozaire. (In 1973 and 1974 international bank loans had financed the conversion of these same companies into publicly owned fiefdoms of the president's family and friends.) And the welcome mat for foreign investors was rolled out, with free repatriation of profits permitted for the first time in a decade.

With reprivatization appeasing the creditors, it was time for opposition leader Nguza-Karl-I-Bond, who had been so active in denouncing Mobutu's looting operations, to return home warmly endorsing the new economic program. With unemployment and the price of basic goods rising sharply, and the black market legalized, Ronald Reagan publicly expressed his 'admiration' for Zaire's efforts.[79]

However, generating foreign investment, either for new projects or to purchase the reprivatized companies, was still something of a problem. Mobutu responded in two ways. He curried favor with the old colonial power, Belgium, perhaps helped by his alleged gift of ivory and rare chimpanzees to King Baudouin, though such gifts contravene international wildlife-conservation conventions.[80] He also solicited investment from Israel and from British and American Jewish businessmen. Pleading that restoring ties with Israel had cost him $350 million in Arab aid, Mobutu signed with Israel technical cooperation agreements and a deal giving special legal protection to Israeli investments. In return, the Israel lobby in the US pushed Congress to step up American aid money to Zaire.[81]

Bernie Cornfeld's Revenge

The US government fanned the debtor countries' reprivatization mania[82] and their undignified rush to welcome any itinerant capitalist jingling spare change. It called on Latin America to hasten policy changes toward foreign investors, but warned that the region should expect no increases in US foreign aid or in US imports of its products. When George Shultz insisted that government direction could damage the economies of developing countries as surely as could natural calamities, he probably had his own government's experiences in the front of his mind. The World Bank concurred, establishing a subsidiary to insure direct foreign investment in developing countries, while the US lobbied the Inter-American Development Bank to reorient lending to favor private foreign investment.[83]

But foreign investment as a 'solution' to developing-country financial problems neglected a few facts. First, the transformation of existing debt into equity did nothing to increase the net financial resources of the developing countries. At best it allowed them to defer some payments because profits on equity need not be paid as regularly as interest on loans.[84] Second, new inflows of investment money were not going to be easy to generate, no matter how many concessions were squeezed out of the debtors, for the US transnational firms in general had no desire to raise their equity stakes in Latin America.

In vain, local economists had pointed out to their mendicant governments that the US had become a net importer of direct investment funds; that US investments in Latin America had long been self-financing, using their borrowings in host countries to transfer profits back to the US; and that any new wave of US investments overseas would focus not on resources and manufacturing but on financial services. Such investments go where the hot money is; and that no longer included Latin America, where US banks had been losing money and scaling down their operations.[85]

Perhaps there was another way. What if the investment funds for Latin America and other developing countries came not through the established US corporations but through recycling the hot money that had fled? The new right-wing French government of Jacques Chirac led the way; for, after instituting the greatest loosening of exchange controls since 1968, it put a full amnesty for black money and tax-evaders' hoards, along with a major tax cut, prominently on its political agenda to draw flight capital back from Switzerland while it put fifty state companies on the auction block.[86]

In a similar spirit Treasury Secretary Baker spoke of the need for developing countries to create a favorable environment for private investment. He also tried to attack the twin US deficits – the budget deficit and the merchandise-trade deficit – by advocating lower interest rates, a lower dollar, and therefore a reduced need to cover the deficits with inflows of flight capital. Both policies pointed toward the return of the prodigal son. Although much of the capital that had fled Latin

America had entrenched itself in physical assets – particularly real estate in Miami, New York, San Diego, Houston, and other favored localities – Latin American liquid financial resources (estimated in late 1984 at $60 to $75 billion) were still available abroad.[87] Tiny Haiti alone boasted about $500 million in its citizens' foreign bank accounts, even without counting the Duvalier family loot.[88] How much more existed in financial assets that could be readily, if quietly, liquefied was anyone's guess. Nor was the phenomenon limited to Latin America. The Philippine finance minister estimated early in 1986 that there was $10 billion in flight capital ready to come home if the environment were made sufficiently inviting.[89] And most important of all, bankers began to see the return of flight capital as the only long-term hope for the developing countries to service their debts.[90] How could those funds, for whom anonymity remained the paramount concern, be given enough security to induce them to return? One expert had already given a compelling answer.

In the late 1960s capital-flight scandals rocked and weakened Investors' Overseas Services. Country after country closed down its local operations. In an attempt to refurbish the firm's image, Bernie Cornfeld hired James Roosevelt, son of the late American president, and sent him on the road to sell a New Deal for the Third World. Cornfeld envisaged a national mutual fund for each country, by which local savings would be invested in local enterprises in order to spread equity ownership throughout the population. It was essentially what General Pinochet would later call *capitalismo popular*. Actually, for Cornfeld, the national funds were a public relations caper – not one was actually established[91] – but in the 1980s, they were an idea whose time had come.

Among Henry Kissinger's schemes for solving problems he had done so much to create was one that the World Bank, late in 1985, implemented with the enthusiastic backing of the Reagan administration. It was an international mutual fund to invest in the equity of companies listed on developing-country stock exchanges. The countries involved were Argentina, Brazil, South Korea, Thailand, Malaysia, Chile, and, of course, Mexico.[92] Initially, participation was to be limited to a handful of sponsoring institutions. But the trillions of dollars washing around Western institutional investors on one side, and the vast resources represented by Third World enterprises on the other, inspired bold dreams about the scheme's possible future. Those banks contemplating accepting equity in developing-country companies in exchange for debt were, no doubt, delighted; for it opened up a potential outside market where the shares could be dumped, should the need arise. Delighted, too, would have been those who had spirited assets out of the debtor countries.

Once the mutual fund became open to the general public, they would have a discreet, safe way of reinvesting them back home.

It was perhaps the perfect loan-back scam. First, capital flight wrecked the debtor-country finances, forcing emergency borrowing from the banks in which the flight capital was deposited. Then, to service the resulting debt, debtor countries were forced to impose severe austerity measures and massive currency devaluations. Then the banks through which the flight capital had passed forced the debtor governments to shed public assets at fire-sale prices. Then the flight capital, whose value had been increased many times in terms of local purchasing power by depreciation of the local currency, could go home again, laundered through an international mutual fund, to repurchase the public assets on the auction block.

But where would interested investors go to purchase shares in the new mutual fund? Certainly it could not be headquartered in London or New York; there, disclosure requirements were too tight. The obvious place was Luxembourg, where so many similar international mutual funds – starting in 1960 with Bernie Cornfeld's International Investment Trust – had found a warm and discreet welcome.[93]

Epilogue

Developing-country debts to the West are getting perilously close to a trillion-dollar question, of which the commercial-bank portion is perhaps $400 billion and growing. How that debt emerged and came to bear its current interest load is a question evaded in refinancing negotiations. In fact, a major objective of those negotiations is to whitewash the debt. First they aim to assure that the governments of the debtor countries assume obligations incurred by private companies and citizens, or by officials who used their public power to accumulate private wealth. Then the negotiations ensure, through long-term rescheduling, retroactive public approval on the disposition of the funds and on the resulting debt.

Undoubtedly, part of the euromarket borrowing by developing countries in the 1970s was 'wasted'; but most went into genuine development projects, whose capacity to be self-amortizing was undermined by events outside the developing countries' control. After 1981 much additional borrowing was undertaken simply for purposes of balance-of-payments financing.

Part of the need for balance-of-payments financing resulted from the deterioration of developing countries' terms of trade with respect to their northern suppliers of capital goods – a phenomenon perhaps not entirely unrelated to phony invoicing for purposes of capital flight. This, and sharp recession in the industrialized countries, resulted in the worst dip in developing-country export receipts since the 1930s. Part of the balance-of-payments financing was necessitated by interest-rate increases, and part came from the need to replenish foreign-exchange reserves drained by capital flight.

Faced with a collapse of developing countries' export earnings, one could argue a moral responsibility of the West to step up concessionary aid flows to help offset the cyclical downturn, particularly as such flows would rebound to the advantage of the West in creating new export markets. But the counterargument, that when the welfare state is under siege at home industrial countries should give priority to the needs of their own citizens, cannot be dismissed out of hand.

However, it is difficult to see why the cost of decisions taken exclusively by the unelected Federal Reserve Board of the United States should be passively accepted by citizens of the US, let alone those of the developing debtor countries. The dramatic fluctuations in world interest rates between 1979 and 1984 cannot be simply imputed to the 'magic of the market.' At least part of the responsibility lies with the conscious sorcery of a few individuals, for which the government that appointed them must take part of the blame, and should, if necessary, assume part of the cost.

Until hard-money dogmatism seized the centers of financial power in the West, real rates of interest over long periods of time averaged about 1.5% to 2%. Those were the rates that both lenders and borrowers came to accept as reasonable, equitable, and, not least, sustainable. They should also be the reference point for renegotiations and refinancing of existing debt loans, allowing a real rate of interest of 1.5% to 2% above the inflation rate in the country to which the payment is destined.

Furthermore, it is a relatively simple exercise to factor out of the debt loads incurred since 1973, and from the debt-service payments already made, a sum to compensate for the actual real rates over that historical norm. The net result might be that, in certain cases, the banks would owe money to the debtor countries.

To the extent that American monetary policy contributed to the appreciation of the US dollar, thereby adding to the burden of developing-country debt, that, too, is grounds on which to base a case for restitution. Even a dollar that has lost 30% of its value in a year still leaves a legacy of years of 'overvaluation' that added enormously to the debt load. If the impact of the excess of interest rates above historical real levels can be factored out of debt-service obligations (and even from the principal of the debt to the extent the excess interest rates were de facto recapitalized), and if the stream of payments made since 1973 can be reestimated to calculate any refund due, the same can be done with respect to the impact of unexpected appreciations of the US dollar. This is particularly true given the role of the flight of capital to the US in pushing up the dollar. Indeed, some of the 'mystery' of the dollar rising in the face of a huge commodity-trade deficit can be solved simply by reference to the phenomenon of developing-country exporters leaving the proceeds of the sales of their goods stashed in US bank accounts instead of repatriating them.

Despite widespread consternation at Fidel Castro's poking his lit cigar into the tinderbox of the regional debt question, what he actually suggested was not simply repudiation. Castro asked for the reclassification of the burden of repaying the debt into a legitimate portion, representing interest at the real rate prevailing at the time of negotiation, and an illegitimate part, due to terms-of-trade deterioration and usurious increases in real rates of interest. He called for the illegitimate portion to be assumed by Western governments, which could compensate the banks out of money saved by reducing military budgets. This, he claimed, would enhance both peace and prosperity – debtor countries could spend the foreign exchange no longer going to interest payments on imports from the industrialized countries, thereby easing the unemployment problem.[1] Such an argument cannot be dismissed, particularly when it comes from the head of state of one of the model debtors of the Americas, one who could draw on the expertise of Robert Vesco.

Part of the answer to the question, whence came the huge debt burden, lies in the nature of the governments in the debtor countries. To the extent that the proceeds of loans were 'wasted' – by military dictatorships with an appetite for arms imported from the war machines of the West or by thugs with insatiable appetites for Swiss chateaux and Bahamian bank accounts – responsibility is inevitably tied to political legitimacy. Insofar as these regimes were kept in office by the Western powers, there is a clear complicity of the Western governments in the looting, and therefore a responsibility for bearing at least part of the resulting cost. At a minimum, the burdens should be shared, not fobbed off on the victims.

In that spirit the Inter-American Development Bank recently called for reclassification of the debt. Debt incurred purely for consumption or for military expenditure should be separated out; half the interest on this part should be channeled into a special trust fund out of which would be made investments in foreign-exchange-yielding projects. Reinvesting current interest to assure a future flow of foreign exchange is scarcely a radical idea – one of the Polish debt deals, for example, had made similar provision for half of its repayments to be recycled back, in this instance as new trade credits. Nonetheless, the bank's plan brought an angry rejection from IMF chief Jacques Delarosière,[2] presumably because classifying the purposes for which the debt had been incurred would raise again the legitimacy question.

That question is all the more urgent because an enormous part of the problem derives from the participation of the international banking community in the fomenting of, and profiting from, capital flight. There would be no 'debt crisis' without large-scale capital flight. It is true that part of the cause of capital flight lies in the social and political conditions in the country where the funds originate. Although a case can be made for accommodating persons seeking to flee desperate circumstances, a case can also be made that such accommodation should not involve passing the cost to those who remain behind, either because they choose to stay to combat those circumstances or because they lack the political and business connections to facilitate their own flight.

Moreover, the political environment that encourages capital flight cannot be divorced entirely from policy decisions of Western governments with respect to the leadership of their client states. And to the extent that Western governments, particularly that of the US, used the flight of funds to avoid politically unpopular decisions with respect to their own budget deficits, they share responsibility.

Furthermore, because at least some Western banks have been not passively accommodating but actively encouraging the international flight of funds, they can be held to account just as they are found to be openly complicit in domestic money laundering: they should absorb part, if not all, of the resulting social cost. That bankers periodically open their front doors to delegations from developing-country governments in search of loans to replenish foreign-exchange reserves while their back doors are never closed to flight capital – which will then be 'recycled' to the countries of origin – borders on the obscene. The US government at least *tried* to put Meyer Lansky in jail for doing something similar.

When Castro and the Inter-American Development Bank raised the dreaded legitimacy question, they focused only on debt-service payments. But it is more important to scrutinize the origins of the debt principal in order to do what Argentine politicians cozened their population into thinking they would do – assess how much of the debt *per se* (rather than just the debt-service cost) is legitimate. If the Argentine civilian government has a moral and legal right to roll back the military budget and sell off military industries to the private sector, including foreign investors, why does it not also have a right to write off the debts military officials incurred for clandestine arms imports or to create retirement funds abroad? If China, which repudiated its pre-1949 debt – on the grounds that the government that incurred it was illegitimate – can be welcomed back into the international capital market, why should not the democratic regime in Argentina be able, without penalty, to repudiate part or all of the debt incurred by the preceding military regime?

It was in 1979, the year when interest rates began their dizzying climb and the global pool of hot money began whirling out of control, that two of the most unfortunate precedents were set on that question. The first occurred in the Persian-Arabian Gulf, where the shah of Iran sat on his Peacock Throne while David Rockefeller stood watch over the Imperial Treasury.[3] Through Chase Manhattan Bank flowed the deposits of the National Iranian Oil Company (NIOC) at a time when the country was the world's second-largest oil exporter. Chase also controlled the business of issuing letters of credit for Iranian oil exports. In fact, Chase held the bulk of the foreign-exchange reserves of the Iranian central bank, on which it apparently paid somewhat less than market rates of interest. Chase functioned as banker to the Pahlavi Foundation, established by the shah in 1960 to defuse criticism of the amount of wealth being accumulated by him and his immediate family. By the time of his fall, this charitable organization allegedly controlled one oil company, twelve sugar refineries, one electronics firm, a football club, four cemeteries, and interests in mining, industrial bakeries, banks, and General Motors, among others. The foundation's assets were allegedly enhanced by money diverted from the NIOC into Pahlavi Foundation accounts. In the late 1970s the gap between the earnings from Iranian oil exports and the money recorded as entering the national income accounts was allegedly in the billions.

In 1978, when the government budget went into deficit, Chase was on hand to lead-manage loans necessary to maintain Iranian military and development spending levels. That some of these loans seemed to have been negotiated by the shah personally, and might therefore have been contrary to Iranian law, did not deter the bank. As long as the shah remained in power, there would be no questioning of their legitimacy. And the entire arrangement seemed to be backed up by the ultimate security – US government commitment to the shah as its policeman of the Persian-Arabian Gulf, and Soviet support of the shah's regime until a few weeks before his fall.

The new regime initially did its best to remain on good terms with the banks – with one important exception. The business of letters of credit for oil sales was opened up to all banks; the central bank spread its reserves among several banks; and the NIOC began searching for alternative depositories. Chase's position had been unusually privileged in yet another respect: Iranian deposits in Chase greatly exceeded the value of the bank's loans to Iran. But if deposits continued to be drained out, this position could be quickly reversed. Furthermore, there was the danger of revolutionary Iran repudiating its debts to Chase.

But Chase had precedents in Middle East dealings on which to draw for a possible solution. In 1966 when Yousef Beidas's Intra Bank came crashing down, Chase froze deposits Intra held at Chase New York, refusing to release them until Intra repaid debts due in Beirut.[4] Similarly, if Chase were able to call Iranian loans into default, it could legally seize deposits to offset its loans before the deposits migrated to the competition.

After David Rockefeller and his sidekick, Henry Kissinger, persuaded President Carter to admit the deposed shah into the US, Iranian militants seized the US embassy in Tehran. The US retaliated by freezing Iranian assets. The American freeze meant that Iran could not meet loan payments on the due date; Chase called Iran into default and seized assets, offsetting the deposits against outstanding loans, and wiped its books clear of Iranian exposure – while the rest of the banking world looked on in growing outrage.[5]

Probably the most important though unappreciated aspect of the ultimate settlement of the dispute was that the terms for the release of the hostages also made academic questions about the legitimacy of the shah's debts. Iran accepted responsibility for them; yet the US did not accept responsibility for locating and returning a fortune that the Khomeini regime insisted totaled $25 billion. The US claimed that the shah took out only $60 million, and it was in Switzerland. Given the hostility toward the Khomeini regime, it is not surprising that virtually all subsequent suits against the shah's estate in the US were dismissed.[6]

Switzerland responded to the demands of the new government (as it had done when Haile Selassie was deposed) by refusing to freeze the absconding monarch's assets, insisting that the Iranian government work exclusively through the courts. And although one lawyer acting for the Iranian government insisted that the shah alone had $3.25 billion in Switzerland, little was ever found, as the search was legally restricted to deposits in the major banks, ignoring the private banks and bypassing the issue of how much had transited Switzerland. Except for some fiduciary deposits of the central bank, Switzerland released nothing; and the question of recovery of the looted national assets effectively vanished from the political agenda.[7]

Another bad precedent was set by the revolutionary government of Nicaragua. During the 1970s Nicaragua borrowed from the international banking system through Ultramar Banking Corporation, which was partly owned and controlled by the Somoza family. One reason for the growth of debt was that the bank took more than 5% as a 'fee' for its services. Another reason was the need to finance the import of arms to defend the regime. A third was the need to replenish foreign-exchange reserves drained by capital flight, not least that of the Somoza family.

In September 1979 the head of the revolutionary junta, Daniel Ortega, declared before the United Nations that Nicaragua would pay all the debts except those associated with the import of arms or with 'corruption.' He denied any responsibility for 'repaying' loans where the money had never entered Nicaragua.

Alas, two months later, international and domestic pressure and unwarranted optimism about future flows of aid and trade to rekindle the war-stricken economy caused the government to accept full responsibility for all the debts.[8]

There were two separate but closely related issues involved. One was the legitimacy of the debt, and the second was the location and retrieval of diverted money to facilitate repayment once responsibility had been accepted. Location is difficult and often impossible because of the machinery of peekaboo finance. And even when the assets are found, their new host government must be forced to regurgitate them. However, there have been some glimmers of hope.

Shortly after the Second World War, Swiss banks were forced to make some restitution for their holdings of looted gold. Granted, the restitution was very small in relation to the probable total that had been stolen and then laundered in Switzerland; but the precedent was set.[9] For the disappearing Iranian money, too, there was a useful precedent. Although the mullah-cracy of Iran accepted the legitimacy of the debt, the government also coaxed the Swiss into a partial departure from their hitherto sacrosanct secrecy rules. A further departure came in 1982, when Costa Rica defaulted on payments on its 'cuckoobonds' (bearer eurobonds issued through Swiss banks), and one of the bondholders tried to have his bank sue on his behalf. The Swiss courts refused the suit, arguing that bank secrecy cannot serve as cover for a client's identity when bona fide legal proceedings are in progress.[10] US-government-imposed agreements with Switzerland on drug money and insider-trading cases also helped to erode the capacity of Switzerland to erect stone walls in front of foreign probes.

Such chinks in the armor of Swiss bank secrecy mean that there may be some hope, however modest, of recovering the assets of another absconding autocrat. In February 1986 Ferdinand Marcos decided to follow the lead of his late friend the shah of Iran. He was helped by the US Air Force, which supplied the planes to take him into exile and loaded them with a few of his personal effects: twenty-two crates of gold, currency, stocks and bonds, jewelry, and, perhaps most important, the videotaped documents that could possibly unscramble the maze of ghost companies and peekaboo bank accounts in which his already exiled fortune was held.

The size of that fortune was a matter of considerable speculation. Dewey Dee is a Philippine financier who had apparently fronted for some

Marcos flight-capital operations. He had absconded to Vancouver in 1981, after wrecking the Manila money market and leaving $100 million in unsecured debts behind. Dee resurfaced to claim that Marcos was worth $3 billion. The CIA estimated the total at more than $2 billion. That claim must be taken seriously. After all, current CIA chief William Casey was head of the Export-Import Bank of the United States when it was funding the acquisition by the Philippines of 'one reactor for the price of two.' However, some members of the Commission on Good Government established by the new regime to probe the size, distribution, and nature of the Marcos fortune put the total at $5 to $10 billion, not to mention the offshore hoards of those cronies who bolted with him. Apart from a Marcos real estate empire in the US, most of the family wealth, the commission felt, was in Switzerland.[11]

As befitting a regime that is essentially a joint venture of the IMF, the Pentagon, and the Vatican of John Paul II, among the first acts of the new government was to reassure the IMF and the creditor banks of its fiscal and financial responsibility, and implicitly to guarantee that questioning the legitimacy of the Philippine foreign debt was not on its political agenda. Recovery of the Marcos money ostensibly was, but it is not clear how serious about it the new government really is. Playing up the corruption of the old regime serves, as it has in many other debtor countries, to prepare the public mind for the austerity necessary to pay the debt. It tells the population that they have been plundered mainly by their own former rulers rather than by the international banks. It helps to coax more aid money from the US government; aid money will, in effect, go straight from the US Treasury to the US banks. And it deflects attention from the character of the new government, riddled by former Marcos cronies and/or partners in the enterprises through which the looting took place. Within weeks of Marcos's fall, pressure was mounting inside the Philippines for the government to call off the treasure hunt.[12]

Prior to any assets being recovered they must be located. Central to the location process are the videotapes carried out of the Philippines by Marcos. These tapes, like the cash and jewelry that accompanied them, were seized by US customs; this set off a major legal wrangle. Moreover, securing the release of anything located is not a straightforward matter, for it must be demonstrated that the assets were illegitimately acquired.

Even before securing access to those documents, the Commission on Good Government launched an action under the Racketeer Influenced and Corrupt Organizations Act (RICO), alleging that Marcos and his cronies ran not so much a government as a criminal enterprise, which was of direct interest to the US courts: much of the money allegedly diverted came from US government programs, US-based corporations, and Philippine citizens resident in the US; much of the take transited or came to rest in the US. Such an argument would have made it logical to name a series of US administrations as co-conspirators. Nonetheless, the notion of treating a foreign government as a criminal enterprise so excited a California judge that she tried to impose a worldwide freeze on the assets of Marcos and his associates! Whatever the outcome of the dispute, there hangs over the proceedings the 1984 decision of a New York judge, rejecting a similar action by the government of Iran against the late shah's regime, on the grounds that the US courts are not the logical forum in which to conduct a general review of the conduct of a foreign government.[13] Inside the US the Philippine government is aided by a 1982 tax treaty that calls for the exchange of information on tax-law violations; but the US has never enforced another country's exchange controls. The Reagan administration is understandably reluctant to frighten other client regimes, present and future, by helping to trace secret retirement funds and political war chests, and there is a deep-rooted fear among financiers that if the money is found and recovered, the US will lose its long-cultivated appeal as a flight-capital haven.[14]

As to the Swiss component of the Marcos money, allegedly some $800 million in bank deposits, the Swiss government did set a precedent by ordering the assets of Marcos and his cronies frozen, a precedent later extended to the supposed $350 million deposited by Baby Doc. Swiss bankers were upset at the government's action, for the freeze occurred before the new regime in Manila formally charged Marcos with offenses that were also crimes under Swiss law. The Swiss actions were apparently prompted by efforts to shift some Marcos money out of Switzerland to the benefit of other peekaboo centers.

One apparent aspirant was Costa Rica. After Marcos was rebuffed in his efforts to buy a Panamanian island that had once housed the shah of Iran, he allegedly offered to deposit one billion dollars in the central bank of Costa Rica in exchange for sanctuary. Costa Rica made a public show of refusing, on the grounds that Marcos and his money were tainted; but the real reason likely had more to do with the preemptive Swiss freeze.[15]

Furthermore, the Swiss action may have reflected a fundamental change in the nature of the country's banking business. During the 1970s and 1980s, the major Swiss banks had greatly internationalized their operations – actively participating in loans syndications, accepting increasing amounts of international institutional business, and extending their overseas-branch networks, not least in the US. It was a far cry from the days when the valise carried by their cash couriers represented the bulk of their international exposure. This meant that the major Swiss banks had something important to lose should scandal chase them out of major markets and their overseas assets face sequestration.[16] After all, the Marcos and Duvalier fortunes represented in good measure the loot from US foreign aid at a time when the US government was under the control of aggressive budget-cutters. The Marcos and Duvalier freezes, coupled with the absence of similar moves in the US,[17] might well represent the final triumph of the US over Switzerland as the world's premier hot-money haven.

Not that the freeze necessarily means a return of the money to the Philippines. Once again, the money belonging to Marcos and his cronies must be specifically identified. Despite some patchwork 'tightening' of disclosure provisions in 1982 to head off the bank-secrecy referendum, it is still lawful in Switzerland for deposits to be held in the name of attorneys and trustees acting on behalf of anonymous depositors. All they must do is declare that to the best of their knowledge their clients are not engaged in unlawful behavior. Furthermore, much of the money, if it exists, will likely have been deposited in the name of Panamanian and Hong Kong ghost companies capitalized by bearer shares, by Liechtenstein 'foundations,' and by South Pacific island instabanks; such assets will likely be unidentifiable from existing documentation. Finally, it remains to be proved that anything Marcos did was actually a crime under Swiss law. Within a few weeks of the imposition of the freeze, the Swiss banking commission was already talking down estimates of the amount of Marcos money frozen in Swiss accounts.[18]

Is there an alternative procedure? Perhaps, though given the 'reform' governments proliferating in developing debtor countries, the political will to do the technically possible is likely lacking. Still, the precedent set in 1979 is a sword that cuts two ways. If, when Iran 'defaulted,' Chase could seize Iranian deposits and 'offset' them against loans outstanding, why cannot developing debtor countries do the same? Why can they not calculate the amount of money illegally siphoned out with the active collaboration of the international banks, and 'offset' such illegal capital exports (including an estimate of subsequently accrued interest) against debts allegedly owed syndicates comprised of those same banks? It may well have been such thoughts that cost the head of the Venezuelan central bank his job early in 1984.

For many years Venezuela was regarded as wonderfully solvent, because of its huge flows of oil revenue. But in 1982 its financial situation suddenly and sharply deteriorated; capital flight became epidemic, and foreign-exchange reserves dropped from $20 billion to $11 billion within a year. Furthermore, the international banks began pressuring the government of Venezuela to guarantee the private-sector debt.

The head of the central bank, Leopoldo Diaz Bruzual, objected, charging that in 1982 the private sector put $5 billion of its borrowings offshore and brought back only $500 million. To that date there had been an estimated $12 billion in capital exported by the private sector, $8 billion in Miami bank accounts, not to speak of real estate holdings. He contended that the private sector could repay the private foreign debt and still come out ahead. And he insisted that, 'We overborrowed. But the international banks are guilty, too.... They must suffer some damage, make some sacrifices, or at least share them....' When the government went ahead with a de facto guarantee of the private-sector foreign debt, it prompted a major feud between the finance ministry and the central bank chief.

The central bank chief also took aim at the national oil company, which held huge cash surpluses abroad while the government was forced to borrow heavily on the euromarket; and he agitated for the direct control by the central bank of all the hard-currency holdings of the oil company. This time he was successful, unfortunately, as it turned out.

The presidential elections in February 1984 produced a victory of the Social Democratic party of Jaime Lusinchi. In his inaugural speech Lusinchi stated that, with respect to the foreign debt, 'Venezuela will pay ... to the last cent.' He was not kidding. In short order he showed his commitment to the principles of social democracy by imposing a massive austerity program. He also fired the central bank chief who continued to resist using state foreign-exchange holdings, now enhanced by the oil-company surpluses, to repay private debtors' international bank loans.[19]

Yet the issues raised by Venezuela's central bank chief remain unresolved. For if it is permissible for the state to use its foreign-exchange holdings belonging to the population as a whole, to discharge the international-bank debt belonging to a few private citizens and companies, why should the process not work in reverse? Why shouldn't the state use the offshore resources of a privileged few of its citizens to offset the debts that those citizens dumped on the public? A useful precedent was set when the US government ordered US companies to leave Libya, and froze Libyan financial assets in the US. It then threatened to offset against these financial assets the value of the physical property the US companies were forced to leave behind, should Libya expropriate it.[20] In a similar way, why should not Mexico, for example, estimate the value of real estate illicitly held in the US by its citizens and offset it against the value of US financial assets – bank loans – effectively frozen in Mexico?

The obvious retort is that netting flight capital against outstanding debt would lead to massive insolvency of major international financial institutions, as the debts they would be forced to write off would greatly exceed their capital. That, in turn, would cause a freezing of the global flow of payments, making trade dry up and setting off runs on banks all over the world. Out of such a crisis could come either a world depression like that of the 1930s (if Western governments did not respond) or hyperinflation (if they responded by creating the liquidity necessary to keep their banks from collapsing). A frightening scenario, indeed. But it is not the only one. After four years of crisis, the major international banks have certainly built up enough officially recognized reserves of capital to ride out a partial repudiation;[21] in addition, there are informal reserves of capital on which they can draw.

Bernie Cornfeld had a secret, which he did not share with the other directors of Investors' Overseas Services. That secret was the ultimate cause of Cornfeld's downfall, as the other directors reacted to a non-existent liquidity crisis by dumping him from control. The secret was and is that there is a difference between hot money and cool, between the widow's mite and the heroin trafficker's hoard, between a temporary corporate working balance and a tax-evader's secret offshore bank account. Although IOS was a mutual fund, not a bank, its shares, like bank deposits, were theoretically redeemable on demand. But between 10% and 20% of the money in IOS was felt to be not subject to demands for redemption, for it could not risk exposure. Such examples are not merely of antiquarian interest, for in 1980, when Nugan-Hand Bank came crashing down with a $50 million hole in its accounts, no depositor turned up to claim the missing money. Similarly, when a high-living employee of Morgan Guaranty Bank was investigated, in the spring of 1986, for possibly having illegitimately diverted foreign clients' money, the speculation was that the funds in question were Brazilian flight capital, whose owners were in no position to protest, at least in public.

Flight capital appearing on a bank's balance sheets is, in accounting terms, no different from other deposits. But, as some of the banks came to realize, it does not always behave like other deposits. It is, like the hot money on the IOS books, de jure a deposit but de facto part of the capital of the banking system. In effect, it is debt that insists on behaving like equity; and it is easy enough to modify accounting procedures to conform to this economic reality.

If the exchange of debt into equity is legitimate for creditor interests to demand of debtors, it is equally legitimate for debtors to demand of creditors. And the augmented capital of the creditor institutions, which possess the information to determine which deposits are effectively frozen into capital, thus provides a major cushion against which bad debts can be written off without imperiling the solvency of the banking institutions. If those bad debts are those that the debtor countries can identify as illegitimate – deriving from phony invoicing or the looting of the national patrimony by persons enjoying power without responsibility, or caused by the need for borrowing to offset the drain from capital flight – the circle is complete. The 'debt crisis' is resolved by eliminating it at source, leaving the world with a smaller, but considerably wiser banking system, and leaving it free from the overhang of paper obligations that currently blight the economic futures of debtor and creditor countries alike.

July 27, 1986

Bibliography and Sources

Principal Periodicals Consulted

Les Affaires
Afrique-Asie
American Banker
Arab Banking and Finance
Arab News
Asian Wall Street Journal
The Bank for International Settle-
    ments, Annual Report
The Banker
Barron's
The Boston Globe
Business America
Business Week
Cambio 16
The Christian Science Monitor
The Congressional Record
Counterspy
Covert Action Information Bulletin
The Daily Telegraph
Le Devoir
Dun's Business Monthly
The Economist
L'Espresso
Euromoney
L'Exprèss
Facts on File
Far Eastern Economic Review
Federal Reserve Bulletin
Le Figaro Magazine
Finance (Montreal)
Finance & Development
The Financial Post
The Financial Times (London)

The Financial Times of Canada
Foreign Affairs
Foreign Exchange
Foreign Policy
The Gazette, Montreal
The German Tribune
The Globe and Mail
The Guardian
IMF Survey
Inquiry
Institutional Investor
Intelligence Digest
International Banking Report
International Currency Review
The International Herald Tribune
International Money Line
The Jerusalem Post
Jeune Afrique
Jeune Afrique Economique
Labour, Capital and Society
Latin America Commodities Report
Latin America Political Report
Latin America Regional Report:
    Andean Area
Latin America Regional Report:
    Brazil
Latin America Regional Report:
    Caribbean
Latin America Regional Report:
    Mexico and Central America
Latin America Regional Report:
    Southern Cone
Latin America Times

Latin America Weekly Report
Liberation
London Currency Report
Maclean's
Manchester Guardian Weekly
The Miami Herald
The Middle East
Middle East Economic Digest
Middle East International
Middle East Research and Intelli-
    gence Reports
Le Monde
Le Monde Diplomatique
An-Nahar Arab Report & Memo
The National Journal
New African
The New Republic
The New Statesman
The New Yorker
The New York Times
Newsweek
Le Nouvel Observateur

The Observer
The Ottawa Citizen
Pacific Islands Monthly
El Pais
Pakistan & Gulf Economist
Panorama
Paris Match
La Presse, Montreal
Proceso
South
Spotlight
The Sunday Telegraph
The Sunday Times
Time
The Times (London)
The Toronto Star
The Village Voice
The Wall Street Journal
The Wall Street Transcript
The Washington Post
World Press Review

Secondary Sources

Australia, Commonwealth–New South Wales Joint Task Force On Drug
    Trafficking. Report Volumes II, IV. Canberra: 1983.
Blair, John M. The Control of Oil. New York: 1978.
Bloch, Jonathan and Patrick Fitzgerald. British Intelligence and Covert Action.
    Kerry: 1983.
Blum, Richard H. Offshore Haven Banks, Trusts, and Companies. New York:
    1984.
Boettcher, Robert. Gifts of Deceit. New York: 1980.
Boyer, Jean-François. L'Empire Moon. Paris: 1986.
Bresler, Fenton. The Chinese Mafia. London: 1981.
Buendia, Manuel. La Ultraderecha en Mexico. Mexico City: 1984.
Cecchi, Alberto. Storia della P-2. Rome: 1985.
Chambost, Edouard. Guide mondial des secrets bancaires. Paris: 1984.
Charbonneau, Jean-Pierre. The Canadian Connection. Montreal: 1976.
Clark, Evert and Nicholas Horrock. Contrabandista. New York: 1973.
Clarke, Thurston and John J. Tigue. Dirty Money. New York & London: 1976.
Conway, Barbara. The Piracy Business. London: 1981.
Cornwell, Rupert. God's Banker: An Account of the Life & Death of Roberto
    Calvi. London, 1982.
Davis, L. J. Bad Money. New York: 1982.

Delpirou, Alain and Alain Labrousse. *Coca Coke*. Paris: 1986.

Demaris, Ovid. *The Last Mafioso*. New York: 1981.

Derogy, Jacques. *Israel Connection: La Mafia en Israel*. Paris: 1980.

DiFonza, Luigi. *St. Peter's Banker: Michele Sindona*. New York: 1983.

Drosnin, Michael. *Citizen Hughes*. New York: 1985.

Effros, Robert C., ed. *Emerging Financial Centers*. Washington: 1982.

Eisenberg, Dennis, Uri Dan and Eli Landau. *Meyer Lansky: Mogul of the Mob*. New York & London: 1979.

Epstein, Edward J. *Agency of Fear*. New York: 1977.

Eringer, Robert. *The Global Manipulators*. Bristol: 1980.

Faith, Nicholas. *Safety in Numbers: The Mysterious World of Swiss Banking*. New York: 1982.

Faligot, Roger and Pascal Kop. *La Piscine: Les Services Secrets Français 1944–1984*. Paris: 1985.

Franco, Victor. *La Fuite des capitaux*. Paris: 1979.

Garwood, Darrell. *Under Cover: 35 Years of CIA Deception*. New York: 1980.

Goulden, Joseph. *The Death Merchant*. New York: 1985.

Gurwin, Larry. *The Calvi Affair*. London: 1983.

Hammer, Richard. *The Vatican Connection*. New York: 1982.

Higham, Charles. *Trading With The Enemy*. New York: 1983.

Hougan, Jim. *Spooks: The Haunting of America*. New York: 1978.

———. *Secret Agenda*. New York: 1985.

Hudson, Michael. *Global Fracture: the New International Economic Order*. New York: 1977.

———. *Superimperialism: the Economic Strategy of American Empire*. New York: 1972.

Hulbert, Mark. *Interlock*. New York: 1982.

Hurtado, A. G. *The Political Economy of the Rise and Fall of the Chicago Boys*. Cambridge University Centre For Latin American Studies: 1983.

Hutchison, Robert A. *Vesco*. New York: 1974.

Knight, Stephen. *The Brotherhood: The Secret World of the Freemasons*. London: 1984.

Kruger, Henrik. *The Great Heroin Coup*. Montreal: 1980.

Kwitny, Jonathan. *Vicious Circles: The Mafia in the Marketplace*. New York: 1979.

Laya, Jean-Marie. *L'Argent secret et les banques suisses*. Lausanne: 1977.

Lernoux, Penny. *In Banks We Trust*. New York: 1984.

Le Vaillant, Yvon. *Sainte Mafia*. Paris: 1971.

Lo Bello, Nino. *The Vatican Papers*. London: 1984.

Manhattan, Avro. *The Vatican Billions*. Chino, Calif: 1983.

Martin, Malachi. *Rich Church, Poor Church*. New York: 1984.

Mayer, Martin. *The Bankers*. New York: 1974.

———. *The Fate of the Dollar*. New York: 1980.

———. *The Money Bazaars*. New York: 1984.

McCoy, Alfred W. *The Politics of Heroin in Southeast Asia*. New York: 1972.

McNamara, Robert. *The Economic Challenges For SubSahara Africa*. Washington: World Bank, 1985.

Mendelsohn, M. S. *Money on the Move*. New York: 1980.

Messick, Hank. *Lansky*. New York: 1973.

———. *Of Grass and Snow*. New York: 1979.

Mills, James. *The Underground Empire: Where Crime and Governments Embrace*. New York: 1986.

Mobillard, Max and Roger de Weck. *Scandale au Crédit Suisse*. Geneva: 1977.

Moffitt, Michael. *The World's Money*. New York: 1983.

Mumcu, Ugur. *Papa, Mafya Ve Agca*. Istanbul: 1984.

———. *Silah Kacakciligi Ve Teror*. Istanbul: 1983.

O'Callaghan, Sean. *The Drug Traffic*. London: 1967.

Pean, Pierre. *V: enquête sur l'affaire des 'avions renifleurs.'* Paris: 1984.

Raw, Charles, Godfrey Hodgson and Bruce Page. *'Do You Sincerely Want To Be Rich?'* New York: 1971.

Reid, Margaret. *The Secondary Banking Crisis*. London: 1983.

Reuter, Peter. *Disorganized Crime*. Cambridge, Mass.: 1982.

Robbins, Christopher. *Air America*. New York: 1985.

Sampson, Anthony. *The Money Lenders*. London: 1981.

———. *The Sovereign State: The Secret History of ITT*. London: 1973.

Sher, Julian. *White Hoods: Canada's Ku Klux Klan*. Vancouver: 1984.

Sobel, Lester (ed). *Corruption in Business*. New York: 1977.

Thomas, Gordon and Max Morgan-Witts. *Pontiff*. New York: 1983.

Torrie, Jill (ed). *Banking on Poverty: The Global Impact of the IMF & World Bank*. Toronto: 1983.

United Nations, Conference on Trade and Development. *Financial Solidarity for Development*. New York: 1984.

United States Senate. Permanent Subcommittee on Investigations. *Crime and Secrecy*. Washington: 1983.

United States, President's Commission on Organized Crime. *The Cash Connection: Organized Crime, Financial Institutions, and Money Laundering*. Washington: Oct. 1984.

Whittemore, L. H. *Peroff: The Man Who Knew Too Much*. New York: 1975.

Yallop, David. *In God's Name*. London: 1984.

Ynfante, Jesus. *Une crime sous Giscard*. Paris: 1982.

———. *Las fugas de capitales y los bancos suizos*. Barcelona: 1978.

Ziegler, Jean. *Une Suisse au-dessus de tout soupçon*. Paris: 1976.

Notes

Abbreviations Used

AA Afrique-Asie
AB American Banker
AF Arab Banking and Finance
AH An-Nahar
AN Arab News
AW Asian Wall Street Journal
BA Barron's
BI Bank for International
    Settlements, Annual Report
BW Business Week
CA Cambio 16
CM Christian Science Monitor
CR Congressional Record
CS Counterspy
DP Le Monde Diplomatique
DT Daily Telegraph
EC The Economist
EM Euromoney
EP El Pais
ES Espresso
EX L'Express
FE Foreign Exchange
FF Facts on File
FM Figaro Magazine
FP Financial Post
FR Far Eastern Economic Review
FT Financial Times, London
GM Globe and Mail
GU Guardian
GW Guardian Weekly

GZ Montreal Gazette
HT Herald Tribune
IB International Banking Report
IC International Currency Review
ID Intelligence Digest
II Institutional Investor
IM International Money Line
JP Jerusalem Post
LA La Presse, Montreal
LC Latin America Commodities
    Report
LD Le Devoir
LI Libération
LM Le Monde
LP Latin America Political Report
LR London Currency Report
LT Latin America Times
LW Latin America Weekly Report
MD Middle East Economic Digest
ME Middle East
MH Miami Herald
MI Middle East International
NA New African
NJ National Journal
NS New Statesman
NT New York Times
NW Newsweek
OB Observer
PG Pakistan & Gulf Economist
PI Pacific Islands Monthly

PN	Panorama	SG	Sunday Telegraph
RA	Latin America Regional Report:	SP	Spotlight
	Andean Area	ST	Sunday Times
RB	Latin America Regional Report:	TB	The Banker
	Brazil	TI	The Times
RC	Latin America Regional Report:	TM	Time
	Caribbean	TS	Toronto Star
RM	Latin America Regional Report:	VV	Village Voice
	Mexico and Central America	WP	Washington Post
RS	Latin America Regional Report:	WS	Wall Street Journal
	Southern Cone	WT	Wall Street Transcript

Prologue

1. HT 2/8/83; IMF, *World Economic Conditions*, 1984.
2. WS 30/7/85, 23,30/9/85, 8/10/85.
3. See the views of Italian sociologist Pino Arlacchi in *LM* 4/4/85.
4. Canada, Senate, Standing Committee on Banking, Trade and Commerce, Proceedings, October 2, 1985, 11:24.
5. Blum, *Offshore Haven Banks*, vii.
6. Cf. the views of *Le Monde's* Paul Farba, WS 24/7/85.

Chapter One

1. Raw, 102.
2. FT 11/2/83. More recently Tamil refugees have been accused of being a major source of heroin for the European market. The heroin apparently is used partly to fund a new life abroad and partly to pay for arms for guerrillas battling the Sri Lankan government. (GW 11/8/85.)
3. Cf. the view of Alex Cockburn, WS 4/8/83.
4. The still-prevailing view of 'organized crime' in the US as an essentially Italian phenomenon was challenged long ago by one of America's best-known crime writers, Hank Messick. See especially his work on Meyer Lansky. More recently the work of Peter Reuter not only casts doubt on the centrality of the 'Mafia' in organizing crime in America (see also the symposium in *Attenzione*, Feb. 1980) but even questions the very notion that crime is 'organized.'
5. On the transition in the 1930s, see Messick, *Lansky*, 156 et passim, and more recently his *Of Grass and Snow*, 156.
6. Chambost, 31.
7. Further details on Lansky's career are in Eisenberg et al., and Wismer, who traces the Canadian connections.
8. Faith, 218-19; NT 28/9/85. It was a prophetic arrangement. Huey Long ruled Louisiana much in the fashion of a modern Latin American dictator: civil liberties were virtually suspended and $100 million worth of highways cost the taxpayer about $150 million.
9. See especially Messick, *Lansky*, Chapters 14-16; Wismer, Chapters 3, 6, 10;

Clarke, 93–94. The role of the Bank of Miami Beach, established in 1955, was as a depository for the take from Cuban casinos. In 1958 the Miami National Bank was taken over by the Teamsters' Union on the advice of its 'financial adviser,' Allan Dorfman, as a place through which the skim from Las Vegas casinos could be moved. In Nassau, mob-linked interests allegedly controlled the Bank of World Commerce until the US government forced the Bahamian authorities to delicense it in 1965.

10. Clarke, 62.
11. Clarke, 115; Faith, 221; Eisenberg, 250–51. The loan-back could actually be legal in the US until as late as 1970.
12. Faith, 215; Eisenberg, 270–81; Messick, *Lansky*, 248–49, Derogy passim. It was ICB's Bahamian affiliate, Atlas Bank, that replaced the Bank of World Commerce in 1965 when the US government forced its delicensing.
13. Throughout the late 1950s and 1960s, American corporations invested heavily abroad in a search for raw material supplies (particularly in Latin America, the Middle East, and sub-Saharan Africa) and in branch plants to serve local markets (particularly in western Europe). One of the best and most comprehensive works on the rise and operation of the transnational corporation is that of Barnet and Müller.
14. The phrase 'Pentagon Capitalism' was coined by Seymour Melman. On the financial mechanics see Hudson, *Global Fracture*.
15. Related to the author by Michael Hudson, to whom Kahn's outburst was directed.
16. Clarke, 64–70; Hutchison, 47–48. On Lefferdink's subsequent fate, see Sobel, 40.
17. Cornfeld's career is traced in the works by Raw, Faith, and Hutchison, and in Hougan's *Spooks*, among others.
18. In the US mutual funds were all the rage in the 1950s. Offshore mutual funds were the rage of the 1960s; they promised both the gains from mutual-fund investments (and the supposed reduction of risk from investing in a diversified 'fund' of securities) and a better chance of hiding those gains from the tax collector. And IOS went one better. It offered investors participation in the Fund of Funds, an offshore mutual fund investing in other mutual funds. To the traditional mutual-fund advantage of liquidity (a share in a mutual fund could, in theory, be resold to the company at any time) was added the new advantage of diversity among diversity.
19. Raw, 100.
20. See especially Clarke, 44 et passim.
21. Cf. Hutchison, 79–80.
22. Peroff's story is related by Whittemore; see also Hutchison, 411–12 and Hougan, *Spooks*, 212, 216, 225 on its effects on the Vesco affair.
23. Hutchison, 78; Faith, 215; Raw, 106.
24. Raw, 103–9; Hougan, *Spooks*, 170–72.
25. Hutchison, 82ff; Raw, 114.
26. Raw, 359, makes no estimate about the size of the 'sump' of black money; Hutchison, 82, puts the 'mug's money' (as it was called at IOS) at $150-250 million; while Hougan, *Spooks*, 175, relying on more up-to-date revelations, places it at $500 million.

Chapter Two

1. The Chase memo was given to the author by a former Chase balance-of-payments economist. On the Intra Bank affair, see BW 22,29/10/66; EC 22/10/66, 12/11/66, 24/12/66; NW 31/10/66. Officially Beidas died of cancer in a Geneva hospital. Others claim he died of a heart attack in his hotel suite; still others allege murder. See Hougan, *Spooks*, 213–15.

2. Stories also circulated alleging that Beidas was funding the narcotics traffic out of Beirut. (O'Callaghan, passim; Kruger, 103n, 184–85). Such traffic was substantial; but it taxes credibility to assume that the Lebanese warlords who ran it would call on the Palestinian banker for financial assistance – or that Beidas would have helped had they come calling. However, it is possible that some managers of the Intra-controlled Casino du Liban used the casino for laundering mob money. (Hougan, *Spooks*, 213.)

3. Moffitt, 57.

4. In general, see Mendelsohn for an overview; and Sampson, Chapter 7.

5. Franco, 215–16; Mabillard, 13.

6. That the Cuban Revolution occurred at all owes something to the intrigues of the Lansky-Luciano mob. In 1938 Batista legalized the Communist party, but Lansky pressured him to reverse the decision, warning of possible problems with the US government. When Batista came back to power, in a 1952 coup, he heeded the warning, driving the Communist party into guerrilla action. (*DP*, March 84.)

7. Hutchison, 81–82; Hougan, 160, 169, 179.

8. Vesco used the front of Butler's Bank in the Bahamas to 'lend' IOS some of its own money in a deal whereby, in return for such 'assistance,' the other directors would dump Cornfeld from control.

9. Hutchison, 346, 421; WS 13/9/84.

10. Hutchison, 314–17; NT 17/10/83; WS 8/3/83.

11. Hougan, *Spooks*, 206.

12. WS 14/7/84.

13. Kruger, 26n.

14. Messick, *Lansky*, 244.

15. OB 3/10/83.

16. WerBell may have taken at least part of his pay for arms in drugs, though an American indictment against him for conspiring to import 50,000 pounds of marijuana failed to convict after the principal prosecution witness died in a plane crash before he was to testify. (Commonwealth-New South Wales Joint Task Force on Drug Trafficking. Report IV, 679–82; Hougan, *Spooks*, passim.) WerBell claimed that both the drug-smuggling and later machine-gun-smuggling charges were part of a CIA campaign against him.

17. According to WerBell, the failure of the operation was planned from the start. The US government and CIA simply wanted to frighten Papa Doc into good behavior without losing such a staunch ally in the war against communism. After the abortive invasion, WerBell got a contract to retrain Papa Doc's security forces, and Lansky moved to Haiti some of the casinos that had been closed in Cuba.

18. Hougan, *Spooks*, 208. In 1976, yet another scheme was afoot, led by a group

of American mercenaries, to invade Haiti and establish a free-trade zone for gambling and tax-evasion schemes. But an exposé by *Washington Post* columnist Jack Anderson appears to have aborted it. (Goulden, 316.)

19. Hutchison, 353.
20. In Costa Rica, as in several other Latin American states, the army was the main pillar of the political left. Hence, among Don Pepe's first acts as president was the abolition of the armed forces, replacing them with a heavily militarized police force and a personal paramilitary guard. That eliminated most of the danger of coups and permitted the US government to hold up Costa Rica as a shining example of democratic principles working in the Americas.
21. Hutchison, 356–57, 360; Hougan, *Spooks*, 156; Sobel, 164–67. Vesco claimed to have invested $25 million in various Costa Rican enterprises, many of them government controlled.
22. Hougan, *Spooks*, 67.
23. *PI* June, July 80; Hougan, *Spooks*, 95.
24. *PI* June 80.
25. Messick, *Grass*, 82–84, 168–69.
26. *PI* June, July 80; *FR* 3,20/6/80; *CS* Nov. 80-Jan. 81. French participation in the expedition appears to have been less than enthusiastic. French policy in the region appears to have been equally motivated by a desire to upstage the British and the Americans, whom it suspected of attempting to undermine France's nuclear independence. Furthermore, France may well have seen the destabilization of Vanuatu as a means of discouraging independence movements in its other Pacific colonies.
27. Hougan, *Spooks*, 235; Hougan, *Secret*, 129; Blum, 98–99; Drosnin, 204, 317, 360–61, 410, 439, 524. See *Hughes Tool Co. v. Meier*, 1977. D.C. Utah. Apparently Meier was then arrested by the Mounties in Vancouver and extradited to the US, where he was convicted of tax evasion. (*GZ* 12/12/78; *Vancouver Sun* 25/8/79.)
28. *WS* 17/11/78; *PI* Sept. 78, Jan. 79.
29. Senate Report: 70-72.
30. Sher, 167–69, 175, 179. A similar fate awaited another group of entrepreneurs active in the Indian Ocean. In 1981 a gang of South African, British, French, and Australian mercenaries, led by Congo veteran Mad Mike Hoare (and allegedly with the backing of some American businessmen and the South African government), set out to improve standards of hospitality afforded to modern financial enterprise by the left-wing government of the Seychelles. This government had quarreled with France, Britain, and the US over the militarization of the Indian Ocean, with Japan over fishing rights, and with South Africa over the islands' close relations with the African National Congress and the South West African People's Organization. Several earlier mercenary invasion attempts had failed. Then, late in 1981, a Royal Air Swaziland flight arrived, carrying a rugby team that played by its own rules. When an alert customs official found a pistol in a false-bottomed suitcase, the mercenary team seized the airport, but little else, before they were captured. (*AA* 5/1/81, 17/8/81, 12/10/81, 17,21/12/81.) A subsequent enterprise of the arms dealer in the Dominica operation, Charles Yanover, to take $400,000 from North Korea to assassinate South

Korean strongman Chun Doo Hwan, and then to collect $1.5 million from South Korea or the CIA for exposing the plot was no more successful than his island-collecting campaign. (*GM* 17/2/84.)

Chapter Three

1. See for one of a virtually unlimited number of examples, the views expressed in *New Leader* 17/9/84, a magazine of US organized labor, which states (p.13) 'the story begins in the Persian Gulf where the sheiks found themselves drowning in money.'
2. Moffitt, 83.
3. The classic account of domestic price fixing by the US oil companies is Blair, *Control of Oil*.
4. Copetas, 115-18.
5. See the excellent account in Hulbert's study, *Interlock*. On the CIA project, see Goulden, 40.
6. An excellent brief survey is in *HT* 12/12/83.
7. *BI* 1975 132.
8. A superlative biography of this amazing character is by DiFonza; but see also Gurwin, Cornwell, Lo Bello, Martin, and Yallop. Sindona's Canadian capers are examined by Philip Mathias in *FP* 12/4/86.
9. Kwitny, 202-203. Several bank failures had been at least partly attributable to looting by the mob – when the party was over, it was the Federal Deposit Insurance Corporation (FDIC) that picked up the tab.
10. Lo Bello, 196; DiFonza, 6.
11. Actually Giannini founded the Bank of Italy in California, later merging it with an institution called the Bank of America.
12. *DP* Oct. 82.
13. Gordon, 144-49; Gurwin, 10; DiFonza, 32.
14. Yallop, 110, 129.
15. See DiFonza, Chapter 9. The primary purpose of the bear raid on the lira seems to have been to allow Sindona to avenge himself on the Bank of Italy for its role in checking his Italian ambitions; the secondary purpose was enormous profits. But when Sindona refused to give Moneyrex's manager, Carlo Bordoni, the $4 million that had been promised to him as a reward for helping to wreck the lira, he made a fatal mistake.
16. DiFonza, 77-79, 81, 83, 89; *FF* 8/9/79.
17. *EC* 6/7/74, 21/12/74; *TM* 8/7/74; *NR* 12/4/75; Sampson, Chapter 9; *WS* 17/2/84.
18. *TB* Aug. 82.
19. *IC* Oct. 82.
20. Reid relates the story of the crash in the British money market.
21. One exception to the drying up of aid funds was the OPEC group. Between 1973 and 1981 the main Arab members gave nearly $70 billion in financial assistance, 77% in outright grants, virtually all with no strings with respect to its use. (United Nations, Conference on Trade and Development, *Financial Solidarity For Development*, New York: 1984.)
22. See the excellent survey by J. Frieden in MERIP, Sept. 1983.

23. The banks also cooperated by inventing techniques of 'country risk analysis' that, like the international trade theory taught at the universities where the country risk analysts were trained, started by deleting from the scope of the analysis most of the potentially useful information.
    LW 24/10/80 examines a controversy over the 'best' method of calculating country risk that sprang up between the two most prestigious English-language international financial magazines, *Euromoney* and *Institutional Investor*. Moreover, the 'credit ratings' awarded to certain countries ultimately reflected the political priorities of NATO as much as the numbers racket being played by bank research departments. Strategic importance of a borrower meant the likelihood of Western government financial aid if it ran into trouble.
24. See the interesting dissection of OPEC's 'power' by Epstein in *The Atlantic* March 1983, reproduced in *TS* 7/3/83.

Chapter Four

1. *NT* 2/10/82.
2. There was an element of statistical illusion about these figures. For while the petroboom produced rapid growth in urban employment, it coincided with a deterioration of the rural economy (*LD* 9/12/82). Mexico had a dual agricultural economy – traditional peasant farms producing for the domestic market in the south, and rich capitalist agribusinesses oriented toward the American market in the north. Like other oil exporters – Nigeria was an obvious example – Mexico in the 1970s became a net food importer, while a cost squeeze on traditional agricultural areas in the south drove the rural population toward the urban areas. There huge slums fed cheap labor into industry on both sides of the border, with latent social upheaval kept in check by government subsidies to keep down the price of basic foodstuffs. On the agricultural crisis, see *Science*, 18/2/83, Vol. 219.
3. *WS* 15/5/84. Mexican developments are surveyed in *II* Nov. 82; *DP* Oct. 82.
4. *WS* 11/10/85 provides an excellent assessment.
5. *NT* 14/8/82; *EC* 20/8/83.
6. *WS* 22/10/82.
7. *OB* 15/8/82; *WS* 19/8/82; *NT* 21,31/8/82.
8. *BA* 20/9/82.
9. *WS* 7/5/85.
10. *EC* 21/8/82; *FT* 5/11/82.
11. See the commentary of William Safire (*NT* 23/8/82) and Susan Purcell of the Council on Foreign Relations (*NT* 24/8/82).
12. *IB* April 82.
13. *BA* 23/8/82.
14. *WS* 26/9/85.
15. Kruger, 177–79, 182–83. Interestingly, Sicilia-Falcon's security chief was a former US navy commando who had participated in the Phoenix Program. At one point Sicilia-Falcon made a deal, which never materialized, to manufacture in Mexico special American assault rifles. However, they may have been destined for export, given Sicilia-Falcon's alleged ties to a number of

European secret services – not least those of Portugal, which were scheming a coup against the country's revolutionary government. (Mills 99, 325, 358–59, 363–64.)

16. *AN* 18/9/82.
17. *WS* 1/9/82.
18. *FT* 25/7/84.
19. *FT* 18/9/82, 4/10/82; *GU* 21/9/82; *HT* 22/9/82; *AN* 28/11/82.
20. *FT* 9/9/82; *WS* 17/9/82. Mexican banks during the oil boom moved from straightforward commercial banking to investment banking, overseeing a fusion of industrial and financial capital that was a new phenomenon in Mexico, at least on that scale. There was little or no state interference, for although the Mexican state has a major stake in industry, it had traditionally kept out of the financial sector. Even the central bank was partly owned by private-sector institutions.
21. *EM* Oct. 82; *GM* 1/9/82; *GU* 12/10/82.
22. *GM* 4/9/82.
23. *GM* 3/9/82; *GM* 14,25/9/82.
24. *FT* 9/9/82.
25. *WS* 9/10/85.
26. *AB* 7/9/82.
27. *LD* 3/9/82.
28. *WS* 1/10/82, 16/11/82; *NT* 16/9/82; *GM* 4/9/82. See the comments of Jim Jeffries, *CR* 16/9/82; Jesse Helms, *CR* 13,15/9/82; Larry MacDonald, *CR* 1/10/82.
29. *FT* 1,19/11/82; *WS* 24/11/82. There was another possible twist to the nationalization scenario. In 1980 the US Congress passed the Monetary Control Act, giving the Federal Reserve the power to buy securities issued by or guaranteed by foreign governments. It was under the terms of the Act that the Fed was able to participate in the emergency package for Mexico. Once the loans and credits made to Mexican banks by American ones ceased to be private-sector obligations and became those of the Mexican government, then, under American law, those loans presumably became eligible for rediscount purposes at the Fed should the issuing bank or banks face an extreme crisis of liquidity.
30. *GM* 4/9/82.
31. *AN* 12/9/82.
32. *WS* 11/10/85.
33. *GM* 7/9/82.
34. *FT* 28/11/82; *WS* 29/12/82; *NT* 25/11/82; *LW* 2/12/82.
35. *AB* 23/11/82; *NT* 19/11/82; *FT* 11,17,18/11/82.
36. *NT* 3/7/84. Charged with tax evasion, influence peddling, embezzlement, smuggling, drug trafficking, slaving, and murder (*LW* 3/2/84), he was later arrested in the US and extradited back to Mexico. (*NT* 3/4/85.)
37. *BW* 28/2/83; *LW* 4/11/83.
38. In general, see *RM* 28/10/83; *AN* 12/9/83; *FT* 11/10/83; *NT* 18/1/84; *WS* 14/5/84. On the career of El Trampas, see *Informacion Sistimatico*, Aug., Sept., Oct., Nov. 1983 and April, May, June 1984; *Proceso* 15,29/8/83, 19/9/83, 17/9/84, 16/12/85.

39. *LW* 8/7/83; *NT* 18/1/84. At press time, Diaz Serrano was still in jail.
40. *WS* 9/10/85.
41. The major casualty of the moral renovation campaign may well have been not the top-level financial pirates but Mexico's best-known investigative reporter. At the end of May 1984, someone sporting a military haircut shot and killed Manuel Buendia. In his column in *Excelsior*, Buendia had frequently denounced ex-President Lopez Portillo and his regime for plundering the public purse; and he published exposés of the alleged drug dealing and other enterprises of the former chief of the Mexico City police. The bosses of the petroleum union also numbered among his targets. But those targets had also included the Mexican neofascist paramilitary organizations, Opus Dei, the CIA, the World Anti-Communist League, and Miami-based Cuban-exile terrorist organizations, one of which had threatened to kill him after he had met with Fidel Castro. (*RM* 8/6/84; *LM* 9-10/6/84; *FT* 7/6/84.)
42. Actually La Quina emerged from the moral renovation process stronger than ever, even becoming the object of de la Madrid's fulsome praise at the union's annual congress in November 1984, where de la Madrid declared him morally renovated.
43. *FT* 2,8,17,30/12/82; *NT* 15/12/82; *WS* 6/12/82; *EC* 18/12/82; *GM* 25/2/83.
44. *WS* 29/5/84.
45. See for example the editorial in *FT* 15/9/83.
46. The political key to the financial miracle was the structure of the PRI and its control over the Mexican labor movement. This assured the cooperation of organized labor in implementing austerity programs. However, there was a limit. Even before the severe austerity measures were introduced, one-third of the labor force drew the minimum wage. It was estimated that an average family needed four times that income to meet basic needs. As the austerity measures reached the point at which the beans-and-corn diet of the peasant became middle-class staples, there was a danger of losing control of the union rank and file.
47. *NT* 19/3/83; *AN* 18/7/83.

Chapter Five

1. There are now available a number of excellent accounts of the Vatican as an off-shore financial center, focusing particularly on the Banco Ambrosiano scandal. See especially those of Cornwell and Gurwin. Very useful additional information is in DiFonza, Yallop, Manhattan, Lo Bello, and Martin.
2. Manhattan, Chapter 19; DiFonza, 33; Martin, 38.
3. Martin, 14, 32–46.
4. On the rapprochement with Mussolini that yielded the Vatican its rights as a sovereign power, see Manhattan, Chapter 19; DiFonza, 33; Martin, 38. On financial relations with Hitler and Franco, see Lo Bello, 35.
5. In reply the Italian spy agency informed CIA chief William Colby that it had already planted the bug! (Cecchi, 133–34).
6. Gurwin, 13.

7. Gordon, 146.
8. On the role of the IOR, see, for example, *TB* Sept. 82; *DT* 8/8/82; *EC* 14/8/82; *OB* 15/8/82; *EM* Oct. 82; *FT* 17/11/82; Gordon, 139ff. On top of the banking activities come the IOR's trust company functions, exercised on behalf of an array of Catholic institutions. It also runs its own investment portfolio, separate from that of APSA.
9. Cornwell, 52.
10. Cornwell, 28.
11. *EM* March 83.
12. Apart from the general references cited in (1) above, on the Ambrosiano affair see also, among an enormous volume of material available, *PA* 28/6/82, 19/7/82; *FT* 29/7/82, 6/8/82, 1/10/82, 17/11/82, 31/3/83, 19/11/83, 30/11/83, 13/1/84, 7/3/84; *DT* 30/3/83; *AB* 5/1/83; *EC* 14/8/82, 12/3/83; *AN* 22/7/82, 30/7/82, 31/7/82, 7/8/82, 21/8/82, 25/8/82, 11/10/82; *OB* 19/9/82; *GU* 12/3/84.
13. *FT* 17/11/82; *ST* 27/5/83.
14. *II* Oct. 82.
15. Similarly, the KGB allegedly infiltrated British Freemasonry to gain for its agents positions of importance with the help of Masonic brothers. See *GU* 5/2/84 and the interesting investigations of Knight, although Knight's conclusions about P-2 as an arm of the KGB seem inherently implausible.
16. Cecchi, 132ff.
17. See in general the preliminary report of the Italian government enquiry, published as 'Il Complotto di Licio Gelli' in *Espresso*, Supplemento Speciale, 20 Maggio 1984. An interesting contrast is provided by Alberto Cecchi, the vice-president of the parliamentary enquiry, who disassociated himself from parts of the official account and published his own. An excellent and concise account of the phenomenon is in DiFonza, 66-74. The press generated a flood of information and a deluge of speculation about P-2, some of the more outrageous and seemingly impossible facets of which were later confirmed by the Italian parliamentary inquiry. On the other hand, there is the danger that the P-2 has become a handy scapegoat for all of Italy's problems since the late 1960s, thereby deflecting the search from deeper root causes. See for example, *LM* 19/3/83, 21/1/84, 25/4/84, 12/5/84, 27-28/5/84, 29/5/84, 13/7/84; *FT* 13/8/83, 11/5/84, 12/5/84; *GM* 19/8/83; *TS* 19/8/83, 28/8/83; *AN* 19/3/83, 11/8/83, 15/9/84; *WS* 15/8/83, 10/7/84; *GU* 14/3/83, 30/5/83, 12/5/84, 28/5/84; Yallop, 115 et passim; DiFonza, 66-74; *EX* 9/8/85.
18. These activities were apparently coordinated through the so-called Monte Carlo Lodge. *OB* 19/9/82; Gurwin, 133.
19. Cornwell, 68.
20. Such a shift in strategy may have brought it into competition with the Israeli secret service, which allegedly offered arms to the Red Brigades in order to destabilize Italy. Once Italy was weakened as a southern cornerstone of NATO, the US would be forced into greater strategic and military dependence on Israel. *HT* 4-5/6/83.
21. Among the worst of the P-2-related drains was the support Calvi's bank provided for the Rizzoli Group, the most prestigious publishing house in Italy

and proprietors of the daily newspaper *Corriere della Sera.* The paper had taken a leftward lurch in the early 1970s, but had found itself in financial difficulties. The Rizzoli Group then took it over, but the financial problems intensified. The big state-run banks refused to lend to it, for they, under the influence of the Socialist and Christian Democratic parties, did not like its politics. At that point Umberto Ortolani, the P-2's media expert, entered the picture, introducing the principals of the Rizzoli Group to Calvi, whose bank subsequently became de facto owner of the operation and therefore loaded down with even more bad debt. On Rizzoli finances and the P-2, see *HT* 16/3/83; *EC* 26/2/83; *NT* 8/3/83; *FT* 4/3/83, 11/3/83, 2/4/83; *LM* 21/2/83, 9/3/83; *GM* 2/6/83; *WS* 25/8/84.

22. Sindona claimed that the Latin American activities of P-2 had the support of the church, particularly superhawk and fervid anticommunist Paul Marcinkus, who concurred with Sindona that 'Where there was economic order ...there would be no room for revolution or subversion.' In such worthy pursuits Somoza was a natural ally. See *NT* 11/10/82, 27/12/82; *AN* 3/10/82; *WS* 23/11/82.

23. *LM* 15–16/9/85.

24. Banco Ambrosiano's Nicaraguan activities were long shrouded in mystery until some light was shed in the summer of 1986 by former Calvi aide, Francesco Pazienza. See *ES* 6/7/86. According to Pazienza, Calvi's courtship of the Sandinistas soured his relations with Marcinkus. Perhaps it was to restore those relations that Calvi shut down his Managua affiliate, though he reputedly carried a valid Nicaraguan diplomatic passport until his death in June 1982.

25. *IB* Aug. 81.

26. *FT* 17/11/82; Gurwin, 94.

27. Cornwell, 23.

28. *ST* 13/2/83.

29. *NT* 30/7/82; *TB* Sept. 82; *FT* 31/3/83; *HT* 26/7/82, 26/4/83; *EM* Oct. 82.

30. *TB* Aug. 82; *AN* 11/8/82; *NT* 11/8/82; *FT* 9/5/83, 22/11/83.

31. *TB* Sept. 83; *FT* 27/4/83; *HT* 9/6/83, 13/6/83; *WS* 9/6/83.

32. *EC* 9/10/82; *FT* 20/12/83; *HT* 14/5/84.

33. *HT* 3/6/83; *FT* 27/8/83.

Chapter Six

1. In general see 'The Coup and its Aftermath,' Committee for Human Rights in Turkey, New York: 1981; 'Is Democracy a Luxury Item for Turkey,' *Labour, Capital and Society*, Vol. 13, No. 2 Nov. 1980.

2. *IB* Oct. 82; *EC* 16/4/83.

3. *LM* 15/10/82.

4. *TB* Aug. 82.

5. See especially McCoy's superlative work on the politics of heroin.

6. Turkey, with India, produced the bulk of the world's legal pharmaceutical supply. The suppression of opium production in Turkey did more to cause a crisis in the world's legal supply of codeine than it did to affect the global flow of illicit drugs. As a supplier of illicit drugs, Turkey accounted for 3%

to 8% of the world's total at the peak of its trade. (Epstein, 243; Peter Dale
Scott in Kruger, 2.)

7. On the Golden Crescent heroin traffic see, *WS* 16/11/82, 6/4/83;
AN 4/8/83, 31/1/84, 18/6/84; *EC* 16/6/84; *FR* 29/3/84; *CS* Nov. 80–Jan. 81;
LM 22/12/83; *CM* 28/2/84; *HT* 21/2/84; *ME* May 83; *GU* 8/10/83;
ST 24/3/85. Pakistan periodically floats stories about the suppression of the
trade, but the main result of its efforts has been to concentrate control in
the hands of a few politically well-connected dealers. (*GW* 10/11/85.)

8. Kruger, 222–23.

9. On the export routes see *FR* 26/5/83; *ME* Aug. 83; *SG* 4/4/83; *NT* 12/4/84;
EC 28/1/84; *AN* 18/5/83, 23/7/83, 5/3/84; *LM* 11/12/82.

10. On the Turkish underworld see the books of Ugur Mumcu; see also
LM 11/12/82; *New Yorker* Oct. 15, 1984, carried a long interview with
Mumcu.

11. A good survey of these developments is in *South*, March 1985.

12. See especially Epstein's brilliant and entertaining work on Nixon's war on
heroin for information on the misinformation that is rife about the heroin
business. Among those political antagonists blamed by the US government
for the illicit drug traffic have been Germany in the First World War, Japan
during the Second World War, the People's Republic of China during the
Korean War, Iranian nationalists during the nationalization of the Iranian
oil industry in 1951, Castro in the late 1950s, and North Vietnam during
the period when the CIA was openly transporting opium on behalf of its
Southeast Asian mercenaries. (Epstein, 26, 33, 81.) More recently heroin has
become a KGB conspiracy, and Castro is blamed for the cocaine traffic.

13. *WS* 13/5/83. The highest estimated portion of US-consumed heroin reaching the US market via Bulgaria is about 10%; even that may be an
exaggeration.

14. See especially the work of Gordon Thomas and Max Morgan-Witts.

15. *AN* 28/3/83; *WS* 20/12/82, 10/8/84, 9/4/85; *NT* 24/1/83, 7/2/85;
LM 3/1/83.

16. *GM* 1/5/84.

17. See Mumcu, *Papa Mafya Agca*; *LM* 21/4/84.

18. *LM* 11/12/82; *LD* 10/12/82.

19. *LM* 21/9/85.

20. *LD* 26/11/82; *IB* Dec. 82; *GM* 26/11/82; *FF* 3/12/82.

21. *LM* 11/12/82.

22. *FT* 26/11/82; *NT* 24/11/84; *TS* 27/11/82; *SG* 4/4/83; *LM* 8/6/84.

23. *PN* 13/12/82; *GU* 1/2/83; *AN* 15/4/83. The figure of $690 million for the
value of the seized heroin is another example of how the traffic has been
sensationalized. As Epstein points out, valuing seized heroin according to
the price it might fetch on the streets is akin to valuing a rustled cow
according to the price of a steak dinner in New York's fanciest restaurant.

24. Further delays might have resulted from the number of 'accidents' and 'suicides' that afflicted earlier investigators of the P-2. *AN* 6/6/83; *GU* 30/5/83;
LM 4/12/83.

25. *LM* 16/12/82. Some confirmation of this possibility would be available if, as
some claimed, some of those arrested in the Stibam bust were not only

former members of the Italian secret services but also people who, like Hanafi Arslanyan himself, were still on the payroll of the US Drug Enforcement Agency at the time of their arrest.

26. *AN* 13/11/83.
27. *AN* 17,19,24/3/83, 2/4/83, 6/8/83; *HT* 16–17/4/83; *FT* 6/4/83, 20/8/83.
28. On the Kastelli bubble see *AF* July 82; *FE* July-Aug. 82; *TB* Aug. 82; *MG* 25/6/82, 23/7/82, 6/8/82, and the Special Report Oct. 82.
29. *FT* 30/7/82; *AN* 10/8/82.
30. Ziraat Bank's ostensible purpose was to provide agricultural credit. Apparently agriculture in Turkey is broadly defined to include the harvesting of hot money buried in fields and gardens. On the laundry operation see *FT* 20/4/83.
31. *FT* 8/11/82; *WS* 27/12/82.
32. *AN* 18/8/82.
33. *WS* 18,22/8/83; *FT* 8/9/83, 25/11/83; *GM* 5/11/83.
34. *AN* 28/8/82, 5/12/83; *FT* 2/4/83, 11/8/83.

Chapter Seven

1. The pope plot story began with two accounts, one by Claire Sterling and the other by a former CIA Istanbul station chief, Paul Henze. (See, for example, *WS* 22/12/82; *CM* 13/3/83, 18/3/83, 21/3/83, 25/1/84; *GM* 11/6/84.) It was rendered more respectable by the extensive and undoubtedly well-motivated research of Gordon Thomas and Max Morgan-Witts. See also *Newsweek* 3/1/83. However, there were, to put it mildly, certain difficulties of fact and logic from the start. (See *NT* 4/12/82, 3/1/83, 27/1/83; *LD* 9/11/82; *LM* 10/11/82; *WS* 21/12/82, 1/2/83. But also see Claire Sterling's defense of the thesis in *EX* 15/2/85.)
2. A curious premise of the theory is that the KGB would choose as its key hit man someone who, after being sprung from jail – to which he was sent after the murder of Apdi Ipekci – publicly announced his intent to kill John Paul II in a letter to the editor of one of the most widely read newspapers in Turkey. But then again, maybe theorists of the Bulgarian Connection believed Ali was advertising for sponsors.
3. *LM* 8/6/85; *NT* 7/6/85, 12/9/85. Celik is rumored to have been spotted in Miami in the company of Stefano Dalla Chiaie, Italy's most notorious right-wing terrorist, who was sought for the bombing of the Bologna railway station. If this is true, the Bulgarian intelligence agent is keeping very odd company.
4. Celenk admitted trafficking in Bulgarian arms, but denied that he knew Ali Agça, let alone gave him money. (*LM* 16/10/85; *NT* 25/12/85.)
5. It remains to be explained how Ali Agça and his alleged key Bulgarian contact, Sergei Antonov, planned the assassination without a common language in which to communicate. Under interrogation, Ali Agça was asked to write down the name of the street on which Antonov lived. He did so, duplicating the misspelling of the street name in the Rome telephone directory. When Ali Agça was asked to describe Antonov's apartment, in which they presumably met to plot in sign language, he described it perfectly,

right down to the French doors in the living room. The only problem was that Antonov's apartment was the only one in the building that did not have such doors. Maybe Ali Agça was confusing it with another apartment in the same building, which according to the Roman press, housed a Franciscan monk who doubled as a local CIA operative. (GU 27/10/83, 5/1/83; VV 5/7/83; LM 7/1/83.) But Ali's 'evidence' was deemed credible enough to keep Antonov in jail for four years on the Alice-in-Wonderland principle of first the sentence, then the trial.

6. Once the trials actually started, the credibility of the story was further undermined by Agça's contradictions. (E.g., LM 8,14,19/6/85; WS 7,8,26/8/85; NT 29/5/85, 17,18/6/85, 12/9/85; GU 25/5/85, 25,27/6/85; LD 28/5/85, 13/6/85; GM 19/6/85.)

7. HT 26/7/82.

8. In general, see II Jan. 82.

9. Moffit, 112–13.

10. Somewhere in the KGB disinformation mill, an energetic and ambitious officer should be busy concocting a tale of a group of international bankers, infiltrated by CIA men, planning to hire Turkish underworld figures to train them with the Contras in Central America and then to put them to work with agents of the West German secret service active in Rome to plan the murder of the pope in order to create chaos in Poland, thereby destabilizing the northern flank of the Warsaw Pact.

11. Manhattan, Chapter 7.

12. NS 27/9/85.

13. On Opus Dei see le Vaillant, Maffia Sainte; NS 1/3/85; PN 19/7/85; Yallop, 263–64; WS 30/12/83; LM 17/1/84, 6/12/84; ES 16/3/86. According to Spain's prestigious El Pais, by 1979 Opus Dei members controlled 604 newspapers, magazines, and specialist publications, 52 radio and television stations, 38 public relations and advertising firms, and 12 companies involved in production and distribution of films. L'Espresso puts Opus Dei's Italian income at 50 billion lire per annum.

14. The thesis of David Yallop in In God's Name is that Pope John Paul I was murdered, likely through arrangements made by Licio Gelli, to prevent a cleanup of Vatican finances and a purge of the Freemasons who had infiltrated the Vatican. It is an intriguing story, but a great deal more noncircumstantial evidence is necessary before it can be granted much credibility. There is an obvious difficulty in the thesis in that, if P-2 was responsible for the 'murder,' would it not also have been concerned about the succession? Why eliminate one anti-Masonic pope, just to have another of even stronger anti-Masonic tendencies? See also Manhattan, 256, on the conflict between Opus Dei and the alleged Freemasonic faction in the Vatican. Yallop's impressive digging did churn up a great deal of new and highly credible information on scandals around the Vatican's finances.

15. ES 2/3/86 puts Karol Wojtyla praying at Belaguer's tomb before the conclave that elected him pope.

16. GM 14/9/83; VV 5/4/83; DP June 84; NT 4/10/84, 24/11/84; Gurwin, 177; LD 23/4/84; LM 1/10/84, 6/12/84. Opus Dei had its autonomy from local bishops, who might have been sympathetic to liberation theology, formally assured, thereby undermining the spirit of Vatican II, which had aimed to

increase the power of national episcopates. Inside the Vatican it was upgraded to a personal prelature, reporting directly to the pope, a status that John XXIII had explicitly denied it. Within the Vatican, one of Opus Dei's Spanish adherents became press spokesman, the first time the position had gone to a non-Italian; and Opus Dei was also rumored to be in line to replace the Jesuits in control of the Vatican radio. Nor have its aspirations to control the Vatican finances abated. (*ES* 8/6/86.)

With the serious illness of Father Pedro Arrupe, the 'black pope' who headed the order, John Paul II overruled the choice for interim successor and picked his own. The Vatican followed up by lobbying in the subsequent elections for a new head of the order who would agree to keep the Jesuits out of politics, except where the Vatican wanted them involved. (*LM* 14/8/83, 5/9/83.)

17. *GM* 1/3/81, 3/10/81.
18. *EM* Aug. 81.
19. *LD* 11/11/81.
20. *FT* 15/9/82.
21. *FT* 26/10/82, 22/2/83; *NT* 28/10/82, 25/3/83, 3/4/83; *WS* 25/3/83; *GU* 22/3/83; *AN* 31/10/84.
22. *WS* 7/1/86; Yallop, 189, 298–300, 307.
23. Cecchi, 226–27; Manhattan, 254.
24. *PN* 28/6/82, 5,19/7/82.
25. The Vatican also seemingly bowed to Opus Dei influence by renewing its attacks on Freemasonry as being incompatible with Catholicism. This set off a round of verbal warfare with France's powerful Grand Orient, whose leadership was accused by the Vatican of fomenting a campaign against the social doctrines of John Paul II. Between Opus Dei and the Grand Orient of France, there had long been a vicious feud. (*LM* 28/2/85; Pean, 48.) The Vatican seems also to have set off a worldwide anti-Masonic paranoia that recalled the witch-hunts of the 1920s. Its participants included non-Catholic denominations, Scotland Yard, and the Ayatollah Khomeini. A 1985 report to the British Methodist Church by a working party concluded that Methodists should not join the Masons because of the excessive secrecy of their rituals and their anti-Christian doctrines. The Baptists took the report under consideration, too. (*GU* 13/6/85.) A year earlier Scotland Yard declared membership in the Masons to be detrimental to police integrity after a major corruption scandal in the London police force, historically strongly Freemasonic. (*OB* 9/9/84, 7/10/84, and the work of Knight.)

While the Grand Orient of France was condemning John Paul II (whom some Italians referred to as 'our Ayatollah') as a 'dangerous reactionary' (*NS* 27/9/85), it also found itself battling Khomeini's followers, particularly in Africa. French Freemasonry had long been strong in Africa, north and south, and had given the former French colonies much of their post-independence leadership. With prominent masons in powerful positions in the Mitterrand government – Defense Minister Charles Hernu, for one – the battle against French influence in Africa came to be associated with an attack on Masonic influence. (*LM* 11/9/85.)

26. On the Calvi 'suicide,' see *FT* 28/9/82, 13/1/83, 30/3/83; *AN* 22/8/82; *ST* 5/12/82; *DT* 29/3/83, 30/3/83; *GU* 14/1/83, 29/3/83, 30/3/83;

OB 16/1/83; WS 30/3/83; TI 29/3/83. Calvi's widow persists in accusing those in the Vatican opposed to the Opus Dei deal of being the architects of his death. (ES 13/4/86.) It is interesting to speculate whether three years earlier, when Calvi allegedly switched sides in Nicaragua, he did so in an effort to curry favor with the Jesuits in the Vatican, then likely more powerful than Opus Dei.

27. FT 24/7/84, 21/12/84; WS 4/8/84.
28. WS 8/8/83. For more recent activities of black marketeers operating in the tourism sector, see FT 8/8/85.
29. HT 6/8/85.
30. LD 9/7/84.
31. The bulk of the funds was to come from the West German Catholic churches which, as a result of a 1933 agreement with Hitler, had access to the proceeds of a special tax on the German population. Thus, to the degree the foundation succeeded in making more foreign exchange available for Poland to pay on its debt service arrears (the biggest slice of which was due to West German banks), it did so by passing off part of the burden onto the West German taxpayer. (LM 8–9/4/84; GM 7/4/84.)
32. WS 17/4/85.
33. GM 6/10/84; NT 26/7/84.

Chapter Eight

1. WS 9/12/82; NT 18/12/82.
2. AN 23/8/82, 23/10/82.
3. Initially the Vatican just claimed that its letters of comfort did not imply any responsibility on the part of IOR. Then came the appointment of the blue-ribbon committee, whose members included Philippe de Weck, head of the Union de Banques Suisses, to search for a loophole. These experts obligingly noted that the letters of comfort had been issued after the transactions to which they referred had been completed; therefore the IOR did not have to honor them! The Vatican subsequently added an equally convincing argument: as the IOR itself received no money from any of the transactions, it was not responsible for the matters referred to in the letters of comfort. And it further insisted that, although the IOR technically owned the shell companies that had incurred the debts, it did not know it owned them and therefore was innocent.
   The problem with these arguments was that they were all false. The letters of comfort were issued while transactions were still going on; the Vatican received direct benefit from the borrowings through the shell companies; and the IOR had taken an active role in establishing at least some of those shell companies. FT 8/10/82, 22/11/82, 27/11/82; WS 22/11/82, 23/11/82, 29/11/82; NT 22/11/82.
4. GU 16/4/84; FT 17/11/82, 25/10/83, 22/11/83, 3,20/12/83; AN 3/8/82; LD 4/6/84; LM 13/1/83; DT 14/4/84; EC 2/4/83; HT 14/5/84.
5. FT 18/3/85.
6. LD 2/12/82; FT 3/3/83.
7. See especially Lo Bello, Chapter 18; Manhattan, Chapters 9, 35.

8. *LM* 6/3/85.
9. *FT* 28/3/83; Manhattan, Chapter 34.
10. *WS* 10/4/84; *GU* 2,9,10/4/84; *LM* 5,11/4/84; *FT* 2/4/84.
11. On the Lateran Treaty revision, see *HT* 26/1/84, 20/2/84; *LD* 26/1/84, 28/1/84; *LM* 27/1/84; *FT* 15/2/84, 26/3/84; *GM* 26/1/84.
12. *FT* 15/2/84; *NT* 15/2/84.
13. Ynfante, *Crime*, 44; *LM* 2/2/85.
14. *II* July 84.
15. Hutchison, 292; see also Hammer, passim, and Clarke, passim.
16. *FT* 5/12/83.
17. In general on the sMH collapse, see *EM* Jan. 84.
18. On Esch and his relations with the banks, see *FT* 25/11/83; *HT* 20/12/83; *EC* 3/12/83; *WS* 2/2/84.
19. On the crash and rescue, see *FT* 3/11/83; *NT* 4/11/83; *WS* 4/11/83; *AN* 10/11/83; *HT* 14/12/83; *EC* 21/1/84; *IB* 25/11/83. On the aftermath, see *WS* 28/3/84, 18/7/84, 11/6/85; *HT* 29/12/83. The Lloyd's purchase is covered in *NT* 13/12/83; *HT* 6/12/83; *FT* 6,13/12/83; *WS* 15/12/83.
20. While six officers of Herstatt had already been jailed (*FF* 14/10/83), there was still a trial of its principal owner in progress. Early in 1984 he was also sentenced. (*WS* 17/2/84.) For the impact on Luxembourg, see *II* June, July 84.
21. *FT* 9/2/84; *HT* 9/2/84; *II* June 84.
22. *FT* 22/11/83.
23. *FT* 28/3/83.
24. *FT* 26/3/84.
25. The new Mafia tended to cooperate more than in the past with the Neapolitan Camorra and the Calabrian N'drangliata. (*EC* 23/7/83.) However, in some of its activities the Mafia did remain true to its origins and loyal to its former allies, as witness the continued role of the allegedly Mafia-controlled Bank of Sicily in overseeing the administration of Vatican holdings on the island. (Lo Bello, 202.) Similarly, the Mafia's traditional hold on the Sicilian produce trade was simply adapted to modern commercial conditions, especially in light of Italy's integration into the European Common Market; and it therefore became a vehicle by which the Mafia could siphon off money in the form of fraudulent claims for subsidies under the EEC's Common Agricultural Policy. (*FT* 15/2/85.)
26. *AN* 8/5/83, 17/8/83; *EC* 23/7/83; *WS* 4/1/83; *LM* 31/7/83; *GU* 12/1/84; *GM* 26/4/84; *FT* 4/12/84, 10/8/85.
27. *WS* 27/9/83; *CM* 26/4/83; *HT* 14–15/5/83; *GM* 26/4/83; *GU* 30/5/83, 7/1/84; *NT* 11/2/86. Among the prominent journalists murdered in Sicily in the early 1980s was Giuseppe Fava, who denounced the Mafia and decried the militarization of the island. Just before his assassination, his review had published a map of the proposed military bases, earning him the enmity of the NATO authorities and of the Mafia, which had been quietly buying adjacent land partly with recycled heroin money. Actually, the traditional Mafia had never been entrenched in the parts of Sicily where the cruise-missile bases were being built; the beneficiaries were apparently part of the new, drug-trade-based criminal elite.

28. DiFonza, 242–57. There remains the interesting question of why the P-2 membership lists were sitting in an open briefcase, as if waiting for the police to find them, though the explanation of Knight, viz., that it was all a KGB plot, seems hard to take seriously. Gelli long insisted that, though a P-2 list did exist, the list found in his office was merely a collection of his friends and business associates. Perhaps so, but that would put Gelli in a friendly and commercial relationship with some curious people: the heads of intelligence agencies, top politicians, commanders of death squads, overseers of the Bolivian cocaine trade, arms peddlers, and so on. He later changed his story, claiming that the list was, indeed, that of P-2.

29. *AN* 22/10/84; *NT* 25/3/85; Gurwin, 69–70.

30. *ES* 30/6/85; *EP* 18/6/85; *LM* 19/6/85; *WS* 7,8,26/8/85, 19/9/85; *NT* 17,19/6/85, 12/9/85, 3,8/10/85. Pazienza denies calling on Ali Ağça in jail.

31. *WS* 7,8/8/85. Pazienza was indicted, late in 1985, along with Gelli and Stefano Dalla Chiaie, in conjunction with the 1980 Bologna railway station bombing. The prosecution seems inclined to the view that Gelli ordered the bombing, Pazienza 'masterminded' it, and Dalla Chiaie carried it out. Pazienza seems insistent on the association of Dalla Chiaie with Oral Celik in Miami. (*NT* 13/12/85.) In May 1986, Gelli was one of twenty persons Italian magistrates recommended for trial for the bombing. (*TI* 15/5/86.)

32. *DP* Oct. 82.

33. The law led to a large amount of cash being pulled out of Sicilian banks in anticipation of the probes; and it set off a mini building boom in Sicily, as the money made a lunge into the sanctuary of the real estate market. (*LM* 19/11/84; *WS* 1/3/85.)

34. *WS* 18/3/85. Italy finally succeeded in using a new extradition treaty with the US to get Sindona back to stand trial. Curiously enough, faced with a fifteen-year jail sentence, and in spite of his bombastic declarations that, if he survived to stand trial, he would name names, Sindona said nothing to implicate prominent politicians in his various affairs. (*WS* 14/10/83, 26/9/84; *NT* 26/9/84; *LM* 8,9,10/10/84, 21,24/11/84.) However, he was also charged with arranging the murder of Giorgio Ambrosoli, liquidator of his failed Italian banks, as well as attempted extortion from Roberto Calvi. (*FT* 5/6/85.) See Chapter 21.

35. *AN* 15/9/82.

36. *ST* 9/9/84.

37. *OB* 21/8/83; *AN* 17/8/83; *LM* 11,12,18/8/83; *LD* 11/8/83; *WS* 11,15,18/8/83; *HT* 11,18/8/83; *FT* 11,12,13/8/83; *GU* 11,12,13/8/83; *NT* 13/8/83.

38. *FT* 27/9/83; *EX* 9/8/85.

39. *GZ* 21/2/85.

40. *HT* 28/5/84; *FT* 18,29/2/84; *WS* 10,31/1/84, 27,29/2/84; *TB* June 84; *GU* 26/1/84.

41. *FT* 27/1/84, 13/2/84, 21/4/84, 9,26/5/84; *GM* 27/2/84; *HT* 9/3/84; *WS* 11/5/84.

42. The appeal for public aid for religious schools was timed for the US presidential race, during which Reagan was toying with the idea of reversing one of the principles for which the Freemasonic founders of the American

NOTES **403**

republic had stood, namely, the separation of church and state, by reintroducing tax credits for parents whose children went to religious schools. (WS 27/11/84; LD 1/12/84.)

43. FT 2,3/4/84, 24/7/84; WS 1/8/84, 24/9/84. After five years of inquiry, Marcinkus and the other top managers of the IOR were cleared of involvement in the apparent embezzlement scheme. (WS 10/6/85.)
44. Le Vaillant, 225-26, 357-60. He notes that from 1947, 'les constitutions secrètes precisent que les banques sont un moyen privilégié d'apostolat.'
45. Le Vaillant, 284; NS 1/3/85.
46. Ynfante, Fugas, 189-90; Le Vaillant, 195-96, 198.
47. Ynfante, Fugas, Chapter 3.
48. Le Vaillant, 345; Ynfante, Crime, 34,40 et passim.
49. Raw, 153-55.
50. CA 12/8/85. About one-fifth of them ended up in Brazil; the rest scattered.
51. See in general Il Dec. 83; WS 21/3/83; FT 22/3/83, 12,14/10/83.
52. Ynfante, Fugas, 43. Ruiz Mateos insisted that the problem was merely one of 'delays' in the receipt of payment for exported wine.
53. LW 3/6/83. A 1985 estimate scaled down his alleged capital flight to $125 million. (CA 12/8/85.)
54. GU 1/3/83; FT 5,9/5/83, 6/10/83, 13/4/84; HT 2/7/84; CA 4/2/85, 12/8/85; EP 2/6/85.
55. On the Banca Catalana affair, see DP July 84; LM 1/6/84, 11/7/84; LD 30/5/84; NT 24/5/84; HT 21/6/84; FT 5/9/82, 27/4/84, 24,29,31/5/84, 8/6/84, 24/7/84.
56. EP 14/2/85; CA 23/5/85.
57. GU 7/3/83; FT 25/2/83, 1/3/83; LD 28/2/83; NT 25/2/83; NS 1/3/85. The theory that the Socialist party (where Spanish freemasons found a congenial home) sought to reduce Opus Dei's influence in the banking system (NS 1/3/85) is superficially plausible. Apart from Ruiz Mateos, members of Opus Dei headed several banking companies, the Confederation of Savings Banks and the Association of Private Banks, as well as holding positions of influence in the central bank. (ES 4/5/86.) However, by that time, Opus Dei financiers had had a major falling out with Ruiz Mateos, refusing him aid and, he feels, perhaps even engineering his downfall. The cause of the rift is unclear. Perhaps Roberto Calvi could have clarified it.
58. NT 20/4/84. The lack of an extradition treaty worked both ways. By late 1985, when such a treaty was finally signed, there were about one hundred British fugitives in Spain, living mainly near Marbella, dubbed the 'Costa del Crime.' (GW 8/12/85.)
59. AN 10/4/83; FT 5/5/83.
60. EP 6/1/85. The later total put diversion from employee payroll accounts at 5.2 billion pesetas, tax evasion at 8.5 billion, and social security evasion at 10.7 billion.
61. GU 30/4/83; FT 7,30/3/83; HT 7/3/83; WS 28/2/83; TI 28/2/83.
62. TB Nov. 83; FT 20/4/83, 12/5/83, 1/6/83, 2/9/83; NT 2/6/83, 8/7/83; GU 11/5/83; AN 22/4/83, 15/7/83; WS 28/9/83; HT 6/6/83, 17/11/83.
63. FT 26/4/84, 29/5/84, 1/6/84, 24/7/84; AN 26/5/84; GU 26/4/84; WS 27/4/84.

64. *CA* 13/12/85; *ES* 4/5/86, 8/6/86.
65. *FT* 6/3/85.
66. *CA* 9/9/85; *NT* 2/12/85. He could only be tried on charges of inventing credits to cover losses and overvaluation of the assets, because the terms of the West German–Spanish extradition treaty left him immune from the charges of capital flight, and tax and social-security fraud. The Spanish government later dropped the fraud charge. (*WS* 6/6/86.) But whatever the precise charges, the trial is likely to become a political circus; Ruiz Mateos has been adopted as a far-right folk hero standing against many of the most important policy initiatives of the Socialist government, including Spain's entry into the EEC. (*FT* 5/12/85.)
67. *CA* 9/9/85.

Chapter Nine

1. *GU* 5/3/83; *FT* 14/5/83; *RS* 9/3/84; *OB* 7,16,23/9/84.
2. On Gelli in Argentina, and the Argentine P-2, see Cecchi, 77–78, 82, 139; *LW* 5/6/81; *FT* 17/8/83; *TS* 28/8/83; *OB* 21/8/83, 19/9/83; *GU* 14/2/83; Gurwin, 52; Yallop, 307, 310.
3. *LW* 19/6/81; *HT* 17/11/83; Kruger, 85.
4. *LP* 27/6/75, 12/9/75.
5. *LP* 30/5/75, 12/3/76.
6. *LP* 26/3/76, 16/4/76, 21/5/76, 2/7/76.
7. Kruger, 113. *LP* 18/5/79 described El Brujo as 'probably the most important narcotics operator in Argentina at the time.' However, during his long stay in the US no drug charges were laid. Nor do they seem to have figured in the extradition proceedings in 1986. (*GW* 13/7/86.) They may well have been an invention of the military to discredit him. Argentinian exiles asked by the author profess never to have heard of Lopez Rega's alleged drug dealing.
8. The story of the ABT is traced in *BA* 28/9/81. US District Attorney Robert Morgenthau still issued an indictment against Graiver, insisting that there was reason to believe he was still alive. (*FF* 5/5/78.)
9. *South* Dec. 83.
10. Cecchi, 82. Massera was later accused by former finance minister Juan Alemann of having accumulated 'unjustified wealth' during his tenure in office. (*LW* 24/6/83.)
11. *WS* 23/4/84.
12. *WR* 21/11/80.
13. *WS* 17/5/84.
14. By 1980 seven major banks controlled 58% of all deposits; 200 other financial institutions held some 3%. Thus, Argentina got the worst of both worlds: high concentration of control of savings and a proliferation of high-cost, inefficient, and vulnerable institutions. The result was waves of collapses when trouble struck, as it did in 1980.
15. *IB* June 80.
16. In retrospect, it appeared as if Britain had undertaken the façade of negotiations in order to gain time to get its task force into position. The *Belgrano*

had been shadowed for more than a day before Thatcher ordered its demise.

17. When threats from the AAA forced the owner of the Abril publishing group to flee the country, Gelli and Ortolani arranged for Italy's Rizzoli Group to take it over. See Chapter Five, note 21.

18. *LW* 29/5/81; *FF* 10/12/82.

19. *LW* 5/6/81.

20. *PN* 4/1/82.

21. *PN* 28/6/82; *RS* 14/10/83; Yallop, 311; Cecchi, vice-chairman of the P-2 enquiry in Italy, ascribes a high probability to the view that Calvi was assassinated by British intelligence. (Cecchi, 226.)

22. *LD* 26/8/82; *NT* 25/8/82; *GU* 25/8/82; *GM* 25/8/82, 11/9/82; *LD* 26/8/82; *FT* 30/9/82, 16/5/83.

23. Reputedly Argentina threatened to repudiate its debt in May of 1982, but by September it was publicly denying any intent to default.
LR 17/5/82; *WS* 20/9/82.

24. *FT* 9/9/82.

25. See Chapter 21.

26. *FT* 8/11/82.

27. *FT* 9/11/82; *GU* 25/11/82, 8/2/83, 12/8/83; *LD* 16/8/83; *WS* 13/7/83.

28. *WS* 18/10/82, 29/10/82; *FT* 28/10/82, 6/12/82, 16/12/82, 23/2/83; *NT* 28/10/82, 17/10/82; *HT* 28/10/82; *LD* 18/12/82; *GU* 29/3/83; *GM* 28/3/83.

29. *FT* 16/2/83.

30. *HT* 11/3/83, 11/10/83; *RS* 9/3/84.

31. *LM* 17/12/82.

32. Argentine citizens with funds lodged in Panamanian, Uruguayan, Swiss, or American bank accounts also drew dollars from banks inside Argentina on security of those accounts. Then they would sell the dollars to the Argentine central bank, repaying the bank loan in pesos, and creating another foreign-exchange credit at the central bank on which they could draw. Some three billion dollars of the foreign debt was estimated to have emerged from such back-to-back loan arrangements. (*NT* 17/10/83, 7/4/84; *GM* 11/8/83.)

33. *LW* 13/1/84.

34. *WS* 7/10/83; *FF* 21/10/83.

35. *LW* 25/11/83; *WS* 10/10/83; *GU* 3/10/83; *FT* 17/10/83; *LS* 25/11/85. These charges appear to have come to nothing, and may well have reflected a quarrel between Martinez de Hoz and the military over control of the Argentinian steel industry.

36. On the Kramer coup, see *WS* 4/10/83; *FT* 3/10/83, 4/10/83, 5/10/83; *HT* 3/10/83, 8–9/10/83, 10/10/83; *GU* 4/10/83; *NT* 4/10/83; *LD* 5/10/83; *CM* 5/10/83; *RS* 14/10/83.

37. *RS* 9/9/83; *LW* 20/5/85.

38. *NT* 7/10/83; *GM* 7/10/83.

39. *WS* 5/10/83.

40. *LM* 11/10/83; *LW* 7/10/83.

41. *WS* 6/10/83.

42. *FT* 21/10/83; *LD* 28/10/83.

43. *IB* 11/11/83; *FT* 2/11/83; *SP* 14/11/83.
44. *LW* 25/3/83, 3/6/83, 24/6/83; *FT* 26/10/83; *GU* 25/8/83; *LD* 26/8/83. On the 'amnesty' question, see *LW* 7/10/83; *ST* 5/12/82; *FT* 23/2/83.
45. *LW* 15/4/83; *RS* 23/12/83.
46. *RS* 18/11/83.

Chapter Ten

1. Hougan, *Spooks*, 333.
2. *WS* 24/2/83.
3. *FT* 18,23/3/83; *WS* 24/2/83; *GM* 9/8/82, 16/3/83.
4. *LW* 4/5/84. The only real result was to make American military aid flow through more covert channels, and to open up a new market for Israeli arms salesmen. Subsequently Israel peddled to the Contras, the Central American juntas, the Afghan resistance, and so on, arms captured from the PLO in the Lebanon war.
5. *VV* 5/11/85; *WS* 30/10/85; *NT* 8/1/83; *GU* 8,10/1/83; *LM* 10/1/83; *GM* 20/12/82; *FT* 23/3/83.
6. *GM* 1/2/83, 16/3/83; *WS* 12/8/83.
7. Since the 1960s, the officer corps had been a uniquely privileged profession, and an upward socioeconomic path for those not from the traditional landed class. The commissary stores made available to the officer corps luxury imports at low prices. Militarization of educational institutions assured that the offspring of the corps would get privileged entry, and the corps penetrated deeply into the civilian economy. The military owned banks and other credit facilities and asserted a strong presence in agribusiness and the property market. If Rios Montt were to take seriously the IMF prescriptions for tax hikes and domestic austerity, the economic privileges of the military caste could be threatened. (*RM* 25/10/85.)
8. In addition, there is a possibility that dispensing with Rios Montt, who took a strong stand on Guatemalan sovereignty over Belize, was also a concession by the US in return for Britain not protesting the renewal of military aid to Guatemala. *WR* 31/3/83, 19/8/83; *RM* 19/8/83, 3/5/85; *FT* 13/10/83; *WS* 12/8/83; *LW* 31/3/83. By late 1985, with the state coffers empty, capital flight endemic, 50% of the working population unemployed or underemployed, industries at 60% capacity, and a foreign debt load of $2.5 billion, it seemed time for a civilian government to brush up the country's image and encourage foreign investment. (*LM* 6/9/85.)
9. *RC* 2/3/84.
10. *GU* 25/7/83, 2/4/84; *GM* 9/12/82, 12/5/83; *CS* June–Aug. 83; *LM* 3/4/84; *FT* 2/10/84.
11. *WS* 2/11/84; *WP* 2/11/84.
12. On the Moonies in general, see the work of Boettcher and the interesting survey in *SP* April 83.
13. *FR* 19/4/84.
14. *FR* 12/1/84.
15. On Sasakawa's career, see *VV* 4/10/83; *FT* 10/8/85; also Hougan, 455 et passim.

16. Hougan, *Spooks*, 446, 450–55; Sobel, 106–12. Leslie Deak later commented, 'We made the payment. The fact that the money was used for bribes is Lockheed's shame, not ours.'

17. According to *Spotlight*, a newspaper of the American radical right, Moon was arrested several times, including once by the South Korean vice squad for performing 'purification rites' on underage female converts.
(*SP* April 83.) The source often recycles bizarre and dubious information, but its Moonie survey has the ring of sound research.

18. Boettcher, 8 et passim.

19. *NT* 23/8/85.

20. On Moonie cash movements, see Boyer, 149, 169–70. Mind control was subsequently supplemented by the hiring of private detectives to bring back to the fold young converts lured away by deprogrammers working for their concerned parents. (*WS* 23/5/85.)

21. Boettcher, 169; *DP* Feb. 85; Hougan, *Secret*, 106–7n puts their ownership at 46%. The nominal shareholders, thirteen low-level Moonies, were allegedly fronting for Korean and Japanese sect directors, who were the real owners. See *SEC v. Diplomat National Bank* (*IC* No. 2, 1983; Senate Report 169).

22. See, for example, *ME* Sept. 83. Apart from Latin America, the Moonies have moved into publishing in the Middle East with their *Middle East Times*, published out of Cyprus. In Washington the Moonies' oracle is the *Washington Times*, set up to combat the *Washington Post*, which is accused of being excessively 'liberal.' Of course, it may also represent Moonie revenge on the *Post* for breaking the Watergate scandal. The paper is in good editorial hands, those of cold war ideologue Arnaud de Borchgrave.

23. *DP* Feb. 85.

24. Endorsement of that position was by no means universal. Opponents of the liberation theology insisted that the real reason for the growth of cults was that the Brazilian church spent so much time on the social well-being of its flock that it left a spiritual void that the Protestant sects and religious cults could exploit. (*RB* 9/8/85.)

25. *LW* 19/7/85.

26. In Italy the leaders of a new Catholic fundamentalist movement were exerting increasing power inside the Christian Democratic party, and working to assure that there would be no repetition of the late Aldo Moro's policy of political dialogue with the Communist party.
(*WS* 17/10/84, 16/9/85.)

27. *RC* 22/8/85.

28. The pontiff went on the offensive against those who 'see the poor as a class or as a class in struggle' and who forget that the 'first liberation to reach for is the liberation from sin' (*GW* 21/10/84). Although Father Boff was silenced (*GU* 15/5/85; *NT* 8/5/85), talking very loudly was the American Enterprise Institute, which had sponsored the drafting by prominent American Catholics, including Alexander Haig, of a document that asserted publicly and without evident Vatican rebuke the compatibility of Catholicism and capitalism. (*NT* 13/9/84.)

29. *LW* 12/2/85.

30. *LM* 12/11/84.
31. *BW* 11/3/85.
32. *LM* 15–16/9/85.
33. These included Israeli mercenaries and Cuban exiles, recruited by 2506 Brigade in Miami, a Bay of Pigs veterans' organization. (*LM* 27/7/85; *FT* 11/10/85.)
34. *LW* 4/5/85, 14,21/6/85; *NT* 16/11/85; *GM* 30/11/85.
35. From 1981 until the cutoff of funds in 1984, the main distribution point was the US embassy in Tegucigalpa. When official aid was restored in 1985, the Honduran government, minus Chief of Staff Alvarez, refused to allow the continuance of that role. (*LW* 6/9/85.) In Costa Rica, concern over progressive militarization brought even old Don Pepe back into the political arena, to combat the country's progressive integration into the regional maelstrom. (*TS* 18/8/85.)
36. When Mexico responded to its debt crisis and falling oil prices by demanding cash up front from places that formerly got oil on credit, the new policy did nothing for Mexico's cash-flow position, though it was of considerable financial advantage to the Reverend Sun Myung Moon. When in April 1985 Mexico ceased to make oil available to Central America on soft terms, Nicaraguan junta chief Daniel Ortega made an emergency trip to the Soviet Union to coax it into covering the oil gap. He left for Moscow the day after the US House of Representatives refused to approve a bill permitting the Reagan administration to restore funding to the Contras. When the bill failed, Reverend Moon and his allies decided to put up the cash for the Contras. But Ortega's Moscow junket fed the administration's propaganda mill, and several months later Congressional approval of the funding was secured. (*GU* 3/9/85; *WS* 13/6/85.)
37. *WP* 27/11/84; *RM* 3/5/85.
38. Late in 1985 the Dominican Republic Moonie chief and head of the small Partido Popular Cristiano was found murdered. He had been accused of using his political links to make large investments in the country on behalf of the Moonies. (*RC* 1/11/85.)
39. In general, see *BA* 16/7/84.
40. Kruger, 6.
41. *CA* 9/9/85.
42. *GM* 31/3/84.
43. *El Periodista*, 28/6/85.
44. *PN* 19/7/82; Cecchi, 77; *RS* 27/5/83; *LW* 5/6/81; *FT* 27/9/83; Gurwin, 56.
45. *RS* 27/5/83, 1/7/83.
46. *WS* 11/3/83, 29/11/83, 17/1/84; *FT* 8/4/83; *NT* 10/3/83.
47. *RS* 14/10/83; *LM* 15/3/83.
48. Safi was a journalist whose professional credentials included an association with the Lebanese Phalangist party and marriage into the most right-wing faction of Uruguay's Colorado party. He also made a tour of duty generating propaganda on behalf of the military government.
49. *DP* Feb. 85. Boyer (p. 214) claims that Julian Safi was the owner of Kami Ltd.
50. *RS* 13/4/84; *HT* 20/2/84; *NT* 16/2/84.

51. *RS* 2/8/85. In mid-July 1985 the head of the Montevideo municipal government revoked permission to build the center and scuttled the $45 million project. This caused fears of a general pullout of Moonie cash, which had become so important to Uruguay. When a tax revolt broke out against the head of the Montevideo government, threatening the government's very existence, some suspected the hand of the Moonies behind it.

52. The editor selected for that newspaper, Fernando Gomez, was Uruguay's former ambassador to Colombia. His fervid anticommunism may owe something to the fact that, while in Colombia, he was one of a group of diplomats kidnapped by the pro-Cuban M-19 guerrilla group. (*LW* 25/9/81.)

53. *LM* 28/9/83, 14/12/83, 27/5/84.

54. *FT* 24/11/84.

55. *CM* 15/6/84; *LM* 19/6/84; *FT* 27/11/84; *LW* 22/6/84; *LI* 18/6/84. Initially the Colorado party viewed Moonie activity with suspicion; however, since coming to office, they seem to have done nothing to interfere with Moonie business.

Chapter Eleven

1. Cited in *TM* 1/11/81.

2. *WS* 12/9/83.

3. By the mid-1980s, about 10% of the adult population of the US was estimated to have used the drug at some point. (*NT* 7/11/85; *WS* 9/1/86.)

4. For a version of the 'narco-terrorism' story, see *New America* March–April 1985. For a more balanced view see *WS* 9/4/85; though *WS* 10/2/86 contains a version of the communist-subversion-equals-drug-trafficking story that takes both paranoia and fantasy to ethereal new heights.

5. The apt term 'narcocracy' is from Anthony Henman. See *LW* 25/10/85.

6. *FT* 17/2/83; *WS* 25/3/83; *NT* 9/10/85.

7. For the Indians, the nutrients derived from chewing the leaves supplement a sparse diet, and the small amount of active drug in the leaves increase their capacity for physical hardship. This effect had led the Spanish conquistadors to reverse their initial ban on the use of the leaves, once they began the systematic exploitation of Indian forced labor in the silver mines. To this day landlords and mine owners encourage the use of coca, for it stills hunger pangs and thereby helps maintain high productivity in spite of malnutrition.

8. On Barbie and his Bolivian career, see *CS* July–Aug. 83; *HT* 19/3/83; *LM* 19/8/83; *OB* 21/8/83.

9. *AN* 15/3/83; *HT* 29/3/83; *AA* Feb. 85.

10. For example, the CIA-trained Cuban exiles in Florida active first in the heroin and now in the cocaine traffic; the Meo of Southeast Asia, whose opium the CIA flew to market while the men fought as auxiliaries in Vietnam and Laos; the Afghan resistance fighters in Pakistan, within whose ranks a powerful drugs-and-arms mafia operates. Another intriguing example is from Argentina, where Minister of Social Welfare Lopez Rega received automatic weapons from the US for the creation of a special 'antinarcotics force.' This force formed the core of the paramilitary death squad

AAA, which allegedly protected the operations of the local affiliate of the French Connection. See Chapter 9, n. 7.

11. *DP* Feb. 85; Boyer, 216; Delpirou, 137–38, 148.

12. Gurwin, 192–93; *OB* 28/10/84; *GU* 14/2/83; *LM* 3/2/83; *AN* 6/4/83; *FT* 11/12/84; *DP* Feb. 85; *WR* 22/8/80.

13. *LW* 29/5/81.

14. See in general *II* April 81; *EM* Jan. 82; see also *NT* 11/6/84.

15. *FT* 23/12/82.

16. *GM* 24/1/83; *FT* 4/3/83.

17. In little more than a century and a half of republican history, Bolivia has had 191 presidents. Seven of them held office from 1978 to 1980 (when the cocaine business took off) as a result of three general elections, contested by more than seventy political parties, supplemented by four successful coups d'état.

18. See the survey in *DP* Feb. 83. One banker declared 'I wouldn't give Bolivia a wooden nickel, even if it was your nickel.' As, in the international banking game, it usually *is* someone else's nickel, and as bankers are rarely hesitant to throw away other people's money if the bank can turn a profit from the operation, there had to be something particularly rotten in the state of Bolivian finance.

19. *AB* 9/9/82.

20. *FT* 1,5/10/82.

21. Arce Gomez's exile in Argentina was upset by an indictment on charges in Miami and consequent arrest. (*LM* 30/4/83; *NT* 17/5/83.)

22. *AN* 10/4/83; *LM* 29/3/83; *NT* 30/3/83; *RA* 15/4/83.

23. *AB* 5/11/82.

24. *RA* 1/3/85. This dedollarization badly hurt some of the foreign banks, causing them to shut down their local operations. First Bank of America went home in 1982; most recently the Bank of Boston closed its La Paz office in 1985.

    While the emergency regulations also provided for the first increase in the minimum wage since 1956 – Siles Zuazo's previous inaugural year – that increase was more than offset by price hikes in essential products, as subsidies on food, fuel, and essential services were lifted. (*NT* 8/11/82.) Further attacks on general living standards followed shortly.

25. *FT* 29/11/82.

26. *RA* 24/6/83, 29/7/83; *LC* 8/7/83; *AN* 6/3/83, 17/7/83, 8/1/84; *FT* 7/2/84.

27. *LM* 3/2/83; *WS* 17/2/83; *NT* 21/7/84. In the producing areas, there are alleged to be more than 5,000 private runways (undoubtedly an exaggeration), but not a single radar unit controlled by the government (undoubtedly the truth). The main producers have powerful paramilitary forces to back them up.

28. Suarez Gomez is reported to have put his air force to good use on such occasions as in April 1983, when two of his planes forced down a central bank of Bolivia aircraft carrying the payroll for civil servants in a remote area, allegedly because the local agency of the central bank had refused to cash one of his checks. The plane was looted and two of the functionaries abducted. Of course it is possible that the Bolivian government uses Suarez

Gomez as a scapegoat for all that goes wrong, much as the Italian government seems to use Licio Gelli. (*DP* March 84; Delpirou, 153.)

29. *TM* 25/2/85; *AN* 6/3/83, 16/6/83, 17/7/83.
30. On El Niño's impact, see *LC* 24/6/83; *RA* 24/6/83, 29/7/83; *AN* 20/6/83; *GM* 1/7/83. The lack of real progress against the drug dealers was in part a result of Siles Zuazo's concession to realpolitik. The government antidrug agency was a victim of the austerity measures; its staff was halved and the few agents assigned to enforcement were deterred by assassinations and insufficient equipment.
31. *WS* 26/7/83; *FT* 4/5/83.
32. Centered on the Social Democratic party of Siles Zuazo, the coalition also included the Movimiento de Izquierda Revolucionaria (MIR) (some of whose leaders routinely turned up at the US embassy for 'consultations'), the Christian Democrats, and the Communist party, whose ministerial allocation of labor and mines was designed to keep the powerful and largely Communist party-led COB in line. The MIR used lack of progress against the drug trade to beat the government while the Christian Democrats and Communists warred over austerity and debt.
33. On the political dissension, see variously *LM* 28/3/83, 28/4/83; *LW* 25/3/83, 17/6/83; *LD* 25/11/83; *FT* 24/11/83.
34. *RA* 20/5/83, 29/7/83; *LW* 27/5/83, 10/6/83, 12,26/8/83; *South* Jan. 84; *GU* 30/8/83.
35. *LM* 31/8/83.
36. *FT* 30/1/84.
37. *LW* 6/4/84; *AN* 11/4/84; *LM* 12/4/84, 9/10/84.
38. *FT* 17/5/84; *NT* 1/5/84; *LM* 21/5/84, 6/7/84; *GU* 11/5/84.
39. *AN* 2/6/84; *GU* 18/5/84; *HT* 31/5/84; *LM* 11/7/84.
40. Hougan, *Spooks*, 143.
41. *RA* 6/4/84.
42. *LM* 22–23/4/84; *LD* 24/4/84; *NT* 2,17/7/84.
43. On the military plots and their background, see *NT* 5/7/84; *LM* 11/3/84; *AN* 25/11/83, 18/2/84; *LD* 3/7/84; *GM* 13/7/84; *WS* 3/7/84.
44. *FT* 2/7/84; *LM* 3,4/7/84.
45. See the survey in *IC* Dec. 81; as late as one year after the 'debt crisis' broke, Colombia was still described as 'the golden exception,' *EM* Sept. 83.
46. *TM* 25/2/85; *LM* 4/4/85 puts a lower value on the trade, about $3 billion.
47. *LW* 9,16/3/84; *RA* 6/4/84. On the Jamaican trade, see *FT* 24/10/84; *GW* 25/11/84.
48. Clark and Horrock, 16, 80–84, 92, 184–92.
49. *NT* 3/1/85, 25/2/85.
50. *WS* 30/8/85.
51. *LW* 28/10/83. Confirmation of information about Colombian cocaine and black markets is rendered somewhat difficult by the fact that occupational diseases such as assassination strike journalists in Colombia even more often than heart attacks hit the inmates of Italian jails. *RA* 7/10/83; *LW* 12/10/84.
52. *LW* 25/5/84; *WS* 28/11/83; *TM* 25/2/85.
53. *LW* 30/1/81.

54. *IC* July 84; cf. Blum, 67.
55. *FT* 13/2/84.
56. *Latin America Times*, Nov. 83.
57. *WS* 5/4/83, 28/11/84; *LD* 24/3/84.
58. *AN* 19/1/84.
59. Peruvian official quoted in *TS* 27/10/85.
60. Allegedly the Conservative party organizers had depended heavily on cash from the marijuana dealers to buy votes in the party's traditional strongholds. (*AA* 17/8/81; *South*, May 83.)
61. Betancur began his term by publicly delivering his income-tax form to the auditor general for inspection, thus contradicting his populist image by placing himself in a distinct minority among his countrymen, at least of his social class. (*FT* 29/9/82.)
62. The guerrilla movements are surveyed briefly in *DP* Jan. 86.
63. *LW* 9/7/82. For example, the M-19 guerrilla movement began as an urban, middle-class, and reformist organization pushed underground, where it was progressively radicalized.
64. *LW* 28/10/83.
65. *RA* 24/6/83; *LD* 24/3/84.
66. The charges about the guerrillas guarding the airstrips are particularly interesting, coming as they did from an army that had been reportedly helping to load planes with marijuana for export to the US. (*HT* 30/3/84.)
67. *LW* 28/10/83; *NT* 10,15/11/83; *HT* 16/11/83; *WS* 30/4/84, 15/10/84. M-19 had never made a secret of the fact that it had used drug dealers to secure arms; nor is it unlikely that Cuba, like Bulgaria, found it politically and fiscally convenient to ignore the content of cargos passing through its territory. But joining them in a grand plot to control the world's cocaine trade is another matter, especially as the major Colombian dealers are known to hold fanatically right-wing views. Interestingly, one of the major sources of 'intelligence' on Castro's alleged involvement in the drug trade is anti-Castro Cuban exile organizations. See, for example, *CM* 10/11/83. It is common enough for the DEA, which endorsed the anti-Castro report, to be used as cover by the CIA. (*RA* 13/12/85.)
68. *EP* 6/6/85; *CA* 21/1/85, 6/6/85; *LW* 9/8/85. More specifically, he cited a visit from a delegation of Spanish police and a former CIA man seconded, as CIA men often are, to the DEA.
69. *TS* 27/10/85.
70. *NT* 31/10/84; *AN* 3/12/82. Although Shining Path has no relations with outside powers that might provide it with funding, the possibility of any link between the cocaine dealers and Shining Path is greeted with skepticism by observers on the ground, who point out that it would be quite out of character for the fanatically puritanical Shining Path. (*TS* 27/10/85; Delpirou, 181–85.) On the other hand there seems little doubt that Shining Path, like the Colombian guerrilla groups, would seize on peasant discontent at the government's efforts to destroy their coca crop to make anti-government and anti-US propaganda. (*WS* 31/10/85.)
71. *LW* 16/8/85; *DP* Nov. 85.
72. The first raid yielded what was claimed to be the largest seizure of cocaine

in history. Several weeks later another major raid produced an even bigger haul. The complex boasted production capacity of three hundred tons of cocaine per year, about six times previous estimates of the annual output of all of Colombia. (*LW* 20/7/84; *RA* 18/5/84.)

73. *LW* 9/9/83, 6/4/84, 4,11/5/84; *LM* 3/5/84; *HT* 3,23/5/84; *NT* 12,17/5/84; *CM* 3/5/84; *RA* 18/5/84; *LD* 2/5/84; *GM* 4/5/84.

74. Only a partial truce was ever carried out, with frequent interruptions. (*NT* 3/4/84, 24/8/84; *WS* 15,24/8/84; *GU* 29/5/84; *GM* 29/5/84.) Finally full-scale war erupted again. The worst incident came when M-19 stormed the justice ministry in Bogotá in November 1985 and took a number of judges hostage. The bloodbath that passed for a rescue operation could have been planned by Egyptian antiterrorist units. It seems as if the army was itching not only to attack the guerrillas, but also to settle scores with some of the captive judges, at least one of whom allegedly died at the hands of the army after his rescue. The government claimed that M-19 had seized the ministry in order to destroy documents linking them to the drug trade. But this explanation gained little credibility except among babes-in-the-woods of international diplomacy such as Canada's ambassador to the United Nations, who agreed to head an international task force on 'narco-terrorism.' (*LD* 9/12/85.) There were too many copies of ministry documents elsewhere for the explanation to hold water. (*NT* 9/11/85.) Another explanation was that the attack occurred just when the judges were debating the projected extradition treaty with the US, implying that the attack was ordered by the big drug traders, again not a very convincing contention. (*DP* Jan. 86.)

75. *LW* 18,25/5/84.

76. *HT* 30/5/84, 21/2/84. In fact, in 1981 the US DEA publicly described the work of the Brazilian antinarcotics chief for Amazonas state as 'heroic,' only to find, one month later, that his unit was a main beneficiary of the expansion of the coca frontier beyond the borders of the Andean countries, and that it was notorious for extorting money from the coca dealers and absconding with the seized drugs. (*LW* 22/1/82.)

77. *RA* 27/7/84; *LW* 20/7/84.

78. *Latin America Times*, Nov. 83; *LW* 28/9/84; *LM* 10/10/84.

79. *FT* 2/7/84; *LM* 17/5/84, 2,6/6/84, 3,4,7/7/84, 17/10/84; *WS* 24/8/84; *AN* 5/5/84; *GU* 7/6/84.

80. See especially *WS* 13/8/85.

81. *LW* 17,24/8/84.

82. *FT* 14/6/85; *LW* 1/2/85, 1/3/85.

83. *RA* 25/1/85; *LM* 28/2/85; *FT* 21/3/85; *LW* 4/1/85.

84. *LW* 8/3/85, 9/8/85.

85. *LM* 6/8/85; *LW* 16/8/85.

86. *LM* 8/8/85, 21/9/85, 25/10/85; *WS* 30/8/85; *LW* 6/9/85.

87. *LW* 8/11/85.

88. If that is true, the flight capitalists appear to have had some assistance from abroad. In May of 1982 the Colombian ministry of defense had arranged with Chase Manhattan's London branch for a loan of $47 million to finance the purchase of imported military equipment. A year later, some $13.5 mil-

lion was still unspent. But a telex order, based on documents later seen to be fraudulent, was sent to Chase requesting that the money be transferred to Morgan Guaranty in New York. From there the funds were distributed among coded accounts at the Zurich branch of the Israeli Hapoalim Bank. The theft was discovered only in September 1983, when the Colombian government tried to draw on the funds to cover purchases of aircraft, apparently in conjunction with a planned offensive against the cocaine traffickers. The search for the money was scarcely encouraged by a series of murders – first of the chief investigator of the ministry of finance, then of an important witness, then of a lawyer for the Banco de la Republica, then of a congressional investigator, and so on. By the summer of 1985 the death toll had hit seven without a trace of the money. (*GU* 20/11/83; *RA* 26/7/85.)

89. *HT* 21/2/84; *RA* 22/6/84.
90. More specifically the dollars could be traded for bearer certificates of deposit at the central bank, and those CDs converted into pesos in ninety days. In the interim, the CDs could be resold to money-market dealers, who could dispose of them on the stock exchange. (*LW* 29/3/85; *TS* 27/10/85.)

Chapter Twelve

1. In general, see US Senate Report 77–85; Eiffros 799–893; *FT* 16/2/83.
2. *WS* 3/11/83; *AN* 26/5/84. Although its location is not quite as good as that of its leading competitor, the Bahamas, Panama has the advantage of sharing the language of the principal producers of marijuana and cocaine, and of many leading wholesalers in the US.
3. *TS* 27/10/85.
4. *LW* 11/1/80; *RM* 15/7/83; *NT* 17/4/84.
5. Cited in *Boston Globe* special insight report on money laundering, part one.
6. *FT* 12/10/83.
7. Inside Chile, rightist groups plotted the collapse of savings companies to spread panic, while capital flight to Argentina was encouraged, perhaps with the complicity of its government. The wheat growers' association encouraged its members to refuse to plant, and the truckers snarled the distribution system that relied on them. Allegedly cash dollars to support the truckers' strike came through the Banque pour le Commerce continental of Geneva, a bank owned by Chilean exiles, the Klein family. (Ziegler, 78.)
8. On American policy toward the Allende regime, see especially Seymour Hersh, *The Price of Power*, and Sampson's study of ITT, which played a central role in the sabotage of the Chilean government. An illuminating compilation of documents was issued by the Bertrand Russell Peace Foundation in 1972 under the title *Subversion in Chile*.
9. It was agreed by diplomats and intelligence reports that Allende posed no strategic threat to American interests. The decision to undermine and then overthrow him apparently had to do with developments half a world away.

   The real threat was the rising power of eurocommunism in Italy, NATO's southern flank. In 1969 the Christian Democratic premier of Italy, Aldo Moro, began his efforts to create a broad coalition of political forces in which the Communist party would be a participant for the first time in Italian history. The objective of the Nixon White House, and of Secretary of State Kissinger in particular, is reputed to have been to assure that nothing resembling a political legitimation of the Communist party occur in the Americas lest it reinforce the Italian development. On this point, see Hersh.

10. An excellent survey is in A. G. Hurtado.
11. *FT* 1/21/83; *WS* 17/1/83, 11/2/85.
12. That secret military alliance had Argentina as the target. As the British government thundered on about the need to defend democracy against military dictatorships like Argentina, it used Chilean bases for its spying operations, including a planned (though never implemented) commando raid on the air bases from which Argentina was launching its Exocet-carrying aircraft. In exchange, Chile was assured British arms and enriched uranium for its atomic weapons program, and it secured from a defeated Argentina concessions over the long-disputed Beagle Channel. (*NS* 25/1/85.)
13. *WS* 24/11/82; *NT* 5/12/82.
14. *IB* Dec. 81; *AN* 1/6/82; *FT* 15/1/83; *TB* Feb. 83; *LM* 17/2/83; *WS* 21/1/83.
15. *FT* 11/2/83, 4/3/83, 14/4/83; *WS* 11,15/2/83; *GM* 24/1/83.
16. *RS* 9/3/84; *FT* 9/11/83, 31/1/84, 29/2/84; *WS* 3/2/84, 6/3/84.
17. *RS* 9/3/84.
18. Blum, 147–48; Clark and Horrock, passim; *GW* 1/4/84.
19. Epstein, 96–97; Clark and Horrock, 193–94; Farnsworth and McKenney, 83. The controller was tried in Dallas and given a five-year sentence.
20. *LP* 18/5/79.
21. *LP* 27/7/79. Panama was also the first country in Latin America to recognize the new Nicaraguan regime. This may have been in revenge for Somoza's periodic threats to reactivate plans for a competing canal through Nicaragua that would carry five times the freight of the Panamanian one. (Hougan, *Spooks*, Chapter XI.)
22. *LP* 21/5/76.
23. *LP* 7/5/76.
24. *LP* 27/7/79; *LW* 21/11/79.
25. *DP* Jan. 83; *LW* 23/10/81, 25/3/83.
26. When the debt crisis began to hit the country, the National Guard made the intelligent decision to falsify election results and to parachute into the presidency a former World Bank vice-president, Nicholas Ardito Barletta. The gesture was intended to smooth the ruffled feathers of the international banks. But when Barletta imposed the inevitable tax increases, popular unrest mounted. When a former health minister in the Torrijos government, Hugo Spadafora (who had accused General Manuel Antonio Noriega, head of the National Guard, of drug trafficking), was found murdered and decapitated, and Barletta promised an investigation, the National Guard dumped him from office. (*NT* 2/10/85; *LM* 1/10/85; *WS* 30/9/85, 6/12/85.)
27. *WS* 3/11/83.
28. *RM* 15/7/83.
29. *GM* 4/6/84.

30. *NT* 24/12/82; useful material on Colombian banking is in Lernoux, Part II.
31. The economic emergency included a new bank code that scaled down the maximum loan a bank could make to any one client, and strict limits on intrafamily lending. It reduced the permitted concentration of ownership of financial groups, and banned savings institutions from accepting deposits unless the institutions were regulated by the superintendent of banks. All financial institutions operating without specific authorization from the government were to be shut down. But, on the appeal of the Colombian bankers, the Supreme Court subsequently ruled the measures unconstitutional. (*AN* 11/10/82; *LW* 16/11/84.)
32. *LW* 6/3/81; from 1978 to 1980, two GGC mutual funds had been accused of defrauding 37,000 small shareholders of $33 million, and of blocking an investigation through blackmail, bribery, and political stringpulling.
33. *LW* 13/1/84, 17/2/84, 16/11/84; *RA* 26/7/85.
34. *LW* 15/6/84.
35. *LW* 29/3/85.
36. *HT* 28/11/83.
37. *WS* 3/11/83.
38. Jorge Ochoa allegedly worked through the accounts kept by the Colombian coffee growers' association in his First Interamericas Bank. Ochoa and his partner in the bank, Gilberto Rodriguez Orejuela, were jailed in Madrid on charges of drug smuggling and money laundering. The New York accounts of the coffee growers' association were embargoed, and Panama shut down the First Interamericas Bank. (*LW* 29/3/85.)

Chapter Thirteen

1. *GU* 31/3/84.
2. *FR* 21/6/84.
3. *FT* 28/10/85. South Korea 'illegally' conducted trade with China. Its 1985 value could hit $1.5 billion, half of it going via Hong Kong.
4. *WS* 12/11/84.
5. On the Triads, see McCoy, Chapter 6; Bresler; O'Callaghan; Messick, *Grass*, 157–58; *TS* 18/9/83. Their name comes from their triangular symbol representing Heaven, Earth, and Man.
6. Kruger, 115.
7. Cited in *FR* 6/9/84. Mills, 753, observes that Tuan was pulling US legs. Mills claims that he was not remotely interested in fighting 'Communism,' but more than remotely interested in peddling opium.
8. On lateral-transfer techniques, see Clarke, 103. On Chinese underground banking, see Mills, 760, 1135.
9. *HT* 7/3/83; *AN* 20/6/83; *LM* 18/8/83; *TS* 18/9/83.
10. In general, see Effrios, 95–115.
11. Hongkong & Shanghai Bank is actually a federation of banks embracing the original flagship bank of the same name; a merchant bank called Wardley's; the British Bank of the Middle East; the Mercantile Bank of London (with its old imperial India trade connections); Hang Seng Bank, the largest of Hong Kong's 'Chinese' banks; and Marine Midland, America's

thirteenth-largest bank, which was integrated into the group in 1981. With
these affiliates, and an extensive network throughout Southeast Asia, by
the end of 1982 some 70% of its $58 billion in assets were held outside the
colony. But despite such diversification abroad, its domestic position
remains dominant. As a financial intermediary, it funded the diversification of the Hong Kong economy: the shift into manufacturing in the 1950s,
into shipping in the 1960s, and into electronics and real estate in the
1970s. In the process it also financed the rise of a new group of Chinese
entrepreneurs who were challenging the economic hegemony of the old
Anglo-Scottish elite (see e.g., *FR* 1/8/85; *WS* 5/2/86). This practice
undoubtedly earned it the appreciation of the People's Republic of China,
not to mention its 30% share in the business of PRC export financing.
(*AW* 4/6/84, 14,21/5/84; *FT* 1/4/84, 2/5/84; *NT* 168/7/84.) Hongkong Bank
also became the first foreign bank to establish itself in China, specifically
in the Shenzen New Economic Zone, since 1949. (*FT* 22/8/85.)

12. Public regulation of commercial banking activity has been marginal. The
    government historically has had virtually no control over the money
    supply. Two private-sector banks issue the currency notes; a long history of
    budget surpluses has precluded a real secondary market in government
    debt that could be manipulated to affect bank cash reserves; and the cartel
    that controls interest rates is obligated only to 'consult' the government.

13. This undoubtedly delighted the Hongkong Bank, which as lender of last
    resort managed to take control of the troubled Hang Seng Bank, the largest
    'Chinese' bank in the colony, giving Hongkong Bank an even more domi-
    nant position in the local retail deposit market and in the gold market; and
    the moratorium provided insurance against the entry of new competitors.

14. *IB* April 81.

15. More specifically, the DTCs were divided into two groups. Some, mainly
    those already owned by banks, would receive licenses from the government
    that would permit them to accept deposits of any maturity, but with a
    minimum denomination of HK$500,000. The remainder, registered as com-
    mercial companies rather than licensed as financial companies, faced the
    same restrictions on size of deposit; moreover, any deposit they did accept
    had to be of a term of at least three months.

16. *FR* 8/5/81; *EC* 18/12/82; *AW* 2/4/84.

17. In general, see *BW* 5/3/84; *DP* Jan. 83.

18. *FT* 19/10/83.

19. *WS* 9/3/83, 7/4/83, 3/2/84, 6/5/85; *FT* 9/3/83, 7/4/83, 10/9/85; *HT* 3/8/83;
    LD 26/4/84; *EC* 26/2/83; *EM* April, June 85.

20. *FR* 28/7/83, 14/4/84, 3/5/84; *AW* 23/2/84; *FT* 3/3/83, 13/4/83;
    WS 13/12/82, 2,3/3/83; *LM* 13/10/83; *GU* 13/4/83, 7/6/84.

21. *WS* 11/4/83.

22. *WS* 19/12/84, 22/1/85. Private clubs in general followed. (*WS* 22/10/85.)

23. Decentralizing control of businesses' financial flows and the opening of the
    retail sector to private enterprise caused state company managers to join
    local governments and private merchants in massive tax frauds. Further-
    more, corruption among public officials grew with the increased opportuni-
    ties. (*WS* 12/11/85; *FT* 28/11/85.)

24. Currency black markets ceased to involve simply selling foreign exchange illegally obtained from tourists to factory managers in need of imported parts. In 1984 and 1985, the country was hit by major scandals around black-market-currency dealings and associated contraband trading worth hundreds of millions of dollars. (FT 19,22/3/85, 2/8/85; FR 2/5/85; GM 25/5/85.)
25. HT 1/4/83; GM 11/4/83.
26. In general, see FR 10/2/83; EC 26/2/83; FT 22/1/83; WS 24/1/83; NT 18/1/83.
27. IB 13/4/84.
28. ST 22/4/84.
29. WS 22,29/12/82, 28/2/83.
30. GU 20/9/83.
31. WS 8/4/83.
32. WS 28/7/83. Lloyd's Bank had grown from a sleepy representative office to a billion-dollar operation, in part on the basis of the property market, in which the local manager allegedly participated for personal profit at the bank's expense. Among other activities, he is accused of setting up a Hong Kong company that in turn owned a Panamanian company that held interests in several operations of the Lo family, who were prominent textile manufacturers-turned-property speculators. Among their deals was one in which the Lo firm sold Lloyd's a floor of an office building for a new headquarters. The price was outrageously inflated. But the Lloyd's manager did not object, as he and the Los allegedly split the profits. When the Lo family firm fell in a spate of lawsuits, the manager of Lloyd's took off to an Argentine exile, where he continued to proclaim his innocence, leaving criminal charges behind him and his chief partner in jail.
33. EC 3/9/83; FR 3/8/83.
34. FT 30/3/83; WS 18/5/83, 20/7/83.
35. FT 9/12/85.
36. The Carrian affair generated an enormous amount of publicity. See, for example, WS 1,17/3/83, 18/6/83, 19/8/83, 10,11/10/83, 7,23/5/84; AW 19,26/3/84, 2,30/4/84, 28/5/84, 9,16/7/84, 12/11/84; SG 27/5/84; IB 30/3/84; FR 17/2/83, 28/7/83, 20/10/83, 31/5/84; FT 2/2/83, 1/3/83, 13/4/83, 15/9/83, 10/10/83, 4/7/84, 3/1/85; AN 8,16/11/83; GU 10/10/83; HT 8–9/10/83.
37. FR 28/4/83; WS 3/1/85.
38. Until the raid there had been agreement, reluctant on the part of many, to scale down and stretch out debt, and to sell assets: properties in Singapore, a shipping company, and an insurance company that had come under CIL's control. The shipping company was successfully unloaded; but the murder of Jalil Ibrahim undermined the final rescue operation for the parent. (WS 14/9/83; AW 26/9/83; FR 29/9/83; GU 4/10/83; NT 11/10/83.)
39. FT 4/10/83.
40. AW 17/10/83; GU 11/10/83; GM 19/6/85; FT 2/4/85.
41. WS 14/9/83.
42. FR 24/11/83.
43. There were also some odd legal maneuvers. The lawyer originally assigned

to defend Mak was yanked off the case by the director of the Hong Kong legal-aid department for reasons the director claimed were 'too sensitive to be revealed.' Then George Tan and his lieutenant made an unsuccessful attempt to have the trial held in camera – a curious move given that there had been no legal link made between the Carrian affair and the murder trial. (*FR* 22,29/3/84.)

44. *FR* 26/4/84, 17/5/84.
45. *AW* 7/5/84; *WS* 3/5/84; *II* May 84.
46. *FR* 7/9/83, 24/2/83; *EC* 9/7/83.
47. *AW* 4/6/84; *WS* 4/5/84; *IB* 11,25/5/84.
48. *WS* 26/8/83, 1,11,13/10/83, 3/11/83; *FR* 20,27/10/83, 17/11/83; *FT* 17/8/83, 13/10/83.
49. *FT* 28/2/84. The government was faced with the prospect of either cutting back on the progress of the New Economic Policy or taking a loss in a state-run mutual fund, also an instrument of the NEP, in which 1.3 million bumiputras had been invested at a guaranteed 10% dividend. Any such loss could have provoked a grass-roots explosion. Hence, the government covered the hole by borrowing in Singapore from a syndicate of international banks. But the banks demanded as part of the price that the government shelve the part of the NEP that called for Malays to buy out a majority share in the foreign-owned banks operating in the country. This concession must have been particularly pleasing to the big commercial banks of Hong Kong, such as Hongkong & Shanghai Bank, which had a branch network in Malaysia second in extent only to that of Bank Bumiputra itself.
50. *WS* 17/9/84.
51. *FT* 17,18/4/84, 12/5/84; *WS* 17,18/4/84; *AW* 23/4/84, 14/5/84; *FR* 17,31/1/85.
52. *AW* 21/5/84.

Chapter Fourteen

1. *AW* 21/5/84.
2. *FT* 16/5/83; *GU* 24/9/83.
3. Also helpful were the Hong Kong bank inspectors, who upgraded the status of Dollar Credit from a 'registered' to a 'licensed' company. That permitted it to sell CDs of any term to maturity and engage in a new round of speculative lending. (*FT* 2,8,17,25/2/83; *WS* 17/2/83.)
4. *FT* 12/9/83; *WS* 14/12/83; *FR* 21/6/84.
5. *WS* 10/3/83.
6. *FT* 10/3/83; *WS* 22/11/83.
7. *FR* 8/12/83, 24/10/85; *WS* 1/10/85.
8. *WS* 5,12/10/83; *FR* 13/10/83.
9. *WS* 13/3/85.
10. For example, Current Finance seemed to feel that its major responsibility was to the current financial position of its owners. Although the 'rules' insisted that no more than 10% of a DTC's total loans could go to firms controlled by directors, those who ran Current Finance simply falsified the books and borrowed a sum greater than the total of the public deposits in

the DTC. After its collapse in February 1983, the directors were convicted of fraud. (FR 17/5/84.)

11. *GU* 3/3/83, 28/4/83; *FT* 18/3/83.
12. *FR* 21/7/83; *FT* 11/2/83, 9/3/83, 14/4/83; *WS* 29/8/83.
13. However, lest anyone suppose the government was preparing the ground for a nationalization of the banking system in anticipation of Chinese rule, the new management was drawn from the biggest private-sector banks. The authorities took great pains to emphasize that, once public money had set the bank right, it would be returned to the private sector. (*FR* 6/8/83; *AW* 23/1/84; *WS* 28/9/83; *FT* 28/9/83; *HT* 28/9/83.)
14. *TB* May, June 82, Sept. 83.
15. *FT* 1,3/10/83, 23/3/85; *HT* 4/10/83; *FR* 21/7/83, 9/3/85. Fung King Hey walked out as the largest shareholder in Merrill, Lynch. His shares had been puffed some 200% by an American bull market, while the shares of SKH that he had traded for those of Merrill, Lynch had depreciated by a factor of two-thirds.
16. *FR* 27/10/83; *HT* 18/10/83; *FT* 12/9/83, 17,22/10/83; *WS* 30/9/83, 17/10/83; *AN* 15/10/83; *GU* 1,18/10/83, 31/1/84.
17. *FR* 5/5/83; *GU* 11/5/84; *GM* 22/11/83; *AN* 18/5/84; *FT* 20/1/84; *WS* 22/6/84; *HT* 10/1/84.
18. The obvious question, raised by Stephen Solarz, head of the House of Representatives Subcommittee on Asian and Pacific Affairs, was whether this drug deal, if it existed, could have involved the complicity of the Taiwanese authorities. Assuming the query was not merely rhetorical, Congressman Solarz might begin his search for an answer, not in New York (where the drugs were allegedly to be sold), or in Las Vegas (where, presumably, the take was to be laundered), or in California (where Henry Liu was gunned down), or even in Taiwan. Rather, he might look at the KMT-patrolled border area between Burma and Thailand, whence the heroin came. (*FR* 4,18/4/85, 2/5/85; *NT* 9,18/4/85, 17,19/9/85, 28/10/85.) Taiwan rejected American requests for Chen's extradition. However, other members of the Bamboo Union are currently on trial in the US for various racketeering offences.
19. *BW* 14/1/85.
20. *NT* 12/11/85, 13/12/85; *FT* 31/10/85.
21. *FT* 23/11/82. On games Singapore bankers played to evade reserve requirements, see *FR* 21/4/83; *FT* 16/5/83; *WS* 27/7/84. Once the Singapore regulatory mechanism was tightened, among the first acts of the regulators was to expel Jardine-Fleming, the merchant banking arm of Jardine-Matheson, from the country. (*WS* 5/10/84.)
22. *AW* 17/10/83, 23/1/84; O'Callaghan, 193.
23. First came the Pacifico Bank affair. Then came a major run on Tai Fung Bank, the unofficial financial agent of the People's Republic of China, the banker to the gambling syndicate that provides much of Macao's public revenues and, in the 1960s, the alleged center of the gold-for-opium traffic that used to run through the island. (*FR* 6/10/83; *GU* 25/10/83; O'Callaghan, 193.) Then came Hong Kong's abolition of the withholding tax that had assured the routing of so much business through the Macao banks.

When that cozy relationship ended, Macao decided that its future might well lie as an offshore financial center for the New Economic Zones in southern China. It therefore set out to forge for itself a new role as a regional peekaboo center, which it did with sufficient energy to set off several more runs on its banking system before 1985 was out. (FT 10/4/85; GU 17/9/85.)

24. AW 5/3/84.
25. See Chapter 20, 'Hawaii's Worst-Kept Secret.'
26. GM 20/1/84.
27. FR 9/6/83.
28. WS 25/10/84.
29. RC 14/6/85; Taiwan was also busily investing in the region in the hope of gaining political support in its battles against China. Even Ulster got into the game, perhaps hoping to see itinerant Hong Kong textile sweatshops fulfill its own aspirations for industrial glory, which had been shattered by civil war and the collapse of the automobile enterprises of John De Lorean. (FT 25/4/84, 3/7/84; AW 4/6/84.)
30. NT 25/3/86; FT 2/3/84, 10/1/85; GM 22/11/83, 11/4/86. On Paraguay's long history of operating a profitable refugee service, see Clark and Horrock, 87 et passim.
31. FR 20,27/6/85; NT 11/6/85; GU 13/6/85; WS 11,12/6/85; FT 7,8,13/6/85.
32. SG 22/4/84; WS 28/2/83, 23/1/84; FT 25/1/84, 25/4/84, 3/7/84; AW 4/6/84, 16/7/84; GM 27/1/84; HT 14/6/84; GU 11/1/84, 3/10/84; NT 26/5/84.
33. To guard against further takeover threats by aspiring Chinese entrepreneurs, Jardine-Matheson and Hong Kong Land engaged in a major cross-purchase of shares, out of which they emerged owning nearly 40% of each other. That set the stage for the simultaneous collapse of the shares of the two companies.
34. FT 29/3/84, 9/10/84; FR 20/1/83, 15/3/84, 28/6/84; WS 14,28/1/83, 24/8/84, 8/11/85.
35. WS 5/3/83, 3/8/83, 10/8/83; FR 13/10/83.
36. FT 30/3/84, 5/4/84, 15/5/84; FR 12/4/84; GU 29/3/84; NT 29/3/84, 2/4/84; LM 30/3/84; AW 2/4/84; WS 29,31/3/84; LD 30/3/84; HT 29/3/84. Although by 1985 Hong Kong Land returned to profitability (FT 15,18/3/85), the conglomerate was forced to sell off its shipping fleet and to withdraw from the oil service industry. (FT 30/3/85.)

Chapter Fifteen

1. Cited in NT 14/6/84.
2. General treatments of the subject of Swiss banks, especially the seamier side of their activities, are by Faith (who blows the myth about the origins of Swiss bank secrecy), Clarke, and Ziegler. Mabillard's is the classic account of the Chiasso scandal; Franco's is a superb exposé of the mechanics of capital flight out of France, and Ynfante's does similar service for Spain.
3. Clarke, 22.
4. WS 30/11/83; FT 29/5/84. HT 3/6/86 cites the total of Swiss bank foreign

assets as $142 billion. This seems to refer to assets held by the Swiss banks overseas – quite a different thing than the total holdings of foreign assets. It also cites a figure of $50 billion for loot from developing countries hidden in Switzerland.

5. *NT* 5/10/84.

6. Franco, 16.

7. *GU* 19/9/85.

8. Blum, 161.

9. Faith, 49–80; see, for example, US Senate Report 7, where the myth is repeated. A parallel myth about Swiss banking is that much of its capital expansion after the war came from the absorption of the fugitive fortunes of German Jews who did not survive to reclaim their money. (Franco, 14.) This is also false, as very little Jewish refugee money ever went to Switzerland. (Faith, 200.)

10. Even after he was sprung from jail, Adams's problems did not end, as the Italian banks, who formerly were willing to finance his business, harassed him, evidently to oblige their Swiss colleagues, and he wound up in jail once more, with his goods seized. (*LI* 6/8/85.)

11. On Swiss banking activities in the war, see Higham, as well as Faith. Also *VV* 26/4/83. Some of the activities with respect to gold were finally admitted by the Swiss central bank in 1985. (*GM* 21/6/85.)

12. Franco, 167.

13. *WS* 21/11/84, 4/3/85; *FT* 20/11/84. That certainly did not end the Soviet presence in the Swiss gold and foreign-exchange markets, for the bank would be replaced by a branch of the Soviet Foreign Trade Bank. (*BW* 25/3/85.)

14. *GU* 9,10/9/85; *FT* 29/9/85; *NT* 16/9/85; *WS* 27/9/85, 13/1/86.

15. *FT* 2/8/85.

16. See especially Eisenberg, 'The Synagogue in Geneva'; also *EC* 14/12/74; Faith, 214–17, 222, 283–85; Hutchison, 68, 80, 400; and references in Raw, Messick, Derogy, and so on. In 1975, Israel sentenced to fifteen years Rosenbaum's chief associate for illegally funneling millions in state funds to ICB. (*FF* 31/5/75.)

17. *VV* 5/11/85.

18. *GW* 13/7/86; Faith, 191; Hougan, *Spooks*, 109n. Garwood, 107, claims the CIA estimated Trujillo's fortune in the upper range, around $800 million; but that seems hard to credit, given the time and context.

19. Spanish flight capitalist Julio Munoz aspired to create a special Swiss facility for managing the runaway money of latino strongmen Trujillo, Batista, Peron, and General Arbenz (of Guatemala). When the Swiss banks would not cooperate in moving the Trujillo fortune to Switzerland, he simply bought a couple of remarkably short-lived banks of his own. (Faith, 193; Laya, 86.)

20. Ziegler, 48.

21. Ziegler, 51; Sobel, 121.

22. *GM* 19/5/84; Franco, 145. Nor did fortune smile on the Swiss banks in 1975 with the fall of Saigon. For when General Thieu and Cambodian dictator Lon Nol tried to load sixteen tons of gold onto a Swissair flight, they were

refused permission; the plane was scheduled to stop in Bangkok and Bahrain, and Swiss airline officials were fearful that the gold would be seized before it got safely to its final destination. (Ziegler, 51.)

23. Copetas, 115.
24. The Swiss banks were finally forced by the Iranian government to reveal a total of $2 billion, mainly from the Iranian central bank, deposited during the shah's regime. (Faith, 334.) It was far short of estimates by the antishah forces (Franco, 11), but it did not include the portfolios managed by the private banks and any money sent initially to Switzerland and then shipped on to the US or elsewhere for real estate and similar investments. Perhaps because of the shah's ties to Swiss banks, the Khomeini government allegedly prefers to run through secret bank accounts in the Channel Islands the money needed for covert action, including assassination of representatives of the old order. (LM 10/1/84; LD 21/1/84; GM 11/1/84.)
25. Sampson, 150–54.
26. FT 9/7/85.
27. FT 30/7/82, 22/12/82, 30/12/83; WS 6/10/83.
28. AA 9/11/81, 21/12/81. On Mobutu's alleged manipulations of food import deals, see BW 12/12/83.
29. In general, see DP Nov. 82; South Jan. 83; Jeune Afrique Economique Dec. 82; AN 7/3/84; WS 22/2/83.
30. According to New African, the firm was once suspected, with a Montreal broker, of having been the inadvertent conduit for AIDS moving from Africa to North America; but medical opinion later rejected the hypothesis.
31. See the book on this subject by Conway; also BA 29/11/83; FT 13/2/85.
32. Nigeria's contract with SGS was abruptly terminated in 1984. (NT 20/8/84; FT 3,5/10/84.) The reasons remain obscure, but the event did cause Nigeria some problems with its creditors.
33. FT 30/11/82; NT 19/1/84; Copetas, 115, 120.
34. AN 26/10/82; NT 1/2/83; WS 2/11/83; FT 25/10/83, 9/11/83.
35. GU 5/2/83.
36. WS 26/4/83.
37. FT 22/11/83; FT 29,30/12/83; GU 30/12/83.
38. WS 3/1/84; GM 3/1/84.
39. FT 3,5,6/1/84; AN 4/1/84; LM 17/1/84; CM 3/1/84; WS 9/3/84.
40. FT 5/4/84; HT 23/1/84; AN 24/2/84; GU 10/1/84; NT 19/1/84.
41. AN 25,27/4/84, 8,19/5/84; LM 25/4/84; FT 25/4/84, 9/5/84; LD 24/4/84; GM 24,25,26/4/84. There were precedents for such a move. During the civil war of the 1960s that so delighted IOS salesmen, the Nigerian federal government successfully used a forced conversion to wipe out the treasury of the Biafran secessionists. That inspired President Mobutu in 1979 to obliterate the savings of hundreds of thousands of Zairians through a similar currency coup.
42. WS 1/5/85.
43. OB 10/11/85, 1,8/12/85, 5/1/86. The Bank of England injected £200,000,000 into the bank after the takeover, while publicly declaring that no fraud or malpractice was involved in the bank's operation or demise. Nine months later, they called in the fraud squad. (GW 14/10/84, 11/8/85, 17/11/85.)

44. *WS* 19/7/84.
45. *ME* Jan. 85.
46. *Jeune Afrique* 18/7/84; *OB* 17/2/85; *FT* 7/7/84; *GM* 7/7/84; *New African* April 85; *GW* 15/7/84. Copetas claims that under Dikko, the rice landed at $35 per 100-pound sack, and was then sold for $217.
47. *FT* 13,25/2/85.
48. *OB* 15/7/84, 2/9/84.
49. *JP* 15–21/7/84; *GM* 7,9/7/84; *NT* 11/7/84.
50. *OB* 16/6/85; *NA* April 85. Another theory holds that the government, dominated by Muslim northerners, did not want Dikko back, for fear that he would incriminate too many top-level people, and that the kidnapping was planned by members of the southern elite, in collaboration with Israel, to embarrass the northern politicians. (*NS* 22/2/85.)
51. Late in 1985, Ralph Bernstein, whom Nessim Goan had trained in the business of investment in foreign real estate, was cited for contempt of the US Congress for refusing to answer questions about Imelda Marcos's New York real estate empire. (*NT* 17/12/85.) See Chapter 22.
52. *ME* Nov. 82.
53. Cornwell, 194, 195, 196, 203; Gurwin, 114–17, 136, 137.
54. *ST* 28/10/84. On a similar exchange negotiated with the Marxist regime in Ethiopia, and the bribing of the Nimeiry government in the Sudan to cooperate in the movement of Ethiopian Jews, see *EX* 18/1/85; *OB* 21,28/4/85.
55. *TS* 18/8/85.
56. *AN* 5/5/83. While Tabatabai was taking action against the Swiss arms dealers, he was also defending himself against narcotics-possession charges in Germany, on which he was ultimately found guilty in absentia. (*FF* 14/1/83; *NT* 20/2/83; *TI* 10/3/83.)
57. *OB* 26/8/84; *Middle East Executive Reports*, Feb. 86.
58. *LM* 11/6/85; *GU* 13/6/85.
59. *GU* 10/7/85.
60. Conway, passim; *WS* 26/4/85. The captain of the ship was found guilty early in 1986 of embezzlement and causing a shipwreck. (*WS* 14/2/86.)
61. A general survey of the Marc Rich affair is in *BA* 19,26/9/83. See also *NT* 18/8/83, 20,21/9/83; *FT* 20,21/9/83; *HT* 22/9/83; *WS* 22/8/83, 2,20,22/9/83, 6/10/83. There is an excellent recent account of the firm's checkered history by Copetas.
62. Copetas, 124.
63. Copetas, 145. Marc Rich had hired away from Phibro an expert in smuggling tin concentrate; and it was his close relationship with the prime minister and the finance minister of Malaysia that led to the price-rigging scheme.
64. Copetas, 119–20.
65. *FT* 17/10/85. The Swiss Federal Court finally ruled the transaction contrary to Swiss banking law, but by then the issue was academic.
66. *WS* 30/9/83.
67. *HT* 20–21/8/83; *CM* 22/8/83; *FT* 22/9/83; *BA* 11/6/84; *WS* 3,31/2/84, 26/9/84, 12/10/84; *NT* 14/10/84.
68. Rich can legally do business in the US, and in the autumn of 1985 he

attempted to purchase a Houston refinery; but he cannot personally go to the US for fear of arrest. (*WS* 6/12/85, 4/4/86.) The US had previously dropped the charges of trading with the enemy (Iran), but persisted with the others.

Chapter Sixteen

1. Mabillard, 33.
2. Manhattan, 141.
3. Faith, 187ff.
4. Mabillard, 59.
5. *FT* 8/11/83, 4/8/85.
6. Faith, 279.
7. DiFonza, 57–58.
8. Lo Bello, 231, 238.
9. In 1920 Eugenio Balzan, proprietor of the prestigious daily *Corriere della Sera*, was chased out of Italy by the rising Fascists. However, he managed to take his fortune with him to exile in Lugano. His daughter subsequently endowed a foundation, whose funds were administered by Finter Bank. Certain 'donors' to the Balzan Foundation paid in, in lire, and received back a large part of their 'donation' in Swiss francs. (Raw, 205–13.)
10. Mabillard; Faith, passim; Laya, 27–28; FF 3/3/78.
11. *LM* 26/11/84. One theory holds that all the charges being levied against Andreotti with respect to P-2 and Mafia links were an American-government-inspired plot to discredit him and to prevent him from succeeding to the presidency. Allegedly Andreotti had undergone a change of political faith and was swinging toward a position like that of Aldo Moro. (*NS* 25/1/85.)
12. *LM* 8/6/84, 25–26/11/84; *FT* 14/2/83, 28/3/83, 7/6/84; *LD* 21/2/83; *WS* 14/2/83. In the autumn of 1985 about 123 persons went on trial in the case. (*FT* 10/9/85.)
13. *FT* 24/10/84, 29/11/84. The protests by shopkeepers were met by counter-protests by unions, whose members were taxed at source and who therefore could not take advantage of facilities for tax evasion. (*LM* 23/11/84.)
14. Italian authorities seem to have had little success in policing the casinos, though in April 1985 one of the chief alleged money launderers in northern Italy was arrested in Milan. (*LM* 28/4/85.)
15. For an overview see Ynfante, *Las fugas*.
16. *ES* 4/5/86. Interestingly enough, a former lawyer for the Ruiz Mateos empire turned up in Switzerland to meet the new Spaniard Marc Rich, and to offer his services in the fight against American extradition procedures. (*CA* 3/6/85, 9/9/85.)
17. *CA* 11,18/2/85, 3,17/6/85, 11/11/85; *EP* 8,9,10,11/2/85, 10/5/85, 5/6/85; *FT* 15/1/85, 7/2/85, 30/3/85; *LM* 6/6/85.
18. *CA* 11/2/85.
19. *CA* 9/9/85.
20. *CA* 18/2/85.
21. Franco, 30. In 1983, a French National Assembly Committee estimated at

$4 billion the amount of money sitting in the illegal Swiss accounts of French private citizens. (*HT* 3/6/86.) This figure seems very conservative.
22. Pean, 67.
23. Laya, 20.
24. Franco, 30, 111.
25. Actually gold plays a double role in the French flight-capital business. Apart from being a vehicle for spiriting assets across the border into Switzerland, gold also functions as the principal instrument for internal capital flight: French private gold hoards are estimated to total 7,000 to 8,000 metric tons. (Franco, 37, 42, 111–14.)
26. The declared need for 'medical services' abroad, especially in Switzerland, is a common ploy for moving small amounts of money out of countries with exchange controls.
27. See the account of Israeli journalist Jacques Derogy.
28. *LM* 29/1/84.
29. *ES* 13/4/86; Cornwell, 83–85 et passim; Gurwin, 37–40; DiFonza, 228–30. On Cavallo's earlier career, including an arrest (and an acquittal) for coup-plotting, see Anselmi, 41; Cecchia, 166–69.
30. *LM* 16/1/86.
31. *IB* Dec. 81.
32. On the 'sniffer' airplane affair, see Pean; also *LM* 6,10,21/1/84, 29,30/3/84, 17/5/84, 14/6/84, 24/7/84, 22/11/84; *LD* 3/5/84.
33. Bonassoli spent his time in merry pursuit of such projects as making images of satellites and flying saucers appear on television screens and inventing death rays for the Italian army.
34. Some elements of Violet's career are outlined in Faligot, 193–98.
35. Pean, 90.
36. Perhaps the project was inspired by a contemporary invention deployed in Marseilles at the peak of President Nixon's war on drugs. This was an American-invented 'sniffer' device to smell out clandestine heroin refineries. Unfortunately it got confused by the smell of cooking oil, and careered about, accurately plotting the locations of neighborhood restaurants. (Epstein, 141–43.)
37. There has long been a suspicion that French intelligence was responsible for the death in an airplane 'accident' of Italian state oil company chief Enrico Mattei, who allegedly procured weapons for the Algerian revolutionaries in exchange for a deal whereby Italy, rather than France, would exploit the Algerian oil fields after independence. (Faligot, 217–19; Kruger, 47, 106.)
38. Violet denied that Ambrosiano's Ultrafin or Opus Dei's Banco Occidental were involved in the project whose ultimate raison d'être was to rectify the French balance-of-payments situation. (*LM* 6,10/1/84.) On the general situation of French finances, see *LM* 21/3/84, 5–6/5/85; *FT* 8/3/83, 21/4/83; *HT* 8/3/83; *CM* 19/4/83; *NT* 21/4/83.
39. *LM* 19/8/83, 15/11/83, 5/6/84, 15–16/7/84.
40. *FT* 17/1/85.
41. *HT* 10,18/5/83; *WS* 7/5/83; *FT* 10/5/83; *NT* 10,24,26/5/83; *LM* 15–16/5/83.
42. *LM* 20/4/83, 15/7/83, 17,24/3/84; *FT* 28,29/3/83, 6/5/83, 9/8/83;

WS 30/3/83, 2/8/83; *HT* 29/3/83, 12/4/83; *NT* 22/3/84. The government reacted to the increased *internal* flight of capital by abolishing anonymity in the purchase and sale of gold. (See n. 25 above.) The government also tightened up the enforcement of rules requiring the use of traceable checks instead of cash for payments greater than Fr. 10,000. On the fiscal assault on the French Moonies, see Boyer, 10, 71, 102.

43. *TB* Nov. 81; *LM* 27/1/84, 26/5/84; *FT* 26/4/84; *WS* 25/4/84.
44. *GU* 6/10/83; *AN* 29/1/84; *GM* 12/3/84.
45. *FT* 25/5/84, 5/7/84; *II* May 84. Three former officers and a range of clients were fined a total of $20 million.
46. *FT* 18/6/85; *LM* 5–6/5/85; *WS* 19/9/85.
47. *EX* 17/1/86.
48. *LM* 31/12/85, 5,6/1/86; *FM* 4/1/86.
49. *Nouvel Observateur* 16/1/86; *Paris Match* 17,26/1/86, 14/3/86. Curiously enough, the man who declined the Perrot contract had seen service not only with 'Mad Mike' Hoare in the Congo, but also, he claimed, with the Sandinistas in Nicaragua. He subsequently left the mercenary trade, declining – sensibly, with hindsight – to join 'Mad Mike' in his abortive Seychelles operation in 1981. See Chapter 3, n. 30.
50. *EX* 17/1/86; *FM* 11,18/1/86. All such speculation must be viewed in light of the right-wing press's distaste for and eagerness to embarrass the Socialist government. On the other hand, the government did succeed in effectively suppressing the affair very quickly after it broke into public view.
51. *FT* 8/11/83.
52. Pean, 67–68.
53. Ynfante, *Une crime* ..., 107, 177 et passim.
54. Leclerc was convicted in 1985. *GU* 20/5/85.
55. *La Jornado* 18/8/86; Mills, 822, 871. Sicilia-Falcon recently published a full-page ad in *Excelsior* (5/8/86) protesting his ill-treatment after ten years in prison. After all, all he had done was export 'vegetables' to the US.
56. *FT* 1/10/83, 19/4/84; *GU* 4/4/84; *TB* June 84.
57. *GU* 1/3/84; *TS* 20/5/84; *GM* 19/5/84; *AN* 15/5/84; *HT* 13/5/84.
58. *LM* 22/5/84.
59. *AN* 21/10/84; *WS* 31/1/85, 12/4/85.

Chapter Seventeen

1. In general, see *IC* Feb. 85.
2. *WS* 30/3/85, 9/4/85, 3/10/85. Thus, the Association of Old Crows, created in 1964 by a group of Second World War veteran intelligence and electronics officers, evolved by the 1980s into a 20,000-strong lobby group – comprising industrial figures, research scientists, and military men – to push for the development of high-tech warfare and to function as a conduit for information flows between the Pentagon and private industry. Defense contracting, too, absorbed 2,151 former Pentagon officials between 1982 and 1984.
3. *WS* 4/4/85; *NT* 18/3/85, 1/4/85.
4. *WS* 10,20,24/5/85, 4/9/85. The trick was to impute to arms costs an infla-

tion factor 30% higher than the GNP deflator, when in fact the two rates were about the same.

5. *NT* 10/5/85.
6. *LD* 2/4/85; *NT* 8/4/85.
7. *WS* 15/1/85; *NT* 18/3/85.
8. *NT* 29/4/85, 2,14,15/5/85, 31/10/85; *WS* 16/5/85, 29/8/85, 3,29,31/10/85, 29/11/85, 12/6/86; *GW* 2/6/85, 15/12/85.
9. See the survey of shady corporate practices by Amitai Etzioni, summarized in *NT* 15/11/85. 62% of the firms on the Fortune 500 list were involved in illegalities between 1975 and 1984.
10. Cf. *HT* 26/3/85. The calculations were done for the period up to and including 1980, but there seems no *a priori* reason to assume a radically different result would emerge for the more recent period.
11. *LM* 20/3/85.
12. *HT* 21/5/85. According to the BIS, what was involved in the dollar appreciation was a rush *not* to the dollar *per se* but to the US. Given the emergence of a eurodollar market, it was no longer true that a preference by investors for dollar assets also meant a preference for US assets. But with the crisis of the 1980s the geographical preference came to dominate.
13. See especially *LM* 16/2/85; *FT* 22/3/85; *WS* 1/4/85, 1/5/84.
14. *DP* May 85; *LM* 11/4/85; *NT* 18/11/84.
15. *GW* 31/3/85; *GU* 17/9/85; *LM* 1/8/85; *WS* 17,18/12/85; Boyer, 160.
16. *FT* 11/1/85; *WS* 1/4/85; *NT* 1/4/85; *HT* 18/7/85.
17. *WS* 2/10/85; *HT* 2/1//86.
18. *WS* 7/5/85; *LM* 7/5/85.
19. *WS* 4/2/85.
20. *Federal Reserve Bulletin*, March 84; *AN* 12/12/83; *Finance & Development*, Dec. 83. For the year 1983, the estimates range from a low of $225 billion to a high of $900 billion. The IMF estimates put the figure in the high range, equal to some 25% of measured GNP or about $700 billion. They also show that the underground economy was growing faster than the overground one.
21. See, for example, the data cited in Blum, 48.
22. *WS* 9/1/86.
23. See variously Reuter, 183; Messick, 121–22; *NT* 18/12/82, 3/5/85; *WS* 11/1/84. On the homegrown marijuana boom, *NW* 25/10/82.
24. Those intent on dodging taxes might, for example, join Posse Comitatus, a militant tax-protest group linked to the National Commodities Barter Association, which has been accused of establishing facilities to convert cash into bullion without receipts. (*WS* 11/4/85; *NT* 11/4/85.)
25. In the late 1970s, the IRS estimated that 41% of self-employed earnings were undeclared, along with 50% of rent and royalties, 22% of capital gains in property, and 16% of interest and dividends. (*WS* 15/4/86.)
26. *WS* 15/4/85.
27. *WS* 26/4/85; *NT* 26/4/85.
28. *WS* 17/10/85.
29. *NT* 6/7/83; Boyer, passim, has a detailed account of Moonie oceanic enterprises.

30. A few weeks later, the French government moved to charge the French Moonie organization with fiscal fraud. (*LM* 23/5/84, 22–23/7/84; *NT* 19/7/84, 23/8/85; *GM* 15/5/84; *WS* 17/12/85.) Boyer contends that the White House *did* telephone the Justice Department on Moon's behalf; others claim the administration lobbied the Supreme Court *not* to review the conviction. Both might be true.
31. *LD* 3/4/85; *La Presse* 3/4/85.
32. *HT* 12/7/84; *LM* 10–11/3/85; *GM* 29/1/86; *NT* 29/1/86. See the defense of Hubbard in *NT* 4/2/86. If Hubbard did indeed funnel 'church' money through Switzerland, he was not a pioneer. It was through a Swiss account in a Panamanian bank that the cult around the 'Reverend' Jones moved its funds prior to the infamous massacre of its followers in Jonestown, Guyana. (Blum, 12, 89, 155.)
33. *HT* 23–24/6/84; *WS* 19/4/85.
34. Clarke, 79.
35. *FT* 8/11/83; *EM* April 85; *WS* 2/1/84, 18/12/84; *NT* 6/12/84.
36. For example, *NT* 12/12/85; *EM* April 85. The insider-trading issue really blew up in 1981 in conjunction with a takeover bid by a Canadian liquor conglomerate, Seagram's, for St. Joe Minerals in the US. The SEC claimed that American clients of the Lugano-based Banca della Svizzera Italiana used inside information about the projected takeover to earn more than $1 million. A New York judge froze the assets of the bank in retaliation for its refusal to cooperate in the investigation. Finally a fine of $50,000 a day persuaded the bank to get Seagram's permission to turn over the documents. A similar case came out of a takeover bid for Santa Fe International. After five years the Santa Fe case was successfully prosecuted. (*NT* 17/1/86; *WS* 17/1/86, 27/2/86.)
37. *BW* 29/4/85. The spring of 1986 saw a string of major scandals around insider trading through Caribbean and Swiss banks. (*HT* 14/5/86; *WS* 15,23/5/86; *LI* 18/5/86.)
38. *LD* 1/12/84; *WS* 11/2/85; *FT* 23/4/85.
39. *HT* 1/2/84.
40. Raw, 241.
41. *NT* 12/4/83.
42. *WS* 6/7/84.
43. *II* May 84; *WS* 10/7/83.
44. *WS* 9/7/84; *LM* 12/9/84.
45. *LM* 20/5/84.
46. *TB* June 84; *FT* 2/7/84; *WS* 25/6/84; *NT* 14/8/84.
47. *II* Feb. 85.
48. *WS* 13,17/8/84, 10/9/84.
49. *WS* 15/10/84, 24/5/85; *NT* 25/10/84, 7/11/85; *LM* 28–29/10/84; *FT* 24/4/85.

Chapter Eighteen

1. 'System' is perhaps a misnomer, for the US banking 'system' is a legal and regulatory jungle. Nearly 5,000 banks are incorporated under federal law,

regulated and insured by understaffed federal agencies; nearly 10,000 more exist under state law. There are, as well, more than 3,000 savings banks, divided between federal and state jurisdictions, and variously covered by federal, state, or private deposit insurance.

2. *IB* Aug. 82.

3. *WS* 2/7/84, 28/9/84; *HT* 19/7/84; *NT* 15/5/84, 18/6/84.

4. On the early history of Continental Illinois, see the references in Hammer, Yallop, DiFonza, Cornwell, and Gurwin; an interesting, if idiosyncratic, treatment of its relations to the Vatican is in *SP* 4/6/84.

5. It had major loans outstanding to International Harvester, Massey, Braniff Airlines, Canada's Dome Petroleum, Mexico's Alpha Group, and others. (*FT* 30/11/82.)

6. *FT* 29/5/84.

7. On the bank debacle, see *AB* 18,31/5/84; *IB* 25/5/84; *TB* June 84; *FT* 14,19/5/84, 5/6/84, 10/7/84; *GU* 11/5/84; *EC* 2,16/6/84; *BW* 4/6/84; *HT* 5,25,28/6/84; *GM* 19/5/84; *LD* 4/6/84; *NT* 15,16,17,18,19,21,23/5/84, 4/6/84; *WS* 11,15,16,18,23,25/5/84, 5/6/84, 19,26,27/7/84, 23/8/84, 5,12,15/10/84; *IC* July, Sept. 84.

8. *HT* 29/5/84; *WS* 20/9/84.

9. *FT* 23/10/84; *LM* 5/6/85; *NT* 24/10/85, 16/11/85.

10. On the farm crisis, see *WS* 6/6/85, 26/8/85, 4,25/9/85, 7,31/10/85, 14/10/85, 4/11/85. During the 1970s much farm lending was effectively collateralized on expected capital gains from the land, rather than the value of future expected production. Hence, in the early 1980s, with low inflation, high interest rates, and low commodity prices, the crisis was acute.

11. *NT* 4/10/84, 16/11/84; *WS* 16,19/11/84.

12. Clark, 133.

13. On casinos, mob links, and the role of union pension funds, see *NT* 12/10/83, 28/1/84, 4/12/85, 8,16/1/86; *WS* 17/3/83, 12,22/10/83, 8/11/85. Because the casinos did not have to report transactions, drug dealers and tax evaders could run millions in cash through them, and have the casino wire the money to an offshore bank. In 1983, Allan Dorfman, a mob expert in the business, finally seemed willing to cooperate with the FBI in revealing the secrets, but he was gunned down in a Chicago street.

14. In the summer of 1984 a major bust revealed a drug-dealing organization that used a network of banks across the US to convert cash into cashiers' checks and money orders in sums of less than $10,000 – on which transactions the banks were not required to file a report. The money was then redeposited in the Florida offices of several banks, in accounts registered to the Panamanian branches of a number of international banks.

15. *NT* 10/4/84.

16. *WS* 12/11/84.

17. For example, in September of 1983 three members of an alleged Colombian drug-trafficking group were charged with depositing $11 million in cash with the People's–Liberty Bank and Trust Company of Kentucky, converting the money into cashiers' checks, bank drafts, and so on, shifting it to other US banks, and then sending it on to Panama, Colombia, and Canada. No bank officers were named in the indictment. (*AB* 28/9/83.) Also in

1983, a former officer of Riggs National Bank of Washington was indicted on charges of laundering cocaine money. (*WS* 12/12/83.)

18. *WS* 8,26/2/85, 4,5,7,12/3/85, 4/4/85, 25/7/85; *RS* 1/7/83; *RA* 1/3/85; *Boston Globe* 14/2/85; *LM* 20/3/85; *FT* 6/3/85; *NT* 8,13,14,15,26,28/2/85, 6,29/3/85; *BW* 25/2/85, 18/3/85.

19. That was scarcely the end of the list. Also in 1985 the Metropolitan National Bank of Texas was named in an indictment of a trafficking ring that had allegedly imported 250,000 pounds of marijuana from Mexico. (*NT* 13/12/85.) And DEA raids in Puerto Rico led to the arrest of fourteen bankers on charges of having laundered hundreds of millions in dirty money. (*RC* 27/9/85.)

20. *LM* 20/3/85; *WS* 13/3/85, 8/11/85; *NT* 18,19/6/85, 16/10/85; *CM* 19/6/85. The ABA later claimed only four or five banks were seeking immunity from prosecution.

21. *IC* July 84; *WS* 6/5/85; *TM* 3/12/84.

22. The culmination came with the scandal over First United Fund, one of the country's largest money brokers, which was alleged to have contributed to twenty bank failures as a result of tied-in loans. (*WS* 3,25/7/84, 20/9/84, 16/11/84, 9/4/85; *NT* 16/5/84, 3/7/84; *HT* 4/7/84.)

23. To some degree the distinction between insured and uninsured deposits had been merely theoretical. But in the late 1970s the FDIC decided to tighten up and remove the 'unintended' 100% insurance. In 1984 the Continental Illinois disaster, which threatened to drain enormous sums out of the insurance fund, and the scandal over First United Fund prompted yet another tightening of the regulations.

24. *NT* 27/3/84; *WS* 21/3/84. The FDIC tried to counteract these legal games, but was blocked in court. It also tried to force banks to disclose how much of their deposit money came from money brokers, hoping to embarrass banks into limiting their use of the volatile money-for-hire with strings often attached. (*WS* 7/8/84; *NT* 21/6/84.) In June 1985, for the first time, the FDIC withheld automatic payment of insured deposits while it investigated possible fraud in the relations between the broker and the bank. (*WS* 17/6/85.) It also considered implementing a rule to force brokers to reveal the identity of owners of CDs (*WS* 30/7/85), something that would not only reveal deceptive packaging and unpackaging, but also incidentally interfere with the laundromat function that brokering of deposits sometimes played. See also the complications arising from the failure of the Golden Pacific Bank in New York's Chinatown in June 1985. (*NT* 25,26,27/6/85; *WS* 28/6/85, 1/7/85.)

25. *NT* 14/3/85, 25/4/85.

26. First Interstate found a novel way of circumventing interregional and interstate barriers by franchising use of its electronics facilities to a host of smaller local banks, who would preserve their nominal independence. (*WS* 19/2/85; *NT* 15/10/84.)

27. *NT* 2,11/6/85; *WS* 23/5/85, 11/6/85.

28. *NT* 23/5/85, 27/1/86; *WS* 23/1/86.

29. *WS* 25,30/4/84, 22,23/5/84, 6/6/84; *HT* 22/6/84; *NT* 23/4/84, 25/5/84, 6/6/84.

30. *WS* 28/8/85.
31. The SEC charged that the auditor took $125,000 in payments; and the auditor, though not admitting to the SEC's charges, did plead guilty to grand theft and obstruction of justice. (*WS* 18/12/85.)
32. Arky, who committed suicide in the summer of 1985, still protesting his innocence in the ESM affair, had a long association with hot-money operations, including the Tennessee banks of the Butcher brothers, which crashed with a loss of $700 million. (*WS* 22/8/85.)
33. *NT* 5,7,12,14,16/3/85, 22,29/5/85, 10/6/85, 23/10/85, 5,9/11/85, 14/12/85; *WS* 7,12,15/3/85, 18/12/85; *BW* 8/4/85.
34. *NT* 15,16,17/5/85; *WS* 15,17/5/85.
35. *GU* 15/5/85; *WS* 6,9/1/86. By then another major crisis had swept the Maryland thrift industry, after the collapse of a big real estate tax shelter operation pulled down a thrift it had bought to fund its speculations. (*WS* 20,26,30/8/85, 23/9/85, 25/11/85.)
36. *EM* Jan. 84.
37. *NT* 17/1/85.
38. *LW* 29/5/81; Kruger, 130.
39. *LW* 29/8/80.
40. Senate Report, 35.
41. *LW* 4,11/7/80.
42. *NT* 13/4/83, 24/11/84.
43. *LT* Nov. 83.
44. *LW* 20/2/81, 12/7/85; *GM* 14/12/82, 16/6/84; *NT* 8/1/85; *WS* 13/2/81, 14/12/82, 17/4/84; *BW* 18/3/85. Three years after Botero Moreno was first charged, so, too, was the head of another Miami-based Colombian exchange house, who allegedly ran his cash through a branch of the Miami Capital Bank, paying heavy laundry fees to assure that no questions were asked and that the required paperwork was faked.
45. *WS* 22/8/85; *EM* Jan. 84.
46. *FT* 27/10/83.
47. *NT* 6/11/84. The Florida banks soon had powerful allies. The bill tightening up on penalties for money laundering was stalled in Congress by pressure from, among others, the American Civil Liberties Union and the American Bankers' Association. (*WS* 13/6/86.)
48. Senate Report, 1–2; 'Cash Connection,' 45–46.
49. Interesting material on the seamier side of Florida banking is in Lernoux, Chapters 5, 6, 7, 8.
50. *LW* 2/9/83.
51. On the attempted takeover of the Sunshine State Bank by an accused marijuana dealer working through a Panama-based instant-company dealer, see *WS* 5/8/85, 22/4/86.
52. *WS* 17/11/82. Orozco was allegedly laundering funds for wealthy Colombian coffee merchants to enable them to evade taxation, as well as washing cocaine money. Commodity dealers are well placed to launder money: holders of illegal cash work through them to buy and sell the same commodity, then pay the broker to tear up the losing ticket. The only record is a gain, which can be presented as legitimate market earnings. Orozco was

sentenced to eight years and fined $1 million. (President's Commission, 35.)

53. *NT* 13,15/3/84.
54. *OB* 4/11/84; *CM* 20/1/84; *WS* 30/11/83, 13/1/84, 23,24/5/84, 12/2/86; *MH* 25/2/86.
55. *FT* 27/10/83.
56. *NT* 13/4/83.
57. *AB* 16,24/5/84.
58. *WS* 26/6/85. Those regional mergers may represent a leap from the frying pan into the fire, for they also threaten to transfer control of Florida banking to Atlanta.
59. *NT* 17/2/86.

Chapter Nineteen

1. *BA* 11/7/83; *FT* 16/3/83; *GM* 15/3/83; *IC* No.3 1983, Dec. 84; *II* Jan. 85; Senate Report, 34; *HT* 1/2/84, 26/11/85.
2. *TB* May 84.
3. *IC* Vol. 15, No. 2; *HT* 16/3/83; *NT* 15/3/83; *WS* 16/3/83.
4. Effrios, 5–14; Senate Report, 54–62; Blum, Chapter 10.
5. Hutchison, 58–60.
6. Kruger, 187n; Charbonneau, 434. The accusations about Vesco and heroin came from mob hot-money expert Frank Peroff (see the work of Whittemore). While some writers such as Kruger take the heroin story seriously, Charbonneau argues that it was a fraud invented by the Montreal mob to arouse Peroff's interest in a heroin deal. A 1975 US government report also raised the possibility of Vesco's involvement in heroin deals (*FF* 20/4/84.) But it must be remembered that Costa Rica had refused a US request for Vesco's extradition on securities charges. Drug charges would have facilitated extradition proceedings.
7. *AN* 13/1/84; *LM* 8/8/85.
8. *NT* 19/3/86.
9. Mills, 1127, asserts that Vesco and Lehder jointly bribed Pindling to obtain use of Norman's Cay.
10. *FP* 3/9/83. Another explanation for the tightening is that in 1979 the Canadian government began probing in a tax case.
11. *FT* 19/7/85; *EC* 12/10/85; *GZ* 23/12/85.
12. *GZ* 22/10/85, 21/12/85.
13. *NT* 24/11/82; *WS* 8,31/3/83; *NT* 17/10/83. Vesco acquired Columbus Trust through Butler's Bank, which was itself merged into Bahamas Commonwealth Bank a short time later. According to the *Wall Street Journal*, US government records claim that drug dealers, as well as tax evaders, were clients of the firm. One of the indicted officers fled US justice; another, a Bahamian attorney, defied a US subpoena. (Blum, 75.)
14. Senate Report, 99.
15. *FP* 13/8/83, 3/9/83; *Ottawa Citizen* 14/6/83; *AN* 15/6/83; *GZ* 23/9/83.
16. *FP* 3/9/83, 14/1/84.
17. *GZ* 23/12/85. An interesting examination of Scotiabank's Caribbean activities was aired on CBC's *fifth estate*, 25/5/86.

18. *TS* 23/9/83; *GM* 23/9/83; *GZ* 24/12/85.
19. *GM* 11/1/84.
20. *FP* 17/12/83; *GM* 17/11/83, 13/12/83; *NT* 13/12/83.
21. Senate Report, 90.
22. Senate Report, 5, 176.
23. *TB* May 84; *WS* 11/1/83.
24. Indictment papers issued by US District Court for the District of Colorado, US Justice Department 9-30-82, *United States v. Kilpatrick et al.* See also *Maclean's* Oct. 82. The indictments were dismissed on August 25, 1983. The government appealed the dismissals, but the appeal was also dismissed on September 24, 1984.
25. *Les Affairs* 5/5/84; *FP* 3/9/83, 19/11/83, 14/1/84; *TB* May 84; *GM* 23,25,29/11/83, 3/12/83. The bank eventually lost its appeal against the fine. (*GZ* 8/1/85.)
26. *WS* 24/7/84; *GM* 3/12/83.
27. *FT* 26/3/85.
28. *FT* 4/7/84; *WS* 13/9/84; *GZ* 24,25/2/86. A Scotiabank official stated, 'We have acknowledged that money launderers had access to our bank in the Caribbean in the past. We have taken extensive, and we believe effective measures to assure this sort of thing doesn't happen [in the future].'
29. *NT* 1/6/84; *WS* 10/12/84, 31/10/85. See the letter from the Caymans attorney general pledging cooperation with the US in *WS* 7/5/85.
30. *LW* 16/9/83; *FT* 8/9/83. An agreement to allow the US three military bases followed, the next spring. (*FF* 20/4/84.)
31. *TB* Nov. 83; *FT* 19/10/84.
32. *FT* 3/7/84, 18/12/84; *WS* 25/7/84, 6/8/84; *NT* 15/12/84; *GM* 22/2/84; *AN* 17/7/84.
33. *NT* 13/2/85; *WS* 27/2/85.
34. *WS* 27/9/84, 15/10/84.
35. *GZ* 22/10/85, 23/12/85. There is also some controversy over a $110 million loan to the Bahamian government that the Bank of Nova Scotia had lead-managed. The US Congress Permanent Subcommittee on Investigations suggested that the loan may have reflected political pressures rather than commercial considerations, as if US bank loans to Turkey, Zaire, Israel, and others didn't. Senate Report, 56; *FP* 3/9/83.
36. *FT* 25/6/85, 8/10/85.
37. *FT* 7/3/85; *OB* 17/3/85; *GW* 17/3/85. At least he had the pleasure of the company of his peers. A month later a former cabinet minister from Belize also wound up in a Miami jail, charged with conspiracy to import some of Belize's burgeoning marijuana crop into the US. (*NT* 9/4/85.)
38. *WS* 10/12/85.
39. *LW* 5/4/85; *RM* 16/8/85; *WS* 31/10/85.
40. On the new Mexican drug boom, see *HT* 24/5/86; *LM* 17/5/86. For New York, the negotiations with California bankers were a great success, producing an agreement that after 1990 California should be open to full interstate banking, provided the legislature can also be convinced. (*WS* 3/3/86.) Among the Hong Kong banks that sent billions in unreported cash to Crocker Bank in San Francisco were Hang Lung and Overseas Trust Bank.

41. *GM* 23/11/85; *TS* 20/10/85.
42. *WS* 8/2/83; Senate Report, 11.
43. *GM* 3/3/84.
44. *WS* 29/1/86. Convictions followed. (*WS* 1/8/86.)
45. *WS* 27/2/85.
46. *WS* 10/1/86; *GM* 5/4/86.
47. *FR* 30/10/81.
48. Clarke, 81.

Chapter Twenty

1. Cited in the excellent survey of the geopolitical background to the
   Nugan-Hand affair by James Nathan, 'Dateline Australia,' *Foreign Policy*
   Winter 1982–83, 170. A mass of detail is available in Volumes II and IV
   of the Commonwealth–New South Wales Commission of Enquiry into
   Drug Trafficking. A good summary is available in the exposés of John-
   athan Kwitny, *WS* 24/8/82, 16,17/8/83; *GM* 10/11/82; Lernoux, Chapter
   4; Nancy Grodin in *Covert Action* March 1982; and Jonathan Marshall
   in *Inquiry* 24/11/80.
2. Kruger, passim; *GW* 25/8/85, 29/9/85, 13/10/85. One result of the
   decreased domestic demand for their services for 'intelligence' work is
   that French criminals have been hiring on with foreign governments.
   Spain's secret police have apparently hired them to assassinate ETA guerrillas, and Israel's Mossad was reported to have used them to knock
   off Palestinian targets. (*GW* 1/17/84, 25/8/85.)
3. *ST* 24/2/85.
4. *FT* 7/3/84; *GU* 12/3/84. See Pazienza's further revelations in *ES* 6/7/86. If
   he is telling the truth, an IOR-controlled Panamanian ghost company
   ERIN S.A. *may* have been the conduit for funding the purchase of arms for
   the IRA from German arms dealers. Pazienza's speculations are based
   partly on an alleged British intelligence report dating from 1981, and
   partly, no doubt, on the support some in the Church have given the
   cause of Irish reunification.
5. *NT* 21/12/82. The defense easily demolished the allegation. (*GU* 23/4/84.)
6. *ST* 24/2/85.
7. On Mafia gunrunning to the IRA, see *TS* 9/9/83. The alleged CIA involvement broke into the public domain after an FBI sting operation broke a
   New York gunrunning ring run by a man who insisted he was working
   at CIA orders. (*CS* March–May 1983; *WS* 14/5/83.) The alleged ties
   between the CIA and the IRA took a more spectacular turn in early 1984.
   Maverick right-wing Ulster MP Enoch Powell claimed that the CIA had
   prompted the IRA to murder Lord Mountbatten, who had just delivered a
   strong antinuclear speech. According to Powell's theory, the CIA backs
   the IRA because the CIA long ago realized that the only way to get the
   Irish Republic to abandon its neutralist foreign policy stance and join
   Britain in NATO was to successfully reunify Ireland. (*GU* 9,10,11/1/84.)
   Ireland would then play a vital part in NATO defenses against Soviet submarines in the North Atlantic.

8. Tad Szulc, 'The CIA and the Banks,' *Inquiry* 21/11/77.
9. *WS* 7/11/85; *GW* 22/4/84, 20/1/85, 13/4/86; Garwood, 210.
10. To be sure, occasional problems emerged when spooks haunted establishment financial institutions. See, for example, the uproar in 1983, when a former aide to Alexander Haig was charged with embezzling CIA secret funds from Swiss Bank Corporation and Lloyd's Bank International in Geneva. Claiming to have handled millions of dollars earmarked for CIA operations, he threatened to reveal the details of the covert operations for which he laundered the funds if the government persisted in prosecuting him. (*CS* June–Aug. 83, citing *Miami Herald* 2/10/83.)
11. Commonwealth–New South Wales Commission of Enquiry into Drug Trafficking (hereinafter cited as CNSW), Vol. IV, 682; Hougan, *Spooks*, 202.
12. Franco, 215, states that the CIA uses a Liechtenstein *anstalt* for purposes of funding coups and revolutions. On the growth of the CIA's air arm, and other facets of proprietaries, see Robbins, *Air America*. An excellent account of the use and abuse of CIA proprietaries is in Goulden's exposé of renegade spook Edwin Wilson. See also, Garwood, 222, 225 et passim.
13. *NT* 15/10/84.
14. According to the recollections of Jimmy 'The Weasel' Fratianno, the Florida mob accepted the arms and money and imaginative assassination devices with which the deed was to be conducted, then sold off the equipment and poured the poisons down the sink, all the while regaling their CIA contacts with tales of heroic shootouts with the Cuban coast guard. (Demaris, 224, 233–38, 315, 389–90.)
15. *NT* 23/2/86.
16. *NT* 10/12/84. On the question of CIA operations through other US corporations, see Sobel, 133, 156–61.
17. Hougan, *Spooks*, 70, 73, 181.
18. Yallop, 99, 130; DiFonza, 35, 100, 102, 104; *GU* 14/12/83. There is also a story, denied by the US embassy in Rome, that when the CIA, under congressional pressure, moved to sell off its Roman newspaper, *The Daily American*, it wanted to ensure that any new owner would be friendly to the agency's purposes. Michele Sindona was.
19. Goulden, 26–27, 145–55, 160, 163, 178, 188.
20. *NT* 25,26/9/85.
21. The basic account is by Hammer; but see also Yallop, 41, Martin, 65–66, and a quite different version in Lo Bello. The essence of the story is that in the early 1970s, Marcinkus was involved in some way in a deal with a group of American experts in hot and counterfeit paper, by which the Vatican bank would purchase counterfeit American securities with a face value of nearly $1 billion. For these securities the IOR was allegedly willing to pay about 45% of their face value. Where there is smoke in the Vatican, there is usually a towering inferno; and the existence of a deal of this nature seems not to be in doubt, though its purposes remain

vague. Furthermore, someone at the Vatican had not done his home-
work, because, if the details of the story are true, the IOR was going to
pay for the counterfeit securities about 900% above the market rate.
Counterfeit securities normally sell for about 5% of face value. (See
Clarke, Chapters 9, 10.)

22. Gurwin, 194.

23. More specifically, the prospective buyer was made out to be Fiduciary
Investment Corporation, whose sole function was to administer funds
for a Catholic order, the Passionist Fathers of New Jersey. And apart
from the order's endowment, funds for the purchase were to come from
Banco di Roma per la Svizzera, a bank 51% owned by the Vatican.
According to Gurwin, 174, the only conceivable attraction of the tiny
New Jersey bank seemed to be its list of 300 FBI agents with financial
problems. However, another advantage would be the capacity to funnel
hot money via the bank into the Vatican's international financial network, through the accounts of the Passionist Fathers, in much the same
manner that French police suspected the mob used the accounts of the
Missions étrangères de Paris.

24. Messick, *Grass*, 176–79.

25. Eventually WFC collapsed, costing investors $55 million and saddling
Hernandez with convictions for tax evasion and money laundering.
(NT 24/12/82; Senate Report, 161.)

26. When Wallace Groves, a former Wall Street financier who had served
time for mail fraud, set up his Intercontinental Diversified Corporation
to run a real-estate and harbor-management business in the Bahamas
(where Groves had extensive interests in gambling), his company also
ran, from 1965 to 1972, money for the CIA. (WS 18/4/80.)

27. WS 18/4/80.

28. Clarke, 166; Faith, 249.

29. Kruger, 187n.; Hougan, *Spooks*, 389–91. Hitchcock was never indicted in
the LSD affair, but he gave testimony against his former associates. See
United States v. Sand 541 F 2nd 1370 (1976), Clarke, 166–69, Senate
Report, 164. That was not quite the end of the story. After the LSD expo-
sures, the operator of one of the Brotherhood of Eternal Love's California
laboratories departed for Italy where he had a curious subsequent career
that apparently gained him the confidence of both the Red Brigades and
the US embassy in Rome. (LM 26/1/83; GM 27/4/83; HT 27/4/83;
AN 28/4/83.)

30. Hougan, *Spooks*, 239, 390.

31. CM 9,24/5/83; LM 26–27/5/83.

32. Kruger, 145–46; CS Dec. 83–Feb. 84, March–May 84. On Task Force 157,
see *Foreign Policy* No. 49, *op. cit.*, and *Inquiry* 23/11/81.

33. CS July–Aug. 82, Dec. 82–Feb. 83. Bob Hawke, the new Labour leader,
whose background included a place in the *Guinness Book of Records*
for his beer-drinking exploits at Oxford, proved his worth in the
summer of 1985 when the *Rainbow Warrior* scandal, like the ship itself,
blew up in the South Pacific. He whipped up a Red Scare to cover for

French intelligence, sided with Reagan against New Zealand on the nuclear issue, and talked about Cuban and Libyan plots against the South Pacific islands! (*NS* 4/10/85.)

34. See, for example, McCoy, passim; *WS* 9/4/85.
35. CNSW II, 293.
36. *EM* Jan. 82.
37. CNSW II, 316.
38. *CS* March–May 83; *WS* 24/8/82.
39. CNSW II 320, 326.
40. CNSW II 281, 306, 379–84. The actual form taken by the proposal for a bail fund is subject to some dispute. See the account of the then-president of the bank, Admiral Earl Yates, formerly of US Naval Intelligence, who opposed a bail scheme on the grounds that it would give the bank a bad reputation! (CNSW IV, 780.)
41. *CS* Dec. 82–Feb. 83; CNSW II, 443–456, IV, 661–685, 718–730; *WS* 24/8/82.
42. *IB* May 80.
43. Perhaps also a belated victim of the Nugan-Hand collapse was one of the region's main heroin traffickers, Martin Johnston. Known as 'Mr. Asia,' Johnston is sometimes thought to have been one of the bank's most illustrious clients (though investigations have never confirmed this). About the time of the Nugan-Hand collapse, Johnston shifted his operational headquarters to England, where he was found murdered, with his body mutilated to hamper identification, about a year later. Apparently Mr. Asia had been about to reveal information to the police about some of his colleagues, including Alexander James Sinclair (known in the trade as 'Mr. Big'). Sinclair was arrested and imprisoned, and parts of his personal fortune of about $40 million – invested in Sydney businesses, a silver mine in Indonesia, a plantation in Fiji, and several accounts in those Swiss banks that claimed to be no longer accepting drug money – were frozen. In July 1983, Sinclair declared that he, too, was willing to cooperate with the authorities, including revealing how laundered money from drug sales was used to purchase arms for the IRA. One month later, the thirty-nine-year-old Sinclair suddenly collapsed and died on his way to lunch. (CNSW II, 372–74, 393, where Sinclair's Christian name is given as William; *GW* 21/8/83.)
44. CNSW IV, 793–98.
45. *FR* 21/4/83.
46. CNSW IV, Chapter 38.
47. CNSW IV, 829; *NT* 5,8/3/85; *OB* 17/3/85. Subsequent plans for offshore banking were arrested along with the chief minister of the islands in Miami in 1985.
48. CNSW IV, 725.
49. See the accounts in *FR* 20/10/83; *WS* 11/8/83, 9,14/2/84, 18/4/84; *HT* 17/4/84; *AN* 17/4/84.
50. *WP* 2/11/84; 27/17/84.
51. *NT* 3/9/85, 23/10/85.
52. *OB* 4/11/84; *RA* 14/12/84.
53. On the crisis at Deak's, see *FT* 8,22,27,31/12/84, 8,9,11/1/85;

WS 17,26/12/84, 2,9/1/85; *GM* 27,28/12/84, 5/2/85; *NT* 10,25,28/12/84. Nicholas Deak had refused to testify before the Presidential commission on money laundering – which had no subpoena power.
(*NT* 13,15/3/84.) Officers of Deak & Co. called the charges against the firm, 'gross distortions.' (*WS* 9/5/86.)

54. On Deak's murder, see *NT* 19/11/85. One factor never explained was how Deak's and the Colombian money launderer Eduardo Orozco made their first business contact. Curiously enough, Orozco formerly ran his commodity-trading firm in partnership with Alberto Duque; and when Duque purchased the City National Bank of Miami, he hired to run it Donald Beazley, the former manager of the Miami office of Nugan-Hand Bank.

55. *FT* 13/1/86.

56. *FT* 5,19/2/85; *WS* 28/3/85; *FR* 3/1/85.

57. *WS* 9/5/86.

Chapter Twenty-One

1. *South* July 83; *EC* 30/4/83; *NT* 21/8/83.

2. *LM* 8/8/85.

3. *AN* 18/11/83.

4. *CM* 6/4/84; *FT* 26/3/84.

5. *ECLA* 'Notas sobre la economia y la desarrolla de America Latina' Jan. 84.

6. *South* July 85; *FT* 17/4/85; Robert McNamara, 'The Challenges for Sub-Sahara Africa,' Washington: 1985, 27 et passim, *LM* 29/5/86.

7. *FT* 6,7,8/2/85; *LD* 30/4/85.

8. BIS Annual Report 1985, 112.

9. *GU* 16/9/85.

10. *WS* 14/8/84.

11. *WS* 15/4/85.

12. *WS* 18/11/85; *NT* 11/11/85; *FT* 7/11/85. Officials at the Mexican central bank claim that 1985 capital flight totaled only $1 billion.
(*WS* 24/1/86.) To put it mildly, this is nonsense. Private estimates range as high as $12 billion, with the elections of the summer of 1985 alone sending $4 billion fleeing. See the views of the Mexican chief debt negotiator, interviewed in *LI* 11/6/86.

13. *AN* 28/8/83.

14. On Paraguay, *RS* 2/8/85; *NT* 14/1/86. Added to the invoicing episode was another scandal around the smuggling of timber to evade export duties and to hide abroad the foreign exchange earned. (*RS* 15/11/85.) On the general problem of capital flight from South America, see *HT* 3,29/4/86.

15. *LC* 2/9/83; *AN* 8/6/83.

16. *FR* 27/11/81, 1/8/85; *OB* 15/7/84, 5/7/85; *WS* 13/11/85; *GM* 30/11/85.

17. *FT* 10,13/12/83.

18. *GU* 6/9/85.

19. Belgium may have found Antwerp's position in the global diamond trade

good for its balance of payments, but not for its fiscal position, as the diamond district is notorious for fostering tax evasion. (*NT* 31/1/86.)

20. *WS* 25/9/84.
21. *LW* 27/7/84; *GW* 24/6/84; *LM* 29/1/86; *New Leader* 17/9/84. On the problem of definition, see *HT* 12/6/86.
22. *FT* 1/5/84, 1/12/84; *HT* 3,29/4/86.
23. *WS* 11/10/85.
24. *EC* 30/4/83.
25. *RS* 6/9/85; *HT* 29/4/86.
26. *NT* 25/2/86; *HT* 4,29/4/86.
27. *LP* 21,22/3/86; *NT* 21/3/86. The official inquiry ruled suicide. Needless to say, the finding was greeted with some skepticism, not least by José Maria Ruiz Mateos, who added fear of murder by poisoning to his night-mares about the sight of the undersides of London bridges. (*WS* 6/6/86.)
28. On the OPEC deficit, see *AN* 2/10/84; *EC* 5/2/83; *WS* 16/3/83; *FT* 20/12/83. On the UAE financial debacle, see *AN* 2,23/11/83, 24/10/84, 12/11/84; *MG* 30/11/84; *WS* 22,23/11/83, 8/2/84; *FT* 30/11/83.
29. On the Souq el-Manakh collapse in Kuwait, see *ME* Feb. 83; *EC* 19/2/83; *FR* 3/3/83; *AF* July 82; *South* Feb. 83; *FT* 25/9/82; *SG* 19/9/82. Detailed treatments of aspects of the crisis are in *AN* 22/4/83, 8/5/83, 11,23,27/2/83, 25/3/84, 8/5/84, 4/7/84; *AH* 30/1/84, 14/5/84; *FT* 23/2/83, 21,26/3/84, 1,2/5/84; *WS* 18/1/83; *HT* 25/4/83; *GU* 28/5/84. On capital flight, see *FT* 26/3/84; *AN* 27/2/84, 26/3/84, 4/7/84; *WS* 18/1/84. On the windup, see *FT* 21/3/84, 1/5/84; *AN* 11/2/84, 21/3/84, 14/5/84; *GU* 28/5/84.
30. IMF *World Economic Outlook*, Sept. 84.
31. *HT* 2/8/83.
32. *WS* 6/2/85.
33. *WS* 11/10/85. See the recent scandal at Morgan Guaranty over what appeared to be Brazilian flight capital diverted by a bank officer. (*HT* 24–25/5/86; *NT* 23/5/86.)
34. *IB* 30/3/84.
35. *AN* 28/10/83.
36. In general, see *EM* April 82 Supplement; *CS* Sept.–Nov. 82; *DP* Jan. 83; *IC* March 84.
37. On military corruption, see *LM* 16/5/86. On cronyism, see *FT* 25/2/83, 11/3/83; *WS* 24/2/83, 4/11/83; *FR* 30/6/83; *EC* 5/3/83, 23/4/83; *II* Dec. 83.
38. *NT* 7/3/86. One interesting example of cronyism is provided by a rela-tive of Imelda Marcos, who borrowed funds from foreign banks with a guarantee from the Philippines government in order to create an empire of fifty companies. Among them was one that produced 75% of the cigarette filters used in the local market, which may not be completely unassociated with a presidential decree that lowered the tariff rate paid on imported inputs for his firm.
39. *NT* 20/3/86.
40. *LM* 18/5/85.
41. *FR* 7/6/84, 4/4/85; *WS* 23/5/86. Among Cojuangco's enterprises was a

private militia, trained by Israeli advisers and armed with weaponry allegedly diverted from US military aid flows or directly smuggled in from the US. On arms smuggling, see *NT* 22/11/85.

42. *NT* 24/3/86.
43. *NT* 7/3/86; *GW* 23/3/86. Westinghouse admits paying 'fees' to a crony, but denies knowledge of any subsequent disbursement of the money.
44. *LM* 1–2/9/85.
45. *WS* 17/3/86; *NT* 20,26,27/3/86.
46. *FR* 23/2/84, 18/7/85, 15/8/85; *WS* 18/9/85; *VV* 15/10/85, 12/11/85 (letter of Ernesto Macedes); *NT* 19/9/85, 12,13,17/12/85; *GW* 11/8/85.
47. *NT* 6,11/12/85.
48. *NT* 16/12/84; *FT* 16/12/84; *WS* 23/4/84; *IC* July 84. While many military leaders were put on trial, others, including Suarez-Mason, had already fled. (*LW* 20/1/84; *RS* 24/5/85.)
49. *NT* 19/6/84, 2/7/84.
50. *FT* 12,26,28,30/3/84; *NT* 8,19/3/84, 2/4/84; *WS* 26/3/84; *GU* 8,19/3/84.
51. *TB* Feb. 83; *FT* 12/4/83.
52. *II* June 83; Higham; *FT* 5/4/84; Swiss Bank Corporation, *Investment Study* Nov. 83.
53. *South* Sept. 82; *FT* 14/11/84, 4,11/12/84; *LW* 7/12/84. Argentina, Brazil, and Mexico were all forced to restructure their central banks. Not to be outdone was the People's Republic of China, which followed its successful introduction of Club Med and Coca-Cola on to the Chinese road to socialism by converting the Bank of the People into an orthodox central bank and ceding to it responsibility for issuing currency and controlling the foreign exchanges. (*LM* 11/10/83.)
54. *WS* 19/11/84.
55. Also on the roster of creditor collective bargaining tools was the alumni association of the World Bank, whose members – Turgat Özal of Turkey, Cesar Virata of the Philippines, Nicholas Barletta of Panama, among others – occupied, sometimes briefly, positions of financial power in their home countries.
56. *WS* 1/4/83.
57. *EM* Jan., Aug. 82; *TI* 29/9/81; *LD* 9/2/82; *FT* 2/11/82, 21,25,26/1/83, 1/2/83; *NT* 8/12/82, 3/11/83; *DP* Jan. 83; *HT* 24/8/83; *EC* 26/2/83. See also the Union Trust case and the panic it engendered when it seemed to confer Chapter-Eleven protection on sovereign debtors such as Costa Rica. (*FT* 30/4/84; *NT* 27/4/84; *WS* 12/6/84.)
58. *GM* 10/9/82, 14/9/82; *SG* 15/8/82; *TI* 24/8/82; *FT* 29/7/82, 14/9/82.
59. *FT* 23/9/83; *HT* 26/9/83, 10/1/84; *AN* 19/9/83; *GW* 4/8/82, 19/9/82; *WS* 1,27/12/83, 3/2/84. The Vesco deal likely had the support of certain elements in the US government anxious to wean Cuba from the USSR. But US customs and, evidently, the Reagan administration felt differently.
60. *EC* 10/12/83; *FT* 6/12/83, 7/6/84; *LM* 9–10/6/84; *RM* 8/6/84; *LW* 19/8/83; *WS* 10/5/83, 15/8/83.
61. *FT* 17/1/84; *WS* 24/1/84, 23,28/2/84; *IC* March 84; *FR* 29/3/84; *II* June 84.

62. *IB* Nov. 82; *WS* 28/10/82; *FT* 27,28/10/82, 11,13/1/83, 28/10/83; *NT* 26/10/82, 9,10,12/1/83, 24/6/83; *GU* 11/1/83; *CM* 3/11/83; *TB* Nov. 83.
63. *AN* 13/1/83.
64. *FT* 19/8/83.
65. *GU* 22/8/83.
66. *FT* 26/8/83; *WS* 12/9/83.
67. *Il* Oct. 82.
68. On the collapse of the concept of a debtors' cartel, see *WS* 2,9,12/9/83; *FT* 2,12/9/83; *GU* 7,9,10/9/83; *NT* 9,10/9/83; *LM* 6,9,11–12/9/83. On the Quito conference, see *FT* 12/1/84, 7/2/84; *HT* 10/1/84; for that of Cartagena, *LW* 29/6/84; *GU* 22,23,25/6/84; *LM* 23/6/84; *NT* 22/6/84; *FT* 23/6/84. Particularly harmful to the prospects for the cartel idea was the stance of Venezuela, which, having taken the lead, then explicitly repudiated the idea. (*FT* 15/5/84, 6/9/84.) Mexico and Brazil also put their enormous weight behind the anticartel forces. (*FT* 23/6/84.)
69. *NT* 17/4/84.
70. *LW* 20/4/84. Prebisch died during a North American tour in the spring of 1986. His final public position seemed to consist of illogical efforts to reconcile traditional Latin American critiques of the free market with IMF orthodoxy.
71. *FT* 2,4,17/4/84; *WS* 2,4,12,23/4/84; *NT* 3,12/4/84; *HT* 3/4/84.
72. *WS* 1/10/85.
73. *WS* 29/5/84.
74. *NT* 19/7/84.
75. *WS* 10/9/84.
76. Apparently picking up on revelations made by the late Manuel Buendia, Anderson unveiled his story of de la Madrid's alleged $162 million retirement fund in the *Washington Post* on the morning of an official visit by de la Madrid to Washington. (*NT* 3/7/84; *IC* Sept. 84.)
77. *HT* 16/7/84; *WS* 6/6/84, 11/7/84; *FT* 7/6/84.
78. *WS* 24/9/84, 10/10/84; *NT* 11/11/84; *LM* 11/9/84.
79. *WS* 26/6/84; *NT* 12,28/6/84; *GM* 12/6/84.
80. *HT* 29/5/84; *NT* 8,9/6/84.
81. *GU* 13/6/84; *NT* 16,30/6/84; *WS* 15/6/84, 25/7/84; *FT* 21/7/84.
82. *WS* 2/8/84, 26/9/84; *NT* 26/9/84.
83. *WS* 4/12/84.
84. *WS* 3,31/12/84, 10/1/85; *FT* 27/11/84.

Chapter Twenty-Two

1. *GU* 16/9/85; *Il* May 85.
2. *LC* 3/9/83; *Business America* 19/9/83; *BW* 10/1/83; *NT* 2/5/84. US exports to Latin America fell 37% during the first year of the crisis. Lost markets in Mexico alone cost the US more jobs than three years of recession in the automobile industry. And the United Nations Conference on Trade and Development (UNCTAD) estimated in 1985 that three years of debt crisis had cost the West eight million jobs. (*FT* 5/9/85.)

3. *LM* 24–25/3/85; *WS* 1/5/85; *FT* 19,26/3/85; *NT* 13/2/85, 25/3/85.
4. *RC* 1/2/85; *LM* 20/2/85; *GU* 1/5/85; *FT* 1,5/2/85, 2/3/85; *NT* 21/2/85; *WS* 4/3/85, 21/5/85, 17/6/85.
5. *FT* 12,14,28/6/85, 17,20/7/85, 13,15,18,20/6/85; *WS* 10,17/6/85, 1,5/7/85; *LW* 19/7/85; *RS* 28/6/85; *LM* 17/9/85.
6. *NT* 26,29/10/85, 15/1/86; *LM* 28/10/85; *WS* 28/10/85, 5/11/85, 4/12/85.
7. *NT* 26/9/85.
8. *FT* 13/12/84; *NT* 18/1/85.
9. *FT* 8,14,15,20/3/85; *RB* 23/11/84; *NT* 19/3/85.
10. *WS* 17/5/85.
11. *FT* 27,28/8/85; *WS* 27/8/85, 8/10/85, 5/12/85; *GU* 5,24,26/9/85; *OB* 26/5/85; *NT* 19/12/85.
12. *WS* 7/6/85, 26/9/85, 1,4,11,24/10/85.
13. *GU* 21,24/9/85; *OB* 13/10/85; *WS* 2/10/85.
14. Interview with Castro in *World Press Review* August 1985; *GU* 30/7/85; *OB* 4/8/85; *WS* 12/6/85, 30/7/85.
15. *RC* 23/8/85; *OB* 13/10/85; *LW* 9/8/85.
16. *LM* 9/10/85; *FT* 8,9/10/85.
17. *FT* 6/6/85; *LM* 21/6/85; *LW* 26/7/85; *WS* 23/7/85.
18. *LW* 15/11/85; *WS* 30/8/85, 24/9/85, 11,29/10/85; *NT* 24/9/85, 11/10/85; *LM* 21/9/85; *HT* 30,31/7/85; *GU* 29/11/85. Garcia subsequently clashed with the US oil companies in Peru and pulled Peruvian reserves out of US banks; but he also ceded to creditors on interest-rate issues, dropped his threat to pull out of the IMF, and imposed an Argentine-style emergency austerity package. (*LD* 31/12/85; *MH* 25/2/86; *WS* 25/2/86.)
19. *GU* 19/7/85.
20. *FR* 18/7/85. These notes were undoubtedly better than the bills CIA counterfeiters had left behind in South Vietnam after the fall of Saigon, hoping that the North Vietnamese would try to use the sloppy counterfeits and have their credit rating adversely affected. In fact, the only people to lose credit standing from the bills were those fleeing South Vietnamese officials and generals who added the counterfeit money to their loot and tried to pass it in the US.
21. *WS* 24/3/83. Such plans assumed incorrectly that inflation was the sole reason that interest rates were so far above historical norms, and that inflation in financial markets proceeded at the same rate as inflation in international commodity markets.
22. *IB* 11,25/5/84; *EC* 2/6/84; *HT* 15/6/84; *NT* 7,9,13,24/5/84; *GU* 9/5/84; *GM* 8/5/84; *FT* 2/5/84. One problem with rate capping was that the capped rate might be insufficient to keep the loan current. In such a case it would be necessary to talk US bank regulators into allowing the US banks to count the value of the interest arrears being capitalized as current income. (*EC* 2/4/83; *FT* 3/4/85.)
23. *FT* 28/4/84.
24. *NT* 14/5/84. In 1985 Manuel Ulloa proposed converting one-third of Latin America's $360 billion in bank debt into long-term, low-interest bonds. All debt incurred for balance-of-payments support and nonproductive infrastructure (i.e., public works that did not pay for themselves) could be so

treated. Presumably the bonds would be held by a major international institution such as the World Bank. Their cost would ultimately be dumped on the taxpayer of Western countries if sufficient money could not be coaxed out of the public sectors of the developing countries over time. The loans for self-financing projects would be handled separately. (*GU* 24/5/85.)

25. *LW* 6/4/84; *AN* 29/3/84; *FT* 27/3/84, 12/4/84.
26. *BW* 28/2/83; *FT* 5/3/83.
27. *WS* 3/3/83. A similar scenario was pushed by the US Treasury Department's developing-country-debt troubleshooter, Tim McNamar. He called for debtors to mortgage future export receipts, selling bonds backed by future flows of income from primary-product exports, and using the discounted prepayments on these commodities to balance seasonal and irregular cash flows.
28. *EC* 9/7/83; *GU* 10/5/83; *OB* 16/9/84.
29. *FT* 12/10/85.
30. *OB* 23/6/85; *LW* 28/6/85. 'Low' to Kissinger meant a real rate of 3%.
31. *FT* 3/10/85.
32. *FT* 12/10/85.
33. *WS* 30/7/85, 23/9/85, 8/10/85; *NT* 27/9/85.
34. *FT* 22,28/10/85; *WS* 30/9/85, 1,3,4,7,22/10/85, 23/12/85;
    NT 1,4,8,9,22/10/85.
35. The Reaganites had long accused the bank of financing the growth of 'socialism.' Hence, the new plan, which called for a shift in the direction of World Bank lending, also required a purge of its top management.
36. *WS* 1/4/85.
37. *WS* 18/4/84.
38. *LW* 9/3/84. The US government agency that insured private direct investment refused to extend investment insurance to countries in Latin America that insisted on the final authority of local courts.
39. *WS* 16/12/85; *TS* 15/12/85; *GW* 6/4/86. Thatcher denied Labour's allegations.
40. *GU* 8,11,13/5/85, 11/7/85; *WS* 7,13/11/85, 6/2/86.
41. *WS* 30/8/85.
42. The domestic black market in gold was legalized, a tax amnesty planned, and the government announced the pending end of restrictions on the use of cash payments. *LM* 1/10/85; *WS* 12/11/85; *GM* 3/2/86; *NT* 7,11/4/86; *LI* 23/5/86; *WS* 23/5/85; *LM* 24/5/86. Interestingly enough, François Mitterrand also endorsed the idea of a new initiative on international debt during his 1985 state visit to Brazil, blaming the US for damaging debtor countries by its financial policies, and calling for greater 'flexibility' in dealing with the debt. (*LW* 18/10/85.) Needless to say, the 'cohabitation' of a socialist president and a right-wing prime minister was soon on the rocks.
43. *LM* 28/10/83.
44. *FT* 11/10/85; *NT* 16,18/12/85; *WS* 23/12/85.
45. *LW* 22/3/85; *OB* 28/7/85.
46. *WS* 19,27/11/84, 2/5/85; *FT* 28/12/84; *II* May 84; *DP* March 85. The swaps carried the danger that bank regulators would force the banks to carry the

paper on their books at its discounted, rather than its face, value, which would force massive writedowns.

47. *LW* 24/2/84.
48. *LW* 17/2/84.
49. *LW* 27/1/84.
50. *LD* 12/12/83, 10/2/84; *WS* 27/1/83, 20/12/83, 31/7/84; *LW* 6/1/84; *FT* 23/11/83.
51. *LW* 10/2/84.
52. *LD* 30/4/85; *FT* 18/3/85; *NT* 21/3/85, 1/5/85; *WS* 18/3/85.
53. *LW* 6/9/85; *WS* 9/10/85, 23/12/85. Naturally Argentina began by selling off profitable companies. (*NT* 6/3/86; *WS* 17/1/86.)
54. *FT* 11/4/85, 16/9/85.
55. *LM* 8/8/85, 21/9/85, 25/10/85; *WS* 30/8/85; *LW* 6/9/85; Delpirou, 162.
56. *LW* 23/12/83, 24/2/84, 22/6/84, 2/11/84, 21/6/85; *LM* 11/6/85.
57. *LW* 22/3/85, 23/8/85; *FT* 6/8/85; *WS* 5/12/85.
58. *WS* 3/1/86.
59. *RS* 20/12/85.
60. *LW* 22/3/85; *RS* 11/10/85. Chile was also a pioneer of Baker-style borrowing arrangements. For when it finally signed a deal for a $7 billion refinancing of its bank debt, effectively wiping out any question of its legitimacy, part of the refinancing had a World Bank guarantee. (*FT* 4/7/85.)
61. *WS* 17/12/84; *FT* 14/3/85.
62. *RM* 2/12/83.
63. *AN* 22/3/84. More recently Cuba has considered reviving the drive to attract foreign investors as part of a contemplated scheme to shift the Cuban planning model in the direction of the 'market socialism' of Hungary. (*LW* 15/11/85.)
64. *WS* 7/4/83, 30/11/84, 20/8/85, 11/4/86; *FT* 12/12/84, 18/1/85; *LW* 24/2/84, 4/1/85, 20/9/85.
65. *NT* 17,20/2/86; *GM* 8/2/86; *GW* 9/3/86.
66. *FT* 9/5/83; *LW* 22/6/84, 1/2/85, 8/3/85; *RM* 25/10/85; *WS* 8/2/85, 16/12/85.
67. When the plan to swap debt for equity in the public sector was unveiled, US National Security Agency economist Norman Bailey remarked, 'To the extent [the debt conversion] can be done, it obviously makes the whole debt situation more manageable.' (*FT* 18/3/85; *WS* 15/3/85; *RM* 16/8/85; *LW* 22/3/85.) A study recommending the debt-equity swap for Pemex was done by the Royal Bank of Canada in 1984.
68. *NA* March 85; *FT* 16/8/83; *NT* 4/5/85.
69. *AW* 24/3/84, 18/6/84; *FT* 3/1/85; *WS* 17/12/84, 22/1/85, 12,18/3/85; *GU* 27/5/85; *FR* 5/5/83, 1/8/85.
70. *AW* 9/7/84; *FR* 31/10/85; *WS* 27/2/86, 5/3/86; *NT* 26/2/86, 7/3/86; *FT* 7/1/86; *LI* 5/6/86; *HT* 14/5/86. While Cardinal Sin and the Philippine church hierarchy went over to the opposition, Marcos was not abandoned by all ecclesiastic opinion. As the heat began to mount on the house of Marcos, Moral Majority leader Jerry Falwell, fresh from a trip to South Africa, heartily praised the Marcos regime. (*FR* 22/8/85; *MT* 12/11/85.)

71. *NT* 17/1/85, 28/9/85, 25/10/85; *FT* 8/8/85; *LM* 5–6/5/85.
72. *LD* 17/9/85. A somewhat similar scheme was also to be tried in Jamaica, again with a Rockefeller trust and AID money involved. (*The Gleaner* 21/7/84.)
73. *AN* 14/12/83; *FT* 13,20/12/83, 6/1/84; *LM* 10/1/84; *GM* 3/1/84; *WS* 20/12/83; *II* Jan. 84.
74. *GM* 5/7/84; *AN* 18/5/84.
75. *WS* 20/9/84; *GM* 28/5/84, 9/10/84, 5/11/84; *MI* 19/8/83; *LM* 21/7/84; *FT* 8/1/85.
76. *AN* 29/2/84.
77. *MD* 27/7/85, 3/8/85; *FT* 2/8/85. None of this did much to alleviate the crisis of unemployment and declining investment endemic since 1980. (*AN* 10/8/83, 2/12/83, 21/8/84; *FT* 11/8/83, 21/3/84, 29/5/84, 9/10/84, 24/12/84; *GM* 12/3/84; *ME* May 85.)
78. *MD* 4/1/85.
79. *FT* 9/7/85.
80. *GU* 12/7/85.
81. *Jeune Afrique* 13/2/85; *LD* 25/8/84; *LM* 12–13,16/5/85.
82. See the survey in *FR* 25/7/85; *FT* 2/8/85, 13/9/85.
83. *LM* 23,29/5/85; *NT* 22/5/85. The US AID went into the business of helping developing countries unload state companies. (*NT* 20/2/86.) And more calls were heard to shift US foreign-aid flows away from foreign governments toward private-sector concerns. See, for example, *WS* 12/6/86.
84. Under the Glass-Steagall Act of 1932, US commercial banks were forbidden to underwrite securities. This restriction prevented them from repeating in the 1980s a ploy to shed bad international debt that they had used in the early 1930s, namely, selling it to the general public. It might be possible for them to circumvent possible Glass-Steagall restrictions on debt-equity swaps by working through investment companies. The big banks might eventually evolve into international investment trusts. (*II* Jan. 85; Mayer, *Money Bazaars*, 223, 308, 335; *FT* 8/10/85.)
85. *RA* 30/8/85; *WS* 25/6/85. Although their Latin American operations are being cut back, US banks have been actively pushing against barriers to foreign entry into the domestic banking business that many, perhaps most, countries, developed and developing alike, have traditionally erected. To further this development, the US government is lobbying through the General Agreement on Tariffs and Trade (GATT) for an international accord that would free international trade in services, such as banking and insurance. Moreover, US banks and the IMF seize upon successive credit crises in developing countries to press for 'deregulation' and 'liberalization' of their financial sectors. US banks successfully entered Turkey, after the Kastelli crash, Spain, during its great banking crisis, South Korea, in the wake of crises on its curb market, and also Australia, New Zealand, and Canada. (See, for example, *WS* 13/5/85, 25/7/85, 4/11/85; *FT* 22/8/85.)
86. *LI* 23/5/86; *LM* 16/5/86; *HT* 14/5/86; *GW* 27/4/86. The 10% laundry fee planned for returning flight capital would have been more than compensated for by recent devaluations of the French franc against the Swiss franc.
87. *NT* 15/2/85, 17/4/85.

88. *NT* 17/2/86. There was also an unknown amount in stocks, bonds, and real estate, as well as bank accounts of Haitians with dual citizenship.
89. *WS* 5/3/85.
90. *HT* 3,29/4/86.
91. Raw, 113, 144; Hutchison, 85–87. In a similar spirit, when Robert Vesco, hiding out in Costa Rica, was charged by the SEC with looting $225 million from IOS, his defense was that he planned to invest the money in the development of economically backward countries. (Hutchison, 352, 413.)
92. *NT* 20/12/85; *FT* 18/12/85; *FR* 31/10/85. *Far Eastern Economic Review* even titled its announcement of the enterprise 'Enter the Fund of Funds'!
93. Hutchison, 28.

Epilogue

1. Interview with Castro in *World Press Review* Aug. 85.
2. *FT* 21,23,25/9/85.
3. Two excellent accounts of the Chase-Iranian coup are in Davis, Chapter 4, and in Hurlbert; Sampson, Chapter 17, gives a different version of events. See also the interview with the former Iranian central bank chief in *EM* Feb. 82. There is an odd account in *SP* 4/2/80, reflecting the obsessive suspicion with which the American radical right regards the Rockefeller family.
4. *BW* 22/10/66; *NW* 31/10/66.
5. For two interesting post-mortems, see *IC* Sept. 81 and Peter Brimelow's commentary in *BA* 13/12/82. Although the issues were settled in principle, there was still much controversy to come over specifics of the negotiations. See *WS* 1,7/2/83, 4/10/83, 11/11/83; *AN* 10/4/83, 25/7/83, 24/8/83; *HT* 19/5/83; *FT* 15,29/10/83; *GM* 25/8/83. The American banks actually walked away from the incident with a profit, perhaps the first time in history that kidnappers paid a ransom to supposed friends of the victims. Thus, it seems only fitting that when in mid-1985 the last installment of Iran's debts to the American banks was paid off, the bank that received the final payment was European-American, custodian of the wreckage of Michele Sindona's Franklin National Bank. (*MD* 15/6/85.)
6. *GW* 23/3/86; *WS* 17/3/86.
7. *LD* 16/11/79; Faith, 336–37.
8. See especially Oscar Ugarteche, 'Nicaragua: the Risks of Debt Renegotiation,' in Jill Torrie (ed.), *Banking On Poverty*, Toronto: 1984.
9. Faith, 141. An interesting sidelight to the saga of the looted gold came when the former chief of the Italian secret services, General Ambrogio Viviani, confessed that the secret services had collaborated in the 'escape' of former SS colonel Herbert Kappler from an Italian military prison in 1977. According to Viviani – and denied by the then-serving minister of defence – the 'escape' was arranged in exchange for information on the Swiss hideout of eighty tons of gold bars looted from the Bank of Italy in 1944. Kappler, stricken with cancer, wanted to die in his homeland – which he did, six months later. (*LM* 16/5/86.)
10. *EC* 26/2/83.

11. *GZ* 5/3/86; *WS* 3,5/3/86; *NT* 22/1/86, 7/2/86, 14/3/86, 1/4/86.
12. *NT* 24/3/86; *HT* 2/5/86. Using tales of looted aid money to coax yet more aid money can prove to be a dangerous game, for it might increase the conviction of an increasingly redneck Congress that increases in foreign aid are a waste – unless they go to Israel.
13. Because of its public image, the new Philippine government has a greater probability of success than had Khomeini's regime in battling in the courts for the return of assets. Even before the grandiose California freeze, the New York Supreme Court froze Manhattan real estate apparently belonging to Imelda Marcos, and the Filipino government has launched a $1.5 billion suit against Marcos in a Texas court to gain control of Texas property he allegedly bought with illegally diverted funds. (*WS* 21/3/86; *NT* 4,21/3/86.) But it will likely be a long and uncertain battle. On the customs seizure, see *Azurin v. Von Raab*, N.86–2154, Court of Appeals for the 9th Circuit, brief of amicus curiae, Republic of the Philippines, in the Appeal from the mandamus order issued by the District Court of Hawaii; and the reply brief of the appellant. On the PNCO case, see *Republic of the Philippines v. Marcos et al*, CIV 86–3859, amended complaint and the appeal from the freeze order 86–6091, 86–6093, District Court, District of Columbia.
14. *WS* 3,17/3/86; *NT* 13/3/86.
15. *TM* 15/5/86; *WS* 22/4/86.
16. *HT* 3/6/86.
17. Despite pledges, the US government did very little to help the new regime in Haiti recover the money. And unlike the case of Marcos, in which US customs confiscated documents – just by the remotest chance – important paper clues to the Duvalier fortune were lost when mobs ransacked the homes of Duvalier and his close associates. (*HT* 13/5/86.)
18. *GM* 26/3/86; *LD* 27/3/86; *NT* 1/4/86; *WS* 10/6/86.
19. *AN* 18,28/9/83; *HT* 13/2/84; *FT* 7/12/82, 29/9/83, 5/11/83, 8/2/84; *EM* Jan. 84; *WS* 21/2/83.
20. *MD* 10/5/86. One effect of the freeze was partly to undermine the process of convincing Arab investors that the US was a safe haven. In its wake even the government of Kuwait announced its intention to diversify its reserves away from the dollar. (*HT* 14/5/86.)
21. Cf. *FT* 20/2/86.

Index